MARRIAGE AND FAMILY

In Diverse and Changing Scenario

MARRIAGE AND FAMILY

In Diverse and Changing Scenario

AMITESHWAR RATRA
Consultant, Department of Women's Education,
School of Continuing Education,
Indira Gandhi National Open University,
New Delhi

PRAVEEN KAUR
Professor, Department of Human Development and Family Studies,
IC College of Home Science, CCS Haryana Agricultural University,
Hisar, Haryana

SUDHA CHHIKARA
Professor, Department of Human Development and Family Studies,
IC College of Home Science, CCS Haryana Agricultural University,
Hisar, Haryana

Foreword by

Tej Verma
Principal Scientist/Additional Director-General (Home Science),
Krishi Anusandhan Bhavan, Pusa, New Delhi.

Preface by

Prabha Chawla
Professor, Department of Women's Education, School of Continuing Education,
Indira Gandhi National Open University, Maidan Garhi, New Delhi.

DEEP & DEEP PUBLICATIONS PVT. LTD.
F-159, Rajouri Garden, New Delhi - 110027

MARRIAGE AND FAMILY
In Diverse and Changing Scenario

ISBN 81-7629-758-5

Typeset by THE LASER PRINTERS
8/15, 3rd Floor, Subhash Nagar, New Delhi - 110 027

Printed in India at MAYUR ENTERPRISES
WZ Plot No. 3, Gujjar Market, Tihar Village, New Delhi - 110 018

Published by DEEP & DEEP PUBLICATIONS PVT. LTD.,
F-159, Rajouri Garden, New Delhi - 110 027
Phones : 25435369, 25440916
E-mails : deep98@del3.vsnl.net.in • ddpbooks@yahoo.co.in
Showroom :
2/13, Ansari Road, Daryaganj, New Delhi -110 002 • Telefax : 23245122

To the Holy Spirit who has cherished me,
To the Greatest Teacher of creation,
To the light of God who enlightens our path at every moment,
To the Mother India who has nourished me,
To the Motherland for her rich cultural heritage,
To the land of deep familial cohesiveness and strong moralistic attitude,

I pay my abysmal obeisance.

Contents

Contents

Foreword

Families are the crucibles in which our humanity is born, nurtured and fulfilled. From cradle to grave, man and woman exist in an institution called family, though changing in structure. This is an exciting time in the field of family science, for the institution of marriage and family is undergoing rapid change. Our own perspective on the marriage and family has developed and changed during the past few decades. In the book "Marriage and Family: In Diverse and Changing Scenario," authors do a comprehensive task in covering the changing philosophy from the past to the present days while holding on to the common thread of marriage and family. The book highlighting the Indian traditions also delves into the research literature and at the same time contains the global perspective of marriage and family. The book has beautifully filled up these two ends by giving various fillers to join the common thread.

This book has made a serious attempt of building a conceptual framework and succeeded in reaching the higher levels of standards that can help to strengthen the marital relationships. This book comprehensively provides personal direction and guidance in simple and easy to understand language and content to nourish intimate relationships. It helps prepare students who as future professionals will promote the overall goal of family life education and also who have no professional interest in family, but all of whom will have a life-long personal investment in family.

An undisputable strength of this book is its in-depth

coverage of a surprising array of varied and neglected topics. The authors give an exhaustive detailed description of various marriage customs of Indian societies. This book encompasses both personal and intellectual understanding. The book has virtues of both functional approach and academic approach. Reading this book will enrich both professional and layman.

I heartily congratulate the authors for exhibiting an in-depth insight into the subject matter. I am hopeful that readers will derive maximum benefit through this script.

DR. TEJ VERMA
Principal Scientist/
Additional Director-General (Home Science),
Krishi Anusandhan Bhavan, Pusa, New Delhi.

Preface

The book on "Marriage and Family: In Diverse and Changing Scenario" is authors' original contribution to the society. The language used is simple but effective, sequence of chapters is well thought of as it traces the historical evolution of the institution of marriage and family. Though a routine subject it has been dealt with a subtle philosophical approach to keep the interest of readers intact. Step-wise analysis of the society, relationships and firm bondage helps the reader to appreciate the development of the institution of marriage.

The text is not devoid of myths and mythologies to make the reading interesting, simultaneously it provides scientific basis and understanding to make things acceptable to society. The placement of chapters has been done keeping in mind the thread of continuity and understanding. Like in Chapter One and Two in-depth meaning of marriage and its types are provided. Chapter Three outlines various meanings of love in both the Indian and Western contexts. Chapter Four and Five discusses the importance of readiness for marriage and methods of mate selection. Chapter Six contains an exhaustive and authentic guide to the ways in which a traditional Indian marriage is conducted. Chapter Seven enlists the components of marital harmony and personal compatibility in detail.

Chapter Eight provides alternatives to marriage which have come into existence with an advent of modernism and traditional outlook taking a back seat. Chapter Nine describes marriage and family structures across various Indian tribes and foreign societies.

Chapter Ten and Eleven discusses the meaning of the family and outlines the tasks and problems of family life cycle. Chapter Twelve portrays the typical and atypical forms of family existent in the society in the present times. Chapter Thirteen gives a detailed overview of laws on marriage and divorce in India. Chapter Fourteen provides an overview on conflicts, divorce and re-marriage. Chapter Fifteen and Sixteen addresses the role of mass media and sex education and emphasizes the role of marriage and family counselling and in the end provide illuminating guidance on how to save the marriage.

I congratulate the authors for taking this initiative in bringing out this excellent work of research, which is much needed in the society.

DR. PRABHA CHAWLA
Professor,
Department of Women's Education,
School of Continuing Education,
Indira Gandhi National Open University,
Maidan Garhi, New Delhi.

Acknowledgements

We want to thank some of the many people who helped us. We dedicate this book to the Almighty and our motherland India for her rich and diverse cultural heritage.

We want to express our admiration, respect and gratitude to Dr. B.S. Yadav, ex-Professor, Department of Mathematics, North Campus, University of Delhi, Delhi; Dr. Neerja Chadha, Associate Professor, Department of Women's Education, School of Continuing Education, Indira Gandhi National Open University, New Delhi; Mrs. Ranjeet Sharma; Mrs. Chand Chawla; Mrs. Rashmi Gaud; Dr. Taruna Khemani; Dr. Mahavir Singh, Documentation Officer, National Social Science Documentation Centre (NASSDOC, ICSSR), New Delhi and Dr. Jayanti Datta, Reader, Lady Irwin College, Department of Child Development, New Delhi whose beatific expressions inspired us at times when we were bereft of hope while writing this book.

We are highly grateful to Dr. Devender Saini, Ms. Hem Lata, Mrs. Valerie Sophie, and Ms. Meenakshi Ohlan for their valuable contributions and sincere efforts put forth to help in the completion of the book.

We wish to thank the academic staff of the Department of Human Development and Family Studies, Chaudhary Charan Singh Haryana Agricultural University at Hisar in Haryana, Dr. Shakuntla Punia, Dr. Shanti Balda, Dr. Sheela Sangwan, Dr. Santosh Sangwan , Dr. Bimla Dhanda, Dr. Anju Manocha, Dr. Anju Aneja and Ms. Krishna Duhan for their valuable suggestions in select areas of the manuscript.

The authors acknowledge the efforts put forth by various researchers, authors, and websites especially their work done in the field of marriage and family. The authors want to especially mention a vote of thanks to all the learned people of various Indian communities consulted.

We are also deeply indebted to Mr. Rajesh Kashyap, Mr. Dharmesh Kumar and Mr. Gulshan Sharma for typing and re-typing the manuscript neatly and efficiently.

We express our appreciation to Mr. G.S. Bhatia, Managing Director of Deep & Deep Publications Pvt. Ltd. at New Delhi who has overseen the entire project with great competence.

Finally, the authors want to thank their respective families. We are unconditionally grateful and give our undying love to them for their understanding and acceptance of our passion to complete this complex, difficult and time consuming task than originally perceived. Dr. Amiteshwar Ratra wants to specially thank for the adultation provided by her family, her father Mr. Sujan Singh's infinite best wishes and blessings, her mother Mrs. Ravinder Kaur Singh's earnest prayers, enthusiasm and encouragement, affection of her brothers and loving support of her sister-in-laws, Pramod & Santosh, Harpinder & Jasveen, and Tejinder & Harnam, and lively tit-bits provided by Mansimar, Harnoor, Kanjnoor, Yamini and Mayank lightened the mood while writing the book. Dr. Praveen Kaur recalls the inspiration provided by her late husband Mr. R.P. Singh. Dr. Kaur fondly praises the love and affection of her sons and their wives, Harmeet & Manleen and Ardaman & Madhvika and angelic smiles of her grandson Gurmehar. Dr. Sudha Chhikara thanks her husband Dr. B.S. Chhikara for his ever willing co-operation and love and affection of her children Abhimanyu and Abhilasha.

Deep in our hearts, we appreciate the help received from those whose names we might have missed.

DR. AMITESHWAR RATRA
DR. PRAVEEN KAUR
DR. SUDHA CHHIKARA

1

Marriage

The evolution of concept of marriage is difficult thing to trace because birth of man is the birth of marriage. Marriage is a practice that seems as old as the human race itself. Marriage and family are closely associated with the being of each other. Man is social animal hence enjoys the company of his fellow human beings. He shares his happiness and sufferings with other fellow beings and at the same time competes and want to gain power on his neighbour. To enjoy the various fruits of life, it was essential to regulate the behaviour of group members for which he has developed various institutions.

UNDERSTANDING THE INSTITUTION OF MARRIAGE

Institution is a term used for any social structure instituted for the welfare of others. It is governed by certain values, rules, regulations, laws, customs and traditions. It is well organized in its structure and functioning. Institutions once started continue for a long time and therefore, it is characterized by permanence. Groups are different from institutions as groups may be temporary which may be organized for good or bad purpose. It may or may not have the welfare motive behind its formation. In groups, members are important, but, in institutions, welfare motives are important than the person or his motives. Institutions continue to live for ages and were created by our ancestors. The term institution is also different from organization on the basis of motives, permanence and membership. In organizations motives may be destructive and membership essential. Rules and regulations change with leadership, whereas, changes in institutions are not easy to occur.

Thus, institution is formulated with a welfare motive, is governed by the rules and regulations and is permanent and continued relationship in nature. There are many institutions in society. Marriage is one of them. The physical union must have existed from the very beginning of life to satisfy sexual need. The Old Testament states bond of Adam and Eve started life on Earth. As the humanity developed and transferred itself from nomadic life to settled life, gave rise to psycho-social needs in order to satisfy these needs, need to systematize relations, to stabilize society our ancestors must have developed rules, regulations which became customs and traditions. Thus, the marriage system was instituted. The main primary goal of marriage is preservation of human race. It is a social institution designed to perpetuate the human race. Personal gain is the secondary aim. For preservation of race, we not only, reproduce children but also rear, protect and educate them. Parents for life long take responsibility of their children till they are fully grown up to take their own care. In early history of marriage, we find dharma and progeny the primary aims and rati (sex or personal satisfaction) as the tertiary goal. However, in recent history, sex for personal satisfaction has grown so large. In all cultures, the social roles were dominant in past, signifying rearing, protecting and educating. Marriage leads to family and related religious, moral, sociological, psychological, physical, economic, legal, recreational and educational relationships. Any society not dedicated to the social purposes of the marriage is likely to extinct. It is the social task imposed by nature that makes marriage an institution—a social relationship tending towards permanence. Without its stability and perpetuity healthy child rearing is not possible.

Almost in all cultures, marriages are performed with religious ceremonies. Religion imposes certain controls through rules and traditions. Sociological relationship makes it to celebrate it in presence of many people, following social customs and traditions. Marriages have to be governed by laws. All these aspects contribute towards the stable and happy marriages. It is the knowledge and mastery of these relationships, which constitutes the art of a successful and happy marriage.

MEANING AND DEFINITION OF MARRIAGE

Marriage is one of the deepest and most complex web of human relations. It is the most essential part of society and social system as well. Radha Krishanan (1956) writes, "marriage is not a mere convention but an implicit condition of human society. It is an adjustment between the biological purposes of nature and the sociological purposes of man."

Marriage is union of man (or men) and woman (or women) in a rite defined by social custom and law and carrying with it specific economic, sexual and child-care responsibilities. This definition of marriage is very ancient which holds true even to day. In other words, a marriage is a legally recognized union between a man and a woman in which they are united sexually, cooperate economically, and may give birth to, adopt or rear children. The union is assumed to be permanent although in reality it may be dissolved by separation or divorce. According to Edward Westermarck (1891) marriage is a universal human institution that had been part of the social structure of all settled societies—a flexible institution existing in many forms. He also issued a famous dictum, "marriage is rooted in the family, not the family in marriage" (Mace, 1991). Therefore, marriage must be legally controlled and safeguarded by the community to assure continuity of the family. In Dictionary of Sociology, Duncan Mitchell (1978) defines marriage as, "socially sanctioned sex relationship involving two or more people of the opposite sex, whose relationship is expected to endure beyond time required for gestation and the birth of children."

Marriage has been more recently defined as a legally binding contract between a woman and a man that conveys certain rights and privileges including sexual exclusivity, legitimating of any children born of the union, and economic responsibilities. While most marriages involve an emotional commitment on the part of the two persons, this is not a requirement for a valid marriage (Axelson, 1985). Some are against the marriage. According to them, marriage has been thought of as mental illness. Therapist Karl Whittaker mused, "marriage produces hateful demons out of perfectly nice people while on the other hand, it is the only way to get a Ph.D. in interpersonal relationships" (Beavers, 1985). James Framo more seriously states, "aside from its alleged inherent absurdity, marriage is an incredibly intricate phenomenon, simultaneously existing on multiple levels, stretching back to the past and built on uncommunicable experiences" (Beavers, 1985).

PURPOSE, MOTIVES AND FUNCTIONS OF MARRIAGE

Marriage is a communion, getting together of two sexes for enjoyment and fulfilment. In the early stages of human history woman was 'truth' and the man was 'opinion' with respect to their progeny (Narayan Karan Reddy, 1978). In the middle ages, marriage was a clan-kinship and herd-relationship and in the later years, marriage has been viewed as a caste and a class barrier or a bondage. In the recent years there is evolution of marriage as a holy bondage of two souls. The existing patterns of marriage arrangements are quite different from those of the earlier forms. With the changing needs of the people in our dynamic society the purpose, motives and functions of marriage have kept on changing and evolving with the demand of its constituent members. Our Indian society is so complex in its structure, norms and values that it becomes difficult for social scientist to discover the real facts objectively. Marriage is a social agreement governed by social custom and tradition. Purposes and motives of marriage have been different at all phases of society. It cannot be said whether marriage institution started because of romantic love or animal lust.

CONCEPT OF MARRIAGE IN INDIA

In primitive form, marriage was based on two opposite needs or desires of men and women. Men are more independent and power controlling. Women, on the other hand, are more dependent and have desire to submit. Thus, the union of two satisfied each other's enduring needs. The primitive form of marriage was different from what we see today.

In Hindu Dharma, marriage is viewed as a sacrament and not a contract. Hindu marriage is a life-long commitment of one wife and one husband, and is the strongest social bond that takes place between a man and a woman. Grihastha Ashram (the householder stage), the second of the four stages of life begins when a man and a woman marry and start a household. For a Hindu, marriage is the only way to continue to family, and, thereby, repay his debt to his/her ancestors.

In Hindu view, marriage is not a concession to human weakness, but a means for spiritual growth. Man and woman are soul mates who, through the institution of marriage, can direct the energy associated with their individual instincts and passion into the progress of their souls, union of mind and personality in pursuit of Dharma, Kama and Moksha. The base of happy marital union is love, harmony and respect for the partner.

In ancient India, marriage was considered necessary for the complete fulfilment of the purpose of life of men and women without which it was believed they could not achieve "Moksha." It was considered necessary for women due to tradition and culture and above all because of the complete economic dependence of women on men. A necessity, because of the tradition and culture to which she must adhere to or because of the financial and social security. Later on, women realized the need for genuine companionship, emotional and biological needs. Promilla Kapur (1973) in her study writes that there is a shift in the need for educated Indian women to marry from need for social security, physical security, need for belonging to a husband, home and children, to fulfil one's sacred and social duty, for mutual love to mutual companionship, material comforts, satisfaction of emotional and physical needs, for personal advantages outweighing the disadvantages of living alone, for personal convenience and for possessing a husband, home and children and have desire to perpetuate ownership.

Traditional Hindu marriage was based on absolute trust, mutual affection, capacity to adjust and sharing the responsibilities equally. At every stage of the wedding ceremony when the incantations (Mantras) from the Vedas were uttered, prayers were offered to ensure a smooth life. The duties were demarcated and freedom given to both. The union being sacred, the vow did not give room for separation. There was no scope for differences of opinion and should an occasion arise, both should respect the sentiments of the other, thereby, ensuring that no confrontation takes place.

In the ideal form of marriage laid down by the Indo-Aryan culture, "marriage was and is considered a ceremonial gift of the bride by her father (or other appropriate relative) to the bridegroom, in order that both may together fulfil three of the standard four purposes of human existence." According to the Hindu Philosophy and religion, marriage is to propagate family, 'Vivha' is meant to propagate 'Kutumba'. Brahmashastras specify that marriage is followed by 'grihastha-ashrama' meaning the householder's life. The four purposes of human existence according to Hindu religion are Dharma, Artha, Kama and Moksha. Dharma means religious duty towards society, Artha means economic duty or earning, Kama means satisfaction of sexual desires and Moksha means salvation, the end of life and union of atma (soul) with Parmatma (God). Thus, according to Hindu view of life, it is very necessary for a man and a woman to marry, in order to achieve the four purusharthas—Dharma, Artha, Kama and Moksha—the four great ideals of life. The aims of Hindu marriage are 'dharma' meaning righteousness, 'praja' meaning progeny and 'rati' meaning pleasure. In Indian thought, though sex is given an important place as a necessary function of marriage but not very important function. Sex is the least desirable aim of marriage in orthodox Hindu thought. Traditional Hindu concept of marriage is that of religious sacrament. There are many sacred rites to be performed during a Hindu marriage which enables one to fulfil religious as well as social obligations, religious and moral on the one hand, and social and economic on the other hand. Various rites performed are like homa, panigrahan, saptapadi discussed in Chapter 6 in detail. For a Hindu, marriage is a 'Sanskara' and as such it is a sacrament which could be broken only by death. According to Hindu philosophy, marriage is a union of two souls and not simply of two bodies. It is a religious bond which cannot be dissolved at will. The ideal form of Hindu marriage is a means of fulfilment of life, the true purpose being, a complete companionship in fighting the battle of life together. It is richly rewarding relationship in life, if stable, endures till life's end. Kapadia (1958) writes, "traditional Hindu marriage was a social duty towards the family and the community and there was little idea of individual interest."

The Hindu marriage was ideally monogamous. Prabhu (1954) while referring to the Sutras of Apastamba and Gautama, Vol. II, writes, "so long as the householder (grihastha) has already a wife who is liable to take part with him in his religious duties as a grihastha, and, also has borne him issues, he must not take another woman for his wife." The Vedic Gods are monogamous. The rules for the performance of domestic religious rituals do not allow for the possibility of an additional wife. Mutual conjugal fidelity is emphasized in the wedding hymn and in philosophical discussions of marriage (Goode, 1963). Divorce was permissible to the wife if husband is of bad character or is long gone abroad or is guilty of high treason or is dangerous to his wife or has become an outcast or has lost virility (Radha Krishnan, 1956).

With the passage of time, change in the roles of individuals enacted in the society, purposes to marry, among the young generation is taking place. Earlier marriage was between the two families—the bride and the groom's family. Families took initiative in searching for a matrimonial alliance in accordance with their family status, caste, character, and education. Unlike the prevailing custom now, in olden times the eligible boy's father used to go in search of a girl from a noble family and seek her parent's approval. Marriage was considered to be a partnership especially for wife even after her husband's death. Widow remarriage was prohibited and sati system (wife burning in her husband's pyre) gained approval of the society.

In the present form, marriage is more between two individuals rather than two families. Both the bride and the groom practice more free will as opposed earlier. In this, they can either get the approval of their elders and get married or marry without their permission and get their marriage registered under the law of the land.

As the purposes of marriage change so does the forms of marriage. The ideal Hindu marriage is a lifetime commitment, the true purpose being a complete companionship in fighting the battle of life together. Dr. Radha Krishnan (1956) further added, "marriage is an institution, is a device for the expression and development of life."

The religious point of view calls marriage as sacrament and spiritual binding not in one but in all births. It was believed that marriages are made in heaven. The social point stresses it as union of two families and not only two persons. Ideally, therefore, its purpose is not only the generation and nurturing of children into socially useful citizens but it is the enrichment of the personality of husband and wife. Each supplements the life of the other, to achieve completeness. It aims at the individual's biological, emotional, social and spiritual fulfilment and development through a relationship, which neither could achieve in isolation. It is for the development of whole mankind to produce useful members of future society. Many times individual interests and pleasures are sacrificed for the sake of others. Kapadia (1958) writes, "marriage was a social (and religious) duty towards the family and the community, and there was little idea of individual interest." Manu, the lawgiver, accepted marriage as a duty and not enjoyment. He rejected romantic marriages as unworthy because it is based on lust. Romantic love leads to sexuality, encourages unwise choice and threatens the stability of the family. Divorce and remarriages were not allowed and are still not encouraged in the Indian society.

Marriage ideally provides for love, security, companionship, social acceptability, legitimized sex, love, homogeneity of age, race and sex, a stability of environment and identity for children, an opportunity for personal growth, a division of labour, ego support, an opportunity for commitment to each other and for the attainment of common goals, more organized life and time saving arrangement. These are the positive goals achieved for the welfare of society and has been the traditional concept of marriage.

In India, traditional marriages fulfil many of the criteria of social institutions. It provides marital satisfaction, social and personal happiness. Marriage had a more social origin and reason rather than individual origin and purpose. Through marriage, children are born of this relation who in return brings happiness. Though, couples may find some disturbances, dissatisfactions and problems in their life but these are temporary. Both partners and families make adjustment, though it is mostly the wife and her parental family who does most of the adjustment to make a marriage succeed.

Society being in a dynamic state has brought about change

in concept of marriage. In the present times, it has resulted in loss of social individuality, loss of privacy, dissatisfaction with spouse, feeling of being trapped, not accommodating with each other, sexual frustration due to mismatch, being tied down, problems with in-laws, influence and interference of wife's parents.

The Western ideology of marriage is finding its way in India now. Like in the West, people here also regard marriage as a personal matter concerned with love making, home making and living together. Most of the marriages in India are still performed by sacred rites and rituals but the reasons of marriage are changing. The traditional concept of love was complete submission of wife to her husband, Pati is Parmeshwar, husband is God and wife was given the status of Ardhangini, the other half of man. Both, man and woman are said to be incomplete without each other. The Indian philosophy views it as fulfiling obligations towards the family, society and mankind, whereas, in the west, marriage is considered essential for the fulfilment of personal needs and happiness.

THEORIES OF MARRIAGE AND THE FAMILY

A theory is a set of general principle or concepts used to explain data and to make predictions that may be empirically (experimentally) tested (Miller, 1986). Theories are important because they can suggest directions for research according to the questions they raise. The theories we discuss in this chapter are symbolic interaction theory, social exchange, structural functionalism, conflict and family systems.

Symbolic Interaction Theory

Symbolic interaction is a theory that looks at how people interact with each other. Symbolic interactionists are concerned with relationships. When we feel that our partner really understands us (or doesn't), that we communicate well (or don't), that we live in harmony with each other (or don't), we are expressing feelings which form the core of symbolic interaction research. Symbolic interactionists study the interactions that make up a relationship.

An interaction is a reciprocal act. Interactions are the everyday words and actions that take place between people. For an interaction to occur, there must be at least two persons who both act and respond to each other. These interactions are conducted through symbols, words or gestures. During interaction we interpret or define these symbols and then react to them. In the 1920's Ernest Burgess (1926) defined the family as a "unity of interacting personalities." This definition is critical to symbolic interaction theory and in the development of marriage and family studies. Marriage and families consist of individuals who interact with one another over a period of time which then define the nature of our family as loving family, conflict-ridden family, emotionally distant family, high-achieving family, and so on.

A social role is an established pattern of behaviour that exists independently of a person such as the role of wife or husband existing independently of any particular husband or wife.

Symbolic interactionists study how the sense of self is maintained in the process of acquiring these roles. Families are "created" by their members, according to symbolic interactionalists. Each family has its own unique personality and dynamics created by its members' interactions. Structures are significant only in so far as they affect family dynamics.

Critique

This theory suffers from several drawbacks. The theory tends to minimize the role of power in relationships like understanding of resolution of conflict. Symbolic interaction doesn't fully account for the psychological aspects of human life, especially personality and temperament. The theory emphasizes individualism. It encourages competence in interpersonal relationships, and it values individual happiness and fulfilment over stability, duty, responsibility and other familial values. The theory does not place marriage or family within a larger social context. It disregards economic discrimination against minorities and women.

Social Exchange Theory

Social exchange theory measures our actions and relationships on a cost-benefit basis. People maximize their rewards and minimize their costs by employing their resources to gain the most favourable outcome. An outcome is basically figured by the equation, Reward-Cost=Outcome. When the emotional cost outweighs the benefits of the relationships, the relationships will end. In personal relationships, resources, rewards and costs are more likely to be things such as love, companionship, status, power, fear, loneliness and so on.

As people enter into relationships, they have certain resources—either tangible or intangible—that others consider valuable, such as, intelligence, warmth, good looks or high social status or huge bank balance.

A corollary to exchange is equity: exchanges that occur between people have to be fair, to balance out. Some researchers suggest that people are most happy when they get what they feel they deserve in a relationship (Hatfield and Walster, 1981). When partners recognize that they are in an inequitable relationship, they generally feel uncomfortable, angry or distressed.

Critique

Social exchange theory assumes that individuals are rational, calculating animals, weighing the costs and rewards of their relationships. In reality, we are sometimes rational and sometimes not. Sometimes we act altruistically like parent-child relations, true love relations without expecting any reward. The theory also has difficulty ascertaining the value of costs, rewards and resources, for these can be highly individualistic.

Structural Functionalism Theory

Structural functionalism theory explains how society works, how families relate to the larger society and to their own members. The theory is used largely in sociology and anthropology, disciplines that focus on the study of society rather than individuals. It discuses what functions the family serves for society, what functional requirements are performed by family members for the family and what needs the family meets for its individual members.

Society is like a tree, in so far as, it has different structures that perform functions for its survival. These structures are called sub-systems. The sub-systems are the major institutions, such as the family, religion, government and economy. The family provides new members for society through procreation and socializes its members so that they fit into society. According to structural functionalists, the family molds the kind of personalities it needs to carry out its functions. It encourages different personality traits for men such as instrumental traits like competitiveness, coolness, self-confidence and rationality, and, in women, expressive traits like warmth, emotionality, nurturing and sensitivity.

Critique

Although structural functionalism has been an important theoretical approach to the family, it has declined insignificance in recent decades for several reasons. Firstly, this theory cannot be empirically tested for being 'right' or 'wrong'. Second, the functions of a particular system are not clear. Third, structural functionalism has a conservative bias against change. Aspects that reflect stability are called functional, and those that encourage instability are called dysfunctional. Traditional roles are functional, but non-traditional ones are dysfunctional. Finally, structural functionalism looks at the family abstractly. It looks at it formally, from a distance far removed from the daily lives and struggles of men, women and children. It views the family in terms of functions and roles, the very life of family, family interactions are absent.

Conflict Theory

Conflict theory holds that life involves discord. Conflict theorists see society not as basically cooperative but as divided, with individuals and groups in conflicts with each other. They try to identify the competing forces. Conflict theorists would agree that love and affection are important elements in marriages and families, but they believe that conflict and power are also fundamental. Marriages and families are composed of individuals with different personalities, ideas, values, tastes and goals. Each person is not always in harmony with every other person in the family. Conflict theorists do not believe that conflict is bad, instead, they think it is a natural part of family life. Families always have disagreements. Families differ in the number of underlying conflicts of interest, the degree of underlying hostility, and the nature and extent of the expression of conflict. Family members have different resources and amounts of power. Power could arise from legitimacy—the belief that the person is entitled to prevail by right like authority because of being head of the family or being your parent, money, physical coercion, and, the power of love.

Everyone in the family has power, although the power may be different and unequal.

Critique

A number of difficulties arise in conflict theory. First, conflict theory derives from politics, in which self-interest, egotism and competition are dominant elements. The theory does not emphasize on people's behaviour is also characterized by self-sacrifice, cooperation and love or bonding which distinguish the family from all other groups in society. Second, conflict theorists assume that differences lead to conflict. But differences does not necessarily/always imply conflict it may also be accepted, tolerated or appreciated. Third, conflict in families is not easily measured or evaluated. Families live much of their lives privately, and outsiders are not always aware of whatever conflict exists or how pervasive it is. Also, much overt conflict is avoided because it is regulated through family and societal rules.

Family Systems Theory

Family systems theory combines two sociological theories, structural functionalism and symbolic interaction, to form a psychotherapeutic theory. Mark Kassop (1987) notes that family systems theory creates a bridge between sociology and family therapy. Family systems theory views the family as a structure of related parts or sub-systems. Each part carries out certain functions. These parts include the spousal sub-system, the parent/child sub-system, the parental sub-system, and the personal sub-system. For the family to function well, the sub-systems must be kept separate (Minuchin, 1981). When the boundaries of the sub-systems blur, as in incest, or spill over into each other, as in parent's conflict affecting child, the family becomes dysfunctional.

As in symbolic interaction, interaction is important in systems theory. A family consists of its members, their interactions, communication, roles, beliefs and rules. The structure of marriage is determined by how the spouses act in relation to each other over time (Lederer and Jackson, 1968). Researchers and therapists believe that interactions must be studied in the context of the family system. The family has a structure that can be seen in its day-to-day interactions. The family has a purpose, it has a goal to remain intact. It seeks homeostasis or stability. A well functioning family constantly changes and adapts to maintain itself in response to its members and the environment.

Critique

The basic concepts of the family systems theory are still in dispute, even among the theory's adherents (Melito, 1985). Family systems theory originated in clinical settings in which psychiatrists, clinical psychologists and therapists tried to explain the dynamics of dysfunctional families. Although its use has spread beyond clinicians, its greatest success is still in the analysis and treatment of dysfunctional families.

2

Types of Marriage

The evolution of marriage is a difficult thing to trace for the birth of man is the birth of marriage. Marriage is a union of man and woman. It indicates relationship between one or more men to one or more women. Marriage indicates a long lasting bond between the husband and the wife. Marital relationship between man and woman lasts even after the sexual satisfaction is obtained. Marriage requires social approval. Marriage is one of the universal social institutions. A union of man and woman becomes a marital bond only when the society gives its approval. When marriage is given the hallmark of social approval, it becomes legal contract. Marriage imposes certain rights and duties on both the husband and the wife.

Marriage is an institution of society, which can have very different implications in different cultures. Cultures vary according to whether they emphasize marital solidarity over lineal solidarity or *vice versa*. Societies with strongly developed extended family systems emphasize lineal solidarity over marital solidarity. Marriage may be defined as a culturally approved relationship of one man and one woman (monogamy) of one man and two or more women (polygyny), or of one woman and two or more men (polyandry) in which there is cultural endorsement of sexual intercourse between the marital partners of opposite sex and, generally, the expectation that children be born of the relationship. Therefore, marriage must be legally controlled and safeguarded by the community to assure continuity of the family.

India is a composite society. It is a mixture of different religions, races, tribes, cultures and castes. Hindus and Muslim traditional marriage systems have been persisting in India from so many centuries; to some extent there is a fusion of these two religions in India bringing a mixed and composite character of Indian society in general. These marriage systems have experienced some changes with the passage of time similar to the changes in other facts of life of these people. It has been due to the influence of western culture and philosophy dominated by democratic and secular values and thinking brought some changes in the deep-rooted social and cultural institutions of India society as a whole. The renaissance, reformation, French revolution, American revolution, Russian revolutions brought lot of changes in the social fabric of the entire modern society of today. Indian society has also been influenced by British rule and its freedom struggle. The rise of industrial revolutions and urbanization brought a new modern culture based on free will and thinking. The emergence of scientific thinking and mass media collaboration across the world in the twentieth century brought lot of changes in each and every facet and walk of human life across the world. The mechanization, urbanization, and modernization have oriented people to materialism, individualism and self-orientation, which have resulted to changes in the marriage and family systems in the Indian society in the twentieth century.

The aims and forms of marriages in the past and present times have changed. The existing patterns of marriage arrangements are quite different from those of the earlier forms. Earlier it was a necessity, now it is a need. Earlier it was sexual and economic. Now it is for psychosocial order. Hence, its forms have remained changing.

TYPES OF MARRIAGES IN THE INDIAN CONTEXT

Manu describes eight forms of marriage as approved in India. The recent forms of marriage have replaced the earlier forms of marriage. Classification of ancient Indian marriages included Brahma, Daiva, Prajapatya, Arsha, Rakshasa, Asura, Gandharva and Paisacha.

Brahma Marriage

'Brahma' is the form of marriage in which the father of the bride invites the bridegroom. The bride decorated with ornaments was given as a gift to the bridegroom after enquiring his family status, health, character and learning.

Brahma or ceremonial form of marriage, in this the parents seek and secure a boy for their daughter and invite him to accept her as his wife. This is the most ancient marital form still prevalent in the country. The union is sanctified by a well-defined series of rituals, including the gifting of the girl (panigrahana), acceptance by the groom who makes solemn with fire as witness (saptapadi), oblations and offerings (homa), and the propitiation of the assemblage of elders on the occasion (sabhapuja).

Daiva Marriage

In the 'Daiva' or divine form of marriage, the bride is given to the priest who performs sacrifices for her father; in this the bride is given as a sacrificial fees. The bride has no choice for her husband. Wife is well dressed and heavily ornamented at the time of marriage.

Arsha Marriage

In 'Arsha' or priestly form of marriage, the bridegroom presents a pair of cattle, which is, a cow and a bullock to the father or elders of the bride. It is not considered as sale of the bride but it is compensation to the dowry given by the bride's parents at the time of the marriage. In the above three marital forms rituals and solemn ceremonies form an important ingredient, the parents of the girl take an active role.

Prajapatya Marriage

The 'Prajapatya' implies a form of marriage which is a gift of the bride to the bridegroom on the condition that they should never cease to practice the principles of 'dharma' that is, social righteousness in Manu-dharmashastra. In this, the girl is given away to the young man of her choice with a simple farewell prayer that the two may live happily ever after. It is the girl here that takes the initiative for choosing her spouse and her parents passively participate in the function.

Gandharva Marriage

In the 'gandharva' or clandestine type of marriage involves romantic elopement. In this type, parents are altogether dispensed. When the boy and the girl have agreed to marry, they retire, unknown to people around, to a secluded woody retreat and there in the presence of the fire brought from a learned Brahmin's house get married by simple affirmations of love and fidelity. As the marriage is taken place in the presence of the sacred fire, it is binding on the parents of both the parties. It is obligatory for the bride's parents later to recognise and ratify the marriage by a formal function or else face legal proceedings. This marriage may also take place through a simple ceremony of an exchange of garlands. Vatsyayana in Kama-Sutra has considered this an ideal type of marriage. This marriage took place for fulfilment of carnal desires. Though, it was not a popular form of marriage but was a sanctioned form of marriage. This marriage took place after the consent of both bride and the bridegroom. Kalidasa's great drama Abijnana Shakuntala deals with this type of marriage between Dushyanta and Shakuntala.

Asura Marriage

The 'asura-vivaha' or mercenary marriage is the marriage by purchase. In this, the bride's people receive monetary gratifications from the bridegroom's people; bride price is decided upon by mutual consultations. Marriage by bride price was common in Vaishyas and Sudras than among Brahmins and Kashtriyas.

Rakshasa Marriage

In the 'Rakshasa' or diabolical form of marriage, a girl was forcibly carried away from her parents house much against her will. Neither romance nor sacraments played any role in such marriages; might and force were solely on the scene.

Paisacha Marriage

In the 'Paisacha' or ghastly marriage, maiden is abducted

while she is asleep or intoxicated and then raped and rogue/rapist was allowed by custom and law to have there after the girl as his wife.

Marriage by Capture and Swayamvara

The other traditional forms of marriages, which though not clearly mentioned in Rigveda but existed were the marriages by capture and swayamvara. The former is when one king attacks the other king and captures his kingdom; he would marry with him the daughter of the vanquished. In the case of swayamvara marriage, there are many competitors; the bride is asked to garland a person of her own free choice. The bride had the choice to select her husband amongst the worthy men selected by her parents. In this case there could be competition and the would-be-grooms were expected to show exceptional acts of bravery. In the Epics of Ramayana and Mahabharata, the marriages of Sita and Draupadi are exemplary under this category. In the former, Lord Rama breaks the bow, and in the latter, Arjuna aims at the eye of the fish to win the hands of their respective brides.

These above forms of marriage have undergone various stages of transitions and modifications. Though, the basic sanctions of the Hindu marriage have been maintained. It is still considered marriage until death do us part.

Besides, these traditional forms of marriages, India also illustrates the universal types such as polygamy and endogamy. Monogamy is the ideal marriage form universally approved and widely practiced in India as elsewhere in the world. At a given time, there is only one spouse, the husband and the wife. Polygamy is the practice of having more than one wife or husband at a given time. Polygyny is the practice of having two or more wives, prevails in several communities and tribes, especially among the Nagas, the Bhils, the Gonds, the Todas and the Lushais. Polyandry is the practice of having two or more husbands, is common among the Botas, the Khasas and the Todas. The polyandrous practices of the Jaunsari Bawar in Dehra Dun, the Himalayan tribes and the matriarchal Nair society in Kerala are well known. Tibetan communities are also predominantly polyandrous.

Considering the high divorce rate, monogamy may no longer be the best way of describing the today's marriage forms, especially of the western society. They may be called as serial monogamy or modified polygamy, because one person may have several spouses over his or her lifetime.

Polygyny is of two types: sororal polygyny and non-sororal polygyny. Sororal polygyny is a type of marriage in which the wives are invariably the sisters. The Latin word 'soror' stands for sister. When several sisters are simultaneously, or potentially the spouses of the same man, the practice is called 'sororate'. Non-sororal polygyny is a type of marriage in which the wives are not related as sisters. Polyandry is also of two types—fraternal polyandry and non-fraternal polyandry. Fraternal polyandry or adelphic polyandry is when several brothers share the same wife. This practice of being mate, actual or potential, to one's husband's brothers is called 'levirate'. It is prevalent among the Todas. Non-fraternal polyandry is when the husbands need not have any close relationship prior to the marriage. The wife goes to spend some time with each husband. So long as a woman lives with one of her husbands, the others have no claim over her. Nair polyandry is of this type. Tibetans too have this type.

Group marriage means the marriage of two or more women with two or more men. Here, the husbands are common husbands and wives are common wives. Children are regarded as the children of the entire group as a whole. Some of the tribals in Australia, India, Tibet and Ceylon are believed to have practiced group marriage.

Endogamy is a rule of marriage in which the life-partners are to be selected within the group, and the group may be caste, class, tribe, race, village or religious group. Thus, we have caste endogamy, class endogamy, sub-caste endogamy, race endogamy, tribal endogamy and such other forms. Endogamy prohibits marriage outside the group. Exogamy is a rule of marriage in which an individual has to marry outside his own group. It prohibits marrying within the group. The rule of exogamy insists that the so-called blood relatives shall neither have marital connections nor sexual contacts among themselves. Near relatives are not supposed to marry among themselves. But the degree of nearness differs from community to community. Exogamy assumes various forms in India. The Hindu practice of one marrying outside one's own 'gotra' is gotra exogamy. Parvara exogamy is that those who belong to the same 'parvara' (uttering the name of a common saint at religious functions) cannot marry among themselves. Village exogamy is the practice of marrying outside their village like among Naga, Garo, Munda. Pinda exogamy is that those who belong to the same 'pinda' (or sapinda) cannot marry within themselves (Pinda means common parentage or immediate ancestors).

It may be noted that endogamy and exogamy are not mutually exclusive. In some societies both the rules may co-exist. For example, in India, both are practiced by the Hindus, castes and sub-castes are endogamous in nature. But 'gotra' a small unit of sub-caste is exogamous. Such rules differ from society to society. Today, there is a greater trend towards exogamous marriages. Endogamy is said to be conservative. It is widely criticized. Exogamy is appreciated as progressive and more scientific. Exogamy has brought peoples of various castes, races, religious groups and tribes together. It can effectively reduce social distance among people and, encourage and support social solidarity and communal unity.

Hypergamy, man belonging to the higher castes marrying the girl belonging to the lower caste was permitted, while hypogamy, man belonging to the lower caste marrying the woman belonging to the higher caste was severally condemned in the Smriti texts in India. In today's present age, the most common criteria of mate selection among the youth is homogamy. Homogamy refers to the fact that most persons select a marriage partner who resembles themselves in certain ways.

Arranged Marriages

After an explosion of love marriages in the 1970's and 1980's, arranged weddings are back in fashion among India's growing bread of busy professionals. Many Indians who spend the better part of their day with just a computer for company are turning to their parents to arrange their marriages through family connections, newspaper ads, marriage bureaus and wedding Web sites.

A recent survey by the Family Planning Association of India published in the *Times of India* (2001) newspaper found almost 60 percent of India's urban youth age 15 to 29 chose arranged over love marriages. The difference between now and when their parents were tying the knot is that arranged marriages today don't just look at traditional factors. In fact, with increasing westernization, a number of families are shedding their obsession with family backgrounds, words like compatibility and relationship have entered the lexicon of arranged marriages. Education, professional status and income are often more important than family background.

Two decades ago, love marriages were frequently a form of rebellion against Indian's traditional lifestyle. Today, people are prizing arranged marriages as part of the country's heritage. The popularity of arranged marriages is not just a fallout of the hard-nosed professionalism that has left people little time. It is also influenced by a burst of films romanticizing arranged marriages and the extravagance surrounding the traditional wedding rituals.

The custom of arranged marriages in India has survived migration and modernization remaining central to the fabric of society. The need to marry someone in your minute sub-caste is still followed by many of the people involved in arranged marriages.

In Indian society, the emphasis on the family is much stronger than in the Western world. Indian often live with their extended family, so in a practical sense the mate of an adult child must be a fit for the whole family, not just the individual. Additionally, there is the common cultural idea that love follows a marriage, that love is learned as your ties to your marriage partner grow. Many Indians believe that you chose a marriage partner based on a variety of compatibility factors like family, caste, job, education level and that with time love then grows. They believe that love alone is an immature, romantic frivolity and, that is, a poor foundation on which to base a life-long partnership.

Arranged marriages have been around in India as long as probably the institution of marriage itself. Aunts, purohits, nais or middle persons have always played an intrinsic and pivotal role in it, from its conception to implementation. As times have progressed, they proved that they could adapt to the changing times by updating themselves with the latest jargons, terminologies and sometimes even, technologies, necessary to perform this 'task'. The underlying task here is, of course, "arranging" a marriage.

Until recently, messengers attached to a particular caste, were ideal matchmakers for all families since they were professional news carriers of the community. They would deliver invitations for weddings and festivals, announce births and deaths, and intimately knew all the families in the community. Families with children of a marriageable age would approach them for help in finding spouses.

These days a family friend or distance relative approaches a family for a match. This ensures that no direct insult or humiliation is conferred upon the family which makes the first move, should the proposed match not be amenable to the other family. Advertising in daily newspapers remains a well-established tradition for parents of prospective brides and grooms to state their requirements. In cities such as New Delhi, the seat of Indian middle class families, the advertisements echo the same requirement for girls and boys, university graduates who are tall and fair of complexion. Parents with dark-skinned daughters have a harder task getting their daughters married.

While to many people raised in the west, this might sound odd. It is important to remember that, in India, arranged marriage be seen as an act of love. Since, marriage is one of the most important decisions and because divorce is not accepted among most Indians, it is imperative that the marriage choice is carefully planned. How can a young person make such an important decision on his/her own? Instead, the parents and family look for certain traits in a marriage partner. Some desirable traits looked for in both male and female are matching levels of education, matching cultures, close parental cities, matching religions, and matching eating patterns to just name a few. Potential bridegrooms come under close scrutiny for several areas of the matching process. Can they support the bride? Can they appear to be men who will make good husbands and fathers? Often, the bride and her in-laws after marriage is what are called a joint family. Because of this, the groom's family is also brought under scrutiny. Do the women of the household seem well cared for? Do they have a big enough house for another grandchildren? Does the family have a good reputation? Potential brides also come under scrutiny by the boy's parents. Since it is a commonly held belief that bride has to uphold family's honour and pride, the girl must be from good family and have good manners, respectable and have no taint on her name. She has the makings of a good wife and mother. Will she work after marriage or stay at home? There are so many factors to weigh, that we cannot list them all.

Often, this turns into an interview process where photos are provided of the boy/girl in question along with his/her life and family. If that meets with approval, arrangements will be made for the parents to meet the family. Traditionally, however, the bride and the groom would not even see each other until the day of marriage or after. Today, while most marriages are still arranged, times have changed. There is usually a small courtship period, bride and groom can meet and talk under the careful watch of a guardian. Also, if either one of the two does not approve, the marriage is likely to be cancelled. Very few families today "force" marriages upon their children.

The arranged marriage has adjusted to modernization. Prospective grooms were once not even allowed to see the photograph of their prospective brides so as to preserve an unmarried woman's purity, her most valuable asset, by the 1930s, the couple exchanged photographs, in order to decide if they liked each other. Now, the couple meets, talks and discusses important issues before deciding to marry or not.

Of course, with any society, you have those people who will not just adapt and change. There are places time has not moved forward. For those people, they carry on their lives as their parents have. Shockingly, there are still some forced marriages and child brides.

Many Indians contend that arranged marriages are more successful than marriages in the West, particularly given the latter's staggering divorce rates. Romantic love does not necessarily lead to a good marriage, and often fails once the passion dissipates, they argue. Real love flows from a properly arranged union between two individuals.

It goes without saying that no marriage, not even an arranged one, is inured from basic incompatibility or abuse. But the arranged marriage does have its advantages. Living with the extended family—daughters traditionally live with their in-laws including, brothers-in-law and their wives and children—means a free staff of child minders. Apart from the economic savings of a family home, shocks such as a death or the loss of a job can be absorbed. The system cares for elderly parents and grandparents who are generally isolated in western societies.

Also, because the arranged marriage tends to be a union of two families of strong moral and cultural values it provides checks and balances against areas that may splinter it, such as infidelity. Above all, it is a buffer against one of the biggest modern day ills—the despair of feeling isolated in a cold world.

With most unions between individuals from the same background, the arranged marriage reflects and reinforces the social, economic, geographic and historical diversity of India itself. More like a continent than a country, India is made up of many states, with as many languages, thousands of dialects, major world religions, hundreds of sub-religions, an outlawed but still practiced caste system amongst Hindus, and an informal class and economic differentiation amongst Christians and Muslims.

The Indian girl-child and boy-child remain just that, the property and extensions of their families, until they are married. For the female, ownership changes hands from father to husband to son. But, for millions of women from India, an arranged marriage is not a matter of choice. It is about the union of two families, in a community, in a caste, in a religion, in a province, and in a country. It is what defines India's *status quo*, which is ultimately male-dominated. A girl is marriageable from age 18, and parents get worried if she remains unmarried past 24 or 25. It is acceptable for a boy to remain unmarried till his late 20s, but after that questions are asked about his desirability as a husband. This age criteria does not necessary apply to a growing urban middle class population, in metropolitans specially, New Delhi or Mumbai.

Most people tend to equate Indian marriages with arranged marriage. The parents in order to meet this domestic obligation prepare themselves mentally and, more importantly, financially when their child reaches marriageable age. They search for a suitable partner keeping in mind the societal rules regarding caste, creed, natal chart, and financial and social status of the family. Traditionally, it is the girl's parents who bear the cost of the wedding and to jumpstart their daughter's married life they shower her with gifts and ornaments to take to her in in-laws family. Unfortunately, this has aggravated people's greed culminating in the many evils of dowry system.

It is incumbent on the girl's family to make the first move towards a matrimonial union. Many young women have to have huge dowries attached to them to ensure marriage. A price is placed on the boy's head based on his education, economic and social status. Many fathers go heavily into debt, even bankrupt, trying to pay for the dowry. In villages, dowries are given in the form of cattle, land and jewelry. In the towns and cities, dowries are given in the form of hundreds of thousands of rupees (Indian currency), furniture, jewelry, and expensive household items and even homes and expensive foreign holidays.

The deal is completed either discreetly and subtly in the upper class educated families, or more crudely in lower-income homes. The phrase "bride burning" was coined in India after several young brides had their saris lit on fire in front of a gas stove either by their husbands or in-laws because of their father's failure to meet demands for a bigger dowry.

In Indian Muslim families, the boy's family takes the first step to ask for the girl. First, a respected family of equal status of the girl's family is selected; its antecedents are examined for insanity, felon, and undesirable behaviour. A girl is then selected from that family. A third party is sent discreetly to inquire whether the other party is interested to save face in the event that they are not. The couple meet, and the nikah (marriage) is arranged. The boy has to give her a marriage gift (dower) so she is independent financially.

Arranged marriage ceremonies in India differ from community to community and from place to place. These ceremonies are indispensable, highly religious and significant. The rites of marriage are also social and are meant to increase intimacy between the two families. However, with a little variation, the usual custom and rituals are more or the less the same throughout India (For details, see Chapter 6).

As in India, other parts of the world like South Eastern Europe, Asia and Africa parents arrange their children's marriages. In arranged marriages love is expected to grow between the couple after the marriage. Indeed, marital love may be highly valued. In India, parents typically check prospective partners' astrological charts to assure future compatibility (Ingoldsby, 1995). Arranged marriage was practiced throughout most of the world into the twentieth century and Western Europe well into the eighteenth century.

Arranged marriages developed in collectivist societies are based on strong extended family ties. In these societies marriage is a union between two families or kin groups rather than just two young persons. Selection of a suitable mate is a huge responsibility on the elders of the family rather than the young people themselves. Love is said to be more likely infatuation and blinds right judgement of good spouse. Love marriage is thought to be a part of individualistic society which does not value family ties, ignoring obligations to the family and kin group for personal goals (Ashraf Uddin Ahmed, 1993). Ahmed (1993) concludes that arranged marriage performs the following functions, among others, arranged marriage affirms and strengthens parents' power over their children, helps keep the family traditions and value systems intact, helps consolidate and extend family property, enhances the value of the kinship group and helps young people from getting into the uncertainty of searching for a mate.

In Arranged marriages, marriage may be fixed by the prospective bride and groom's parents or elders taking into consideration various things, like for selecting groom-man's height, weight, education, family background, age, income, house and health, and, for selecting bride—appearance, health, wealth, height, weight, age, education and family background.

Earlier in arranged marriages, the prospective groom and bride possibly meet on their wedding day itself or after as per the social customs. Now both (sets of) parents want that their children choose their prospective partner from few selected good matches they see. Both boy and the girl meet each other along with their parents and are sometimes given an opportunity to interact with each other separately. In present day, most of the time, parents give an opportunity to their children to select partner of their choice, though now also in some social norms boy and the girl meet each other on wedding day itself.

In arranged marriages, love is expected to grow after wedding. For them, marital relationship is not so much about finding the right person but creating the right relationship, it is not how much love you have in the beginning but how much love you built till the end.

DIFFERENCE BETWEEN LOVE MARRIAGE AND ARRANGED MARRIAGE

	Love marriage	*Arranged marriage*
1.	Free-will to choose life partner.	May or may not have freedom to choose life partner.
2.	Parents' will not considered.	Parents' will is essential.
3.	Based on an instant desire for each other.	Based on desirable qualities.
4.	Love may decrease over time.	Love deepens and grows over time.
5.	Leaves areas that you don't want to question.	Accepting of each other even with imperfection.
6.	Trusting and secure.	Trusting and secure.
7.	Support of friends and parents may or may not be present.	Support of both family and friends present.
8.	Increased fear that the relationship may end.	Allows time to build the relationship.
9.	Increased feelings of guilt.	Freedom from guilt.
10.	Allows growth of romantic love, which may or may not change to mature love.	Allows growth of mature love.
11.	Increase divorce rate.	Comparatively low divorce rate.
12.	Marriage without traditions takes place.	Marriage with traditions takes place.

Love Marriages

Despite the strong hold arranged marriages still have on the minds of young people where it is practiced in the world, with acculturation and world culture becoming more westernized or Americanized, adoption of their cultural beliefs, norms and values is evident. People are moving from collectivist society to individualistic society. Change from thinking and doing for others welfare to thinking and doing for one's own welfare is being more encouraged.

The average Indian anchored to the age-old rules of an arranged marriage-would hardly embark on a love marriage. Even today, love marriage is looked down upon and the orthodox priests interdict a love marriage. This is mainly because such wedlock usually defies the barriers of caste, creed and age. However, Indian history is witness to the fact that time and again, Indian princesses chose their life mates in Swayamvaras—an occasion when princes and noble men from all over the kingdom were invited to assemble in a bridegroom choosing ceremony. It is also interesting to note, that, Bhishma, in the greatest of Hindu epics—the Mahabharata (Anusashana Parva, Section XLIV)—perspicaciously hints at 'love marriage', after the appearance of puberty, the girl should wait for three years. During the fourth year, she should look for a husband herself (without waiting any longer for her kinsmen to select one for her).

With global westernization, "love marriage" are replacing arranged marriage as the preferred way to select mates throughout the world. People want freedom to choose their own mates and at the same time want approval of their family, parents and elders for their marriage. This love-*cum*-arranged marriages is becoming more popular these days especially among the urban Indian culture. Love marriages are those in which both or either set of parents don't approve the wedding of their child with their chosen beloved and the young couple has to marry against the wishes of either or both parents and, therefore, forego the traditional wedding ceremony. A wedding is an ancient ritual that symbolizes a couple's commitment to each other. The wedding marks major transitions in life as the man and woman take on marital roles.

Throughout history, people have written about the actions and feelings that go with love. We will discuss this in detail in Chapter 3. In India, Shah Jahan, Emperor during Mughal India period built a monument called Taj Mahal in memory of his beloved wife Mumtaz Mahal.

TYPES OF MARRIAGES IN THE WESTERN CONTEXT

John Cuber and Peggy Haroff (1974) in their study found several distinct types of marriage representing different kinds of adjustment and different conceptions of marriage. These types of marriage were classified as: (i) Conflict-habituated marriage, (ii) Devitalized marriage. (iii) Passive-congenial marriage, (iv) Vital marriage, and (v) Total marriage. Partners give their own personal meaning to their "normal" marriage.

Devitalized Marriage

The devitalized marriage is most marked by the contrast between its earlier years and its present. In earlier years, husband and wife were deeply involved with each other, loved and cared for partner's small needs, had good sex and closely identified with each other. Soon after the honeymoon is over, even the "deeply in love" couple find strain in their relationships. To them marriage is dull and boring. The marriage appears to be lifeless. However, no conflict appears. Now, that earlier closeness is not seen but whatever they do is in regard to sense of duty. They do not contemplate divorce as they get along well enough with each other.

Passive-Congenial Marriage

The passive congenial marriage expects that the couple never be highly emotionally attached. Couples begin their marriages with low expectations, which change little over the years. Partners do not gain satisfaction from each other but from their varied roles like father, mother, career and friend. Partners don't adjust to each other rather to their careers.

In the first type there is loss of interest and happiness but in this type passivity is from the very start. The mates are not in illusion with the marriage. Life together is adequate with little conflict. The couple shares common interests. It is more cool calculated marriage. It may be called rational marriage. Marriage was a reality to them and not the idealized or romantic notion.

Conflict-Habituated Marriage

In the Conflict-Habituated marriage, conflict not harmony is the most distinguishing characteristics. Couples fight and fight, abuse each other physically and emotionally, but does not believe that fighting is a reason for divorce.

This style has substantial but controlled tension and conflict. There is extensive quarreling, nagging, and bring up of past misdeeds. The couple may be polite in the presence of other people. There is no physical violence, but extensive verbal attacks. Tension prevails in the atmosphere. This is probably their need to make others feel their presence. This goes on life long.

Vital Marriage

The vital pair are happy. They live in harmony. They have well-established good homes; love their children, busy with jobs, proud of their careers. They are bound together in important life matters. They share everything they hear togetherness. They enjoy sharing things and work. They leave promotions and excellent job opportunities because they cannot separate from each other. Their family life is more important than a career.

In vital marriage, the partner's lives are closely inter-wined through matters that are important to both of them. Being together brings mutual excitement, satisfaction and pleasure. Conflict is not central to their relationship. They experience a strong, positive psychological bonding.

Total Marriage

The total marriage is similar to vital marriage, except that both husband and wife participate in each other's lives more completely and on more levels. Total marriages have few areas of tension because difficulties are resolved as they arise. These are the total relationship. All parts of life are intimately shared. Wives and husbands are friends and partners as well. They are inseparable. They have nothing private from each other. One understands other's feelings, even without expressing. They work for each other's welfare and one's pinch is another's pain.

Cuber and Haroff view the first three types of marriages as utilitarian marriages. These marriages are based on convenience and lack of better alternatives. The last two are viewed as intrinsic marriages, the marital interactions are inherently rewarding. These five types of marriages have one thing in, is that they are all enduring. They do not represent degrees of marital happiness and satisfaction.

3

Love

Why study love? In a very real sense, to do so is an attempt to examine the un-examinable and to know the unknowable (Peck, 1978). Some claim study of love violates love's mystery. Love is an essence of life. There is no subject as central to the human experience and at the same time as incomprehensible as human love (Kazak and Reppucci, 1980).

Love has always been a favourite subject of philosophers and poets. The arts in many forms have reflected the world's fascination with the meaning of love. A few decades back, love was discovered by family scientists. To understand the nature of love depends upon one's hands on experience in life. People in a variety of ways invariably use this term. Love is used to describe the selfless altruistic nature of parents for their infant or child, sibling concern for each other, child's idealizing of his or her parents, mutually supportive or cooperative relationship between friends, erotic, passionate, romantic attraction between two people for each other, for your pet animal, or chocolates, even for one's country and this ubiquitous word is also used frequently in connection to one's preferred God of worship.

Love does not necessarily depend upon similarity of tastes

or interests. It can be inspired by physical or spiritual attraction—as in The Bhagavata Gita and The Guru Granth Sahib where references of the love feeling are expressed as a form of devotion, as a means to attain salvation. The kinds of love, with which, people can build a firm basis for marriage, one that combines the essence of all three components, unconditional acceptance, friendship and erotica. Although the emphasis tends to change from passionate to compassionate love, as persons grow older, love itself remains an important part of couple relationships; with romantic symbols love often remains unchanged over the life cycle.

Love, by whatever name, is the most often sought quality in a relationship. Therefore, understanding how love develops, its role in commitment, and how it grows and changes over time is significant to healthy relationship.

Erich Fromm (1956) defined love simply, "love is an art." He perceived love as the overcoming of human separateness, the fulfilment of the longing for union. As such, it is an attitude or orientation of character that determines a person's relatedness to the world, not one's object of live. "If I truly love one person I love all persons, I love the world, I love life (Fromm, 1956). Sullivan (1947) defined the state of love as "when the satisfaction or the security of another person becomes as significant to one as is one's own security. The love of a person implies not the possession of that person, but the affirmation of that person. It means granting him gladly the full right to his unique humanhood. Both May (1969) and Peck (1978) include the concept of will in their treatises on love. Peck defined love as, "the will to extend one's self for the purpose of nurturing one's own or another's spiritual growth."

Love was defined by social scientists as "a set of positive feelings targeted toward another person", "an emotion that follows from our decision to cooperate with our partner." Love is perceived to include friendship, devotion and intellectual compatibility and passion-related elements.

Fromm (1947) coined the term "productive love." The essence of productive love is the same whether it is mother's love for her child, love of human kind or an erotic love between mates. Maslow's hierarchy of developmental needs (1943) offers additional insight into love as it relates to the satisfaction of human needs. The developmental needs are identified as physiological hunger and thirst; safety; security and order; belongingness and love—affection; and identification; esteem—prestige, success and self-respect; and self-actualization—desire for self-fulfilment. Love is viewed as satisfying two human needs. Caring is placing another's needs before your own. Valuing your partner for simply being himself or herself.

Love is an intense, affectionate, loyal emotion. Love takes many forms. Parents love their children, people love their country, friends love each other, husband and wife loves each other. However, different these and many other types of love, all involve similar feelings and attitudes. Love takes many different forms and we will review several of these in this Chapter.

LOVE IN THE INDIAN CONTEXT

According to Goode (1959) apart from poets and storytellers, Vatsyayana, Ovid, Capellanus and others have written books which are more or less "how-to-do-it" books and tell one how to conduct oneself in love relations and how to satisfy one's sex-partner. Freud (1922) said, "Love is aim-inhibited sex."

Love is considered to be sexual whenever the genitals are directly or indirectly stimulated but whenever they are not involved, love is non-sexual. Indian ancient classical literature has idealized sensuous and romantic love. It is only later literature that one finds a shift towards a somewhat more prosaic attitude towards love. In ancient India, the erotic art of Khajuraho was supposed to teach people the art of making love.

In India, the concept of love is as old as the Hindu mythology itself. Among various Hindu deities, there is a God of love also. The mythological Hindu beliefs give an important role to Kama, the god of love. Kama, is the lord of love. The Hindu God of carnal love, who is said to arouse physical desire. Born out of the heart of creator Lord Brahma and Lakshmi. Kamadeva is depicted as a youthful being with a greenish or reddish complexion, decked with ornaments and flowers, armed with a bow of sugarcane, string with a line of honeybees and floral arrowheads. His consorts are the beautiful Rati and Priti, his vehicle is a parrot, his chief ally is Vasanta, the God of Spring and he is accompanied by a band of dancers and performers—Apsaras, Gandharvas and

Kinnaras. He is young, winged man who uses a bow and arrows made of flowers. He is also called Kama Ananga (Kama the bodiless) as well. Kama's body was destroyed when he fired his weapon on at God Shiva, the destroyer, in order to disrupt his meditations. God Shiva then opened his third eye with the gaze of which Kama's body was reduced to ashes. For the sake of Kama's wife, Rati, Goddess of Passion and lust and daughter of Rishi Daksha, Shiva restored him, but only as a mental image, representing the true emotional and mental state of love rather than physical lust. Kama means pleasure. The term Kama also refers to one of the four goals of life according to Hindu traditions, Purushastras, these include dharma, artha, kama and moksha.

No history and study is complete without elevations from the past and ancient. No culture is complete without its basics being assessed. In the Middle East, 2000 yeas ago, the Jewish, Christian and later the Islamic faiths seemed to question sexuality. The sexual drives of women and men needed careful regulation. In contrast, Hinduism in India talked about a journey through this life that may be different for every person. It is your Karma, inevitable fate that decides one's destiny like to be poor, idealistic or lascivious. Western religious tradition often divides that which is sexual and physical form that which is spiritual and divine. In contrast, Hinduism attempts to integrate sexuality with all aspects of life.

Perhaps, the most famous writing that has survived from antiquity that is specifically sexual in content is the Hindu book, the Kama Sutra by Vatsyayana. Kama Sutra means love percepts for he believed that even exciting and pleasurable as sexual intercourse is, it is an art that must be diligently studied to obtain the greatest joy by both men and women.

In India, though one finds a lot of frank and scientific treatment of love and sex in ancient classical literature, it was Vatsyayana who in Kama Sutra gave a vivid account of the various facets of sexual life and attraction portraying those stirrings of the human heart that make life so full and poignant. This whole account, with its ardent love of life and passionate spiritual serenity, has nothing in common with the abstinence solicited by the votaries of suffering. Spiritual freedom is to be secured, not by the arbitrary suppression of desires, but by their judicious organization (Radha Krishnan, 1956).

Kama Sutra is a divine ancient Indian text on sex, widely considered the standard work on love in the Sanskrit literature written by Vatsyayana. The author is believed to have lived sometime between 1st to 6th centuries AD, probably during the Gupta Period. The Kama Sutra contains 35 chapters, organized into 7 parts, each of which is written by individual expertise in the respective fields. There is a discussion of kissing, various types of foreplay, orgasm, a list of sex positions, oral sex, paraphilia, ménage-a-trois, courtship, marriage, seduction, proper conduct of a wife, courtesans' means of attracting others to oneself. The book contains 64 sexual positions and depicts positions as art. Vatsyayana believed there were 8 ways of making love, multiplied by 8 positions within each of these. However, 20% of the book is devoted to sexual positions. The remainder gives guidance on how to be a good citizen and insights into men and women in relationships. It, also, contains certain norms and disciplined actions necessary to achieve one's goal. The Kama Sutra describes making love as a divine union. He believed that sex itself was not wrong, but doing it frivolously was sinful. It is a technical guide to sexual enjoyment. Some believe that Vatsyayana was in 1st to 4th century AD and belonged to Benaras now called Varanasi in Uttar Pradesh in the Northern India.

A certain sage, Babhravpanchal, is also believed to have compiled a treatise, called Kama Shastra, which is not available now. It is said to be a very huge collection. Kama Shastra means pleasure treatise contains specialized knowledge or technique about sex, was a document also written by Nandi, the disciple of Lord Shiva. It consisted of about 1000 chapters. The collection is unfortunately lost. It deals with human sexuality in a frank and forthright manner and was written almost two billion years ago.

Kama Sutra revelations are remarkably modern and progressive. Women are as sexual as men, and men should work to provide women with erotic pleasure, including orgasms. Kama Sutra literally means treatise on sexual pleasure.

Unlike the Christian view, that, the sole purpose of sex is procreation, in the 4th century Hindu world that gave birth to the Kama Sutra, the cultivation of sexual pleasure, independent of procreation was considered one of life's highest callings. Kama Sutra written by Vatsayana Mallanaga, upper class man, had written his treatise in chastity and the highest meditation. Kama

Sutra is ancient world's most famous sex book. The ancient Hindus believed that life had three purposes—religious piety (dharma), material success (artha) and sexual pleasure (kama). All three were equal and the erotic was celebrated as the seat of earthly beauty.

The Chinese had sex manuals 500 years earlier the Kama Sutra, and Ovid's 'Ars Amatoria', a hand book for courtesans, preceded the Kama Sutra by some 200 years. The Kama Sutra is not even the first Indian sex guide. Vatsayana mentions several sages who troded this erotic path before him. What makes the Kama Sutra unique in world literature is that it's the first comprehensive guide to living an eroticized life. The sexual culture it describes is surprisingly modern.

Although Vatsyayana was a man writing for men, some of the Kama Sutra speaks directly to women, tells how virgins attract husbands, instructs women how to be good wives, deals with skills required of courtesans, recognizes women as full, lusty participants in sex and exhorts men to learn ejaculatory control to last long enough to bring them to orgasm.

Kama Sutra is very attentive to women's pleasure, a view that arrived in western culture only a few decades ago, a view lost on many men. Kama Sutra is all about love, lust, flirtations, courtship seduction, rejection, infidelity and marriage, its about sexual power, manipulation and deceit. It contains safe sane and erotically rich life in an ancient mirror.

Over a period of time, lots of changes have occurred in various Hindu sects. Yet, due to various social and ethical inhibitions, some time after Vatsyayana's Kama Sutra was written, sex began to be considered beyond scientific enquiry and was almost tabooed for discussion and remained so until recent times. Today, India, in comparison with the United States is a modest and conservative society though some of the erotic realism and acceptance of early Hinduism are still apparent in Indian Society.

Khajuraho sculptures is the boundless expression of romance in creativity through hands, the sculptures enchant the living past. It is a voyage hundreds of years back and sweep the shores of imagination. Originally, there were 85 temples, only 22 famous for their erotic sculptures.

Tajmahal stands on the bank of River Yamuna. The fifth Mughal emperor, Shah Jahan in 1631 in memory of his second wife Mumtaz Mahal, a Muslim Persian Princess, built it. Mumtaz's real name was Arjumand Banu, she was the daughter of Asif Khan, brother of the emperor Jahangir's consort Noor Jahan. It was after the death of her father-in-law Jahangir she was bestowed with the name Mumtaz Mahal and her husband Khurramm with Shah Jahan. Mumtaz was so pretty that prince lost his heart to her in their very first meeting. Taj Mahal's construction began in 1631 and was completed in 22 years. It is a symbol of eternal love. It is the mausoleum of the Mughal Empress Mumtaz Mahal. Shah Jahan is said to have made this monumental piece in love for his wife.

Perhaps no other faith glorifies the idea of love between the sexes as Hinduism. This is evident from the amazing variety of mythical love stories that abounds sanskrit literature, which is, undoubtedly one of the richest treasures and contains hoards of exciting love tales. Kalidasa's—Meghadutam, Abhijnanashakuntalum; Surdasa's—Lyrical rendition of the legends of Radha, Krishna and the Gopies of Vraj.

Classical love legends from Hindu Mythology and folklore of India are both passionate and sensuous in content. The beautiful truth is that, for centuries the saga of the folk lovers which immortalizes the memory of Heer, Sohni, Sahibaan, Sassi and others has been handed down from generation to generation, for they have immortalized a woman's love for her lover. Their memories are still alive as they had died for love and not because their lovers had died for them at the alter of love. They rebelled against the conventional norms of society. These women who loved, did not treasure their body or soul, they sacrificed everything for love. The roots of this philosophy has been embedded in the poetry of various great poets like Waris Shah, Amrita Pritam, and many others who believed that the world existed on love.

Syed Hashim Shah (1735-1843) a highly learned, prolific and multilingual writer who flourished during the Sikh Supremacy in Punjab and who has been mentioned in terms of esteem even by eminent Western Scholars. In Punjabi, he versified the popular love—tragedies of Punjab to describe and acclaim the "Kamal Ishq" meaning perfect love of their heroes and heroines (viz. Sassi and Punnu, Heer and Ranjha, Sohni and Mahiwal, Mirza-Sahibaan and Shirih and Farhad).

Maulvi Ghulam Rasul (1813-1874) wrote about tragic romance of Sassi-Pannu. Sassi Punu is a very famous folk love story in Punjab and Sindh now in Pakistan and one of the favourite scribs for producers in the sub-continent. It was written by Nawab Mir Mohammad Maasoom as "Masnawi Husn-O-Naz" in Akbar period (1556-1605). Qazi Soorthi rewrote this story in Mohammad Shah Rangeela's period (1719-48). Hashim Shah (1753-1833), a very famous Punjabi poet, wrote this story in his classic book "Sassi" and Shah Abdul Latif Bhattai (reh.) included this story in his spiritual classic Sindhi literature.

Indian sub-continent culture and history is full of passionate folk love-lore of love and passion.

Spiritual Love

The Radha-Krishan amour is a love legend of all times, has served as a model for male and female love in a variety of art forms and since the 16th century appears prominently as a motif in the North Indian paintings. The allegorical love of Radha has found expression in some great Bengali poetical works of Govinda Das, Chaitanya Mahaprabhu and Jayadeva, the author of Geet Govinda.

Love in all its form finds its epitome in the dual—unity of Lord Krishna and his beloved Radha. Krishna is seen as the universal symbol of the lover and the ideal hero, while, Radha as the universal symbol of the beloved and the ideal heroine (Nayika-nayak).

Radha's utterly rapturous love for Krishna and their relationship is often interpreted as the quest for union with the divine. This kind of love is of the highest form of devotion in Vaishnavism (a religious sect in Hindus) and is symbolically represented as a bond between the wife and the husband or the beloved and the lover.

Suradasa, the great poet, in his Radha-Krishna lyrics relates the various amorous delights of the union of Radha and Krishna in their ceremonious Gandharva form of wedding in front of 560 million people of Vraj. Worship of Lord Krishna is incomplete without the deification of Radha.

The Guru Granth Sahib (also known as the Adi Granth) is truly unique among the world's great scriptures. It is considered the supreme Spiritual Authority and Head of the Sikh religion, rather than any living person. It contains writings from other faiths also. It glorifies love of the immortal, to the supremacy to God. It contains hymns like, "Jin Prem Kiyo tin hi Prabh Payo"meaning "the one who loves only finds the God."

IMMORTAL LOVE LEGENDS

Indian folklores contain not only love histories of unrequisited love but also contains existence of love among husband and wife. Below a few of such folklores are described.

Savitri and Satyavan

Savitri and Satyavan tale highlights the love and care of a woman for her husband. Savitri was the beautiful daughter of a wise and powerful king. The fame of Savitri's beauty spread far and wide, but she refused to marry, saying that she would herself go out in the world and find a husband for herself. So, the king chose the best warriors to protect her and the princess wandered throughout the country searching for a prince of her choice.

One day she reached a dense forest, where dwelt a king, who had lost his kingdom and fallen into his bad days. Old and blind he lived in a small hut with his wife and son. The son, who was a handsome young prince, Satyavan, was the sole comfort of his parents. He chopped woods and sold it in the countryside, and bought food for his parents and they lived in love and happiness. Savitri was strongly drawn towards them and she knew her search had come to an end by meeting Satyavan, famous for legendary generosity.

Savitri's father agreed with a heavy heart to marry his daughter to the penniless Prince who had been cursed to die within a year. They lived happily. When only four days of his age were remaining she undertook a vow to defeat death. On the fourth day Satyavan died with Yamaraja (the God of death) walking away with his vitality, Savitri walked purusing Yamaraja. As they walked one behind the other, on the way there occupied a question-answer between them. Yamaraja was very impressed by the gentle behaviour of Savitri, her wisdom, her one pointed devotion (dedication) to her husband, getting pleased by her he asked Savitri to ask for boons. Savitri asked for such boons which helped not only to obtain for the well-being of both her father's and her husband's families but Yamaraja had also to return the vitality of Satyavan. Savitri with the power of her chastity and fidelity protected her good fortunes. She is mentioned among the great chaste and faithful goodly women, who took Satyavan as her husband knowing fully well that he would not live long.

Shakuntala and Dushyant

Kalidasa, the great ancient Indian poet wrote Abhijnan-a-Shakuntalam. It contains the legend of the exquisitely beautiful Shakuntala and the mighty king Dushyanta. It is a thrilling love story from the epic Mahabharata. While on hunting trip King Dushyanta of the Puru dynasty meets the hermit girl Shakuntala. They fall in love with each other. Marries in the absence of her father in Gandharva form of marriage by mutual consent with mother nature as the witness. As the time comes for departure he promises to send envoy to being her to his castle and gives her his signet ring. After Dushyanta left, Shakuntala was always engrossed in his thoughts. One day a hotheaded hermit Durvasa stops at her hut, lost in love thoughts fails in hospitality. Durvasa curses her, that, for the person Shakuntala has lost all senses and has failed in hospitality should forget her. Hearing this, Shakuntala's friends ask forgiveness and then the hermit said he would remember her only on produce of a significant souvenir. Shakuntala lost the signet ring. Fisherman along with fishes found it. The ring was so costly and had the king's stamp, the fisherman gave the ring to king Dushyanta, who became free of the curse on seeing the ring. Then, he called for Shakuntala and they are reunited happily. She gives birth to a male child who is called Bharat, after whom India gets her name.

Anarkali and Salim

The royal romance of Prince Salim (later known as Jahangir) and Anarkali has resulted into a lot of literary as well as cinematic lore. It is believed that the original name of Anarkali was Nadira or Sharfunnisa and that she received the name or the title of Anarkali (literally meaning pomegranate bud) for her beauty.

The popular version of the story runs thus, Anarkali was a dancer at the court of Emperor Akbar. The emperor's eldest son and heir apparent, Salim, fell in love with her. Akbar did not approve of the relation as the dancer was of lowly birth and, hence, considered not fit to be the queen of the would-be emperor of Hindustan. But, the lovers did not pay heed to Akbar's disapproval. At last Anarkali was sentenced to death—she was bricked alive in a wall. Anarkali suffered cruel decimation at the hands to Akbar, the great, but did not forsake her love for Shahzada Salim.

Sassi and Pannu

Sassi means moon-beautiful, was the only daughter of King Adam Khan of Bhambour, Sindh, Pakistan (40 miles south of Karachi on the right coast of Indus river, which was discovered in 1958). At her birth, astrologers predicted that she was a curse for the royal family's prestige. She was put in a wooden chest with jewellery and thrown in Indus river. Atta Dhobi, a washer-man, saw the chest. Later, the king decides to remarry. When the king heard that the daughter of Atta, the washerman, was as beautiful as the angels, the king summoned her to the palace. Sassi was still wearing the tabiz (amulet), which the queen mother had put around her neck, on seeing the tabiz the pent-up feelings of the parents flowed into tears. They wanted their lost child to return to the palace and bring joy and brightness into their lives but Sassi refused and preferred to live in the house she had grown up. The king presented her with abundant gifts, land and gardens. As all the rare things of the world were within her reach she wanted to acquire knowledge and sent for learned teachers and scholars. Makran trader brought prince Pannu's painting, son of King Jam Arao, the ruler of Turbat. He was so beautiful that Sassi fell in love with him at sight. There was a flutter within the business community of Sassi's love for Pannu. They met and fell in love with each other. Pannu's Baluchi brothers developed an enmity for Sassi. They followed him and on reaching the town, when they saw the marriage celebrations of Sassi and Pannu in full swing, they could not bear the rejoicing. That night the brothers pretended to enjoy the marriage ceremonies and forced Pannu to drink different types of liquor. When he was dead drunk the brothers carried him off on a camel's back and returned to their hometown Kicham. The next morning, when Sassi realized this, she ran barefoot towards the city of Kicham. To reach this city she had to cross miles of desert land, the journey through which was full of dangerous hazards, leading to the end of the world. Her end was similar to the end of the Kaknoos bird. It is said that when this bird sings, fire leaps out from its wings and it is reduced to ashes in its own flames. Similarly, Pannu's name was the death song for Sassi.

Sohni and Mahiwal

Sohni was the daughter of a potter named Tula, who lived in Punjab near the banks of the Chenab River. As soon as the Surahis (water pitchers) and mugs came off the wheels, she would draw floral designs on them and transform them into masterpieces of art. Izzat Biag, the rich trader from Balakh Bukhara, came to Hindustan on business but when he saw the beautiful Sohni he was completely enchanted and, instead of making floral designs on earthenware she started building castles of love in her dreams. Izzat Baig sent off his companions to Balakh Bukhara. He took up a job as a servant in the house of Tula, the potter. He would even take their buffaloes for grazing. Soon he was known as Mahiwal (potter). When the people started spreading rumours about the love of Sohni and Mahiwal, without her consent her parents quietly arranged her marriage with another potter. Suddenly, one day her barat (marriage party) arrived at the threshold of her house. Sohni was helpless and in a poignant state. Her parents bundled her off in the doli (palanquin), but they could not pack off her love in any doli (box). Izzat Baig renounced the world and started living like a fakir (hermit) in a small hut across the river. The earth of Sohni's land was a dargah (shrine) for him. He had forgotten his own land, his own people and his world. Taking refuge in the darkness of the night when the world was fast asleep, Sohni would come by the riverside and Izzat Baig would swim across the river to meet her. One day, as he could not catch a fish, so he cut a piece of flesh from his thigh and roasted it for Sohni. Seeing the bandage on his thigh, Sohni opened it, saw the wound and wept. From the next day, Sohni started swimming across the river with the help of an earthen pitcher as Izzat Baig was badly wounded. The rumours of their romantic rendezvous spread. Sohni's sister-in-law replaced the hard baked pitcher with an unbaked one, at night when Sohni tried to cross the river with the help of the pitcher, it dissolved in the water and Sohni was drowned. From the other side of the river, Mahiwal saw Sohni drowning and jumped into the river.

Mirza and Sahibaan

Mirza-Sahibaan is a love lore and a treasure of Punjabi literature. They were cousins and childhood playmates. When her parents were forcibly wedding Sahibaan to someone else, she calls Mirza and asks him to protect his self-respect and love by keeping his promises and sacrifice his life for truth. Mirza, a young full-blooded man, who had self-esteem took Sahibaan on his horse and they rode away. But, soon Sahibaan brother's followed them with swords in their hands. Sahibaan did not want her hands drenched with blood instead of henna. She thought Mirza would not miss his target, if he strikes, so her brothers would die. She puts away Mriza's quiver on a zand trees. She presumed on seeing her, her brothers would feel sorry and forgive Mirza and take him in their arms. But, the brothers attack Mirza and kill him. Sahibaan takes a sword and slaughters herself and thus bids farewell to this world.

Heer and Ranjha

Heer was the daughter of a feudal landlord Chuchak sial from Jhang. Before her sacrifice for Ranjha, she proved herself to be a very courageous and daring young girl. Ranjha was romping about, teasing the girls and breaking their pitchers. They fall in love with each other. But, Heer's parents arranged her marriage much against her wishes with a member of the house of Kaidon, Heer questions her marriage with Kazi, as she believed her first marriage had been performed in the presence of Nabi (Prophet). Heer is forcibly married to Kaidon but could not forget Ranjha. She elopes away with Ranjha. When Heer's parents hear about this, they repent and send for both of them promising to get Heer married to Ranjha. But Heer's uncle Kaidon betrays them and poisons Heer.

Nal and Dayamnti

Nal and Dayamnti love, affection and concern for each other has been mentioned in detail in the Mahabharata. Raja Nal of Naisadha had its capital at Narwar and Damoh had got is name from the name of the Queen of Narwar, Rani Dayamnti, wife of Raja Nal. They portray an ideal couple that share pleasure and sorrow, face problems together and don't think of separation even at difficult times.

Baz Bahadur and Rani Roopmati

Mandu is a celebration in stone of life and joy, of the love of the poet, prince Baz Bahadur for his beautiful wife, Rani Roopmati. Mandu located at an altitude of 2000 feet, Mandu, in Madhya Pradesh, was originally the fort-capital of the Parmar rulers of Malwa. Towards the end of the 13th Century, it came under the rule of the Sultans of Malwa. Mandu is a celebration of life and love, a tribute to the tender love of the poet Baz Bahadur for his consort, Rani Roopmati. The balladeers of Malwa still sing of their love, and perched atop a hill, Roopmati's pavilion still gazes down fondly upon Baz Bahadur's palace.

LOVE IN THE WESTERN CONTEXT

Every mythology that existed on earth has its own set of Gods and Goddesses for various purposes. Sanskrit has 96 words for love, Ancient Persian has 80 words for love, and Greek has 3 words for love—eros, agape and philia. The ancient Greeks used three words to distinguish between the various meanings of love: agape, philos and errors (Crosby, 1991). Agape, the unconditional love, believed to represent the ideal, best reflected in a parent's love for her/his child. It is love "in spite of" rather than "because of," love that is unearned and undeserved. Philos, the brotherly love, is love of friendship or love between equals. Eros, the sensual, physical emotion of lust, is the drive toward intimacy with another being.

And, English has only one word for love. Amor or Cupid is the God of love in Roman Mythology. Venus is the Goddess of love in Roman Mythology and is equivalent to Greek Aphrodite and Etruscan Turan. Suadela in Roman mythology was a Goddess of persuasion particularly in romance, seduction and love. She was strongly associated with Venus. Aphrodite is the Goddess of love, sex and beauty in Greek Mythology. Greek mythology refers to the collected legends about Greek (Greece) Gods and Goddesses and ancient heroes and heroines, originally created and spread within an oral-poetic tradition. Aphrodite is risen from sea foam. Eros is the God of love in Greek Mythology. Freya is the Goddess of love in Norse Mythology. Freya, the sister of Frey and the daughter of Niord is usually seen as the fertility Goddess of Norse Mythology, Goddess of love, sex and attraction. She may be the same Goddess as Frigg and might be considered the counterpart of Venus and Approdite. Kama is the God of sensual love in Hindu Mythology. Xochipilli is the God of love in Aztec Mythology, Tlahuizcalpante cuhtli in Aztec Mythology, Kukulan in Maya Mythology and Vanadiṣ in Norse Mythology is the God of love. Norse Mythology represents the early pre-Christian religion, beliefs and legends of the Scandinavian people. The name also refers to Germanic Mythology in general, as it is part of the old Germanic belief system. Frigg in Norse mythology, Frigg, Frige, Frigga or Frea was the mother of Goddess and wife of Odin or Odr. Considered the queen of heavens, the Goddess of motherhood, fertility, love and housework. Freya became Frigg after she lived with Odin. Wotan, Wodan, Woden, Oden or Adin is usually considered the Supreme God of Germanic and Norse mythology.

Xochipilli (flower prince) was the god of love, games, beauty, dance, flowers, maize and song and his wife was Mayahuel, a human girl, given the ability to love and return his love, in Aztec mythology, Ehecati is the wind god in Aztec mythology. The Aztec civilization recognized many Gods and supernatural creatures. The Aztecs were a Mesoamerican people of central Mexico in the 14th, 15th and 16th Century. It was tribe with a rich mythology and a cultural heritage. Macuilxochitl is the God of love. Tlazolteotl represents the earth, sex, childbirth and a mother Goddess and Xochiquetzal is the Goddess of flowers, fertility, games, dancing, prostitutes and pregnant women.

The great Greek thinker Aristotle, about 2000 years ago wrote that both men and women had powerful sexual drives and described orgasm as a pleasurable climatic occurrence. He described sexual interaction as natural mammalian events.

Victorianism

Victorian era called for purity of thought and act but also for ignorance. No boy or girl, nor most women, were to know anything about sexuality. Victorianism succeeded in convincing generations of women and men that sex was a dirty business. It was best not to know or think about it and get it over with swiftly and efficiently.

Romanticism is viewed as idealized love and emphasized emotion. It is an emphasis on the non-physical, spiritual and ideal aspects of love and sexuality. The fable of innocent boy and virginal girl falling hopelessly in love, the eternal "Romeo and Juliet" created by Shakespeare grew and prospered.

The romantic notions of sensual innocence coupled with adventure to win one's true love gave birth to thousands of legends. The two lovers caught in intrigue and drama, eventually emerge triumphant and stand proudly at the marriage altar. They will live, the myths assert, happily ever after.

TYPES OF LOVE

Romantic and Mature Love

Romantic love is the exhilarating feeling that one feels while the other, is the long-lasting, caring and giving type of love that is called mature love. For some couples, the romantic love sparks the relationship that then grows into mature love. Sometimes, a caring and giving friendship grows into a romantic relationship. And at times, romantic love dies and the relationship ends.

Family sociologists have traditionally viewed romantic love as a carefully conditioned social product (Waller and Hill, 1951). That is, people fall in love because they are socialized to do so. Although persons are socialized to idealize the loved one and to view him/her as a uniquely perfect individual, this period of euphoria inevitably results in conflicts and adjustments. A classic definition of romantic love suggests that love exists at the point when a person's sentiment overcomes her/his objectivity (Waller and Hill, 1951).

Romantic love is seen as couple walking hand-in-hand, staring into each other's eyes, being focused on each other, and spend all their time together. These blissful feelings lead them to think about marriage. Romantic love alone is not enough to build a long lasting relationship. At times, these feelings will increase and other times will decrease.

Romantic love, the idealization of the other, is perhaps the most complex manifestation of emotion of love. Values in romantic love are personal while values in marriage are familial. Romance is private, tumultuous, idiosyncratic and characterized by intense experience and awareness, while, marriage is public, stabilized routine and often mundane (Saxton, 1970).

Mature love is characterized by a giving, unselfish attitude.

Each person is concerned about the well being of the other person. They like to do things that please each other. They are committed to finding and doing what is best for each other. They may give up personal desires to bring benefit to the loved ones. Mature love grows with relationship and time. It is not 'falling' in love. It takes both time and effort to develop mature love in a relationship.

Mature love grows in stages. At the start, the couple develops rapport. They care about each other and enjoy being together. They want to spend time to know each other. As rapport develops, couple begins to share more personal thoughts, ideas and feelings. Trust develops and leads them to get dependent on each other for support and encouragements. They miss each other when apart and look forward to being together. This leads to the last stage, in which, both feel their personal needs are being met in the relationship, their need for acceptance, respect, caring, understanding and belonging. The couple feels important and valuable to each other. Mature love grows deeper and continues to grow throughout the life cycle.

Erotic Love

Erotic love is physically and emotionally intense. It is sexual and emotional intimacy with another. There seems to be biological "chemistry" that binds the two lovers together and leads them to marry or establish another form of enduring partnership (Fisher, 1982).

Dorothy Tennov (1979) invented the term limerence for sexual, passionate and romantic love. It is not a widely used term for erotic love. Individuals are preoccupied with their love, thinking constantly about each other, may become emotionally uneven. They are happy and buoyant when the loved ones reacts favourably, down cast and depressed when the loved person seems disinterested or rejected. As erotic love ages, its intensity declines. However for some couples it is sufficient to keep them together for life.

Over the years several different scientific and literary descriptions of erotic love based on sex and attraction, physical and emotional have emerged. Based on the works of various writers who have applied both statistical analysis and insight to the understanding of love, erotic love involves companionship, caring, intimacy, romance, sex and commitment, which would more appropriately be called mature love.

Platonic Love

Platonic love is the love that does not include sex. It is just friendship between man-woman. However, such friendship may slowly evolve to include sexual relations. Love between friends may be deep and intimate yet it is not physical. Friendships between members of the same sex, lovers are different from friends in sexual intimacy, in exclusiveness and fascination though both these relationships are deep and committed to each other.

Devotional Love

Profound and caring emotions may center about faith, country and group identity. People speak of loving their God, their nation or their ethnic groups. This is devotional love that does not involve physical contact.

The love between parent and child is the first encounter for all of us with love. Parental love and altruistic love, a selfless concern for the welfare of others are similar to some and for some parental love is a special case of altruistic love.

Infatuation

Infatuation has been defined as foolish, unreasoning love or passion. A person usually becomes infatuated with someone who appears to fit her/his image of sexual and/or social desirability. A strong feeling of attraction between a male and a female is called infatuation. It is self-centered and one-sided. Both the partners need not share the same feelings. It is not long lasting. It begins and might end quickly. Infatuation is based on a person's good traits like looks, manners, nice voice, brilliance, shows confidence, tops in class, has leadership quality, stands up against oppression. These feelings may leave as quickly as they came for any other person rating higher on their like traits list. Marriages based on such love leaves both partners hurt and disappointed when their feelings fade. Their disagreements produce unkind thoughts, harsh words or actions.

Infatuation often involves such "love" feelings as eye appeal, fantasy projection and partner dependency (Hine, 1980). It is irrational attraction, which is based on less than adequate knowledge of the person, will adversely affect the development of an interpersonal relationship. Most authorities consider infatuation to be unstable and short-lived, thus forming a poor basis for establishment of a long-term relationship (Miller and Siegel, 1972; Uday, 1974).

LOVE, CHILDHOOD AND ATTACHMENT

Love is very complex emotion, which has attracted man since his earliest days, but it has only recently been subjected to scientific scrutiny. There is the prevalent belief that love is fundamentally unknown and unknowledgeable and that the nature of love is beyond human comprehension.

No one is born with the ability to love nor does love result from mere growth. Instead, it is a complex product of many life experiences. Love in later life is affected by the quality of life in early life. Therefore, it is imperfect for adults because it was imperfect for them as children.

Attachment theory maintains that the degree and quality of attachments experienced in early life influence our later relationships. It has been used to explain personal relationships such as personality traits (Shaver and Brennan, 1992); loneliness (Shaver and Hazan, 1987); conflict styles (Pistole, 1989); religious commitment as a form of attachment to God (Kirkpatrick and Shaver, 1992); and is useful in studying sexual bonding and the dynamics of gay and lesbian relationships (Feeney and Raphael, 1992).

Its most important contribution to date is in study of love. It examines love as a form of attachment that finds its root in infancy (Hazan and Shaver, 1987; Shaver *et. al.*, 1988). Research suggests that romantic love and infant/caregiver attachment have similar emotional dynamics.

Mary Ainsworth and Colleagues (1978) indicated that there are three styles of infant attachment: secure, anxious-ambivalent and avoidant. In secure attachment, the infant feels secure when the mother/caregiver is out of sight. He or she is confident that the mother will offer protection and care. In anxious/ambivalent attachment, the infant shows separation anxiety when mother leaves. He or she feels insecure when the mother is not present. In avoidant attachment, the infant senses the mother's detachment and rejection, when he or she desires close bodily contact. The infant shows avoidance behaviours with the mother as a means of defense. In Ainsworth's study, 66 percent of the infants were secure, 19 percent were anxious/ambivalent and 21 percent were avoidant.

Some researchers (Feeney and Noller, 1990; Shaver *et. al.*, 1988) believe the styles of attachment developed during infancy continue through adulthood. Hendrick and Hendrick (1994) however, question the validity of applying infant research to adults as well as the stability of attachment styles through out life. Secure adults were most likely to value intimacy in their relationships (Mikulincer and Erev, 1991). They experienced greater relationship interdependence, commitment, trust and satisfaction (Simpson, 1990). Anxious/ambivalent adults were the most likely to idealize their partners (Feeney and Noller, 1991). Not surprisingly, they were often dissatisfied with their ability to find and sustain warm and secure relationships (Mikulincer and Erev, 1991). Avoidant adults were most likely to experience a relationship break up (Feeney and Noller, 1992). They were also less likely to achieve intimacy (Mikulincer and Erev, 1991).

In adulthood, the attachment styles developed in infancy combine with sexual desire and caring behaviours to give rise to romantic love. And the likelihood of being optimistic about love relationships is related to attachment style (Carnelley and Janoff—Bulman, 1992).

MAN, WOMAN AND LOVE

When the term "romance" is used in the context of the courtship process, women more common than men are likely to say romance is important to their relationships (Rubenstein, 1983). Another basis for concluding that women are more pragmatic about romance relates to the earlier finding that women tend to express their inner feelings more directly, whereas, men tend to rely on non-verbal communication. Women, when compared to men, are more likely to report experiencing both positive and negative emotions, contentment and joy as well as anger, depression, insecurity and loneliness. They also understand their feelings of joy and liking for their partner while over expressing sadness and hurt (Sprecher and Harfield, 1986).

LOVE AND MARRIAGE

Turner (1970) observes all kinds of family love-marital, parental, filial and sibling have certain basic character in American middle class culture. Love is enduring, pervasive, intimate, trusting, altruistic, compassionate, consensual, responsive, admiring, spontaneous and valued. Saxton (1970) points out in the paired relation of marriage, love has four major components: altruistic love, companionate love, sexual love and romantic love. Altruistic love emphasizes the well-being of the other; providing for the other brings the lover more satisfaction than providing for his or her own physical well-being. Companionate love refers to the satisfaction derived simply from being with the other person, from sharing his presence, whether talking, playing, working or building together. Sexual love is the fusion of love with sex, the sex-object and the love-object are the same person at the same time. Obviously, either love or sexual satisfaction may occur without the other, only when a person experiences the two together is the phenomenon described as sexual love. In its ultimate fruition, sexual love may yield a satisfaction and depth of involvement almost mystical in intensity. All these four components of love leads to a healthy marital life.

SEX AND PROCREATION

Vatsyayana's concept of sex was that it was not only meant for procreation, but was also source and means of deriving one of the greatest earthly pleasures, and which every individual has a right to experience and enjoy. According to the Roman Catholic view, sex is sacred and inherently good. It is sacred by virtue of being the specific means of reproduction. But, whenever, it is attempted just to secure the pleasure of the sex act and avoiding the sacred purpose of reproduction, it is sinful (Thomas, 1956). Russell (1959) points out that sex is a natural human need like food and drink. It is true men can survive without it, whereas they cannot survive without food and drink, but from a psychological stand point the desire for sex is precisely analogous to the desire for food and drink. Radhakrishnan (1956) maintains, it is not right to think that a man and a woman should not take physical delight in each other for its own sake and should do so only for sake of children.

LOVE AND COMMITMENT

Love creates bonds that unable us to endure the greatest hardships, suffer severest cruelty and overcome any distance. Love is essential to our lives. Love is both a feeling and an activity. We feel love for someone and act in a loving manner.

Love and commitment are closely related to each other in our intimate/close relationships. They create and sustain each other. Love reflects the positive factors such as caring and attraction, which draw people together and sustain them in a relationship. Commitment reflects the stable factors such as love obligations and social pressure that help maintain the relationship for better or worse.

In A Midsummer Nights Dream, William Shakespeare said, "love looks not with the eyes but with the mind." Beverly Fehr (1988) conducted a research to discover people's prototypes (that is, models) on love and commitment. They listed 12 attributes each to both love and commitment. The attributes of love are: trust, caring, honesty, friendship, respect, concern for the others well-being, loyalty, commitment, acceptance of the other the way he or she is, supportiveness, wanting to be with the other, and interest in the other. The attributes of commitment are: loyalty, responsibility, living up to your word, faithfulness, trust, being there for the other in good and bad times, desertion, reliability, giving your best effect, supportiveness, perseverance, concern about the other's well-being

Researchers have found that love and commitment are correlated to satisfaction in romantic relationships (Hendrick, Hendrick and Adler, 1988). Zick Rubin (1973) found that there were four feelings in identifying love: caring for the other—wanting to help him or her, needing the other—having a strong desire to be in the other's presence and have the other care for one, trusting the other—mutually exchanging confidences, and tolerating the other—accepting his or her faults. Of these, caring appears to be the most important, followed by needing, trusting and tolerating (Steck, Levitan, Mc Lane and Kelley, 1982).

THEORIES OF LOVE

The Wheel Theory of Love

Sociologist Ira Reiss (1980) calls the process through which love is developed and maintained as the wheel theory of love. The love is developed and maintained through four processes: rapport, self-revelation, mutual dependency, and fulfilment of the need for intimacy. A reduction in any one affects the development or maintenance of a love relationship, as they are interdependent. The process flow into one another in one direction to develop and maintain love '+' and they flow in the opposite direction to weaken it '–'. All these four processes are influenced by role conceptions, which define what a person should expect and do in a love relationship. The socio-cultural background of the individuals affects all this.

Six Basic Styles of Love

Sociologist John Lee (1973, 1988; Borrello and Thompson, 1990) describes six basic styles of love. These styles, he cautions are relationship styles not individual styles. The style of love may change as the relationship changes or when individuals enter different relationships. The styles are:

Eros—Love of Beauty

Erotic lovers delight in the tactile, in the sensual lines of the body, its feel and touch. They are attracted and fascinated by beauty. This love does not last long.

Ludus—Playful Love

For ludic lovers, love is a game, something to play at rather than to become deeply involved in. Love is for fun, encounters are casual, carefree and often careless.

Storage—Companionate Love

Storage (pronounced STOR-gay) is the love between companions. It is a love without fever, tumult or folly, a peaceful and enchanting affection. It begins usually with friendship and deepens into love. If this love ends, it is gradual and couple often becomes friends.

Mania—Obsessive Love

The word mania comes from the Greek word for madness. For manic lovers, nights are marked by sleeplessness and days by pain and anxiety. The slightest sign of affection brings ecstasy for a short while, only to have it disappear. Satisfactions last but a moment before they must be renewed.

Agape—Altruistic Love

Agape (pronounced AH-ga-pay) is love that is chaste, patient, selfless and understanding. It does not expect to be reciprocated. It emphasizes nurturing and caring as their own rewards.

Pragma—Practical Love

Pragmatic lovers are first and foremost logical in their approach. They look for someone with compatible background, education, personality, religion and interests. If they meet a person who meets their criteria, erotic or manic feelings may develop.

Lee believes that to have a mutually satisfying love affair, a person has to find a partner who shares the same style and definition of love. The more different the people are in their styles of love, the less likely it is that they will understand each other's love.

The Triangular Theory of Love

The triangular theory of love is developed by Robert Sternberg (1986; Chojnacki and Walsh, 1990), seeks to emphasize the dynamic quality of love relationship. This theory sees love as composed of three elements, as the points of a triangle. These elements are intimacy, passion and decision/commitment. Each can be enlarged or diminished in the course of a love relationship and their changes will affect the quality of a relationship. They can also be combined in different ways and each combination offers a different type of love.

Intimacy refers to the warm, close feelings of bonding we get when we love someone. According to Sternberg and Grajek (1984), there are ten signs of intimacy: wanting to promote your partner's welfare, feeling happiness with your partner, holding your partner in high regard, being able to count on your partner in time of need, being able to understand each other, sharing yourself and your possessions with your partner, receiving emotional support from your partner, giving emotional support to your partner, being able to communicate with your partner about intimate things, and valuing your partner's pressure in your life.

The passion commitment refers to the elements of romance, attraction and sexuality in your relationship. These may lead to increased self-esteem, to be sexually active or fulfiled to affiliate with others, to dominate or to subordinate.

The decision/commitment component consists of two parts, one short-term and one long-term. The short-term part refers to your decision that you love someone. The commitment represents the long-term aspects; it is the maintenance of love. Decision may or may not be taken consciously. But it usually occurs before you decide to make a commitment to that person. But a decision to love someone does not necessarily entail a commitment to maintaining that love.

The Different Combinations of Kinds of Love

According to Sternberg, the intimacy, passion and decision/ commitment can be combined in eight basic ways. These combinations form the basis for classifying love:

Liking-Intimacy Only

Liking represents the intimacy component alone. It is the basis for close friendship but is neither passionate nor committed.

Romantic Love—Intimacy and Passion

Romantic love combines intimacy and passion. It is more intense than liking as a result of attraction. It may begin with an immediate union of the two components with friendship that intensifies with passion or with passion that develops intimacy.

Infatuation—Passion Only

Infatuation is love at first sight. It is the kind of love that idealizes its object, it rarely sees the other as a "real" person. Infatuation is marked by sudden passion and a high degree of physical and emotional arousal. It tends to be obsessive and all consuming. It is rarely returned equally.

Fatuous Love—Passion and Commitment

Fatuous or deceptive, love is whirlwind. It begins the day

couple meets and quickly results in cohabitation, engagement and then marriage. It is fatuous in the sense that a commitment is made on the basis of passion without the stabilizing element of intimate involvement, which takes time to develop. Passion fades soon enough and all that remains is commitment, with neither passion nor intimacy, the commitment wanes.

Companionate Love—Intimacy and Commitment

Companionate love is essential to a committed relationship. It often begins as romantic love, but as the passion diminishes and the intimacy increases, it is transformed. Some couples are satisfied and some not with such love. Those who are unsatisfied with this love may seek extra-relational affairs to maintain passion in their lives.

Consumate Love—Intimacy, Passion and Commitment

Consumate love is born when intimacy, passion and commitment combine to form their unique constellation. It is the kind of love we dream about, but, do not expect in all our love relationships. It may be achieved but it is difficult to sustain it. To sustain it, we must nourish its different components, for each is subject to the stress of time.

Non-love-Non-existent Love

In non-love there is absence of intimacy, passion and commitment. Non-love can take many forms, such as attachment for financial reasons, fear or the fulfilment of neurotic needs.

The Geometry of Love

The shape of the love triangle depends on the intensity of the love and the balance of the parts. Intense love creates traingles with greater areas. Just as love relationships can be balanced or unbalanced so can love triangles. The greater the match between each person's triangles in a relationship, the more likely each is to experience satisfaction in the relationship (Sternberg and Barnes, 1985).

A recent study on three components of love found that commitment was a more powerful predictor of relationship satisfaction than passion or intimacy for men and women of all ages (Acker and Davis, 1992).

Unrequited Love

Unrequited love is that which is not returned. Jealousy is an aversive response that occurs because of a partner's response that occurs because of partners real, imagined or likely involvement with a thick person (Bringle and Buunk, 1985; Sharpsteen, 1993).

4

Readiness for Marriage

When you go to a shop to buy garment you select one out of many. When you want to buy a book, you read, evaluate and then buy. But, marriage is a different story. You cannot make choice; you cannot try and change. It is a lifetime decision; once it is taken it cannot be reversed. There is also no freedom for trial. Reasons are many. Once you have developed a relationship, it is difficult to get away completely. One of the partners may get involved emotionally then break up will be disastrous. Hence, selection should be proper, matching to each other's qualities and requirements. Second important thing, behind happy and enduring marital life, is that, both the partners and their families should be prepared to accept the changes emerging out of this new wedlock. Not only girls, but boys, also need to be prepared for marriage. Besides, families from both sides should also be prepared for accepting the changes. Preparation may be of various types—physical, mental, psychological, social, culture/moral values and economic. Both the partners should be physically fit, emotionally healthy and social-culturally ready to participate.

PHYSICAL PREPARATION

This aspect is related to physical growth and maturity. Age is an important factor. Early marriages are harmful so is the case with late marriages. Child marriages have been abolished in India a long time back. But, in some states, like Rajasthan and among lower socio-economic class, some instances of child marriages are still reported. According to the Indian law, the minimum age for a girl at marriage should be 18 years and for a boy it should be 21 years.

Males and females have different genetic combination of sex chromosome pair, which determines their biological sex. Secretion of certain hormones amount is different in both male and female. They have different internal and external reproductive organs. Genetic differences are evident from the time of conception itself. In a normal conception, the female parent contributes an 'X' chromosome and the male parent contributes either an 'X' or a 'Y' chromosome, together they form a chromosome pair which determines sex of the child. An XX combination results into a female child, while XY combination leads to a male child.

The action of hormones determines the sex of the child. Hormones are chemicals that act as signals from one part of the body to another. Here, we will discuss two major types of hormones, androgens and estrogens. Both, females and males produce both types of hormones, but their amount of secretion is controlled by the sex of the child. Male child produces more androgens, sex hormones that contribute to the development of typically male features (like the growth of body hair) and females produce proportionately more estrogens, sex hormones that aid in the development of typically female features (like the development of breasts). Till the first six weeks after conception, sex difference among female and males fetuses is identical. Hormonal effects start to show up in the fetus about seven weeks after conception, the Y chromosome causes the secretion of the androgen testosterone which results in the male internal organs to enlarge and grow while other rudimentary female organs shrink with the chemical processes. The relative lack of androgens in female fetuses causes the development of female internal organs beginning at about the twelfth week of prenatal development and leads to the shrinking of the incipient male organs. The development of external reproductive organs follows some time later, during the fourth month of pregnancy (Archer and Lloyd, 1985).

In India, we recognize a "third sex" and define a corresponding third gender role (Nanda, 1990). Third sex individuals belong to a special religious sect called hijras, are individuals born with ambiguous—looking genitalia (probably because of unusual prenatal hormone production) or are males whose male organs fail to function. They undergo the removal of their penis, testicles and scrotum and take up a specialized gender role in their society. Nanda (1990) describes them as neither men nor women, function as an institutionalized third gender role, their ambiguous sexual nature accounts for their traditional occupation, that of performing after the birth of child, at weddings and at temple festivals.

The eunuchs are usually gay men, who for many people in India are associated with prostitution and sexual deviance. They are now also members of parliament in India. Unique recoverities the credit agency run by B. Raguram Shetty sends the eunuchs to collect money owned by shopkeepers and traders, who often are so embarrassed they pay up immediately.

The eunuchs, the people of the third sex are born neither male nor female. Indian society uses a series of titles for them like 'chhakka', 'double deckers' or 'hijra', such people never gain the affection or support of their families. Their parents hide their gender and try to contradict the truth of their sexuality. They live amongst themselves in a separate world called the 'hamaam' (bath house). Here, there are no hostile glares, no violence and no ridicule or contempt. They develop deep emotional ties among themselves.

When an infant is born whose sex cannot be easily determined by looking at the external genitalia it poses a dilemma for medical staff and the baby's parents. It's not difficult to imagine the consternation for parents, if something we all take for granted, i.e. declaring 'it's a boy' or 'it's a girl', can't be stated at the moment of birth.

Because of the complexity of fetal development, things can and do go wrong. There are many different types of genital abnormality. The female baby for instance, can be born with ovaries but male external genitals. Female pseudohermaphroditism—males can be born with undescended testicles (testicles still contained within the pelvis) but with female looking genitalia, male pseudohermaphroditism. Babies can have ovaries and testicles as well as ambiguous looking genitals and this is what is known as hermaphroditism. Hijras and hermaphrodites are not, of course, confined to South Asia. But in the West, it is routine to rectify such perceived abnormalities by surgery.

Biological maturity and physical health are first requirements for sex relations in marriages. Sex relations are essential as it has special value in establishing close and affectional relationship between husband and wife. Though, it is not common in our culture, but medical check-up before marriage will be helpful as many later on problems could be averted. Some individuals may suffer from serious problems like blood group incompatibility, RH incompatibility, infertility, HIV infection, venereal diseases or other infectious diseases, which should be cured before marriage instead of hiding to avoid later on problems. Divorces due to infertility have adverse effects. We have heard divorces in western culture due to some peculiar habits like snoring, clumsiness, sluggishness, too much talking or not talking. Appearance, grooming, make-up, dressing sense also helps in adding to the love between the spouses. Physical attractiveness often leads to marital relationship. Though, such type of marriage may not last long. Partners may not find life long happiness with each other. Alcohol, smoking and drugs are other aspects, which may distort the family relations.

Gender Role in Society

Every culture provides guidelines for how its members should participate in the society and defines the role-played by specific members. The process through which new members of a culture learn its language, values, beliefs and behavioural expectations is known as socialization. The young boys and girls learn about masculinity and feminity from the society they live in and, this shapes their own behaviour as well as their expectations from the opposite sex. Identifying psychologically with one sex or the other is developing a sexual identity. Sexual identity is the psychological identification of an individual as either male or female. This leads to the development of gender identity. Gender identity is the extent to which an individual has learned and incorporated the behaviours and expectations associated with a gender role into his or her own personality (Stover and Hope, 1989). Establishing and development of a sexual identity and gender identity are both psychological processes. Most of the time biological sex and gender identity correspond. But, there are incidents in which they might be inconsistent. Some people choose an androgynous way of life in which there are a few differences in how females and males act or dress. Androgyny is the term used to describe a type of personality that combines the positive aspects of both masculinity and feminity. Research on androgynous personalities found that androgynous individuals are more adaptable (Bem, 1975) and competitive (Alagna, 1982). Androgynous fathers are more loving and responsive to, but less of demanding of, their children than masculine fathers (Baumrind, 1982).

De Lucia (1987) reported university students behaviour related to dating. All students engaged in some cross-gender type behaviour, but students scoring high on masculinity tended to engage in masculine dating activities (for example, opening the door, making reservations, paying, deciding when and where to go out to eat and verbally expressing sexual desires) while students scoring high on feminity tended to engage in feminine dating activities (for example, sensing the other's disturbance about something, giving into the other's wishes, watching the other participate in activities outside the relationship, avoiding decision-making and non-verbally letting the other know they would like to have sex). Androgynous students were less restricted in their dating activities; both male and female androgynous students felt free to engage in either masculine or feminine dating behaviours (De Lucia, 1987). While the enthusiasm for androgyny as a social science concept has faded (Giele, 1988), it still communicates a very powerful idea—that feminine and masculine attributes are not opposite (Weitzman, 1984) rather both sets of attributes can be combined in one individual at a given time in one situation (for example, both be caring for their child) or either be masculine or feminine in any situation. There are growing expectations that married mothers should help provide for the family and that married fathers should take an active part in caring for their children (La Rossa, 1988).

MENTAL PREPARATION

Individual should be mentally prepared for the marriage in which they are getting involved by willingness for its own sake rather than as a gateway from loneliness in old-age, to marry as to have company during old-age, avoid being left alone, social pressure from the parents or society in which one lives. Like, in our society, singlehood is not approved but at the same time just marrying under the social pressure would lead to marriages that are more stressful. Marrying for economic advancement (Lott, 1987) occurs among all but this alone as a feature, later leads to conflict in the relationship and also if what a spouse had expected and does not get also leads to disentanglement of the marital ties. In India, dowry (economic commodities, either in cash or kind) is still given by brides parents to the bridegroom and his family, though the law of the state bans it.

Girls and boys, both, along with their family members must be prepared mentally. Both, should have positive attitude towards marriage. They should view marriage not as a compulsion but, there should be willingness on their part. They should be prepared emotionally to appreciate their spouse and accept their in-laws as their own parents. Girls should be taught about many things like how to respect elders, how to bear responsibilities and how serve and sacrifice. Sharing and caring will help her to make her own place in new family. When girls make too many demands in the beginning or avoid taking household responsibilities, they take longer time in making their place in the hearts of their husband and in-laws. Faithfulness and honesty are other characteristics, which will help, in building-up happy marital relationship. All these things must be taught before marriage. Teaching such things these days are more essential because of small and independent families. In large families, girls and boys get ample opportunity to learn through watching, others or discussing with elders, friends or cousins. Husbands and their parents too must learn—how much to expect from each other, how to express their expectations, how to honour the qualities of brides instead of pin pointing weaknesses and how to avoid frictions, and ignore smaller things.

Girls and boys, both, should be able to change their behaviour or habits if need be, if daughter-in-law get up late in the morning or sleep late in night this may be disturbing to others. Being religious also helps in adjustment process. All persons involved try to find out some common goals, interests in life. In all together, girls should be taught to be active, interesting and social (to some extent), too. She should know the appropriate ways of entertainment and enjoyment. Boys should be taught to keep a balance of relationship between parents and wife. He should try to develop amicable relationship between his parents, especially mother and wife and try to integrate his wife into her new role healthily.

Mental Health

These days due to increased tensions, the mental problems are being increased. Excessive worries, tensions, depressions, delusions, hallucinations or compulsive behaviour are some sort of abnormal behaviour, which may disturb the married life. Hence, if any of the person, girl or boy suffers from any of such or other related problems, they should be cured first. For emotional well-being, it is essential that they should learn proper control and proper expression of emotions. Bad temper, moodiness are also unhealthy ingredients for marriage.

SEXUAL PREPARATION

Proper sex education about the sexual needs, sex behaviour, pregnancy, childbirth, etc. is also essential for girls and boys, both, before the marriage. Instead of family members or friends, the doctors or family counsellors can guide in a better way by giving scientific knowledge and also information about family planning.

Knowledge regarding laws about marriage, divorce, dowry, property, sex determination and abortions should be given to face any eventuality. Though, it should not be heightened, much.

Some girls have notion that child's birth will spoil their youthfulness and also spoil their figure and cut freedom. Boys many times are scared of responsibility of children or extra burden. They need to be educated in this regard, too.

SKILLS LEARNING PREPARATION

Skill Learning

It will always be helpful in marital relations if girls are equipped with certain skills to run their family smoothly. Developing expertise in cooking, stitching, knitting, maintaining house, gardening, decoration or beautification will certainly help her in making her own place in the in-laws family. Developing expertise in cooking, house-hold care responsibilities and sharing of home-care responsibility by husbands would lead to happy functioning of their family life.

Education

Sound academic qualifications alongwith some professional courses will equip the girl with better qualities. It will help her to maintain her confidence, respect and, if need be, she can add to the family income. Education and professional skills among boys is necessary. Boys, still being the primary bread-winner in the family, this skill will boost their earning capacity and, as well as increase their confidence and respect.

Dowry

Though, dowry is not viewed positively but, it is observed and experienced that gifts given or articles prepared by her, brings appreciation to the girl's family. It boosts up her confidence. Dowry in form of gifts, small easily afforded by the family should not be viewed negatively. Huge dowry in the form of expensive materialistic gifts, cash or property should be discouraged by both boy's and girl's family. Also, under the law of the land this is a non-bailable crime. It has also been seen, that, dowry demands have lead to bride-burning by the in-laws or girls committing suicides because of the torture they face from their in-laws hands and, at times, their parents not in the capacity to fulfill their in-laws demands. Dowry giving and taking, both, should be discouraged from youth's young age itself.

PSYCHOLOGICAL PREPARATION

There are certain behaviours or habits that hinder proper getting along with others in married life. These are—holding grudges, gossiping, jealousy, laughing at or making fun of others, boasting, arguing and combating others, and sarcasm and cutting remarks.

The person who holds grudges tends to keep looking for more wrongs. They make themselves and others unhappy without cause. Gossiping is viewed as a means of hiding weaknesses of self. They try to put others down to build themselves up. They may fall into the habit of repeating unpleasant things about others and praising themselves up. A generous attitude attracts people, whereas, jealousy drives friends away. The jealous person is seldom happy himself. To overcome it, it is suggested that one should try to overlook the faults and develop appreciation for other persons. Those who make fun of others, in fact show a lack of confidence in their own standing in the world. People avoid company of such persons who ridicule the ideas of others or laugh at their mistakes. Boasting is not appreciated in civilized cultures, however, in some people this tendency still persists. Boasting of possessions is boring to others. One who talks about what he/she has or what his/her parents or relatives own is not likely to win good relationships. Healthy differences of opinion are not bad, but, doing it with family members, often, widen differences in relations. Sarcasm always hurts feelings and, hence, upsets relations. Some habits worth cultivating are like dependability by being punctual, by borrowing only when necessary and are careful to return by keeping your word. Cheerfulness, giving honest compliments, good sportsmanship, consideration for the rights of others and being prepared for coming moments or events helps to foster healthy familial and marital relationships.

Dependability

Dependable and reliable persons are always respected and appreciated. One should be punctual, and remember that borrowing is bad. If borrowed do return things in time without damaging it. Keeping words and keeping promises lead to appreciation and avoid wrathfulness. Carefulness in these and other matters adds up to dependability.

Cheerfulness

Cheerfulness is one of the most attractive traits of all. Laugh and the world laughs with you. Being cheerful is a great quality.

They have active sense of good humour.

Honest Compliments

All of us know the feeling of warm pleasure and appreciation when someone gives us an honest compliment. We develop appreciation for person who gives compliment. It is not flattery. Flattery is not sincere. Compliments on looks, appearance, dresses are not bad but more graceful are compliments given on actions or behaviour.

Good Sportsmanship

It is a quality to recognize the importance of the group, in present case they are members of family. They are supportive to each other, less fault finding and accept their mistakes easily, and without criticism.

Consideration for the Rights of others

Instead of always demanding things from others, having high expectations from others, it is better to recognize what others deserve. What I can give to others and what is his/her right to get. Being prepared in advance even for routine work will help you. One should plan in advance; streamline your routine so that you have more time and energy for enjoying life.

MARRIAGE AS REVOLT AGAINST PARENTS

Marriages taking place just to show rebellion against parents and elders of the family, also, does not last long. Social-psychological theory and research show that parental interference can increase feelings of romantic attraction between partners (Katz and Liu, 1988). Any parental interference in the relationship is likely to increase the romantic attraction between the two persons, leading to the so-called Romeo and Juliet effect and further rebellion against the parents (Driscoll, Davis and Lipetz, 1972). If the primary reason one partner wants to get married is to escape from parental authority or to establish independence, this should be recognized as an unhealthy motivation for marriage (Rubin, 1976).

PREGNANCY AS A REASON FOR MARRIAGE

Unintended pregnancy becomes a reason for a couple to hasten marriage. Marriages that are precipitated by an unintentional pregnancy have a much greater risk of marital dissatisfaction and ultimate divorce than marriages not having pre-marital pregnancy (Kraus, 1977). Pre-marital pregnancy is often associated with subsequent marital break-up (Teachman, 1983; Teti and Lamb, 1989). The reasons for this could be several like the marriage is forced to occur at a time not planned, pregnant brides are often teenagers. Babies are expensive and a couple not financially prepared for the costs can be overwhelmed. These babies shatter their parents' goals. For teenage parents are less likely to attain educational goals, have low income and occupational status and have more children than they would like and to go on welfare (Hayes, 1987). In, in-laws relationships may be marred if parents resent their child's marital partner for having brought about a marriage they did not want or viewed as too early.

Knox (1975) lists companionship, emotional security and desire to parent and raise children as positive reasons for marriage. Marriage is a socially approved union for developing closeness with another human being. Legitimate needs for companionship, to love and to be loved by someone else can be satisfied. Marrying for emotional security implies that a person seeks the stable structure of marrying to help ensure the maintenance of a close interpersonal relationship over time. Although most people do not marry only to have children (and this alone may not be a positive reason for marrying), many regard children as a valuable part of married life. The benefits of love, sex, companionship, emotional security and children can be enjoyed without marriage. But marriage provides the social approval and structure for experiencing these phenomena with the same person over time (Knox, 1975).

DATING

Dating is not common in our culture but very common in western culture. During dating boys and girls fix up time to meet, where they talk to each other, understand each other and also understand their own self. It helps in many ways. Boys and girls, both, should know the limits of their relation at this stage. It should not be crossed. One should also not make haste in developing love relationship, as, if after sometimes you want to leave partner, he/she may not want to let you go with others. Secondly, if one partner gets emotionally involved then separation will be very difficult on him or her. Dating has several functions. It helps to:

Discovering Oneself

During dating one can explore good things in self. They get to know about self through the eyes of others who is friendly and close. Many times, parents keep on criticizing and do not appreciate as a result children do not develop positive self-concept. During dating, they can develop positive attitude towards their own self. Adolescents now develop independent identity and, they also do self-evaluation and self-analysis.

Becoming Realistic about the other Sex

Dating provides the first good opportunity to become well acquainted with someone of the other sex outside one's own family. They also know how people of other sex think, feel, expect and behave, their emotions, reactions, limitations or plus points. This will help in later life when they get married.

Discovering Families

Normally girls may make mistake in expecting same level of freedom, love, protection, and independence in their in-laws house, as they used to get in their parent's families. During dating, people have an opportunity to get acquainted with other kinds of families in a new way. If parents cooperate, dating couples may spend a great deal of time in each home. Dating has positive as well as negative roles depending upon understanding and cultural context.

Engagement

Dating is a form of friendliness, where there is no commitment, whereas, engagement is a step towards marriage. In our culture, it is performed in presence of many people with religious ceremonies. Here, begins the process of understanding each other and developing emotional ties. There should be sufficient time between the engagement and marriage for mental preparedness, in our culture; such decisions are taken by elders keeping in mind various aspects. The engagement is in reality a period of serious courtship; a time during which the couple can make a careful check to see whether they have chosen someone with whom they can live the next 40 years or more. Engagement is not simply a time for having fun—although enjoying the same interest is one strong bond for a happy marriage. Engagement is a healthy way of preparation for marriage.

5

Mate Selection

With the rise in divorce rate, preparation for a happy healthy marriage is gaining importance. Young people need to learn how to avoid conflict in marital relationships. Planning and preparing yourself for a happy marriage is the first step in making it happen in your own life.

The family environment in which one grows up is strongly influenced by one's cultural heritage. Every culture has its own way of life. Cultural heritage is a learned behaviour that is passed on from one generation to another. Family guidelines and beliefs are part of one's heritage.

In a happy marriage, both the partners, feel satisfied in the relationship. Many factors influence happiness in a marriage. The life journey of a person is full of thorns. To cross this path such a companion is needed who helps when in trouble, gives courage when faced with problems and is able to proceed with heart and soul together in life. Our heart desires to establish contacts with the other heart and both desire to love each other. Both the hearts are brimming with sweet feelings and, when both of them are bound together in a string, the society calls it, the institution of marriage.

A person's life is said to be complete only when his or her other half is beautiful, wise, full of loving feelings and, both hearts are capable of complete union with one another. An old saying among Indians is that, if a man has a gentle, beautiful, healthy and educated wife than such a house is more comfortable than the palace of God Indra or abode of Heaven. There are some eco-psycho-social factors that are related to couple's happiness. Personal qualities include the ability to give and receive love, empathy, emotional stability, trustworthy, sensitive, caring, flexible, logical, reasonable, thoughtful, dependable and responsible.

Arranged marriages had been the common way of marriage till twentieth century in India and still have hold on the society. Though its form to certain extent has changed. In the good olden days, in India, marriages were confined to a limited caste and sub-caste, sometimes, also, to a particular geographical area or regions and, sometimes to a particular vernacular language of the people. Family ties and blood relations played a tremendous role in the most rural families. At times, family purohit (priest), or a known mid-wife or barber acted as a mediator for marriage alliances. Even today, these people along with newspaper advertisement and website networks have an appreciable role in formation of marital alliances. Though, mass media like radio, 'Mujhe Se Shaadi Karoge' on Radio at 98.3 FM on Sunday at 12:30 PM is running fast to catch up in the race of search of eligible marriage partner. Lately on, Sony TV channel a serial named 'Kahin Na Kahin Koi Hai' (June 2002) was started, as matchmaking serial but was not very successful.

Our Indian society is rooted conspicuously in the traditional religious rural background. In the present, dynamically changing Indian society, religious orthodoxy, its conventions, customs, social attitudes, behaviours, and acceptable social norms have come in conflict with the growing ideals of new social life. The ancient ways of marriage and kinship are slowly giving place to the new forms and patterns. In the contemporary society, there is a definite revolution in reforms of marriage, their rites and rituals. The age-old wedding ceremonies are conspicuously simplified.

If we analyze, there were negligibly few inter-caste marriages in the past. We see inter-religious, inter-community and inter-lingual marriages are increasing in numbers. Introduction of democratic ideals, secular ideas, western ideology, technological advancement and westernization of the modern society has resulted in attitude change among all sections of the society. Industrialization has resulted in rural work force shifting to urban and semi-urban areas in search of work and, thereby, acculturalization of the rural people. The rise of literacy rate, explosion of mass media and general progress of the society has all accumulated together to bring a resultant attitude change in the people of Indian sub-continent.

Profession and occupation greatly influence the matrimonial alliances in every country. Generally, man is supposed to be the earning breadwinner member, while woman is supposed to be responsible for house keeping and chosen as a dependent member. With, more and more women, having entered into various professions, the likelihood of them to be only housekeeper has remarkably reduced. The needs of the modern society has resulted into an increase of dual career families.

'Gotra' is an important component in the Indian marriages. The gotra in Hindus is considered as the common line of descent. If the 'gotra' is common, the alliance is prohibited. This implies that people of 'sagotra' or same gotra are blood relations. They are supposed to be brothers and sisters, so the marriages among these are prohibited. The traditional Hindu society, thus, presents a peculiar genetical objection. People coming from the same origin do not prefer to marry each other. If, at all, there is any marriage links between them, the offering will not be healthy or may not even survive. From scientific angles also the persons having the same genes are prohibited from marriage.

Religious consciousness pervades every walk of life. No social problem remains in isolation without being influenced by religious sentiments of the concerned individual, directly or indirectly. India is a secular country and, its sovereigns have diverse faiths and religious beliefs. Religious groups tend to discourage interfaith marriages, believing that such marriages may weaken individual beliefs, lead to children being reared in a different faith or secularize the family. Some, who are from different religious backgrounds, however, do convert to their spouses' religious faith (Sander, 1993).

Krishnamoorthy and Audinarayana (2001), studies data from the 1992-93 National Family Health Survey, to find a high consanguinity in the South Indian States of Andhra Pradesh, Karnataka and Tamil Nadu. In Kerala, the frequency of consanguineous marriages, is very common type of preferred marriage of the Dravidian marriage system, uncle-niece marriages are observed. In the other states of South India, consanguinity a coefficient of inbreeding is high. While no change in consanguinity is observed during the past three to four decades in Karnataka, a definite decline is observed in Andhra Pradesh and Tamil Nadu. Due to recent changes in the demographic situation in these states, this decline in consanguinity is likely to continue.

The language controversy is more prominent in the South India than the North India. Men are more particular about the local or regional language in the South. There is lot of socialization process in the North with respect to language. The North has witnessed several struggles and movements in pre-independence days. Apart from this, their local language is their national language. For this reason the North poses comparatively less problems of language than the South (Report of the Education Commission, 1964-66). The particulars of 'Horoscope' and 'Star' in general are more 'desired' by the 'Southerners' than those of 'Northerners' (Reddy, 1978).

Marriage forms have, however, changed during the long course of human history, but they always remained an important social institution with mankind, which embraced all the sexual and productive aspects of human life. Marriage is a holy union between man and woman. Indians define marriage as a sacrament or a holy bondage. Marriage is grouping of two sexes. Above all, a communion of two souls. According to Freudian psychology, marriage is to release of libidinal energy. Marriage is a biological need. It is, also, the fulfilment of life aspiration (Lundberg, 1958).

Marriage is a communion, getting together of two sexes for enjoyment and fulfilment. In the early stages of human history, woman was truth and man was opinion, with respect to their progeny. In the Middle Ages, marriage was a clan-kinship and herd-relationship and, in the later years, marriage has been viewed as a caste and a class barrier or a bondage (Reddy, 1978).

The existing patterns of marriage arrangements are quite different from those of the earlier forms. The present forms of marriage are also fast changing with time. With the change in time, there is the emergence of new social ideas, which invariably influence the marriage relations in a given society. In arranged marriage, mate selection is a procedure in which parents or other older people select marriage partners for members of younger generations. Elders of the family control the initial and sometimes the final decision of the marriage proposal. Marriage is based on practical criteria than emotional ones. The development of emotional and physical intimacy takes place after marriage.

Day-by-day, arranged marriages are decreasing in our society, although, there is some hope of their future survival due to the age long traditional social stability. Recent past is again seeing revival of arranged marriages, which were at its decline in 1970's, 1980's and early 1990's. Even arranged marriages are now based on personal liking of the spouses based on higher education, income and personal characteristics of age.

Today, most of the marriage alliances are based on academic qualifications and earning capacities of the males especially, with working middle class community looking forward to earning female counterpart also. Monogamy is a marital union of one man to one woman at any given time. But, monogamy is a minority preference among world cultures, practiced by only 24 percent of the known cultures (Murdock, 1967). The preferred marital arrangement worldwide is polygamy, the practice of having more than one wife or husband. One study of cultures throughout the world found that 75 percent of the cultures studied (representing, nevertheless, a ministry of the world's population) preferred the practice of having two or more spouses.

THE STAGES OF MATE SELECTION—STIMULUS-VALUE-ROLE THEORY

The Stimulus-Value-Role-Theory of mate selection has been given by Bernard Murstein (1976, 1987). Murstein developed a three-stage theory. The stimulus-value-role theory explains the development of romantic relationships. This theory is based on exchange. Each partner evaluates the other, if the exchange seems more or less equitable, the two will progress to the next stage. According to the theory, couples go through the following stages in a defined sequence.

In the stimulus stage, each person is drawn or attracted to the other before actual interaction. This attraction can be physical, mental or social; it can be based on person's reputation or status. This stage according to him is the most prominent on the first encounter, when one has little information with which to evaluate the other person.

In the next stage, the value stage, partners weigh each other's basic values, trying to determine if they are compatible. Each person tries to figure out the other's philosophy of life, politics, sexual values, religious beliefs, and so on. In the role stage, each person analyzes the other's behaviours or how the person fulfils his or her role as lover, companion, friend, worker and potential husband or wife, mother or father.

People most often marry others of the same race, as they are likely to have more in common. Sometimes, people of different races are also attracted to each other. These couples face many challenges but their mutual love for each other helps the relationship to grow. Marriage takes place usually from the field of eligibles, those whom our culture approves as potential partners. The field of eligibles is defined by two principles endogamy (marriage within a particular group) and exogamy (marriage outside a particular group).

Endogamy strengthens group structure. People usually marry from the group to which they identify—nationality, ethnic group, religious affiliation, or socio-economic status because they share common assumptions, experiences and understandings. The principle of exogamy requires us to marry outside certain groups. Exogamy is enforced taboos that are deeply embedded within our psychological make up. Marriage in Hindus among same sagotras is considered incestuous.

Homogamy refers to the tendency to choose a mate whose personal or group characteristics are similar to ours. Heterogamy refers to the tendency to choose a mate whose personal or group characteristics differ from our own. The homogamous considerations of a mate choice generally apply to heterosexuals, gay men and lesbians alike in their choice of partners. The most important elements of homogamy are race and ethnicity, religion, socio-economic status, age and personality characteristics. These elements are strongest in first marriages and weaker in second and subsequent marriages (Glick, 1988). They also strongly influence our choice of sexual partners, as our sexual partners are often potential marriage partners (Michael, Gagnon, Lauman and

Kolata, 1994). Marriages that are homogamous tend to be more stable than heterogamous ones (Burr, 1973).

Researchers who have studied marriage relationships have formed a principle called homogamy. This principle suggests that people who have many similarities, or much is common are more likely to have a satisfying marriage. People are more likely to be attracted to some one who has similar interests, goals and values like them, belongs to similar background and share similar life goals.

Sometimes, a person is attracted to another who is quite different. When these differences benefit the relationship. They are called complementary qualities. That means the strengths of one person make up for the weaknesses of the other (Leone Johnson, 1998).

SELECTION OF MARRIAGE PARTNER

Social scientists refer to the process of searching for, finding and choosing a marriage partner as mate selection. Mate selection is the first step in assuring society a continual supply of new people, which is an essential component of every society. A person selects the individual by virtue of background or birth and are most likely to make compatible marriage partners. This is also called pool of eligibles. Mate selection is important to individuals for it determines with whom to live, love, share and work with for the years to come in future, with the notion of till death do us part.

Mate selection procedures vary from society to society. One of the major variations is in terms of who does the selection. Is it done by the partners themselves ? Is it done by the elders and parents of the partners ? Is it done by mutual agreement of both partners and parents? Is the agreement for economic reasons? Is it necessary to wait for marriage to have sex?

Although women tend to marry those with the same socio-economic status and cultural background, men tend to marry women slightly below them in age, education, and so on. Constantine Safilios—Rothschild (1976) found that many women expect men to bring more expressive, affective, and companionable resources into marriage.

The use of advertisements in magazines and newspapers, for

mate selection, has existed in our society from quite long time. These personal advertisements have become match-makers. Typically, a person places an advertisement in matrimonial column in the newspaper and then waits for the responses to be sent to the newspaper publisher who, in turn, forwards them to the advertiser or directly to the person who has applied. The content analysis of advertisements show that the exchange/ bargaining system is very much evident. Each individual makes an offer for something in return. More specifically, women were likely to offer attractiveness while seeking financial security with partners who were older than them. In contrast, men were more likely to be seeking attractive partners who were younger than them and to be offering financial security (Harrison and Saeed, 1977).

FACTORS IN SELECTING A LIFE PARTNER

Today we can learn the art of spouse selection from understanding the nature of true love, the nature and purpose of marriage, the conditions for marriage, the nature of men and women, the role of expectations, background factors, psychological factors for happiness, and the reasons for breakdown in marriage.

Love as a Basis

At the core of marriage is love and at the core of love is the craving and bodies. It is a merger of two human personalities. Both act and feel, as one though may not be one.

Marriage Goals

Being in love is so dominant that other factors are ignored. But, if we select partners in marriage with an eye on their ability to serve marital goals, we would have fewer unhappy and unsuccessful marriages. In marriage willingness to raise a family, fondness for children and many other goals and functions are to be fulfiled.

Similarity or Complementary

Men and women are called the efficient cause of marriage since they are the parties to it. They can act as complements to each other, supplying each other's deficiencies, moderating each other's weaknesses, and developing each other's points of strength. One study reported in mate selection that each individual seeks within his or her field of eligible that person who gives the greatest promise of providing him or her with maximum need gratifications.

Fulfilment of Expectations

Each partner should also have similar expectations of marriage. These expectations live at the basis of marital success or failure. These are conditioned (associated) by early education and environment. The religion, ethnical caste group, social class, economic group and general culture all contribute to these expectations. But, today in mixed cultures marriages are taking place with different cultures and varying expectations. Marriage counsellors report that marriages are being broken because of different expectations.

Background Factors

Many studies have explored the factors in childhood, adolescence, and adult premarital life, which are linked with a successful marriage. Generally, we found that one who was from a small town, or the country, raised in a large family, belongs to religious creed, had happy childhood, had warm and affectionate relationships with his family, such a person would be raised with discipline, would have adequate sex education and would marry with the approval of his parents.

Psychological Traits

The following traits are important in happy marital life. The negative traits are—Being touchy, losing temper easily, fighting to get one's own way, being critical of others, being careless of others' feelings, chafing under-discipline, rebelling against orders, showing dislikes, being easily affected by praise or blame, lacking self-confidence, dominating the opposite sex, having little interest in old people, children, charity, upliftment activities, most of the time excited, and having alternate moods quickly.

THERE ARE CERTAIN HURDLES OF FILTERS IN PROPER MATE SELECTION

Propinquity

Propinquity means physical proximity or closeness. You are likely to meet people who live near you, working in the same office or sit near you in class. One should not limit to these aspects rather should increase exposure to different environments. Propinquity helps to overcome the hesitations in interactions with strangers; it explains why people marry within their own social class because our place of residence, school and work environment is correlated with socio-economic status.

Attractiveness

Some people whom you become more familiar are more attractive to you than others. Personal preference plays role here. Generally, you select someone whose physical attractiveness is similar to your own.

Similarity

People tend to marry those similar to themselves in terms of age, physical attractiveness, personality traits, attitudes, cognitive abilities, education and social class background.

Reciprocity

The other person is judged to be attractive and to have desirable characteristics, signs that attraction was mutual. Reciprocity boost self-esteem reduces likelihood or rejection.

Complementarily

When a potential partner possesses desirable characteristics and shows evidence of reciprocal attraction, that individual may be perceived an opportunity for self-expansion. You can enhance the self, by incorporating the resources of the other person, through establishing a close relationship. So, you may fall in love with those who possess what you lack but value those people who complement you in some way.

The Right Person at the Right Time

The main hurdle in mate selection may be whether the person

who is able to make all the preceding cuts shows up at the right time. Temporal readiness refers to the fact that people often marry within a limited time frame.

Happily married men show evidence of an even and stable emotional tone. They are cooperative in money matters, saving, cautious, conservative and have religious bend. Happily married women are characterized by kind attitude towards others and by the expectation of kind attitude in return. Do not easily take offense and are not unduly concerned about the impressions they make upon others. They are cooperative, do not object to subordinate roles, and not annoyed by advice from others. They have missionary and ministering attitude. They enjoy activities that bring educational or pleasurable opportunities to others also, and work for dependent and underprivileged. In religion, morals and politics they are conservative and conventional. They are self-assured and optimistic in outlook.

Many consider the factors whom not to marry. Factors which are considered here include those persons having little preparation for marriage, being immature, irresponsible and selfish, undue attachment to parents, incorrect attitude towards sex, heavy drinking, inability to handle money wisely, tendency to nag, being affectionate and a spoiled child, suspicious, jealous, being perfectionist and irreligious. Desirable characteristics for marriage partners are willingness to rear a family, high moral standards, same religion, desired stability and dependability, emotional maturity, good grooming and manners, and affectionateness.

The selection of a partner in marriage is one of the most important decisions of lifetime. Other decisions can be revoked but this one cannot. We can change our career, occupations, our names, our friends—but we cannot change our life mates; they are partners until death do us part, even when separation takes place, the intimacy of marital life has traces on one's personality which are not easily erased. Most broken marriages have their seeds of failure planted before the marriage is over.

Desirable qualities in spouse include honesty, loving and caring attitude, congenial personality, respectful, intelligent, mature/responsible, ambitious, loyal and trust worthy, and physical attractiveness. In studies it has been revealed that unattractive man if married to attractive woman has something to offer other than looks, such as fame or fortune. Hatfield and

Walster (1981) write that although we prefer more desirable qualities than ourselves but matching considerations influences our actual choices. We all tend to end up with partners of approximately our own social value. Thus, our selection of a mate appears to be a delicate compromise between our desire to capture an ideal partner and our realization that we must eventually settle for what we deserve.

Marriage takes place usually from the field of eligibles, those whom our culture approves as potential partners. The field of eligibles is defined by two principles—endogamy (marriage within a particular group) and exogamy (marriage outside a particular group).

Physical Attractiveness

Physical attractiveness is particularly important during the initial meeting and each stages of a relationship. If you don't know anything else about a person, you tend to judge him or her on appearance.

We unconsciously infer qualities based on looks. This inference is based on halo effect, the assumption that good-looking people possess more desirable social characteristics than unattractive people. Dion *et. al.* (1972) from their research concluded that attractive men and women were assumed to be more sensitive, kind, warm, sexually responsive, strong, poised and outgoing than others, they were assumed to be more exciting and to have better characters than "ordinary" people. Research indicates that overall, the differences between perceptions of very attractive and average people are minimal. It is when attractive and average people are compared to those considered to be unattractive that there are pronounced differences, with those perceived as unattractive being rated more negatively (Hatfield and Sprecher, 1986). Hatfield and Sprecher (1986) demonstrated that good-looking companions increase our social status.

Others rate good-looking people as smarter, healthier, more desirable and more important. Attractive people are viewed as being happier, more sensitive, more interesting, warmer, more poised, and more sociable and as having better character than their less attractive counterparts (Cash and Janda, 1984; Margolin, White, 1987). Characteristics often mentioned as attractive for both sexes include slimness, clear skin, smiling features and clean appearance. In men, average height or taller and a beard often are considered to add to appeal. In women, a feminine figure and breast size were considered important. We tend to rate our own attractiveness as high, medium or low and seem to choose potential lovers whose physical appeal we evaluate as similar to ours. Today, people travel alot because of their jobs and education and are likely to meet people from all parts of the country and world. Propinquity, meaning nearness plays a leading role in mate selection process especially if done by the individual itself.

Physical attractiveness may bring people together initially, but they are more likely to stay together if they are physically similar. White (1980) found that daters who had been most similar in physical attractiveness stayed together for a long time. Dating couples that end up, as marriage partners are similar to one another in other ways as well, their attitude towards war, birth control, various political issues, technological growth and sex roles are strongly similar (Buss, 1985). Daters who become spouses also tend to be closely matched in terms of social background characteristics such as race, socio-economic class and religious denomination.

Age at Marriage

The age at which people marry depends heavily on social standards and expectations. In technologically advanced nations, where economic independence is stressed marriage often occurs relatively late. In order to limit population increase the official government recommended age in the People's Republic of China is 28 for men and 25 for women (McWhirter, 1988).

Adults are waiting longer to marry today, than in previous generations. Increasing age at time of marriage probably results in young adults beginning marriage with more maturity, independence, work experience and education. These are important assets to bring into marriage. Adolescent marriage and late marriages are likely to end in divorce. Youthful marriages are good. Older you are when you marry the greater the likelihood of marital happiness. Men usually marry slightly younger women. Though, a trend of men marrying older women is seen among the celebrities like Sachin Tendulkar—Anjali, Aizhruddin—Sangeeta Bijlani, Saif Ali Khan—Amrita Singh.

Socio-economic Status

People tend to marry those of the same socio-economic status because of shared values, tastes, goals, occupations and expectations and same educational background. Women in our culture marry to a higher status men than men from lower status, and daughters are send to higher status family for better adjustment of their child.

Level of Education

It seems to affect both marital adjustment and divorce. It may give us additional resources such as income, insight or status. It also provides help to carry out marital roles.

Childhood Environment

Childhood environment includes attachment to family members, parents' marital happiness and low parent child conflict is associated with one's own happiness, in marriage and resultant adjustment to the new role, new life, to the spouse and their family members.

Personality Factors

Cate and Lloyd (1992) reviewed various studies and found that those who had been psychologically healthy in college were more likely to be maritally satisfied than those who had been psychologically unhealthy; gifted, emotionally stable children were more likely to feel satisfied in marriage; higher impulse control, lower neuroticism and greater conventionality predicted both husbands' and wives' marital satisfaction. Social scientists like Antill, 1983; Buss, 1984; Kurdek and Smith, 1987; Lesnick—Oberstein and Cohen, 1984 found that people tend to choose partners who share similar personality characteristics, like impulsive, accurate reasoners, quarrelsome and extrovert. Old saying that the opposites attract sometimes come true.

INTER-CASTE, INTER-RELIGION, INTER-CLASS AND INTER-RACIAL MARRIAGE

In India a girl is traditionally married to a man of her own caste, province and religion and sometimes because of this constraint it becomes difficult to find a suitable match for her.

Inter-caste and inter-provincial marriages have arisen. This change towards the acceptance of inter-caste marriage was observed long ago by Ghurye (1950), "formerly marriage outside one's caste was not to be even thought of today many educated young men and women are prepared to leak though the bonds of caste if mutual love or attraction demands it." Also, other Indian researchers/ scientists have also reported an increase in inter-caste marriages since 1917 but the increase had escalated after 1946, thereby, indicating that opposition to inter-caste marriage has substantially decreased (Kannan, 1963; Desai, 1945, Kapadia, 1958, Das, 1971 and Mehta, 1970).

Cormack (1961); Prince (1971); Cavan (1971) in their various studies found that college and university students opined that one should marry within one's faith (religion) by Catholic university students in the United States; Jewish students in the United States. Differences over religious matters could lead to other marital problems.

People's religious faith strongly influences his or her beliefs and practices. Marrying someone of a different faith can cause problems, unless the couple discusses the issue first. A religious difference among the couple becomes evident in raising a child in a certain religious faith. Each partner may wish to raise the child to follow his or her religious beliefs. In India, various inter-religious marriages have surfaced since long past. History shows various examples of inter-religious marriages of which Emperor Akbar's marriage to Rajput Princess Jodhabai is quite famous and it is also an exemplary of happy marriage.

Marriages are less homogamous, if, we consider couple's religion before the wedding. Many partners who originally differed in religion change their religion to make it the same as their future spouse's (Glenn, 1982; Shatzmiller, 1996). This may happen because partners agree with the widely held belief that inter-religious marriages tend not be as successful as homogamous ones—a belief supported by research (Ortega, Whitt and Williams, 1988; Heaton and Pratt, 1990; Manekar and Rankin, 1993). Religious homogeneity improves chances for marital success involves value consensus. Religious orientation may come into play when deciding about leisure activity, child rearing, spending money, and many other facets of marital interaction. Religious homogany may create a more integrated social network of relatives, friends and religious advisors (Heaton and Pratt, 1990).

Interclass marriages are also prevalent among different sections of the society. Researchers have defined the concept of hypergamy as improving one's social and/or economic status by marrying up. The opposite, hypogamy, involves marrying down. Pearlin (1975) found that partners experienced more stress in these class heterogamous unions. Moreover, the spouse who had married down was more stressed than the one who had married up. The relationship between stress and marrying down existed only when status striving was important to the individual. Those people for whom status was important and who had married down perceived their marriages more negatively—as less reciprocal, less affectionate, less emotionally supportive and with less value consensus than those who had married up. For people for whom status was not important, neither marrying up nor down produced any difference in their evaluation of their marriages.

In an interracial marriage, the greater the differences between the spouses, the more likely they will experience conflict. If they are very different, there will be more areas of conflict. They would need to adjust more than persons who marry in the same race, also acceptance of the spouse in the in-laws family might take some time.

COURTSHIP

The period before marriage is especially important, because couples learn about each other and themselves. Courtship sets the stage for marriage. Many of the elements important for successful marriages, such as the ability to communicate in a positive manner and to compromise and resolve conflicts, develop during courtship. They are often apparent long before a decision to marry has been made (Cate and Lloyd, 1992).

Premarital factors correlated with marital success include (1) background factors (age at marriage, length of courtship, level of education and childhood environment), (2) personality factors, and (3) relationship factors (communication, self-disclosure and inter-dependence). Length of courtship is related to marital happiness. The longer you date and are engaged to someone, the more likely you are to discover whether you are compatible with each other.

Dating is a social activity in which a couple spends time together getting to know each other. Dating may be either formal or informal. Formal dating is when one person invites another to a planned event. It is more structured in nature than informal dating. Informal dating is when two or more people agree to meet and spend time together in a relaxed environment. Dating helps the partners to know each other and provides them companionship. Dating is the prevailing mate selection procedure popular in the United States and Canada. As a mate selection procedure, dating maximizes individual choice while minimizing parental control, emphasizes emotional factors over practical ones, and assumes intimacy prior to long-term commitment.

The engagement period is the final stage in the dating process leading to marriage. It is also the time period from fixing of marriage to the wedding day. It signifies the start of a couple's plan for a married life. It provides time for a couple to discuss important issues as they continue to develop their relationship. Appropriately, it should be the time when the couple discuss the role expectations from each other, their commitment to the relationship, understand and accept each other as the person really is. Now-a-days, couples also plan about their career goals, housing needs, finances earlier. The couples should be aware of their own emotions and be able to express them to each other. An engagement period provides time for continued evaluation and growth in the relationship. It allows time for planning future needs, discuss role expectations, finances, housing, career goals and sexual expectations.

Advent of modernization, education, social consciousness and increasing awareness of individual rights, especially among women, invasion of satellite television, advances in telecommunication, rapid urbanization and industrialization, increased travel within and abroad, migration from rural to urban areas, the decline of support of joint family, better educational facilities, our young people are exposed to a wider issues that affect and alter their behaviour. Parents are giving increased choice and freedom to youngsters to choose their life/marriage partner. There is change from not seeing the marriage partner till marriage to seeing, talking and understanding the would-be before marriage. In India, marriage takes place among the two families and not the two individuals only. But, now elders are giving younger generations more freedom to choose the marriage partner than earlier times.

6

Marriage Customs in Different Indian Societies

Indian marriages are deemed almost necessary in the Indian society. Arranging a marriage is the responsibility of Indian parents and other relatives of both bride and groom. Indian marriage alliances entail some redistribution of wealth as well as building and restructuring social realignments, and, of course, result in the biological reproduction of families. In India, there is no greater event in a family than a wedding. In arranging and conducting of marriages, the complex permutations of Indian social systems best display themselves. Some parents begin marriage arrangements on the birth of a child, but most wait until later. After marriage arrangements are completed, rich panoply of wedding rituals begins. Each religious group, region, and caste has a slightly different set of rites. Generally, all Indian marriages involve as many kin and associates of the bride and groom as possible. The bride's family usually hosts most of the ceremonies and pays for all the arrangements for large numbers of guests for several days, including accommodation, feasting, decorations, and gifts for the groom's party. Essentially, India is divided into two large regions with regard to Hindu kinship and marriage practices, the north and the south. Additionally, various ethnic and tribal groups of the central, mountainous north, and eastern regions follow a variety of other practices.

THE RITUALS AND THEIR RATIONALE

The Indian wedding ceremony has a number of rituals and customs most of which are often labelled as superstitious or time wasting. It is believed to be nothing but rituals and more rituals. But have we asked ourselves what a "Ritual" is? A ritual begins as a creative rational action to express a sentiment or idea—like the lighting of lamp to dispel darkness at twilight or folding of hands into a "Namaste" to greet an elder. As more and more people, succeeding generations, repeat the action it becomes a convention—then a ritual. A ritual is thus an action on which time has set its seal of approval. The Ritual of the Indian weddings, too, is each symbolic of beautiful and noble sentiments. Unfortunately, today many parents and couples perform them without an awareness of the rich meaning behind them. A modest attempt has, therefore, been made to briefly describe the meaning and significance of the rituals.

MEANING OF THE SEVEN PHERAS

Hindu marriage ceremonies involve elaborate rituals, one of the most important being the "saat phere" or the seven steps to marriage. This ritual involves the bride and groom circumambulating around the sacred fire seven times while the priest chants the holy mantras. With every step, the couple invokes the Gods to shower their blessings on them. This chapter deals with explanations of the significant Indian marriage customs prevalent in the Indian society today. The significance of each sacred "phera" is described below:

Saptapadi, or the taking of seven steps by the bride and the bridegroom before the sacred fire, is considered to be the rite of prime importance in solemnizing a marriage. According to Paraskar Grahaya Suktram and various other prominent Smritis, marriage has no strength or recognition if this rite is not duly performed. Until the bride has performed the Saptapadi she is considered unmarried. The Saptapadi is the only ritual that gives the right to a girl to choose her husband in front of the sacred fire (Agni).

A question that often comes to the mind is why seven steps? Seven has a very deep spiritual, philosophical and divine significance in it. There are seven matrikas or seven aspects of mother energy. The sacred fire has seven flames, there are seven porous pious rivers, seven phases in the life of a woman, seven elements of body, seven notes of music, seven rays of the sun and seven main planets. Therefore, seven is always considered to be a mystic number that bestows long life. In the famous Puranic story of Savitri and Satyavan, Savitri mentions to Yamaraj (Lord of Death) that I have moved with you for seven steps, so we are already friends. As a friend, how can you make me a widow by taking away my husband Satyawan's soul. Hence, the concept of Saptapadi is very closely related with our mystic legends in the tradition of fulfiling the four ends of human life, i.e. Dharma, Kama, Artha and Moksha in the family life (grahasta). While performing this rite, the bride, bearing in mind all previous ceremonies of Kanyadaan and Laja Homa, agrees to take the seven steps as the beginning of her life together with the bridegroom.

It is important to mention here, that this ceremony, i.e. Saptapadi is mostly confused with pheras or agni pradakshina. The agni pradakshina or pheras is a totally different rite of four, three or seven circuits round the sacred fire, three of which are led by the bride and rest by bridegroom. The Saptapadi on the other hand is the rite of seven steps taken together by the bride and the bridegroom, at a slow and measured pace side-by-side and step-by-step in the north-eastern direction. While moving forward the bride is always on the right side so that the bridegroom's right hand is on her right shoulder. He says to her "Let not your left foot surpass your right foot." With each step, the bride and the bridegroom take a pledge together.

First Step

Bridegroom says, "Om esha ekapadi bhava iti prathaman", "My beloved, our love becomes firm by your walking one step with me. You will offer me food and be helpful in every way. I will cherish you and provide for your welfare and happiness and that of your children. Bride says, "Dhanam dhanyam pade vadet",

"I humbly submit to you, my lord. Kindly give me the responsibility of the home, food and finance. I promise you that I shall fulfil all responsibilities towards the welfare of the family and the children.

In simple words, in the first step, the couple invokes the Gods for plenty of pure and nourishing food. "With God as our guide, let us take the first step to live with honour and respect. Let us walk together so we get food," the couple prays.

Second Step

Bridegroom says, "Om oorje jara dastayaha", "My beloved, now you have walked the second step with me. Fill my heart with strength and courage and together we shall protect the household and the children." Bride says, "Kutumburn rakshayishyammi sa aravindharam," "My lord, in your grief, I shall fill your heart with courage and strength. In your happiness, I shall rejoice, I promise you that I will please you always with sweet words and take care of the family and children. And, you shall love me and me alone as your wife."

In other words, with the second step, the couple prays to the Gods to give them the mental, physical and spiritual strength to lead a healthy life. "Let us be happy and enjoy life. Let us walk together so we grow together in strength," they pray.

Third Step

Bridegroom says, "Om rayas Santu joradastayaha", "My beloved, now you have walked three steps with me. By virtue of this, our wealth and prosperity are going to grow. I shall look upon all other woman as my sisters. Together, we will educate our children and may they live long." Bride says, "Tava bhakti as vadedvachacha", "My love, I will love you with single minded devotion as my husband. I will treat all other men as my brothers. My devotion to you is that of a chaste wife and you are my joy. This is my commitment and my pledge to you."

The third step is for preserving wealth and prosperity in life. The chant at this stage means, "let us share joys and pains together. Let us walk together so we get wealth," they pray.

Fourth Step

Bridegroom says, "Om mayo bhavyas jaradastaya ha", "My

beloved, it is a great blessing that you have walked four steps with me. You have brought auspiciousness and sacredness into my life. May we be blessed with obedient and noble children. May they live long." Bride says, "Lalayami cha pade vadet." "My lord, I will adorn myself from head to toe with flowers, garlands and ornaments, and anoint myself with sandalwood paste and fragrance for your sake. I will serve you and please you in every way I can."

With the fourth step, the bride and groom invoke the Gods for attainment of happiness and harmony by mutual love and trust in all walks of life. "Let us not forget parents and elders. Let us walk together, so we get happiness by sharing our joys and sorrows," they say.

Fifth Step

Bridegroom says, "Om prajabhyaha Santu jaradastayaha", "My beloved, now that you have walked five steps with me, you have enriched my life. May God bless you. May our loved ones live long and share in our prosperity." Bride says, "Arte arba sapade vadet" "My Lord, I will share your joys and sorrows. Your love will make me trust and honour you. I will carry out all your wishes."

In the fifth step, they pray for the welfare of all living beings in the Universe and pray for virtuous, noble and heroic children." Let us observe all acts of charity. Let us walk together so we have family," they say.

Sixth Step

Bridegroom says, "My beloved, you have filled my heart with happiness walking six steps with me. May you fill my heart with joy and peace at all times and seasons." Bride says, "Yajne home shashthe vacho vadet." "My Lord, in all acts of righteousness, in material prosperity in all enjoyment and divine acts, I promise you I will participate and I shall always be with you."

They ask the Gods to give them a long, joyous life and togetherness forever. "Let us live a long and peaceful life. Let us walk together so we have joy," the couple prays, in the sixth step.

Seventh Step

Bridegroom says, "Om sakhi jaradastayahga." "My beloved, as you walked the seven steps with me, our love and friendship became eternal. We experienced spiritual union in God. Now you have become completely mine and I offer my life to you. Our marriage will be forever." Bride says, "Attramshe sakshino vadet pade." "My Lord, as per the law of God and the holy scriptures, I have become your spouse with the taking of the seventh step. Whatever promises we gave, we did so with a pure mind. We will be truthful to each other in all matters. We will love each other forever."

With the seventh, and the last step, the couple prays for understanding, companionship, loyalty and unity. "Let us be friends with love and sacrifice. Let us walk together so we have friendship," the holy chants signify.

After the seventh step has been taken, the groom says to the bride: "With seven steps we have become friends. Let me reach your friendship. Let me not be severed from your friendship. Let your friendship not be severed from me." With completion of the saptapadi, the two are pronounced husband and wife.

Following are the different marriage customs and rituals in different Indian societies, existent in the present times.

ARYA SAMAJ WEDDING

Swami Dayanand Saraswati founded The Arya Samaj in the nineteenth century, when the soul of mother India was crying for freedom from foreign domination. Swami Dayanand Saraswati propagated the teachings of the Vedas, believing that they are a perennial source of Divine Knowledge. Vedic 'gyana' or Divine knowledge is like the sacred Ganga river whose waters purify the body and the soul. Vedic gyana is for purification, elevation and sublimation of one and all, irrespective of colour, caste or creed. Members of any Hindu community can have an Arya Samaj wedding. The other wedding ceremonies, which precede the Vedic marriage rites, can be typically of that region, caste or community. In other words, the Arya Samaj wedding can be clubbed together with a Punjabi, Sindhi, Gujarati, or any other community's wedding.

Shaadi

The vidhi or rites of Arya Samaj wedding rituals.

Madhuperk

Once the bride and groom have entered the 'mandap' the Vedic rites begin, the first one being the 'madhuperk'. The bride gives the groom water three times. The first time he sprinkles it in his feet, the second time he sprinkles it all over his body and the third time he drinks the water. 'Madhuperk' is a mixture of curds, 'ghee' or clarified butter and honey. The groom sprinkles a little bit of this in all directions and then eats it three times.

Kanyadaan

The bride's parents offer their daughter's hand in marriage to the groom and he accepts it.

Havan

To invoke the blessings of 'Agni' or the God of Fire, the 'pujari' lights a sacred fire or 'havan' to the chanting of Vedic mantras. There are two types of 'havans'—the 'sadharan' (ordinary) or 'vishesh' (special). The 'vishesh' havan is the chanting of mantras and praying to all the 'Divyashaktis' or forms of God. The main 'prarthana' or prayer during the lighting of the 'havan' is the 'prarthana' of 'grahast jivan' (married life).

Pani Grahan Sanskar

The groom stands up and takes his bride's hand in his and chants mantras, promising to look after her till her old-age and keep her happy at all times. He accepts her as his 'poshya' (meaning that he will provide for all her needs). The bride and groom now take one 'parikrama' (circumvention) around the fire.

Shilarohan

The bridegroom chants a 'mantra' and the bride's mother places her daughter's right foot on a stone. The rock is a symbol of stability, permanence and firmness. The bride's position in the groom's home is now permanent and together, the couple will face all of life's challenges like two solid rocks.

Lajahom

'Laja' is puffed rice, a symbol of prosperity. The bride's brother stands behind the couple while the couple faces each other. The bride places both her hands into the groom's and her brother then puts the puffed rice into them. Together they offer this 'laja' as an 'ahuti' or sacrifice into the fire amidst the chanting of mantras. This ritual is performed three times and each time the mantras chanted have a different meaning.

Parikrama

The couple goes around the sacred fire four times, each 'parikrama' (circumvention) strengthening the bond between them. The first three times the bride must lead the groom, as she is the embodiment of Goddess Lakshmi. It is only after the fourth 'parikrama' that she becomes the 'ardhangani' (wife) and is now her husband's responsibility. After the completion of the 'parikramas' the 'pujari' ties the bride's sari 'pallav' to the groom's 'angavastra' (a scarf tied around the shoulders), with three knots.

Saptapadi

These are seven steps taken by the bride and groom together, each step has significance. After the 'saptapadi' the couple takes one 'parikrama' around the fire together with neither of them leading.

Sprinkling Water on the Couple

Older members of the groom's family sprinkle water on the couple while four 'mantras' are chanted by the 'pujari'. These prayers are recited to invoke the blessings of all the deities in the couple.

Hriday Sparshmantra

The bride and groom place one hand on each other's hearts and chant 'mantras' together. The meaning of these 'mantras' is— ' I am installing you in my heart from this day onwards; I will be loyal to you; this alliance is made in Heaven; let us ask the Almighty for His blessings'.

Sindoor

'Sindoor' or vermilion powder is the sign of a married Hindu lady. The groom applies 'sindoor' in the center parting of the bride's hair and also ties the 'mangalsutra' around her neck. The bride and groom feed each other sweets and the 'mantras' chanted at this time hold good for both and are not one sided. It is not only the wife's duty to ensure that her husband is fed; he in turn also has to see that she has been looked after.

Dhruvnakshatra

The couple is now instructed to look towards the Pole Star ('Dhruvnakshatra') amidst the chanting of 'mantras'. The Pole Star is always firm in its place and the vow means that 'I will live permanently with you'.

Arundhati Nakshatra

An invoking blessing from Arundhati and Vashisht. 'Arundhati' was the wife of the sage 'Vashisht'. The 'Arundhati' and 'Vashisht Nakshatras' are two stars joined together and appear as one at all times.

Ashirwaad

Now that the marriage rites have been completed, the newly weds are blessed by all the elders. Everyone present showers coloured rice or 'akshat' on the couple.

SINDHI MARRIAGE CEREMONY

Pre-marriage Ceremony

"Kuchcha Shagun" is solemnised by the parents of the bride and bridegroom where the couple get to see each other and rings are exchanged. Thus, after this ceremony the couple is engaged. The parents of the bridegroom give gifts and presents in the form of clothes, money and jewellery to the bride and *vice versa*. Mehendi ceremony, which is performed 3-4 days earlier to the marriage, is celebrated amidst songs and fan fare. An interesting ritual is "Sath" where the bride and the groom a day before the wedding have to break the cover of a small earthen pot in one shot with the shoes they have been wearing since morning. The same shoes then has to be worn on the wedding day.

Marriage Ceremony

The marriage begins with the "thread ceremony" of the bridegroom if he has not done it before. The bride and groom are seated next to each other and then the bride's mother washes the feet of the couple placed in a plate while the pundit chants mantras. The couple then takes the phera's round the holy fire. Here there is an option of phera's, the couple can take either three, four or seven phera's. The marriage comes to an end after parents and elders bless the couple.

Post-marriage Ceremony

After the marriage, the bride opens the lock of the groom's house, establishing her entry into the new house. She sprinkles milk all over the house and puts salt in the hands of her in-laws, who return it to her in the belief and hope that she will mingle freely with her new family. The bride is then lavished with gifts, cash, clothes and gold.

SINDHI (HYDERABADI) SANATHAN DHARAM WEDDING

A Sindhi marriage is very exuberant and extremely lavish. A ceremony typical to this community is the 'dattar' or salt ceremony, wherein the bride is brought to her new home and made to sit by a mound of salt. She fills her hands with as much salt as they can hold and slowly showers the same into the recipient's hands. This salt exchange is performed three times each with every member of her husband's family, to ensure harmony between the family members and her.

Janya

Sacred yellow thread is put on the groom, and the 'pujari' or 'maharaj' (Brahmin priest) chants the 'guru mantra' (the 'gayatri mantra') into the groom's ear. The sacred thread or 'janayu' is the symbol of a Hindu male. A red 'dupatta' or veil is used to cover the groom and his parents when the 'pujari' is chanting the 'guru mantra'. The groom is given a 'tokri' (basket) to beg for alms from all the relatives present. He goes around saying 'bhiksham dehi' and everyone present puts money into the basket, which is then handed over to the 'pujari'. The Sindhi community normally addresses the priest as 'Brahman' or 'maharaj'.

Kacchi Misri

This is a symbolic acceptance of the alliance between the parents of the bride and groom, wherein 'shagun' (token gifts) is exchanged. The 'shagun' consists of five types of fruits and 'kharchi' (money) for the bride and groom. The bride's family gives the groom's family 'kharchi' and *vice versa*.

Pucci Misri

This ceremony is usually performed in the Sindhi Temple, but in some cases it is also performed at home in the presence of a 'pujari'. 'Ganesha Puja' is performed first followed by the 'Ardaas' (reading of the Sikh Holy Book—the Guru Granth Sahib). The couple exchanges rings. The bride's family brings five kilograms of 'misri' (unrefined sugar with 2 crystals joined together) in a clay pot, which Misri in the gurudwara is opened by the groom's mother. The groom's family brings a 'thali' or platter containing cosmetics and a red ribbon. The groom's sister and sister-in-law then beautify the bride with these cosmetics.

Mehendi

The 'mehendi' ceremony is a light-hearted occasion with no religious connotation. Nevertheless, it is devoted to an important aspect of any marriage—the beautifying of the bride for the forthcoming nuptials. Professional 'mehendiwaalis' or henna artists apply the henna paste on the hands and feet of the bride and her female friends and relatives. 'Sangeet' usually follows the 'mehendi' celebration where traditional wedding songs and popular songs are sung to the beat of the 'dholak' (drum). Cocktails and dinner follow the celebrations.

Navgrahi Puja

The 'Navgrahi Puja' is performed on the morning before the wedding. It is imperative for the bride's 'mama' (maternal uncle), 'chacha' (paternal uncle) and brother to be present. As per Sindhi tradition, all 'pujas' are performed in the groom's home first and only then in the bride's. The 'pujas' performed on this day include the 'Ganesha Puja', 'Omkar Puja', 'Lakshmi Puja', 'Kalash Puja', followed by the 'puja' of the nine planets or the 'Navgrahi Puja'.

Sagari

After the 'Navgrahi Puja' the ritual of 'sagari' follows the same evening. Members from the groom's family come to the bride's home or any other chosen venue and decorate her with a floral headdress, floral bracelets, and garlands. The groom's sister then presents the bride with cosmetics, five types of fruits, and 'misri', along with a 'thali' of dried coconut, sweets, 'batashe' (sugar candy) and 'attar' (perfume). The bride's family has to then give lavish gifts to each person who has decorated her.

Garhi-Bukhi

This ritual is conducted in the homes of the bride and groom simultaneously. For the 'garhi'—the mother places a 'matka' (clay pot) full of water on her head assisted by her son-in-law. The pot of water is taken outside the house and the son-in-law carries a 'katti' or knife with him at all times to protect his mother-in-law from evil spirits. He is now referred to as 'aner'. The pot of water is then brought back into the house and every person present, garlands the mother and the father of the bride or the groom (as the case may be). This 'matka' is now placed in the 'pujasthan' (shrine) inside the home.

The son-in-law or 'ghor' as he is now addressed, gives money to the priest after circling it around the pot of water and the bride or the groom. Next, seven married ladies or 'sumangalis' have to pound 'haldi' (turmeric) sticks in a jar or 'okhli', seven times each. The bride and the groom then do the same. After the 'puja' the mothers receive gifts and money from their relatives. The mothers give the 'aners' either gold guineas or money and a red 'dupatta' (2 metres long veil) as tokens. For the 'bukhi' five kilograms of wheat is brought, which the bride and groom (separately in each home) cup in their hands and offer to the 'pujari' 21 times each. The entire quantity of wheat should be over within the stipulated 21 actions.

Vanwa

The 'vanwa' is held immediately after the 'garhi-bukhi' if the wedding ceremony has been fixed for the next day. The 'pujari' ties a 'challa' or anklet around the right foot of the groom and the bride (once again in their respective homes) and performs a small 'puja'. After this the parents apply oil to the foreheads, palms, feet and backbones of the bride and groom. The mother then takes two 'vicks' of cotton and burns them in oil; she, then circles them around the head of her child who is to be married to remove any bad spirits which may be present at the time. The bride and groom are then supposed to wear a new shoe on the right foot and break a 'mitti ka diya' (earthen lamp) with it.

Shaadi

On the morning of the wedding day, the bride's sister, sister-in-law and a young male child go to the groom's home in a decorated car carrying 'muras' (money, sweets, 'misri' and a coconut). They leave the bride's trousseau in the groom's house and the bride's sister-in-law performs a small ceremony whereby she has to apply some cosmetics on the faces of the groom and his mother. The priest puts a red 'dupatta' on the groom and the groom then proceeds to the bride's home. Before he can enter the house, the bride is escorted outside and both of them then place one foot each on the others. The bride and groom are given water to drink and something to eat because after this their hands are going to be tied together with the sacred thread or 'mouli'. Some money and a dried date are placed between their palms before their hands are tied. After the chanting of 'mantras' the couple and their relatives leave for the wedding venue.

The actual wedding rites are known as the 'Sanatan Dharam' rites and the 'pujas' conducted include the 'Ganesha Puja' (invocation of the elephant God Ganesha), 'Omkar Puja', 'Lakshmi Puja' (invocation of the Goddess of Wealth), 'Kalash Puja' (God of Water or Varun Devta), and the 'Navgrahi Puja' (puja of the nine planets). All the deities are called upon to bless the bridal couple and if conducted in detail, these 'pujas' could take upto three hours! It is not uncommon these days to have the rites shortened keeping the essentials 'mantras' intact. Once all the deities have been worshipped, the 'havan' or sacred fire is lit to invoke the blessings of the God of Fire or 'Agni Devta'. In Sindhi weddings it is customary for the couple to take only four 'parikramas' (circumventions) around the sacred fire. The bride leads in the first three and the groom in the last. After the fourth 'parikrama', the bride has to sit on the left of her husband. The wedding rites now complete, the bridal couple and guests are ready to proceed to attend the wedding reception or the 'satavaro'.

Satavaro

The Sindhi community normally hosts the reception on the same day as the wedding. This celebration is for the family, friends and well wishers of the bridal couple to come and bless the newly weds and shower them with gifts.

Dattar

A ceremony typical only to the Sindhi community, it is performed after the bride is brought back home after the wedding, but sometimes even takes place at the venue of the reception. The groom's family brings two kilograms of salt in a steel 'parat' or platter. The bride's family brings a hand fan or 'pankha' decorated in red velvet with some silver trimmings. The hands of the bridal couple are untied and the 'mouli' or sacred thread and the dried date are placed in the 'pujasthan' (shrine). The husband is the first one to place some money and a gift in the salt for his wife as a blessing for a healthy lineage and a happy married life. The bride fills her hands with as much salt as they can hold and slowly showers the same into her husband's hands. This salt is exchanged three times. The next person to perform this ritual with the bride will be her father-in-law, followed by her mother-in-law and then one by one each person from the groom's family. After the salt ceremony the couple is fed the dried date, which was earlier, tied between their hands and the groom breaks a coconut in front of the 'pujasthan'.

SINDHI (HYDERABADI) ARYA SAMAJ WEDDING

Janya

Sacred yellow thread is put on the groom, and the 'pujari' or 'maharaj' (Brahmin priest) chants the 'guru mantra' (the 'gayatri mantra') into the groom's ear. The sacred thread or 'janayu' is the symbol of a Hindu male. A red 'dupatta' or veil is used to cover the groom and his parents when the 'pujari' is chanting the 'guru mantra'. The groom is given a 'tokri' (basket) to beg for alms from all the relatives present. He goes around saying 'bhiksham dehi' and everyone present puts money into the basket, which is then handed over to the 'pujari'. The Sindhi community normally addresses the priest as 'Brahman' or 'maharaj'.

Kacchi Misri

This is a symbolic acceptance of the alliance between the parents of the bride and groom, wherein 'shagun' (token gifts) is exchanged. The 'shagun' consists of five types of fruits and 'kharchi' (money) for the bride and groom. The bride's family gives the groom's family 'kharchi' and *vice versa*.

Pucci Misri

This ceremony is usually performed in the Sindhi Temple, but in some cases it is also performed at home in the presence of a 'pujari'. 'Ganesha Puja' is performed first followed by the 'Ardaas' (reading of the Sikh Holy Book—the Guru Granth Sahib). The couple exchanges rings. The bride's family brings five kilograms of 'misri' (unrefined sugar with 2 crystals joined together) in a clay pot, which Misri engagement is opened by the groom's mother. The groom's family brings a 'thali' or platter containing cosmetics and a red ribbon. The groom's sister and sister-in-law then beautify the bride with these cosmetics.

Mehendi

The 'mehendi' ceremony is a light-hearted occasion with no religious connotation. Nevertheless, it is devoted to an important aspect of any marriage—the beautifying of the bride for the forthcoming nuptials. Professional 'mehendiwaalis' or henna artists apply the henna paste on the hands and feet of the bride and her female friends and relatives. 'Sangeet' usually follows the 'mehendi' celebration where traditional wedding songs and popular songs are sung to the beat of the 'dholak' (drum). Cocktails and dinner follow the celebrations.

Navgrahi Puja

The 'Navgrahi Puja' is performed on the morning before the wedding. It is imperative for the bride's 'mama' (maternal uncle), 'chacha' (paternal uncle) and brother to be present. As per Sindhi tradition, all 'pujas' are performed in the groom's home first and only then in the bride's. The 'pujas' performed on this day include the 'Ganesha Puja', 'Omkar Puja', 'Lakshmi Puja', 'Kalash Puja', followed by the 'puja' of the nine planets or the 'Navgrahi Puja'.

Sagari

After the 'Navgrahi Puja' the ritual of 'sagari' follows the same evening. Members from the groom's family come to the bride's home or any other chosen venue and decorate her with a floral headdress, floral bracelets, and garlands. The groom's sister then presents the bride with cosmetics, five types of fruits, and 'misri', along with a 'thali' of dried coconut, sweets, 'batashe' (sugar candy) and 'attar' (perfume). The bride's family has to then give lavish gifts to each person who has decorated her.

Garhi-Bukhi

A special 'puja' for the mothers of the bride and groom. This ritual is conducted in the homes of the bride and groom simultaneously. For the 'garhi'—the mother places a 'matka' (clay pot) full of water on her head assisted by her son-in-law. The pot of water is taken outside the Garhi-bukhi house and the son-in-law carries a 'katti' or knife with him at all times to protect his mother-in-law from evil spirits. He is now referred to as 'aner'. The pot of water is then brought back into the house and every person present, garlands the mother and the father of the bride or the groom (as the case may be). This 'matka' is now placed in the 'pujasthan' (shrine) inside the home. The son-in-law or 'ghor' as he is now addressed, gives money to the priest after circling it around the pot of water and the bride or the groom.

Next, seven married ladies or 'sumangalis' have to pound 'haldi' (turmeric) sticks in a jar or 'okhli', seven times each. The bride and the groom then do the same. After the 'puja' the mothers receive gifts and money from their relatives. The mothers give the 'aners' either gold guineas or money and a red 'dupatta' (2 metres long veil) as tokens. For the 'bukhi' five kilograms of wheat is brought, which the bride and groom (separately in each home) cup in their hands and offer to the 'pujari' 21 times each. The entire quantity of wheat should be over within the stipulated 21 actions.

Vanwa

The 'vanwa' is held immediately after the 'garhi-bukhi' if the wedding ceremony has been fixed for the next day. The 'pujari' ties a 'challa' or anklet around the right foot of the groom and the bride (once again in their respective homes) and performs a small 'puja'. After this the parents apply oil to the foreheads, palms, feet and backbones of the bride and groom. The mother then takes two 'vicks' of cotton and burns them in oil; she, then circles them around the head of her child who is to be married to remove any bad spirits which may be present at the time. The bride and groom are then supposed to wear a new shoe on the right foot and break a 'mitti ka diya' (earthen lamp) with it.

Shaadi

On the morning of the wedding day, the bride's sister, sister-in-law and a young male child go to the groom's home in a decorated car carrying 'muras' (money, sweets, 'misri' and a coconut). They leave the bride's trousseau in the groom's house and the bride's sister-in-law performs a small ceremony whereby she has to apply some cosmetics on the faces of the groom and his mother. The priest puts a red 'dupatta' on the groom and the groom then proceeds to the bride's home. Before he can enter the house, the bride is escorted outside and both of them then place one foot each on the others. The bride and groom are given water to drink and something to eat because after this their hands are going to be tied together with the sacred thread or 'mouli'. Some money and a dried date are placed between their palms before their hands are tied. After the chanting of 'mantras' the couple and their relatives leave for the wedding venue.

The Wedding Ceremony

Madhuperk

Once the bride and groom have entered the 'mandap' the Vedic rites begin, the first one being the 'madhuperk'. The bride gives the groom some water three times. The first time he sprinkles it in his feet, the second time he sprinkles it all over his body and the third time he drinks the water. 'Madhuperk' is a mixture of curds, 'ghee' or clarified butter and honey. The groom sprinkles a little bit of this in all directions and then eats it three times.

Kanyadaan

The bride's parents offer their daughter's hand in marriage to the groom and he accepts it.

Havan

To invoke the blessings of 'Agni' or the God of Fire, the 'pujari' lights a sacred fire or 'havan' to the chanting of Vedic mantras. There are two types of 'havans'—the 'sadharan' (ordinary) or 'vishesh' (special). The 'vishesh' havan is the chanting of mantras and praying to all the 'Divyashaktis' or forms of God. The main 'prarthana' or prayer during the lighting of the 'havan' is the 'prarthana' of 'grahast jivan' (married life).

Pani Grahan Sanskar

The groom stands up and takes his bride's hand in his and chants mantras, promising to look after her till her old age and keep her happy at all times. He accepts her as his 'poshya' (meaning that he will provide for all her needs). The bride and groom now take one 'parikrama' (circumvention) around the fire.

Shilarohan

The bridegroom chants a 'mantra' and the bride's mother places her daughter's right foot on a stone. The rock is a symbol of stability, permanence and firmness. The bride's position in the groom's home is now permanent and together, the couple will face all of life's challenges like two solid rocks.

Lajahom

'Laja' is puffed rice, a symbol of prosperity. The bride's brother stands behind the couple while the couple faces each other. The bride places both her hands into the groom's and her brother then puts the puffed rice into them. Together they offer this 'laja' as an 'ahuti' or sacrifice into the fire amidst the chanting of mantras. This ritual is performed three times and each time the mantras chanted have a different meaning.

Parikrama

The couple goes around the sacred fire four times, each 'parikrama' (circumvention) strengthening the bond between them. The first three times the bride must lead the groom, as she is the embodiment of Goddess Lakshmi. It is only after the fourth 'parikrama' that she becomes the 'ardhangani' (wife) and is now her husband's responsibility. After the completion of the 'parikramas' the 'pujari' ties the bride's sari 'pallav' to the groom's 'angavastra' (a scarf tied around the shoulders), with three knots.

Saptapadi

These are seven steps taken by the bride and groom together, each step having significance. After the 'saptapadi' the couple takes one 'parikrama' around the fire together with neither of them leading.

Sprinkling Water on the Couple

Older members of the groom's family sprinkle water on the couple while four 'mantras' are chanted by the 'pujari'. These prayers are recited to invoke the blessings of all the deities on the couple.

Hriday Sparshmantra

The bride and groom place one hand on each other's hearts and chant 'mantras' together. The meaning of these 'mantras' is—'I am installing you in my heart from this day onwards; I will be loyal to you; this alliance is made in Heaven; let us ask the Almighty for His blessings'.

Sindoor

'Sindoor' or vermilion powder is the sign of a married Hindu lady. The groom applies 'sindoor' in the center parting of the bride's hair and also ties the 'mangalsutra' around her neck. The bride and groom feed each other sweets and the 'mantras' chanted at this time hold good for both and are not one sided. It is not only the wife's duty to ensure that her husband is fed; he in turn also has to see that she has been looked after.

Dhruvnakshatra

The couple is now instructed to look towards the Pole Star ('Dhruvnakshatra') amidst the chanting of 'mantras'. The Pole Star is always firm in its place and the vow means that 'I will live permanently with you'.

Arundhati Nakshatra

Invoking blessings from Arundhati and Vashisht. 'Arundhati' was the wife of the sage 'Vashisht'. The 'Arundhati' and 'Vashist Nakshatras' are two stars joined together and appear as one at all times.

Ashirwaad

Now that the marriage rites have been completed, the newly weds are blessed by all the elders. Everyone present showers coloured rice or 'akshat' on the couple.

Satavaro

The Sindhi community normally hosts the reception on the same day as the wedding. This celebration is for the family, friends and well wishers of the bridal couple to come and bless the newly weds and shower them with gifts. The reception is usually held in a hotel or banquet hall.

Dattar

A ceremony typical only to the Sindhi community, it is performed after the bride is brought back home after the wedding, but sometimes even takes place at the venue of the reception. The groom's family brings two kilograms of salt in a steel 'parat' or platter. The bride's family brings a hand fan or 'pankha' decorated in red velvet with some silver trimmings. The hands of the bridal couple are untied and the 'mouli' or sacred thread and the dried date are placed in the 'pujasthan' (shrine).

The husband is the first one to place some money and a gift in the salt for his wife as a blessing for a healthy lineage and a happy married life. The bride fills her hands with as much salt as they can hold and slowly showers the same into her husband's hands. This salt is exchanged three times. The next person to perform this ritual with the bride will be her father-in-law, followed by her mother-in-law and then one by one each person from the groom's family. After the salt ceremony the couple is fed the dried date, which was earlier, tied between their hands and the groom breaks a coconut in front of the 'pujasthan'.

HARYANVI JAT WEDDING

The marriage rituals are full with lot of traditions. Their weddings are colorful and celebratory. The celebrations begin several days before the actual wedding ceremony and consist mainly of singing and dancing to the beat of the 'dholak'. As per custom, a man/woman should not marry a woman/man belonging to his/her own gotra, his/her mother's gotra and his/her grandmother's gotra.

Puchkarna

When the bride's family finds the groom, a good match, than they invite the bridegroom's family. The elders from both families meet and on reaching a favourable decision, on the spot presents small gifts and maan or money to the bride. Then the bride's parents along with sweets give double amount of maan and gifts to the groom's family. This symbolizes a relationship between the two families and they fix a thiya to be given by the girl's family to the boy's family on every marriage ceremony.

Sagai

Several weeks before the wedding, the bridegroom's family come to girl's house in a group who are ceremonially greeted by the girl's family and presented with thiya, maan and other gifts and food.

Sawa

An auspious date for the wedding is agreed upon by both the parties after consulting the priest. The bride's father sends a letter written on paper stained yellow to the boy's family suggesting the date of marriage.

Lagan

Lagan is sent 9 or 11 days prior to the wedding, the bridegroom's mother and grandmother alongwith the bridegroom are given gifts, clothes and maan by the girl's family.

Byah Bhejna

The marriage date is fixed and girl's family sends byah consisting of bridegrooms clothes and maan for all members of his family. In return, the bridegroom's family sends clothes and gifts for the bride.

Bhaat Nyotna

The mother of both the bride and the bridegroom's visit their respective maternal families to invite all her brothers and her nephews. She takes one coconut, sweets and bheli of 5 kg. gur or jaggery for her brothers. This ceremony takes place with a lot of dance and folksongs. Mother exchanges her old dupatta with brother's wife's new dupatta.

Baan

The number of baans or days for worship are fixed by the family purohit or priest, which generally constitute for 5-7 days. It is held in the evening in the respective homes of both the bride and the groom's family in which seven suhagin women perform "teil chadana", the food is given by neighbours or the parental family members. On the day of marriage is "teil utarna" again done by seven suhagin (married) women.

Bhaat Lena

On the day of marriage bhaat is taken by the respective bride's and groom's family from their maternal uncles and their family. Maternal uncles and their family come along singing and dancing on dholak beats and are warmly greeted by the sister and her sons, aarti is performed of the brother. They bring the clothes to be worn by the bride or the groom, respectively. Along with it they bring gifts, sweets and give maan to all the family members of their sister's family. Bhhati gives maan for all the panchayat members also. They are served with special food called 'khand-kasar'.

Ghori Chadai

The groom is dressed in the clothes brought by his maternal uncle. The kangna or seven-knotted sacred thread is tied on his right wrist. Maternal uncle helps the boy to sit on the ghori or mare.

Shayi Dalna or Kajal Ghalai

Groom's bhabhi puts kajal in the eyes of the groom's eyes and for this she gets maan also.

Lagam Pakrai or Bag Pakrai

Bridegroom's sister's husband holds the lagaam of the ghori while the groom sits on the ghori and he is given maan for this.

Chuchi Piloi

Before the departure of the barrat, the groom's mother feeds groom for the last time and then barrat departs amidsts music.

The barrat consists of the grooms friends dancing in front of the ghori, with groom sitting on the ghori, followed by the ladies singing folk songs. The groom is presented with 'noto ki mala', maan, milk and sweets by the girl's community and family members.

Chawal Marna

Groom's sister throws chawal or rice throughout the barrat procession on the groom till he is sitting on the ghori. She has diya, rice, sindoor, sweets and other manglik items on her thali and keeps on throwing little amount of rice on her brother and she is given maan for this.

Milni

The milni ceremony takes place where boy's father and girl's father embrace each other and the latter gives gifts and maan to the boy's father and his family.

Barothi

Barothi is the threshold ceremony; the boy is taken to the threshold of the girl's house mounted on the mare where he strikes the toran (a small wooden frame suspended over the door).

Neem Jhadna and Aarta

Girl's younger sister sprinkles neem water on the groom and gets maan from the groom. The bride's elder sister performs Aarta; it consists of diya, money, and sweets. She also gets maan from the groom.

Chawal Marna

Bride fills both her hands with rice and throws it on the groom.

Jai Mala

Garland of flowers, jai mala is put by the bride around the neck of the bridegroom and *vice-versa*. After this colorful ceremony, the bridegroom is taken inside the house of the bride and the baratis are then entertained to delicious and sumptuous dinner amidst merriment and festivity.

The actual marriage ceremony takes place at the auspious time decided by the purohit in the bride's house where a canopy is erected. Sacred fire or hawan is lighted and the marriage is performed around it. Bride's maternal uncle seats the bride for the phere. Groom's sister ties the knot between boy's chaddar and girl's duppatta. While bride's brother gives Kheel to the couple to perform the marriage ceremony.

Kanyadaan

The father of the bride formally gives away the girl to the groom amidst mantras alongwith some money or gold ring.

Phere

The boy and the girl both circle slowly four times round the sacred fire keeping their right sides towards it, the boy leads in the first three and the girl in the last.

Bidya

Bride's father give details of daan-dahej or dowry in front of the panchayat after the marriage.

Thappa

Bride and groom go for thappa, by pasting mehendi and ghee handprints on the wall.

Jawahari

All members of the bride's family gives gifts to the groom.

Thappa

An elder male member is selected from the baratis by the groom's family who wears the thappa given by an elderly woman of the bride's family. If man selected is groom's grandfather then bride's grandmother gives the thappa. She gets maan for this ceremony.

Now barrat departs with the bride. Bride is given two earthen pots full of sweets. One she will throw at the starting of the groom's village and, the other she gives to her mother-in-law on reaching home.

Bahu Utarna

Mother-in-law performs this ceremony by receiving the bride at the threshold of their house.

Bar Rokai

Grooms sister stands in front of her brother and his wife and stops them from entering the house and lets them in only after taking some gifts.

Thappa

Bride and groom go for thappa again, by pasting mehendi and ghee handprints on the wall.

Then, later in the day kangana is opened with fun.

Diya Silayi

Bride with groom's female members go to the village pond and perform diya silayi, they throw all the diyas used in the baan in the village pond. They go and come back by singing folk songs.

Phere

The bride visits her parental family and is presented with gifts. Later, the couple starts their married life together.

PUNJABI MARRIAGE CEREMONY

Punjabi Wedding Ceremony is basically a very simple and lively function and is celebrated with lots of zest and fan fare. The wedding ceremony consists of many rituals, which have a distinct significance and charm.

Pre-Wedding Ceremony

Roka

Roka ceremony is performed on a mutually convenient date backed by 'shubh muhurat'. This is a simple function, which is attended by family members and close friends. There is normally an exchange of gifts and cash. After this roka ceremony, the girl and the boy are considered engaged to each other and are also allowed to court. The wedding date is fixed after roka.

Sagan

The ceremony usually takes at the groom's house or it may be at a banquet hall, hotel or club, if the number of guests is large. During the ceremony, the pandit performs "havan." The girl's father applies the "tikka" (made of kesar, rice grains and flower petals) on the boy's forehead who takes the blessing from the girl's family members. Each of the relatives and friends present from the girl's side then offers mithai to the boy and gives cash.

Chunni Chadana

On this occasion, the boy's parents and relatives visit the girl's house. The boy's sister or sister-in-law meets the girl first and traditionally presents her a red "chunni" or a red sari. After dressing the girl in clothes brought by the boy's family, they then lead her to the venue of the ceremony where her future mother gives her gifts and adorns her with jewellery. The boy and the girl exchange rings and the girl is then given gifts, in cash and kind, by all those present from the boy's side.

Sangeet

One of the attractive and interesting part of the marriage ceremony is "sangeet." After sagan on every night till the wedding day, the relatives and friends get together for singing sessions both at the boy's as well as the girl's house. One day is fixed for special sangeet session which is attended and celebrated by both the sides together.

Mehendi

Mehendi is applied on the bride's hands and feet either by a family member or by a professional but the important factor is that the Mehendi is sent by the boy's side as part of the kwar dhoti, sent by the boy's family on the wedding day.

Wedding Ceremony

This is done in two parts. Ceremonies are performed

separately at the bride's house as well as the groom's house.

Ceremonies at the Girl's House

The "chuda" ceremony begins with a "havan" or "puja" performed by the pandit. The oldest mama and mami (or those performing this ceremony) keep a fast till chuda. The chuda, i.e., the set of cream and red ivory bangles, is not shown to the girl, she sees it just before the ceremony. After the puja, everybody present is supposed to touch the chuda, in a manner of offering their good wishes to the girl. The chuda preceded by a mauli which is tied by the pandit on the girl's wrist. Four lamps are lit and the bride-to-be is made to sit in front of them. Oil is constantly added to the diyas so that the glow will be reflected on her face and she will look more beautiful on the wedding eve. A paste of turmeric powder and mustard oil is applied to her body and then the bride is given a bath with holy water. The bride then wears her bridal attire, which is as per tradition given by the maternal uncle.

Ceremonies at the Boy's House

The bridegroom is applied a paste of turmeric and mustard oil and is bathed by water brought by his sister-in-law from the temple. His maternal uncle presents his attire. Thus maternal uncles play an important role in Punjabi marriages. After he has bathed and changed into his new clothes, puja is performed. The boy's father or an elderly relative is given the honour of tying the "sehra" on his head. A pink colour turban is first touched by all the relatives present before it is tied on the boy's head. The groom then leaves for the venue. As the time of the mahurat approaches, the boy is led to the "vedi" where the pundit performs puja for the boy. The first few mantras are recited by the boy only. This is the time for the mischievous pranksters from the girl's side to make a grab for the boy's shoes, which they later exchange for money. Thereafter, the girl is led to the "vedi". Then the ritual of "kanyadaan" takes place where the girl's father puts a ring on the boy's finger before placing his daughter's hand in his. Thereafter the couple take the seven phera's round the holy fire.

Post-Wedding Ceremony

As per tradition on her first day in her new home, the bride is made to cook something, preferably a sweet dish like halwa or kheer. The parents and relatives of the groom give gifts and presents to the bride. The first day after the wedding is also an occasion when the newly weds visit the girl's parents. Both the girl and the boy are given gifts of clothes and jewellery by the girl's parents and relatives.

PUNJABI HINDU (SANATHAN-DHARAM) WEDDING

Rokna or Thaka

'Rokna' is an important part of the Punjabi wedding, although, the 'shagun' now could be any amount of money—instead of the customary Rs. 1.25, which was so common in the olden days.

Sagai

Rings are exchanged between the bride and the groom to be, in the presence of a 'pandit' or 'pujari', close friends and relatives. The wedding day would normally be fixed after the 'sagai'.

Chunni Chadana

Close female relatives from the groom's home go the bride's home with what is known as the 'suhag ki pitari' (a decorated basket containing gifts from the groom's mother for the bride). These gifts usually consist of 'mehendi' (henna), clothes, jewellery, fruits, dry fruits, dried coconut, 'chuaare' or dried dates, bangles, 'sindoor' (vermilion powder) and a red 'dupatta' or veil. During this ceremony the ladies sing wedding songs to the beat of a 'dholak' or small drum and decorate the bride-to-be by dressing her up and draping the red 'dupatta' on her.

Mehendi

The 'Mehendi' celebration is a lighthearted affair with no religious connotation. It is usually held at the bride's home and is a daytime function. Professional 'mehendi' artists or 'mehendiwallis' make intricate patterns on the hands and feet of the bride and her other female friends with the henna paste. Another, modern day custom practiced at 'mehendi' functions is to have a bangle seller or 'chudiwalla' adorn the hands of all the ladies present with colourful 'chudis' or bangles.

Kangna Bandhana

On the morning of the wedding day, the bride and the groom (each in their respective homes), has to have the sacred thread or 'mouli' tied to their right wrists. The 'mouli' has an iron 'challa' (bracelet) tied to it along with turmeric sticks, 'supari' (betel nut) and 'kaudis' (shells). The thread has to have as many knots as possible in order to make it difficult to untie later!

Chuda Chadana

Only the bride's family celebrates this ritual. The bride's maternal uncle or 'mama', gifts her a red ivory bangle or 'chuda', which the maternal aunt or 'mami' will adorn her wrists with. These days ivory has been replaced with acrylic or plastic. Four unmarried girls of marriageable age surround the bride and drape a red 'dupatta' on her, while the 'mami' puts on the 'chuda' for her. The girls also adorn the bride's hands with 'kaleeras'. 'Kaleeras' are traditionally supposed to be made from pure silver but these days people usually prefer to use the ones made from foil because 'kaleeras' are never used after a marriage.

Uptan

One day before the actual wedding, the bride and groom (in their respective homes) are cleansed with turmeric paste. This daytime ceremony prepares both of them for the nuptials. 'Uptan' is a paste made from sandalwood, turmeric and rose water and is applied by seven married female members of the families, to the faces, hands and feet of the bride and groom. After this ceremony the bride and the groom are barred from stepping outdoors until after the wedding ceremony. During the entire seven days of 'sangeet', which follows, they must remain indoors and are not allowed to meet each other.

Sangeet

'Sangeet' is usually held after the 'mehendi' ceremony and is more of a ladies function, when all the ladies and unmarried girls from both sides congregate to have fun and frolic by dancing and singing traditional wedding songs.

Ghodi Sajana

In most Punjabi weddings, the groom travels to the bride's

home mounted on a mare. The mare or 'ghodi' is traditionally decorated for this wedding procession. The mare's hair is plaited with sacred thread or 'mouli' and the groom's sisters feed her with Bengal gram, which has been soaked in water the night before. The groom's sisters are given a 'shagun' in the form of money for their efforts! The groom's sister-in-law applies 'kajal' or kohl in the groom's eyes, before he departs for the bride's home, and for this she is also given a shagun.

Sehra Bandhi

Just before the groom can mount the mare—married ladies from his family tie the 'pagadi' or turban, the 'sehra' or floral veil, which covers the groom's face, put 'shagun' in his 'jholi' or lap and bless the groom. The 'shagun' usually consists of a red 'dupatta', dried coconut and dried dates or 'chuaare'. Then the groom's nephew or 'sarbala' as he is referred to, mounts the mare along with the groom, and, the two are ready to leave for the wedding procession.

Agwaani

The bride's family receives the 'baraat' at the entrance of the bride's home.

Milni

This is probably the first time that all the relatives from both families are seeing each other and the 'milni' is to help them get acquainted. It is very typical for each relative to embrace his counterpart—grooms and bride's fathers, maternal uncles (mamas) and paternal uncles (chachas), in the other family at least 3 times each. Throughout the 'milni' the groom and the 'sarbala' remain mounted on the mare. Once all the relatives have greeted each other, the bride's brother and/or another male relative help the groom off the mare. The groom is then escorted to the threshold of the house and the bride's mother performs the 'aarti' (traditional Indian welcome ritual with a lamp or 'diya' placed on a platter or 'thali') to welcome her son-in-law.

Jaimala

After the bride's mother has performed the 'aarti' for her son-in-law, the bride is escorted to the threshold to welcome her beau in the traditional manner by garlanding him. The groom in turn garlands his bride. This exchange of garlands is known as the 'jaimala'.

Shaadi

The actual wedding rites are known as 'sanatan dharam' rites and the 'pujas' conducted during the wedding ceremony include the 'Ganesha Puja' (invocation of the elephant God, Ganesha), 'Omkar Puja', 'Lakshmi Puja' (invocation of the Goddess of Wealth), 'Kalash Puja' (invocation of the God of Water or Varun Devta), the 'puja' of the nine planets or the 'Navgrahi Puja'. Once all the deities have been worshipped, the 'havan' or sacred fire is lit to invoke the blessings of 'Agni Devta' or the God of Fire. Fire forms an integral part of all Hindu customs and rituals, as it symbolizes purity and also acts as a witness to the marriage—in other words, 'Agni Sakshi'. All the vows between the bridal couple are exchanged in the presence of this 'witness'. During the entire process—the 'pujas', the 'havan' and the 'saath pheras' (seven steps around the sacred fire) the couple's hands remain tied.

Bidaai

Before the bride leaves for her marital home, she either lights a 'mitti ka diya' (earthen lamp) in her parents home or turns on all the lights. What follows is the most touching and sensitive ritual of Hindu weddings, the 'lajahom'. 'Laja' or 'phulian' is puffed rice (a sign of prosperity), which the bride has to take in both her hands and shower on all her family over the top of her head. She does this all the way to the palanquin or decorated car, which is waiting to take her to her new home. By doing this she is repaying all her debts to her parents for having looked after her all these years. On reaching her marital home, she is welcomed at the entrance, by her mother-in-law, who performs the traditional 'aarti' for her. After this, the newly wed sprinkles a little coconut oil near the door.

Kangna Kholna

The bride and groom untie each other's bracelets in the presence of all the relatives. There is a lot of teasing and fun and frolic at this time. The bride is required to untie her husband's bracelet first.

Mooh Dikhai Ki Rasm

Literally translated this means the 'showing of the bride' to the groom's family members, but in reality it is actually a form of introduction. The mother-in-law showers her 'bahu' (daughter-in-law) with jewellery, clothes and money at this time. The other close relatives of the family also offer her gifts and money.

Reception

A wedding reception is a concept borrowed from the West and is now an integral part of many Indian weddings. The parents of the bride and groom host a lavish dinner and invite as many friends and relatives to introduce the newly weds to the rest of the community. The reception is generally hosted in a hotel or banquet hall.

PUNJABI-HINDU (ARYA SAMAJ) WEDDING

The marriage ceremonies in the Punjabi-Hindu Sanathan Dharam wedding differ from the Punjabi-Arya Samaj Wedding in how the actual wedding is conducted. Their pre-wedding ceremonies like rokra or thaka, sagai, chunni chadana, mehndi, kangna bandhana, chuda chadana, uptan, sangeet, ghodi sajana, sehra bandhi, agwaani, milni, jaimala and post wedding ceremonies like, bidaai, kangna kholna, mooh dikhai ki rasam and reception are same. The actual Arya Samaj, wedding has been described early in this chapter.

PUNJABI SUNNI MUSLIM WEDDING

The Punjabi Sunni Muslims are originally from Kashmir and had migrated to the Punjab centuries ago. Owing to this Punjab Sunni Muslims have many similarities in dress, social customs, ceremonies and food habits to those of the Hindu community. Their weddings are colorful and celebratory and the food is legendary for its exotic taste. The celebrations begin several days before the actual wedding ceremony and consist mainly of singing and dancing to the beat of the 'dholak' (durm).

Mangni

The groom's family makes an offer for the bride's hand in

marriage. On reaching a favourable decision, elders from both families meet and decide on a suitable date for the wedding. The groom arrives with his entourage at the bride's home. Leading the procession are several traditionally dressed young girls carrying clay pots containing 'mehendi' (henna), herbal oil, 'uptan' (a paste of turmeric, sandalwood powder and herbs) and each one has an oil lamp lit on it. The groom's mother gifts her future daughter-in-law several sets of clothes complete with accessories, toiletries and as many as five sets of jewellery all artistically gift-wrapped. In affluent families, a set of diamond jewellery is considered essential. The groom's mother slips the engagement ring on the bride's finger though in liberal families the groom may do this himself. The bride's parents gift the groom a suitcase full of clothes, accessories and toiletries. After the ring ceremony, a cake is cut, the 'dholak' (small drum) brought out and Punjabi songs sung with gusto!

Jora Katai

Several weeks before the wedding, the female relatives gather at the bride's home. The tailor is called into take her measurements and the first garment for the trousseau is cut. Later in the evening the men folk join in the celebration of this event and dance and sing to the beat of the 'dholak'.

Haldi Ceremony

Two days prior to the wedding, the ladies of the family gather at the bride's home. The older women apply herbal oil on her head and braid her hair into a series of fine plaits. 'Uptan' is applied on her body as a purification rite. In the evening the plaits are opened and the bride has a ritual bath. A simpler ceremony with a symbolic application of 'uptan' is performed for the groom on the same day.

Mehendi and Shukrana

This ceremony of blessing the couple is conducted in the groom's home first, and, then in the bride's. The bride's family takes decorated clay pots with lighted oil lamps on top containing 'uptan', 'mehendi' (henna) and oil to the groom's house. 'Mehendi' is symbolically applied to the groom's little finger while professional 'mehendi' artists apply fine designs of 'mehendi' on the hands of the ladies present. The bride's family also takes clothes, accessories and gifts for the groom.

The groom's family reciprocates by arriving at the bride's home later, carrying decorated pots in quite the same manner as was done by the bride's family. The clay pots contain 'uptan', 'mehendi' and oil and have lighted lamps on top. They also bring with them the bride's trousseau consisting of several sets of clothes (always an uneven number), footwear, accessories, nightwear, undergarments, towels and toiletries.The bride may not meet the groom that evening. She remains seated inside the house while professional 'mehendiwallis' trace intricate designs with henna on her hands and feet.

Nikaah

On the morning of the 'nikaah', the groom gets dressed in traditional attire and visits the mosque accompanied by his 'baraat' (male friends and relatives). A representative of the 'maulvi' (Muslim priest) and a 'gavaah' (witness, usually an uncle) take the 'Nikaahnaamah' (marriage contract) to the bride's house for her to read and sign. This document includes the amount of the 'mehr' (literally, bride's price), which was given earlier by mutual consent. She must read the whole document and give her 'qabool' (acceptance) and only then sign on it. The 'Nikaahnaamah' is then taken back to the mosque where the groom and his 'baraat' are waiting.

This signed marriage contract is read aloud to all the men folk present, the groom gives his 'qabool' and signs it as well. The 'Agadh-e-nikaah' is then read out to give the contract religious sanction. The groom and his 'baraat' then leave for the bride's home where they are ceremonially received by the men folk in her family. A black goat is brought to the groom around which, the groom waves some money to ward off the presence of any evil. He is then taken to meet his wife and is allowed to sit beside her.

Ruksati

The bride's maternal aunt feeds the groom milk and, then feeds the bride from the same tumbler. The groom reads out the first page of the Holy Quran. Members of both families view the bride and groom as a married couple for the first time and shower them with gifts of money. This is called the 'mooh dikhai' (literally translated it means 'showing of the face').

Valima

While the 'nikaah' may be a small, private affair, the 'valima' must be celebrated with great pomp and splendour and in large numbers. The bride and groom are now recognized as a married couple and all the guests are a witness to this union by Islamic law. This celebration is replete with a grand feast consisting of the traditional Muslim 'biryani' (rice cooked with lamb).

KASHMIRI MARRIAGE CEREMONY

Kashmiri Pundits are tradition preservers and cling on to their legacy with determination.

Pre-Marriage Ceremony

Horoscope Matching

The first important ritual is the matching of horoscope of the boy and the girl. Importance is also given to the status, fame and moral character of the family and their close relatives. This is followed by "Kasamdary", which is a formal commitment on the part of both the girl's and boy's families to the marriage.

Engagement

The date of the engagement is fixed by the family purohits, according to the Kashmiri calendar. On this day, the maid servant of the boy's family goes to the bride's house with gifts and presents for the bride and also has to feed cream and dry fruits to her with a silver spoon. On the same day, either the sister-in-law or the brother-in-law of the girl, along with one or two children, visit the boy's house with presents for him. Both families hold a music session in the evening, wherein, Kashmiri marriage and folk songs are sung.

Devgon

The girl's "Devgon" (Havan) ceremony starts with "Kanishran" (Bath). In this ritual, a veil held by young girls is placed over the bride's head and a mixture of water, rice, milk and curd is showered along with flowers by the relatives present with a rendering of mantras by the purohit. Fully dressed in traditional clothes and headgear, she is draped in the famous Kashmiri shawl. The shawl is draped over the bride's head and is appropriately pinned below her chin. The boy also starts with a bath and comes fully decked for the ceremony.

Marriage Ceremony

The actual marriage is fixed either during the day or at night. All invitees first assemble at the groom's residence. The groom normally wears the pheran and his waistband. Other embellishments include a sword, which is adjusted in his waistband, and embroidered slip-on shoes on his feet. The eldest paternal uncle ties the turban. A plate of rice containing some money is touched to the left shoulder of the groom while the turban is being tied. The groom rides a horse in the marriage procession to the bride's house. They are greeted and welcomed with the blowing of "shankhs." The bride's maternal uncle has to carry her out to the place where the groom is made to stand. The marriage ceremony start with slokas read by the pundit. The bride and the groom are told about their duties towards one another. The couple has to cross their arms one over the other and hold hands covered with cloth. This ritual is called "Aathwas." Kashmiri folklore holds that the first one who manages to pull out the other's engagement ring plays a dominating role in the married life of the couple. A golden thread (Mananmal) is tied to their foreheads. Stepping on seven one rupee silver coins placed in a circle makes the first round around the sacred fire. The next six rounds are done to the chanting of mantras. The bride and the groom finally feed each other some food. They are considered man and wife now. Then comes the "Bidaai" a time when the bride leaves her parent's house to take on her responsibilities to her husband and in-laws.

Post-Marriage Ceremony

The same evening of her wedding the bride accompanied by her husband and two children has to go to her father's house for dinner. This ceremony is called "satraat". As a part of the "satraat" ceremony, the couple is presented new clothes by the bride's parents, which they have to wear before returning home. "Phirlath" is a tradition where the couple is invited again for lunch or dinner by the girl's parents. "Roth Khabar"—Roth is a one-meter long and half-meter wide cake decorated with nuts and sent to the groom's family on a Tuesday or Saturday following the wedding.

KASHMIRI HINDU BRAHMIN WEDDING

The Brahmins of Kashmir are a handsome and gifted people. The Raija Pandits follow a non-vegetarian diet, while the Shaka Pandits follow a vegetarian one. In the earlier days, they never married outside their community, but now, of course, there are inter-caste marriages. The elders of the families usually arrange the Kashmiri marriages, the preparations for which begin six months in advance. Traditionally a cook, known as 'vaza' is hired during the marriage to make all the delicacies and special snacks for the ceremonies to mark the beginning of the celebrations.

Gota

The making of thin flakes of pistachios, almonds and betel nuts.

Bhandawar

To announce that a wedding is going to take place in the family, mango leaves are strung on a strong cotton string and hung at the entrance of the home. This string of mango leaves is known as the "bhandawar." Multani Mitti or white clay soaked in water and mixed with different colours, is used to paint floral designs called "krool" on the entrance wall to mark the auspicious occasion.

Badia Ceremony

'Badias' are small, sun-dried salted cakes with holes in the center. These are made out of 'urad dal' (lentil) flour, mustard seed oil and spices like coriander, 'jaivitri', 'saunf' (aniseed), nutmeg, etc. Silver coins are placed in the holes of these 'badias' and the bride's family, as an acceptance of the wedding between the two families then sends them across to the groom's house.

Shagun

For the Shagun ceremony, the Vaza or cook, prepares a

porridge made from rice and finely chopped intestines of the goat. This special delicacy is fed to all the guests and relatives. During the 'Shagun', 'badias' are cooked once again. The lady who prepares the dough for the 'badias' has a special task—in a terracotta dish she places the rice, 'badias', salt and money and holds this on her shoulder while she kneads the dough for the 'badias'. This spread of rice, 'badias', salt and money is known as the "zung." The Zung is then given away to the poor and needy as a gesture of goodwill.

Mehenzeraat

The ceremony of applying henna on the bride and the groom is always performed in the night. In the earlier times, the henna was applied only on the palms and the nails of the bride, with a mere blob dabbed on the feet. These days, however, intricate patterns are created by professional 'mehendiwallis' all over the palms, forearms and on the feet right up to the ankles. The feast after the henna ceremony is a gala and grand dinner with several dishes made of sheep or goat meat. The Kashmiris consider chicken meat as taboo. No meat other than that of a goat or a sheep is served.

Phoolon ka Gehn

The first formal acceptance of the confirmation of the wedding is sent from the groom's family to the bride's home in the form of jewellery made entirely from flowers. Fresh red roses and jasmine flowers are used to create necklaces, earrings, the 'tikka', braids for the bride's hair, anklets, waist bands, also known as "tagadis", arm bands or "bazubands", and a special thumb ring called "arsi." The "arsi" has a small mirror embedded in it to enable the bride to look at herself. Young relatives from the groom's family, proceed to the bride's home in a ceremonial procession, replete with a band playing traditional 'shehnai' music and carrying the floral jewellery and a brand new sari for the bride, all on a silver platter.

Devgun

This ritual is held simultaneously in the homes of the bride and the groom. Six unmarried girls tie 'curds' or yogurt in a muslin cloth and hold it over the heads of the bride and the groom and pour water through this to bathe them. The Pundit or Guru performs a puja around the sacred fire during which the bride-to-be has to wear 'Dejeharooh' or gold tassels strung on a sacred thread and passed through the middle ear cartilage. These holes are pierced in the ears of all Kashmiri girls when they are 2 or 3 years of age. The significance of wearing the Dejeharooh is, that the bride is now ready for matrimony.

Sanzvaru

This is typically an evening function where the groom's family sends a carved wooden chest containing a pashmina shawl and cosmetics for the bride. 'Sanz' means decorative and 'varu' means 'things'. The wooden chest is wrapped with a heavily embroidered satin or velvet cloth with the words "Sada Suhagan" (wishes for the bride to live a long and happy married life with her husband) embroidered on it.

Flakes of almonds and pistachios or 'gota' as they are traditionally known, wrapped inside betel leaves, along with 'varak' (thin coating of silver) are sent on a silver platter or 'thaal'. An extra large betel leaf with rose syrup and gold 'varak' is also sent especially for the bride. All these items are taken to the bride's home in a procession accompanied by a live band and the Guru.

Sehrabandi

The groom's brother-in-law ties the traditional 'pagadi' or headdress and the 'sehra' or floral veil for the groom. The 'pagadi' is stitched from 'banarsi silk' fabric. During the tying of the 'pagadi' and 'sehra' the groom is made to stand on the entrance of the home where colourful designs have been made on the floor—this is known as the 'Veghu'. All the elders of the family shower coins on to the 'veghu' after having taken them around the groom's head a few times. This is done to keep away the 'evil eye' from the groom!

Baraat

The bride is adorned with all the jewellery given to her by her parents. They also present her with an ensemble called the 'pucca panch daan', literally translated, means 5 of everything: e.g. 5 bangles, 5 sets of earrings, 5 necklace sets and a 'tagadi' or waistband. A 'veghu' is created in the bride's home and her maternal uncle or 'mama' carries her up to it. The groom arrives in a decorated car (horses do not form a part of Kashmiri weddings) up to the 'veghu' and is welcomed with the sprinkling of rose water. The couple is then escorted to partake of the grand vegetarian feast, hosted by the bride's family. The groom eats on a silver plate and after that, the bride is fed from the same plate. The bride's parents usually fast during this occasion.

Lagan

After the gala vegetarian meal, the Guru performs the wedding ritual around the sacred fire. The couple takes the 'pheras' or seven steps around the fire, after which they are made to sit facing each other under a pashmina shawl. This is the same shawl which was sent to the bride's home by the groom's family for the 'Sanzvaru' ceremony. They can now view each other in a silver mirror. The wedding ritual is very long and sometimes lasts the whole night! Midway during the ritual the couple is allowed to rest for about a half hour.

Posh Puja

'Posh' means flower in Kashmiri. The morning after the wedding ritual, the couple is made to stand up to receive blessings from all the relatives. Members from the groom's family stand near the bride and members from the bride's family stand next to the groom. The couple is then blessed by one and all with the showering of rose petals.

Bidaai

The bride stands on the 'veghu' and takes a few coins in her hands, which she throws over the top of her head. She is now ready to be escorted to her new home.

Dahi Bhaat

On arrival at the marital home the couple is made to sit on large, sturdy, upturned baskets and feed each other sweet rice and curd. At this point, the 'Dejeharooh' is removed and the bride is adorned with silver tassels or 'Atahroo', signifying that she is now a married lady.

Garasun

The bride's brother and sister come to the marital home and escort the bride back to her parent's home for one day. This ritual is known as the 'garasun'. The bride wears all the jewellery given to her by her in-laws and proceeds to her parent's home. The bride's family prepares a lavish spread of non-vegetarian delicacies for the relatives from both homes. After the grand meal, the bride and groom return to the marital home, carrying with them all the gifts presented to the bride by her parents.

KASHMIRI SHIA MUSLIM WEDDING

Kashmiri Shia Muslim weddings are rich in social customs and ceremonies. For a whole week before the wedding, festivities are held in the homes of the couple. Kashmiri men are tall and well built and their women beautiful and lively. Liberal-minded, they are fond of fun and amusement this is reflected in their weddings.

The Engagement

Traditionally, the groom's parents ask for the bride's hand in marriage. Before confirming the alliance, 'Istakhara' or divine consent is sought. All Muslims may revert to the 'Istakhara' when faced with an important decision and Kashmiri Muslims always observe this before confirming a matrimonial alliance. A note, written to Allah asking for direction for this very important decision is handed over to a 'maulvi' (Muslim priest). He may or may not read the note, but offers prayers opens the Holy Quran at random and reads aloud the first verse on the page on the right. The verse is translated and interpreted. Based on this, a verdict is given which could be: 'very good', 'good', 'better after some time', 'miyaneh' (in between), 'bad' or 'very bad'. When the 'rishta' (alliance) is confirmed, the groom's parents and close family members visit the bride in her home and gift her a piece of jewellery. The bride's relatives reciprocate and a visit is made to the groom's home.

Naabad Nishani

'Naabad' means 'mishri' or unrefined sugar. After consulting a calendar both families decide on a 'saat' or an auspicious day, which must exclude the days of 'Moharram' and 'Safar', which are periods of austerity. The chosen date will be written on the 'saat naamah' by the groom's father and officially handed over to the bride's father, thus confirming the wedding date. This is followed by a 'wazwaan' or traditional banquet.

Nishaani

The 'Nikaahnaamah' is a marriage contract and the 'Nikaah' is the signing of this contract. Kashmiri Shia Muslims sign the contract well before the actual wedding day—even months before! The 'Nikaahnaamah' includes the amount of the 'mehr' (literally, bride's price), which was agreed upon by mutual consent of both families. Four 'shahids' (witnesses) take the 'Nikaahnaamah' to the bride's house for her to accept and sign. With witnesses from her family present the 'Nikaah' is read aloud and the 'mehr' cited. The bride accepts the terms of the contract, says 'qabool kiya' (I have accepted) and signs the document.

The document is taken back to the groom and read aloud to him in front of his family. He, too, confirms his acceptance by saying 'qabool kiya' and signs it. A few verses from the Holy Quran and the 'Agadh-e-Nikaah' are read aloud to give religious sanction to the marriage. The contract of the marriage is now complete and the couple is officially married; but until the wedding is conducted some time later the bride and groom continue to live in their parents' homes and are not allowed to meet each other. They may, however, exchange photographs!

Manziraat

This ceremony is held one day before the wedding. It is mainly a ladies function and is attended by the bride's friends and relatives. Family and friends bless the 'mehendi' (henna) after which, it is applied on the hands and feet of the bride by professional 'mehendiwallis' (henna artists). It is washed off after a few hours leaving a deep red colour, which can last up to a few weeks. A similar ceremony, though not as elaborate is held for the groom in his home. This ritual is followed by the 'wazwan'.

Vardaan

One day before the wedding the groom's 'mama' (maternal uncle) and a few other male relatives take the 'vardaan' (the trousseau prepared for her by the groom's parents) for the bride. It consists of a complete set of clothes and jewellery, which will be worn by her on her wedding day.

Reception of the 'Baraat'

The groom usually arrives on horseback and is referred to as the 'maharaaz' at this time. The bride's family offers him a ceremonial welcome; the bride's mother helps him dismount and leads him to the 'masnand' (a platform set with comfortable cushions) where he and his friends are seated. The groom's female relatives and friends retire to an inner hall where they are made to feel welcome. 'Vaan vun' or songs appropriate to the function are sung to the rhythm of the 'tumbak nari' (a clay drum) and hot, spiced tea is served. What follows is the wedding feast or 'wazwan', which is prepared in both homes for seven days—but tonight's menu will excel itself!

Ruksati

After the feast the 'baraatis' leave, though a few stay back to escort the bridal couple back home. The groom's maternal uncle goes inside and asks for the bride. She bids farewell to her family, an emotionally charged moment! Her own 'mama' (maternal uncle) escorts her out, her face still covered and rides with the bridal couple in the decorated car all the way to the groom's home. Escorted by the groom, the bride enters her new home to be received by her mother-in-law. Outside, a 'qurbaani' (sacrifice of a sheep) is performed in her honour and in the name of Allah. The mother-in-law lifts the bride's veil and gifts her a ring and 'husk kaanth' (a broad gold bangle) on seeing her for the first time as a married woman.

The Khabbar

All through the following day, the groom's family and friends meet the bridal couple and give them their wedding gifts. The bride's family, except her parents also visits the couple and partakes of the 'wazwan', a feast, which is an integral part of any Kashmiri celebration.

Phirsaal

Seven days after the wedding, the bride's family invites the bride, groom and close family members to their home. The 'wazwan' is served and the bride and groom stay back here for three days, during which, the bride's family and friends take the opportunity to meet and wish the groom.

UTTAR PRADESH KAYAST WEDDING

Bariksha

Once the parents of the bride and groom have mutually decided that a wedding will take place between their son and daughter, the bride's family sends a silver bowl full of rice, turmeric and 'supari' (areca nut) to the groom' s family along with an envelope containing money. These items are sent as a symbolic gesture to confirm the alliance.

Sagai

The formal engagement takes place after the 'bariksha', where the groom's family proceeds to the bride's home laden with gifts for the bride. These gifts usually include a sari, set of jewellery and the engagement ring. The groom's mother places all these in the bride's 'kodi' (sari pallav) and applies the traditional 'tikka' (vermilion mark) on the bride's forehead. Family and close friends are invited to attend this ceremony, which is followed by a lunch or dinner hosted by the bride's parents.

Haldi and Tel

These are ritualistic ceremonies signifying the cleansing of one's mind, body and soul before embarking on the path of marriage. The bride wears simple clothes and all the older women of the household apply oil on her face, arms and legs. A paste called 'uptan' is made from pure vegetable oils, fresh milk curds, henna and turmeric and also applied on the bride's face, arms and legs. Her sisters or cousins then lead her for her bath. A similar ceremony is held for the groom at his home.

Tilak

The bride's parents, brothers, sisters, uncles and aunts along with their spouses go to the groom's home carrying clothes, jewellery, electronic items, fruits, sweetmeats, and the 'tilak' (paste made from rice and vermilion). The gifts are presented to the groom in the 'puja room' or in front of the family deity and each member of the bride's family applies the 'tilak' on the groom's forehead, thereby blessing him.

Mehendi and Sangeet

Traditionally, this is a function meant only for family and close friends and is light hearted affair. These days, however, it has evolved into a mega event and probably most looked forward to! Professional Mehendiwallis make intricate patterns on the hands and feet of the bride with henna paste. Amongst U.P. Kayasts, henna is applied on the hands of the groom as well. This is done amidst singing of traditional songs as well as parodies based on popular songs. Members of both families join in to sing and dance in celebration.

Bhaat

The 'mama' or bride's maternal uncle plays a major role in any Kayast wedding. He is expected to give lavish gifts to his sister and niece. On the day of the 'bhaat', he comes to the bride's home bringing saris, jewellery and other gifts and also hosts a lunch for the groom's family and gives them gifts as well.

Baraat

This is a very colourful and grand ceremony. The groom is dressed in a white and gold 'achkan' (long jacket with a Nehru collar), and 'churidars' (fitted trousers). On his head, he wears a 'safa' (turban) with a 'kalgi' (brooch) pinned onto it. A sword or dagger is tucked in his waistband. Before he departs, all his relatives apply the ceremonial 'tikka' on his forehead (vermilion). Traditionally, he would depart on horseback, but these days a decorated car is a popular choice. The 'baraatis' (groom's party) are received by the bride's family and at the 'darwaza' or entrance to the wedding venue the bride's mother welcomes the groom by applying 'tikka' on his forehead.

Jaimala

The bride is led in to the wedding hall by her female relatives and friends. Before entering the 'mantap' (platform erected to perform the marriage rites) the couple exchanges garlands signifying their acceptance of each other as husband and wife.

After the 'jaimala', the wedding rites will commence when the couple will be seated at the 'mantap' along with their parents and the 'pujari' (Brahmin priest).

Havan

All auspicious ceremonies are performed in the presence of the God of Fire or 'Agni Devta'. The sacred fire is lit by the 'pujari' amidst Vedic chants and the couple's parents offer prayers to Lord Ganesha and all the other deities so that they can fulfil the aims of 'dharma' (duty), 'artha' (worldly prosperity) and 'kama' (physical desires). The 'pujari' adds clarified butter or 'ghee', wood and 'samaghri' (a mixture of herbs, clarified butter, rice grains) to the sacred fire amidst Vedic chants.

Kanyadaan

This is one of the most important rites of a Hindu marriage. The bride, groom and the bride's parents stand up in front of the 'agni'. The parents join their left hands and the groom places his right hand over theirs. The bride, then places her right hand over that of the groom's. The bride's parents then lock their right palms and place them over the hands of the bride and groom. The bride's father asks the groom if he accepts the responsibility of being his daughter's husband. The groom accepts and then the bride is 'given away' by mentioning the names of the fathers and forefathers of both families.

The marital knot is tied by taking the end of the groom's scarf and tying it to the sari 'pallav' or 'dupatta' (veil) of the bride to signify the coming together of the couple. After the tying of the marital knot, the couple sits in front of the sacred fire and promises are made between the two.

Phere

The bride and groom walk seven times around the sacred fire, taking their seven wedding vows. For the first three 'pheras' the bride leads the groom around the fire and during the last four 'pheras' the groom has to lead her. All throughout the 'pheras', the 'pujari' recites mantras and offers 'samaghri' to the fire.

Bidaai

A most touching ceremony, the 'bidaai' is full of emotionally charged moments, when the bride leaves her parental home and bids farewell to her parents, family and close friends. She leaves for her marital home in a decorated car accompanied by her husband and one male member from her family, usually her brother.

Parchan

The groom's mother receives her daughter-in-law at the entrance and performs an 'aarti' for her. The 'aarti' is performed to remove the 'nazar' or evil eye and, also to welcome the bride into her new home. On entering the home, she is taken to the family 'puja room' and made to sit in front of the family deity.

Mookh-dekhai or Vadu Milan

'Mookh-dekhai' literally means 'show your face' and since the bride generally has her head covered through most of the ceremonies, this is actually the very first time that the family gets to see her. She is seated and each relative comes in and showers her with gifts and gets acquainted with her.

Reception

The reception has become mandatory in several families. A grand dinner is hosted and, the bride and groom are introduced as a married couple to the community at large.

UTTAR PRADESH KHATRI WEDDING

Sagaai

Once, both the families decide that an alliance will take place, the bride, her parents, brothers, sisters and their spouses go to the groom's house laden with gifts. This is done to 'confirm' the alliance. The elders in the groom's family apply 'Tilak' to the groom's forehead and an auspicious day is fixed for the wedding.

Godh Bharai

A day or two before the wedding, the groom's family members go to the bride's home, carrying gifts for her. The bride sits down while the groom's mother places all the gifts (saris, jewellery, cosmetics, accessories, silver, sweetmeats, all laden on silver platters) in her 'godh' (lap). This is called 'godh bharai'

(bharai is to fill). The groom's family applies 'tilak' on the bride's forehead.

Tilak

Applying vermilion on the groom's forehead. This ceremony usually takes place on the day preceding the wedding. The bride's brother and other relatives go to the groom's home laden with gifts for him and his entire family. The bride's mother applies the ceremonial 'tilak' on the groom's forehead, and, the family returns carrying gifts given by the groom's family for the bride's brother.

Sangeet

The festive sangeet function and a grand dinner follow the tilak ceremony. There is a lot of singing and dancing by members of both families, especially the youngsters at the sangeet. Music is considered to be the soul of Hindu marriages. In many families the 'ladies sangeet' begins almost one week before the wedding and takes place every day till the day of the wedding!

Kangana

This ceremony is an important one and is performed under the guidance of a 'pujari' (Brahmin priest). Two small bundles are made with betel nuts, tamarind and tiny shells (cockles) and tied to the sacred thread or 'mouli' and blessed by the pujari. These bracelets (kanganas) are then tied to the wrists of the bride and the groom and remain tied till the completion of all the wedding rituals. The 'kanganas' are a symbol of 'protection' for all the wedding rites.

Mehendi

The henna ceremony. Professionals 'mehendiwallis' or henna artists are called to apply the henna paste making intricate designs on the palms and feet of the bride and the other ladies and young girls who wish it. This is typically a ladies function and usually takes place a day or two before the wedding day. Though the applying of 'mehendi' is a laborious process especially for the bride, the singing and dancing by the other ladies present, makes it a fun filled occasion.

Seedhe Haath Tanni Kadai

This ceremony is held simultaneously in the bride and groom's homes. Each member of the family dips 'doob' (special blades of grass) into mustard oil and touches the bride's and groom's toes, knees, shoulders and foreheads with it. A paste called 'uptan' is made from chickpea flour, mustard oil, fresh milk curds and turmeric and applied on the faces, arms and feet of the bride and groom. After the 'uptan', the bride and groom proceed for their regular baths.

Chooda

'Choodas' are traditionally a set of cream and red ivory bangles with inlay work, presented to the bride by her 'mama' (maternal uncle) and 'mami' (maternal aunt). These days, however, ivory is replaced with either plastic or acrylic. The ceremony begins with a puja performed by the pujari. The bangles are blessed by everyone present and then slipped on the bride's wrist by her aunt and uncle.

Vivah

In preparation for the 'vivah' or wedding ceremony, the U.P. Khatri bride wears a heavy Benares silk sari or a heavily embroidered 'lehenga choli' (full length skirt and blouse). The colours are usually red/magenta/bright pink. Her ears, neck, arms, wrists and ankles are adorned with traditional 'kundan' jewellery (uncut rubies, emeralds and diamonds set in gold). The groom's attire consists of off-white or cream coloured 'sherwani suit', a 'safa' (head gear) and a jewelled sword (a family heirloom), which is fixed in his waistband. For all Hindus, 'vivah' is one of major 'samskaras' (sacraments), which binds not only the bride and groom, but their families as well.

Baraat

The groom leaves for the marriage venue in a ceremonial procession. As in several other Hindu weddings, here too, the groom is mounted on an elaborately decorated mare, and proceeds to the marriage venue accompanied by a live band playing music and all his family and close friends. The family and friends accompanying him, dance all the way to the venue! The bride's family receives the groom in a ceremonial fashion on his arrival.

Jaimala

Her close friends and cousins escort the bride to receive the groom. The pujari performs a small puja, after which, the couple exchange garlands symbolizing their acceptance of each other as life partners and enter the 'mandap' (temporary) temple or altar erected for the wedding ceremony. The bride also performs the traditional 'aarti' for the groom.

Dinner

In all U.P. Khatri weddings, dinner is served to the guests after the exchange of garlands, because the wedding rites are usually conducted after midnight and may last till the wee hours of the morning! Only a very few close family friends and relatives remain to witness the wedding rites.

Lagna

Two pujaris, one from each family, officiate during the lagna. A special puja is performed for the groom when he enters the mandap. The ceremony consists of several rituals performed by the couple and their parents and close relatives.

Havan

Fire plays an important role in all Hindu marriages. It is a symbol of purity and also acts as an 'agnisakshi' (witness) to the marriage. To the chanting of Vedic mantras, the sacred fire is lit and prayers are offered for good health, prosperity and long and happy married lives for the couple. Fresh flowers, rice, clarified butter or 'ghee', sugar, grains and 'kumkum' (vermilion) are used to perform these Vedic rites.

Kanyadaan

Kanyadaan is the giving away the bride by her parents and is one of the most important rites of Hindu marriages. The bride stands facing the groom, holding betel leaves, betel nuts, rice grains and one flower in her cupped hands. The pujari touches the foreheads of the couple with the 'kalash' (pot of water). The bride's father touches her hands and asks the groom if he will accept the responsibility of becoming her husband. The groom accepts and pledges to protect and look after her by grasping both her hands.

Gath Bandhan

To solemnize the pledge taken earlier, the bride's sari 'pallu' or 'dupatta' (veil) is tied to the grooms scarf/shawl symbolizing the joining of their hearts and binding the two families together in a lifelong relationship.

Pheras

The bride and groom go around the fire seven times, taking their marriage vows. The pujari recites mantras and offers 'samaghri' (mixture of herbs, clarified butter and rice grains) to the fire. After the 'pheras' the bride must shift to the groom's left, the side closest to his heart!

Bari Palang

The bride and groom are escorted to the room wherein lies the nuptial bed. While they sit on it, a small puja is performed and the bride takes fistfuls of rice and throws it over her head without looking back. Family members standing behind her try to catch as many grains as possible in their sari pallus and dupattas! It is a sign of good luck for the person who manages to gather the most!

Bedi Lutna

After the wedding rites are completed the young cousins and other children from families remove all the toys and decorations from the mandap and take them home. Literally translated, 'bedi' is the small platform where the fire was lit, and 'lutna' is to plunder! Now that all the marriage ceremonies are completed, the parents of the bride and groom embrace and congratulate each other.

Many families follow the tradition of sending the bride to the groom's home at this time (it is now close to daylight!) Her brother goes to fetch her, the groom and his immediate relatives the next morning and brings them back to the bride's parental home to partake of a sumptuous breakfast!

Vidaai

The bride leaves her parental home. The bride's parents, close friends and relatives bid her a tearful farewell, all the while showering her with flowers and gifts. She leaves in a decorated car for her new home.

UTTAR PRADESH PATHAN SUNNI MUSLIM WEDDING

Their marriage are steeped in tradition and the ceremonies begin several days before the signing of the marriage document or the 'nikaahnamah'. The bride and groom are always resplendently dressed in richly embroidered clothes and wear heavy traditional jewellery. The groom arrives on horseback and after the wedding rituals are completed it is customary for the bride to be carried a few yeards in a richly decorated 'palki' (palanquin). The Muslim community is famous for its lavish cuisine and grand feasts follows most of the ceremonies.

Nizbat

The groom's family sends a proposal to the bride's family. The bride's consent to the engagement is absolutely necessary. The 'nizbat' takes place as soon as the decision is made so that the community knows that the couple is spoken for. The groom's mother, sisters and a few close female relatives go to the bride's home laden with gifts for her. A high tea is served. The groom does not attend this ceremony. To fix a date for the wedding, older members of both families get together shortly after the 'nizbat' and an auspicious date is decided upon with mutual consent.

Mangni

A few days prior to the wedding, the groom, his family and close friends are invited to the bride's home. The groom's mother takes a set of clothes, jewellery, accessories, toiletries and footwear for her future daughter-in-law along with platters of fruits and sweetmeats. The bride is blessed by the groom's mother and is permitted to come out and meet the guests.

Milaad Sharif

'Majlis' is a religious gathering, and the 'milaad sharif' is a 'majlis' held in thanksgiving for the joyous occasion of marriage. Female relatives and close friends attend this ceremony attired in festive clothes and fine jewellery. 'Milaad Sharif' prayer books written in Urdu are read out aloud in 'taranum', a classical plainchant.

Mayun and Uptan

About eight or fifteen days before the actual wedding the bride enters a state of 'mayun' which indicates that she is now in seclusion and her movements are restricted. A yellow sheet is drawn across the corner of the room and this is her special abode until the wedding. The groom's mother brings the 'uptan' (a paste made from turmeric, sandalwood powder, herbs and aromatic oils) for the bride. After blessing her and removing 'nazar' (evil eye) the groom's mother and his sisters apply the 'uptan' on the bride's hands and face. Each day till the wedding, a 'dai' (local midwife) will come in and massage the 'uptan' into the bride's skin and leave it on for most of the day. A similar ceremony is held for the groom, where the bride's mother brings the 'uptan' for him and the bride's sisters, cousins and friends apply it on him, teasing him mercilessly all throughout!

Mehendi

One day before the wedding the groom's mother sends a decorated clay container with 'mehendi' (henna paste) for the bride. Platters of sweetmeats and fruits covered with pretty silk 'rumaals' (silk handkerchiefs) are also sent. Seven 'sumangalis' (married ladies) come and bless the bride and then apply 'mehendi' on her palms and fingernails. These days it is customary to engage the services of professional 'mehendiwallis' to apply the henna paste. The groom goes through a similar ritual in his home.

Sehrabandhi

The 'sehra' is a short veil of either golden thread, strings of pearls or just flowers, which is tied to his turban by the groom's mother after seven married men bless it. The groom leaves with his 'baraatis' (male relatives and friends) for the bride's home, which he must reach before sunset or 'magreeb se pehle'. The 'baraat' or procession is led by a troupe of men carrying gaslights and a uniformed band playing popular film music.

Nikaah

After the 'baraatis' are given a ceremonial welcome by the bride's family they are seated and the Qazi (Muslim priest) or his 'vakil' (representative) and two 'gavaah' (witnesses) take the 'nikaahnamah' (marriage document) to the bride and read it aloud. She accepts by saying 'qabool kiya' (I accept) and signs the contract. The 'nikaahnamah' makes a mention of the 'mehr' (bride price), which was decided earlier by mutual consent.

The document is then taken back to the groom and read aloud to him. He too gives his assent by saying 'qabool kiya' and signs the contract. Verses from the Holy Quran (aiyetain) are read, followed by the 'Agadh-e-Nikaah' to give the marriage religious sanction. The 'sunnat' or announcement of the marriage is made immediately by distributing 'chuaare' or dried dates and 'mishri' or unrefined sugar.

Aarsi Mussahaf

After the 'nikaah' the groom's mother and sisters go inside to greet the bride and on seeing her for the first time as a married lady, ('mooh dikhai') gift her jewellery, bless her and put a sweetmeat in her mouth. The bride changes into new bridal attire and is led out by her mother-in-law and sisters-in-law. Her face is completely covered by the 'dupatta' (veil). Four young girls hold an embroidered cloth as a canopy under which the bride and groom are then seated. The groom's mother slips, what is known as an 'aarsi' (large silver ring finely worked with enamel, with a piece of mirror embedded in it) on her thumb. 'Aarsi Mussahaf' is when the groom takes her hand and positions the ring so that he can see her face for the first time as his wife! The trousseau brought by the groom's family for the bride is now presented to her, while the groom receives gifts from her parents. The ceremony is followed by a grand, festive meal.

Vida

As always, this is the most emotional moment in a bride's life. She bids a tearful farewell to her parents, family and friends and is helped into a 'palki' (palanquin) along with her sister. In urban cities the traditional send-off in a palanquin is a symbol of the past and it is merely carried a few yards out of the house from whence the bride, groom and 'baraat' step into waiting cars. A few yards away from the groom's house the bride is once again helped into the 'palki', which is carried into the compound. When she steps out the gallant groom sweeps her up in his arms and carries her over the threshold of the house! This is called 'dehleez paar', literally translated means 'crossing the threshold'.

Valima

While the 'nikaah' may be as intimate a ceremony as the family desires, for the 'valima' it is essential that as many guests are invited as can be afforded by the families. The groom's parents host the event and the venue is usually a banquet or marriage hall. A noted poet or 'tarcaif' is requested to compose verses in honour of the occasion. These verses or 'sehras' cleverly weave in the family's history and extol the virtue of the bride and groom. The dinner is a lavish spread with the special 'biryani' (rice cooked with lamb) and a wide variety of meat and chicken dishes.

GUJARATI MARRIAGE CEREMONY

Pre-Wedding Ceremony

The first ceremony performed is called Mandap Mahurat which is performed by the Pandit a few days before the wedding at the house of the bride and the groom. The next ceremony is the Griha Shanti. The puja for Griha Shanti is conducted by an acharya with the family members and relatives of the bride as well as the groom. The purpose of the puja is to bring peace among the stars so that the couple can live a happy married life. The actual wedding day begins with what is known as the Pokavu, the arrival of the groom. The mother-in-law at the entrance to the wedding hall greets him. A small ceremony is performed and then she tries to pinch the groom's nose. This playfully reminds the groom that he has come to their door to ask for their daughter by rubbing his nose on the door.

Wedding Ceremony

In a Gujarati marriage ceremony, the bride and groom exchange garlands twice. This is known as "Jaimala." The first time the groom is placed higher than the bride. The second time again at the Mandap but on equal ground. During the "Madhuparka", the groom's feet are washed and he is fed honey and milk. During this time, the bride's sisters try and steal the groom's shoes, adding mischief and humour to the ceremony. At the end of the day, the groom retrieves his shoes by offering his sister-in-law's money. The bride is then carried to the Mandap by her maternal uncle in a ceremony that is known as "Kanya Agamana." At this point, the "Antarpat," or the curtain separating the bride and groom, is lowered and the couple again exchange garlands. It is now time for the bride to be given away in a ritual known as "Kanya Daan" or "Hasta Milap." In Gujarati Marriage Ceremony, phera's are not taken seven times but it is taken four times. This ritual is called "Mangalpheras," when the couple circles the holy fire four times which symbolizes "Dharma," "Artha", "Kama" and "Moksha." The "Sapta Padi" is performed with a variation in which the groom helps the bride touch seven betel nuts with her right toe, while they recite the seven vows. After the ceremony is over the couple take blessings of the elders.

Post-Wedding Ceremony

After the departure of the bride and groom amidst tears of joy and grief, which is known as the "Vidai," the couple returns to the groom's house where they play a game called "Aeki-Beki." This game is played by placing a ring and several coins in a tray filled with water, which is coloured, by "sindoor" and milk. It is said that the person who finds the ring four out of seven times, will rule the household.

GUJARATI PATEL HINDU WEDDING

The Patels or Patidars of Gujarat are ambitious, intelligent, hardworking, hospitable and excessive on occasions like marriages. Their weddings are arranged on a grand scale and are bright and colourful. The bride and groom receive huge amounts of clothes and jewellery and the groom is given cash gifts at almost each ceremony; in fact after each 'parikrama' (circumvention around the sacred fire) his palms are crossed with gold!

Chandlo Maatli

The 'chandlo' (applying the vermilion mark on the forehead) announces the acceptance of the alliance between the two families and the consent of the bride and groom to come together in holy matrimony. 'Chandlo' is the 'tikka' and 'maatli' is the clay container in which 'mithais' (sweetmeats) were packed in the olden days. The bride's father and four other male members from her family visit the groom carrying auspicious items and the bride's father applies the 'chandlo' on the groom's forehead and gives him a 'shakun' (a blessing symbolized by a token sum of money). An astrologer is consulted and the wedding date is fixed. The 'chandlo maatli' ceremony is usually followed by a high tea or dinner.

Ganesh Sthapan

Lord Ganesha is always the first deity to be propitiated at any significant event. His blessings are invoked before the preparations begin for the wedding so that no obstacles present themselves and all goes well. This 'puja' is attended by close family members and is performed in both homes simultaneously on an auspicious day. After the 'puja' a vegetarian meal sans onion and garlic is served along with a sweet called 'khansaar'.

Mehendi

This is an intimate gathering of the bride's female relatives and close friends two days before the wedding. 'Mehendi' (henna) is ground into a paste and applied by professional 'mehendiwallis' (henna artists) in fine patterns on the palms and feet of the bride. Songs specific to the occasion are sung and lunch is served.

Garba and Dandia Raas

On the evening of the 'mehendi' family and friends gather together dressed in traditional finery and sing and dance to the beat of the 'dhol' (drum). The women form a circle to dance the graceful 'garba' and the men join in later in an energetic 'dandia raas' (dandias are sticks).

Prenuptial Ceremonies

Mandva Mahurat

A day before the wedding, Lord Ganesha is worshipped once again, this time his blessings are sought for the ground on which the wedding canopy will be installed. Though, family and close friends attend the 'mandva mahurat', only the women of the household observe the 'puja'. The 'pujari' performs a brief 'puja' at the shrine inside the house then puts 'tikka' on the foreheads of five men from the family. He goes on to give them a small stick with 'nada chari' (red thread) wrapped around it. The men link their hands and carry this to the site of the 'mandva' and embed it into the earth. This stick is symbolic of one of the poles of the 'mandva', which will support the canopy.

Pithi

A shrine is arranged with a picture of Lord Ganesh set in it. The bride sits on a 'bajat' or low stool, palms upturned. It is the perogative of the 'kaaki' (paternal uncle's wife) to mix the 'pithi' (a paste of sandalwood powder, herbs, rosewater and 'German mogro') (a type of 'attar' or perfume). She then arranges the 'pithi' on a decorated platter and has it blessed by the priest. The women of the household apply the 'pithi' on the bride's skin. The bride keeps this on until the next ceremony (the 'griha shanti') is completed. A small ceremony called the 'ookarhi nautarvi' is conducted after the 'pithi', wherein, the 'kaaki' places an iron nail, a whole 'supari' (betel nut) and a one-rupee coin in a shallow hole dug by the 'pujari'. This is done to ensure that no evil spirits enter the venue of the wedding.

Griha Shanti

This is a very important religious ceremony. Both sets of parents are the primary figures in the invocation. On behalf of the parents, the officiating priests ask the deities to ensure stellar harmony and peace during the period of their son and daughter's wedding. The bride takes a coconut to her parents who are seated on 'patlas' (low stools) in front of the sacred fire and seats herself beside them. While the priest is performing the 'puja', which can take upto two hours—she hands this 'shriphal' (coconut) to her parents, who in turn hand it over to the priest for 'ahuti' (sacrifice). The coconut is consigned to flames, thus propagating peace and harmony between all the nine planets. Similar ceremonies are conducted in the groom's home.

Mameru or Mosaalu

The custom of 'mameru' originated centuries ago, when there were no legal rights existing for daughters. It was customary for the parents to start making provisions for their daughter by gifting her with things on occasions like 'rakshabandhan' or 'bhaidheej'. These gifts accumulated as 'streedhan' (daughter's wealth). When the girl grows up and gets married, the 'mama' or maternal uncle comes with the 'mameru' consisting of clothes, jewellery and other gift items including the traditional 'paanetar' (silk wedding sari—usually white with red border) and 'choodo' (ivory bangle—now replaced with acrylic or plastic). The 'mameru' ceremony takes place one day before the wedding.

Varghodo

On the evening of the wedding, the groom, dressed in all his finery and carrying a 'katar' (small dagger) prepares to leave for the wedding venue. The priest gives the groom's sister a small bowl wrapped in cloth and containing coins on which the Hindu Swastika has been etched. She rattles this over her brother's head to ward off the evil eye and also to warn him that even though he is getting married, he must not forget his sister! The groom's father's sister-in-law garlands him and gives him a cluster of flowers. After being blessed by all he mounts a richly caparisoned mare and leaves for the wedding venue accompanied by his relatives and close friends.

Var Ponke

The bride's mother receives the groom and his 'baraat' (procession) at the entrance of the wedding venue. She performs the traditional 'aarti' for the groom, applies the 'kumkum' (vermilion) and rice 'tikka' on his forehead. Before the groom can enter the premises, he is made to step onto a 'bajat' (low stool) where the bride's mother performing the 'aarti' and applying the 'tikka' for him once again accords him a ceremonial welcome. The clusters of flowers given to him earlier by his aunt are now exchanged for a coconut decorated with red thread. One of the groom's aunts goes inside to call on the bride who is worshipping at the shrine of Lord Ganesha and presents her with the 'kanya shelu' (a platter with a sari, some jewellery, pretty slippers, and a 'mangalsutra' made from black beads and strung on red thread). This is the last gift she receives as a maiden. The sari is draped around her shoulders, the 'mangalsutra' tied around her neck and she is led outside to receive her groom. The bride garlands the groom signaling her acceptance of him as her husband and is led back inside the shrine to continue her worship of Lord Ganesha. The bride's mother places two clay pots filled with rice on the ground and the groom breaks them before entering the wedding 'mandva'.

Lagna

The wedding ceremony—divided into following segments:

Varmala

The bride's 'mama' (maternal uncle) escorts her to the 'mandva' where she garlands the groom and he reciprocates. She now sits facing him. The priest puts the 'tikka' on both their foreheads and blesses them.

Kanyadaan

The bride's parents apply 'tikka' on the couple and the bride's father performs the 'kanyadaan'. This is done by tying the hands of the bride and groom together in a marital knot known as the 'hast medap'. The bride's right hand is placed in the groom's right hand and they both reach out over the unlit fire below. With this gesture the father of the bride symbolizes this promise; "I offer you this most precious gift of my daughter to take as your own, to cherish and to protect." The bride's mother connects the couple by tying the 'varmaala' (a length of sacred red thread) across them and looping it like a garland over their hands. After the ceremony the 'varmaala' is removed and put around the bride's neck like a garland.

Mangal Pheras

The 'pujari' lights the sacred fire amidst Vedic chants. The couple circles the fire four times. The groom leads the bride the first three times and the fourth time he is led by her. These circumventions are called 'mangal pheras'. After the last 'phera' there is a small tussle to see who gets back to the seat first!

Saptapadi

After the 'mangal pheras' the couple takes the seven steps around the fire and with each step a vow is taken. After the completion of all these ceremonies the couple is seated and blessed by all with the showering of rice.

Vadava Vanu

The bride bids a tearful farewell to her parents, family and friends. The 'pujari' performs a small 'puja' for the decorated car by applying 'tikka' to the hood. The bride's mother breaks a coconut in front of the car, invoking blessings for a safe journey for the couple. The bride and groom leave accompanied by at least three others (it is necessary to have a minimum of five people in the car). The bride's brother usually escorts her to her new home.

Var Ghodyu Pokvanu Che

The newly weds are received by the groom's mother and sisters. The groom's mother performs a small 'aarti' and puts the traditional 'tikka' on their foreheads. She also gifts her daughter-in-law a piece of jewellery.

Reception

This is an event borrowed from the West and is not mandatory. The reception can be as simple or as elaborate an affair as desired by the families. The purpose is to introduce the bride and groom as a married couple.

GUJARATI NAAGAR BRAHMIN WEDDING

Gujarat is the home of the Naagars but many Naagar families are settled in Uttar Pradesh, West Bengal and Punjab. A progressive community, their girls are often married off with no expectations of wealth from the in-laws side. This is called 'kanku-kanya', meaning that the bride is welcome only with a vermilion mark on her forehead. One ceremony which forms an integral part of any Naagar Brahmin wedding is the 'mosaalu', wherein the bride's 'mama' or maternal uncle brings the 'choodo' (ivory bangel-now replaced with acrylic or plastic), 'paanetar' (silk wedding sari usually white with red border) and a colourful basket containing gifts for his niece one day before the wedding. Naagar Brahmin marriages are very colourful and the traditional Gujarati folk dance called the 'Garba' forms an integral part of the celebrations.

Chandlo

The 'chandlo' (applying the vermilion mark on the forehead)

announces the acceptance of the alliance between the two families. This ceremony is usually observed after the matrimonial alliance is fixed but before the wedding date is fixed. A priest or 'pujari' officiates at this ceremony and blesses the couple by applying the 'chandlo' on their foreheads. The couple then exchanges garlands and the families exchange gifts given for the bride and groom.

Ganesh Sthapan/Ganesh Matli

The Ganesh 'puja' signals the start of all the festivities. The 'Ganesh Sthapan' is a small family function wherein the priest invokes the blessings of Lord Ganesha. The 'puja' is performed in both homes by the paternal aunts or 'phois'. In return for their efforts the 'phois' receive lavish gifts.

Garba

The 'Garba raas', a graceful Gujarati folk dance captures the essence of celebration and is performed in large circles by women singing and dancing to the beat of the 'dhol' (drum). The men join in for the 'dandia raas', a rhythmic dance performed with sticks or 'dandias'. The Garba is normally held after 8 p.m. up until midnight.

Pithi

The 'pithi' ceremony is performed simultaneously in both homes and prepares the bride and groom for the nuptials. A paste called 'pithi' made of sandalwood powder, turmeric, herbs, aromatic oils and rose water is prepared and applied on the faces, arms and legs of the bride by members of her family. The groom undergoes a similar ritual in his home.

Mandva Mahurat and Griha Shanti

This ceremony bears a deep religious significance because the parents of the couple seek the blessings of Mother Earth and ask permission to commence with the digging of the soil to erect the 'mandva' or 'mandap' (platform erected for the wedding rites covered with a canopy). A priest conducts the ceremony where a pole is erected to symbolize the consecration of the 'mandva'. 'Griha Shanti', a ceremony conducted to seek the blessings of all the nine planets, immediately follows the 'mandva mahurat'.

Mosaalu

The custom of 'mosaalu' originated centuries ago when there were no legal rights existing for daughters. It was customary for the parents to start making provisions for their daughter by gifting her with things on occasions like 'rakshabandhan' or 'bhaidheej'. These gifts accumulated as 'streedhan' (daughter's wealth). When the girl grows up and gets married the 'mama' or maternal uncle comes with the 'mosaalu' consisting of clothes, jewellery and other gift items including the traditional 'paanetar' (silk wedding sari—usually white with red border) and 'choodo' (ivory bangle—now replaced with acrylic or plastic). The 'mosaalu' ceremony takes place one day before the wedding.

Lagna

The 'lagna' or wedding ceremony is broken up into the following segments:

Varghodo

The groom, dressed in all his finery and accompanied by his close friends and family proceeds to the bride's home in a decorated car. Here, the modern day vehicle has replaced the traditional mare! The groom's sister is his constant companion and keeps jingling the 'looni' (small steel bowl filled with betel nuts) near his ear all throughout the procession! This is to keep him alert about Mama carrying groom everything that is happening around him. On disembarking at the wedding venue the groom is greeted by the bride's family and accorded the traditional 'aarti' welcome.

Mangalsutra Varmala

The groom is welcomed by the bride's mother with an 'aarti' and 'pookhana' (4 small sticks). The bride is then escorted to welcome the groom and proceeds to garland him and he reciprocates. The groom is then led to the wedding 'mandap' while the bride returns to her room. The priest begins the wedding rites with the bride's parents seated around the sacred fire.

Mangalastak

These are a series of four lined verses with eight stanzas glorifying Lord Ganesha. The singing of the 'mangalastak' is a very distinct feature of marriages in the Naagar Brahmin community.

Kanyadaan

Before the 'kanyadaan' can begin, the bride's parents renew their own marriage vows. The bride is then led into the 'mandap' by her 'mama' or maternal uncle. She is seated opposite the groom on a 'paatla' or 'aasan' (low stool) and her parents perform the 'kanyadaan' ceremony by placing her hands into those of the groom's.

Hasthamilap

The bride and groom's hands are tied with a cloth in a symbolic marital knot and they take vows to honour their commitment to each other.

Pheras

Also known as 'saptapadi', the 'pheras' are performed immediately after the 'hasthamilap' ceremony. Here, the bride and groom walks around the sacred fire seven times repeating their marital vows. At the beginning of each 'parikrama' or circumvention, a vow is taken. The couple is then proclaimed man and wife and the ceremony is completed with the groom tying the 'mangalsutra' on the bride. The couple then leaves the 'mandap' to seek the blessings of the elders of both families by touching their feet.

Vidai

After the 'lagna', the bride leaves her parental home in a 'doli' or palanquin. These days a decorated car usually replaces the palanquin. A ceremony wrought with emotion it is symbolic of the severing of the bride's rights in her parent's home as she now belongs to her 'sasural' (in-laws home). As she leaves, her brother presents her with a shawl, which is worn by her for the journey. Before leaving for the marital home, the bride and groom apply wet 'kumkum' (vermilion) on their palms and put their imprints on the outside wall of the house or near the 'Ganesha Sthapan'. It is important to conduct the 'vidai' ceremony at an auspicious time.

Reception

Though a Western concept, the reception has become an integral part of the most Indian marriages. The couple's parents host a lavish banquet for their families and friends, wherein, the bride and groom are introduced as a married couple and are congratulated by all.

MARWARI MARRIAGE CEREMONY

Pre-Marriage Ceremony

The engagement ceremony or the "Sagai" takes place at the house of the groom. This is strictly all male affair. On this day, the bride's brother puts "tilak" on the groom's forehead. A sword, clothes, sweets, etc. are given to the groom. "Ganapati Sthapna" and "Grih Shanti" is the second-most important ceremony performed a few days prior to the wedding. An idol of Lord Ganapati is installed and a "havan" is performed. This sthapana is important as all ceremonies commence only after this. A few days prior to the wedding the "Pithi dastoor" ceremony starts. It consists of the application of turmeric and sandalwood paste to the bride and the groom who cannot leave the house once the pithi starts. This ceremony continues until the day of the wedding. "Mehfils" are an integral part of every Rajasthani wedding. 'Ladies' mehfils as well as 'gents' mehfils are organised. The traditional dance—'ghoomar' is performed in the ladies mehfil, while men have their own parties. The "Janeu" (sacred thread ceremony) is performed a day before the wedding. The custom of Palla Dastoor is typical to the Marwaris. On the day of the wedding or a day prior to it, the groom's family brings the Palla Dastoor to the bride's house. It consists of clothes, jewellery and gifts from the groom, which the bride has to wear during the wedding ceremony. A Marwari "barat," consisting entirely of male members, which proceeds to the wedding grounds.

Marriage Ceremony

As soon as the "Barat" reaches the bride's house the groom is taken to the ladies section where the bride's mother receives the groom with the traditional "aarti" and he is then taken to the "mandap." The bride is brought to the mandap by the maternal uncle dressed in traditional marwari costume, which is sent to her by the groom's parents. The "kanyadan" ceremony is then performed, wherein, the bride is given to the groom for life. "Saat Phreras" are taken round the scared fire, while the pundit chants mantras.

Post-Marriage Ceremony

The barat returns with the newly weds, the girl is bid farewell by her family and is accepted into her new family. When the bride enters her new home a small ceremony called Grihapravesh takes place. Puja and other ceremonies also take place on this day.

MARWARI AGARWAL WEDDING

The Marwari Agarwals though orthodox and tradition bound are still full of life, drive and initiative. For them, marriage is an occasion for great extravagance, pomp and splendour. Vast amounts are spent on decorations, food, jewellery, clothes and gifts. The ceremonies are bright and joyous and the lavish wedding celebrations can carry on for several days.

Mudha-tikka

On an auspicious day, decided by an astrologer, the groom's family call on the bride, taking with them, a platter filled with rice, jaggery, dry fruits, sweetmeats, a diamond ring and sometimes a garland for the 'tikka'. They also carry gifts for the bride, which may include clothes and other items.

Godh Barai

On an elaborately decorated tray, the groom's sisters carry gifts, jewellery, toys, clothes and sweets and place these on the bride's 'jholi' (lap). The toys are presented to her with a wish that she may have many children!

Sangeet

The bride sits on a silver 'chowki' or low stool, in all her finery, wearing the jewellery gifted to her after the 'mudha-tikka' ceremony and is surrounded by all the ladies from both families. They all sing traditional wedding songs and the occasion is filled with gaiety and laughter.

Naandi

Approximately ten days before the wedding ceremony, the family 'pujaris' (Brahmin priests), perform the Ganesha puja in the bride's and the groom's homes. The significance of this puja is to ward off any evil and negate the effects of any deaths in the family, so that the marriage may take place without any obstacles.

Bhaat

In most Marwari Agrawal families, the 'mama' or bride's maternal uncle plays a crucial role in the marriage. The custom is, for the 'mama' to bestow lavish gifts on his niece at the time of her wedding and she would not then make any further claims on her father's wealth. For the 'bhaat', the 'mama' is called to the bride's home, where he is given the honour of being formally invited to the wedding. He and his sister partake of a meal consisting of rice and lentils after which, his sister feeds him some sugar. He gives his sister a traditional 'tie-dye chunri', which she keeps with her for the rest of her life. The 'mama' also leaves behind gifts for the bride and the groom.

Tel Baan

The ladies of the families 'prepare' the bride and groom (in each respective home) for the forthcoming wedding. They apply a paste made from vegetable oils, fresh milk curds, henna and turmeric on the faces, arms and feet of the bride and the groom. This is followed by a regular bath.

Mehendi

This ceremony is usually held one day before the wedding ceremony and takes place in the afternoon or early evening. Amidst friends, music, singing and dancing, the bride allows professional 'mehendi' artists to paint intricate designs on her arms and feet with henna paste.

Korath

When the bride is ready and the auspicious time for the wedding ritual is nigh, male members from the bride's family go to the groom's home, carrying an invitation card and other gifts and officially invite him to come to the wedding venue.

Baraat

The groom, in all his splendour and armed with a sword (a Rajput tradition), mounts an elaborately decorated mare and proceeds to the marriage venue. All his relatives and a live band playing popular music accompany him. Throughout the groom's procession known as the 'baraat', the people accompanying him dance to the beat of the music. At the entrance of the marriage venue, hangs a small shrine with seven birds carved on the top and a small idol of Lord Ganesha inside it. The groom hits this with a stick and then enters the venue.

Baraat Swagat

The bride's father receives the groom on his arrival at the marriage venue. A welcome prayer is conducted and the groom gives his word that he will perform the sacred rites of marriage according to his prescribed religious duty. The bride's mother honours him by performing the traditional 'aarti'.

Varamala

The bride, in all her finery is escorted to the wedding mandap by her family and amidst Vedic chants; she garlands the groom, accepting him as her husband. The groom reciprocates.

Pheras

After the varamala, the pujari (Brahmin priest) lights the 'homa' or sacred fire. Offerings are made into the sacred fire as a form of thanksgiving and purification. The bride's 'dupatta' or veil is tied to the grooms waist band, and the couples goes around the fire seven times, repeating their marriage vows.

Kanyadaan

A silver or gold coin is placed in the bride's palms, which are held together by her father, who then places them in the hands of the groom. Amidst prayers, the pujari pours water over their joined hands and blesses them. The bride then moves to the left of the groom and he puts 'kumkum' or vermilion in the center parting of her hair.

Seer-guthi

The groom's sister or 'nanand' braids the bride's hair with sacred thread or 'mouli, which was blessed earlier at the Naandi Ganesh Puja. She then fills the bride's parting with vermilion; in other words, the 'maang bharan'. A traditional 'nath' or nose-ring is gifted to the bride by her mother-in-law.

Chuda

The groom's mother adorns the bride with colourful glass or lac bangles.

Mooh-dekai

Literally translated, 'mooh-dekai' means to 'show your face', but it is really a ritual by which the bride makes her acquaintance with all the members or her husband's family. She sits alone and each member of the family comes in to meet her and shower her with gifts.

The Jua

The first of the two fun filled ceremonies, which follow the wedding rituals. Here, a ring is put into a silver dish filled with milk and the bride and groom dip their hands into the bowl to search for the ring. Whoever finds the ring first is said to be the dominant partner in the marriage!

Muti-Bund

The groom closes his hand in a tight fist and the bride tries very hard to open it! Then the bride does the same and it is the groom's turn to unlock her fist.

Vidaai

In all Hindu weddings, this is considered to be the most emotional ritual, when the bride leaves her parents' home and makes her way to her husband's. Family and friends, who also shower her with blessings and gifts, give her a tearful farewell. The male members of the bride's family bid farewell to the groom by applying the traditional 'tilak' (vermilion) on his forehead and shower him with gifts. The couple leaves in a decorated car.

Vadhu Pravesh

When the bride arrives at her new home, her mother-in-law, who welcomes her with the traditional 'aarti', helps her out of the car. At the entrance, she puts her right foot onto a tray of vermilion powder, symbolizing the arrival of good fortune. With both her feet now covered in the red powder, she kicks over a vessel filled with rice and coins to denote the arrival of fertility and wealth in her marital home.

MARWARI JAIN (OSWAL) WEDDING

The Oswals, who are mainly Jains, hail from the town of Osian, near Jodhpur in Rajasthan. The Oswal Jains celebrate their festivals with great regularity, gaiety, colour and song. The Marwari bridegroom carries a sword and is regally clad in a turban, jewellery and a coconut is tied to his side. He is mounted on a lavishly decorated mare and led in a procession to the bride's house. It is customary for him to touch a decoration fixed on the door with a 'neem' twing or perhaps his sword before entering.

Khol Barana

Once an alliance has been arranged the groom's family comes to the bride's home carrying coconuts and gifts on a silver platter. Neither the bride nor the groom is present at this ceremony.

Tikka

The bride's family goes to the groom's home carrying lavish gifts; usually, cash, jewellery, suit lengths, electronic items, watches, etc.

Bathse

The mothers of the groom and the bride, each in their respective towns or cities, visit all their close relatives and extend personal invitations to each one of them. Along with the invitation, they also gift them sweets.

Mayara

Just before the wedding, the bride's parents, brothers, uncles and other family members go to the groom's house, carrying gifts for all his family members. The groom's family reciprocates in like manner.

Bana Betai

This ritual is performed to 'prepare' the bride and the groom for the forthcoming wedding. The bride and groom (in their respective homes), wear old clothes and 'channe ka atta' (chick pea flour), is applied on their faces, arms and feet. This paste is traditionally used to beautify the skin. This is purely a ladies function.

Nikasi

This is a very grand and colourful ceremony. The groom is made to sit on a richly decorated mare and is accompanied by a band playing music. All the young members of his family join the procession, singing and dancing all the way to the wedding venue!

Padla

The groom's sisters, gorgeously attired, present the bride with a richly woven and embroidered lehenga (full length skirt), or a rich sari along with jewellery. The bride will wear this on her wedding day. The traditional Marwari jewellery is 'jadhau' (uncut diamonds set in gold).

Varamala

On reaching the wedding venue, the groom is received by the bride's father and led to the 'mandap' (platform erected for the wedding rites). The bride is literally 'carried' to the mandap, by her maternal uncle where she showers flowers on the groom. The other relatives present there, circle the groom three times while the bride is showering him with flowers. The bride's uncle then puts her down in front of the groom and the couple exchange garlands. The jewellery worn by the bride at this ceremony consists of a 'nath' (nose-ring), a 'mangtika' (piece of jewellery worn in the center parting) and silver anklets. It is imperative for brides to adorn themselves with these pieces of jewellery even in the simplest of Marwari Jain weddings.

Phera

This is the main wedding ceremony performed by a 'Pujari' (Brahmin priest). The bride and the groom sit at the mandap, which is beautifully decorated with flowers. The bride's parents perform the 'kanyadaan' (giving away the bride). This is a very emotional moment for the bride and her parents. The bride's sari 'pallu' or 'odhni' is tied to the groom's waistband and the couple's hands are joined and tied with a piece of cloth. The 'pujari' ignites the 'homa' or sacred fire, and amidst Vedic chanting, the couple goes around the fire seven times. Each circle around the fire is known as a 'phera'. The 'pujari' chants aloud the wedding vows, which the couple repeats after him.

Bidai

This is the most emotional moment in a bride's life, when she is blessed with the showering of flowers by all her family and close friends and prepares to leave her parents home to join her husband. A decorated car is kept ready to carry her to her new home.

BENGALI MARRIAGE RITUALS

The Bengali marriage is totally focused on the age-old Vedic customs, complete with chants and the 'yagna' or the holy fire. It is also accompanied with some social customs.

Pre-Wedding

The Ashirbaad: The Engagement

The engagement ceremony is not a religious function and priests are not required. It is a gathering of both families with an emphasis on the exchange of gifts, discussions, negotiations and the fixing the date for the marriage. The elders bless the couple by showering them with 'dhaan' (husked rice) and 'dooba' (three bladed grass).

Ai Buddo Bhaat

The bride's last meal as a maiden in her parental home. The Al Buddo Bhaat celebrates the last meal of the bride as a maiden in her parental home. The bride's mother prepares a feast of Bengali delicacies for her daughter, which is shared by the extended family.

Dodhi Mangal

This ceremony is performed at the crack of dawn on the day of the wedding in the house of the bride and of the groom. About ten married women accompany the bride/groom to a nearby pond. They invite the Goddess Ganga to the wedding and bring back a pitcher of water from the pond to individually bathe the bride and the groom.

Then they offer food to the bride/groom. The meal consists of mach bhaja (fried fish) followed by rice cooked in water. Curd and chiruya complete the meal.

Tattva

Tattvas or gifts are exchanged between the families of the bride and the groom during the pre-wedding and post-wedding ceremonies. The Gae Halud Tattva is sent before the haldi or turmeric ceremony. It is for the bride from the groom's house. The gifts include clothes and cosmetics. Also among the gifts are fish, assorted sweets, curd, paan, dhaan and durba (holy grass). A relative of the groom arrives at the bride's house bearing the gifts. Adhibas Tattva are the gifts coming from the bride's house. It includes a saree for the groom's mother, and fish, sweets, curd, paan, dhaan, and durba.

Snan

A few married women apply turmeric and oil on the hair and body of the bride/groom. After bathing, the bride and groom must wear a new set of clothes presented to them by their in-laws. The old clothes are later given away to a napit (barber).

Gai Halood/Haldi Uptan

The 'Gai Halood' takes place on the dawn of the wedding day. The groom is anointed with a paste of turmeric and scented oils. It is an intimate function filled with fun and laughter, where his relatives, especially the girls, mercilessly tease the groom!

The same paste is then sent across to the bride's home for her 'Gai Halood' ceremony, which is much more elaborate. Before sunrise, on the wedding day, the bride is fed Dahi Mangal' (natural yogurt), after which she fasts until the marriage ceremony is over.

The blowing of the conch, signals the arrival of the 'haldi paste' and gifts from the groom's home. The pride of place amongst all the gifts is a large 'rohu' (fish)!

Shaka Paula

The bride is adorned with coral and shell bangles by 'sumangalis'. Amidst the chanting of Sanskrit 'shlokas' (verses) by the priest, seven married women or 'sumangalis' adorn the bride with coral and shell bangles. The groom sends an iron and silver entwined bangle for the bride, symbolizing a tough and enduring relationship.

Dressing up the Bride

The bride adorns herself in all her bridal finery. Her hair is tied into a bun and covered with a veil. The mukut is placed on her head and secured in place by pinning it to the veil. After her bridal makeover, a design of the mukut is traced on her face using the chandan paste. The bride must sit with the gaach kouto and kaajal laata for the ceremonies that follow.

Bar Jatra

According to Bengali customs the groom travels to the bride's home in order to marry her. Many 'Stri-Achars' are performed when the groom sets for the bride's place. A little boy, preferably a relative, would be the 'nit bar' (little groom) and accompany the groom. This is basically done to outwit the evil eyes, which is said to harm the groom when he travels alone. In the yester years the groom used to travel in a palanquin alone, with the rest of the family following, to the bride's place. The bride and the groom are made to dress up like Lakhshmi-Narayan.

Wedding

Boijotri: The Wedding Procession

The bride's maternal uncle comes to fetch the bridegroom, his family and friends and escorts them to the wedding venue. The groom is resplendent in a 'sherwani' (long silk coat) or suit or even the traditional 'dhoti kurta'.

With the blowing of the conch, the 'boijotri[1] or 'baraat' (wedding procession) sets off for the wedding venue.

Potto Bastra: Welcoming the Groom

On his arrival, elders from the bride's family receive the groom with the 'boron' (straw colander) containing a lamp, honey, yogurt and betel leaves. He is then presented with a shawl and a 'dhoti', which he is supposed to wear for the wedding ceremony.

The groom and his relatives arrive at the bride's house to the ringing of bells, blowing of shankh (conch shells) and ululation. The baran dala is held by an elder female relative of the bride and the plate is first touched to the groom's forehead, then to ground, and back again to his forehead in a gesture of part blessing, part-reverence.

The mothers of the bride and of the groom do not attend the wedding.

The 'Chadnatala', bounded by banana plants, is decorated with 'alpana' or designs. The groom is brought here and is made to wear a new dhoti by the relative of the bride who gives the bride away to the groom. He is made to stand on a 'piri' (a very low wooden stool). The bride is then brought, sitting in another 'pin', carried by her relatives, and is circled clockwise around the standing groom for seven times, seven being an auspicious number for the Hindus. Hence 'shat paake bandha'.

Shubh Dhristi/Exchange of Garlands

The bride walks up to the groom, eyes lowered and goes around him seven times, welcoming him and then stands in front of him. Her face is covered with betel leaves, which are moved apart to enable the couple to make eye contact for the 'shubh dhristi' (auspicious 'viewing' of each other).

The couple now exchanges garlands and the groom proceeds to the 'mandap' (marriage platform) followed by the bride. Just after the 'shuvo drishti' the bride and the groom exchange the garlands they had been wearing. This is called 'malabodol'. The origin of 'malabodal' comes from the 'swayamvar sabha', which was a common practice among the princesses who chose to garland the princes they wanted as their husbands.

'Chadnatala' the barber plays an important role. He recites poems to drive away evil spirits from the place of the marriage. This is known as 'gourabachan'.

All through the ceremony a white cloth is held over the couples. The bride and the groom are made to sit together in front of the priest. The groom is given 'bistor'. It is a collection of fourteen 'kush' (types of grass). A puja is performed with 'padyo', 'argho', 'modhuparko' and 'aachomonio'. On the groom's right palm the bride's right palm is placed. The priest then places a cloth, five fruits and 'kush' and ties around with a garland of flowers.

Kanyadaan

Amongst Vedic chantings the bride's parents symbolically hand over their most precious gift, their daughter, to the bridegroom.

Hasta Milap

The hands of the couple are tied together in a symbolic knot and the bride is officially handed over to her husband-to-be.

Saptapadi

The couple takes the seven steps of matrimony around the sacred fire. With each step the bride leaves her family and with the seventh step, she finally becomes a member of her husband's family. The bride and groom take a vow with each step.

Sindoordaan

Performed at the end of the marriage rituals, this ceremony is the preserve of a husband. He applies the 'sindoor' or vermilion powder on the parting in the hair of his bride to establish her marital status.

Bashar Ghar

In accordance with Bengali tradition, after the wedding feast, the groom's family, friends and guests leave but the groom stays back in the bride's home. The following day is spent at his in-laws amidst a lot of teasing and entertaining by the younger generation in the 'bashar ghar' or ceremonial room.

Vidaai

In one of the most poignant moments of her life, the 'vidaai', the bride takes leave of her parental home. For her it symbolizes the changing of her 'gotra' (ancestral lineage) and allegiances in one stroke! The groom's father comes to fetch his son and daughter-in-law, carrying gifts for them.

Bride's Reception: Welcoming the bride in her Marital Home

Her mother-in-law gives the bride a warm welcome. On entering the home, she gives her daughter-in-law a fish (in the olden days is used to be a live fish!) to hold, while she waits for the milk to boil over (symbolizing a house overflowing with food and affection).

The bride then steps onto a platter containing 'alta' (vermilion water) and walks into her new home leaving her foot imprints on the floor of the house. She is then taken straight into the kitchen and blessed by all the elders.

Bahu Bhaat

The following day is a very important one for the bride as it is on this day that she is formally accepted by all her husband's relatives through the formality of the 'Bahu Bhaat'.

The bride personally serves elaborate rice dishes to all the elderly members of the family for lunch. It is at this time that the groom avows to take on the 'bhaat' and 'kapood bhar nilan' (literally translated it means—taking on the responsibility of providing food, shelter and clothing for his wife).

Sampradan

The purohit conducts the wedding ceremony. The bride and groom exchange garlands while the purohit chants mantras. Her paternal or maternal uncle gives the bride away. This particular part of the ceremony is called sampradan.

Post-Wedding

Basar Ghar

The bride and groom are welcomed inside the bride's home. The couple is served dinner. Jokes and music by friends and relatives keep the couple awake all through the night

Bashi Biye

The next morning, the groom adorns the forehead of his bride with vermilion. The newly-weds worship the Sun God in the presence of the purohit.

'Konokanjoli'

Another ritual known as 'Konokanjoli' is performed, where the bride throws a handful of rice grains behind her indicating the clearance of her debts to her parents. This ritual is of course obsolete.

Bou Baran

This ritual is performed to welcome the bride and groom to the latter's home. The groom returns home with the bride, the day after the marriage. The mother in law welcomes the bride while she sets her feet in her new home in a traditional Bengali style. The alpana or the design which is applied to decorate the grooms's place is known as 'Bouchatra'. The bride groom sets her feet on the alpona holding a fish in one hand and a pot of water on the other. These outdated rituals were tests to gauge the bride's capability to perform household chores and hold the husband's attention with an underline tone of sexuality. The women of the house pour water on the ground beneath their vehicle when they alight.

The groom's elder brother's wife holds a plate containing lac dye and milk under the bride's feet. Having imprinted the soles of her feet thus, she leads her by the arm into the house. The elders of the house bless the newly weds.

Kal Ratri

The night after the marriage is called Kal ratri. This night the bride is not supposed to meet the groom. This custom probably has been derived from the myth of Lakhinder and Behula in the Manasamangal Kavya, in which Lakhinder died of snakebite on this day due to the curse of Devi Manasa.

Bhat Kapar

The day next, the groom offers new garments and food in new utensils to the bride. The groom promises to take care of his better half till death through this ceremony.

Bou Bhat

It is during this ceremony that the bride has her first meal in the home of her in-laws. Until now, her meals usually arrive from a neighbor's house. A day after the marriage day is the "Bou Bhat". This is the day when the new bride serves the guests a delicacy called 'Ghee bhat' (a mixture of rice with ghee). This ceremony is followed by a reception in the evening, hosted by the groom's father.

Reception

The groom's family generally hosts the wedding reception, which is a formal function to introduce the newly weds to family and friends.

Traditionally it was a simple domestic affair, but in modern times it has become customary to host the reception in a hotel or banquet hall and invite as many guests as the family can afford.

Phool Sajjaya

The bride is bedecked with jewellery made from flowers. On the third night after the wedding ceremony, the bride is bedecked with floral jewellery, a custom very special to the Bengali community.

The last of the wedding ceremonies, this occasion sees the bride in a new sari and the groom in a new dhoti and kurta. Their nuptial bedroom is decorated with flowers. The flowers, clothes and sweets for the occasion usually arrive as gifts from the bride's house.

The bridal bed is also decorated with flowers and the marriage can now be consummated.

Dwiragaman

Eight days after the marriage, the bride returns to his father's home, accompanied by her husband. This is also known as "Ashtomongola" or Dwiragaman . On this day the 'Gat chara' is unknotted. The newly wed couple spends the night at the home of the bride. The Ashtomongola marks the end of the Bengali marriage ceremony.

BIHARI KAYAST WEDDING

The Kayast (Kayastha) community can be found in several states of North India. The nomenclatures and adaptations of various ceremonies may differ depending upon the state in which they are domiciled for many generations.What is common however is the important role of the 'pujari' at most ceremonies, giving and receiving of lavish gifts, the 'tilak' ceremony, the 'saath pheras' and the important role played by the maternal uncles in the marriage rituals.

Cheka

An auspicious day is selected for the 'cheka' and 5, 7, 9 or 11 members from the groom's family accompanied by the groom go to bride's home with some jewellery, a sari, sweetmeats, dry fruits and cash gifts. These gifts are known as the 'cheka'. The bride and groom exchange rings and after the ceremony the bride's family reciprocate the gesture by taking gifts for the groom.

Shagun

On the day of the 'shagun' the 'pandit' or 'pujari' (Brahmin priest) from the bride's family takes the following items and goes to the groom's home accompanied by the bride's brother, the 'hajaam' (barber) and four other male members. Rice from the 'pujaris' house, a yellow cloth, rice dipped in turmeric, cash, 'doob' (a special type of grass, considered very auspicious as it is the symbol of Lord Ganesha), 'supari' (betel nut), 'paan' (betel leaves) and coins. All these items are also dipped in turmeric and put inside a yellow cloth, which in turn is put inside a metal container known as 'kasha'. This pot is known as the 'shagun ka katora'. The 'pujari' hands over the 'shagun ka katora' to the 'pujari' from the groom's family and receives 'shagun ka samaan' (consisting of the same ingredients) from him in return.

Tilak

The bride's brother has to perform the 'tilak' ceremony for his future brother-in-law. He carries with him a 'gaggara' (stainless steel or copper utensil used mainly for storing water in Indian homes) in which the auspicious coconut and mango leaves are placed. He also carries three 'parats' (stainless steel or brass platters). The first 'parat' contains 'dhan' (husk covered rice) coloured red or yellow, one and a half or five kilograms of 'supari' (betel nuts) dipped in turmeric, and 'haldi' sticks (turmeric) which have to be the same quantity as the 'supari'. The second 'parat' contains yellow rice and Rs. 51 also coloured yellow.

The third 'parat' contains dry fruits and sweetmeats. At this time the bride's brother takes the 'kasha', which was used for the 'shagun' ceremony and 'chandi ke bartan' (silver ware) consisting of plates, spoons and bowls as gifts for his brother-in-law. Every gift and 'puja' item being carried for the 'tilak' ceremony has to be touched by the bride before it leaves the house. Before the 'tilak' ceremony can commence (it usually takes place on the night of the arrival of the bride's family), all the gifts sent by the bride's family are displayed in the courtyard of the house and the 'pujari' performs the action of purifying the groom by sprinkling holy water or 'ganga jal' on him amidst the chanting of Vedic mantras. The ceremony can now begin. The bride's brother holds a 'katora' (silver or copper bowl) containing 'dahi' (yogurt) and 'sindoor' (vermilion). He applies a vertical 'tikka' or 'tilak' (mark) on the groom's forehead with the 'dahi' and garlands him with the 'zari' (brocade) garland brought by him earlier. He then holds a 'kalash' (silver or copper container), which contains the auspicious coconut, mango leaves, rice and 'supari'. The 'pujari' makes the groom touch this 'kalash' and put it down. In like manner each and every gift brought by the bride's brother is touched by the groom and put aside one by one. After all the gifts have been 'offered' to the groom and put aside, the entire gathering blesses him by showering 'akshat' or coloured rice. All the five males from the bride's family (in most cases this group consists of the bride's brother, the 'hajaam', two servants and the 'pujari') receive gifts in the form of new sets of clothes and money from the groom's family just before they leave. These gifts are known as 'samang' and the farewell as 'bidaai'.

Lagan Mahurat

The day chosen by the 'pujari' to commence all marriage rituals is known as the 'lagan mahurat'. On this day the bride wears an old sari and the married ladies of the household apply 'uptan' (a paste made from mustard seeds, milk, saffron and turmeric paste) on her hands and body. This is typically to beautify the bride before her big day! The 'pujari' from the bride's family now goes to the groom's house to collect half the quantity of husked rice and half the quantity of the 'haldi' paste, which has been kept aside by the groom's people to gift to the bride's family for the 'lagan mahurat'. The remaining 'dhan' (husked rice) is later roasted with sand over the fire and made into what is known as the 'lava'. This 'lava' is later used for the wedding ceremony. After the 'uptan' paste is washed off from the bride's body, 'haldi' (turmeric) paste is applied and kept on for a few hours before it too, is washed off. On the day of the 'lagan mahurat' ladies get together to make the 'lagan ki badi' (small balls made out of 'urad dal' (lentils). Special songs are sung during this occasion.

Haldi Ka Din

In most Bihari weddings the 'haldi' ceremony (beautifying the bride with turmeric paste and fragrant oils) lasts for four days. The first of these four days is known as 'haldi ka din'. The 'pujari' conducts the 'Satyanarayana Puja' simultaneously as the married men and women apply the 'haldi-uptan' paste on the bride. Kohl is applied in the bride's eyes. Throughout the ritual the bride has rice in her cupped hands and a 'katora' filled with 'dahi' on top of the rice. The groom begins the same ceremony in his house and the 'Satyanarayana Puja' is performed in his house as well.

Madva Bandhana

One day before the wedding ceremony, the married male members from the bride's family construct the wedding 'mandap'. The barber brings nine bamboo rods and cuts them for the roof and the frame. In this, he is assisted by at least 5, 7, 9 or 11 males. Each bamboo rod is tied to the other with 'kaccha dhaaga' (raw cotton thread) by the married males. The barber, later ties the same rods with stronger thread. Throughout the tying of the bamboo rods the 'pujari' chants mantras. These days, it is not uncommon to hire professional help to construct the 'mandap'. The 'madva bandhana' or making of the 'mandap' has to happen on the same day as 'haldi ka din'. A 'diya' or lamp burns continuously in the 'mandap' till the wedding. The 'madva bandhana' ceremony takes place separately in the groom's house as well, the only difference being that the 'mandap' constructed there is on a much smaller scale because the actual wedding rites are not performed in the groom's house.

Baraat Ka Din

Arrival of the groom's procession is divided into the following segments:

Ghidhari

Ancestor worship and invoking their blessings for the marriage.

This is a day of fasting for the bride, her parents, uncles and aunts. The 'pujari' offers prayers to all the deities and then to the ancestors seeking their blessings for the union. The bride is required to sit between her parents during the 'puja'. 'Pind-daan' or offering of ground rice is made to the ancestors. The bride's mother and other 'sumangalis' (married ladies) grind the rice before the 'puja'. On completion of the 'ghidhari puja', the bride's parents ask their elders for their blessings by touching their feet.

Kumarpet Ka Bhaath

On the day the groom's procession is due or 'baraat ka din' the second ceremony, which is performed, is the 'kumarpet ka bhaath'. The bride's sister and/or her father's sister (bua) prepare a meal fed only to the bride and either 5, 7, 9 or 11 unmarried girlfriends.

Haldi Ceremony

On the morning of the wedding day, the bride once again prepares herself for the 'haldi-uptan' paste application in exactly the same manner as was done earlier on 'haldi ka din'. Only this time, married ladies do the honours. In the evening, after her bath the bride is dressed and decorated for her wedding by all the married women in her household. At the groom's home the same ritual of applying the 'haldi' paste on him is performed, after which he is dressed for the 'jaimaal' ceremony. The ceremony involving the dressing up of the groom is called 'joda pehanana', which is the same as 'sehrabandhi' in other North Indian communities. The groom's sister's husband or 'behnoi' has to perform the honours of dressing the groom.

Darwaza Lagna

The procession from the groom's house proceeds to the bride's home with a great amount of gaiety and singing and dancing along the way. When the 'baraat' is at the entrance of the wedding venue, all the important members from the bride's family wait with garlands of flowers in their hands to welcome the 'baraatis'. Each person from the groom's family is welcomed with a garland by his counterpart in the bride's family (i.e. the bride's father garlands the groom's father, the bride's 'mama' (maternal uncle) garlands the groom's 'mama' and so on and so forth). The ladies also garland their counterparts from the groom's family. This ritual is called 'darwaza lagna'. While his 'baraat' is being welcomed the groom remains seated in the decorated car and awaits the arrival of the 'pujari' from the bride's family, to come and welcome him by applying the 'tilak' on his forehead and to help him out of the car. The bride's father performs a small 'puja' for the groom at this time to bless and welcome him. The 'puja' is performed with a 'kalash' (pot) filled with water and decorated with a coconut and mango leaves. The bride's father then leads the groom to a decorated chair reserved especially for him.

Jaimaal

The bride is escorted to the wedding site to welcome and garland her groom. Two young unmarried girls holding the 'aarti ki thaali', a platter with 'kumkum' (vermilion) and 'diyas' (small clay lamps) and two other girls carrying garlands for the couple precede the bride. The bride performs an 'aarti' for the groom and then the couple exchanges garlands. The 'jaimaal' accomplished, the bride is escorted back to her chambers and all the 'baraatis' leave for the 'janvaasa' (literally translated it means the place where people rest before the wedding ceremony).

Galsedi or Parichavan

After having his dinner at the 'janvaasa' the groom returns to the 'mandap' for the wedding rites, but before allowing him to proceed, the bride's mother and all the other married ladies stop him at the door for the 'galsedi' ceremony. The bride's mother holds a 'thaali' (platter) containing a lighted 'diya' (lamp), 'paan' (betel leaves) and small lumps made from cow dung. Each of the women comes forward one at a time, heats the betel leaves on the 'diya', foments the groom's face, forehead and eyes a minimum of five times each, always using the left hand. The remaining women simultaneously throw the cow dung lumps behind the groom. In case there is a shortage of time and the 'shubh mahurat' (auspicious time) of the wedding rites is likely to get delayed, the 'galsedi' is performed by only five or seven ladies. The bride's brother or brother-in-law now arrives to escort the groom or the 'nause' as he is now referred to, to the wedding 'mandap'.

Kangna Bandhana

For this ceremony the bride changes into a yellow silk sari with 'zari' or gold borders and removes every piece of jewellery worn by her and is led to the wedding 'mandap' by her relatives. She is made to sit between her parents on a low stool or 'peedha'. The groom is already seated opposite them, alone. Both the 'pujaris' (one from each family) are also seated. Though the actual wedding rites will be performed by the 'pujari' from the bride's family, both may chant the mantras. The first ritual on her arrival is the tying of the bracelets made out of mango leaves, 'kaccha dhaaga' (raw cotton thread), 'akshat' (coloured rice), 'haldi' and money, on her and the groom's right hands. The 'pujari' ties these bracelets to the chanting of mantras. This is called 'kangna bandhana'. These symbolic bracelets have to be worn by the couple for the next four days. The 'hajaam' (barber) who is also sitting in the 'mandap' has to now cut the finger and toenails of the bridal couple while they are seated in the 'mandap'.

Kanyadaan

'Kushk' is a type of grass, which, is used to make rings for the bride, her parents and the groom at this time. Before the 'kanyadaan', the 'pujari' slips these rings onto their fingers. For the 'kanyadaan' ceremony the 'pujari' asks the bride's father to stretch out his right hand, on top of which the bride's mother places her right hand, next the groom places his right hand on top of his mother-in-law's and lastly the bride, holding a conch, places her right hand on top of the groom's. The 'pujaris' chant mantras throughout and in this manner the bride is 'given away' by her parents to the groom eliciting a promise from him to look after and cherish their daughter. The 'pujari' sprinkles holy water on all of them. After the 'kanyadaan' ceremony the bride is seated to the right of the groom.

Kanya Nirakshan

After the 'kanyadaan' ceremony the groom retires to the 'janvaasa' while the bride goes in to change for the next ritual, the 'kanya nirakshan'. Literally translated it means viewing the bride. The groom's father accompanied by the groom's elder married brother or 'bhaisur' now arrives to adorn the bride with the jewellery sent by her mother-in-law. This ritual is called 'bhaisur nirakshan'. This is the only time during the entire wedding that the 'bhaisur' is allowed to touch the bride or even enter the 'mandap'. His head must be covered with a 'rumaal' (handkerchief) or a 'topi' (cap) at this time. He first blesses the bride by placing his hand on her head and then presents her with two saris (one is the wedding sari and the other is the 'gouna sari'), two 'chunris' (veils) and a set of 'lehenga-choli' (long ethnic skirt with a blouse). He then adorns the bride with all the jewellery sent for her by her in-laws.

Shaadi Ki Rasm

When the bride is escorted back to the 'mandap' after she has changed into the wedding sari sent by her in-laws, the 'pujari' seats her beside the groom and begins chanting mantras to purify the couple. At this time, only the couple is seated in the 'mandap' along with the priest; the parents and other relatives are standing around watching this ceremony. The priest first performs all essential 'pujas'—the 'kuldevta puja', a 'puja' for all the other Hindu deities and then a special 'puja' called the 'damad ki puja'. 'Damad' means son-in-law. He then asks the couple to repeat a series of vows after him keeping the sun, moon, stars, earth and sky as witnesses to this union.

Lava Chidakna/Pheras/Parikrama

Amongst Bihari Kayasts it is considered inauspicious to have a 'havan' or fire burning inside the 'mandap', so a 'bedi' or a small provisional open air base is created with an earthen pot having a fire lit inside, and surrounded with wooden logs (preferably sandalwood), outside the 'mandap' for the next important ceremony—the 'pheras'. Half the quantity of 'lava' or roasted husked rice is sent from the groom's mother (this is the same 'lava' which was kept aside for this purpose on the day of the 'lagan mahurat'), for the 'lava chidakna' ceremony; the other half of the 'lava' is from the bride's family. Both are mixed together by the bride's mother. The entire lot of 'lava' is carried by the bride's younger brother in a cloth tied on his shoulder like a hammock. He then puts fistfuls of it into a cane 'supra' or 'soop' (a 3-sided conical cane basket), which is held by the bride with both her hands. The groom stands behind her and lends support by holding her elbows and together they go around the fire seven times, to the chanting of mantras. As they walk around the fire the bride keeps tilting the 'soop' and showering the 'lava' into the fire as an 'ahuti' (sacrifice). Her brother keeps re-filling the 'soop' with fresh 'lava'.

Sindoordaan

After the 'pheras' are over her relatives who hold a long cloth to cover her face completely and shield her from the eyes of unmarried girls and widows surround the bride. It is considered an ill omen if unmarried girls and widows look at her at the time of 'sindoordaan'. Her mother or her sister-in-law, who is referred to as 'bidakari', covers her eyes. The groom holds the 'sindhora' (a special container made out of 'lac' and painted prettily in red) in his hand. The 'sindhora' contains the 'sindoor' or vermilion powder, 'sanghauli' (coins with holes in the center made out of shell), sacred thread or 'mouli' and the 'taagpaag dholna' (the 'taali' or 'mangalsutra'—sacred thread with gold and black beads—the sign of a married lady). The groom takes a pinch of 'sindoor' in his fingers and starting with the tip of the bride's nose begins to apply it in the bride's center parting. This is called 'maang bharana'—'maang' literally means the center parting. This is done at least five times and all throughout the bride's eyes remain closed. After the groom has finished applying the 'sindoor' all the married ladies proceed to do the same, i.e. apply 'sindoor' in the newly wed bride's hair and offer her blessings for a happy married life.

Kohvar

Now that the couple is well and truly married, all the post-wedding celebrations begin. The bride is escorted to her room where she sits on the beautifully decorated bridal bed ('kohvar') and awaits her husband's arrival. After a lot of teasing and fun and frolic the groom manages to extricate himself from the clutches of the bride's sisters and cousins and is led to the shrine in the 'kohvar' room to perform a small prayer along with his wife. The 'puja' over, the couple now feed each other 'kheer' (sweet dish made from rice, milk and dry fruits). This act of feeding each other is called 'mooh jhoota'.

Kangna Kholna

The fourth day after the wedding rites have been performed is considered an auspicious day to untie the symbolic bracelets. The bath that the couple has on this day is called 'chauthi ka nahn' and the day itself is referred to as 'chauthi ka din' (fourth day). Amidst chanting of mantras the 'pujari' unties the bracelets and blesses the couple. The bride's sister-in-law opens the symbolic knot or 'gaanth', which was tied earlier in the 'mandap'.

Kaccha Khana

If the groom and his 'baraatis' have stayed back after the

wedding, the day after the 'sindoordaan' they will be served a special meal consisting of 'dal' (lentils), rice, five different types of vegetable dishes, 'dahi-bhade' (fried lentil balls dipped in curds and garnished with spices), 'kadi' (gravy dish), 'papad' (roasted savoury wafer made from lentils or potatoes and spices).

Bidaai Ki Rasm

If the groom has stayed back in the bride's maternal home, he will leave with his bride either after two days or after performing the 'kangna kholna' ceremony which takes place on the fourth day after the wedding as explained earlier. The bride sits while her mother fills her lap with gifts. She receives the 'bidaai ki sari' and in her 'khoicha'/'jholi' or lap, her mother puts half a kilo of yellow rice, money, 'sindoor', 'haldi' and 'doob'. The groom is gifted a new set of clothes and 'salaami' (going away presents) which consist of money from all the bride's relatives and some jewellery.

Kaleva

A couple of days after the bride has left, her brother or brother-in-law goes to the groom's home to invite her back to her parents home for a few days. He carries gifts with him for the bride and her in-laws. The bridal couple returns with him carrying gifts for the bride's family and stays in the bride's maternal home or 'maika' for some time.

MADHYA PRADESH RAJPUT WEDDING

The word Rajput means king's son or Prince, Rajputs claim that they are the direct descendants of the Kshatriya clan, who were the original Aryans. Rajput marriage have to be seen to be belived for their extravagance ! Rajputs are a colourful race and marriage in this community are resplendent in colour, pomp and spelndour and more often than not, very traditional.

Tilak

The first agreement made by both the families, that their son/daughter will enter into holy matrimony, is signified by the bride's brother going to the groom's home with gifts and sweets for the groom and his family.

Pili-Chitthi

A 'patra' or letter with the symbol of Lord Ganesha, dabbed with 'haldi' (turmeric) and 'kumkum' (vermilion) powder, is sent by the groom's family to the bride's, confirming the acceptance of the forthcoming alliance between both the families.

Mandap Aarohan

About a week before the wedding, all the sons-in-law and brothers-in-law from the bride's family, help to erect the marriage 'mandap' (canopy held up with wooden posts where the actual wedding rites will be performed) and elaborately decorate it with flowers and silver or gold paper. The pillars of the mandap are painted in alternate red and white bands.

Haldi Ceremony

About a week before the wedding, the haldi ceremony begins and is performed each day till the day of the wedding. The ladies from the bride's family apply a paste of haldi (turmeric) and oil on the bride's face, arms and feet.

Mehendi

This bridal ceremony is held on the morning before the wedding. A paste of henna and 'alta' (a red liquid to mark the auspicious occasion) is applied in traditional designs on the palms and feet of the bride by professional 'mehendiwallis'.

Maira

The bride's maternal uncle plays an important role in most Hindu weddings. Like in most other weddings, here too, he presents his niece with lavish gifts and goes on to host a sumptuous vegetarian lunch in honour of the bride.

Padla

On the afternoon of the wedding day, all the gifts given by the groom's family are displayed in the bride's home.

Baraat

Mounted on an elaborately decorated mare, along with a young male child, the groom leaves for the wedding venue, accompanied by other male members from his family. A band playing popular music often accompanies this procession. On his arrival at the marriage venue, his future mother-in-law who greets him with the 'aarti' offers the groom a traditional welcome.

Saat Pheras

A 'pujari' (Brahmin priest) officiates at this ceremony. A sacred fire is lit and amidst Vedic chantings, the groom's shawl is tied to the bride's 'dupatta' or veil, and the couple goes around the fire seven times. Each circle around the fire is known as a 'phera'. After the 'pheras', the groom adorns the bride's wrist with green glass bangles.

Kunwar Kaleo

On the morning after the wedding ceremony, the groom and other members from his family, are invited to join in a festive meal hosted by the bride's family. This is usually a lavish breakfast, consisting of an array of sweets and dry fruits amongst other delicacies.

Bidaai

As in all Hindu weddings, this is a tearful ritual, when the bride bids farewell to her parents and siblings and other members of her family. She is blessed with the showering of flowers and coins by the groom's family—thus reassuring her family that even though the 'Laxmi' or goddess of wealth is leaving her parents home, prosperity will remain. She leaves for her new home in a decorated car, accompanied by her husband. On entering her new home she must put her right foot forward first.

Mooh Dekai

Literally translated, 'mooh dikhai' means 'show your face', but this is a ritual, which helps to introduce the newly wed to members of her husband's family! The bride is made to sit alone and each member of the groom's family comes in turn to make her acquaintance and shower her with gifts.

MARATHI WEDDING

Marathi Wedding requires flowers, fruits, sweets, coconut, camphor, scented sticks, kumkum. Lord Ganesha's idol is decorated with flowers, fruits, sweets and coconut is given as offering, scented sticks are lighted at the time of puja, and harati is given by the bride and the bridegroom.

Dev Brahman Puja

Three mugs of water is placed in front row and 2 mugs of water is placed at the back row. These mugs filled with water and are known as Pancha Loka Pala. (Pancha Loka Pala means Ganeshji, Durgamata, Akash, Vayu and Ashwani). A thread is tied around 5 mugs. The girl parents, the girl and a co-bride sit in the centre without touching the Mugs and thread. 5 married ladies (suhagan) give them a bath (first oil is applied then haldi is applied before giving bath). The girl's hands and feet are decorated with 'Melwat'. The girl's mother's eye brows are decorated. Cookery: Puran poli, Methkut (prepared of gehu, rye, sont, haldi), pud chatni (prepared by all type of dal like moongdal, urad dal etc., imli, putana fried and prepared), payasam. Muhurat: Around the chakki 5-7 supari packets, beetel leaves on which jagri is put is placed around the chakki wheat is ground in chakki and channa dal is ground in the grinder by the would be bride. 4 bamboo sticks are placed at four corners with the thathi on top. Puja: Lord Ganesha's idol is prepared out of wheat and haldi abhishek is performed. Puran poli, Payasam, Methkut, Pudchatni is offered as 'BHOG' to God. The idol is later on placed on the Mandap in front of the house. This puja is performed at the groom's place too. Sloka: Mano Jyothi Riti Pratistapa Vivah Ang Bhutah Deva Prathisth a Aham Karishath.

Nandi Shradh or Pitra Pujah

This takes place after the Dev Brahaman Puja. In the memory of the elders who have passed away meals are offered to friends, guests and relatives.

Sod Munj

'Sod Munj' means the boy is leaving behind bachelorism and entering marital life. Rice, wheat, etc. is tied in a cloth. The groom wears new clothes, holds an umbrella in his hand, and carries with him the bundle of rice and wheat. Pujari performs 'Hom'. The groom's maternal uncle pleads him to enter into marital life. After this 'Dev Brahman' puja is performed.

Seemanth Puja

This takes place one day before the wedding. The girl's parents give new clothes to their son-in-law's. After that the would be son-in-law's feet are washed by the bride parents in a new bucket. Kumkum is put on the forehead of the groom, his parents and other family members. The girl's parents give him his wedding clothes. Five suhaagan ladies give him 'harti'. A coconut is passed on to all the family members of both the parties which is ultimately received by the girl's parents. This form of greeting is to know each other.

Dev Pratishta

An age old belief is that as the idol of Lord Ganesh and the family Diety are moved from the residence to the wedding hall, the power of the Lord is reduced. Hence, puja is performed to restore the lost power. A garland of flower is put around the deities, agarbathi is lighted, coconut and sweets are offered to God and harti is given. This puja is performed by both the parties separately. The bride's uncle gives the bride a yellow colour sari while the groom's uncle gifts him with new clothes. No wedding ceremony takes place without this custom. Sloka: Mano Jyothi Riti Pratistapa Vivah Ang Bhutah Deva Prathistha Aham Karishath.

Gauri Har ka Puja

4 rows of earthen pots are put at 4 corners each row consists of 4 earthen pots placed one on top of the other with a lid on the top. The bride performs puja by putting haldi and kumkum and seeks Goddess Gauri blessings for a happy married life.

Tying of Mangalsutra

The mangalsutra along with the kolipoth is tied around the girls neck by the groom 4 silver toe rings are put on the girls toes on the 2nd and 4th toe of both the feet. Sloka: Mangalyam thanthuna nena mama jeevana hetuna kante rudraya shubade thwam deeya sharadam shubam.

Laxmi Puja

Goddess Laxmi's face is decorated with nose ring and tilak, etc. In front of Goddess Laxmi rice, wheat and gold ornaments are placed. The purohit performs puja to the Goddess of wealth.

If the bride's name has to be changed then the renaming ceremony takes place here itself.

Saptapadi/Vivah Hom

A bin to light fire, beetel nut, a stone puffed rice, ghee is required. Around the sacred fire, 7 beetel nuts and a stone is placed. While, the girl's brother puts ghee and puffed rice in the fire the young couple goes around the sacred fire. After each round, a beetel nut is kicked out. At the end, the bride puts her feet on the stone and the groom touches her feet which is placed on the stone, which means that in difficult times and times of need he bows his head to her for support.

MAHARASHTRIAN KONKANASTHA BRAHMIN WEDDING

Weddings in Maharashtra spell joy, hope and permanence for everyone involved. For the families of the couple, this day is the fruition of months of planning, buying and collecting items for the wedding. Great care is taken to ensure that the elders are respected and proprieties adhered to. The bride's family hosts the wedding after consulting the groom's relatives about any special preferences.

The Engagement

After the horoscopes of the bride and groom are matched and the decision is made for them to marry, a formal engagement ceremony is held. An auspicious date is determined by the 'pujari' (priest), and the bride's parents host the event. This is called the 'mahurat'. Their home is decorated with flowers and mango leaves and 'rangoli' patterns are made on the floor. 'Rangoli' is coloured powder. The groom arrives with his family and perhaps some close family friends and the bride's parents welcome them. The groom's parents bless the bride and gift her a 'sari', some jewellery and flowers for her hair. The bride leaves to change into the 'sari' and wear the jewellery gifted to her. The bride's parents also bless the groom and give him a suit, a watch and other gifts. They also have gifts for his parents, usually clothes. The bride now returns, adorned in all her finery. The couple exchanges rings after which, five 'sumangalis' (married ladies) perform the 'aarti' for them and all the elders present bless them. The groom's parents distribute 'pedhas' (traditional Maharashtrian sweetmeats) to the guests. Depending upon the time, light refreshments or a vegetarian dinner is served.

Vyahi Bhojan

On any auspicious day, before the wedding, the groom's parents invite the bride's parents and other family members for a meal. If the family lives in another city, then this event takes place one day prior to the wedding and is hosted in a marriage hall.

Grahamak/Nav Grahi Shanti Puja

This 'puja' is performed separately in both homes. A 'homa' or sacred fire is lit and the 'nav grahi shanti puja' (puja of the nine planets) is conducted.

Bangdi Bharan

This ceremony is held two days before the wedding, in the bride's home. The 'bangadiwala' or bangle seller is called home. The bride's mother gives him edible leaves, a coconut and one coin. He first slips the green bangles on the bride's wrist. The bangles have to be uneven in number. The bride's parents may also present her with gold bangles, which are also slipped onto her wrist by the 'bangdiwalla'. The other ladies present at this occasion also adorn their wrists with green glass bangles.

Mehendi

Though this is not a traditional Maharashtrian ceremony, it is popular and incorporated into wedding celebrations by many families. Henna paste is applied on the palms and feet of the bride by professional henna artists or 'mehendiwalis' in intricate patterns and left on for several hours to dry and for the colour to develop into a deep red. The bride's female friends and relatives also have the henna paste applied to the palms of their hands.

Kelvan

The bride is seated at a table which has been decorated with 'rangoli', patterns made from coloured powder and lentils, in the midst of which is a silver 'thaali' (platter) specially laid out for her. Her mother probably makes her favourite dishes on this day.

The families of the bride and the groom are ceremonially invited by various friends and relatives to have a meal at a get-together known as `Kelvan'.

Seemant Pujan and Vaang Nischayam

On the day prior to the wedding, the bride's mother washes the groom's feet in a silver platter or 'thaali'. The 'varadakshina' or groom's offering is given to him. Married ladies from the bride's family perform an 'aarti' for him. His mother's feet are also washed and she is presented with a sari. The fathers of the bride and groom formally agree to the alliance and the elders from both families are introduced to each other and gifts are exchanged. If the bride has an older, married sister, her husband's feet are also washed and both of them receive gifts. The groom's parents gift a sari, jewellery and 'saubhagya abhushanas' (ornaments for a married lady) to the bride. The married ladies from the groom's family perform an 'aarti' for the bride.

Ghana Bharan and Haldi

On the morning of the wedding day, the bride and her parents are seated on a wooden plank or 'pat'. Married ladies or 'sumangalis' pound wheat with a wooden rod called 'musal'. The bride and her parents offer prayers to the deities to ensure that the wedding rituals are devoid of any impediments and everything goes smoothly. After that, a mixture of 'haldi' (turmeric) and oil is applied on the hands, feet and faces of the bride and groom (separately in both homes). The paste is applied with mango leaves dipped in it. Next, the bride and groom bathe and dress up for the Dev Devak 'puja'.

Dev Devak

The days leading up to the wedding are filled with religious and social customs. As with any auspicious occasion, divine blessings are sought before embarking on festivities. Each of the families has one particular deity they worship and the worship of this family deity is called 'Devkarya'. The bride and her parents and the groom and his parents in their home perform this 'puja' separately.

Gauri Haar Puja

The Goddess Gauri (Parvati) was considered the perfect wife. As an Aryan princess marrying a non-Aryan, Lord Shiva, she merged herself completely with an alien culture and the unfamiliar lifestyle of her husband's family. When the bride is ready for the wedding, she sits on a low stool at the shrine and begins a continuous worship of Lord Shiva and his wife Parvati. On a 'chowki' (low stool) in front of her is a platter of rice on top of which rests a small silver figure of Parvati. The bride collects rice in her hands and pours it over the idol saying 'Gauri, Gauri sowbhagya de' (Gauri, Gauri, bless me with a lifelong marriage). She repeats this ritual until the 'mahurat', the auspicious time for the wedding. This ritual is performed at the venue of the wedding.

Varaat

In preparation for his wedding, the groom wears a silk 'dhoti' (a waist to ankle length silk fabric with borders) and an 'angavastram' (stole) across his shoulders. Traditionally, he is supposed to go bare chested, but these days most men prefer to wear a 'kurta' (long shirt) along with the 'dhoti'. Like the bride he also wears a 'mundavali' framing his face. His headgear is the Maharashtrian cap or a turban. On his arrival at the bride's home he and his relatives are awarded the traditional 'aarti' welcome.

Rukhavat

After the 'aarti' the groom and his procession are served a traditional Maharashtrian breakfast called 'rukhavat'.

Lagna Mahurat

The wedding ceremony—divided into following segments:

Varmala

The couple exchanges garlands.

After the 'rukhavat', the bride's mother puts some 'ghee' or clarified butter in the groom's palms, which he is supposed to eat. He is then given a decorated coconut and escorted to the 'mandap' (platform erected for the wedding rites). The bride's parents and other members from her family wash the feet of the groom, his parents and close relatives before the wedding ceremony can begin. The bride is brought to the 'mandap' while her mother retreats to the shrine where her daughter was praying to the Goddess Gauri and continues the worship of the deity. The bride's mother is not allowed to witness the couple garlanding each other. The bride stands on the 'pat' (wooden plank) in the west, facing east. The priests begin the chanting of the 'mangal ashtaka' (eight wedding verses), a narrative especially written for this wedding, explaining the process of the wedding, introducing the bride and groom and also containing advice for the couple on how to live a happy married life. Each of these recitations ends with a 'shubha mangala savdhan', which alerts everyone that the 'shubh mahurat' (auspicious time for the wedding) is approaching. The priest then chants a 'mantra' from the Vedas invoking power from the forces of nature, strength from the planets and blessings from the Almighty. The silk cloth, which was separating the couple, is pulled away by the priests towards the north and the bride garlands the groom, who in turn garlands her. The guests assembled, shower them with rice mixed with 'kumkum' (vermilion).

Kanyadaan

According to rites prescribed in ancient Vedic texts, the bride's father takes the groom's right hand with his own right hand and places it over his daughter's right hand. The priest trickles water on the connected hands, symbolic of 'the gift' being handed over. Bride's father: "I give you this goddess-like daughter of mine to take as your own". Groom, placing his right hand on bride's right shoulder: "I accept your daughter for the fulfilment of my life". Bride's father: "Do not exploit my daughter while fulfiling your life". Groom, "I shall not exploit her." This he says three times, affirming his vows.

Mangalsutra

At the exact auspicious time indicated by the priests, the groom's ties the 'mangalsutra' around the bride's neck. The necklace of black beads strung on gold is symbolic of the perpetual union of the couple. While tying the necklace, the groom says, "With this sacred thread I entrust my life to you and will protect and care for you for a hundred years."

Paani Grahan

The bride and groom face each other and he places his palm on hers while he invokes the gods and the forces of nature saying: "Blessed bride, I accept your hand—may we prosper and grow old together".

Lajja Hom

The bride's brother gives his sister two fistfuls of 'lahaya' (puffed rice). The groom guides the bride's hands and the puffed rice is consigned to the sacred fire, while the priests invoke the Gods by chanting Vedic hymns. This signifies the bridegroom asking the bride to merge completely with her new family.

Saptapadi

Seven handfuls of rice are placed in the northern periphery of the 'mandap'. As the groom leads the bride to each pile, she places her right toe on it.

Ashirwaad

The couple is showered with rice again while the priests continue the recitation of prescribed Vedic hymns, repeated by the groom. The couple touches the feet of all the family members who are older than them and accept blessings from them.

Wedding Feast

Even if the lunch is served buffet-style, special arrangements are made to seat the groom's family. The newly wed couple first go around and greet all the guests, serving them sweetmeats, and only after that do they proceed to partake of the meal. A Maharashtrian wedding feast is worth waiting for! After the marriage is solemnized, guests sit down to a traditional meal served on banana leaves. Most 'mahurats' are scheduled for the morning therefore the meal served is usually a lunch. The feast is a vegetarian one devoid of onions and garlic and consists of a selection of vegetables prepared in coconut gravy and accompanied by green mango chutney, cucumber and peanut salad, rice, 'puris', golden 'dal' (lentils) called `varan' and a sweet dish like 'jalebi', creamy 'basundi' or saffron-scented 'shrikhand'. 'Mattha' or coriander-flavoured salted buttermilk complements the meal, which ends with a sweet `paan' called `vida'.

Vidaai

The groom goes to the shrine where his bride had earlier worshipped Goddess Gauri and takes the figure of the deity with him. The couple bid farewell to the bride's parents and family and leave in a decorated car. A few members from the bride's family escort her to her marital home.

Griha Pravesh

The groom's mother and sister receive the bridal couple at the doorstep. His older sister performs a brief 'aarti' with a lighted oil lamp for them. The bride is then made to kick over a grain measure filled with rice. This symbolizes her bringing prosperity into the house. A little sugar is put into her mouth as a good omen.

Reception

Though this is not a social requirement, many families choose to host a reception to celebrate the wedding and introduce the bride and groom to their friends, family and even business associates. This may either be a simple affair or as elaborate an event as desired, hosted in a hotel venue with a live band and gourmet food.

Panch Pavan

On the fifth day, after the marriage, the bride's family invites the groom's family for a big feast.

RAJPUT WEDDING

The engagement ceremony is organized at the groom's place which is attended only by the bride's father, brother and close relatives. Women are altogether prohibited and not even the bride is allowed to attend her engagement—"tika"—ceremony! The bride's brother makes the alliance official by applying "tilak" to the groom's forehead and by giving him gifts, clothes, sweets and sword. Then a few days before the actual wedding "Griha Shanti" and "Ganpati Sthaapana" are performed, wherein, either the bride or groom's parents perform a "Havan" to please the Gods and install an idol of Lord Ganesha. Only after the "Sthaapana" do other ceremonies commence.

Then comes the "Pithi Dastoor" during which the bride or

groom cannot leave the house. It consists of relatives applying turmeric and sandalwood paste to the bride or groom. The bride is brought under a silken canopy dressed in the traditional Rajasthani dress—orange "poshak"—and is then applied the paste by women. Four ladies belonging to the same clan as the bride hold the canopy at the four corners with the help of swords. At the groom's place too a similar ceremony is performed, but it is less elaborate. The entire time the ceremony is in progress the "Dholnas"—women singers with "dholaks" sing pre-wedding songs.

An integral part of Rajasthani Weddings are "Mehfils" which are usually held in the evenings seperately for the men and the women. At the "ladies' mehfil" the women dressed in dazzling clothes gather in an enclosed courtyard and perform a special dance in group called the "Ghoomar." If being held at the groom's place, only the groom is allowed to attend this otherwise all-women affair. The "gents' mehfil" is again a strictly male affair with the singers performing. Another important ceremony is the "Mahira Dastoor" which is common to both the houses wherein the maternal uncle of the bride or groom along with his entire family is received with much respect and joy by the groom's or bride's mother and given a traditional welcome who in return gifts sweets, jewellery and clothes to the entire family. After this the "Janev Ceremony" is performed only on the groom. He dresses like and ascetic and performs a "havan" before wearing a sacred thread—"janev."

A typical Rajasthani tradition requires the "baraat" to cinsist only male members where the groom dresses in a gold "Achkan" with a "churidar" or "jodhpurs" with "jootis" and the traditional orange turban on which is adorned a piece of jewellery specially meant for the turban called "Serpech." Around his waist is tied a "Cummerband" and a necklace adorns his neck. The members of the "baraat" are also dressed similarly with colourful turbans—"Safas." There is absolutely no dancing and the "baraat" looks regal and royal with the groom and other members carrying swords. The groom usually rides a horse or an elephant. Upon reaching he is received by the bride's mother in the ladies' section who performs the traditional "aarti" and then takes him to the "mandap" for the wedding ceremony. At this point only one married male relative and, maybe a younger brother or cousin accompanies the groom to the stage. After "bidaai" before the bride lifts her veil for the groom, a coconut is placed below the wheel of the vehicle in which the couple is seated. The groom then gives some jewellery to his bride.

The "Griha Pravesh" takes place at the groom's residence after the couple return during which the bride wears her veil until all the "pujas" and ceremonies are taking place after which the bride and the groom play a few games. The next day the "Paay Laagan" takes place wherein the bride in a veil is blessed by all the family members of the groom and is given gifts. The traditional veil is then finally removed and this marks the end of the joyous wedding.

MARRIAGE CEREMONIES AMONG SOUTH INDIANS

Ushering-in of the Bridegroom

On the evening prior to the wedding day, the bridegroom is to be brought in a procession from a temple in a flower decorated car. He is escorted by the bride's parents, and welcome at the marriage mandap, which is the bride's abode. Nadaswaram band leads the way along the streets, the flower decorated car jam-packed with children. This is a social function, called jana vasam in south India and baraat in north India. Through such a parade, public approval is sought of the groom, chosen by the family. After reaching the marriage hall, there is a formal ceremony of betrothal.

On the Wedding day—The Preliminary Invocation

Ganapati Puja

As in an inauguration of any function so also in a marriage—Ganapati, the God of Initiation is invoked, to keep away all impediments.

Nandi Devata Puja

There are several presiding deities—the Nandi Devatas. To propitiate them, a leaf-laden branch of the pipal tree is installed, and an ablution with milk is performed by five Sumangalis (housewife, with husband living). This puja is followed by a presentation of a dhothi, and a saree to the marrying couple.

Navagraha Puja

This is performed to propitiate the nine astral planets that rule over man's destiny.

Vratham

The marriage ceremonies begin with the Vratham performed separately by the bride and the groom. For the bride, it means the tying of the KAPPU—the holy thread on her wrist which is meant to ward off all evil spirits. It symbolises a kind of the protective armour for the bride. For the groom, the various Gods—Indra, Soma, Chandra, Agni. From there on, the groom prepares himself for a new chapter in his life as a householder or Grihasta. The days of his bachelorhood or brahmacharya are now over and the acceptance of this is all what the Vratham is about.

Kasi Yatra

This a very important part of the ceremony. Immediately after his student-life, the young bachelor has two alternatives before him—Married life (Grihasta) or asceticism (Sanyas). Being by nature escapist, he prefers the ascetic life to the tribulations of married life. He, therefore, 'makes his way' to kasi (Varanasi), complete with slippers, umbrella, bamboo fan, etc. On his way, the bride's father intervenes and advises him of the superiority of married life to ascetic life. He, also, promises to give him his daughter as companion to face the challenge of life. The umbrella is to remain with groom, to remind him in the future, of this advice the real tradition. (However, there are different view points on this aspect. Given below is an observation by Sri. Narayan of Malaysia: During the wedding ceremony the groom is welcomed as Mahavishnu Svarupaya varahaya i.e. maha vishnu himself (or the Siva the equivalent in the Adi Saiva tradition) and the bride as Lakshmi. Thence, it is imperative he knows no sin, thence, he needs to perform a yatra to Kashi, submerge in Ganges and comes and does the wedding purified.

In the days of yore, when a man after education takes a yatra like this (it takes up some months, sometimes a year on foot), he gets to see the world, otherwise which he would not have been exposed to, thence from Brahmacharya, before moving to grahasta ashrama he come experienced and purified, disiplined (goal-oriented) and fit to take up the challenges of married life. And those days the groom would have been engaged (nischya dartha), and proceeds on this yatra and is welcomed back by the father-in-law etc. after coming back, with this words Maha Vishnu Svarupaya, and given the kanya dhana. Samnyasa and Grathasta ashrama are both pillars of the society, which is still relevant and have positive contributions to society. This has to be clearly understood.

Vaaku Nichaya Muhoortham

At the marriage hall, the bride's father and the bridegroom's father facing each other, solemnise the final betrothal ceremony, the vedic priest chanting the relevant hymns—in which the names of the bride, the bridegroom, as well as the names of their three generations of ancestors, are cited in presence of friends, relatives, and invitees. The mantras say: "O God Varuna, Be she harmless to my brothers and sisters? Oh Brihaspathi? May she no evil to her husband? O Lord Indra? Bless her to be a good guardian of her children? O Surya? Bless her with all wealths?"

Exchange of Garlands

The bride and the groom are lifted on the shoulders of their respective uncles; and in that position the two garland each other thrice for a complete union. A garland worn by a person, should not be used by another, ordain our shastras. Here the exchange of garlands symbolises their unification—as one soul in two bodies. It is inward acceptance by each of the very fragrance of the other.

Oonchal-swing, Ride and Singing of Laali

Then, the marrying couple is seated on a swing (oonchal); they rock forth and back, as the ladies around sing—laali, songs to praise to the couple. The chains of the swing signify the eternal Karmic link with Almighty above; the to-and-fro motion represent the undulating sea-waves of life; yet, in mind and body they shall move in harmony unperturbed, steady and stable.

Paalikai Seeds Sowing

This is fertility rite. Paalikais are earthen pots prepared a day earlier—pots spread at the base with hariali grass and Bael leaves (Vilvam); nine kinds of pre-soaked cereals are ceremonially sown in these pots by Sumangalis. After the marriage, the sprouted seedlings are released in a river or pool. This ritual invokes the blessings of the eight-direction-quartered guardian angles, for a healthy life and progeny to the couple.

Vara Puja

The feet of the bridegroom is washed in milk, and wiped off with silk. Water, and lighted lamps are circulated around the swing in order to guard the couple against demons and ghosts. Coloured globules of cooked rice are waved in circular motion, and thrown away—to propitiate the evil spirits.

Kanya Dhaanam

The bride is made to sit on her father's lap and is given away as gift by him, to the bridegroom. On the girl's head, a ring made with Kusa, the sacred grass called darbha, is placed, and over it, is placed a yoke; the gold mangal sutra (or thaali) is placed right on the aperture of the yoke, and water is poured through the aperture. The mantras chanted at this time, say:

> "Let this gold multiply your wealth? let this water purify your married life, and may your prosperity increase, offer yourself to your husband?" The bride then is given an auspicious ablution, and an exclusive new koorai saree is draped around her—this is done by the sister of the bridegroom. To bride in her new saree, a belt made of reed-grass is tied around the waist. The mantras chant: "She standeth here, pure before the holy fire, as one blessed with boons of a good mind, a healthy body, life-long companionship of her husband (sumangali bhagyam) and children with long life. She standeth as one who is avowed to stand by her husband virtuously. Be she tied with this red-grass rope, to the sacrament of marriage?" Thanks giving vedic hymns follow to the celestial caretakers of her childhood: the Deities of soma, gandharva and agni. Having attained nobility, the girl is now free to be given over to the care of the human—her man. The Vedic concepts underlying this ritual is figuratively this: that in her infant stage, soma had given her coolness of the moon, and strength; in the next stage, gandharva had given her bodily beauty; and lastly

agni gave her passions. The father of the bride, while offering his daughter chants: "I offer ye my daughter, a maiden virtuous, good-natured, very wise, decked with ornaments to the best of my ability—that she shall guard the Dharma, Wealth, and Love?"

The Bridegroom's Assurance

Thus, offering her daughter, her father gets a word of assurance three times that the bridegroom shall remain for ever her companion in joy and sorrow—in this life, and after death too?

Kankana Dharanam

The bride ties a string fastened to a piece of turmeric, around the wrist of the bridegroom—to bind themselves by a religious vow. It is only after tying the Kankanam that the bridegroom gets the right to touch the bride. A little later, the bridegroom ties a Kankanam on the bride's wrist.

Maangalya Dharanam

Next, timed to exact auspicious hour, is the tying of the Mangala Sutra (Thaali). The bride seated over a sheaf of grain-laden hay, looking eastward, and the bridegroom facing westward, ties the gold Mangala Sutra around the neck of the bride. As he does so, the Nadaswaram drums are beaten loud and fast, so as to muffle any inauspicious sounds at the critical hour. This is called Getti Melam; as it sounds, the Sumangali ladies sing "gouri kalyaname, vaibhogamay?" Three knots are tied—the first one by the bridegroom, the other two knots by his sister to make the bride a parts of the boy's family. The Vedic hymn recited by the bridegroom when he ties the knot, is: "Praying the Almighty that I be blessed with a long life, I tie this knot around your neck, oh soubhaygavati, may providence bestow on you a fulfiling life of a 'Sumangalis' for a hundred years to come?"

Paani Grahanam

This means "holding hands." The groom holds the hand of the bride. The Mantras say: "The Devas have offered you to me in order that I may live the life of a householder (grihasta); we shall not part from each other even after we grow old?"

Saptha Padhi

Holding the bride's hand, the bridegroom walks seven steps with her. This is the most important part of the marriage ceremony, and only when they walk seven steps together (i.e. perform saptha padhi) is the marriage complete legally. The belief is that when one walks 7 steps with another, one becomes the another's friend. The mantras recited then, mean: "Ye who have walked seven steps with me, become my companion, where by I acquire your friendship. We shall remain together inseparable. Let us make a vow together; we shall share love, share the same food, and share the strength, the same tastes. We shall be of one mind, we shall observe the vow together. I shall be the sama, you the rig: I shall be the upper world, you the earth; I shall be the sukhilam, you the holder—together we shall live, beget children, and other riches, come thou, o sweet-worded girl?"

Pradhaana Homam

A crucial part of the wedding is the homage paid by the couple to agni, the fire-God. They circle around the fire, and feed it with ghee, and twigs of nine types of trees, as sacrificial fuel. The fumes that arise, are supposed to possess medicinal, curative and cleansing effects on the bodies of the couple. Agni, the mightiest power in the cosmos, the sacred purifier, the all-round benefactor, is deemed as a witness to the marriage (agni saakshi).

Treading on the Grindstone

Holding the bride's left foot toe, the bridegroom helps her tread on a grindstone kept on the right side of the fire. The Mantras says: "Mount up this stone. Let thy mind be roc-firm, unperturbed, by the trials and tribulations of life?"

Showing her the "Arundhati" Star

Next he shows her the star arundhati (of the saptha rishi constellation), as also dhruva the polestar. Arundhati, the wife of Vasishta Mahrishi, is exemplified as an ideal wife, the embodiment of chastity. Dhruva is the one who attained immortality through single-minded devotion and perseverance—virtues to be emulated throughout married life.

Laaja Homam

This'shall comprise the bride's own offering to the sacrificial fire. As she is forbidden to do it herself, her brother helps her. He gives her a handful of parched rice grains which she hands to bridegroom who on her behalf, feeds it into the fire. Through this food offering, the bride seeks a long life for her husband, and propagation of the family. Participation of the bride's family members indicates the continuance of links between the two families, even after marriage. The couple circle around the fire, three times, and the feeding of the fire with parched rice, is repeated thrice.

Showering of Akshadai

Akshadai, i.e. rice-grains coated with turmeric and saffron, are showered on the couple, by elders and invitees—as benediction.

Griha Pravesam

Taking with her, fire from the Laaja Homam, the bride takes leave of her home, and enters the new home of her in-laws. The vedic hymns now sound likes the mother's words of advice to her daughter: "Be the queen of your husband's home. May your husband glorify your virtues; conduct yourself in such a way that you win your mother-in-law's love, and be in the good books of your sister's-in-law."

Nalungu

The evening of the marriage day is the time to relax and play. The newly wed wife calls her husband for play, inviting him through a song. Much to the merriment of one and all gathered, there follows list of playful items: the bride anointing the groom's feet with colour paste; fanning him, showing him a mirror; breaking papads over each other's head; wrenching the betel pack from each other's hand; rolling the coconut from one to another as in ball-play; and so on. During these items, the ladies sing songs poking fun at the bride, groom and the in-laws. These events brings out many qualities of the bride and the groom—sporting spirit, kindness, strength, co-operative nature, etc.

The Night Time Homams

The jayaathi homam is performed to propitiate the Gandharvas and deities.

Pravesa homam is done to solemnise the bride's entry into the husband's home. The sacrificial fire is brought along by the bride.

Sesha homam is Fire oblation with the residual ghee, a little of which is sprinkled on the bride's head four times.

Thaamboola Charvanam and Bala Dhaanam

The girl's brother gives the ceremonial first betel to the couple to chew. Certain other gifts are made to bless the couple with children and long life.

Mangala Arathi

A solution of lime and turmeric powder, and in colour, is prepared on a plate, and circled around, and thrown away to ward off evil eye. This is done a number of times during the entire wedding ceremony, and at the end.

Shanti Muhoortham

The consummation of the marriage at night—the nuptials?

MALAYALI MARRIAGE WEDDING

Pre-Wedding Ceremony

A traditional Hindu Kerala wedding starts with exchanging and matching of horoscopes by the parents of the boy and the girl. "Muhurtham" or the auspicious date of the marriage is then finalized in consultation with the astrologers. The day before the wedding, a traditional dinner is served to the bride at the bride's residence. She is seated facing the east, and has a traditional five-course vegetarian meal with her family.

Wedding Ceremony

The Groom arrives at the bride's house in a traditional "dhoti" and "angavastram." He is seated in a north-western room where the bride's father washes the groom's feet and welcomes him. The groom then gives him the off white sari that has to be worn by the bride for the nuptials. The "Veli" or the nuptial ceremony is performed around the "agni" (fire). The bride and the groom circle the sacred fire thrice, after which the bride's father ties the "Taali," which is strung on a yellow thread around the neck of the bride. Thereafter the bride's father gives her hand to the groom in a ceremony called "Kanyadaanam." After the Kanyadaanam, "Sparsham" takes place wherein the groom sits in front of the bride and tilts his head backwards, to touch her forehead. After this the girl offers "Laja" (puffed rice) to the fire to the chant of various mantras. Her palms are placed in her husband's hands and she performs the "hom." After this, the groom lifts the bride's foot and places it on the "Ammi" (grinding stone) signifying breaking of her ties from her old family. The groom then moves the bride's foot forward seven times with his hand symbolizing her entry into his family.

Post-Wedding Ceremony

After the wedding a feast is arranged and thereafter the bride leaves for her husband's home. "Grihapravesh" ceremony is performed at her new home to welcome her arrival.

TAMIL MARRIAGE WEDDING

Pre-Marriage Ceremony

Once the horoscopes are seen and matched and the match is fixed, the pundit fixes an auspicious day for marriage. Till then the boy and the girl are forbidden to meet each other. One day prior to the marriage a ceremony called "Jaanavaasam" is celebrated. The groom's party arrives at the bride's place amidst fanfare, like in a Barat and Ganesh Puja is performed. On the dawn of the wedding day the boy and the girl have an auspicious bath called "Mangala Snanam."

Marriage Ceremony

For conducting the actual marriage ceremony, there is a "mandapam" with a sacred fire. The "mandapam" is decorated with kokam and flowers. Also, there are containers with different varieties of sweets and savouries. The father of the bride welcomes the groom and washes his feet. The groom's family presents the bride with the wedding 9-yard sari, which his sister helps her wear. She wears the saree and comes back where "Kanyadanam" is performed, i.e. the groom and the bride are symbolically united by the bride's father. In this ceremony, the girl's father is made to sit on a sack of paddy, and the girl is seated on his lap. The paddy symbolizes material and spiritual plentitude in the marriage. Then the yoke of a plough is touched to the bride's forehead symbolizing that just as two bullocks are required to carry the plough for tilling the fields, so, also will she and her husband remain side by side to go through life. The bride's father gives away the bride to the groom. The priest performs the havan and the paanigrahan, whereby, the boy accepts the girl and promises to look after her forever. Then, the bride and the groom go around the sacred fire seven times in a ritual called "Saptapadi." The bridegroom takes hold of the right foot of the bride and makes her take seven consecutive steps where the bride touches her feet to a grinding stone "ammi." This symbolizes that their union be as steady, solid and steadfast as a stone. In Tamil Marriage garlanding is done thrice. Most importantly, the boy ties a yellow thread with a pendant called the 'Taali' to the girl's neck.

Post-Marriage Ceremony

In the evening "Nalangu" is performed in which the boy and the girl are given a coconut to play with. It is performed just for fun. An exchange of gifts takes place between members of both families and flower petals are showered on the couple. After this, the "Grihpravesh" is performed, in which the bride is formally received and welcomed into her new home and family after taking a leave from the bride's family.

ANDHRA VAISHNAVA BRAHMIN WEDDING

The most important aspect in marriage in the Andhra Vaishnava Brahmin community is the 'matching of horoscopes', although the family background and tradition are also looked into. It is essential that the 'gothrams' (ancestral lineages) of both the families are different. If originating from the same 'gothram', the bride and groom are not eligible for marriage. Their relationship instead becomes that of a brother and sister! In Andhra weddings it is important that the 'rishis' (sages) too must have different names. The 'rishis' were the celestial beings from whom the human race is believed to have originated. There were seven 'rishis' in all. The weddings are performed by 'purohits' or 'pujaris' (Brahmin priests) in the presence of the God of Fire or 'Agni Devta'. The 'pujari' chants Vedic mantras while conducting the marriage in all solemnity.

Pradhanam

The engagement ceremony takes place once the horoscopes of the bride and the groom are matched. This function starts with a 'Ganapathy puja', in the presence of elders from both families. The couple's parents exchange 'thamboolams' or platters filled with betel leaves, betel nuts, fruits, flowers, 'kumkum' (vermilion) and 'pasupu' (turmeric) along with the 'lagna patrika' (marriage document). The 'lagna patrika' is read aloud by a 'pujari' to the elders, conveying the acceptance of the alliance between both families, and the date, time and venue for the wedding is finalized at this time.

Kalyana Rata

An auspicious time is arrived at for fixing the first pole of the marriage 'pandaal' (canopy erected for the wedding rites). A 'Ganapathy puja' (invocation of Lord Ganesh) is performed to mark this ceremony. The 'kalyana rata' or pole is adorned with turmeric powder, mango leaves and 'rangoli' (coloured rice flour) designs. The 'pujari' performs a 'puja' by sprinkling turmeric, 'kumkum' powder, yellow rice and flowers amidst the chanting of Vedic mantras. The 'kalyana rata' is then fixed very firmly into the ground and an 'arathi' is performed. Prayers are offered so that the 'pandaal' should remain strong and firm throughout the ceremonies.

Nalugu with Mangala Vyadham

From this day on the 'nadeswaram' (wind instrument similar to the clarinet, only larger) accompanied by a 'melam' (drum) is played for all the auspicious occasions till the wedding ceremony is completed.This is purely a ladies function, and takes place one or two days prior to the wedding. The bride and groom, in their respective homes, are anointed with oil by the elders, blessed and given an oil bath, after which they are dressed in silks and adorned with the 'Kalyana thilakam' (a mark made on the forehead with vermilion). Subsequent to this they are not allowed to move out of their homes until the wedding ceremonies are completed. The same evening, the ladies congregate once again and the 'sumangalis' (married ladies) pound turmeric. The bride gives 'thamboolams' consisting of bangles, 'kumkum', flowers and fruits to the ladies and they in turn bless the bride, wishing her a long and happy married life.

Phalikalu Ceremony

After the 'nalugu' ceremony, the bride is adorned in silks and a small 'puja' is performed. 'Navadhanyams' or nine varieties of grains are sprinkled on nine earthen plates (painted white) filled with soil. These are allowed to germinate for sixteen days. The nine grains can be rice, wheat, 'moong dal', black 'urad dal', gingely, red 'chana', white 'chana', chickpeas, green 'moong dal' and green 'chana'. On the sixteenth day after the marriage, the 'mangalsuthrams' (108 strings of sacred thread twisted together and dipped in turmeric) are strung together and the germinated grains are immersed in a flowing stream.

Snathakam

After an oil bath called 'mangala snanam', the groom, clad in a 'pancha' (dhoti) and 'angavastram' or upper cloth performs a 'puja' before the "agnihotram" (sacred fire). He then embarks on a mock pilgrimage or 'kashi yatra' carrying an umbrella, wooden footwear and a hand fan.

Jeela Kaara and Bellam—The Sumuhurtham

The bride's brother pleads with him to abandon his plan to become a priest and to take his sister's hand in marriage and settle down as a family man instead. After much cajoling, the groom agrees and returns to get married. Meanwhile, the bride is performing the 'Gowri Puja' (worship of Goddess 'Gowri Devi') and asking for her blessings. Her maternal uncles, assisted by relatives carry her to the 'kalyana mandapam' (marriage hall) and the ladies of the household follow this procession. She is seated opposite the groom, and a curtain is held between them forbidding them to see each other till the 'shubhmuhurtham' (auspicious time for the marriage rites).

Kanyadanam

The bride and groom perform a 'Ganapathy puja'. The bride's

father washes the groom's feet while her mother pours the water. The bride's father performs the 'kanyadanam' by holding his daughter's hands in which a coconut has been placed and placing them in the groom's hands and pouring water over them. After the 'kanyadanam', the 'pujari' makes the bride and groom tie a 'kankanam' (the sacred thread), on each other's right wrists. The bride and groom are then given the 'madhuparkams' to wear by the bride's parents. These are white handloom clothes soaked in turmeric water with either a red or green border. The bridal couple is also given a pair of camphor garlands, which they have to wear along with the 'madhuparkams' and proceed to the 'kalyana mandapam'. An auspicious time is fixed for the 'jeela karra+bellam'—this is a combination of cumin seeds and jaggery crushed together and placed on a betel leaf. The 'pujari' recites Vedic mantras and the groom places the 'jeela karra+bellam' on the bride's head and she in turn places it on his.

Mangalyadharanam

Before the 'mangalyadharanam' is tied elderly women remove the curtain separating the couple and hold a yoke between them through which the 'mangalsutras' are passed. The bride now sits on the groom's left and the sacred yellow thread is tied around both their necks by the 'pujari'. A few drops of milk are poured to purify these sutras. When the mangalyam or mangalsutra is tied by the groom around the bride's neck, the first two knots are tied by him and the third knot by the groom's sister. Immediately after this ceremony, the groom ties a 'dharba' girdle around the bride's waist. This is a sacred thread made of dried grass blessed by the 'pujari', for the bride to seek non-widowhood. The groom's sister now performs an 'arathi' to mark the culmination of the main wedding ceremony.

Thalambralu

This is a very beautiful ceremony in Andhra weddings. Rice being the staple food, it is poured in abundance over each other's head by the couple in a joyful manner conveying prosperity and abundance.

Sapthapathy

The end of the bride's sari 'pallav' and the groom's

'angavastram' are knotted together. This is followed by a small 'homam' or 'puja' performed by the bridal couple. The groom leads the bride to take seven steps repeating the mantras chanted by the 'pujari'.

The Traditional Wedding Meal

The wedding feast is served on banana leaves following a particular method. Cooked 'tur dal' (lentils) is served on the right lower corner of the leaf followed by 'halwa' (a sweet dish) 'pachadi' (raita or yogurt), chutney, two dry vegetables, gun powder or curry leaf powder, fryums made of white pumpkin, rice fryums and pappad, pickle and salt. The above items are served all around the leaf till the left corner. Then mixed rice or vegetable 'pulao' is served in the center of the leaf and curd 'vada' next to that. Two dry sweets—'bobatlu', pancakes made of corn flour with cooked 'chana dal' (chikpeas) and jaggery, or boorelu, cooked 'chana dal' and jaggery stuffing made into round balls dipped in 'urad dal' (lentils) batter and deep fried, 'laddus' (round sweets made from gram flour, sugar and 'ghee' or clarified butter) are served in a cup. This is how the leaf is set and made ready before the guests are seated to enjoy the meal. After this elaborate meal, 'paan' (betel leaves) and nuts are served.

Laja Homam

The bride offers puffed rice or 'laja' into the fire, given to her by her brother. The offerings are made three times with the chanting of three different mantras. The bridal couple is then taken to see the 'arundhati nakshatra' (celestial star named 'arundhati') to inspire the bride to lead a glorious and virtuous life like the Goddess 'Arundhati'. The 'dharba girdle' is removed after the 'laja homam', thus marking the completion of all wedding rituals.

Nagavalli

The groom ties black beads, threaded by unmarried girls, around the bride's neck. After this the groom holds the right foot of the bride and places it on a granite grinding stone called 'sanni kallu' as he chants a mantra. The groom then adorns each of the bride's second toes with a pair of silver rings (matti). It is during this ceremony that the groom's family presents the bride with jewellery, sarees, and sweets and these gifts are displayed for all to see.

Appagintalu/Vadigantu Biyyam

After the wedding functions are over, the bride is formally handed over to the groom's family. This is an emotional and tearful event. Before the bride is taken to the groom's home, her mother puts some rice in the upper cloth of the 'madhuparkam', and ties it around the bride's waist. A small silver bowl, a tiny sandalwood doll, the root of yam and a sweetmeat called 'chalmidi' (made out of rice flour and jaggery) are added are also put inside the 'madhuparkam'.

Grahapravesam

At the groom's home, the couple is given milk and fruit by the groom's mother and the bride is made to light the 'venkateswara deepam' (a lamp made out of rice flour and jaggery and filled with ghee) in the 'puja' room. She is also made to boil milk on the stove. In Andhra Pradesh, the 'Satyanarayana Vratham' (fasting till the 'puja' ceremony in front of Lord Satyanarayana) is very important. This 'satyanarayana vratham' is observed either in the 'kalyanmadapam' itself, immediately after all the ceremonies are over or a day or two later. Till the 'vratham' is completed, the couple cannot consummate the marriage.

The Sari

The bride leaves for her marital home taking her trousseau with her. As the custom goes, the first three nights are spent in the bride's house by the couple. The girl is then formally taken to the in-laws' home. When the bride leaves, a bridal trousseau consisting of various gifts, along with a lot of sweets, savories, and turmeric powder and 'kumkum' in large quantities is sent with her

TELANGANA ANDHRA REDDY WEDDING

The Reddys or Reddis, also known as 'Kapus' belong to a Telugu speaking community, split into several sub-sections. Those of them who have settled in different sourthern states like Karataka and Tamil Nadu for several generations have adapted their rituals and ceremonies to suit the local customs, so slight variations will be apparent in the sequence of events in a marriage.

The marriage rituals begin with a promise made by both families to each other that a wedding will be solemnized. After consultations with an astrologer, an auspicious day and time are fixed for the marriage ceremony and both the concerned parties draw up written contracts. These contracts are then placed in yellow cloth bundles along with betel leaf, turmeric, nuts and fruits and blessed by an officiating 'pujari'.

Patrika

This ceremony can be performed even one day before the wedding. Both families make a promise that a marriage will be held between their families. After consultations with an astrologer, an auspicious day and time is fixed for the marriage ceremony and both the concerned parties draw up written contracts. These contracts are then placed in yellow cloth bundles along with betel leaf, turmeric, nuts and fruits, blessed by an officiating 'pujari' and exchanged by the fathers of the bride and the groom.

Nisachaithartum or Pradhanum

The bridegroom arrives at the bride's home accompanied by fifty to hundred family members and 'shehnai' (traditional wind instrument popular at most Indian weddings) players. He brings platters of fruits and gifts for the bride's family. His mother applies 'kumkum' (vermilion) on the bride's forehead and gifts her saris and jewellery, into which she changes and a 'puja' is performed. In many Reddi families the groom does not accompany his family members at this time.

Vara Puja

During this 'puja' the groom is given lavish gifts by the bride's parents, which may include clothes, money, a gold chain, a gold ring and a wristwatch.

Paindlipilla or Haldipaspu

This ceremony literally involves the 'dressing up of the bride' and takes place on the morning of the wedding day. Five, nine or eleven 'sumangalis' (married ladies) perform a small ceremony to drive away evil (dhristi). Each of the 'sumangalis' holds a coin in her palm, circles it around the bride's face and throws the coin into a vessel. They, then, perform the traditional 'aarti' for the bride. Oil is applied on the bride by the 'sumangalis' after which she is taken for the ritual bath or 'mangal snahne'. After the bath, the bride changes into a new sari and adorns herself with jewellery given to her by her family. Her mother applies a touch of 'chandan' (sandalwood paste) under the bride's chin and on her arms. As a gesture of respect the bride hands her mother a 'paldaan' (betel leaf, nut and fruits) and touches her feet to take her blessings. This same ritual is performed by all the 'sumangalis', and the bride is blessed by all of them in a similar fashion.

Vivaham (Muhurtam)

The marriage ceremonies are traditionally held in the bride's ancestral home with two 'pujaris' officiating. A large 'pandol' or canopy is erected outside the bride's home and decorated with mango leaves, banana palms and flowers. Traditionally, this 'pandol' was made from the barks of palmyra trees. The oldest member of the bride's family applies 'kumkum' on the groom's forehead, garlands him and escorts him to the marriage venue in a decorated car. The bride's relatives receive the groom at the entrance to the bride's home welcoming him with the 'aarti' and lead him to the wedding 'mantap' (platform erected for the wedding rites). As soon as, he steps into the 'pandol' the bride's brother washes his feet. The bride's parents are seated in the marriage 'mantap' beforehand awaiting the groom's arrival. The groom performs the 'sita kalyani' (puja invoking the blessings of Lord Rama and his consort Sita).

Kankana Shastra

This is a very important ceremony in the Reddi community. On a silver platter are placed two handfuls of rice. A coconut dipped in turmeric is placed on top of the rice on which are placed two pieces of turmeric sticks, which have been tied to a 'kankan' or double thread. Prayers are offered to all the Hindu deities and the 'pujari' implores them to come and bless the 'kankana' with their presence and remain there till all the marriage ceremonies are completed, traditionally five days. The 'pujari' ties one sacred 'kankan' on the groom's wrist. The bride is led into the 'mantap' and the groom ties the second 'kankan' on her wrist.

Kanyadaan

Two 'pujaris' recite Vedic chants and a coconut is placed on the bride's palms. Her father holds her palms and gently places them on the groom's palms, literally 'giving her away'. The bride's mother pours water from a silver 'chembu' (container with a spout) on the father's palms who in turn directs the flow of the water onto the coconut being held by the bride and groom. This ritual is called 'kanyadaan', whereby, the bride's parents relinquish parental authority over their daughter. The groom ties the sacred 'taali' (two flat pieces of inscribed gold pendants strung on a cord dipped in turmeric and composed of 108 very fine threads closely twisted together) on the bride's neck accepting the gift of 'kanyadaan'. He ties the 'taali' using three knots. Then, the couple exchange garlands after which they sit across each other divided by a platter of 'thalambratu' (rice dipped in turmeric). They take fistfuls of this rice and shower it over each other till the platter is empty.

Saptapadi

The 'pujari' lights the 'homa' or sacred fire and the couple takes seven steps around it saying their marriage vows. The groom's 'angavastram' (shawl) is tied to the bride's sari 'pallav' throughout this ritual. Each step is a promise made to each other for an enriching and purposeful life together. As this is a Vedic rite, not all Reddi families perform it.

Grahapravesham

On their arrival in the marital home, the bride and groom are given a glass of milk from which both must drink. The groom's sisters playfully extract promises of gifts from their new sister-in-law, before allowing her to enter the room!

Reception

The reception is not a traditional concept but has become a common feature in many homes and can be as simple or as elaborate as desired. It is often held at the 'Kalyana Mantap' (wedding hall) where the wedding might have been held or even in a five star hotel or club. Cocktails and music accompany dinner.

Kalyanautsavam

This is an important ritual in many Reddi families. The newly weds visit the Tirupathi Temple and perform what is known as the 'kalyanautsavam'—literally translated it means the marriage between Lord Venkateshwara and his consort Padmavathi. For those of them who are unable to travel to Tirupathi, this puja is performed in a Venkateshwara temple in their own area.

KARNATAKA VOKKALIGA WEDDING

The Vokkaliga community of Karnataka consists of agriculturists and landowners. Many of their marriage rituals are, therefore, steeped in rural traditions. They have, like many other communities adapted these rural traditions to urban ones and most weddings are now performed in marriage halls. The marriages, which are still conducted in ancestral homes, however, are truly interesting.

Nischitartha

This is a function when the wedding date is agreed upon after consulting an astrologer. Elders from the groom's family go to the bride's home carrying auspicious items like rice, jaggery, betel leaves, nuts and an old piece of jewellery for the bride on a copper platter. The couple to be married is not present at this occasion. Once the groom's family leaves, the bride is made to sit on a 'hasemane' (wooden stool) and receive the gifts just brought by the groom's family, in her sari 'pallav'.

Chapparashastra (Achandi)

One day before the actual wedding rituals, a 'mandap' or canopy (also known as 'chappara') is erected with much pomp and care in the courtyard or in front of the entrance to the bride's home. In the center of this 'mandap', in a row are placed traditional instruments—a drum, a 'halege' (trumpet like instrument) and a 'shruti' (a type of harmonium). These instruments are blessed by all the female members of the bride's family, who place a banana leaf, betel leaf, jaggery and 'thanbitu' (a sweetmeat) next to each instrument. They, then perform a 'puja' by applying milk, 'kumkum' and flowers to each instrument and conducting an 'arathi'. This ritual is called the 'chapparashastra' and is performed on days other than Tuesdays or Saturdays. The officiating 'pujari' blesses the entire proceedings by sprinkling holy water on the house and the 'chappara'. A similar ceremony is held in the groom's home on the same day. After the 'chapparashastra' the bride is taken to her family temple and the groom to his, for prayers. On returning from the temple, the bride is seated on the 'hasemane' and in her presence, the elders make little white cloth bundles containing coins in different denominations and after assigning each bundle a purpose hang them up in front of the house. This is done to invoke the blessings of all the deities for all the ceremonies which follow.

Kelneeru

The bride sits on a small stool in an old sari. All the women folk anoint her body with a paste made from 'haldi' (turmeric) and coconut oil. After her bath, three or five ladies accompany her to a nearby well or pond, where she performs the 'Ganga puja' to purify the water. The ladies then carry the purified water from the well back to the house, in small earthen pots. On reaching the house, they perform the 'Gau' (cow) puja, feed the cow rice and jaggery and also conduct the 'tulsi' puja. A jackfruit sapling along with 'navratana' stones (semi-precious stones) is also planted by these ladies. Other women from the household wash the feet of these ladies, bless the earthen pots filled with water and keep them reverently in 'puja' rooms. A similar ritual is performed in the groom's house but with a difference. The groom's family prepares what is known as a 'kuke shastra' (two baskets—one with silver items, gold jewellery and saris and the other with rice, jaggery, nuts and coconuts) and keeps them ready for the next day. The bride and groom are blessed by the elders and receive gifts at this time.

Varapuja

The groom arrives in the bride's home in all his splendour, carrying the 'kuke shastra' and the 'mangalsutra' (small gold pendant strung to a yellow thread or a gold chain). He is received by the bride's father who presents him with a diamond ring and a gold chain and feeds him honey and 'ghee' (clarified butter) and performs the traditional 'arathi' on him. The groom is then led to the marriage 'mandap'.

Lagna

The bride's maternal uncle escorts her to the 'mandap'. The bride and groom stand opposite each other separated by an 'antrapate' (white silk sheet). The 'pujaris' chant Vedic mantras and the couple sprinkle 'jeera' (cumin seeds) and jaggery on each other. The white sheet is removed and the bride and groom garland each other. The bride's parents place the 'mangalsutra' on a coconut and take it around to all the family members and guests to have it blessed. This coconut is then placed on the bride's hands, which in turn are placed in the groom's. This moment is the actual 'muhurtham' or moment of union according to the stars! The groom ties the 'mangalsutra' around the bride's neck. Her sari 'pallav' is tied to his 'shalya' (shawl) in the proverbial marital knot and the couple goes around the 'mandap' three times, after which they go outside to view the sun. The sun acts as a witness to the union.

Saptapadi

In some Vokkaliga families the ritual of lighting the sacred fire or 'homa' and the 'saptapadi' (taking the seven steps around the fire) is followed which is much like that of any other Hindu community. The newly weds touch the feet of all the elders present and take their blessings, after which they leave for the marital home. The bride enters her new home by tipping over a small measure of rice with her right toe and placing her right foot inside the door first.

Reception

A grand dinner accompanied by cocktails is hosted by the families to introduce the newly weds to the rest of the community, friends and colleagues.

KERALA SYRIAN CHRISTIAN WEDDING

The Syrian Christians of Kerala were originally Namboodiri Brahmins and their conversions took place during St. Thomas' visit to India about AD 46. Their Church is the Syrian Orthodox Church, the head of which is known as Catholicos and he resides in Kottayam, Kerala. Although they embraced Christianity, the Syrian Christians retained many of their Hindu customs and till date their marriage rituals follow many of the old Hindu traditions. A typically Syrian Christian wedding is an elaborate affair and is usually arranged by the elders. The bride's family makes the proposal to the groom's family.

Kalyanamaurappa

'Kalyanamaurappa' literally translated means 'arranging a marriage' between the girl and the boy. Once the groom's family accepts the proposal, male members from the groom's family visit the bride's family to agree on a wedding date. Both families take a decision at this time, that the girl will come to into the boy's family along with 'streedhanam' (wealth of a woman), which can include money, clothes, jewellery or property. Henceforth, she will not lay any more claims on her father's wealth. Once an agreement is reached, the two eldest male members from each family hold hands in a symbolic clasp. An 'angavastram' (white cloth) covering their hands, seals the contract. The engagement is announced at the respective churches for three consecutive Sundays in the presence of the community and the families of the bride and groom. On the third Sunday, the bride and groom go to their respective churches for confession and to partake in the Holy Communion.

Madhuramvekal

This ceremony is held in the respective homes of the bride and the groom, a day prior to the church wedding. Barring a few differences, the ceremonies are similar. The groom sits facing the east, while a barber cuts his hair and shaves off his beard. The groom's eldest sister or female cousin anoints his hair with oil amidst a lot of bantering and teasing. The groom's brother-in-law then escorts the groom for his regular bath ensuring that he does this from the westerly direction. The groom returns from the easterly direction, sheltered under an umbrella, held by the brother-in-law. On his arrival, all the ladies clap their hands and yodel! This is called the 'korava', traditionally considered very auspicious throughout Kerala. In the bride's home, she is made to wear a simple sari and her brother's wife performs all the rituals of anointing her with oil and taking her for her bath in the exact same manner as was done for the groom. After her bath, the bride changes into a resplendent silk sari, wears traditional jewellery;

adorns her hair with flowers and puts on a gold chain with a cross on it. After the 'korava', the bride and groom in their respective homes, heads covered, sit on a chair, which has been covered with a white cloth and are blessed by the priest. A sweet called 'madhuram' (banana slices soaked in sweet Palmyra palm juice) is brought to be blessed by the priest. The blessing over, the sweet is fed to the bride and groom by the mother or grandmother.

Mantra Kodi

The sari, which the groom will present to his bride in church the next morning, is called the 'mantra kodi'. The night before the church ceremony, strands of thread are drawn from this sari by the groom's sister and twisted to form a cord. On this cord, is tied the 'taali', a leaf shaped gold pendant with a cross, inscribed on it.

Church Ceremony

On the day of the wedding the priest visits each home separately and blesses the bride and the groom. The groom carries the sari for the bride, the 'taali' and two wedding bands. After the blessing, the bride and groom step out of their homes, preceded by a young girl holding a 'diya' or lamp. In the church, the priest officiates and after the sermon the couple exchange wedding bands. All through the ceremony, the bride's sister stands behind her. Vows are exchanged and the groom ties the 'taali' (symbol of a married woman) on the bride's neck. During the tying of the 'taali', the bride's sister is replaced by the groom's sister. The 'mantra kodi' is placed on the bride's head by the priest and blessed. The couple joins hands and is announced man and wife.

Reception

The reception is a modern day concept, borrowed from the West and is basically a celebration of the wedding. The families involved host a grand dinner and the newly wed couple is introduced to the relatives and guests.

KERALA HINDU NAIR WEDDING

The 'Nairs' of Kerala are the only matrilineal community in

the country. Under the 'marumakkathayam' system, the property rights of the joint family are vested in the female members. Marriage among the Nairs has a somewhat different meaning from marriages in other communities and is not so much a religious as a social ceremony. Temple marriages, especially at the Guruvayur Temple, are popular and inexpensive. There is no chanting of 'mantras' and the ceremony is over in a matter of minutes. It is both, touching and impressive in its simplicity.

Vivaha Nischayam

Announcement of the engagement and the exchange of rings. This ceremony is usually divided into two parts: (a) the 'Pennu Kanil'—the bride and groom meet; (b) 'Mothiram Mattal'—the exchange of rings.

Pennu Kanil

After the horoscopes are matched, both families consent to the marriage. The couple then visits the bride's home. This meeting may be a simple affair or a large celebration. In some communities, a representative of the Nair Service Society (NSS) is always requested to attend, in order to record the lineage of both the families and make a formal announcement in the NSS newsletter about the alliance later.

Mothiram Mattal

The 'nila vilakku' (brass oil lamp) is lit and the couple exchange rings. Rings may also be exchanged later at the wedding ceremony, if both the families so prefer.

Ayana

On the evening before the wedding, the families of both, bride and groom gather in their respective homes to bless them. Though 'mehendi' is not a traditional Nair custom, it is 'borrowed' from the Kerala Brahmins now-a-days. Henna is smeared on the palms and allowed to dry for a couple of hours. In South Kerala, young girls dance in a circle around a brass oil lamp, singing the 'Thiruvathira Kali' (devotional songs connected with weddings), while the others clap in rhythm. In some communities, the older ladies in the family twist fine cotton into a thousand wicks, which will be used at the wedding the next day.

Namaskaram

On the day of the wedding, the bride and the groom separately visit a temple near their homes. Any temple will do except that of Lord Hanuman or Lord Ayappya, as these are bachelor gods! The bride's parents carry the 'mangalyasutram' or 'tali', the necklace symbolizing eternal union, for it to be blessed by the priests. On returning to their respective homes, the bride and groom touch the feet of the elders of the family and receive their blessings.

Kalayanam or Vivaham

The actual wedding ceremony may take place in a 'kalayana mandappam' (marriage hall), a choultry (all-purpose hall), temple or hotel. The bride's family receives the groom's family at the entrance of the marriage venue, to the playing of the 'nadaswaram' (long wind instruments) and the 'thayil' (large drums beaten with curved drumsticks). The groom stands on a wooden plank, while the bride's younger brother washes his feet. The bride's aunts perform 'aarti' for the groom with a 'thaali' (platter), on which are arranged the thousand wicks made the night before. The groom is then escorted to the 'mandappam' (platform constructed to perform the wedding rites), by two rows of young girls. One girl carries the 'changala vatta' (sacred oil lamp), while another carries the 'ashtamangalya' (a small thali or platter containing brightly polished brass miniatures of a spoon), water container, sacred oil lamp, metal mirror, bell, 'kumkum' or vermilion box, and a 'kindi' or (container with a spout). The girls following the first two carry the 'taala phuli' (platters of rice, turmeric, and flowers on which oil lamps made out of coconut shells are placed). With his parents flanking him, the groom follows the girls around the 'mandappam', and seats himself on the right side of the canopy, which is decorated with flowers, fabric, palm fronds and banana stalks preferably with bunches of bananas on them! The bride is then escorted to the 'mandappam', to the rich sound of the 'nadaswaram' and the 'thayil'. All present on the dais stand when the bride arrives. She takes her place facing the east, with the groom facing her. At the precise moment set by the astrologer for the 'muhurtham', (the most auspicious time), the groom ties the 'mangalyasutram' around the bride's neck, to the beating of drums, all the while assisted by the bride's uncle, because on no account must the 'mangalyasutram' be allowed to fall! For some communities, the traditional 'mangalyasutram' is a gold pendant strung on a yellow thread. The bride has to wear this for three days after the wedding ceremony, after which, she replaces it with a gold chain. The groom gifts the bride a sari and a blouse on a platter, conveying to her that he will now assume the responsibility of providing for her. The groom's mother also gifts her with some jewellery at this time. The couple exchange garlands accepting each other as life partners. The bride's father places her hand in the grooms, thus handing over his daughter to him in holy matrimony. The couple is then escorted to a room by their older relatives, who bless them. Traditionally, amongst the Nair community, after marriage a daughter does not go to her husband's home but remains in her own ancestral place (tarawad) and the husband comes to visit her; remaining a member of his own 'tarawad'. This custom and the 'marumakkathayam' (matrilineal) system are both dying out, but a child still takes its mother's family name and is entitled to a share of the matrilineal property, should it be divided. However, in these times, the bride does get a send off. The couple leaves for the groom's house escorted by a handful of people from the bride's family. The groom's mother and older female relatives who perform 'aarti' with an oil lamp, which rests on a platter heaped with rice mixed with turmeric, receive them at the entrance. Both enter, right foot forward. The bride is required to kick over a large measure containing rice, symbolizing prosperity.

The Reception

A wedding reception may be held, if both the families so desire. The celebration may be very simple or as elaborate as desired. The dinner need not be vegetarian and alcoholic beverages may be served.

SARASWAT HINDU BRAHMIN WEDDING

The Saraswat Brahmin community is small, educated and very evolved. They believe that among 'samskaras' (sacraments), marriage is the most important. Horoscopes are a prime factor in marriage alliances, particularly if the match is 'arranged' by the parents. Marriage between families of the 'gotra' (ancestral lineage) are prohibited. Even, though, the Saraswat Brahmins are a highly evolved community with a high level of social awareness, marriage ceremonies are traditional, religious and sombre.

Naandi

This is a simple but important ritual consisting of a 'puja' (prayer) and is performed ten days prior to the actual wedding ceremony. The 'puja' is performed separately in both homes. The purpose being to negate the ill-effects of any deaths in the family so that the marriage ceremonies may carry on without any obstacles.

Urdha-moorthu

A 'kalesha' (silver pot) is placed on a small heap of rice with a coconut on it, which in turn is placed in front of the deity and blessed. The 'kalesha' will remain in the puja room till all the wedding ceremonies are completed.

Nischaithambul

The 'nischaithambul' or engagement announces the acceptance of both the families to the alliance. It is held on an auspicious date fixed by the 'pujari' (Brahmin priest), who performs a brief puja after which both sets of parents exchange silver platters laden with 'phalatambul' (coconuts, bananas, other fruits and sweets). The bride is gifted a silk and gold sari and gold jewellery by her future parents-in-law and the groom in turn is gifted a gold chain or watch and clothes by the bride's parents.

Yedur Kansani

This event is traditionally practiced so that the women from both families may get to know one another. On silver platters, women from both families carry, betel leaves folded in a specific manner, rice, coconut, flowers, 'kumkum' (vermilion), 'haldi' (turmeric) and rose water in a 'gulab dani' (long necked silver jar). The most important item for this ritual is the 'kalesh kanadi'; a silver platter containing a small heap of rice on which is placed a silver pot with a decorated coconut on top. The coconut is decorated with mango leaves and a small mirror and a gold chain are placed on top of it. The two groups of women from each family stand 50 ft. apart, facing each other, at the entrance of the wedding venue. Amongst the chanting of 'mantras' (Vedic chants), the women from the bride's family walk towards the groom's relatives welcoming them with an offering of flowers, 'kumkum', 'haldi' and sprinkle rose water on them. They retreat and then the ladies from the groom's family in honour of the bride's relatives perform the same ritual.

Phool-mudi

The father of the bride receives the groom at the entrance of the 'pandol' and the bride's mother performs the traditional 'aarti' for him. The groom is then seated and the bride's father washes his feet and ties the sacred thread or 'jhanava' on him. The bride is received by the groom's mother, who adorns her hair with flowers, performs an 'aarti' for her and showers her with rice. The showering of rice is known as the 'sesha'. She invites the other married ladies or 'sumangalis' to come and bless her future daughter-in-law.

Urdha-moorthu

Urdha-moorthu is a traditional and religious ceremony performed by the bride and groom in their respective homes. The bride seats herself next to a stone grinder and with the help of other unmarried sisters and cousins grinds the 'urad dal' (type of lentil) and 'moong dal' (type of lentil) on the round stone grinder. The groom and his family are invited to this function. The groom does the same in his house and invites the bride and her family to the function. The family priest performs the puja of the nine planets or the 'navagraha puja' after the 'urdha-moorthu'. After the puja, the groom dresses himself like a pilgrim, wearing a 'veshti' (dhoti), 'chappals' (slippers) holds an umbrella and makes preparations to embark on a 'mock' pilgrimage and remain celibate for life! At this point, the bride's father pleads with him not to go on the pilgrimage and asks him instead to accept his daughter's hand in marriage! After much cajoling the 'pilgrim' accepts and returns to get married!

Lagna

The 'lagna' is the culmination of all the wedding ceremonies and rituals when the couple is finally united in holy matrimony. It consists of many pujas and rituals performed by two priests, one from each family. The bride's brother fetches the groom from his home and brings him to the marriage venue in a decorated car. The bride is dressed in a nine-yard sari in the 'kasa' style, having no 'pallav'. Over her blouse she drapes a white shawl, made from 'mulmul' or georgette and makes certain that it is draped in a V-shape. This is symbolic of her unmarried status. When she enters the 'mantap' (platform erected to conduct the wedding rites) for the first time she performs what is known as the 'mantapratishta' or the 'mantap puja', assisted by the 'pujari'. Her mother adorns her with a string of black beads strung on a gold chain or the 'kare-mani' chain and slips on two 'kare-mani' bangles on her wrists (gold and black bangles). If the bride has an older married sister—the pujari performs the 'vara-puja' for them to honour the older son-in-law. Literally translated 'vara' means groom. The groom is made to sit on a sofa outside the 'mantap' along with a young male child and a special puja known as the 'shibika puja' is performed for him. The bride's father then escorts the groom inside the 'mantap' and ties the sacred thread or 'jhanava' on him. Five ladies from the bride's family enter carrying gifts for her—namely the 'lagna' sari, 'chautanam' sari, two additional saris and the crucial 'mangalsutra' (red corals strung on a gold chain, symbols of a married lady). The bride is carried by her maternal uncle to the 'mantap' and a silk sheet is held between the bride and the groom by the 'pujaris' who chant Vedic mantras and announce the 'gotras' and 'pravaras' (lineage and pedigree) of both families to the gathering. The 'lagna' is divided into many segments and begins with the giving away the bride or the 'kanyadaan' ceremony. The bride's father lifts her and hands her over to the groom—denoting that she is now in the care of her husband. The 'sutra-bandhan' follows in which the couple is encircled with nine yards of thread. Next is the 'kankan-bandhan' where the bride and groom slip bangles on each other's wrists, to ensure that the blessings of all the deities will be showered on them throughout the marriage ceremonies. The 'mangalsutra' ceremony takes place after this when the groom adorns his bride with the traditional necklace, a symbol of her marital status, which she will wear at all times. For the next ritual—the 'vivah-havan' (lighting of the sacred fire), the fire is lit with 'agni' (fire) brought by the bride's mother. For the 'laja-havan', the bride's maternal uncle or her brother adorn her toes with silver toe rings and the couple circle the sacred fire with her sari and the groom's 'shalu' (shawl) tied in a sacred marital knot. The bride is then given handfuls of puffed rice or 'laja', which she offers to the fire. The conclusion of all 'havans' is known as the 'havan-purnavati'. The couple is now pronounced man and wife.

Chautanan

'Chautanan' are a series of light hearted but nevertheless symbolic ceremonies. The first of these is when the bride makes the nuptial bed and places two new saris and two coconuts on the bed. The couple then feed each other a banana. 'Vore ubarche' is when the bride's maternal uncle lifts the groom and his wife, actually carrying them around a little distance! The traditional dropping of a ring into a deep vessel filled with water and making the bride and groom search for it is one of the most fun filled customs. The couple is mercilessly teased and the person who finds the ring first is considered to be the dominant partner in the marriage! Whoever finds the ring has to slip it on the other one's finger. Then there is the 'tulsi puja' followed by the puja performed for the coconut palm, after which the meal prepared by the bride is served to all. The final ceremony is the 'mantap-visarjan' or the conclusion of the lagna. The couple takes the blessings of all the elders by touching their feet. There is another charming ceremony, which takes place when the bride and groom arrive at the marital home. The groom's sister's sit on the doorstep refusing to allow the bride to enter unless they are suitably rewarded! Once all of them receive gifts, the hapless bride is allowed to enter and is made to tip over a small bowl of rice with her right foot. Her mother in law performs a brief 'mangal aarti' (welcoming ritual) for the bride and she also gives her daughter-in-law a new name.

Reception

The wedding reception is a modern day concept borrowed from the West. A grand dinner accompanied by cocktails is hosted by the families to celebrate the marriage and to introduce the newly weds to friends and relatives.

ROMAN CATHOLIC SARASWAT BRAHMIN WEDDING

A Roman Catholic Saraswat Brahmin wedding is always held in a church where a holy Mass is conducted according to the rituals followed by the Roman Catholic Church. The couple exchange wedding rings and vows in the presence of family and friends. The Hindu custom of tying a 'mangalsutra' called 'piduk' in Konkani is also observed and during the nuptials the bridegroom ties it around the bride's neck.

The Mudi

At the 'mudi' or engagement ceremony, the bride and groom exchange rings, blessed by a priest who also says a prayer for the couple. The bride's family draws up a contract, which is signed by both the families as a promise to each other that the wedding will be held within a mutually agreed time frame.

The Roce

On the day prior to the wedding ceremony, members of their families anoint the bride and groom with 'roce' (thick coconut milk). On the completion of this ceremony the bridal couple is not allowed to meet till the church ceremony, which is held the following day. For the 'roce', the bride wears her mother's wedding sari called the 'sado' along with old family jewellery. Her unmarried female cousins sit around her and sing traditional Konkani songs called 'vovio'. The groom wears western style clothes and goes through the same ceremony at his home.

Church Ceremony

The parish priest officiates at the church ceremony held in a Roman Catholic Church. The ceremony is simple and involves the exchanging of wedding bands and marriage vows by the bridal couple. A Holy Mass is conducted and all the Roman Catholic rituals are strictly followed. The priest blesses a black beaded necklace or the 'piduk' and the groom ties it around the bride's neck in the church. The 'piduk' bears the same significance as the traditional 'mangalsutra' (Hindu symbol of a married lady).

Reception

After the church ceremony, the bride and groom proceed for

the grand reception. Friends, relatives and professional colleagues are invited to attend this function replete with a grand feast, music and entertainment! The dinner that is served is usually non-vegetarian and accompanied by cocktails.

TAMIL CHETTIAR WEDDING

Marriage alliances among the Tamil Chettiars of Tamil Nadu are traditionally fixed within a group villages. It is not surprising therefore that all Chettiars are related and marriage within first cousins are common. In fact, the first choice for an eligible groom is his first cousin ! Their wedding are elaborately rich in customs. The traditional jewellery worn by the Chettiars is renowned for its breathtaking beauty; diamonds, rubies and emeralds intricately set in gold.

Nichayadartham

Traditionally, the first choice for an eligible bridegroom would be either his sister's or maternal uncle's daughter. The bride's family informs the groom's family about the gifts or 'seer', which they can give to their daughter for her wedding. This is done through a middleman. Once, the groom's family accepts the proposal an engagement takes place in the bride's home on an auspicious day. The engagement agreement is written in two copies by a 'pujari', and these are then exchanged between the families.

Giving Gold for the Sacred 'Taali'

The bride's family makes the sacred 'taali'. Since, the groom's family has to present the 'taali', they provide part of the gold for making it. The Brahmin or 'pujari' reads the 'panchangam' (calendar with auspicious dates) to select the wedding date.

Fixing the Muhurathakal

On an auspicious day and time, the person who is supposed to build the 'pandaal' (canopy erected to conduct the wedding rites) decorates a bamboo stick with turmeric paste and red earth and ties a bunch of mango leaves at its tip. A hole is dug in the ground, ghee (clarified butter) and coral (a semi-precious stone) are placed in it and milk is poured on top of the bamboo stick, which is then placed and fixed in the hole. Sprouted gram are placed in cups in front of the pole and allowed to germinate.

Formal Announcement of the Marriage

Both families inform the paternal and maternal grandparents of the alliance, thus showing respect for the elders. The parents of the bride and groom do this while they are seated on a seat made from palm leaves, set on a 'kolam' (decorative designs drawn in the center of their respective homes with coloured rice flour).

Registering the Marriage

Three days prior to the marriage, both families go to their respective family temples to register the marriage details. The couple is then accepted as a unit of the temple. The temple staff brings sacred ash and garlands to commemorate this registration. The garlands are very important, as these are the ones, which are used for the actual wedding ceremony.

Padaipu

Also, known as 'koodai akki unmuthal', this ritual is performed in honour of the ancestors. Food is cooked and offered to the ancestors and then eaten by family members.

Manai Poduthal

With the help of a mason, married women help in constructing this brick platform. Wooden seats are placed on this platform and the couple is made to sit on this during different rituals during the wedding.

Arasanikkal

In the home of the bride, the relatives tie the bamboo stick, decorated earlier (during the erecting of the 'pandaal') in front of the marriage platform. This is said to represent the presence of a king at the wedding.

Lighting the Lamp

Next to the 'arasanikkal', a pole is tied horizontally from which a traditional lamp is hung. This is lit on the morning of the wedding and extinguished only after all the ceremonies are over.

This indicates a future full of brightness and prosperity for the newly weds.

Mattru Kattuthal

A cloth ceiling is made to cover the top of the marriage platform, which acts as a protective cover for the couple.

Kolam

All the ladies from both families decorate the homes with colourful designs made from rice flour paste.

Receiving the 'taali'

The groom's family members come to the bride's home to receive the sacred 'taali', bringing along with them auspicious gifts.

Minji

The groom's toes are adorned with silver toe rings called 'minji' by his maternal uncle.

Receiving Garlands from the Temples

Family members bring the auspicious garlands from the temples patronized by both families and hand them over to the bride's family. These garlands are used in the marriage rituals.

Stringing of the Necklace to be Worn by the Groom

Two elders belonging to the groom's family string various gold pendants together for the groom's auspicious necklace. He will wear this ornament for the wedding ceremonies.

Pooram Kazhithal

The bride is bathed early morning and then adorned with golden chains. Neem leaves are placed on her head, shoulders, waist, and feet, and later removed with a stick. The purohit conducts the 'Vinayaka Puja', after which the bride bathes again. This bath is known as the 'Kanni Neeradal' (virgin bath). The 'arasanikkal' is decorated with kolams during this ceremony.

Thumbu Pidithal

The centre of the house is decorated with 'kolam' in the shape of a 'gopuram' (dome). This is to invoke the presence of God.

Adorning the Bridal Couple with Jewels

This ceremony is observed separately in both homes. The maternal uncles of the bride and the groom adorn them with gold jewellery.

Azhagu Arathi

Just before the groom leaves for the bride's home, his paternal grandmother performs the traditional 'arathi' for him and rubs sacred ash on his forehead, bidding him farewell.

Welcoming the Groom

The bride's family brings gifts, auspicious items and a ring placed on a large platter for the groom. The procession is accompanied with the playing of the 'nadeswaram'. The groom is then escorted to a 'Pillaiyar' (Ganesha temple) for a prayer before proceeding to the marriage venue. The groom's mother also carries gift items for the bride, along with the auspicious 'taali'

Poovai Arithal

The groom is brought in a procession, accompanied with the playing of the 'nadeswaram', to the front of the house. The bride's paternal aunt accompanies the bride till she walks up to the groom, and the bride's brothers shower her with flowers. She stands on the 'kolam' in front of the house and her paternal grandmother or aunt performs the traditional 'aarthi' for her.

Bhagavanam

The Brahmin or 'pujari' conducts separate 'Vinayaka' or Ganesha Pujas for the bride and the groom. Each of the maternal uncles puts a silver coin on a red cloth along with a piece of turmeric and ties it on the right wrists of the bride and the groom. These bracelets are called 'kappus'. The elders of the family then bless the couple by showering flowers on them.

Arimna Iduthal

The sprouted grains from the 'arasanikkal' are showered on the couple denoting a life full of happiness and prosperity.

Poomanam Iduthal

Family and friends bless the couple by touching them on the wrists, elbows and shoulders with flowers dipped in milk. This ritual is repeated three times.

Saptapathy

The couple goes around the sacred fire seven times while the 'pujari' chants the marriage rites.

Blessing the Sacred 'Taali'

After the tying of the 'kappus' the 'taali' is brought on a platter and all the elders present, bless it.

Thiru Pootuthal

The bride wears the clothes brought by the groom's mother and stands on the platform facing east with the groom standing in front of her. The groom offers a prayer, smears sacred ash from the temple on his forehead and applies the same on his bride, after which he garlands her with the sacred temple garland. He then takes the 'taali' from an elder of the family and ties the first two knots around the bride's neck. Generally, the groom ties the first two knots and his sister ties the last one. Turmeric and 'kumkum' are smeared on the 'taali' and the three knots. The bride places rice and coconut on a platter and the couple exchange garlands three times. They, then take the blessings of the elders.

Isaivu Pidimanam

After the 'taali' is tied, the fathers of the bride and the groom sit in the hall and sign the marriage agreement; this is called 'isaivu pidimanam' and only after this is the marriage truly official. The agreement is made by the 'pujari'.

Thirupootu Ceremony

The bride is welcomed into the marital home by her husband's sister or mother who conducts the following ceremony: Seven cups are kept on a platter filled with fruits, betel leaves, turmeric, sacred ash, rice, salt, tamarind and cotton. A measure is filled with paddy and on top either a brinjal or betel leaf is kept. This is known as 'nirai nazi'. Water is kept in a vessel with a nozzle. The bride is made to stand facing east. The person conducting the ceremony touches the seven cups three times, and puts sacred ash on herself and then on the bride. Thus, after doing this twenty-one times, the bride is given a betel leaf, and water is poured on it. The person conducting the ceremony touches the leaf to her forehead. This is a welcome for the bride to her new home. The bride also performs 'padapuja' for the mother-in-law (washes her mother-in-law's feet).

Kalyana Vevu and Mama Vevu

The maternal uncle's family brings gifts, normally 5, 7 or 9 in number for the bride. This is considered their contribution towards the marriage.

Manavarai

The 'vevu' is followed by the 'manavarai'. Literally translated 'mana' is the wooden seat and 'varai' means groom. Both the maternal uncles escort the couple to a wooden seat. A 'pujari' performs the Ganesha puja, 'Kumbharapana' puja with sacred fire (puja of the coloured and decorated pot), 'navagraha' puja (puja of the nine planets). The relatives bless the couple. The couple is fed with thickened milk and bananas. To indicate that the bride begins her wifely duties on the marriage day itself, another small ceremony is held. She touches the groom's head with oil, soap nut powder and water. He also repeats this for her. After this she serves him food which consists of rice, 'dal' (lentils), ghee (clarified butter), all of which the groom should taste. She then pours water for him to wash his hands—in some cases she serves him the meal on a banana leaf and eats out of the same leaf. To indicate that from, henceforth, they share everything equally they exchange garlands three times—this is done with the help of the maternal uncle. The bride's maternal uncle gives the groom money for his return journey.

The Turmeric Bath

After all the ceremonies are over, the couple change into ordinary clothes and seat themselves on the wooden seat and oil is applied to both separately. This is followed by a bath after which, they wear new clothes given to them by their respective in-laws. The turmeric bath signifies cooling of the bodies after having gone through so many functions.

Kulam Vazhum Pillai

In the groom's home, the 'kulam vazhum pillai' (small silver statue of a baby) is kept in a water pot. The bride and groom circle the pot and pick up the statue. An 'arathi' is performed with turmeric water; the 'kappu' is removed and the bride's toes are adorned with a 'minji'. All this is done by the groom's mother who then adorns the bride's hand with her own bangle and slips the traditional toe ring worn by married women on her second toe. The significance of this function is to hand over the household responsibilities to the bride. The bride and the groom stand on the 'kolam' and the paternal grandmother performs the 'arathi'. The women folk of the house prepare 'pongal' (a dish made from rice, lentils and jaggery) in front of the house and this is offered to the bride on 3 plantain leaves. On one, there is a coconut plant, on the second, there is a writing instrument, and on the third, there is water. This is done as an acceptance of the bride as a new daughter-in-law.

Thumbu Kattudal

The bride is made to stand on the wooden seat and the mother, sister or aunt of the groom tie the 'thumbu' string (matrimonial thread) around her neck. She is then fed with food brought from her mother's house. Visiting relatives eat fruit and milk and gifts are given to the couple by one and all.

Kaichi Utrrudal

Once all the functions are completed the bride's maternal family hosts a feast in honour of her marital family, which is known as 'kaichi uttrudal'.

Removal of the 'Arasanikkal'

After all the functions are over, the bride's father removes the 'arasanikkal' and takes the sprouts covered in a silk cloth to a nearby tank or lake and immerses them. This ritual is performed to the sounding of the conch. This marks the end of all formal ceremonies of the traditional Tamil Chettiar wedding.

TAMIL IYENGAR (BRAHMIN) WEDDING

A very large community, the Tamil Iyengars (Ayyangars) are

known for their superior intellect, high levels of education and good looks. This community is largely based in Tamil Nadu and Karnataka. Being Brahmins, their wedding rituals are long and elaborate and a typical wedding can last for four or five days. For most ceremonies, two 'Pujaris' officiate—one representing the bride's family and the other the groom's. There are bound to be variations in the ceremonies and rituals depending upon the city or state the Iyengars have been living in for several generations.

Vethalepak

This is a kind of engagement ceremony where the bride and groom exchange saris, suits and gifts. The bride goes to the groom's home carrying a platter laden with two silver lamps, a coconut, fruits and flowers. After the exchange of gifts, she leaves the platter behind and goes back home.

Pandalkal or Chapra

An auspicious beginning to any Iyengar wedding commences with purifying the marriage 'pandol' (canopy). The 'pandol' is made of leaves and branches of trees and it is purified by pouring milk, saffron and 'kumkum' (vermilion) on the base of the bamboo poles placed at its corners. The purification ritual is performed by a 'pujari' or any respected elder of the family who is well versed with the rituals of marriage.

Devar Samardhne

This ceremony is also known as 'perumal thadhyaradhne' and is a puja performed on the morning of the wedding day by the bride and groom separately in their homes. The deities are invoked to bless the marriage proceedings and keep all the rituals free from obstacles.

Varapooje or Janwaasam

On the evening prior to the wedding, the first function is 'mapillai azaizsu' (literally, heralding the arrival of the groom and his party). The groom and his family are garlanded by members of the bride's family and are served refreshments and allowed to rest before the 'varapooje' or 'janwaasam' (puja performed to honour the groom). The groom is ceremoniously led to the marriage 'mantap' and the pujari reads aloud the 'lagna patrike', announcing to the audience the antecedents and credentials of both the families.

Nischathartham

This ceremony is performed as a commitment to the forthcoming wedding and announced to the community. Five 'sumangalis' (married ladies) pound a handful of 'urad dal' (lentils) on a dry grinding stone decorated with flowers, kumkum and turmeric. This is done symbolically to wish the couple a happy married life. A room is filled with stainless steel cooking vessels, silverware, kitchen gadgets, linen, towels and other items the couple would need to run an efficient home. This display is called 'bidadi mane' by the Iyengars belonging to Mysore and 'sheer' by the Iyengars from Chennai. The Chennai Iyengars display the 'sheer' on the morning of the wedding day.

Nandi or Vratham

This ritual is held separately in both homes and usually in the morning. It is the commencement of all marriage rituals, where the groom's hair is anointed with oil and he bathes with soap-nut powder. The bride goes through a similar ritual in her home and after her bath, changes into a new sari, wears flowers in her hair and jewellery and is made to sit down for the 'muth aarthi'—a traditional 'aarthi' performed for her with a lighted 'diya' (lamp), 'kumkum' and flowers.

Kashiyathre

Just before the main wedding ceremony, the groom dresses himself as a pilgrim by wearing a 'veshti' (simple white dhoti), 'chappals' (slippers), carries an umbrella, walking stick and makes an attempt to proceed to Kashi (sacred pilgrimage site in the city of Benaras) to take 'sanyas' and lead a celibate life! The bride's father prevails upon him to give up this line of thought and accept his daughter's hand in marriage instead. After much cajoling, the groom relents and returns to the 'mantap' to be married!

Oonjal or Sambandhmale

The groom enters the 'mantap' discarding his pilgrim's 'avatar' (form) and is garlanded by the bride. He in turn garlands her and, then the couple is seated on a decorated 'jhula' or swing.

'Aarthi' is performed for them and the bride's father washes the groom's feet.

Piddishuttal

While the bride and groom are seated on the decorated swing, rice dipped in turmeric and 'kumkum' are showered on them to drive away evil. After this, they enter the marriage 'mantap'.

Kanyadaan

In Chennai, the Iyengars follow the ritual where the bride and groom hold hands and enter the 'mantap' whereas the Iyengars from Mysore have a custom where the bride and groom have to hold the hand of their respective mothers-in-law. The bride is seated in her father's lap all through the 'kanyadaan' ceremony. The couple together holds a coconut dipped in turmeric and the bride's mother pours water onto the coconut. All through the 'kanyadaan', the 'vollagam' (clarinet like instrument) is played accompanied by the 'tabla' (Indian drum).

Mangalaya Dharane

The sacred 'taali' (a small inscribed gold ornament, strung on a yellow thread) is kept on a silver platter along with a piece of jaggery, rice, a coconut and a heavy nine yard Kanjeevaram sari which is given by the groom's mother to the bride. This platter is taken around to all the guests for their blessings. The bride changes in to the nine-yard sari, wearing it in the 'katche seera' style and returns to the 'mantap'. Amongst Vedic chants, the groom ties the first knot of the 'taali' around the bride's neck and his sisters tie the other two knots.

Akshathe

All the elders present at the wedding are given coloured rice, which they shower on the couple after the 'mangalaya dharane'. The bride's mother gives the groom a 'paan' or betel leaf to proclaim her support of the marriage. The groom slips silver toe-rings on his bride symbolizing that henceforth he will look after and protect her.

Homa or Havan

The 'pujari' lights the sacred fire in honour of the nine planets and the gathering keeps the fire ignited by pouring 'ghee' (clarified butter) into it. The fire is not allowed to go off till all the ceremonies are completed.

Saptapadi

The groom's 'shalu' (shawl) is tied to the bride's sari 'pallav' and the couple takes the seven steps around the fire, repeating their seven marital vows.

Nagoli Vasthra

The bride's family, who present him with a suitcase, new clothes, and a diamond ring, gives the groom a ceremonial welcome.

Grupravesha

On the bride's arrival, an 'aarthi' is performed for her at the doorstep by her mother-in-law and she takes her first step into her new home by tipping over a small heap of rice with her right foot. She must ensure that the rice spills as far as possible, bringing prosperity into her new home! She is then taken to the family 'puja' room where she prostrates before the deity and is given a silver or gold coin which she puts into a silver pot filled with water.

Sambandhi Virandh

To celebrate the successful completion of the wedding the families of the bride and groom exchange lavish gifts. These gifts can range from jewellery, clothes or electronic items—depending on how much each family is willing to spend.

Reception

The reception is not mandatory for the Tamil Iyengar community, though many families do opt for it these days. Friends and relatives are invited to meet the newly-weds and the families' host a grand dinner in a hotel or marriage hall.

TAMIL IYER BRAHMIN WEDDING

An Iyer or Ayyar marriage is a mixture of Vedic ritual and Tamil customs. First, the horoscopes of the perspective bride and groom are matched. Then, an understanding arrived at about assets, jewellery, household goods and other articles to be given to the bride by her parents. Finally, an auspicious day is fixed by the priest for the marriage. Among the non-Vedic rites observed is the tying of the 'taali' around the bride's neck by the bridegroom. This is the most important ceremony in a Tamil Iyer Brahmin wedding.

Janam Kundli

The preliminaries for a Tamil Iyer wedding begin with the matching of the horoscopes of the bride and groom. Once these are matched, an auspicious time is chosen when the bride's family invites the groom's family to come and meet the bride and discuss the marriage details. Once all the preliminaries are taken care of, the engagement follows.

Nischaiyahtartham

Though, the Tamil Brahmins (Iyers and Iyengars) basically follow the same rituals and customs there are slight variations. For instance, the engagement ceremony in the case of the Iyers takes place in the groom's residence, whereas, the Iyengars follow the custom of hosting it in the bride's home. A 'pujari' (Brahmin priest) writes what is known as the 'lagna patrika' specifiying the date, time and venue of the marriage and this serves as a sort of commitment for both families. The bride's family brings fruits and sweetmeats and the groom's people in turn serve them snacks and dinner and present a sari to the bride.

Kalyanam

The bride's family arrives at the marriage venue or 'kalyanamandappam' one day prior to the wedding. The venue is decorated with 'kolams' (attractive designs made with rice powder paste) and flowers. In readiness for the arrival of the groom and his family, the bride's family keeps 'chandan' (sandalwood paste), 'kumkum' (vermilion), rose water, sugar candy, garlands and a platter for the 'aarthi' (traditional welcoming ritual). A vessel containing 'thiraattupal' (condensed and sweetened milk) is also kept ready for the groom's mother. On the groom's arrival, the 'nadeshwaram' (traditional wind instrument) is played and the 'aarthi' is performed in his honour.

Vratham

This ceremony is performed separately for the bride and groom at the marriage venue. The rituals followed for the groom are far more elaborate than those for the bride. Sacred yellow thread is tied on the wrists of the bride and groom and they are not permitted to leave the marriage venue. The 'palika' ceremony (sprinkling of nine varieties of grains) for the prosperity of the couple's new life together is conducted simultaneously with the 'vratham'. To culminate the function, an 'aarthi' is performed.

Janavasam and Nischaiyartham

This is a very important aspect of the marriage where any differences between the families are sorted out. This ceremony takes place in a temple. The bride's family brings turmeric, betel leaves, nuts and clothes for the groom. The bride's brother then garlands the groom, and sugar candy is distributed to all present. The groom is then escorted to a decorated car and the family leaves in a procession for the 'mandapam'. Once the procession reaches the marriage venue, the bride is led outside by her close friends to get a glimpse of her future husband! 'Aarthi' is performed and a coconut broken to ward off evil. The groom is then led to the 'medai' (an elevated place in the 'mandapam' where all the ceremonies are performed). Members of both families sit opposite each other and a 'lagna patrika' (marriage contract) is written and read aloud by the 'pujari'. 'Thamboolams' (platters of betel nuts, dry fruits, nuts, coconuts, turmeric and 'kumkum') and gifts are exchanged. The cone shaped 'parupputhengai' (a special sweetmeat) is an important part of all these ceremonies.

Wedding Arrangements

Early morning on the wedding day, the bride's family sends toiletries, a mirror, a basket filled with sweetmeats and a 'nadeshwaram' to the groom's family. The groom's aunt brings a dish of 'appams' (pancakes made from rice flour and jaggery) for this occasion. The 'pujaris' usually tie the traditional 'dhoti' or 'panchakatcham' for the groom and apply 'vibhuti' or sacred ash in three horizontal lines on his forehead.

Kashi Yatra

Dressed in the traditional 'panchakatcham', holding an umbrella, a fan, a walking stick, and a towel containing 'dal' (lentils) and rice tied to his shoulder, the groom embarks on a mock pilgrimage. As he steps out of the 'mandapam', the bride's father pleads with him not to go to 'Kashi' (a sacred pilgrimage site in the city of Benaras) and marry his daughter instead. After much ado the groom accepts and returns to the 'mandappam' to get married!

Unjal

On entering the 'mandapam' the groom discards his walking stick and all the other paraphernalia and is garlanded by the bride. The groom in turn garlands the bride. The couple is then made to sit on a decorated swing and the women folk smear their feet with a little milk, 'kumkum' and 'chandan' (sandalwood paste). A pot of water and a lamp set inside a measure containing rice are carried by the bride's mother and other elderly ladies around the swing and the couple is fed a mixture of bananas, milk and sugar. After the traditional 'aarthi', the bride and groom are escorted for the next ceremony—the 'kanyadhan'.

Kanyadhan

Amidst the chanting of 'mantras' (Vedic chants), the 'pujari' ignites the sacred fire. The groom is gifted a 'muhurtha veshti' (a 4 metre long silk dhoti) and a 'pattu' (a 2 metre long silk fabric to be used as a stole). The bride is seated on her father's lap for the 'kanyadhan'. The bride and groom together hold a coconut dipped in turmeric, while the bride's mother pours water onto the coconut. This is the actual ritual of 'kanyadhan'.

Mangalyadharanam

The 'kanyadhan' is followed by the 'mangalyadharanam'. The 'taali' or 'mangalsutra' is placed on the bride's head along with a miniature piece of jewellery shaped like a yoke and the groom performs a 'puja' with 'kumkum' and flowers. He then, ties the first knot of the 'taali' around the bride's neck and his sister ties the other two.

Sapthapathi

The bride's sari 'pallav' and the groom's 'angavastram' (shawl) are tied in a knot and the couple hold hands. The groom places his foot under the bride's and helps her to take the seven steps around the fire. Then he, places the bride's foot on a grinding stone near the fire and slips silver rings or 'metti' on her toes. The couple is then shown the 'Dhruva Nakshatra' or Pole Star, a symbol of permanence and the 'Arundhati Nakshatra' or symbol of purity and virtue.

Laja Homam

The bride's brother slings a bagful of puffed rice or 'laja' over his shoulder and keeps giving fistfuls of it to his sister to offer as a sacrifice to the sacred fire. After this ritual, the couple circulate and are blessed by all present.

Sesha Homam

This is a symbolic ritual to invoke blessings for healthy offspring. The groom ties a thread around the bride's hip. This ceremony used to be performed just before the nuptials but these days it is a part of the marriage ceremony itself, so that the couple is ready for the wedding reception.

Gruhapravesam

If the grooms' family lives in the same town, the bride is taken to her new home and made to sit on a 'manai' (low wooden plank) and fed milk and bananas. Her in-laws, also, present her with a sari and she is asked to light the 'kuthuvailakku' (sacred lamp in the 'puja' room). If the groom's family does not live in the same town, this ceremony is performed in the 'mandapam' after completion of all the marriage rites.

Seer Bakshanam

The bride's parents prepare several sweets and savouries for the bride to take back with her to her husband's home. These are known as 'seer bakshanam' and are stored in decorated containers by the groom's family and later distributed amongst friends and relatives.

TAMIL MUDALIAR WEDDING

The Mudaliar community of South India follows a custom whereby, the prospective bridegroom's parents approach the bride-to-be's parents with a marriage proposal. On acceptance of the proposal, a memorandum is signed between both families and an auspicious day is fixed for the wedding. A typical Tamil Mudaliar wedding can last up to three days.

The Engagement

The engagement ceremony is formalized through a memorandum, which confirms the alliance. The groom's family presents the bride-to-be with a sari, some jewellery and 21 platters of fruits and dried fruits. The respective fathers of the bride and the groom sign this contract. During this ceremony, the auspicious date of the wedding is also finalized.

Pandakal

The wedding rituals commence with a Ganesha puja. A bamboo with an odd number of eyes is smeared with 'haldi' (turmeric) and 'kumkum' (vermilion) by nine 'sumangalis' (married ladies). This bamboo pillar is erected for the four legged 'pandaal'.

Nalangu

The bride is seated on a wooden plank on the dais. Underneath this plank a banana leaf filled with a handful of uncooked rice is spread. Three stools are placed in front of the bride; 'kumkum', sandalwood paste and rose water are placed on one stool, betel leaves, betel nut and flowers on the second, and a plate with 'arathi' (a mixture of lime and turmeric mixed in water which turns red) on the third. The married women (sumangalis) apply sandalwood paste on the bride's hands, put 'kumkum' on her forehead, sprinkle rose water on her and, also, perform an 'arathi', thus completing the beautification ceremony.

The Bridegroom's Reception

The bride's uncle or brother carries gifts for the groom to his home. The groom is then invited to marry the bride. 'Nalangu' is performed for the groom. The bridegroom is brought to the wedding venue in a decorated car. On arrival, he is received by ladies from the bride's family and 'arathi' is performed on him. The bride is brought separately, and the 'Nalangu' is performed for her as well.

Preparations on the Morning of the Wedding

The four legged 'pandaal' is now erected and decorated with banana tree stalks on all four corners, tender coconuts, mango leaves and flowers. Before sunrise on the wedding day, the bride and groom come to the marriage 'pandaal' separately. The elders of the family put gingely oil and green gram powder on the foreheads of the bride and the groom and smear turmeric on their hands. The clothes worn by the bride and groom at this time are given off to the 'dhobi' (washer man) after the completion of the ceremony. The bride and groom then have an oil bath to signify the beginning of a new life. A Ganesh puja marks the beginning of the wedding rituals.

Arsan Kal

'Arsan' means ruler, and 'kal' means standard. In the olden days, the king was invited to the wedding, thus setting an honourable standard for the ceremonies. To represent this, another bamboo stick is erected by five 'sumangalis' and all the honours are performed, like bathing the bamboo with milk, sandalwood paste and 'kumkum' and tying a silk scarf around it before performing the 'arathi'.

Padapuja and Kasi Yatra

The bridegroom washes the feet of his parents and takes their blessings. This is known as the 'padapuja'. A Ganesha 'puja' is performed and the 'upanayanam' (sacred white thread) is tied around the bridegroom's chest. The bridegroom then pretends to leave on a pilgrimage to become an ascetic. He is stopped by the bride's brother, who washes his feet, gives him an umbrella, a hand fan ('visiri') and slippers and requests him to come and marry his sister.

Mahalaxmi Puja

The bride performs 'puja' to the Goddess Laxmi, and then performs 'padapuja' for her parents to receive their blessings. The groom's family brings the wedding clothes for the bride and the groom along with the garlands. The bride and groom get dressed after this ceremony and proceed to the 'pandaal'.

Manai Pongal

The groom's parents cook rice in a clay pot while the bride and groom get dressed. On their return, the eldest 'sumangali' of the household greets them with garlands. The couple offers prayers to all the deities before entering the 'pandaal'. The sacred fire or 'omam' is then lit to act as a witness to the marriage.

Kanganam

A sacred yellow thread is tied around the wrists of the bride and the groom by the officiating 'pujari'.

Kanikadanam

The bride takes a coconut in her palms and her parents place her hands in those of the groom, symbolically handing her over to her husband.

Mangalyam

The 'mangalyam' is made out of gold in the shape of a tiger tooth. Legend has it that in the ancient days the bridegroom killed a tiger, pulled the tooth out and tied it round the neck of his bride, proving his valour. Strings of thread (strung 108 times) are dipped in 'haldi' (turmeric) and the gold pendant is strung on them. The groom has to tie the 'mangalyam' thread with three knots. 'Haldi' (turmeric) is placed on the knot and the groom presses his ring on this as a seal. This is done with the 'nadeshwaram' playing in the background, and the couple is blessed with the showering of rice dipped in turmeric, and flowers by all present at the ceremony.

Exchange of Garlands

The bride and groom exchange garlands three times. The mother-in-law and sisters-in-law or aunts tie a piece of gold on the bride's forehead to demonstrate her authority and relationship and repeat the same ritual for the groom.

Omam

The groom and his bride circle the sacred fire three times. The bride's brother gives them puffed rice, which they together offer into the 'omam'. After this ritual, the 'pujari' shows them the 'Arundhati' star so that they can be faithful to each other, since "Arundhati" the mythological Goddess was known for her chastity.

Sesha

A white bed sheet is opened and spread in front of the bride and the groom in the 'pandaal' and uncooked rice is placed on it. Elderly men of the family take handfuls of rice and drop them in front of the couple as a blessing.

Paying Homage to the Arasanikkal

The couple goes around the 'pandaal' three times followed by unmarried girls from the bride's family. When they return to the 'pandaal', the 'kanganam' is removed and this ritual is repeated with unmarried girls from the groom's family. In the olden days, this enabled parents with unmarried eligible sons to look for suitable brides for them. The bride then changes into a white sari, and the groom into a white 'veshti' (dhoti), and they sprinkle 'haldi' water on each other—this is primarily to 'break the ice!

Reception

On the evening of the wedding day, a reception is held where all friends and relatives of both families are invited to congratulate and bless the newly weds. The celebrations are replete with a grand dinner.

CHRISTIAN MARRIAGE CEREMONY

Pre-Marriage Ceremony

The fanfare of the Christian marriage begins with the engagement party. Engagement parties usually given by the bride's family often precede the Christian marriages. The "bridal shower," an informal party is organized by the bride's family or friends and consists of only women. Similarly, the groom enjoys the bachelor party or the stage party, which is hosted by him, the ushers or a friend. It takes place just before the wedding.

The Marriage Ceremony

Tradition demands that the bridegroom reach the church first and await his bride there. The best man—usually from the bridegroom's party—greets the bride with a kiss and her wedding bouquet. The procession to the church is usually in one of these ways: the Priest may greet the couple at the door of the church, bless them, and lead them in; or, the bride may proceed up to her waiting bridegroom at the altar on her father's arm; or and the bride may walk in alone to her bridegroom at the altar, preceded by first the pageboys and flower maids, the bridesmaid—best man pairs, and followed by a single bridesmaid carrying her veil.

The bridal couple kneels before the altar. While the basic celebration of the mass is as usual, there is usually a mention by the priest about the couple who intend to marry and that both of them should treat each other with love and respect. The nuptial section of the mass is well known. In the presence of two witnesses from either side, the groom and the bride declare their intention to take each other as man and wife with the famous lines "I, Y, take you, X, to be my lawfully wedded wife. I promise to be true to you in good times and in bad, in sickness and in health till death do us part," with bride repeating the phrases. The best man usually carries both the rings, which are handed over to the priest who then asks the couple to put them on each other's fourth finger of the left hand. This done, he blesses the couple and declares them as man and wife. And then we have the traditional wedding kiss.

Post-Marriage Ceremony

After the marriage ceremony, the bridal couple proceed either home or to a studio for a photographic session, or straight to the reception to celebrate their wedding.

NORTH INDIAN PROTESTANT CHRISTIAN WEDDING

Mangni

A priest officiates at the ceremony. The groom's family arrives at the bride's home with gifts for her, which include a sari, some jewellery and green glass bangles. The couple exchange rings, while the priest recites prayers.

Uptan

Powdered sandalwood and dried herbs are ground into a paste with jasmine oil and and applied to bride's face, arms, legs and feet. The bride may not leave the house after this ceremony and must certainly not meet the groom again till the wedding day. To the catchy rhythm of a 'dholak' (small drum), ladies sing traditional wedding songs.

Shagan

The groom's family brings gifts in the form of clothes, jewellery and green glass bangles for the bride; and the bride's family in turn presents the groom with a gift of clothes and perhaps a watch or gold chain.

Sangeet

Even, though, it is not a requirement, most families these days prefer to host a 'sangeet' party. It can be a simple gathering of family and close friends or as elaborate an affair as desired. The ladies sing traditional folk songs to the beat of the 'dholak' (small drum).

Holy Matrimony

The nuptials take place in a church usually in the late afternoon. Ushers seat guests separating those from the bride's side from the groom's on either side of the aisle. The groom accompanied by the Best Man takes his place near the altar. Her mother's brother receives the bride at the church entrance. He hands her over to her father who leads her inside the church, preceded by three priests, the flower girls and lastly the bridesmaids. The entire congregation stands up as the organ plays 'Here Comes the Bride'. The guests remain standing until the procession has passed to the front of the church and the bride is handed over to the groom.

The couple kneels before the altar. It is customary for two or three people close to the families to read sections of poetry meaningful to the couple. The priest begins the service with the recitation of The Intention (a reading of specially selected Psalms from the Holy Bible). The priest then asks the congregation if anyone has any objection to this marriage. A reading from the Scriptures follows and then the priest reads out the 13th Corinthians—a passage from the Holy Bible on love and commitment, a popular choice at all Christian weddings. The Best Man hands over the wedding rings to the priest for his blessings. The couple then exchanges marriage vows in English, Hindustani or Hindi as chosen by them. Wedding rings are exchanged and they are declared man and wife and the groom is allowed to kiss the bride—though, some Indian families do not favour the kiss, thinking it to be against Indian culture. Next, the couple proceeds to the vestry along with their parents and the priest to sign the church register.

The Reception

No Christian wedding is complete without the reception, hosted usually by the bride's parents and sometimes jointly with the groom's parents. It is often held immediately after the wedding. The bride may choose to change her attire for this celebration. The couple cuts the rich plum cake, so common to Christian weddings. The wedding reception is replete with the services of a live band playing music and Western style dancing. The dinner menu rarely deviates from the traditional 'yakhni pulao' (cooked lamb served with rice), chicken curry and fish!

Vidaai

If the groom and his family have come from another city, before they depart, the couple visits the bride's parents and bids farewell to all the bride's relatives. Prayers are offered and the couple receives blessings. The bride leaves with her trousseau and all her wedding gifts in a decorated car.

Guidelines for Interchurch Marriages in India

Many circumstances of life, and undoubtedly divine Providence itself, arrange that, at times, compatible members of different Churches develop a desire to be united in a permanent bond of marriage and ask their respective Churches for permission to do so. Since, by marriage both partners are united in love, each of them will respect the faith of the other and his or her belonging to a specific Christian community different from one's own. It is important, that the in-laws, too, share in that sense of respect for the faith of the partner of another Church, especially if she or he lives with them. In case of conflict of faith perceptions the matter should be discussed even before marriage so as to arrive at a vision which is acceptable to the conscience of both partners. At any rate, once married the partners must remember that the stability of the family is a primary obligation of both of them, and the fulfilment of other obligations should not threaten it.

When a mixed marriage is celebrated in the Catholic Church it is equally appropriate and advisable that, with the permission of the Bishop, a minister of the other Church be invited to participate in some way in the celebration, like reading from the Scriptures, giving the sermon and/or blessing the couple.

SIKH WEDDING

Sikhism is a monotheistic religion opposed to idol worship and is against the practice of asceticism, the caste system and ritualism. A Sikh wedding is called an Anand Karaj. The ceremony takes place in the presence of the Sikh Holy Book and Guru, the Guru Granth Sahib. The marriage ceremony consists of the recitation of the Anand Sahib (therefore called Anand Karaj) and the Lavan (wedding songs), which are sung as the couple go around the Guru Granth Sahib.

Thaka or Roka

Once, both families have agreed to the alliance, the groom, with his close relatives goes to the bride's family for the formal announcement. This is an indication to the community, that the couple is spoken for and they will receive no more offers of marriage. A respected member of the family offers the 'Ardaas' (prayer). The groom's mother presents a gift to her prospective daughter-in-law and the bride's parents give the groom's parents a 'shagan' (token gift), usually in the form of money and some sweetmeats.

Mangni, Sagaai or Kudmai

The formal 'asking' of the bride's hand in marriage by the groom's family is known as the 'mangni'. The groom's female relatives go the bride's home laden with a complete ensemble of fine clothes, accessories, jewellery and toiletries. The bride will wear the clothes, jewellery and accessories for the 'mangni' ceremony. The groom arrives with his family and close friends at the venue· refreshments are served after which the ceremony commences with prayers and 'kirtan' (singing of hymns) in the presence of the Guru Granth Sahib.

The bride's mother presents a silver 'thaal' (platter), laden with the symbols of the Sikh faith, sweetmeats, saffron and flowers to the groom. He may, also, receive gifts like a watch, money or a gold chain at this time. The groom slips the engagement ring on the bride's finger and she reciprocates. The groom's family receives gifts in the form of money, sweetmeats, dried fruit and fruit to take back with them. Depending upon the time of day, a high tea, lunch or dinner will be served and not necessarily vegetarian.

Shri Akhand Path

It is the continuous reading of the Guru Granth Sahib, the Holy Book of the Sikhs. This auspicious, uninterrupted reading of the Guru Granth Sahib, over a period of forty-eight hours signifies the centrality of the Guru as the Holy Book in worship and in community life. A relay of readers, either from the 'gurudwara' or from within the family and friends, is organized and vigil is kept through the night for, on no account must there be a break in the recitation of the Holy Book once it commences. This prayer marathon takes place separately in the homes of both bride and groom a few days before the wedding. At the conclusion of the reading, hymns are sung and then all those present stand up for the 'ardaas'. The bride, groom and their families are blessed. The Holy Book is opened at random and a verse read out which is regarded as the 'hukam' (divine message). 'Karah Parshaad' (a delicious sweet made from whole wheat flour, 'ghee' or clarified butter and sugar) is blessed first then served to all those present.

Sangeet

Punjabi celebrations typically comprise of 'gaana, bajaana, khana, peena, (singing, dancing, eating, drinking!). Family and friends sing to the catchy beat of the 'dholak' (small drum) making sure several songs are sung to tease the bride's mother-in-law and other members of the groom's family! In a lot of urban communities, the 'sangeet' is a mixed party held at night, hosted separately by both families on two consecutive evenings. Dinner is served and the celebrations could well continue till the wee hours of the next morning.

Bridal Mehendi

This is an intimate ceremony, mainly for the ladies in the family and the bride's and the bridegrom's friends. The 'mehendi' (henna) is passed around to all present for their blessings and each one leaves a few rupees in the platter. 'Mehendi' is then smeared on the palms of the bride after which she reaches back and leaves the impressions of her palms on the wall behind her. These days a protective sheet of paper is pasted on the wall! The henna is quickly washed off and then the professional henna artists or 'mehendiwallis' take over by decorating the palms of the bride and her friends. The bride's 'mehendi' can take upto hours for the intricate patterns to be drawn and then left to dry to achieve a deep red colour. A simple 'mehendi' ceremony is conducted for the groom at his home. The 'mehendi' is passed around to all to be blessed, then smeared onto his palms and quickly washed off! The women in his family may call in a professional 'mehendi' artist to decorate their palms. In both the homes the ladies sing and dance to the beat of the 'dholak'.

Chooda

On the night before the wedding, the groom's mother sends the 'kuvaar dhoti' (the last ensemble she will wear as a maiden) to the bride. After the ritual application of 'vatnaan' (turmeric and sandalwood paste), the bride bathes with water fetched from a neighbour's house in a decorated vessel carried by the womenfolk who sing songs of blessing. She then removes any bangles she is wearing and wears the 'kuvaar dhoti'. In the presence of the Guru Granth Sahib, a brief prayer is said.

Her mother's brother and his wife ('mama and mami') then adorn her wrists with the traditional ivory wedding bangles (these days ivory may be replaced with plastic or acrylic). The bangles are always uneven in number and are blessed by five ladies in the family who have been happily married for a long time. The bride also wears a steel bangle or 'kada' on each wrist onto which her family and friends tie the 'kaleeran' or dangling golden baubles; symbols of good luck!

Sehrabandhi and Ghodi

A symbolic application of turmeric and sandalwood paste precedes the groom's ritual bath. The 'sehra' or veil of golden threads is taken around to each member of the family to be blessed. His sisters tie the 'sehra' onto his turban. The 'sarbala' (a young boy, usually a nephew of the groom or sister's husband) will act as his constant companion and be with him until the wedding ceremony is over. The groom is escorted to the richly caparisoned mare; the mare's attendant feeds her horse gram and the groom and the 'sarbala' mount the mare.

The groom's brother's wife applies a touch of 'kajal' (kohl) to the groom's eyes to ward off the evil eye and his sisters and female cousins braid the bridle with 'vagaan' (golden tassels) for which they receive gifts from the groom's mother. The women sing 'seheras' or traditional songs appropriate to the ceremony. The groom is now ready to proceed to the bride's home for the wedding ceremony.

Milni

The 'baraat' (groom's party) arrives at the venue and is greeted by the male relatives from the bride's family to the singing of 'Hum Ghar Saajan Aaye' a hymn giving thanks for being blessed by the arrival of the gracious folk. The 'Ardaas' is said. The bride's father greets the groom's father by garlanding him and is garlanded in return. All the male relatives of the bride greet their counterparts in the groom's family in sequence, in like manner.

Anand Karaj or Lavan Phera

The 'Anand Karaj' or wedding ritual takes place at 'anand vela' (early morning, usually associated with peace and tranquility). In case, the ceremony begins a little later, it must conclude before noon. In the presence of the Guru Granth Sahib, a normal Morning Prayer service is conducted, after which the 'Asa di Vaar' (the morning hymn) is sung.

The bride, is escorted in by her father or uncle, her sisters and girlfriends and seated on the left of the groom. Since, the Sikhs do not have an ordained clergy, a respected member of the community or gurudwara may conduct the ceremony. The officiator of the ceremony asks the bride, groom and their parents to stand for the 'Ardaas', after which they all bow down to the Holy Book in assent of the marriage. The bride's father places a corner of the bride's veil or 'pallav' in the groom's hands and over his shoulder into the bride's hands, symbolically connecting them and giving his daughter away in marriage. The groom then leads the bride four times around the Holy Book, each round interspersed with hymns containing blessings and advice. The ceremony concludes with the 'Ardaas' and is followed by the 'vaak' (Guru's counsel). This is done by opening the Holy Book at random and reading out a verse from the page on the right. 'Karah Parshaad' is distributed and the couple is garlanded.

Doli

The groom lifts the bride's veil and seeing her as a married woman for the first time her family blesses her with money. She changes into a set of clothes and jewellery brought by the groom's parents. She feeds the male members of her own family with cooked rice and turning her back on them throws back handfuls of puffed rice, invoking a blessing of prosperity on her father and family. She then bids a tearful farewell to her family and friends—a very emotional moment in any Indian wedding. Her father seats her in the decorated car alongside her husband and her brother escorts her to her new home.

On reaching the marital home, the groom's mother, who pours a little oil outside on the doorstep before they enter, receives the couple. She then attempts to drink water from a 'lota' (steel jar), but the groom prevents her! After the third attempt he relents and she drinks it. This is repeated with six other female relatives.

Doli Dinner

The groom's family and close friends get together the night the bride arrives for the 'doli' dinner. Literally translated 'doli' means palanquin. As a courtesy, they may invite the bride's family and her guests who have come from out of town. This may be a very quiet evening with a home-cooked meal, or a full-fledged celebration with caterers called in and exuberant singing and dancing

Reception

The groom's parents usually host the wedding reception. It is a formal party, presenting the newly wed couple to their extended family and friends. A military band is often requested to play elegant marches and classical tunes during this celebration. The wedding reception is an import from the West.

Phera

This visit is made a day after the wedding, if the bride and groom are leaving to live in another city. Otherwise, it may be made whenever convenient. The couple visits the bride's paternal home and receives gifts and blessings.

JAIN WEDDING CEREMONY

A typical jain marriage initiates with "Vagdana", wherein, the parents of the bride and groom declare the intention to marry them, after which, the "Pradana" takes place, where the bride is gifted with ornaments. Then, the mandap and the vedi are made ready—"Mandapa-vedi-Pratishtha" and also the ornament is installed in a ceremony called "Torana Pratishtha."

The "Vara Ghoda" is taken out, wherein, the groom rides the horse. Upon reaching the destination the "Torana Vidhi" rites of welcoming is performed, which includes "Gotra Occhara", reciting of the genealogies or gotra. Then, the bride and groom are allowed to take a look at each other's faces in a ceremony called "Paraspara Mukh Avalokana" after which the "Varmala" garlanding ceremony takes place and vows are taken in "Vara Pratijna." Then, the couple goes round the fire in "Agni Pradakshina" and the bride's father gives her away in "Kanyadaan."

Thereafter comes the "Deva Shastra Guru Puja", wherein, the Jina, Scriptures and Gurus are worshipped. The knot is then tied between the bride and groom's dresses in "Granthi Bandhana" after which the "Panigrahana" ceremony takes place where the groom holds the bride's hand and takes seven steps "Sapta Padi." The couple then seeks "Ashirvada", blessing from the elders present, after, which the bride comes to her own new house which is called "Sva Graha Aagamana." Lastly, suitable donations are made to the temples, institutes in "Jina Grahe Dhan Arpana."

BUDDHIST WEDDING

Buddhist marriage is very traditional, simple and does not include lot of complicated rituals.

Pre-Marriage Ceremony

Once the horoscope of the boy and the girl match, the family of the groom consult the lama for an auspicious day for proposing the marriage. After consulting the lama (priest), the groom's family chooses an auspicious day to visit the bride's house to ask her parents for their daughter's hand in marriage. "Chessian" is the betrothal ceremony. The maternal uncle of the parent of the bride sit on a raised platform and the lama, or the priest, recites a prayer and distributes a religious drink, "madyan," among those present. The date of marriage is fixed in consultation with the astrologer.

Marriage Ceremony

The marriage ceremony is a very private affair and only very close family friends are invited. A Buddhist lama (priest) presides over the wedding. The wedding ceremony is conducted at the bride's home. The lama leads the couple through the religious rites that include the groom's family offering the mother of the bride the price of milk. After the religious rites, the couple is declared as man and wife. Then depending on the horoscope, the bride accompanies her husband to her new house either on the same day, or the next day.

Post-Marriage Ceremony

At her husband's house she is received by her mother-in-law. A feast is then arranged.

PARSI MARRIAGE CEREMONY

In Parsi community, there is a belief that God revealed to Zarathushtra, the prophet, that, not only is marriage a righteous act, but, it is also a commitment, which makes even the earth rejoice.

Wedding Attire

The Parsi groom wears a traditional white overcoat "dugli," white cotton pants and a hat called "pughdi" or "fetah" especially designed for the occasion. The bride is usually dressed in a white sari embroidered with silver or gold. Her head is partially covered. White is regarded as a symbol of purity in Zoroastrianism. The groom's parents generally gift the jewellery worn by the bride.

Pre-Marriage Ceremony

The engagement ceremony begins by the groom's side gifting a red sari (Adravadu), jewellery and accessories to the bride. The bride's family goes to the groom's house with gifts such as clothes, etc. Inside the groom's home, both the bride and the groom are made to stand on a wooden plank with a "rangoli" design. The bride's mother puts a "tilak" on the groom's forehead, garlands him and offers a coconut to him. Then rings are exchanged.

Mandav Saro

"Mandav Saro" is a Parsi ritual, which is performed four days prior to the marriage ceremony. A flowerpot with a mango plant, planted in it is kept in the house. The flowerpot is placed above a rangoli design. Then a square with a cross in center is drawn on the wall with "haldi" (turmeric) and "kumkum" paste. A plate is decorated with coconut, curd, sugar, betelnut, kharak, a little packet (pudi) of small green and red motis and coins. All these ingredients along with milk, water and a 1.50 paise coin is put into the flowerpot after removing the mango plant. A coconut is circled seven times around the pot and then smashed against the wall or ground. Everyone prays that the marriage should take place peacefully.

Naha

On the eve of the marriage, the bride and groom take a religious bath or "Naha" who bathe with consecrated water drawn from the well in a Fire Temple—"Nirang" or consecrated Bulls urine, which has to be sipped, and a pomegranate leaf which has to be chewed and spat out. The Parsi priest stands outside the door of the bathroom and instructs the candidate. The "Nirang" is to purify the body while the pomegranate leaf is to imbibe wisdom, the fruit being a symbol for wisdom. After the holy bath, the bridal couple dress for the occasion until its time to go on the wedding platform.

The Achu Michu Ritual

This ritual is performed to purify the mind and body of the bridal couple. Female members of the respective families carry two silver platters each containing the following items. The first tray (Achu Michu) contains the following items: egg (symbolizing life giving force), coconut (symbolizing inner and outer worlds), betel leaf and areca nut (symbolizing suppleness and strength), unshelled almond (symbolizing virtue and honesty), dried date (symbolizing resilience), sugar crystal or sugar biscuit (symbolizing sweetness), dry rice (symbolizing abundance), rose petals (symbolizing happiness), a glass of water (symbolizing purity, sanctity and perfection). The second tray contains the following items: silver cone (symbolizing the mountain of sweetness from which good spirits are believed to descend), coconut (symbolizing the inner and outer worlds), grains of rice or wheat (symbolizing abundance), vermilion (symbolizing the receptacle of holiness), sugar crystals (symbolizing sweetness), green leaves (symbolizing nourishment), pomegranate (symbolizing immorality), pistachio nuts (symbolizing firmness), silver and gold coins (symbolizing wealth), garland of flowers (symbolizing joy).

The bride's mother then performs the ceremony. The bride's mother takes an egg in her right hand from the "Achu Michu" tray, rotates it seven times in a clockwise manner over the groom's head and breaks it on a stone placed to the right of the groom's feet. Then the bridegroom's mother takes the betel leaf, areca nut, dried date, and almond and sugar crystal in her right hand and rotates it seven times in a clockwise manner over the groom's head. Then the coconut is rotated over the groom's head and broken on the stone placed to the right of the groom's feet. Afterwards, a few grains of rice and rose petals are taken out of the tray, while water is sprinkled on the remaining rice and rose petals and the tray is once again rotated over the groom's head. The mixture is cast down on both sides of the groom's feet. A handful of dry rice is showered over the groom as a token of invoking blessings. The groom is garlanded and given a fresh coconut to hold. A vertical "tilak" is applied to his forehead in vermilion. The groom then steps onto the stage with his right foot and awaits the arrival of his bride. The bride also goes through the same rituals as undergone earlier by the groom. Upon the completion of all the preliminary rituals, the bride steps onto the stage and is seated opposite the groom.

Marriage Ceremony

Once the bridal couple is seated opposite each other on the stage, a white cloth is held between them so that they cannot see each other. The bride's family makes a bundle of two threads entwined. This is offered to the priest, who holds both the right hands of the couple beneath the cloth and makes seven rounds of thread on their hands. Family members who are married hold this thread from the right and seven rounds are taken on the stage while the priest chants prayers. The couples then throw some rice on one another and then the cloth is removed. The couple then sits facing east and then the priest asks in Persian three times "Do you wish to marry this man/woman" and the couple have to say "Pasande Kardum." After completion of the blessing, rings are exchanged and the priest declares that the couple are officially married and the groom kisses the bride.

Post-Marriage Ceremony

The first task, after the marriage ceremony, is to legalise the marriage. A representative from the office of the Registrar of Marriages is invited as an honoured guest to stay for the marriage feast. The young couple signs the documents of marriage registration and the official seal is then stamped on the paper. After this, the couple head straight for the Fire Temple to offer prayer and take blessings of the God. And, then, the couple attends the reception party. After the party, the bride and the bridegroom leave for home separately guarding a "diya" in a small silver container. The bridegroom reaches home first and carefully places the "diya" on the sidetable in the bedroom. The bride is then accompanied by her aunt or other female relatives and she also guards the flame and on reaching home to her impatiently waiting husband places the lamp next to his in the bedroom. And, this culminates the marriage.

JEWISH WEDDING

Jewish Talmudic law provided for three methods of establishing a marriage. All three had to be performed in the presence of acceptable witnesses. The first was the act of cohabitation. However, this were generally frowned upon as not being a fitting way of getting married. The second method was the delivery of a document by the man to the woman and her acceptance of it. The third was the presentation to the woman of some article of established value and her acceptance of it. The structure of the present day wedding ceremony symbolically involve all three. At the wedding ceremony the groom presents his bride with both, a wedding band and a marriage contract. There are three types of Jewish weddings: Orthodox, conservative and Reform wedding ceremonies. While all the types are recognized in Jewish communities around the world, only the Orthodox ceremonies are recognized in Israel.

Engagement

In ancient Jewish tradition, the groom gave his bride an engagement gift. In modern times, it is customary for this gift to be a diamond ring. The stone specifically indicates that it is not a wedding ring and symbolizes that the bride is as precious to the groom as a diamond.

The Aufruf

'Aufruf', translated literally, means, to be 'called up'. The groom has to be called by the Rabbi (rabbis are teachers specially trained in the law of the Torah or the Jewish Bible, to guide the Jews through life), who invites him to read the Torah in the synagogue, on the Sabbath morning before the wedding. The Sabbath lasts from sundown Friday till sundown Saturday and is known as the day of rest. After the groom is called for the 'aliyah' (blessing God at the reading of the Torah), the entire congregation tosses small packets of candy and nuts on him, while he is returning to his seat in the synagogue. The candy signifies the wish that the couple may have a 'sweet' life and the nuts are a reminder that, before the bride and groom can know each other intimately, they must break away the shells, which surround them.

The Groom's Reception

Before the wedding ceremony, the groom sits at the head of table specially laid out for him, known as the 'Chatan's Tisch' (literally translated, means the groom's table), where he is treated like a king. The elders of the family discuss much legality and the civil marriage license is signed and witnessed. The mothers of the bride and the groom are required to break a china dish, to indicate that even in this moment of celebration, they mourn for Jerusalem and Jewish martyrs. The Rabbi and the couple also sign the 'Ketubah' or the marriage contract at this time. The 'ketubah' is a declaration that the bride and the groom will carry out their obligations as husband and wife according to Jewish law and custom.

The Wedding Day

On the wedding day, tradition has it that all past sins are forgiven as the couple begins a new life together. The wedding takes a certain similarity to Yom Kippur—the Day of Atonement. This similarity is signified by the recitation of the Afternoon Service of the Viddui—the confessional of the Yom Kippur. To further emphasize this similarity, the bride and groom fast on their wedding day.

Mincha

After the couple and the Rabbi sign the ketubah, the family proceeds to the synagogue for the recital of the afternoon Mincha prayers. Preparations are made for the groom to proceed to the reception, which is known as the 'Baddekin'.

Baddekin

This ceremony takes place at the same time as the groom's reception—at the Chatan's Tisch. The bride enters the festive buffet reception accompanied by her family, who is called the 'Hachnasat Kallah' (literally meaning, 'accompanying the bride'). The groom is escorted from his Tisch to the bride's reception, where the 'baddekin' (veiling of the bride) takes place. The groom lifts the veil over the bride's face, while the Rabbi blesses her. As a sign of accepting his obligations and further strengthening the signing of the 'ketubah' earlier, the groom now takes hold of a handkerchief or some other object given to him by the Rabbi. This is the traditional method by which the agreement is considered binding; it is performed in the presence of the witnesses who will also sign the ketubah later. After the 'baddekin', the bride and groom's fathers bless the bride.

The Procession

This procession begins with the entrance of the Mesader Kesushin (presiding Rabbi). The groom enters the 'chuppah' first. The 'chuppah' is a canopy covered with embroidered silk or satin fabric, held up by 4 tall posts, which in turn are held up by relatives or friends and the wedding is solemnized under it. The bride follows, accompanied by her parents.

Kiddushin

The Jewish marriage ceremony is divided into two parts: the 'Kiddushin' or the blessing over wine; and the 'Birkat Kiddushin' or thanking God for the sanctity of marriage. The bride and groom take a sip of the wine and the 'Kiddushin' is completed upon the bride's acceptance of the wedding ring. The acceptance of the wedding ring is called 'Nissuin' (literally, the acceptance of the wedding ring by the bride). During the blessing over wine, a betrothal benediction is recited, when the bride and groom, both, drink from the goblet. After this, the most important part of the marriage ceremony follows. The groom puts the ring on the index finger of the bride's right hand and says: "Behold, you are consecrated to me with this ring according to the Law of Moses and Israel."

Ketubah

To separate the betrothal blessings from the marriage blessings (Sheva Brachot—seven spoken marriage blessings), the 'Ketubah' is read aloud in Aramaic (a Semitic language used after Hebrew). The 'ketubah' is a binding document that details the groom's obligation to the bride. Therein, the groom pledges to 'work for, honour, provide and support in accordance with the practices of Jewish husbands.' The 'ketubah' also confers a number of special privileges upon the bride for the duration of the marriage. The signing of the 'ketubah' shows that the couple does not see marriage only as an emotional and physical union, but also as a legal and moral commitment, which delineates human and financial obligations according to the Jewish laws and customs.

Nissuin

This is the recitation of the seven marriage blessings. As in 'Kiddushin', the first blessing is over wine. The second and the third speaks of creation, the fourth is for Zion's joy, the fifth is for the joy of the bridal couple, and the sixth is a prayer, that the couple should experience the same joy that Adam and Eve had in creation. The last blessing speaks of the joy of the couple together.

Breaking the Glass

It is customary for the groom to smash a glass by stamping on it at the conclusion of the ceremony, with his right foot. Once the glass is broken, there are shouts of 'Mazel Tov', which, in Hebrew means 'Good Stars', 'Good Luck, Congratulations!'

Yichud

After the completion of all the ceremonies, the couple moves to a private room. Before they enter, two witnesses ascertain that no one else is in the room. The bride enters the room first and waits for the groom. The couple breaks their fast on this day, and on emerging after partaking of the meal, they are greeted with music and dancing.

Seudat Mitzvah

During the wedding feast, all the guests and relatives participate in the 'mitzvah' (good deed) of 'Lesameach Chatan Ve Kallah' or celebrating in joy with the bride and groom. In accordance with Jewish law and custom, men and women dance separately, divided by a 'mechitzah' (scarf or handkerchief). At the end of the festive meal, the Sheva Brachot (blessings) is repeated along with the 'Birkat Hamazon' (thanksgiving to God after the meal).

BUNT WEDDING

The Bunt community of South Kanara is neither tied to any religious custom nor bound by any Vedic ritual, but their marriages are elaborate and lavish. Bunt marriages are almost always arranged by the parents. Once the alliance is fixed, the family decides what to give the bride in terms of wealth. Once this is confirmed, the astrologer picks an auspicious date for the wedding and invitations are sent out. Close family and friends are expected to attend the wedding regardless of the distance separating them.

Nischitartham

The men folk from the bride's family proceed to the groom's house carrying a silver platter laden with betel leaves, betel nuts and flowers. An elder from the family is assigned the task of introducing the two families to each other. This visit is a mere formality to confirm the date and time of the forthcoming wedding. The exchange of betel leaves and nuts is a confirmation of the alliance and the elders are a witness to it. These days, the 'nischitartham' might even be a more elaborate occasion, where the bride and groom exchange diamond engagement rings and the family follows this up by hosting a lavish party for close friends and relatives.

Mehendi

This modern day ceremony is held separately in both homes. Traditionally, this used to be a very simple ritual where just a dot of 'mehendi' or henna was applied to the bride's palms and finger tips, but has now evolved into a full-fledged celebration complete with professional henna artists or 'mehendiwallis' being invited to weave intricate designs on the hands and feet of the bride and her close female friends and relatives. Mehendi is applied on the groom as well—but just as a symbolic dot on his palm.

Mangalasnana

The 'mangalasnana' ceremony is held separately in both homes one day before the wedding. The groom's cousins and other close family relatives apply turmeric and coconut milk on his face, body and arms. The barber gives him a haircut and then his sister's husband or maternal cousin leads him for his bath. A similar ceremony is held at the bride's home, where her cousins apply the turmeric and coconut milk on her face and body. Her brother's wife or any other older lady from the family leads her for her bath. After the bath, she completes the ritual by wearing a new sari, gold jewellery, and black bangles. The bride and groom then proceed to their 'puja' rooms and after a brief prayer go to the 'tulsi katta' (sacred tulsi plant) to witness the 'tulsi puja' performed by the 'pujari'.

Murthasaese

This ritual is once again conducted separately in both homes and takes place after the 'tulsi puja'. Primarily a ceremony for receiving blessings, it has, however, turned into an elaborate function where a 'pandol' or canopy is decorated with flowers and banana palms and owing to the number of invitees, it is not possible to host it inside the homes. The bride's maternal uncle and aunt slip silver toe-rings on her feet. The eldest 'sumangali' (married lady) distributes red and green glass bangles to all the women present. The bride has to wear black, red and green bangles. All the elders who shower her with rice then bless her. The groom goes through a similar ritual—where his maternal uncle's wife or his paternal aunt adorns his feet with silver toe-rings. He too is blessed by all with the showering of rice.

Muhurtham or Lagnam

According to the tradition, the elders in the Bunt community usually officiated during the marriage ceremony. These days, however, pujaris do the needful. The groom is escorted to the venue of the wedding by his sister's husband or maternal uncle. The bride's brother receives him at the venue and welcomes him by washing his feet. The bride's aunt performs the traditional 'aarti' in his honour and the bride's mother follows it up by performing the 'deepa aarti' (welcome ritual performed with lighted lamps) for him.

The bride arrives at the venue of the wedding in all her finery and is received by her brother's wife, a cousin or an aunt, who leads her to the 'mantap' (platform erected for the marriage ceremony). Her brother washes her feet as well and a similar type of welcome ceremony is performed for her. The 'pujari' requests the groom's sister and her husband or a cousin to hold the hands of the bride and groom and lead them around the 'diyas' (lamps) and the 'mantap'. After this, the couple enters the 'mantap' and after a 'puja' is performed, they exchange garlands.

Dharemaipuna/Dhareyeruna

The bride's parents in the presence of her maternal uncle, his wife and elders of her family perform this ceremony. A silver or brass 'chembu' (vessel with a spout) filled with holy water is held by the bride's parents and taken to all the elders of both the families for their blessings. A gold coin or 'nanya' is placed on the bride's palm beneath which the groom places his hands and the bride's parents pour the water from the 'chembu' onto the couple's hands. This ritual is called 'dhare'.

The 'mangalsutra' (gold chain with black beads), is blessed by 5 'sumangalis' (married women) and the groom ties it around the bride's neck. The bride then slips a plain gold ring on the groom's finger. The bride and groom are made to hold the 'chembu' and sit down and rise three times in quick succession. This is known as the 'dhareyeruna'. In some families this ceremony is performed without the help of a 'pujari'.

Homam

Though not traditional to the Bunt community, this ceremony has now become a practice amongst many families. The 'pujari' lights the sacred fire and a 'homa' or sacrifice is performed amidst Vedic chants. The bride's brother puts fistfuls of puffed rice into the hands of his sister and the groom, which they in turn offer into the sacred fire each time they go around it, namely three times.

Saptapadi

The groom holds the bride's hands and together they take seven steps around the fire. With each step the bride has to tip over small heaps of rice with her right foot and repeat the seven marriage vows along with the groom.

KODAVA OR COORG WEDDING

Coorg is a small, beautiful district of the Western Ghats of Karnataka. The Coorgis are a marital race and their rituals and customs reflect this. They are a conservative people and parents usually arrange marriages in this community. The Kodava or Coorgi culture is unique and cannot be compared with any other community in the country.

Ponn Pareyuva

Having heard of a suitable girl in the community, a member from the groom's family along with his 'aruva' (an elder and well wisher of the family) proceeds to the bride's home to seek her hand in marriage. It is customary to consult horoscopes of the couple, if they are available. The bride's family may ask for the groom's horoscope but it is not considered fitting for the groom's family to ask for the bride's horoscope. If the horoscopes match and the families are in agreement to the alliance, the day for the betrothal ceremony is fixed.

Kuri Maaduva

An elder from the groom's 'okka' (clan) and his 'aruva' go to the bride's home on the appointed day. On this day, the head of the bride's 'okka' invites his 'aruva' or anyone else he may wish to, to join in the celebrations in his house. If an astrologer is present, he is requested to find an auspicious day and time for the 'muhurtha', which is the most important wedding rite. He writes it down on a piece of paper called the 'lagna patrike' ('lagna' means marriage and 'patrike' means letter) and hands it over to both families. At the betrothal ceremony, the 'nellakki nadu baade' or the central hall of the house is swept and cow dung water is sprinkled all over it to ritually purify it. 'Nell' means paddy, 'akki' is rice; both signifying wealth and prosperity. 'Nadu' means middle or central and 'baade' means hall. The central hall is where the Goddess of Wealth, Lakshmi resides. A 'thaliyathakki bolcha' (an oil lamp which is lit and placed on a bell-metal plate on which some rice grains are strewn) is kept in the central hall. 'Thaliya' is plate, 'akki' is rice and 'bolcha' is a lamp with a burning wick. Both families stand facing each other in front of this lamp. The two 'aruvas' then formalize the betrothal and the agreement is sealed, with promises that the wedding will be conducted in accordance with ancient customs. Then, the groom's 'aruva' or another member of his 'okka' folds his hands in salutation in front of the lamp and puts either five 'panas' (coins) or a piece of jewellery for the bride on the 'thaliyathakki bolcha' signifying a pledge.

Karik Muripa/Panda Pani

One day before the wedding, members from the bride and

groom's 'okka' and villagers assemble for the 'karik muripa'. All the women gather together to cut vegetables in the main courtyard of the house, helping the cooks prepare for the feasts that follow, while the men help to erect the 'pandal'. The marriage 'pandal' is usually erected over the steps leading to the house. At least one post of the 'pandal' should be made from the branch of a tree which exudes sap. Once the posts are erected, banana stumps with clusters of fruit are tied to them. The 'pandal' is further decorated with festoons made out of mango leaves and flowers. After the work for the 'pandal' and the 'karik muripa' is over, the bride and groom (each in their respective homes) prays to the sacred lamp placed in the 'nellaki nadu baade' and seeks the blessings of his/ her parents and all the assembled elders, by touching their feet thrice.

Potti Dumbchiduva

After the villagers depart, it is time to pack the bride's trousseau. Members of her family gather in the 'nellaki nadu baade' and fill the boxes with her trousseau, which may include vessels, money, jewellery and clothes.

Melkattu

On the wedding morning, a washer man ties a freshly washed white cloth under the 'pandal', forming a canopy which stretches all the way up to the main 'nellaki nadu baade'. Following this, a red cloth made of silk is attached under the white canopy at the exact spot where the bride and groom will sit for the wedding rites or the 'muhurtha'. A bunch of ripe bananas hangs from one corner of the red cloth, a coconut from another, a cucumber from the third and three betel leaves hang from the fourth corner. Right in the center of this red cloth, three areca nuts or areca nut flowers are attached and suspended.

Rituals for the Groom

Kshoura (Part of the Muhurtha)

Early on the morning of the wedding the groom is led to the 'kanni kombare' (the sacred room in the southwest corner of the house), where he sprinkles a little rice on the lamp that is kept there and salutes it. Next, he is led to the 'kanni kamba', the sacred pillar in the southwest corner of the inner courtyard of the house. He salutes the pillar and then proceeds to the sacred lamp kept in the 'nellaki nadu baade', sprinkles rice on it and salutes this also. After this, he takes the blessings of his parents and elders by touching their feet thrice. He then proceeds for his ritual shave. Using a brush made out of 'garike' (hariyali grass) the barber applies milk on the groom's face and shaves his facial hair and a part of his forehead. This shave is called the 'kombanjoura'. All the shaven hair is put in a plate of milk, making sure that not a single strand falls on the floor!

Bath

The 'kshoura' over, the bridegroom is led by his 'aruva' or bojakaara' (best man) for his bath. Three 'muthaides' (married ladies) pour water on him for his ritual bath.

Dress

The 'bojakaara' dresses the groom after his bath. Once he is dressed, the groom applies 'vibuthi' (sacred ash) on his forehead and chews betel leaves and areca nuts before proceeding for his 'muhurtha' in a ceremonial walk. A live band (mandatory in all Kodava weddings) now starts playing music to herald the arrival of the groom. The bridegroom holds a 'gejje thand' (a staff adorned with silver bells) and is led by the best man towards the marriage 'pandal'. The 'bojakaara' holds an umbrella covered with white cloth over the groom's head throughout the ceremonial walk to the 'muhurtha' site.

Rituals for the Bride

Bale Iduva

In her house, the bride, dressed in a silk sari and long-sleeved blouse, is led by her 'bojakarthi' or a 'muthaide' from her 'aruva's' family for the 'Bale Iduva'. A mat is spread on the floor and the bride and the bangle-seller sit on it. Glass bangles of various colours, such as red, green and black are slipped onto the bride's wrists by the bangle-seller. Black bangles are believed to ward off evil and have to be put on the bride's hands at this time.

Bath

A lady from the 'aruva's' family or the 'bojakarthi' leads the bride for her ritual bath and three 'muthaides' pour water over her.

Dress

After her bath, the bride's 'bojakarthi' helps her dress for the wedding ceremony. Once she is ready, the bride applies 'vibhuthi' (sacred ash) on her forehead, chews betel leaves and areca nuts, before being led to the 'muhurtha' site in a ceremonial walk. As in the bridegroom's case, the 'bojakarthi' holds an umbrella covered with a white cloth over the bride's head throughout the ceremonial walk.

Muhurtha

Before the bride or groom arrives at the 'muhurtha' site, the 'aruva's' wife lights the sacred lamp in the 'nellaki nadu baade'. She then spreads two or three mats, facing in a North-South direction, at the 'muhurtha' site. The washer man covers these mats with a carpet. In the center of this carpet the 'aruva's' wife places a 'mukkali' (low stool) and covers it with red cloth. Two other 'mukkalis' are placed on either side of the one in the center. A silver or bell-metal plate containing rice is placed on each of these and a 'kindi' (small metal pot with a spout) full of milk is placed on top of the rice on one of the 'mukkalis'. Two tall brass pedestal lamps are lit and placed on either side of the 'muhurtha' site. The bride/groom along with the 'bojakaara'/'bojakarthi' walk thrice around the 'mukkali' kept in the center. Before sitting on the stool the bride/groom, stands behind the 'mukkali', sprinkles rice on it three times and salutes it by touching it with both hands and raising them to his/her forehead and then steps over it with the right foot.

Neeredpa

If the Kodava guests coming to the wedding are older than the person who is welcoming them, the latter honours them by touching their feet and seeking their blessings. It is customary to offer guests water to wash their feet.

Baale Birud

On the path leading to the venue of the 'muhurtha' in the wedding house, nine or more (always multiples of three) plantain tree stumps, each measuring approximately a yard in length, are fixed vertically to small wooden stakes driven into the ground. Only a select few are entitled to have the honour of cutting these plantain stumps. They are usually the maternal uncles of the bride/groom and renowned guests whom the family wishes to honour. When the persons who are to receive the honour of 'baale birud' reach the wedding house, members of the host's family along with the 'aruva' and some villagers, proceed at once to the stumps, singing the 'batte paat' (song of the way) accompanied by a band and carrying a mat, a small pot of water, betel leaves and some areca nuts. The guest who is going to perform the 'baale birud' calls out to the gods and prays with the villagers who may be accompanying him, according to the custom of his village. During the prayers all turbans and headgear are removed as a mark of respect. After the prayers the guest or his representative cuts the three plantain stumps with the 'odi kathi' (knife). Before cutting them he walks around the stumps thrice, gently tapping the arrows made out of bark and the flowers on top, with the 'odi kathi'. Then he cuts the stumps one by one, each with a single stroke, and then dances joyously to the beat of the music. The Muhurtha ceremony: Separate Muhurthas for the bride and groom. The groom's 'odi kathi' and 'gejje thand' are set aside before he sits down on the 'mukkali' for the 'muhurtha'. When the groom/bride sits on the 'mukkali', a red cloth is spread on his/her lap. The 'bojakaara' sits slightly behind the groom to his right, while the 'bojakarthi' stands behind the bride. Women come forward and bless the groom/bride before the men can do so. The mother is the first to bless the groom/bride followed by two 'muthaides'. These three ladies usually give gold coins as gifts. The special mode of blessing and presenting gifts at this time is as follows: a little rice is taken from the plates placed on either side of the groom/bride and this rice is sprinkled thrice on his/her head. The entire process is repeated thrice. That done, they offer gifts, usually money. If the gift is jewellery, no money is given along with it. The groom/bride receives the gifts and keeps them on his/her lap on the red cloth, and then drops them on to a tray or box kept by his/her side for this specific purpose. The wedding song is sung during the 'muhurtha' by four men beating 'dudis' (drums) as they sing.

The Wedding Feast

The Kodavas are renowned for the smorgasbord of sumptuous dishes they serve at their weddings. Many kinds of meat dishes are served (and several different preparations of each type of meat) including pork, lamb and chicken.

The Couple is Served their Meal

The bride and the groom remain in the rooms they were escorted into after the 'muhurtha' and their meals are served there. Two of their chosen friends or companions join them for the meal, and they eat from the same plate as the bride and groom.

Bidding Farewell to Guests after the Muhurtha

In both the 'muhurthas', the special guests who were offered the honour of performing the 'baale birud', are now given the honour of being escorted by the hosts right up to the spot where the plantain stumps are staked, to the accompaniment of the wedding band. After the wedding feast, the bridegroom and his party prepares to leave in a wedding procession to the bride's home to bring her to her new home. These preparations begin with the filling of the 'poliya'.

Poliya

Once the meal is over in the groom's house, the 'aruva's' wife fills the 'poliya' (reed basket with a lid) in front of the sacred lamp in the 'nellaki nadu baade' with foodstuffs. Just before the start of the wedding procession, the 'poliya' is placed on the head of the girl/lady who has been given the task of carrying this basket to the bride's house, by the 'aruva's' wife.

The Wedding Procession

Before leaving for the bride's house, those who go in the procession usually have another meal along with the groom. Then the groom goes to the central hall, sprinkles rice on the sacred lamp and salutes it. He then touches the feet of all the elders, seeking their blessings before proceeding on his journey. After that, the groom and his wedding band go to the 'kaimada' (a shrine near the ancestral home where statues representing the ancestors of the 'okka' are kept and worshipped). The groom sprinkles rice on the lamp in the 'kaimada', salutes it and goes tc the site where the plantain stumps are staked and sits down there. Now the head of the family arrives, offers the groom some advice and sends him and his party off on its journey.

Potti Dumbchiduva

A messenger goes to inform the bride's family of the arrival of the groom's procession, once it has reached the plantain stumps. On receiving this intimation, the bride's boxes, which were packed on the previous evening, are checked in the presence of as many close relatives as possible. (Some families do not follow this custom these days).

Kodiyaal or Koru Arapuvavu

On reaching the plantain stumps, three men from the groom's party go to the bride's house to inform her family of the arrival of the groom's procession. The bride's family offers these three men refreshments and then a chosen few from the bride's family along with the wedding band accompanies them to the spot where the plantain stumps are staked, to welcome the groom's procession.

Baale Birud

The bride's family now gives the honour of cutting the plantain stumps in their house, to members from the groom's family. The procedure of 'baale birud' is exactly the same each time this ceremony is performed.

Welcoming the Groom

After the ceremonial cutting of the plantain stumps, the bride's family offers a traditional welcome to the groom. A young girl washes the feet of the groom and his 'bojakaara' with water. The bride's family then showers him with blessings by sprinkling rice on his head as he enters the bride's house. He and his 'bojakaara' are then led to the central hall of the house and are seated there. The 'aruva's' wife takes the 'poliya' from the lady who has been carrying it all this time and places it under the sacred lamp in the central hall.

A Special Meal is Served to the Groom's Procession

The groom's future mother-in-law feeds him with a mixture of rice, milk and sugar. Then the groom, his 'bojakaara' and one other person are served their meal. Following this, the rest of the people from the groom's procession are served their meal.

Dampathi Muhurtha

After the groom's family has had their meal, the bride and groom are seated together under the canopy for the 'Dampathi Muhurtha'. The groom is seated first, to the bride's right. All the rituals observed here are identical to the ones observed in the earlier separate 'muhurthas', the only difference being, that, here the bride is offered the milk, which was brought in the 'poliya' by the groom's family. After the 'Dampathi Muhurtha' is over, the groom showers rice on the bride's head offers her milk in the 'kindi' and gives her the 'cheela pana' (a small bag made from red silk containing at least one gold, one silver and one copper coin). This signifies that he is sharing his wealth with his bride. The couple then exchanges garlands. Then, the bride is taken to the kitchen. The couple stands on either side of the threshold of the kitchen. The groom then takes his bride's right hand and helps her across the threshold out to the central hall.

Sammanda Paraje or Sammanda Kodupa

The bride receives the 'sammanda' (rights) in her groom's 'okka' at this time. This is a very important part of the formalities that legalize the marriage, even though it is filled with exaggerated comments and much hilarity.

Batte Thadpa

After the bride receives the 'sammanda', it is time for the wedding procession to return to the groom's house with the bride. The bride's cousin, who could have married her by tradition, however blocks her path at the threshold and after much hilarity 'releases' her after her husband gives the cousin a gold coin!

Wedding Procession

The bride and groom along with the wedding party now proceed to the 'kaimada', where they sprinkle rice on the lamp kept there and pray to the ancestors of the bride's 'okka'. Next, they go to the spot, where the plantain stumps are staked, accompanied by the wedding bands of both the families. The head of the bride's family now blesses the bridal couple and returns to his home with the wedding band. One man and one woman from every 'okka' in the bride's village join the wedding procession on its journey back to the groom's house.

Baale Birud

On reaching the groom's house, the same ritual is observed of cutting the plantain stumps, this time by the bride's family.

Welcoming the Bride

After the 'baale birud', the couple is showered with rice on their walk up the steps of the groom's house. Immediately on entering his home, the groom goes to the 'kanni kombare', sprinkles rice on the sacred lamp there and salutes it. Next, he goes to the 'nellaki nadu baade', sprinkles rice on the 'kanni kamba' there and salutes it. Then, he does the same to the lamp in that hall and prays before it. The bride also sprinkles rice on the lamp in the 'nellaki nadu baade' and prays before it. After this, she is made to sit on the 'aimara' of the house (built-in wooden bench bordering the inner courtyard of the 'nellaki nadu baade') and, then she, too, touches the feet of all the elders present, seeking their blessings. The bride is now blessed in front of the sacred lamp in the 'nellaki nadu baade' by the groom's family members. She may also receive gifts from them at this time.

Neer Edpa/Ganga Puja

This ceremony symbolizes the bride's becoming a part of the groom's family and helping in household chores. The entire ritual also tests the stamina of the newly wed bride! After her meal, the bride combs her hair and ties a 'vastra' (traditional headdress generally worn by a married lady in the Kodava community). She then proceeds to remove all the ornaments on her feet and puts on silver toe-rings (symbols of a married lady). Once again she is led to the central where she offers prayers at the sacred lamp lit there and sprinkles some rice on it. She is then led to the well or river for the 'Ganga Puja' (worship of the sacred river, Ganga) accompanied by the wedding band. Four small pots are kept ready beside the well. The bride draws water from the well and pours it into each of these pots. She then places two pots of water on her head, one on top of the other, on a small circular cushion. Two other ladies from the groom's family carry each of the other two pots of water on similar cushions and walk with the bride, one in the front and one at the rear. This procession is now ready to return to the house accompanied by the wedding band playing a slow beat. The bride is supposed to take very small steps ('mangalth mott' or wedding step) to the beat of the music. Members of the groom's family dance in front of her, not allowing her to proceed, thus blocking her path!

Potti Kaatuva

The bride's trousseau and all other items brought by her are shown to all the members of the groom's family.

Feasting

All the members from the groom's family and guests now sit down to partake of a grand meal in which the bride and groom join in.

The Bride is given a New Name

The wedding song is sung now and in the song the singers change the name of the bride to the new name chosen for her by her husband's family. Changing the bride's name is an optional practice these days.

Kombarek Kootavu

Either the 'bojakaara' or the 'aruva' leads the groom to the bridal chamber where the bride is seated with her veil covering her face. Before he can proceed to the chamber, the groom is led to the 'nellaki nadu baade' where he sprinkles rice on the sacred lamp and salutes it. On entering the chamber, the groom lifts the veil from his bride's face and she touches his feet, seeking his blessings. It is now, that the groom presents his bride with an ornament, usually a gold wedding band.

NAGA MARRIAGE RITUALS

The Naga tribes follow the exogamous principle in marriage. Persons of the same clan do not marry and any kind of sexual relations between them is strictly forbidden. The only exception are the Konyak chiefs who are considered so sacrosanct that their principal wife must be a woman of the same clan. The Sema's have a legend about the origin of exogamous clans. It is said, that Nikhoga, the first man, had six sons but was able to find a wife only for the eldest. This led to intrigues between the brothers. Eventually, Nikhoga got disgusted and drove away all the remaining five brothers who, in due course, founded exogamous clans. Among the Angamis, a young man having fixed his choice up on a certain girl tells his father, who sends a friend to ascertain the wishes of her parents. If they express conditional approval, the bridegroom's father puts the matter further to the test by strangling a fowl and watching the way in which it crosses its legs when dying. If the legs are placed in an inauspicious attitude, the match is immediately broken off. Otherwise, the girl is informed of the favourable progress of negotiations. At this stage, she can exercise a power of veto, as if she dreams an inauspicious dream within the next three days, her suitor must search a bride else where; if all goes favourably the wedding day is fixed. Proceeding is begun with a feast at the bride's house and in the evening she proceeds to her husband home; but though she sleeps there, he modestly retires to the bachelor's club. The next day brings more feasting, but night separates the young couple as before. On the third day, they visit their fields together, but not till after eight or nine days have elapsed is the village priest called in, and the happy pair allowed to consummate their wishes. The Mongsen tribe among the Aos had a peculiar custom. After the boy and the girl were engaged, they went on a trading expedition for twenty days. If the expedition was profitable, the marriage preparations were proceeded with, but if there was a loss (it was considered as inauspicious omen) the engagement was broken off. The Naga women are well built, hard working, fairly pretty but short in stature. They are never seen idle. Their chores include fetching water, cutting wood, cooking food, brewing liquor, working in the fields and weaving cloth at home. Most of the tribes shave the girls head until she reaches the marriageable age. The idea is that she is not expected to look attractive and have physical relations with the opposite sex until that age.

Pre-nuptial License Varies from Tribe to Tribe

Among the Angamis, it is normal for a girl to have a lover, but the society is strict and the boy and the girl are not expected to go beyond a reasonable limit. The Sema's guard their girl with the greatest care, the reason being that a girl fetches a handsome price at marriage and this price would be substantially reduced if she got involved in a scandal. The offenders in this respect are made to pay heavy fines. The amount of fine would depend upon the social position of the girl's father and would also be in proportion to the girl's anticipated marriage price. The Ao society is comparatively permissive. In earlier days, the Ao girl as soon a she reached puberty, slept in a separate sleeping house with a couple of other girls, there she would more often than not admit her love at night. Among the Konyaks, pre-martial promiscuity is common.

Marriage Price

Marriage price—differs from tribe to tribe and is highest among the Semas. The daughter of the Sema chief gets a fabulous dowry. Part of this given in cash and part in kind in the form of land, mithun or any other movable or immovable property. The girl's father gives ornaments also to the bride but this is much less than the dowry received. The price of a girl also depends upon her accomplishments, an educated girl will fetch a higher dowry. In the past, her appearance was not an important consideration but today, the boys and girls alike, have become beauty and fashion conscious. The Angamis are monogamous. The Semas are polygamous and take as many wives as they can afford. One of the wives, takes position of the head wife, though she is not necessarily the first wife. Among the Lothas, a rich man may take a second wife. The Changs may have anything like four to six wives. Among the Konyaks, the chief may have several wives and even the exogamous restrictions do not apply to him, but the commoner must be monogamous. The Khemungans may have any number of wives. This is due to their strange marriage custom. A Khemungam boy, wanting to marry a particular girl merely tells his father, brother or other near relatives of his choice. These people raid the girls house one fine morning and abduct her. The boy and the girl, thereafter, live as husband and wife. There is no question of any dowry.

Divorce

Divorce is easy in all tribes. Among the Aos it used to be very common. It was very rare to meet an Ao man or woman who had married only once. The Sema is less inclined to change his partner because of financial obligations which it would be invariably entail. In the case of a woman committing adultery, the husband could abandon her while he would keep with him the ornaments brought by the girl at the time of marriage and also claim fine, from the paramour. If this happened within three years of marriage, the husband could even demand return of the dowry. If the husband ill-treated the women, she could separate and demand the return of her personal jewellery. Among the Khemungans, divorce is as easy as marriage. The girl wanting to separate gets up early one morning, cleans the house, prepares the food and then just walks out. Sex-intrigues are not frowned upon among the non-Christian Nagas. The Angamis and Chakhesangs have three lines of cowries embroidered on their kilt. A fourth line signifies powers not in war but love and could denote any of the following achievements:, an intrigue with a married woman living with her husband, a simultaneous intrigue with two girls of the same name, or with two daughters of one father and or with a mother and her daughter.

An Ao would not hesitate to make advances to a woman whose husband was away. Among the Lothas, if the man was going to be away from the village for a long time he could permit his brother or a near relative from the father's side to co-habit with her during his absence. In Naga, warfare valour was always tempered by caution. To die in battle was not considered glorious but was disaster for the spirit of dead warrior and a disgrace for his family. It was believed that the spirit would remain restless and earth-bound until the victor had died and that it would then follow him as a slave to the next world. The outright flight was considered better than the disgraceful fate of death at the hands of the enemy.

MIZO MARRIAGE RITUALS

Although Christianity brought about a near—total transformation in the Mizo lifestyle and outlook some customary laws have stayed on.

Bride Price

The Mizos are not alone in putting a price on a bride. This custom is a prevalent in a few other Indian Communities as well. When a Mizo boy approaches his fiancee's parents for permission to get married, the first thing he has to do is to settle the bride price. If the price among other things, demanded by him, is acceptable to the parents, the boy and the girl are allowed to get married. Thus, the settlement of the bride price to be paid by the bridegroom is an essential pre-requisite to a Mizo marriage. It so generally, happens that part of the bride price which may be paid on the eve of the wedding, while the part of bride price called 'Thutphah' is held back over the years as a sort of security of paying off the debts fall on the next generation. In case of the death of a husband, his son is obliged to pay the bride price. The principal bride price is known as Manpui the rate which is (mentioned in terms of mithun or sial) Rs. 80 per unit. Besides, there are subsidiary bribe prices like *sumhmahruai* (rate Rs. 20) and sumfang (Rate Rs. 8) These prices are to be paid to the bride's father or brother. Pusum, the rate of which varies from Rs. 4 to Rs. 10 is payable to the nearest relation on the side of the bride's mother who most often than not turns out to be the maternal uncle of the bride. An equivalent amount, known as Ni-ar, is paid to the bride's paternal aunt as well. The elder sister or sisters of the bride are entitled to Naupuakpuan, which is the price received by them for having given the bride their clothes to wear or taken of the bride in her childhood. In the event of the bride being the eldest daughter or an only child, this price is received by other female relations. A sum also goes to the Palal who acts as the bride's foster father and takes on the responsibility of safeguarding her interests throughout her married life. The bride's maid also get a price known as thianman. There are some optional payments as well. Taken together, the bride price adds up to a considerable figure which is often impossible for the bridegroom to pay at one time. However, it would be a mistake to continue bride price with sale or dowry. For all those who get a share of it come under a special obligation to look after the welfare and interest of the bride.

Marriage

A mizo marriage is proceeded by courtship and engagement.

The boy and girl are allowed to mix freely during the engagement period. But an engagement may be broken off midway through if the couple fails who get on with each other. As the majority of the Mizos are now Christians, marriages are solemnized in Church. Both bride and the bridegroom wear wedding dresses in the latest Western Style. But, sometimes the bride is also decked in puanchei, a traditional Mizo costume, and white blouse. The bride bring along to her husband a traditional rug called Puandum in which his body is to be wrapped during burial. This is an integral part of the Mizo marriage and failure to bring the cloth entails punishment leading to a reduction in the bride price. There are other types of marriage as well. In the Makpa chhungkhung type of wedding, the bridegroom does not pay bride price but goes to his wife's house to live her. This type of marriage happens in families where there are no male heirs. Consequently, it becomes the duty of the son-in-law to care for his wife's parents. Another type of Mizo marriage, as Luhkhung, is performed without a social ceremony. If a girl becomes pregnant, she start living quietly with the boy responsible for her condition in his house. However, the marriage of a pregnant girl is sometimes performed in the Vestry instead of the main Hall of a Church. Tlandun is yet another kind of marriage in which a couple runs away from home to get married.

Inheritance

The mizos being patriarchal, property is inherited by men rather than women. The family property usually goes to the youngest son although the father may leave shares to other sons, if he desires. If a man has no sons, his property is inherited by the next kin on the male side. If a man dies leaving a widow and minor children, a male relation (who usually happens to be a brother of the deceased) takes charge of the family and looks after the property until one of the sons comes of age. If no such male relative is around, then the widow acts as a trustee of her husband's property until such times as his son or sons are old enough to inherit it. However, although the youngest son of the family is the natural or formal heir to his father under the Mizo customary laws, in actuality the paternal property is generally divided among all sons. The youngest of them gets a preferential treatment in that he would get the first choice of the articles, and he would get two share of the cash in case of one each for the other brothers. A daughter or a wife can inherit property only if the deceased has no heir on the male side. Women, however, are entitled to their own property. The drowry, called thuam, she gets during the marriage from her parents is exclusively her own property. However, a written 'will' formally executed may now confer woman the right to inherit the family property. This is a happy amendment to the traditional customary laws.

BISHNUPRIYA MANIPURI MARRIAGE SYSTEM

Lohong

The institution of Marriage in Bishnupriya Manipuri society is based on the Hindu pattern and mostly Aryan and non-Aryan elements having certain traditional customs. Out of the eight kind of marriage as referred in the Monu Songhita only Brahma (Based upon Vedic Rites) and Kanya or Prajapatya are prevalent in the Society. The marriage takes place after the proposals made by the Parents or guardians of the would-be bride-groom. During the marriage ceremony, special kind of rules and customs are observed. These customs include Waroupath, Hijapath, Lohong, Koina Thilkarani,Tindinkar Chana, Pachor bhat, Phamlokpa etc. The swayamvara, another kind of marriage that was in vogue in the early period, is unknown to Manipur, but there is the practice of Gandharva (secret union) system. The secret marriage of Arjuna with Chitrangoda, the princes of Manipur, suggests as the Gandharva style of marriage. Marriage is restricted within this community. There is the restriction of marriage among the Gutra's and Swapinda's. Fairly child-marriage was practised. But no more now and widow re-marriage is very rare in the society. What is good, is that, there is no dowry system at all in the modern Bishnupriya Manipuri Soceity.

Arrangement (Lepkorani)

Marriages are performed in accordance with the customs. Before the marriage parents of the boy or their recognized parsons go to meet parents of the girl. The horoscopes are tallied and if both the parents agree then the next date for the meeting is fixed. On the next meeting the consent is given by the girl's parents.

Waroupoth

The next stage is 'Waroipot puba' and the groom's family members bring food and the contract is finally sealed.

Hijapoth

Finally, the engagement is declared amongst the friends and relatives, this is called 'Hijapoth'. Friends and relatives from the boy's side then go to the girl's parents with food, fruits and presents. The girl's parents also invite their friends and relatives.

The Procession

A Bishnupriya Manipuri marriage party is of a great show but little is wasted for giving meals. A marriage attended by a procession of peoples, Band parties and Palki's, considered a status symbol.

The Reception

The men dress in dhoti and kurta with a shawl wrapped around and women in "Lahing" or "Chakshabi"es and white chader. The reception is very formal. At the entrance of the gate, a Sambhasa welcomes the marriage party. Later, the groom is received according to traditional way of reception by the bride side. The arrangement for sitting of the marriage party is commonly made in the house very next to the bride's house.

The Bride and the Groom

The bridal dress is unique. It is obligatory for the bride to wear the Raslila skirt. The groom's dress is white dhoti, kurta and turban.

The Marriage (Lohong)

The whole marriage is maintained and under the charge of the Brahmin. Before the main part a Pala is performed and it continues till the end of the marriage. Kirtana music is started when the bride and the bride make seven rounds round the groom. The bride follows the steps in rhythmic styles with the pala music. She has to perform the role of a gopi. There are many good points in Manipuri marriages. There is no stress on huge expenditure. The kabok, ladoos and sweets are distributed after the marriage ceremony. The guests are given Dakshina. The dowry is not as a compulsion but voluntary. The parents of the girl provide essential items for her use such as utensils, sewing machine, implements, clothes, etc.

ASSAMESE WEDDING

A traditional Assamese marriage ceremony goes on for 3 days. However, nowadays most of the people perform the whole marriage ceremony in just one or two days. Dowry is not practised in Assamese society and the groom does not ask for anything from the bride and her family. But the bride's father, may of his own free will, provide necessary household items which are required in married life. The elders are helped by Ghataks or match-makers in selecting a suitable match. Horoscopes are checked. In case of the Arbeg tribe of Assam, marriageable girl tells about her fiancé to her maternal uncle, his sons. If the boy gets a chance, he can run away. If caught, he is imprisoned in a room. The marriage is settled if the boy is caught three times after running away, but he does not run away the fourth time.

Pre-Wedding Rituals

Juran Diya

Juran diya is the first day of the wedding. From the groom's side, a group of men and women (excluding the groom) go to the bride's place. The groom's party carries bridal dresses, ornaments, make-up box and some essential items for the bride. The items are usually in odd numbers as these are seen as lucky. Along with these items, sweets, fish, betel-nuts and betel leaves are also taken to the bride's house. (Betel-nuts and betel leaves are an essential part of any Assamese religious function.) At the bride's house, the groom's mother presents the bride with sets of bridal dresses (mekhela-sadar), ornaments, a make-up box and some other essential items and puts on vermilion (sindoor). The groom's mother also gives one set of mekhela-sadar to the bride's mother. Then, the bride seeks the blessings of the elders (including her in-laws) one by one and also gives them gifts. In return, they too give money to the bride.

Nowani

Once the juran diya is over, then the bride and the groom have to take nowani (ceremonial baths) for the next two days till the wedding. For nowani, water is specially drawn (pani-tola) from a river or a tank by a group of women, while singing marriage songs.

Marol Puja

In her house, the bride is made to sit on a mandap made of banana or mango leaves. She is asked to look into a mirror. Only this mirror may be used till the wedding day.

Adhivasa

Adhivasa is the night of the second day or the night before the wedding day. On this day, both the bride and the groom and their respective mothers keep a fast. The priest performs a puja, offering gram and pulses to God. These are later distributed as prasad. The bride and groom can eat a vegetarian meal only after eating the prasad.

Gathiyan Khunda

Gathiya Khunda is the purification ceremony. In this ceremony, women pound an aromatic root to pulp inside a cloth enclosure, add oil and then apply it on the heads of the bride and the groom. This is done separately in both houses. The bride, bridegroom and their respective parents, do not take any meal after that night till the marriage is over.

Daiyan Diya

The third day of ceremonies is the wedding day. The ceremony of daiyan diya takes place in early morning of the wedding day. A party from the groom's house carries curd to the bride's house. The bride touches the curd, keeps half for herself and returns half for the groom. The bride and the groom (separately in their houses) are seated on the threshold of their bedrooms. An elderly woman relative, takes 2 betel leaves in her 2 hands, dips them in the bowl of curd and touches the bride's/groom's cheeks, arms and feet with the leaves. Then, the bride and the groom (separately in their houses) take a ceremonial bath with turmeric and mati kalai paste. The women throw rice on the girl.

The shraddha for 9 past generations is performed in both the houses. In the evening, the groom and his party leave for the bride's house.

Welcoming the Groom

At the bride's place, the groom gets a ceremonial welcome at the gateposts of the wedding hall. The posts are made of banana plants with festoons of mango leaves. The groom arrives with his best man who protects him symbolically with an umbrella. They are greeted by a shower of rice to drive off any evil spirit accompanying them. The groom is welcomed by the bride's mother. The bride's younger sister washes the groom's feet with water and wipes them with a new gamocha (towel). The groom in return gives her a cash gift. Then, the groom is led to the place under the pandal where the hom jagya is to be performed.

The Wedding Ceremony

In Assamese society, agni is considered to be the mightiest power and the greatest purifier and is deemed to be the witness to the marriage. At the start of the auspicious hour (lagna), the priest starts the vedic rites in front of the fire (agni). Later, the priest calls the bride near the agni while chanting mantras. One end of the bride's cloth (anchal) is tied to the groom's cloth and the knot is called the logoon gathi. The whole marriage ceremony is performed in front of agni and 101 mango stems are burnt in this agni and this is also called hom pura. The most crucial part of the wedding is the homage paid by the couple to agni devata. The priest chants mantras and both bride and groom follow him and offer popcorn and ghee to the fire. Then, the bride's father places her hand in the groom's hand. The priest chants mantras and the bride's father follows him. This is called the Kanyadaan.

Post-Wedding Rituals

Playing Games

After the marriage ceremony the bride and the groom are led to a room. They are made to sit in the centre surrounded by relatives and friends.

A ring is put into a vessel containing rice and the couple have to put their hands in and search for the ring. Whoever, finds the ring first is the winner and it is said, will dominate over the other. Then food is served to both the bride and the groom.

Departure of the Bride

All the ceremonies are over before dawn. The bride and groom touch the feet of their parents to take their blessings. Then the bride goes to the groom's house.

Ceremonies in the Groom's House

At the gate of the groom's house, the groom's younger sister washes the feet of both the bride and the groom and wipes them with a gamocha and in return the bride gives a cash gift to her. The bride and the groom stay separately and are not allowed to see each other till the next day. On the evening of the fifth day (since the start of the marriage ceremonies), a priest performs the ceremony of khuba-khubuni. Offerings are made to 2 imaginary demons named khuba and khubani for smoothening the path of married life. This day symbolises the start of the new life for the bride and the groom.

8th Mangala

On the 8th day, the bride goes to her parents' house with her husband and in-laws. She gives gifts to all the family members. The bride's mother prepares 8 different dishes for the guests. The bride's family also presents the newly wed couple with gifts. The same day the bride (along with her husband and in-laws) returns to her husband's house.

Kaal-Raatri

Traditionally, the bride and the groom are kept away for the first night, because the first night is considered to be 'Kaal-Raatri'.

7

Marital Harmony and Personal Compatibility in Marriage

Every couple does not have problems but a small amount of friction and clash in personality, outlook and thought process becomes an essential gradient of marriage. Man and woman are not only two different sexual beings but their aspirations and expectations from life at any given time are different. Their emotional stability, display of feelings and emotions to the outer world is very different. Living in a social world and learning the specific gender and sex roles of the society, individuals enact in the world and expect others to do according to their ideal aspirations. The romantic notion of marriage has been a noble and exciting experiment, but the approach generally fails. More and more studies are revealing the importance of a happy, healthy relationship. Happily married people are healthier, better adjusted and more successful than their unhappily married or single counterparts. It is necessary to know how couples and society strengthen the vital institution of marriage.

Marriage entails both the spouses to personally and psychologically adjust to the interdependent style of life that marriage implies. Marriage affects every aspect of one's life, the way they do their jobs, the time they spend with their family and friends, time they spend with their spouse, recreational activities, how and when they sleep and for women in our patri-local society, their place of residence is also changed after marriage. Marriage also requires one's adjustment to social position and status of the spouse, and also the social status of being a married person. Individuality of a spouse is lost and the couple is thought to be one by the family members and others, and also by selves. The early 'I' has to be changed to 'We', for good marital adjustment of the couple. This adjustment to being a couple is called pair adjustment. Marital adjustment refers to the complex set of compromises and changes each partner makes to accommodate the other and to fulfil the obligations of marriage.

Marriage of an individual is to another person having heart, and brain of their own with feelings, thoughts, emotions, idiosyncratic thoughts, logics as well as prejudices. Adjustment is also to in-laws living with or visiting after marriage. It involves adjusting, especially of woman to the new families culture, social norms, set of rules, values, behaviour patterns and language dialect used by the family. Even if, marriage is among alike partners having similar family backgrounds, religious affiliations and values of life, alot of adjustment is required on the part of the married couple. The family in which each partner grew up, called the family of orientation had its own set of rules, values, behaviours, language, eating pattern which may be different in the family one forms or enters by marrying, called the family of procreation.

Marital quality (is also referred to as marital satisfaction or marital happiness) is defined as how good the marriage is according to the spouses at a given point in time. Marriages in which partners say they are happy and satisfied are judged to be of higher quality than those marriages in which partners express unhappiness or dissatisfaction. Marital success (sometimes also called marital stability) refers to what happens to the marriage over a period of time. Marriages that last until the death of one spouse are judged more successful than those that end through divorce or separation (Glenn, 1990).

After marriage, couples that emphasize or develop shared personal traits; a common value system, shared leisure activities and joint friends generally have higher quality marriages. Whyte (1990) observed that women who had severe conflicts with their parents have a more difficult time achieving a high quality marriage, and those who married in opposition to parents experience more marital problems.

ADJUSTMENT IN MARRIAGE

The marriages are celebrated with happiness and begin with high hopes and expectations. It is glorious in the beginning. But, this romantic view soon begins to clash with realities. Though, most marriages are happy and do not end into break-ups. However, all marriages pass through the phase of sweet and sour experiences. Partners have to make adjustments. More they are prepared for adjustment better will be the quality of marital-life. It means that people must acquire the skills in human relationships. It will bring maturity, as we mature, we learn that we have to change and adjust if we wish to be liked. For adjustment, efforts are to be made. If people think that everything will be all right after marriage and ignore the adjustment process, it will not solve the problems. Good relationship would not come as a result of love alone. It has to be accomplished.

Couples and families should be more realistic about the challenges of living together and cooperating in all areas of life. Where they disagree, they must be ready either to ignore differences (if not very serious) or be ready to solve reasonably, caring for each other's sentiments and likings. In other areas, sometimes it is essential that they must either agree or must work to adjust their differences if they are to live happily together.

Areas Requiring Adjustability

There are many areas where adjustability is required. The chief areas are economic, in-laws relationship, sex relationships, social activities, recreation, associating with friends, religious life if from different religions and even within religions—one goes to different to saints, sadhus, other idols or deities, and training and disciplining the children. All couples face problems in these areas. The couples that are happy have met the problems, which arise in these areas. Their marriages are successful because they have accepted the task of adjusting to each other's viewpoint. They have arrived at working arrangements.

Adjustment takes Time

Adjustment and agreement takes time. One should not take hasty decisions about divorce or separation. Neither they should be disappointed or frustrated. Adjustment is the need of both the partners and both the families. It may take couple of years.

A marriage is never presented to a couple as a gift. A happy marriage is an accomplishment, a lifetime task to be achieved at each stage of life. It is evident that two people have to cooperate, each giving up some of the preferences and attitudes in favour of mutual understanding and affection. Delay in accepting reality and making efforts to cope with the demands of married life may find difficulty in adjusting to married life.

ADJUSTMENT TECHNIQUES

The various adjustment techniques used by marital partners are:

Compromise

Compromise is willingness of both parties to sacrifice a part of their position. It is a two-way adjustment in which both must cooperate. Couples should be ready at all times to modify their opinions, attitudes, and behaviour without sacrificing basic life principles, their religious and moral values.

Acceptance

The wisest attitude may be accepting partner as he or she is despite his or her shortcomings. Though, one has the duty to correct other, but you cannot change your partner.

Conversion

Conversion is a total surrender to the partner. Women normally do this. This can be achieved only when one retains an open mind on differences and humbleness to admit own weaknesses. Thus, requires genuine maturity of character.

Sublimation

Sublimation is often the only adjustment possible when all

other methods fail, this works. By it a partner accepts the inevitable in his or her spouse for entirely noble and lofty reasons.

Counselling

It is a useful method of removing differences when one or both parties have lost true perspective on marital relationship. Professionally trained and experienced person provides aid by adopting special techniques of counselling.

Abandonment

It is a strong defense against physical or mental breakdown. This may propel a partner to great heights of holiness in marriage. Faith in God and prayers help the person to use this adjustment technique.

Agreement

The happiest are those who have been able to understand and sympathize with each other's viewpoint on most important matters. Exceptions are the marriages when both are in good agreement right from the beginning. Otherwise in most of the cases efforts are to be made. Probably, the most common adjustment in marriage is a compromise. In compromise, person leaves something to please others. Compromise should be satisfactory to both. Some concessions should be given to the compromising partner.

Adjustment becomes easy if both are willing to do so, if both were prepared for marriage, if both loved each other, if others do not interfere, if you have decided "we will not quarrel," if when one is in bad mood or anger you will persuade and bend, and, if "we" will not separate at any cost. Young couples going into marriage should recognize that the venture is new to both of them. They will encounter some problems as they attempt to live together as one.

TYPES OF MARITAL ADJUSTMENT

Marital adjustment is the process couples use to modify their relationship as needed throughout their married life. The need for adjustment is must to develop and maintain a high level of marital quality. Couples have to adjust with each other to lead a happy and successful married family life. Some would adjust for their children and others for each other. There are many types of adjustments done by the married couples. These are discussed below.

'For' Adjustment

'For' adjustment is mutual agreement on various issues. Here couple instead of enjoying themselves, spent their time, energy and money primary for the rearing of a family. Both make sacrifice for adjustment. Family expenditure takes priority over personal conveniences. Such 'for' adjustments are to be made if the high purpose of marriage is to be attained. This requires strong sense of dedication, religious values, willingness to sacrifice and maturity of character. This is also referred to as vertical adjustment by some social scientists.

'We' Adjustment

Adjustment cannot be complete unless both have learned to adjust to each other—their habits, preferences, needs and values. 'We' adjustment is that which is made between husband and wife. It removes incompatibility. Since, men and women are by nature incompatible, the life together requires the blending of their male and female differences. This is also referred to as horizontal adjustment by some social scientists.

HANDLING MARITAL CONFLICT

All married couples experience conflict in their relationships. Some disagreements definitely crop up when two individuals live together on day-to-day basis. Couples deal with these conflicts by making adjustments through certain methods.

Ways in which a quality relationship can be developed by choosing effective ways to deal with conflicts, learning to balance interpersonal relations and adapting to changes in financial and social areas are discussed underneath.

Aggression

Couples handle conflict sometimes through aggression. They don't agree on solutions but continually quarrel. They may hit, be physically abusive or verbally abusive in their anger and frustration. Unresolved hostility has negative effects on a relationship. Aggression does not give satisfactory solutions to the problems rather weakens the marriage relationship.

Concession

When one partner just gives into the other partner's view without presenting any objection or giving one's side of view it is called concession. If anyone of the partner gives in all the time, it decreases the marital quality, but, if both the spouses give in some of the time, the quality of the relationship may be quite high.

Accommodation

In accommodation, both the spouses accept each other's differences and agree to live with them. They don't obstruct the relationship but, mutual differences exist. This method does not improve quality of the relationship but it helps couples work around their differences.

Compromise

Compromise is a satisfying way to resolve marital differences. Both the partners try to find a solution to which they both agree. It is a give and take to reach an agreeable solution. Marriage brings together two unique individuals each having his or her own personal preference, opinion, belief and attitude towards life. The couple has to learn to live with each other's differences and accept the partner as he or she is, and, thus adjust to each other. The changes they make as they learn to live with each other are called interpersonal adjustments.

One has to start thinking for both of them together as 'we' rather than 'I' or 'me'. One has to accept each other's habits. Some of the habits might be changed but many are difficult to change.

One has to praise the partner and constantly show that he or she is loved, cared and appreciated for their thoughtfulness and for being just one self. A warm hug, thank you, I love you, you are great, give flowers, a soft kiss and small gifts shows appreciation for each other and increases the quality of their relationship. One should try to find and spend time for and with each other. Both need to feel accepted, loved and free to express personal thoughts and feelings.

Use Problem-Solving Skills

In this, both the partners listens to each other's opinion, consider the views of both, mutually discuss and come to a solution agreeable to both. If disagreements build on each other, hostile feelings are more likely to grow. Using problem-solving process is difficult when the couple is tense. Allow time for emotions to calm down and then discuss the issue and resolve it. Good listening skills, patience, respect and acceptance of each other are must for resolving the differences in a way, which benefits the relationship.

Resolving Conflicts

Open communication makes it easier to resolve differences through discussion, sharing of feelings and thoughts, constructive problem-solving, compromise and choosing one solution to which both the partners agree.

Most people marry for a combination of reasons, often including sexual and affectional attraction and a quest for security and companionship. A single factor does not make or break a marriage. Instead all factors work together to influence the relationship. Marriage differs from one culture to another and it has changed historically in our society. The purpose of marriage to a larger context is still the same. Two souls belonging to different families come together with a hope and outlook to stay intact till death does us part. The use of adjustment methods helps to resolve conflicts and strengthen the marital bond.

ADJUSTING TO MARITAL ROLES

A person is born as a grandchild, son or daughter, brother or sister, nephew or niece and then develops into uncle or aunt. Many roles one has before marriage continues to exist even after marriage. After marriage, you are son or daughter-in-law, husband or wife, brother or sister-in-law, and with the birth of a child, you acquire the role of a mother or father. At the same time, you have to be a wage earner, cook and housekeeper, depending on your cultural norms, sex-role expectations and equity of work shared among the couple, various tasks of home-making would be shared. Acceptance of one's roles and responsibilities and appreciation of the same by both the partners leads to a healthy married life.

It is desirable for people to work at developing adjustability, since, life is a continuous process of adapting new situations. The more adaptable a person is, the more likely he is to find happiness in marriage, on the job, and in social life. Those who are uncompromising, rigid, and inadaptable to work out good relationships in marriage, will require a longer time to enjoy happiness in marital life.

Marriage is a relationship that needs deep thought before it is entered into. Adjustments are necessary to make a marriage work. Most young people enter into marriage convinced that they are already well adjusted and they will not have the difficulties in getting along with each other. Everybody has to make adjustments not only in the beginning but, also throughout his or her married life. Adjusting is a conscious and deliberate learning process to understand, accept and change. In marriage, there is always some tension because marriage involves the relationship of two persons of opposite sex. When there is no adjustment it will produce dissatisfaction or total failure. Adjustment is a continuous and never-ending process.

ADJUSTMENT PROBLEMS IN MARRIAGE COULD BE AT VARIOUS LEVELS

Environmental

The environmental factors, which strain marriage, are those which make the family come into conflict with the community to which it belongs. Wherein the presence of outward circumstances is hostile to the harmony and happiness of husband and wife. These factors change constantly. They are not the same for all societies and for all times.

Relational

Where the couple fail for various reasons to achieve or maintain good adjustments to each other. These problems arise in the relationship between husband and wife, at the sexual, personal and parental levels. In an overwhelming majority of marriages that are in trouble, there is some degree of sexual adjustment. This is the root cause of the crises. In the first place, sexual union makes marriage unique and different from all other human relationships and gives it a specially exclusive and intimate quality.

Personal

Wherein, deficiencies in one or both of the individual partners render them incapable of meeting the demands of married life. The personal relationship between husband and wife is conditioned by compatibility and mutual adaptation. Compatibility is the degree to which the two personalities share a natural affinity. Mutual adaptation is the process by which they grow in a loving relationship to each other and develop new affinities to compensate for those lacking in their relationships. Good personal adjustments in marriages are complicated by the fact that the couple must achieve some degree of success at two different levels, firstly, they must be good partners and, secondly, they must be good lovers.

Inter-marriages in Today's Society

With the globalization, in-out movements of people to different places, societies, states, countries, culture and explosion of mass media has resulted in people's marriage outside their in-group of caste, religion, and nation, ethnic or racial group. Such marriages may be a result of couple falling in love with each other or non-availability of a compatible mate in one's own in-group and, therefore, arranging marriage to a suitable person.

These days' marriages are evident among people with varying rituals, customs and languages. These marriages neither can be said as good or bad, but are different, the couple faces challenges together, which may be slightly different from what persons of similar background may encounter.

THE HONEYMOON

The honeymoon is the time for the couple to relax after the wedding. They concentrate on getting to know each other and adjusting to their new roles and new life. During this period, most of the couples spend time together to travel. In India, sometimes couple would start their honeymoon after visiting some holy religious shrines and offering their thanksgiving to the God. The length of the honeymoon varies according to the couple's finances and time schedules. Taking a honeymoon in our society generally represents a romantic interlude in the beginning days of a marriage. It provides an opportunity to begin the adjustment transition to marriage. Honeymoon provides an opportunity for privacy that enables the couple to adjust from being separate individuals to becoming a couple who must share a common space and learn the intimacies of living together. It provides an opportunity for marital sexual activity and the achievement of sexual satisfaction. It also provides for a period of recuperation from the stresses and fatigue associated with the preparation and "staging" of a large wedding and reception. Simply, it provides an opportunity for the newly weds to get better acquainted under extremely favourable and romantic circumstances (Coleman, 1984).

Honeymoon is socially provided as a special adjustment period. It is looked upon as a time of supreme bliss. Honeymoon at its best is enjoyable only if the couple understands the significance of it. When it is unrealistically planned, it can actually become a liability, rather, than an asset to the new marriage. A good planning can be done by considering a number of factors like amount of money to be spent, length of honeymoon, activities both would enjoy, opportunities for rest as well as recreation.

When the honeymoon ends, and reality begins, couple becomes aware of a number of disagreeable issues and disillusionment with the marriage is common (Stanush, 1991). An adjustment in the marriage begins when reality dawns, a mature and fulfiling love and understanding draws on the couple, that for marital harmony it is not essential to agree on all issues. There is an understanding between the couple that differences are resolvable.

A source of irritation in marriage is the tendency of married people to take each other increasingly for granted when the honeymoon is over. The pretty girl who took so much pride in her appearance during the days of courtship becomes careless. She grows indifferent about her diet, eats fats and sweets without any discipline, until she has developed the proportions of a barrel, and then begins to wonder why she fails to attract her husband. Within the house, she disports herself in loose clothes, with her hair in disarray, a sight to make any man eager to leave the house early and return late. The husband, on the other hand, may regard his home as a kind of stable, where he can walk around in his stocking feet and bawl out orders or complaints with no regard for the amenities of civilized living.

This is not to assume that it is possible for all persons to be models of beauty or to retain sylph like figures and employ at all times the exquisite manners and formalities of a courtier. Advancing years take their toll of the charms of youth and within the home, both man and wife are entitled to a reasonable measure of informal comfort. Still, a thoughtful consideration of one's appearance and domestic manners can contribute much to tranquility and enduring respect.

An intelligent and solicitous wife can mean the difference between the success and the failure of her husband in his career. She will know how to keep an eye on his personal appearance, his wardrobe, and bearing. She will manifest real pride in his undertakings. She will give him generous encouragement, when he is low in spirits, as well as when he is walking on top of the world. She will know how to merit and elicit his confidence, with the assurance that she can be trusted to hold her tongue and to give sound counsel, not that type of silly or emotional reaction, which makes a man regret having opened his mouth.

The considerate husband will keep in mind that his wife is a living, throbbing human being, not merely a slave to do his bidding. He will remember anniversaries, bring sweets and/or flowers occasionally, and take his wife out to dinner and the movie. He will notice and praise her clothes and tell her how beautiful she looks, not take these things for granted or make her feel simply extravagant or ridiculous. Upon leaving for work and on his return he will kiss his wife, and exchange pleasantries about each other's welfare. He will frequently take his wife in his arms, and tell her that he loves her, and that she will always be the woman of his dreams. In the world, the happiness and loveliness of his wife will always be his chief concern, as he desires that she shall devote her life as a living flame to enkindle and illuminate his.

In today's dual earner marriages, where both the partners earn either by choice or circumstantial necessity, the fixed roles of man as bread winner and woman as home-maker have changed and intermingled. So, now both need to support each other at the time of stress, encourage the partner when he or she is in low spirits, and praise the partner for their contribution in the household affairs. While at the same time, woman still needs to be praised for beauty and looks, wants to hear 'I love you', 'I care for you', 'You are precious', and so on from her husband; and, at the same time, husband needs to be boasted for his efforts in running the house, be given credit for being a successful man in this competitive time and be praised for being a caring and loving husband.

MARRIAGE AND SEX

The second major adjustment problem in marriage is sexual adjustment. If it is not satisfactorily achieved, then it will lead to marital unhappiness. The attitude towards sex is greatly influenced by sex education received during late childhood years and adolescence. Due to unfavourable attitudes, it is very difficult to make better sexual adjustment. Sexual adjustment is basically a matter of mutual satisfaction. This is not a matter of frequency or intensity of sexual act but differing degrees to which each couple obtains satisfaction and happiness from whatever they had have developed.

Marriage is the one relationship in which intercourse is not only permitted and encouraged but also even required. In nearly all countries, lack of coitus following marriage is ground for annulment of marriage. The marriage has not been consummated meaning sexual intercourse has not taken place, and as far as the government and the major religions are concerned, the marriage is erased as if it never happened.

It is far from a sex issue. It shows intimacy, concern, caring and unselfishness among the couple. The reason it becomes so apparent is because sex to many of us is our way of expressing our deep feelings. When there is no sex, we don't receive confirmation of our partner's feelings and we are deprived of being able to express our own feelings.

Sexual activity is the basics of a marital bond. Sexual satisfaction increases as a couple becomes emotionally bonded to each other. Mutual respect, trust, commitment, enthusiasm and appreciation lead to a satisfying sexual union. Sensitivity to each other helps a couple to meet and adjust to each other's sexual needs.

Sex is an important factor in marriage. Sexual adjustment is must for marital satisfaction. Sexual adjustment among the married couple changes with change in work situations, becoming parents, deals with the family stress and growing old. Sex remains important throughout the marriage. Blumstein and Schwartz (1983) found that both the quantity and quality of sex were central to a good overall relationship for all types of couples—married and cohabiting, heterosexual and homosexual. Both men and women over age 50 consider sex to be very important for marriage and older couples that enjoy having sex are far more happily married than those who do not (Brecher, 1984). For men sex is pleasurable physical activity while for women it is a sign of emotional commitment. These separate meanings lead to miscommunication and misunderstanding among the couple.

In India, as in other countries, married couple is expected to have sex only with one another. Any sexual involvement outside marriage with someone other than the spouse is called extramarital sex, leads to conflict among the couple. Adultery, the legal term applied when a married person has intercourse with some one other than his or her spouse often becomes a reason of divorce or separation among the couple. Sexual monogamy, restricting one's activity to one partner only, in the case of marriage, the partners are spouses, is the most preferred way of living in most societies.

MARRIAGE AND IN-LAWS

In-laws relationship laid the foundation of marriage in most marriages. In arranged marriages and many-a-times in love marriages also, in-law relationships begin long before marriage occurs and a pattern of interaction is formed alongside the marriage. In India and other collectivist societies, marriage is not only between two persons but also between two families. Conflict with or about in-laws strain couple's marital happiness.

With marriage each adult acquires a whole new set of relatives, that is, the in-laws. These are the people of different age, having different interests and different values. Both husband and wife must learn to adjust with their in-laws. Some factors affecting in-laws adjustments are as follows:

Stereotype

The widely accepted stereotype of the typical mother-in-law can lead to an unfavourable mental state. The unfavourable attitude towards mother-in-law is that she is bossy and interfering.

Desire for Independence

The young married couple desire for freedom. They desire for independence. They resent the advice and guidance from their parents.

Family Cohesiveness

Marital adjustments are complicated when one spouse devotes more time to the relatives against the wishes of the spouse. Secondly, if a spouse is influenced by family advice or disturbance created due to relatives coming for an extended visit.

Most family culture features associated with high quality marriages are also present in cohesive families—parents and children who are able to adapt to, deal with and survive the difficulties of family life. After years of trying to understand and help troubled families, family counsellors and researchers, Nick Stinnett and John DeFrain (1985) identified six characteristics crucial for building family strength. These are:

Commitment

Members of cohesive families are dedicated to promoting each other's welfare and happiness. They value the unity of the family. Stinnett and DeFrain say that commitment is the most important of six characteristics. They point out that commitment implies that individual family members put the welfare of the family first and work hard to ensure it remains strong. Such commitment sometimes entails sacrifices by family members.

In in-laws relationship, there is a need for commitment to each and every member of the family. There are times when you need to lower ego and give in your position a little to foster healthy familial relationship with the in-laws.

Appreciation

Members of cohesive families show appreciation for each other a great deal. Family members are like everyone else and they like to be appreciated. They do not assume that others know they are appreciated but demonstrate their appreciation through compliments, praise, thank you, and gifts for each other.

Demonstrating such complimentary behaviour towards your in-laws, shows them that you value their presence in your life and give importance to their viewpoints. This would lead to a happy union among the couple, also when each partner appreciates the efforts put forth by the other partner's parents and family.

Communication

Members of cohesive families have good communication skills and spend a lot of time talking with each other. When the couple discusses their problems, seek solutions with the husband's family it is more appreciated than when the same is done with the wife's family. Involvement of wife's parents is especially considered a more serious interference in couple's married life.

Time

Strong families spend quality time in large quantities with each other. The strong families Stinnett and DeFrain (1985) studied were not convinced that a family could make up for a low quantity of time by achieving a high quality of time. Members of strong families did the same kinds of things that most adults and children do—eat meals, do chores, play, participate in religious activities, and celebrate birthdays and holidays—but did them as a family unit, not as individuals. When you involve your in-laws in such activities they feel satisfied and enjoy the warmth given by the extended family members. This is must for collectivist family's growth.

Spiritual Wellness

Whether they go to formal religious services or not, strong family members have a sense of a greater good or power in life, and that belief gives them strength and purpose. Not all the strong families Stinnett and DeFrain (1985) studied were religious, but a spiritual dimension of some sort was crucial to family strength. This spiritual dimension was important for both family well-being and for individual psychological well-being. Spiritual wellness is important for the well-being of the family because it promotes caring, love, and compassion of each family member for the others. It is important for individuals because it helps them find a sense of purpose and meaning in life, a positive confident outlook, guidelines for living, and a sense of peace and freedom.

Coping Ability

Members of cohesive families are able to view stress or crises as an opportunity to grow. Strong families have the skills, knowledge, and resilience necessary to cope with the problems, disappointments, and disasters of life. It is during the period of stress like sickness, loss of job, birth of a child, old age, and loneliness support and counsel of in-laws is highly appreciated.

MARRIAGE AND FRIENDSHIP

The interaction of friendship and marriage is an important factor that may affect marital happiness. Opposite sex-friendships after marriage are seen as a threat to the marriage as the partner involved may develop emotional and/or sexual involvement with the other person. In the past, once the commitment to marry was made, each partner was supposed to either convert opposite-sex friendships into friendships that could be shared with the intended spouse or to discard the friendships in favour of new couple relationships (Bell, 1981). But the contact with opposite sex continues. Women are also expected to have friendships and intermingle only among the spouse's selected few members for friendships. Same-sex friendships provided more help and loyalty than cross-sex friendships. While men are more likely to view both types of friendships equally, women believed their cross-sex friendships provided less acceptance and less intimacy but more companionship than same-sex friendships (Rose, 1985). Many persons believe that marriage should satisfy all of one's needs for friendship and in fact many partners are good friends. But some have found that the majority of women and men do not consider their spouse as a "good friend". Women are more likely than men to consider spouse as good friends (Bell, 1981).

MARRIAGE AND INTERACTION

The improved technology reduced man power and physical labour. Machines replaced number of men and skilled work was emphasized. Computers make complex jobs simpler. Time and energy for leisure activities increased but with the rise of competition in the job market, increase of unemployment, people work for more hours and drastically reduce their leisure time and time available for the family.

Active interaction produces more growth in relationship than passive interaction. Time spent together helps to keep in touch with each other's thoughts and feelings. With the passage of time, partners continue to grow and change throughout life. Active interaction involves physical and verbal exchanges between two people who are doing something together. In passive interaction one is involved as an observer or listener. Passive activities like reading books or watching television become active when you discuss the programs you watch or the books that you read. Active interaction provides insight into the thinking and feeling of one's spouse. Family functions provide time for active participation and interaction with all family members.

Satisfaction of emotional needs also leads to marital happiness. The primary emotional need met in any type of marriage is the need to be loved and to love. Mutual love grows with time as you share personal thoughts, spend time together, share ideas and feelings, think for each other and respect other persons' view points, opinions and beliefs. Marriage provides a platform to meet the basic needs for respect as well as self-actualization. It makes a person productive, creative and helpful.

MARRIAGE AND POWER

The popular press suggests that a number of attributes contribute to personal power, including beauty, charm, communication skills, cultural attainments, material assets, talents and wit (Marcus and Smith, 1982). Family social scientists suggest coercion, influence and/or the ability to persuade as bases for marital power. Gender also serves as a major determinant of power in view of the effects of traditional gender roles in our society (Nock, 1987).

Social scientists, Raven, Centers and Rodrigues (1975) suggested six basis of conjugal power in an attempt to clarify the various bases of marital power, a typology (classification) of conjugal power was developed by them. The classification of conjugal power suggests:

Coercive power—punish partner by acting or not acting in particular way.

Reward power—provide for partner's economic, psychological or physical needs.

Expertise power—use of knowledge by marriage partner about particular subject or activity.

Legitimacy power—recognize certain wife/husband roles carry legitimate responsibilities.

Referent power—gain emotional satisfaction from thinking or behaving as spouse wishes.

Informational power—accept arguments of spouse concerning some issue or problem.

In view of these different bases of marital power, it makes sense to assign non-major decision-making to one or the other of the marriage partners. Four general power patterns were identified in an early decision-making model: husband—dominant; syncratic (decisions negotiated together); autonomic (each marriage partner makes decisions alone in certain areas based on perceived impertise); and, wife dominant (Centers, Raven and Rodrigues, 1971). Lowest level of marital satisfaction was indicated in wife-dominant marriage and highest level of marital satisfaction was found in autonomic.

In India, husband-dominant marital relationships are more evident than any other. Now, a shift is also towards wife-dominant marriage partnerships, with the changing gender roles in our society, wife is using her individual resources to influence marital power.

Marriages in which the wife is dominant are more likely to be unhappy, while egalitarian couples tend to exhibit the highest levels of marital satisfaction and use of coercive control techniques in marriages leads to marital dissatisfaction (Gray Little and Burks, 1983). Changing gender roles also affects decision-making in families in which the wife is not employed. If the wife was a full-time home maker, joint power sharing was associated with greater marital happiness than a wife-centered or husband-centered authority structure. Further, whenever the actual use of authority approximated the couple's ideal pattern, the greater degree of marital happiness was reported by both wives and husbands (Mashal, 1985). With the change of time, reallocation of social roles to genders is taking place. In the changing gender role patterns, both the partners share the economic responsibility of the house.

MARRIAGE AND WORKING WOMAN

With a lot of pressure from all corners, increased use of amenities and once thought luxury items now becoming things for daily use has resulted in the need for both the partners to contribute more and more economic resources in the marriage. More educated women plan to have career with marriage. Increased employment for married women outside of the home has indirectly been detrimental to their social and psychological status, because career women still tend to retain major responsibility for children and house work (Greenglass, 1985).

During the last few years, many wives and husbands have embraced the trend toward egalitarianism in marriage without accepting its full implications. Women along with earning outside marriage earn in the marriage also. She is both a paid and non-paid worker, paid worker when she works in terms of a job or career and non-paid worker when she bears the responsibility of a house care-taker.

The woman cleans the house, looks after daily household chores, gives children adequate care, prepare meals on time and check laundry. She may do these activities by self or may take outside paid help. They are ready to subordinate the demands of their jobs to those of their husbands and ready to move to a distant location when their husbands receive a transfer or promotion. Today, more women want careers. They want to be full partners with their husbands in the world of work and expect their husbands to be full partners in the household. Some men are able to accept better changing marriage expectations than others. On the whole men tend to lag behind women in their awareness and adjustment to changing role expectations (Kramer, 1991).

Earlier, women worked both outside and inside the home but now role expectations are changing. The principle of equality is fast making them demand more contribution from the man in running the house, demand for his time and attention. This may lead to marital disharmony if the matter among the couple is not resolved amicably. In many of the cases, couple adjusts with the demands of each other, time and work responsibility. Dual-earner couples are not always dual workers in the home.

For marriages to work best, each partner must be prepared to give more than one half in the relationship. To do so on regular basis is difficult and may result in depression, unhappiness and low self-esteem if the other partner does not appreciate the work done by the partner.

MARRIAGE AND MONEY

Different views regarding money management are a major source of conflict in a marriage. Both the partners have the right to know where money is spent, how much is spent and why it needs to be spent. Couples may disagree over how much money is spent or the way it is spent. The amount of income a couple have sometimes produces conflict. Needs of the modern society being liberal, overpass the limited income its members earn, becomes a major concerning issue for a couple. Blaming each other for lack of money, feelings of guilt associated with poor income and poor spending habits of partners result in poor marital quality of partners. Amiteshwar Ratra (2002) reported lower marital quality among low-income women.

MARRIAGE AND COMMUNICATION

Communication is an interactive process in which at-least two people continually send and receive information. Human communication largely involves symbols. Symbol is a word, sound, gesture or object that has a certain meaning because people agree that it should have that particular meaning. Symbols when use words in sending a message are called verbal, when speaking tone and inflection are used then it is vocal and the use of body movement and facial expressions while sending a message it is visual or non-verbal communication. Good family communications involves various forms of expression, including such non-verbal communication as eye contact, facial expressions of smile, anger, warmth, etc. Communication is a completion process. It involves many steps and error in any step may cause misunderstandings and conflict.

Good marital communication takes place in a caring environment and is honest but kind. It requires time, good listening skills and understanding the other person's point of view (Stinnett and DeFrain, 1985). According to them good marital communication requires time together and cannot be hurried. The topics of communication do not matter much, as long as couples take some time to converse with one another. Good marital communication requires that both partners talk and that both listen. It involves each spouse accurately encode message in ascendable form—sentence, gesture, facial expression or all, transmit (send, say as a loud sentence), receives (hears the spoken sentence) and decodes (determines what the message means) the messages accurately. Each spouse is careful to avoid meta-messages, messages that has a meaning other than what it symbolizes on the surface, it is a hidden message or a message behind the message, and each asks for clarification about confusing messages. They suggest that couples avoid mind raping, assuming knowledge about what the other person is thinking without taking the time to find out and insist that people be sure they really know what the other means rather than just assuming they do. Marriage is a union of two persons with unique point of view. Differences in point of view can interfere with good marital communication. Building good communication patterns means trying to understand the other's point of view and taking into consideration when encoding and decoding messages. Spouses in quality marriage value each other and care about what the other is going through. They share their good and bad times together. Creating a caring communication, environment also encourages continued positive communication. Caring environment also helps each member of the couple to "open up" to the other and to disclose innermost thoughts and feelings. Self-disclosure is a major component of intimacy. People often face situations of wanting to be honest with another person but fear that honesty may cause pain or discomfort. Married couples with strong relationships are honest yet kind to one another. They maintain a delicate balance between honesty and kindness. Fear of hurting the spouse does not make an intimate partner from stating the fact. Such honesty is expressed in the caring and sympathetic way of two people who are really concerned about the other's welfare.

Good communication is associated with marital satisfaction

for both younger and older couples (Brecher, 1984). Many studies have found that marital communication and marital quality are clearly related to one another. Good marital communication and high marital quality is generally co-associated. However, there are expectations to it. Some couples are happily married even though their communication patterns are not particularly good (Brecher, 1984). Couples who want to handle marital problems by communicating with one another about them have happier marriages when their communication is good. For these couples, poor communication disrupts marital happiness because they place a high value on good communication (Krokoff, Gottman and Roy, 1988). But some couples, including some who are happily married, feel uncomfortable openly communicating with one another about marital problems and prefer to handle conflict by not communicating about it (Krokoff, Gottman and Roy, 1988). For these couples, good communication and marital happiness are unrelated.

Ideally, in a marriage the couple shares some common values and goals, they have similar or complimentary interests. They respect and value each other as persons and want to share their life with one another. The ability to communicate with each other leads to healthy and successful married life. Problems in married life arise when husband or wife has different interests, values and on the contrary they have no cooperation from each other.

Researchers are finding that how well a couple communicates before marriage can be as important predictor of later marital satisfaction as self-disclosure prior to marriage is related to relationship satisfaction later (Surra, Arizzi and Asmussen, 1988). Self-disclosure is the revelation of deep personal information about self. Self-disclosure is to reveal ourselves and our hopes, self-revelation or fears, our everyday thoughts and feelings. Self-disclosure deepens others' understanding of us and our own understanding, for we discover unknown aspects as we open ourselves to others. Otherwise we remain opaque and hidden.

Communication helps us to exercise some control over the environment, obtain desired objects/activities. It is useful in seeking attention. It helps to build and maintain relationships, share our feelings, thoughts and beliefs and share information as well as learn from others. Communication is an integral part of our lives and is the corner stone in husband—wife relationship.

Communication and intimacy are in extricably connected. There is a distinct difference in the communication patterns of couples in satisfied marriages to couples in dissatisfied marriages (Gottman, 1994; Hendrick, 1981; Noller and Fitzpatrick, 1991; Schaap, Buunk and Kerkstra, 1988).

Marriage often leads to learning new behaviours and establishing new routines. Many everyday behaviours can cause friction as you adjust to living with someone else. It is normal that a few of your habits will irritate your spouse as well. Talking to your spouse about an irritating habit may be enough to resolve it. Some habits are difficult to change. In fact, they may have to be accepted.

Marriage also needs to fulfil one's emotional needs to love and be loved by the partner. It is the primary emotional need which needs to be met in marriage. In arranged marriages, love is said to grow after the marriage among the couple and in love marriages it becomes the first reason to establish the relationship. Mature love continues to grow. Mature love will grow as you spend time together, sharing personal thoughts, ideas and feelings. It cultivates feelings of acceptance, belonging and importance. Showing mutual care for each other helps love keep growing. Marriage also needs to fulfil the need for respect and self-actualization. The need for self-respect and acceptance is met when your spouse makes you feel that you are an important part of his or her life. Once this need is met, you strive to grow and reach your full potential in other areas of your life. You may achieve emotional satisfaction in being productive, creative or learning new things. Each spouse needs to grow as an individual, finding some emotional satisfaction in personal accomplishments as a partner, finding some emotional satisfaction when found by the spouse as a good partner, as good friends, as a parent, finding some emotional satisfaction by being altruistic in taking care of the children and, as a good son or daughter or son-in-law or daughter-in-law by taking care of their own parents or in-laws during sickness, participation in family functions and taking responsibility at times of stress.

GENDER DIFFERENCES IN MARITAL COMMUNICATION

There are gender differences among husbands' and wives' communication patterns is an age old awareness. Recently, researchers have discovered specific gender differences in marital communication (Noller and Fitzpatrick, 1991; Thompson and Walker, 1989). Wives send clearer messages to husbands than their husbands send to them. Wives are more sensitive and responsive to their husbands' both positive and negative messages, both during conversation and conflict. Husbands may not reply at all. Husbands more than wives tend to give neutral messages. Wives tend to set the emotional tone and escalate arguments more than husbands do.

Communication includes both verbal and non-verbal communication. Non-verbal communication is by silence, gestures, and expressions. Non-verbal communication conveys interpersonal attitudes, express emotions, handles the on going interaction and gives meaning to our words.

Expression is discouraged by society for males. People avoid self-awareness through suppressing, denying and projecting feelings. Self-disclosure creates the environment for mutual understanding (Derlega, Metts, Potroio and Margulis, 1993). Self-disclosure is reciprocal. It is based on the love and trust we do with our partner. Love has already been defined in earlier chapter. Trust is the belief in the reliability and integrity of a person. It is must for a relationship to exist and continue. Trust is influenced by the way you are likely to interpret ambiguous or unexpected messages.

MARRIAGE AND RELIGION

A high degree of religiosity has been identified as having a positive relationship with marital satisfaction for wives and husbands. In one study, Hendershott (1986) found that in general, women engaging in religious activities and prayers with others had a higher degree of marital satisfaction than men. While, in another study by Hatch (1986), it was found that church attendance and frequency of prayer did not contribute to marital satisfaction. The findings indicated that lack of consensus about religious practices might lower marital satisfaction, while spousal consensus may increase marital satisfaction. Religious teachings also help to revaluate your relationships, your mistakes and gives strength to take initiative in resolving conflicts.

Marriage is to be viewed as a dynamic growth process in which marital happiness involves the ability to cope, change and adapt to circumstances. In fact, to maintain a high level of marital happiness requires a constant day-to-day effort instead of taking the marital relationship for granted (Bienvenu, 1986).

Strategies such as honesty, listening, openness, physical affection, physical attractiveness, self-concept confirmation, sensitivity, supportiveness and verbal affection help to strengthen the marriage bond. Marriage is a cooperative venture requiring great mutual contributions of care, time and energy. The primary purpose of the relationship is to nurture each of the partner, strengthen and support each other at times of success and stress alike. Such couples have a strong marital coalition of shared power and adapt well to changes in the individual and family life cycle.

MARRIAGE AND PERSONAL COMPATIBILITY

In olden days, adjustment was the sole responsibility of woman. She was either an ornament of the home or an unpaid servant. The early training to keep her at low ebb was effective in reducing the conflict to a minimum. If woman leaves everything for husband to decide and worry, life would have been warm, secure and comfortable (like a bird in cage). But, now the trend of relationship is changing. Now they seek equality and companionship in their mutual relations. Though, this pattern of partnership and companionship is difficult to achieve. It requires many mutual adjustments. If adjustment problems are met fairly and courageously, marriage can and will lead to deep mutual happiness.

Real Partnership

Without a real partnership modern marriage will not be fully satisfying. If they have a dynamic partnership of common purpose, they can enjoy life more. If they can freely communicate and understand each other, life will be richly rewarding. Adjustment and harmony will be required in various fields like sexual, emotional, intellectual, social and religious.

Mutual Trust

Mutual trust and honesty are absolutely necessary for a good and happy married life. There should be frankness and no part of life should be kept secret.

Inter-Personal Communication

Intimate and friendly communication between the two binds them together. This is assessed through: (i) Are they both genuinely fond of each other? (ii) Do they really feel relaxed in each other's company? (iii) Do they confide in each other? (iv) When they disagree, can they talk calmly and come to a mutually agreeable agreement. Generally, in marriage some people are held back from speaking because of the fear that they may hurt their partner. However, communication in partners require efforts, determination, patience and open mindedness. The saddest marriages are those in which two people become room-mates, meal-mates, and bed-mates and still remain strangers. In promoting good communication, an attitude of warm acceptance of each other is most important while discussing if your partner should look hurt, withdrawn, suddenly stop talking, or react with undue anger, stop the conversation right there and then.

Quarrelling

Couples quarrel because of many reasons like having different temperaments, expectations, habits or family background. Both are made different physiological (strength), emotionally and intellectually. The important thing in marriage is, if man and woman mean to stay happily married, it is not so much what they quarrel about as how they quarrel. Counsellors say about quarrelling in marriage: Get it out, don't let it fester, stick to the point and avoid side issues, attack the problem rather than each other, avoid dragging in relatives and avoid public display of marital differences.

When conflicts are directed at issues, they can lead to a more complete understanding between people. Attitude of tearing down the other will break the marriage.

Don't Argue when Angry

Don't discuss when you are angry. Harsh criticism or angry charges will never lead to understanding and acceptance. For marital harmony, a sincere and deep regard for the partner's feeling is essential.

Don't Insist on your Rights

Those who insist more on their own rights and do not look at life through the other's eyes, the matters don't resolve. Be ready to give in that times and look at the problem from your partner's prospective.

Infact, couples must develop a talent for asking—for listening—and for understanding each other. The secret of a happy marriage is a cooperative sharing. Ask question—(i) What would I do, If I were in the same situation? (ii) Would I perhaps do the same thing?

Don't Try to Remake your Partner

People should not try to change over their partner's complete personality, though some faults can be corrected. Most quarrels in marriage are due to wife's attempt to remake her husband to her image and husband's effort to remodel his wife to his image.

Adjustment

It is very essential part in harmony. Instead of being rigid one should try to understand other's view point and adjust to each other. Before marriage we have only a very limited range of opportunities to see our partner in various situations. They are unable to discover the attitudes, behaviour which they may display in stress, conflict or crisis. You know them incompletely. Later on after marriage, a lot of things are discovered and you have to adjust, by accepting. Adjustment means, literally to move toward what is fitting, appropriate, just or necessary for both parties. It is blending, meshing, accommodating and fitting together.

Respectful Consideration

They must be considerate to each other's problems. If wife is overworked with dual career roles, if husband is overstressed due to office-work—both can give relations in their expectations. Disagreements should not be made public.

Acceptance

There must be acceptance of the other person as he or she is, with his or her interests and activities. Those couples are truly happy who have acquired sufficient wisdom not to expect the impossible from their marriage or from each other.

Happiness must be Earned

Both husband and wife must put forth constant effort to stay happily married. It comes through understanding and personal adjustments. This must be planned and cultivated. Each must try to find the other's interests, tastes and wishes. It cannot be achieved through fault-finding and nagging.

Basic Needs

You must understand your partner's needs and should try to fulfil those—physical and psychological needs. Besides, love, affection or physical needs, the achievement need is also important. It is a sense of worthwhile contribution in home and society. It is recognition of one's contribution and achievement. The sense of achievement is strong in men. If he is given a feeling that he is a success in the eyes of his wife, he will not fall a victim to the depressing tensions of the business and economic field. A good wife should be an inspiration to her husband. She should be encouraging and supporting partner. A wife needs constant reassurance that she is a good home-maker and has many other good qualities. The husband's opinion about his wife means really very much to her. Educated wife also needs companionship. The greatest gift that husband can give to his wife is the gift of his time. In today's dual earner and dual career marriages, achievement in the outer world is also becoming must for women and they also need support of their husband.

MAINTENANCE OF MARRIAGE

Finding someone with whom you want to be in a committed relationship is tough but making the relationship last may be even tougher. Men, more than women, clearly displayed their social status and financial success as a tactic to keep their mate interested in them and women were more likely than men to work on their appearance as a tactic to keep their mate interested (David Buss and Todd K. Shackelford, 2004). Dr. Buss reported that the reproductive value of a woman indicated by her youth and attractiveness was consistently linked with a man's increased efforts at staying married. In their research, men also reported other efforts at keeping their mates interested such as making promises of change in order to please their spouse and making threats of sexual betrayal. Women on the other hand, married to men with higher incomes reported being more watchful of their husband's behaviour, more punishing of their infidelity threats, more concerned with their own appearance and more emotionally manipulative than were women married to men with lower incomes.

Marital happiness in the middle-ages years is related to having high self-esteem and a good interpersonal relationship. Intellectual bond, emotional attachment, common interest, delayed sexual gratification, adhering to social traditions and customs, companionship, care and feeling of belongingness leads to a long lasting relationship.

Coping is almost as elusive as the concept has been used to denote all the mechanisms utilized by an individual to meet a significant threat to his/her psychological stability to enable an individual to function effectively or in other words it is the effect to 'master' conditions of harm, threat or challenge. When a routine or automatic response is not readily available, coping traits refer to a disposition to respond in a specific way in situations that are stressful.

Every marriage deserves a fair chance, no matter where it is now, and no matter what you or your spouse have done (or not done). You may have tried to change things with little success. You may be wondering if there is any hope for the relationship. Try not to give up on the marriage! There is a difference between people in happy marriages and those in troubled marriages.

Marriage relationship is balanced when both spouses work to contribute equally to maintain the relationship. Both give as much as they can of themselves to the relationship. Both of them feel that the relationship as well as each other is important for their existence and purpose of life. Each person is unique with special abilities, so mutual respect for each other strengthens a marital relationship. Commitment to cooperate and acceptance of the personal traits benefit a marital relationship.

8

Alternatives to Marriage

Marriage was related to age and race, a stability of environment and identity for children, an opportunity for personal growth, a division of labour, ego support, an opportunity for commitment to each other, attainment of common goals, more organized life and time saving arrangement, economic growth and social support. Marital satisfaction was related to social and personal happiness.

With the advent of modernism, traditional outlook took a backseat in the society. Traditional marriage is now considered as a loss of individuality, loss of privacy, lack of freedom, lack of individual growth, lack of social and sexual variety, boredom and dullness, dissatisfaction with spouse, feeling trapped, not accommodating each other, sexual frustration (due to mismatch), being tied down, work with no pay check to housewife, problems with-in-laws. All these factors have lead to a change in the form and purposes of marriage. These factors have given rise to alternative forms of marriage.

ALTERNATIVE FORMS OF MARRIAGE: THE EMERGING TRENDS IN MARRIAGE

The Intrinsic Marriage

This style of marriage is a relationship in which couples have intense feelings about each other, and each considers the other person to be of central importance. The intrinsic marriage is a merging of two people that is so intimate. People who prefer intrinsic marriage also have other concern in life such as career, kin, friends, and their own individuality. There concerns are always important and they do not want to neglect them.

Utilitarian Marriage

These are those, which are established or maintained for purposes other than to express an intimate, highly important personal relationship between a man and a woman. This marriage is one in which the marriage is desirable and useful but subservient to other aspects of life that have greater value.

Open Marriage

This style of marriage involves a unique balance among intimacy, interpersonal commitment and flexibility. Important aspect of this alternate form of marriage is a recognition that individual change throughout their life, and marital relationship is viewed as sufficiently flexible to permit both members of the couple to change and grow and yet retain a meaningful relationship with each other. Other main characters of this marriage are living for now, realistic expectations, privacy, role flexibility, open companionship, equality, identity and trust. It is also called flexible marriage.

Two Step Marriage/Multistep Marriage

In the first marital relationship the individuals usually live together, cohabit sexually, and form one economic unit, but they do not have children. The second relationship involves a more permanent commitment and includes the bearing and rearing of children. The first relationship is to have a testing or 'try out to see if it is what we want' and usually there is no social pressure on the couples to stay together.

Temporary Marriage

It is one in which couple enters into a relationship for the satisfaction of one or two immediate needs. These couples usually value monogamous relationship, but they do not want to be restricted by legal obligation, long-term expectation and parental responsibility.

Group Marriage

It is defined as a group of three or more persons in which individual consider themselves pair-bounded or married to atleast two other members of the group. The combinations can be couple and single person, two couples, two couples and single person, three couples and so on.

Consensual Marriage

In this, the couple agrees that they may have sexual relations outside their own relationships with prohibition of extended or emotional involvement.

Covenant Marriage

Covenant marriage is a new type of legal marriage, in which the bride and groom agree to be bound by a marriage contract that will not let them get divorced as easily as is allowed presently. This is more prevalent in the United States of America. Under a covenant marriage contract, couples are required to get premarital counseling and may divorce only after being separated for at least two years or if desertion for one year, adultery or domestic abuse, is proved in court. In addition, a covenant couple will have to submit to counseling before a divorce (Olson, 1998).

Commuter Marriage

A marriage in which the two partners live in different locations and commute to spend time together. This is also called two locations marriage. Both the partners are working and career-oriented.

Swinging and Sexually Open Marriage

Swinging is a marriage arrangement in which couples exchange partners in order to engage in purely recreational sex (Macklin, 1987). It is new version of the age-old practice of married couples exchanging partner for sexual activity. This form of marriage usually involves a fairly traditional marital relationship except for sexual behaviour. The couple has high commitment to permanence in their married relationship, and are fairly conventional in the other role they occupy. Exchanging partners with other couples for sexual relations. In a sexually open marriage, spouses agree that each may have openly acknowledged sexual relationships with others while keeping the marriage relationship primary. Unlike in swinging, one or both spouses go out separately and outside relationships can be emotional as well as sexual. Partners in sexually open unions tend to be highly independent, willing to take risks, non-conforming and committed to non-possessiveness and personal growth. Couples usually establish limits on the degree of sexual and/or emotional involvement of the outside relationship, along with ground rules concerning honesty and that details to tell one another (Macklin, 1987).

Extramarital Sex

Extramarital sex is the sexual behaviour or contact outside marriage. Extramarital sex is not accepted among most of the world's culture. Extramarital sex depends on the opportunity to find a partner, willingness to take the opportunity and un-satisfaction in marriage. It also depends on nearness or availability of potential partner. Extramarital sex often leads to jealousy and has an impact on economic resources. This is often a reason of divorce. It goes against the moral and religious standards of most societies. Many a times it may arouse guilt and anxiety in the persons involved. The person while indulging in extramarital sex is anxious and fears the loss of a primary relationship.

The terms family/marriage lifestyles refers to differences in style of living rather than to deviant styles. Life-styles are related to and stem from sub-cultures, social classes, and status groups, but they do not involve the degree of collective consensus or the collectively shared meanings found in sub-cultures and social classes. Empirically, life-styles are related to economic consumption patterns, political beliefs, and moral, ethical and aesthetic standards.

Following are the different life styles of social and sexual alternatives of marriage.

SOCIAL ALTERNATIVES

Singlehood

The emerging style of singlehood represents one of chòice. Single hood is seen as a lifestyle capable of successfully fulfiling human needs.

In today's society, more and more people are choosing to live alone. Single living refers to a household consisting of one person. This trend is more common in the United States and other western countries than the Eastern countries and the Indian sub-continent. Singlehood is a state that may or may not be chosen. People choose single living as a lifestyle for several different reasons such as delaying marriage, choosing not to marry, divorce or death of a spouse. The period of single living may be temporary or permanent. Singles have more time to concentrate on their career and can pursue their hobbies as well.

Types of Singlehood

Stein (1981) developed one way of categorizing single people. His four categories are based on whether single status is voluntary or involuntary and on whether singleness is permanent (stable) or temporary. Psychologist Arthur Shostak (1987) refined the typology somewhat by attaching labels to each of Stein's categories. He refers to those in the "voluntary, temporary" category as ambivalent. The ambivalents are mostly young people postponing marriage; many of them are in cohabitation or dating relationships. Those in the "involuntary, temporary" are called wishful category. They actively seek mates. Further he refers to the "voluntary, stable" singles as resolved, and includes those in religious orders, single parents who desire to remain single, confirmed homosexuals and older heterosexual singles who have come to prefer the single way of life. Lastly, people in the "involuntary, stable" category as 'regretful' tend to be older but regard their singleness as a life sentence" rather than as a choice they consciously made.

Rates of singlehood vary by country to country and ethnicity. In 1993, 42.3 million adult American, 22.6 percent of all men and 26.2 percent of women had never married (Saluten, 1994). Women with high levels of education, income, occupational prestige and intelligence are less likely to marry than the other women (Leppel, 1987).

Single females seem to adjust better than single males. Single females experience less discomfort than do single men, report greater happiness, and show fewer symptoms of psychological distress. Compared with single men, single women are more likely to have a higher education, a higher median income, a higher representation in professional or managerial positions.

Individuals who choose singlehood view it as providing greater freedom, more opportunities to meet people and develop friendships, greater economic independence, more varied sexual experiences (in western culture), and increased opportunity for self-development.

Several factors appear to influence people's choice to remain single today: First, expanding employment opportunities for women allow them greater economic self-sufficiency than ever had in the past. Second, the acceptance of non-marital cohabitation, particularly in Western culture, today permits people to satisfy sexual and emotional needs without getting married. The third factor is women's higher level of education and associated commitment to career goals.

The other reasons why people remain single are an unattractive or sex-inappropriate appearance, an incapacitating physical defect or prolonged illness, lack of success in the search for a mate, unwillingness to assume the responsibilities of marriage and parenthood, and residence in a community where the sex ratio is unbalanced.

There are two other categories of singles. First, men and women choose to remain single following a divorce. Second, higher numbers choose not to marry following the death of a spouse in middle or late adulthood.

Socio-emotional Effects of Singlehood

Single people, regardless of their sexual orientation, usually develop a sense of family that differs from others. Many of them acquire a social network that provides the kind of emotional and psychological support found among other family types. Friendships are very important to single people. Singles also participate in a variety of groups that provide social support and recreation. Many people in our culture doubt that single people can be mentally, emotionally, and physically healthy.

Adjustment to Remaining Single during Early Adulthood

The individual who does not marry is likely to be unhappy, lonely to oppose and thwarted in his normal desires for sex, parenthood, affection from an admired member of the opposite sex, and the prestige that marriage and family living provide. In many communities there is no place for the bachelor or spin our except as an extra person at a party or a baby sitter for married relatives.

There are many reasons why people remain single. These have been discussed in the previous section. By age thirty, most women get married. If they have not married by age thirty, they tend to shift goals and values and find a new life oriented towards work. Thirty is thus a critical age for an unmarried woman and her life may be characterized by stress as she approaches it. Thus, reaches a peak at thirty and then gradually decreases as she makes adjustments to new goals and new pattern of life. The desire for marriage and a family decreases after thirty as the women realizes that she is not likely to achieve these goals. Not all unmarried women, by any means, are willing to resign themselves to being single, nor are they all willing to allow themselves to be lonely because of lack of companionship with members of the opposite sex. They may become active in community service or social organizations; they may join clubs or social activities. It is usually easier for a man to adjust to being single than for a woman. A single man is in a great social demand and has little time to feel lonely. He is usually financially able to pursue a pattern of life that is to his liking.

They can't fulfil his sex needs. Finding a satisfactory outlet for the sex drive, which is especially strong during early adulthood, is the most difficult problem the unmarried person faces. The unmarried man usually finds sexual gratification either by engaging in autocratic practices or by having sexual relationships with women of his acquaintance or with prostitutes. Although unmarried women, like men, engage in autocratic practices, they have less opportunity for sexual encounters, which are still not condoned for women in all segments of society and they must always face the possibility of pregnancy.

Adjustment to being Single during Middle Age

By middle age, most unmarried men and women have

adjusted to being single and are reasonably happy with the pattern of life they have established for themselves. Some however, have not made a satisfactory adjustment to being single and decide to marry during middle age.

Most women are realistic enough to know that they pass forty, their chances for marriage grow slimmer every year. This is far more true in the case of single women than of widows or divorcees. After 45, the single women's chances of marriage are very poor. Knowing that her chances of marriage are poor, the middle aged single woman adjusts her life pattern accordingly and often centers her life around her work.

Most men who are single in middle age are so by preference. They find it socially advantageous to be bachelors, and they can marry whenever they no longer derive satisfaction from being single. If they have high aspirations for vocational success, they may prefer to devote their time and energy to working and getting ahead.

Problems of being Single in Middle Age

Just as marriage creates many problems for men and women in middle age, so does being single. Furthermore, single women, like those who are married, tend to have more difficult problems during middle age than do men. The most complex problems that single men and women must cope with during middle age are:

Problems of Women

Problems related to employment and vocational advancement are even more serious for the middle aged woman than for the man. If she loses her job, she has even less chance of finding another one than middle aged man in the same position. Also, women who hold their jobs through middle age are far less often promoted to positions of prestige and responsibility than men. As a result of these practices, working is not always or satisfactory substitute for marriage, with the security it normally brings. To add to her adjustment problems, it is usually the single woman in a family who is expected to assume the responsibility of caring for elderly parents. This often creates a financial burden in addition to the physical and emotional burden of caring for an elderly person while holding down her job.

Assuming the responsibilities for the care of an aging parent, generally means, that the middle aged single woman must limit her social life. As a result, she often cuts herself off from social contacts and activities in community organizations so drastically that when the care of the parents ends, she is lonely and has to find other priorities to keep herself busy than the widow or divorcee, who may have her children or friends she acquired during the years of her marriage to fall back on for companionship.

Problems of Men

The single man is usually in a more favorable position in middle age than the single woman. Because he has not had the responsibilities of a family through the early adult years, he has been able to devote as much time as he wished to his work, and he has been free to move to areas where greater opportunities were available. Although, success in the business would depend on hard work and a willingness to adapt oneself to new situations the middle aged man is usually better rewarded for his past efforts than the middle aged woman, who has followed the same pattern of hard work and personal sacrifice in the earlier years and he is more likely to be promoted. The middle-aged bachelor is therefore, generally at the peak of his career, and he has little reason to be concerned about unemployment.

Furthermore, a single man is not handicapped by problems of caring for elderly parents unless no other family member can assume the responsibility. When he must take on this burden, he usually provides financial and rather than sacrificing his time and efforts to take care of their needs. Consequently, he is free to lead the kind of life he wants, and he has relatively few of the adjustment problems that the middle aged single woman must face.

Adjustment to being Single in Old Age

The popular belief that an old person who has never married will face an unhappy, lonely old age is not true. The single man has learned over the years to develop interests and become involved in activities to compensate for the lack of companionship of a family of his own. As a result he is less likely to face a lonely old age than the man who married, whose interests centered around his home and family, and who now in old age, may find himself without his wife and children.

The modern single woman builds up a life of her own to suit her as a man does. As a result, she has much to keep her happy and occupied in old age. Even though she is retired, she is still happy and because she never had to devote her leisure time to a family, she has had an opportunity to establish many interests which will keep her from being lonely when she reaches retirement age.

Adjustment to being Single due to Loss of a Spouse

The loss of a spouse, whether as a result of death or divorce, presents many adjustment problems for the middle-aged man or woman, but especially for the woman. The middle aged woman whose husband dies or who is divorced experiences extreme feelings of loneliness. This is intensified by frustration of the normal sexual desires, which are far from dormant but inactive. A person who loses a spouse and remains alone for one or more years generally makes satisfactory adjustments to being single, although he may tend to be lonely and to find the single state unsatisfactory.

Loss of a spouse as a result of divorce affects middle-aged people very differently, depending upon who wanted the divorce. A woman whose husband divorced her to marry someone else will have different reactions from those of a woman who found her marriage intolerable and initiated the divorce herself.

The man whose wife dies or who is divorced experiences a disruption in his pattern of living unless a relative can manage the home for him. A woman who is widowed or divorced in middle age often must give up her home, go to work, and live very differently from the way she did when her husband was alive or before her divorce. The woman alone also encounters social complications that men do not face. She may be unwilling on reluctant to go out by herself, and the problem of entertaining is like-wise awkward. For divorced woman, the social complications are even greater. Not only she is excluded from social activities, but also even worse, she often loses old friends. The most serious problem that loss of a spouse in middle ages presents to women is from the fact that their chances for remarriage become slimmer as they grow older. During old age, long period of loneliness complicated by financial and social problems arises. Loss of a spouse in old age is more likely to be due to death. Because woman marry man of their own age or older than they and because man, on the average, die sooner than woman, widowhood in old age is far more common than widowerhood. Thus, widowhood is a greater problem than widowerhood during old age.

Adjustment to the death of a spouse is difficult for men and women in old age because at this time all adjustments are difficult to make. When a man's wife dies shortly after he retires, this greatly increase his difficulties in adjusting to retirement. Because old age is a period during which interests narrow especially social interests, the elderly person who is left alone cannot compensate for this by developing new interests as readily as he could do earlier. The widow usually has the additional problem of a greatly decreased income. Decreased income often means moving into new smaller house, going to live with a married child; or living in an institution, all of which require adjustment and further complicate adjustment to the loneliness which widowhood brings. For the widower, the economic is far less serious problem than the problem of loneliness.

Problems with Unmarried Single

Many people are satisfied living the single life. But if you're not, the following five points may lend some insight as to why you can't seem to settle down.

You're not Ready for Commitment

If you are a serial monogamist or juggle several relationships at once. You're probably not prepared to commit to one person for the rest of your life. Every single human being, whether male or female, wants both freedom and stability. Finding a healthy balance between the two, experts say, is a major obstacle to a successful relationship.

For men, the option of remaining single indefinitely makes settling down less of a necessity. Men are allowed to roam the earth until they are good and ready to settle down. For them, a major problem is fear of making a permanent commitment. In the past, people worried: Am I going to settle down with the right person? Am I doing this because of social pressure?

Men aren't the only ones afraid of commitment. Experts say,

for most women, being single is a choice, and many are reluctant to give up their territory as well. The steady increase of women in the workforce means that they no longer have to be married for economic reasons.

Men and women who get going from one relationship to another usually have an unrealistic expectation of romance. When the honeymoon stage of the relationship is over, some believe that the love is gone as well. If you only focus on romance, you neglect other areas of love. These and other fears are partly responsible for the increasing number of couples who decide to live together without getting married. With divorce rates soaring as ever, more and more single people question the need to get married when they can live together.

You don't have a Life

Love won't come looking for you if you're renting videos every night or working from dawn till dust. Get out there and meet people. We need to meet 10 people in order to find one who may be an appropriate candidate. Out of these 10, one may be your soul mate.

If you're having trouble for finding potential dates, shake up your routine. Volunteer in your community. Find something you like to do, and you'll increase the odds of finding someone who shares your interests. Nobody likes a workaecholic. Many relationships fail when one partner is obsessed with work. If you're constantly canceling dates due to work-related emergencies, you may be hiding other problems.

You're too Picky to Choose

Assessing what you need and want from a relationship is a good idea, but don't go overboard. Many of us have a checklist of characteristics we look for in a partner and relationship. When an item of that list is not met, we automatically dismiss that individual as a prospect. If you have specific height and weight requirements, or insist that your date drive a certain car and wear certain clothes, you've lost sight of what is truly important. When you find someone you can call your, want to meet and talk to them again, feel comfortable in their company, then it's the right choice. In reality, marriage counselors say, we can't get everything we need from one person. Stop looking for someone to be your everything, and start developing healthy relationships with all the people in your life. Keep your friends and outside interests. When a couple work together as a team instead of melting into a we, a good relationship is possible.

You're not over Past Relationships

We all have baggage, but many people let failed relationships affect their self-esteem. When a relationship doesn't work, it shouldn't distract you from who you are. Women who have been burned several times in relationships may decide it's easier to remain single. Those who have been abused or misused are likely to choose not to be involved even again.

Men have their baggage but tend not to give up easily. A man has to be in a relationship with a real psyche or have been married a couple of times before he thinks about never getting involved again. Take advantage of your time alone to reflect on past relationships. Being single is a time to learn how to make healthier, happier choices. Before getting involved again, determine who you are as a person. Figure out your likes and dislikes and decide what you really want and need in a relationship.

You're getting Sad

For some of us, the pressure to get married starts at age 25. By the mid-30s, people start raising their eyebrows. After 40, people start gossiping about your inability to find someone. By keeping the need for a mate in perspective, we give ourselves more choice. Recognize when you are compatible with a person, when the potential for a healthy relationship is still there.

Single people suffering from marriage anxiety tend to give off signs and signals that frighten prospective partners away. Dating is a chance to get to know someone. When you relax and take the pressure away, love will find you when you least expected it. In the meantime, concentrate on yourself. Love your life and look your best at all times. After all, you never know when you might meet that special someone.

Other reasons why young adults remain single are unattractive or inappropriate appearance, physical defects or prolonged illness, no suitable match, unwillingness to assume responsibilities, too busy in career building process, family responsibilities, imagining unhappy experiences, sexual availability without marriage, an exciting lifestyle, freedom in contacting opposite sex persons, belief that social mobility is easier when single than married, strong and satisfying friendships with members of the other sex, homosexuality, marriage as a hindrance in personal freedom, growth and development, and to keep from routine and boring life.

But, later on, they may realize that they are missing something in terms of continued friendship based on partnership, social disgrace, unacceptability by married or families, loneliness as there is no one to share anything. In Indian culture, men want to get rid of household chores and women of economic tensions, both need emotional support—someone to admire or to support, they feel that they do not need possessions, loneliness in later part of life may cause depression, and no one takes care in distress, illness or old age.

Research provides conflicting answers to this question. One study indicates that having poor relationships or marriages is more detrimental to one's health than not having any love relationship. In India, singlehood is not a preferred why of life. According to Ashrams of Hindu culture, marriage is must to attain moksha and singlehood does not attain a higher social status. Singlehood is on the rise because of liberal social and sexual standards, delayed marriage, employment options and higher educational attainment of women. The mass media is glorifying singles culture especially the western media. Also, our own media is showing the marriage, portrayed on television, abounding in extramarital affairs.

Cohabitation

Cohabitation has been defined as a living situation wherein an adult is sharing living quarters with one unrelated adult of the opposite sex. Children may or may not be present in the household, but no other adult may be living in the residence (Spanier, 1983). According to Ridley, Peterman and Avery (1978) cohabitation may be based on different reasons like living together to test the feasibility of marriage, sexual fulfilment and avoidance of domestic responsibilities attempt to gain independence from parental influence and live according to one's own values, or one partner serves as a dependent partner for the other. These relationships may be long or short-term, permanent or semipermanent alternative to marriage.

Living together is becoming more widespread and accepted in recent years. As, the general climate regarding sexuality is more liberal than it was a generation ago. The moral criterion for judging sexual intercourse has shifted, love rather than marriage is now widely regarded as making a sexual act moral. With dramatic increase in divorce rate, the meaning of marriage is changing. Men and women are delaying marriage longer.

Types of Cohabitation

According to Mecklin (1978) at least five different types of relationships can be described as cohabitation: *Temporary casual convenience* is when two people share the same living quarters because it is expedient and convenient to do so. *Affectionate dating or going together* is when two people live together because they enjoy being with each other; they will continue living together as long as it is mutually satisfying. *Trial marriage* includes persons who are "engaged to be engaged," as well as couples who are trying to discover if they want to marry each other. *Temporary alternative to marriage* is when two people are committed to each other but are waiting for a better time to marry. *Permanent alternative to marriage* is when two people live together essentially as husband and wife but reject the idea of marriage.

SEXUAL ALTERNATIVES

Biological sex of a person is determined at the time of conception as male or female. Male being determined by XY chromosome, of which X comes from the mother and Y comes from the father. While, female being determined by XX chromosome, of which either X comes from both mother and father. In India we accept third sex also.

People's identities are not well defined by their biological sexual orientations. Some may be heterosexuals, sexual behaviour and interest in people of the other sex or a person primarily sexually interested in and active with those of the other sex; homosexuals, sexual contact with individuals of the same sex or a person whose primary sexual interest and activity are with someone of the same sex; bisexual, an individual who is sexually attracted to and active with both women and men; transsexuals are biological women and men who feel like and identify with members of the other sex.

Among all the human beings heterosexual behaviour is most common and accepted norm of the society. Though variations in the acceptable norms are evident in the form of transsexualism, bisexualism and homosexuality.

Transsexuality

Transsexual is a person who is clearly male or female with chromosomes and hormones seemingly in agreement, and yet want to change his or her biological sex. Such persons are unhappy both with their sex and gender roles assigned. They want to join the other sex psychologically and physically. It appears so potent that it motivates a few adults to reorient their physical sex. Transsexual men and women endure the discomforts and a risk of major surgery to bring their sex into line with what they believe is their gender (Bullough, Bullough and Smith, 1983). Transsexual individuals report that they have been trapped into the wrong body. Most homosexual people, like heterosexuals are comfortable and content with their biological sex. Transsexual women and men are not happy with their sex they want to change it.

Many but not all transsexual people seek what is called sex reassignment surgery. It is a major surgery often taking 4 to 6 hours. As in all surgery, complications may occur. They need to attend sex or gender dysphoria program that helps evaluate and guide potential patients. This surgery is not performed simply on demand. The person unhappy with their gender and sex need to be educated about the procedure she or he will undergo and the likely results. They learn that once the penis is removed, or the vagina altered, they have taken an irreversible step. They also need to know that they will not become a fully sexually capable woman or man, but only approximate the physical appearance and function of the sex they wish to be. Neither men nor women can be provided with functioning reproductive organs and they will remain chromosomally XX or XY (woman or man), just as they were born. Such people are encouraged to speak frankly with their families and friends and explore the effect the reassignment surgery will have on their jobs and lives. Such surgery would lead to removal or adjustment of primary and secondary sex organs of the desired sex to which a person want to attain.

Homosexuality

Homosexual women and men identify with their own biological sex. Homosexual people are not transsexual, that is, they do not want to be the other sex. Homosexual men think of themselves as men and homosexual women feel and act like women (Bell *et al.*, 1981; Blanchard, 1988).

Homosexual word comes from the Greek word 'homo', meaning same. A person who is homosexual is interested in others of the same sex. A homosexual person is defined as an individual whose primary erotic, psychological, emotional and social interest is in a member of the same sex even though that interest may not be overtly expressed (Martin and Lyon, 1972). When we say homosexual it may refer to both sexes.

The word Lesbian used for homosexual females, comes from Lesbos, a Greek Island, where in ancient times young women were supposedly schooled in feminine and erotic arts. The master of the school, Sappho, according to surviving literature and poetry, encouraged romantic and sexual preferences for women. Homosexual men have preferred the term gay. They suggest that is a more positive term and affirm a life style.

Judging from ancient Egyptian and some Asian and European illustrations, homosexuality has always been a part of human history. The ancient Eastern faiths such as Hinduism and Buddhism said relatively little about homosexuality. Islam, the Muslim faith, strongly forbids homosexuality and gives death as a possible punishment. Early Christian leaders also outlawed homosexuality. The early Greek and Roman worlds seemed to be more tolerant of homosexuality. In both societies 2000 and more years ago, there were relatively few rules regulating sexuality, though all sexual behaviours were not approved. Much of Plato's writing, particularly in his symposium seems to extol homosexual love among man. Sappho did the same for lesbian affection. In Rome, Emperor Egalabalus, in the third century had a number of homosexual lovers and late in his life he married one of his lovers. The sexual freedom did not last long in these civilizations.

During the adolescent years some teenagers explore sexual and/or affectional relations with members of their own sex. Such homosexual interactions may involve deep emotional feelings as well as mutual genital stimulation by hand or mouth, kissing and caressing and other sexual excitation. They may be involved in necking and petting. Necking is defined as kissing with perhaps an occasional hug, but all-important activity is above the neck. It is kissing and hugging without other erotic touch above the neck. It includes putting arms around the partner or any physical contact confined to the area above the neck. Petting connotes any physical contact below the neck. It is kissing and erotically stimulating another person without having sexual intercourse. Heavy petting may be defined as the manual or oral stimulation of the genitalia. Petting includes any physical contact below the neck, between the parts of the bodies of two people, short of the act of intercourse, and that it includes passionate kissing, and intimate fondling of the body, including the sexual organs, with or without clothing, which may, though not necessarily, produce orgasm, but definitely without coitus (Kapur, 1973). Coitus is the act of sexual intercourse.

For some these early homosexual contacts cause a good deal of anxiety and guilt. For others they are the beginning of an adult homosexual orientation. These teenage homosexual experiences do not necessarily leads to adult homosexuality and are seen as attempts to examine and define sexual and affectionate needs. Homosexuality suggests a broad range of attitudes, affections, social expectations and standards. It is specifically same-sex contact, two men or two women having sexual relations. Some adults over the course of several years, possibly due to circumstances, increasingly drift to homosexuality.

People who are homosexuals may, nevertheless, marry a person of the other sex. This may be due to societal or family pressure, want to have children and conventional family life, disguising their homosexual needs in belief that they can be heterosexual or bisexual. But such people may also continue to have homosexual activity. Heterosexual partner in most cases is usually unaware of their spouses homosexual or bisexual needs (Blumstein and Schwartz, 1983; Hill, 1987). The awareness of this may result in friction in marriage. Fidelity or faithfulness, having sexual relations only with one partner is valued high among couples of both orientations—heterosexual and homosexual couples.

Some homosexuals are more or less exclusively interested in same-sex partners since childhood, whereas, others gradually conclude that their primary attraction/interest is for a person of the same sex (West, 1983). Just because a person has had a same-sex experience, does not mean that she/he is lesbian or gay. Homosexuality needs to be differentiated from homosociality. While homosexuality is the sexual orientation toward members of the same sex, but homosociality is the tendency to associate mostly with members of the same sex. Sometimes people tend to be homosocial, associate with members of the same sex but necessarily not be homosexual, such association may be a result of societal accepted norms. People in the Indian subcontinent tend to be more homosocial as compared to their Western counterparts.

Bisexuality

Some people are not entirely consistent in their sexual behaviour. Many people are bisexuals. Bisexual person has an almost equal of heterosexual and homosexual experience. These peoples' sexual-affectional behaviour appears to be mixed.

Bisexuals are attracted to members of both genders. In developing a bisexual identity, men and women go through several stages such as initial confusion, finding and applying the bisexual label, settling into the identity, of bisexual label, and continued uncertainty. Weinberg, Williams and Pryor (1994) gave the first model of bisexual identity formation. The first stage, initial confusion, may last many years. Many are distressed at being attracted to both sexes, others believe that their attraction to the same sex means an end to their heterosexuality; still others are disturbed by their inability to categorize their feelings as either heterosexual or homosexual. The second stage is finding and applying the bisexual label. For many, discovering there is such a thing as bisexuality is a turning point. Some find that their first heterosexual or same sex experience permits them to view sex with both sexes as pleasurable, others learn of the term bisexuality from friends and are able to apply it to themselves. The third stage is settling into the identity. This stage is characterized at home with the label bisexual. For many, self-acceptance is critical. The fourth stage is continued uncertainty. Bisexuals don't have a community or social environment that reaffirms their identity. Despite being settled in, many feel persistent pressure from gay men and lesbians to re-label themselves as homosexuals and to engage exclusively in same sex activities.

9

Marriage and Family Structure Across Various Indian Tribes and Foreign Societies

The tribe is defined as a collection of families, which have a common name, a common dialect, and which occupies or prefers to occupy a common territory. The tribal population in India is 67.76 million (Census of India, 1991). The tribes formed 8.08% of the country's total population. They are found in almost all the states of the country. They are spread over the length and breadth of the country. They live in isolated terrains of hills and jungles. The main sources of their livelihood are agriculture and gathering of forest produce. They do not cultivate for profit, they still rely upon barter system, and spent a greater part of their earnings on social and religious ceremonies. They are mostly illiterate. The major tribes in India are Khasi, Garo, Munda, Gond, Nairs, Jaunsar Bawar, Mizos, Santhals, Nagas, Muria, Bhils.

A tribe is a collection of families bearing a common name, speaking a common dialect, occupying a common territory and is not usually endogamous (Gazette of India). They have similar occupation, customs, culture, tradition, dresses, manners, relationships, music, dance and oral literature. They are hunters, artisans, herdsman, fishing, art, painting, woodcutting, bird catches; snake charmers, blacksmiths, puppeteers and leatherwork and some are pottery-makers. A caste also is a collection of families bearing a common name, occupying or preferring to occupy a common territory very often speaking a common dialect and always endogamous. Among lower castes endogamy is also not strictly observed and here are some tribes that are strictly endogamous.

Culture conveys social charm and intellectual excellence. The sanskrit term for culture is sanskriti. Both sanskrit and sanskriti are derived from sanskar, meaning a ritual performance. Sanskriti stands for that state of collective life that can be attained only after going through the various sanskars. It is a process of refinement. Sanskrit was the urban tongue of ancient India. The rural speech was Prakrit, which is derived from Prakriti, meaning nature. Man is born as a social being. He attains sociology by going through the Sanskars.

Human beings are unique among all the creatures of animal kingdom in their capacity to create and sustain culture. Each society of men possesses its own distinctive culture so that members of one society behave differentially in some significant respects from the member's of every other society.

The Adivasi marriage system is of particular interest as it throws light on the evolution of the system which comprises practices like winning of the bride by capture, purchase, service to the parent, elopement and negotiation. In course of time, the system of negotiation has come to receive preference. Payment in various forms is made for bride price but with modernization the dowry system has come into vogue. The marriage rites are now performed in the bride's house instead of the groom's house.

Prescriptive and preferential marriages with maternal or paternal uncle's son or daughter prevail among Dravidian Adivasi communities except the Kondhs. Adult marriage is the usual practice. Among the Bondas and Saoras the groom is younger than the bride. Polygamy is prevalent among certain tribes to exhibit prestige and importance. Multiple wives, as with the Saoras, helps in sharing and reducing the burden of labour. Clan exogamy is observed by most tribes and also some observe even village exogamy.

Among the social institutions, marriage appears to be the most important one. The tribal people, the only exception being the hos of Kolhan, practice it almost universally. The extreme cupidity of fathers of kolhan brides and their high sense of family dignity have made them to demand an unusually high price for the hands of their daughter in marriage.

The tribes of India have more advanced views regarding the age of marriage of the young people than their advanced neighbours. The practice has come under the influence of Hindu culture. Among the Gonds, Kulis and Bhumias in Orissa, child marriage was said to be common, because of the influence of Hindu culture.

This law has yielded place to marriage of adults. The Souras, Koyas, Kondhs, Gadabas and Bondas of Koraput district marry at a fair age and infant marriages are unknown among them. The groom is generally older than the bride in the tribal area.

There is enough opportunity for the satisfaction of sex impulses outside marriage among the tribes of India. Pre-marital sexual chastity is not very rigidly insisted upon in a large number of tribes. Among the Murias of Madhya Pradesh, for instance, it is a custom on certain days of the week, for those boys and girls of dormitories who are prefects to spend the nights with each other and have sexual relations. Half a century ago, each Oraon bachelor had a sweet heart in the spinsters house. If the girl refused to accept a lover, she was cut of by the older girls, who refused to dance with her, till she accepted a paramour. Before marriage love affairs and even intimate relationships are permitted and widely practiced among the Bondas, Koyas, Gadabas and Soura women in Koraput region. Even after marriage on some festive post-marital laxity is also found among Hos and Oranos, during important festivals, when men and women freely indulge in sex relations. However, sex activity is not the only objective of marriage. Economic co-operation as found in the division of labour between husband and wife seems to be another important consideration for marital union among tribals.

The selection of mate is an important affair even in primitive tribal society. The rules of endogamy, exogamy, hypergamy, preferential mating and prohibited degrees operative simultaneously, and, there by, considerably restrict the freedom of choice. Among the Koyas and Kondhs, marriage with the maternal uncle's daughter is prevalent and is preferred then marriage with others. However, among Bondas this custom is absent. Marriage within the clan and certain brother clan is strictly prohibited among the tribes in Orissa. Generally, marriage also does not occur with in the same village. The ways and means of acquiring a mate in tribal society are varied and interesting. Eight important ways of acquiring a mate may be listed for Indian tribes. They are:

Probationary Marriage;
Marriage by captures;
Marriage by trial;
Marriage by Service;
Marriage by Purchase;
Marriage by exchange;
Marriage by mutual consent and elopement;
Marriage by intrusion.

Marriage by purchase and marriage by service are accepted way of finding a bride. The amount of bride price varies according to the economic conditions of tribe. The Bhumias, Oraons, Saharas, Juangs, Santals, Hos, Nagas, Bhils and many other tribes pay for their brides as a general rule. A Kondha of Koraput who is not able to pay the bride price is asked to work under the father-in-law's house till his final payment.

Probationary marriage, marriages by trial and intrusion marriage are found in limited cases of tribes in India. Marriages among the Bonda tribe are arranged in an extraordinary manner. About two months before Dushera festival each village Naik dig a hole of about 8 square and nine feet deep and roofed with logs and mud so arranged as to leave one small opening. In this all unmarried girls of the village have to sleep. Any youth desirous of matrimony joins them there a night and next morning leaves his brass bracelet with the girl of his choice. The pair after wards goes together to the girl's people and explains matters. Ultimately with relatives on both the side, they repair to jungles, where a fire is lit and the girl applies it to the boys buttocks. If he cries out in pain the girl refuses him, but if he makes no sound the couple are considered to be man and wife. The system has the advantages of giving both parties a choice in the matter.

The marriage customs and rituals among the tribals are elaborate and vary from tribe to tribe. It affects the economic life of a person, who gets a wife, to a great extent. It is necessary to discuss in brief the marriage customs and rituals, which is generally found among the tribes.

The parents of the bridegroom initiate marriages amongst the Soura. They visit the girl's parents bearing with them a present of a pot containing palm wine. The reason for their visit is not immediately made plain. However, sooner or later, the name of the girl is mentioned and her parents inform her of the proposal. If she consents, they accept the pot of wine and ceremonially drink it before several witnesses. After several such visits the bride price is finalized. The presentation of an arrow and its acceptance by the bride's family is equivalent of an engagement. About a year after the engagement the bride is brought to the bridegrooms house and made to the ancestors by a shahman.

Each tribal marriage is accompanied by a lot of feasting and dancing. These are done at bridegroom's house at his cost. Marriage of a tribal boy becomes very expensive as it becomes a source of exploitation by the money-lenders and land grabbers, who are ready to advance money to the tribals at the time of marriage and charge very high rate of interest.

This chapter deals with description of marriage and family systems prevalent in some of the major tribes in India and other societies of the world.

THE KHASIS OF MEGHALAYA

According to the description, Khasis is the major tribe of Assam and Magalaya of India. It is characterized for being monogamy, matrilineal and matrilocal. Inheritance is the privilege of daughters. Elder daughter gets share at the time of their marriage. The youngest daughter is the custodian of the family. She gets big share of the property and ancestors house. Her husband (only younger daughters) live with her in the ancestors house. Sons have no right and no claim on land and property. They can establish their own house. The mother is under no obligation to divide her property in equal shares among the daughters. Elder sisters can dispose-off their share but not the youngest one without consulting her brothers and maternal uncles. She performs the funeral of her mother and collects the bones of the family members for last rites. The son is expected to die in the mother's house. He is to serve mother. First male is treated only as procreating agent. Marriages within clan are prohibited.

Cross-cousin marriages from father's side are permissible but not from mother's side and neither within gotra. In some, clan or communities of this tribe, the system of visit marriage prevails. Husband lives with his mothers' clan and he can visit his wife only at night with the permission of her mother. Children's bear mother's title as surname. Monogamy is the ideal marriage. Those who are never divorced are respected and are called sati but divorce is very common in them. Extra-marital sex relations are known to exist and when detected divorce may be ensured. Other grounds for divorce are—non-bearing of children and prolonged illness. Khasis are now changing under the influence of Christian, Muslim and other cultural interactions. Basically, they were Hindus. Magic medicine and religion are interlined in the religious system of Khasises.

The Khasis, Jaintia, Bhoi, War collectively known as the Hynniewtrep people predominantly inhabit the districts of East Meghalaya, also known to be one of the earliest ethnic group of settlers in the Indian sub-continent, belonging to the Proto Austroloid Monkhmer race. The Khasis inhabit the eastern part of Meghalaya, in the Khasi and Jaintia Hills. Khasis residing in Jaintia hills are now better known as Jaintias. They are also called Phars. The Khasis occupying the northern lowlands and foothills are generally called Bhois. Those who live in the Southern tracts are termed Wars. Again among the Wars, those living in the Khasi Hills are called War-Khasis and those in the Jaintia Hills, War-Prars or War-Jaintias. In the Jaintia Hills we have Khyrwangs, Labangs, Nangphylluts, Nangtungs in the north-eastern part and in the east. In the Khasi Hills, the Lynghgams live in the northwestern part. But, all of them, claim to have descended from the 'Ki Hynniew Trep' and are now known by the generic name of Khasi-Pnars or simply Khasis. They have same traditions, customs and usage with a little variation owing to geographical diversions.

Social Structure

The Khasis, the Jaintias and the Garos have a matrilineal society. Descent is traced through the mother, but the father plays an important role in the material and mental life of the family. While writing on the Khasi and the Jaintia people David Roy observed, 'a man is the defender of the woman, but the woman is the keeper of his trust'. No better description of Meghalayan matrilineal society could perhaps be possible. In the Khasi society, the woman looks after home and health, the man finds the means to support the family, and the maternal uncle settles all social and religious matters. Earlier in the conservative Jaintia non-Christain families, however, the father only visits the family in the night and is not responsible for the maintenance of the family.

Inheritance

Khasis follow a matrilineal system of inheritance. In the Khasi society, it is only the youngest daughter of 'Ka Khadduh' who is eligible to inherit the ancestral property. If 'Ka Khadduh' dies without any daughter surviving her, her next elder sister inherits the ancestral property, and after her, the youngest daughter of that sister. Failing all daughters and their female issues, the property goes back to the mothers' sister, mother's sister's daughter and so on. The Ka Khadduh's property is actually the ancestral property and so if she wants to dispose it off, she must obtain consent and approval of the uncles and brothers. Among the War-Khasis, however, property passes to the children, male or female, in equal shares but among the War Jaintias, only the female children get the inheritance.

Marriage

Marriage within a clan is a taboo. Rings or betel-nut bags are exchanged between the bride and the brideroom to complete the union. In the Christian families, however, marriage is purely a civil contract.

Religion

The Khasis are now mostly Christians. But before that, they believed in a Supreme Being. The Creator—U Blei Nongthaw and under Him, there were several deities of water and of mountains and also of other natural objects.

The Khasis have matrilocal residence and matrilineal descent. Participation in the family religion and the common sepulcher, where bones of the members of the family are entered after death, are the two elements that bind the members together.

The children of the male do not belong to the family. The youngest daughter, *Ka Khadduh*, in a Khasi family is in charge of the family religion. She cremates her mother and enters her bones in the common sepulcher (a place where the bones are kept with a huge stone over it which is different in shape for males and females).

Marriage is a great social institution among the Khasis, as it determines the system of matrilocal residential pattern among them (Sinha, 1970). Being the followers of a unique social system of matriliny, the Khasi women enjoy a special place of status and dignity (Kyndiah, 1990). A Khasi woman is the guardian and preserver of the family goods. She plays a crucial role in the affairs of the family. However, she is not the head of the family, as this is left to a male member. The father of the family has a definite role to play in the household affairs. However, his role is limited to the final word of the maternal uncle.

THE GAROS OF MEGHALAYA

The Garos of Meghalaya in India are predominantly inhabited by the Garos, belonging to the Bodo family of the Tibeto-Burman race, said to have migrated from Tibet. The Goros prefer to call themselves as Achiks and the land they inhibit as the Achikland. The word Garo has been coined after the name of a small group of the Garos residing in the central part of the southern hills. Besides the Garo hills, there are Garo settlements in the plains of Assam and Bangladesh. The Garos call themselves Achik-mande. In the Garo language Achik means hills and mande, man, so Achik-mande means the hills people. Marriage within the clan is completely prohibited and severely punishable. Marriage is however arranged with the formal sanction of the parents. Death of a person is not only a loss to the family, but is also mourned by the entire community. Elaborate death rituals are held. Before embracing Christiantity they used to cremate the dead body, in the presence of all relations of the deceased. Now-a-days, according to Christian practice, the body is buried.

Bachelors' Dormitories

Till now, the institution of Bachelors' Dormitories which is gradually disappearing amongst the tribes of North-Eastern Region, are found in the Garo villages. In such dormitories, young people stay and live together till they are married. They receive various training in the dormitories like protection of crops, construction of roads, organizing festivals, sports and ceremonies. The descent of an individual either man or woman is always reckoned and traced from the mother alone and through her genealogical tree traces its origin back to the common ancestors.

A'chik-Mandei (Garo) society being a matrilineal society, the mother of the house is very important person. In a purely matrilineal and matri-local society, the position and status of women is much better than that of a patrilineal and patri-local society. Garo social system concentrates power in the mahari system consisting of a group of matrilineal chras and paa gachi. It is the chras who controls and oversee the welfare of the family or respective ma'chong (motherhood). The sanctity of the motherhood was preserved and any sexual relation of a man with another woman outside his marriage is considered as an act of sacrilege and the punishment for such offence in earlier days was beheaded or driven-off from the village and the community.

A'chik Mandei society is organized into matrilineal groups which are known as, "ma'chong" (motherhood). Although, the Garo society is matrilineal society the managerial and custodial authority of the family are vested in man. The oldest man of the family (nokni padot) enjoyed the honor and respect of the family members. All the members of one ma'chong have the innate belief that they all branched from the common ancestors or mother gave them the sense of attachment and a feeling of oneness to the members of one ma'chong.

The mahari system amongst the Garos or A'chik Mandei are very important which has two separate entities—(i) Chra-Pante; and (ii) Paa-Gachi.

Chra-Pante

Consists of all the male members of the family such as maternal uncles, great uncles, nephews and brothers of the same ma'chong. It is the Chra-pante that plays the most important role in sharing and administering the welfare of a family. It is the uncles or sons of a family that exercises their avuncular authority in the decision-making process of their mother's house, especially in the process of selection of Nokkrom or heiress. Their decisions in all matters are important and binding legally and socially provided, and no arbitrary decisions are taken without consulting his fellow uncles, brothers and sisters. The eldest male member of a family has the right to veto in any of the important decisions for the welfare of his mother and sisters and their homes.

Paa-Gachi

Consists of all the husbands of grand mother, mothers, sisters and nieces of the same ma'chong. Their opinions are also respected in all the important decisions and take note of them, if their suggestions are for the welfare of their family or ma'chong (motherhood). If not their decisions can be overruled by the Chras their suggestions becomes mere recommendatory.

A woman cannot divorce her husband out of her own accord. An aggrieved woman first approaches her chras and Nio-sari for redress. A woman cannot raise her head against the decision of her chra, if his decisions are for the welfare of her family members. In the affairs of the mahari, woman can participate and offer their views. In all the major decisions, women are also being consulted and their views are taken into confidence.

Inheritance

The entire A'chik Mandei (Garos) social structure is based on principles of preservation of wealth and family property within the same ma'chong (motherhood). It is this principle that governs the choice of "Nokkrom" (heiress) and the "A'kim" (nephew) that keeps the family bonds together.

No Garo or A'chik Mandei male can inherit family property in the matrilineal society. Whatever property he acquires after marriage belongs to his wife and his daughter after his wife's death. If there is no female issue, another woman of the same motherhood, appointed by her Chras inherits the family property. Once in the motherhood, the property either moveable or immovable cannot pass away from it to another. No man has any right to dispose-off or remove any of family property without his wife's permission. To do so is theft in the eyes of the Garos. Where, homestead joint family exists, duly convened mahari have the sole authority to divide such family property. If husband contemplated second marriage, the consent of his first wife and Chra is necessary. If wife deserts her husband and lives with another, she forfeits her right to claim for her husband's and family property. The second marriage of a different motherhood and clan will not entitle the status of Nokkrom (heiress) and claim family property. The father or husband of a family is simply a guardian, custodian and manager of his wife's property. He has no right to dispose off any property earned as husband and without the prior permission and consent of his wife, children and the Chras.

A'kim Bond

A'kim means the "nephew" (gritang-sokchi). It is the law that binds the two ma'chong (motherhood) together through marriage and following the mutual rights and duties. The Law of A'kim binds the community of the same blood together and establishes a lasting good relationship between the two ma'chong (motherhood) of both the husband and the wife. It is under this law that when a wife or husband dies, he or she is substituted by the deceased wife or husband's ma'chong. A'kim-bifurcation if the ma'chong do not succeed in arranging a husband or wife from the same ma'chong (motherhood), he or she is lawfully free to seek a husband or wife from another chatchi mahari. Customary law of A'kim as the said ligament of the community of blood upholds the holy matriarchism and perpetuates social cohesion. Marriage customs and the laws of the Garos are regulated by the two most important laws of exogamy and A'kim. Due to the very existence of these two laws, no marriage is consummated between the two persons belonging the same motherhood.

ASSAMESE SOCIETY

This joint family system appears to be traditional between both the tribal and non-tribal village communities of Assam; it is based on blood relationship. In the case of inheritance, the Dayabhaga system was followed in olden days, as at present. As long as the father lives, the sons cannot claim any share in the property. So the father is the centre of the family and he rules supreme. There are a few tribal societies, which follow the matriarchal system. The Khasi is one among them. They look upon the mother as the centre of the clan. The mother's property goes to her daughters. When there is no daughter, the property goes to the youngest daughter of the mother's sister. The Garos also follow a similar system in the Garo Hills. Among the Dimasa-Kacharis the prevalent custom is that the sons inherit their father's properties and the girls inherit their mother's properties. When there is no children of their own their relatives inherit the properties. Though Assamese women are given an honoured position, no other community in Assam follows the matrilineal inheritance system. The common paternal system governs general Assamese society.

Manu's Prajapati mode is the usual rule for marriages in Assam. The proposal for the girl's hand comes from the boy's family and then follows the other formalities. Elopement is generally discouraged. The eloping couple is generally accepted in the boy's family after they formally beg pardon of society represented by village elders who after imposing a fine lets them off. In Assam, kinship is treated with great importance. Sons and daughters of uncles and aunts are all brothers and sisters, like those of one's own parents. Child marriage is practically unknown. A boy marries from the age of 16 and a girl from the age of 14. If a young boy likes a girl, he sends his father or both the parents to the girl's father, with betrothal ring or bracelets to the girl. Sometimes a gourd of rice beer is taken and accepted. If after acceptance, the girl gets married to another boy, the village council fines the girl's family. The length of the engagement is not uniform. After a day has been fixed for the marriage, both the families prepare beer and strong drinks. If the bridegroom's party has to go through difficult villages he has to give a gourd of beer to each.

After the proposal comes, horoscopes of the boy and girl are compared. A new ring is put on the girl's finger as a mark of sealing the proposal. The nuptials start two or three days, ahead. The first day is the Jorondiya, when a party of women from the bridegroom's side goes to the bride's house and formally presents her with bridal dresses and ornaments. From this day till the wedding, the bride and groom have to undergo ceremonial baths, every day, known Nowani. For this, water is specialty drawn (panitola) by women who go in a procession singing appropriate songs, to the river or a tank. The night of the second day or the night before the wedding day is Adhivasa. Both the bride and the groom and also their mothers have to observe a fast on these days. A priest is engaged for the rites on this day and he performs the *pujas*, offering grams and pulses to Gods, which are later, distributed as *prasad*, after eating it only a vegetarian meal can be had at night. Women then carry on the ceremony of gathiyan khunda in which, inside an enclosure of cloth, they pound a kind of aromatic root to a pulp and apply it on the boy's or girl's head and add oil to the pulp. This is an act of purification. After that night's meal, there will be no usual meal for them and their parents till the marriage is over. Early in the morning of the wedding day, the ceremony of daiyan diya is observed. The bride or the groom is made to sit on the threshold of the bedroom, an elderly woman relative sits in front, takes two betel leaves in her two hands, dips them into a bowl of curd and touches his or her cheeks, arms and feet with the leaves. Then after a ceremonial bath, *Shraddha* of nine past generations is performed. The groom has to take another ceremonial bath before he gets ready in the evening to start for the bride's house. He and his party arrive at the bride's place a little before Langa or Auspicious hour. His would-be mother-in-law ceremonially receives him at the decorated gate. Fistfuls of rice will be thrown at him to drive off any evil spirit accompanying him. Then the groom is led to the place under the pandal where the ceremony is to be performed. Women continue to sing marriage-songs all the while. At the appropriate hour, the bride is brought out and the priest starts the Vedic rites. After all the ceremonies are over, the bride is taken by the groom's party to the groom's house; she need not stay there from that very day, but she must set her foot that day in her husband's house and may go back home. On the third day's evening with the help of a priest, offerings are made to two imaginary demons named Khoba and Khubuni for smoothening the path of married life. Dowry is not asked for, but the girl's father presents all necessary things, which would be required in married life.

Ahoms Marriage

In the case of Ahoms, no marriage is allowed within the same clan. Many customs followed in an Ahom wedding are common to all Assamese communities. The joron ceremony, daiyan and gathiyan are same as others. The system of Saklang, which means marriage, is the usually accepted norm in Ahom society. A good girl is pointed out and the boy's people go to ask for her hand with the 'Sodhanibhar', consisting of betel nuts and leaves, rice, ducks, etc. If nothing objectionable in the boy's family is found, a day is fixed for the girl's people to come and see how the boy's family lives. Then a date for wedding is fixed.

The bridegroom sits in the courtyard; the bride is brought in and she walks seven times round the bridegroom. She then sits down by his side. After this both rise and proceed to a room screened off from the guests. Here one end of the cloth is tied round the neck of the bride, the other being fastened to the bridegroom's waist. They walk to a corner, where nine vessels, full of water have been placed on plantain leaves, the Siring phukam (or master of the ceremonies) reads from the 'Saklang puthi'; and three cups containing milk, honey and rice frumenty are produced, which the bride and the bride groom have to smell. After the bride and the bride groom have exchanged knives, some uncooked rice is brought in a basket, into which, rings are plunged by the bride and the bridegroom, respectively, unknown to each other—it being the intention that each should discover the other's ring and wear it on the finger. The exchange of knives and rings is the binding part of the ceremony. Bride and bridegroom are then taken outside and do sewa (homages) to the bride's parents and the people assembled, and the marriage is complete.

Two days before the wedding, the priest goes to a river or tank to perform pujas to God Khoakham offering rice, eggs, betel nuts and betel leaves. He then "fishes" with a jokai, a bamboo fishing implement, in the water three times. If any fish is caught, it will be cooked and given to the boy and the girl to eat. This is meant for protection against any untoward happening. The day before the wedding the deoban ceremony is performed to worship various Ahom Gods. The priest gives words of advice to the newly-weds from the Ahom holy books on the rights and duties of married life. The past history of seven generation of the two families is recounted to them. After this, the couple is taken inside the bride's house and the customs of exchange of rings, taking of panchamrita, playing games of dice or cowries are gone through.

Rabhas Marriage

Amongst the Rabhas, both widow-remarriage and divorce are allowed with sufficient liberty, they observe Pan Phala or the system of tearing a betel-leaf as a mark of separation. The Rabhas have the custom of paying bride-money. Even today children assume the name of their mother's clan; on the other hand, the father's properties are inherited by his sons; in all religious functions, the father is the head. Marriage within the same clan is not allowed.

Mikirs Marriage

Amongst the Mikirs, no marriage is allowed within the same clan. The Mikir marriage system is generally like that of other Hindus including the joron ceremony and marriage by elopement. A man having illicit love with an unmarried girl will be punished by the Gaon-burha (village headman); if the man is already married, the punishment will be heavier. A man cannot discard his wife without justifiable reasons. Mikir social life in general is largely free. The proposal for marriage is first discussed between the girl and her elder brother's wife. Then follows the formal proposal with Sodhani bhar, as among the Ahoms. After that the question whether the boy will stay with his father-in-law as ghar-jowain is decided and a date for the wedding is fixed.

Lalungs Marriage

Amongst the Lalungs, some customs followed by them stress the important position of women in society. Women priests conduct Lalung religious rites that concern women. A Lalung girl who remain unmarried or a woman whose husband lives at her father's house inherits a share of the paternal property. In the latter case, the bridegroom loses his right to his own father's property. The Lalungs have embraced Hinduism and their marriage customs are generally same as those of other Hindus, but there is no Homa. Marriage within the same clan is not allowed.

THE IRAVANS

Polyandry now survives particularly in the marginal areas among the less advanced members of Iravans and Kammala castes (artisans) in Malabar in Kerala. The common practice is that the eldest brother goes to the bride's house for marriage. Later on all the brothers are seated in a row on the right of the bride at a ceremony in which all the brothers are given sweet drinks, making brothers the co-husbands of the woman. The eldest brother appears to have been the real husband and all his brothers had a matter of right over the sexual use of his wife.

THE TODAS

The Todas bounded by Nilgiri hills in South India is the society in which nothing is personal including its men and women, where religion and economy are based not on God and gold but on buffaloes.

The Todas is a pastoral, polyandrous Indian tribe. The tribe is divided into two endogamous divisions—'Tartharol and Teiveli'. Each of these divisions are further divided into a number of exogamous clans. In some respects the clan is regulating its own affairs, owning property and having in many cases social and religious rituals peculiar to it.

The Todas are polyandrous who believe in freedom and love. The concept of marriages is a form of group ménage in which every male member of one clan has a claim over every female of other clans within some moetic durations. This regular system of marriages permits precocious behaviour between todas men and women and allows polyandry. When a man marries a woman, all his brothers including those who are born later are regarded as the husbands of that woman.

When a boy is married to a girl, all his brothers including those who are born later are usually regarded as husbands of the girl. Husbands are generally own brothers but some times cousin brothers also. When wife becomes pregnant, the elder brother performs the pursutpimi ceremony, the ceremony of giving the bow and the arrow, which confers social fatherhood. He becomes father of first 2 or 3 children; next husband becomes father of next children and so on. However, all brothers are equally regarded as father of the child.

The Todas treat women as property as they could transfer her to another man on payment. He may marry two women then sell off one to become rich. It is less frequent for the brothers of a family to have one wife in common. Often each brother has his own wife or several brothers have more than one wife between them.

However, all the brothers of the family do not confine themselves to just one common wife, often each brother takes up his own wife or several brothers have more than one wife between them. The adelphic polyandry is not in much trend today.

It may also be possible for woman to have husbands from different clans at one time but usually they are half brothers by same mother. On an average, a woman may marry as many as four times so that after these short-lived marriages she becomes less attractive and has a steady relationship with her husbands. The permissiveness among the Todas society makes it difficult for one to establish who is the actual person responsible for the conception when a woman becomes pregnant. The responsibility of the child to be born is taken by any man who may in the sixth month of pregnancy present a symbolic bow and arrow in an elaborate ceremony known as pursuitpimi, assuming the social paternity. Once a ceremony has been performed all the subsequent children by the woman will be considered the children of the same father until another man performs the ceremony, pay the compensation to the previous husband in form of buffaloes, if a man happens to marry a widow he pays compensation to the children of the woman from the previous husband and rarely to the brothers of the deceased person.

Polyandry has been the characteristic marriage institution among the Todas. The Toda female marries one male and at the same time becomes the wife of his brothers. Should other brothers be born subsequently they will also share equally in marital rights. Only brothers share a wife, the union may more precisely be termed fraternal polyandry. When all live in one household and one of the brothers is with the wife, he places his cloak outside the hut as a warning to the rest not to disturb him. When a wife becomes pregnant, there is no call to determine biological father. A remarkable practice to give the child a "legal" father is carried out. The pregnant woman retires to a wood accompanied by the eldest brother. There he fashions ceremonial bow and arrow from twigs and grass and presents these objects to the wife. By the gesture be becomes the recognized "legal" father.

When infant marriages occur in considerable number, there will be later periods, during which there are few females available for marriage. The Toda male in search of wife is permitted by this practice to seek a mate from among those already married. Having selected one, he may, with the permission of the girl's father, of two elders, and of the husband who has given her the bow exchange a number of buffaloes for the latter's wife.

Todas men and women wear long hair and their appearance is much different from their Tamil counterparts. Todas houses are unique half bamel shaped hamlets. These hamlets are not owned by individual but by the patrilineal clan into which todas society is structured. The clan's men are free to move between different settlements belonging to their descent groups. The Toda is the only tribal society in India that is pastoral. They breed and worship buffaloes, which forms an integral part of their culture. Any person has a right to become chief whose chief occupation is to milk the sacred buffaloes, chim the milk and keep alight the eternal flame that burns inside the temple. Since the Todas are a dairy culture and their life revolves around milking the female buffaloes that are given utmost importance and some of them are sacred to be worshipped. On the other hand, the bull does not have any significant role to play except for the purpose of breeding and sacrifice during religious rituals, which is not much in practice. The male calves are sold soon after their birth. The buffaloes are assigned names, for which elaborate ceremonies are held and buffaloes of diary temples are considered sacred. The degree of importance of dairy temple determines grade of buffalo. The Todas concept of purity and pollution are of utmost importance with regard to their herds. The higher the buffaloes grade the greater the care to prevent its minal different.

In the days of adelphic polyandry, the herd of buffaloes was usually held in common by brothers, their herd was divided only if they quarreled with one another, today brothers sometimes share a herd but most buffaloes of sacred temples as well as secular belong to individual members and to the head of household. Ownership of buffaloes changes rather frequently as they are given in gifts in compensation for taking another man's wife and in payment of fines.

The rites and rituals performed during a Toda lifetime involve buffaloes, dairy or both and conscious or unconsciously they are meant to contain whatever threat is posed to the purity of sacred dairies. These rites and rituals are performed right from the time of conception. A woman's first pregnancy is considered to be ritually contaminating. For purifications the woman has to leave her hamlet during fifth month of pregnancy and spend a lunar month out of her hamlet in a pollution hut. Her husband accompanies her as he shares some of the pollution and cooks for her as the woman is prohibited to cook during these days. The lunar month begins with a new moon day and ends of the next. Elaborate rituals involving the man, woman and the sacred calf, mark the beginning of the end of the period. The head patri clan's men or a priest may perform the ceremonies. These days the women seldom spends their time in the pollution hut but the beginning and of purification period are performed on a new moon day with little or no time gap between them the chief hamlets an recognition of their states to not have any pisas and women belonging to these are moved to pollution huts of subside settlements.

These ceremonies are closely followed by that of bow and arrow ceremony, which takes place in the seventh month of pregnancy. This rite determines the all important social paternity of the unborn child for its place in the Toda society, if a child was born to a women who had not been given a bow it would be a bastard, "Podmos" with no patriclan affiliation which is a great disadvantage to the child. A bastard child has no clansmen upon him to call for formal or informal support in either secular or religious matters. He may also marry a woman who is herself prepared to loose clan affiliation. He and his sons may not enter any Toda dairy temple and neither he nor his wife or off springs may be cremated at a regular funeral place.

But after the first child, the rite need not be performed again for the paternity thus established extends to all subsequent children of that woman even those conceived after the man who gave her bow dies. On the other hand, if a different man performs the rite with her during other pregnancy he will be the father of that child and of all subsequent off springs. The "Pisitt" or bow and arrow ceremony as it is popularly called is performed on the day of new moon and is performed in the presence of large number of people and with the blessings of all elderly people from maternal and paternal side. A Toda woman generally delivers her child in her own house or in a hospital. Childbirth is another event which is considered to pollute the woman, with her child she has to purify herself by staying in pollution hut for certain period of time.

Till the name giving ceremony the child's face is left covered by an adult cloak. Either priest or a senior patriclan performs the face uncovering and name giving ceremony. This is for a boy child not for a female child. The infant who dies before name giving ceremony is of little consequence to the society. There is a second name giving ceremony for the boy child when he is older. The maternal uncle plays an important role and gives gifts to child's families.

Usually parents arrange the marital alliances for their children before they are 2-3 years old. The children remain with their parents until maturity and it is possible that the original alliance will be dissolved and the new one arranged before the young couple can begin to live together. It is not essential on the part of the girl to acknowledge her chosen mate to be her first mate. Independent of her betrothal she has liberty to choose any individual as her mate. The young folks do not at first consult their parents in the matter but carry on a courtship and even have a sexual relationship without any ceremony.

Father and the son travel to the village of the intended wife taking with them a loincloth as a preliminary wedding gift. After that girl will remain at home until she has passed the age of puberty. Twice a year, thereafter, until the girl is ten years old, the boy will bring her a loincloth as a gift. After that he brings a cloak. A strange ceremony is performed before the girl reaches the puberty. A man from the opposite moiety comes to the girl's house during the daytime, lies down beside her, and covers both the girl and himself with a cloak. Two weeks later a virile young man of any division except that of girl comes to the village for one night and has intercourse with the girl. A year or two after the ceremony the girl joins her husband at his village.

The boy's parents consider girl's suitability to be his partner. In evaluations, the reputation of family is given more importance than their financial assets. Once they have chosen the girl, the boy's parents visit her parents with their son. The girl's parents cannot refuse the offer unless the girl has already been promised to someone. The father of the boy presents the girl with loin cloth (white) and she is given cloths to wear every year until she is mature to accompany her husband. If the girl's family wishes to dissolve the relationship compensation to the boy has to be paid in terms of buffalo. When the children are mature enough to take up residence together and the girl's parents provides the couple with a dowry.

Divorce exists among the Todas. A man divorces his wife for two reasons. If a wife is a fool or a wife doesn't work. Baroness is not generally regarded as the reason for divorce as it is not easy for the man to take up second wife. Intercourse between wife and another man is not regarded as a reason for divorce but rather as a perfectly natural occurrence. If a man decides to divorce his wife and despite the interference of Toda council he does not agree to take her back he has to pay a penalty of one buffalo to wife's people.

Woman are excluded from any share in work in dairies connected with sacred buffaloes, they are also prohibited from any part in the milking of dominants buffaloes or in the cheeming of milk which is performed solely by males in the part of the hut in which women has nothing to do. Men grazed the cattle and milked while the female do the household activities like pounding grain, sweeping, cleaning and sewing.

THE NAYARS OR NAIRS OF KERALA

The Nayars or Nairs are matrilineal caste groups lining in South Malabar in Kerela in India. The traditional Nayar taravad is a Matrilineal, matrilocal household consisting of thirty-five to one hundred and fifty matrilineally related kin, all living under one roof and sharing a common kitchen.

The Nairs of India follow matrilineal system, though the residential system among them is duo-local, where spouses lived separately in their natal homes and husband is usually the night visitor to their wife. Its joint family residence is called a Taravad (also spelled tharwad). A Taravad consists of a female ancestor, her children and all such other descendants, however remote, in the female line. The male descendants themselves are its members but their children are not. A person belongs to the Taravad of his or her mother only and the Taravad membership arises by birth in the family. A female member of a Tarawad does not change her family by marriage. Each member of a Tarawad acquires an interest in the Taravad properties by reason of his or her birth alone, and when any member dies, the interest of that member devolves upon the other members of a Taravad. Taravads were the female-lineage joint families (with female-owned properties and residences) of the high-ranking Nair caste of Kerala.

Nair women had greater personal freedom than most women to take decisions regarding marital and sexual relations. Nair women played a crucial role in household decisions, the decision-making role being invested with great authority, as inheritance was through them, and it was they who where the bearers of the family name.

The men lived in their own taravad house, eating all their meals there and attending to the needs of their matrilocally related kin. After the evening meal, they would go to their wives taravads, and their female relatives would be visited by their husbands. Today, in most small taravads, it is common to find the husband of at least one of the women living in her house. Within the household all interpersonal relationships were sharply delineated, role were carefully circumscribed, and every individual always knew how he was expected to act in relation to everyone else. Within the family, a younger person could come before a senior only at certain times, and their he was required to stand in the presence of the senior, with his mouth covered. A boy after sixteen years of age was allowed to go to the female section of taravad only under special circumstances. He was allowed little opportunity to talk to his sisters. All interpersonal relations within the family unit were carefully regulated by principles of age.

An adult could derive satisfaction from belonging to a given taravad and from its social position. For the child, the reward for accepting all the restrictions placed upon him was two fold, the knowledge that he, too, could take pride in being a member of a given family with a good reputation, and the pleasure of the graceful, ritually set round of life, with its many festivals and entertainments.

A good child, in the traditional context, may be described as humble, intelligent, although not necessarily brilliant, kind to small babies and animals, religious, in the sense of going to the temple once a day, monitoring, and well-behaved, not to misbehave and avoiding quarrels with other children. Children are taught to be obedient and respectful to elders. The boy from the age of seven was trained in the use of arms and was expected to show courage under difficult circumstances. Blind obedience to elders, never permitted to talk back to an elder, never permitted to question the word of an elder is seen. Children were continually shown in the course of life, in the taravad, how they were to behave with each of their relatives.

A child is taught to stand in the presence of your 'veliyamma'. Always bathe before touching other people. Listen to elders; their words are 'Amrita' (nectar). When every member of the family order than ego was a potential sanctioning agent for him. Age ranking was so important within the family that, among twins, the child born second not only called the firstborn 'Ettan', or elder brother, but was expected to defer to him on various occasions. Distant kin living in the same household ordinarily would know only their age and generational standing relative to one another, not how they were related. The child was always expected to show humility and never to brag about his accomplishment nor voice his disappointments to his elders.

It was thought that a self-reliant person might endanger the unity of the taravad. The child's dependence on other people was encouraged. Infant's needs were gratified as soon as adults became aware of them. For the first two months the infant was nursed every two hours. Among this group, toilet training started early. Physical contact with older people continued even till the age of six or seven. Children were never left to sleep alone.

Child was never permitted to assert himself. Shyness was considered natural especially in front of elders and strangers. Girls were expected to pretend to be shy especially after puberty. Role memorization was given importance with punishment for mistakes. Fear of not being perfect was inculcated early. Fear of evoking jealousy of higher castes, discouraged children from excelling. Displays of aggression on the part of the child were condemned. Except for regulated matches in the 'Kalari' actual fighting was discouraged.

Traditionally, one reward to which a Nayar child could look forward if he was good was the power he would have later in life over lower caste people. Emotions were seldom expressed freely to others. It was not how the junior felt that mattered but how he behaved. The large matrilineal joint family offered certain securities as well as imposing many restrictions. It offered a place where one belonged; one could always count on a house to live in, sufficient food, adequate clothing, and people to attend to one's needs in case of illness, in exchange for obeying all of the customary rules. A man did not have to work and could rely on his male family head, or 'Karanavan' to provide him with the necessities of life, a woman always had the security of a family, regardless of what happened to her husband or husbands.

Karanavan had control over the comings and goings and behaviour of the junior member of his taravad. An ideal Nayar put welfare of the taravad before his own welfare. One was expected to be neat and well dressed and to be a good conversationalist when the situation called for it. Women were expected to be well mannered, entertaining, and possessed of a great deal of skill and tact in manipulating others. In a large family group, sisters of the mother normally cared for the child when mother was busy or in disposed, and mother's mother also cared for her grand children. Mother was child's primary source of emotional solace and the primary disciplining agent.

The child feared head of the 'tava' or grandmother a little. She saw that people followed the rules and brought no disgrace. She was also one of the main story-tellers. Traditionally, the father had little to do with his children due to the institutions of visiting husbands, polyandry, and hypergamy. He had obligations towards his nephews and nieces. The only interpersonal relationship a child had which were not associated with some degree of tension, "respect" and control were those within the peer group or "set."

Social norms and values may be taught and enforced either their direct prohibitory action on the part of socializing agents or indirectly through internalization. An individual in a given culture does what he is expected to do. He has so internalized the particular norms and values involved that they have become a part of his own psychic make up. He is aware of the external punishment he would receive if he did not obey that particular rule. He makes the conscious decision to follow a particular rule. Nayar's express the opinion that children must be trained to be "proper adults." It is the mother who administers most of the punishment although any older family member of taravad can hit him. The age at which physical punishment begins is dependent on the "temperament and character of the mother" and the "health and stubbornness" of the child. Another form of physical punishment common for older children is called 'etham idal'. The child is made to hold his left ear with his right hand, his right ear with his left hand and in this position to bend to the ground a specified number of times. Punishment is considered absolutely necessary.

Teasing or ridicule of various kinds is perhaps one of the most frequently used methods of bringing about social conformity. It might be just saying 'ayo, ayo' or laughing at a child. Teasing as a mechanism is also used by peer group. In the rigidly ordered large taravad situation, an individual knew what his duties and responsibilities were and that if he did not fulfil them, if he broke the social mores, he had no place to go, that is, he was in a sense bound by the rigidity of the social structure.

The mother is the first person to induce guilt reactions. The mother does not tell the child how much she is suffering, but she lives it out before his eyes. The child becomes aware that if he is self-willed in his choice of profession or marriage-partner this is "an attack on the parents." A crying child is a poor reflection on the mother so as soon as the child starts crying efforts are made to stop him. Not eating is a child's most effective weapon against his mother. It is considered the height of selfishness to be concerned about ones own happiness without "considering everyone else first." If one achieves satisfaction it must be kept hidden for to make it public risks arousing every other and thus exposing one self to the "other's eye." Marriage among Nayars is defined as "a union between a man and a woman such that children born to the woman are recognized legitimate off springs of both parents."

Nayar men were trained as professional soldiers and were for part of each year absent from the village in wars against neighbouring kingdoms. The Nayars of the village or of two adjacent villages formed a neighbourhood group of some six according to kin lineage. The linked lineages played their most important role at the pre-puberty marriage rites (taliketukalayanam) of girls. At a convenient time every few years, a lineage held a grand ceremony at which all girls who had not attained puberty, aged about seven to twelve, were on one day ritually married by men drawn from their linked lineages. After various ceremonies, each tied a gold ornament (tali) round the neck of his ritual bride. After the four days ceremony each husband left for his house and had no further obligations to their brides. A bride had only one further obligation to her ritual husband, that, at his death she and all her children, by whatever biological father, must observe death pollution for him. In Cochin, even if their mother's ritual husband never visited his wife again her children must refer to him by the kinship term.

The tali rite marked various changes in the social position of a girl. It brought her social maturity. After the tali rite, a girl must observe all the rules of etiquette associated with incest prohibitions in relation to men of her lineage. After the tali—rite and as soon as she becomes old enough a girl received as visiting husband a number of men of her sub-caste from outside her lineage, normally most from her neighbourhood. In addition, she might be visited by any Nayar of the higher sub-castes of village headsmen, chiefs or royalty, or by Nambudin Brahman. All of these relationships were called Sambandham.

After the ritual marriage, the bridegroom need have no further contact with his ritual wife, though he might if both parties are willing. There appears to have been no limit to the number of wives of appropriate sub-caste whom a Nayar might visit concurrent. While a woman customarily had a small but no fixed number of husbands. A husband visited his wife after supper at night and left before breakfast next morning and placed his weapons at the door while he is there.

Although, the visiting husband made regular gifts so far at festivals, in no sense of the term did a man maintains his wife. The gifts continued to be made at festivals only while the relationship lasted. No man had obligations to a wife of past.

In these circumstances, the exact biological fatherhood of a child was often uncertain, although of course, paternity was presumed to lie with the man or among the men who had paid the delivery expenses. But even when biological paternity was known with reasonable certainty, the senior had neither economic, social, legal or ritual rights nor obligations to his children after he had once paid the fees of their births. And neither the wife nor her children observed pollution at the death of a visiting husband, who was not the ritual husband of the wife.

Among the Nayars, the interpersonal affinal links, patrilineal links were not invested with customary legal, economic, or ceremonial functions of a kind which would periodically bring members of different lineages together in mandatory forms of co-operations and in place of it the Nayars had the hereditary institution of linked lineages whether or not, at a particular time. Sexual relationships existed between individuals of linked lineages; these linages must fulfil their obligations at household ceremonies and give neighbourly help at times of birth and death.

In relations between spouses of the tali-rite, the important rights are those of the woman. She had first the right to have a ritual husband of her own of a superior sub-caste before she attained maturity. Her second right was that of observing pollution at the death of her ritual husband. The tali-tier had no rights in his ritual wife's children except that they should observe pollution at her death.

In Sambandhan unions, the husband had no exclusive rights to his wife. If acknowledged the child of a woman as his, he had to pay delivery expenses. However, the child had one right to his passable biological fathers, that one or more of them should pay the expenses associated with his birth and, thus entitled him to enter the world as a member of his lineage and caste. The elementary family was not institutionalized yet we find that the Nayars did institutionalize the concept of marriage and of paternity and gave ritual and legal recognition to both.

The property belong to the tarwad is the property of all the males and females that compose it. But as the property of a tarwad is importable and as the individual members are not entitled to enforce position, the oldest male member of the tarawad is entrusted with the management of its property and affairs and he is known as karanavan. Theoretically, portion may be affected be common consent; but as any member can resist partition the tarwad continues to be joint and no member can claim division as a matter of right. The rights of the junior members of the tarwad are in practice the rights of maintenance. They are co-owners, however with a right to see that the tarawad property is duly consumed. The junior members are not entitled to maintenance unless they live in a family house. To qualify for maintenance when they live separately they must prove that it was mistreatment by the Karanavan that forced them to live outside the tarawad.

When a tarawad grows, it often splits into smaller family units called tawazhis, the number of which depends on the main female lines, with the consent of the members of the tarawad. A tawazhi in relation to a women is 'the group of persons consisting of a female, her children and all her descendents in the female line'. The property of the tarawad is divided equally among the tawazhis per strips. The tawazhis so formed are thus family units within community property. While the members thus cease to have legal right to the property of the parent tarawad, their kinship ties with it continue. All members of the tawazhi retain the tarawad names. As members of the tarawad, they observe the rules of exogamy and marry outside the tarawad. Similarly, they observe the rules of pollution and consider themselves impure for fourteen days on the death of any member of the tarawad. A partition made in this manner, for the sake of convenience, thus does not affect the right of an individual member to his tarawad or lead to the severance of his kinship ties with the paternal tarawad.

A Nair woman who lives with her people has the right of maintenance in her tarawad property. But she needs many more things besides maintenance, and the tarawad is not legally bound to provide her with all of them. She looks to her husband for the satisfaction of many of these needs, and as the century progresses and standards of comfort become higher so her reliance on her husband increases. Husband and wife are thus drawn closer to each other, and relations between them, which were formal under the old matrilineal organization, become more personal. Their children also bring them nearer to each other. The tarwad being unusually large, it is difficult for the karanavan to see that all children in the tarawad receive proper care and education. Human nature being what it is, judicious distinctions bound to be made between the children of the karanavan himself and those of other members. It is more pronounced. When the karanavan is weak and is guided by more selfish members of the tarawad. Children theoretically belong to the lineage of their mother and take the name of their mother's tarawad.

The whole question of sex relations among the Nairs may be approached from a different angle. Nair marriage is generally known as Sambandham. Nairs also perform the ceremony called tali-ketu-kalyanam. A Nair girl could have sambhandham not only with a Nair man of her caste or of a caste above her, but with a Brahmin and Kshatriya as well. It was considered an honour to be allied to a Nambudiri family by marriage. When the suitor was Brahmin he told the Karanavan, the head of the Nair tarawad, of his desire to marry the girl of his tarawad, then on an auspicious day the suitor would bring some pudakas (clothes which the wife bears) and hand them over to the girl in the presence of her relatives and neighbours, and it would be duly announced that they were married.

It is more nearly a form of marriage than the sambandham, the essential element of both being the giving of cloth. But the sambandham is a personal affair, conducted in privacy, while the tali-ketu ceremony was performed with all pomp and show. In a community where the marriage was loose, publicity was an essential element of marriage. The marriage partner was generally a member of the group who stood in the relationship of a father's sister's son. The tali tier was paid something for tying the tali, and this might have been to compensate him, if he were a cousin, for surrendering his preferential right over the bride.

Socially, the girl who did not go through this ceremony before puberty was considered impure and was excommunicated. Before the girl attained puberty and became fit for consummation, she was ceremoniously married to a person who had preferential claim over her. His right over the girl was then bought off and the girl was, thereafter, allowed to live a free life in regard to sex.

THE ORAONS

The Oraons inhabit the northern part of village Karkara. They are largely concentrated in the Ranchi region in India. Their neighbourhood is divided into 'Unch tola' (upper) and 'Neech tola' (lower tola). In which, upper tola comparatively are well-to-do people and have their dwellings, while in lower tola, the poorer sections of Oraons, have their huts and live in mud huts, thatchat with grass and bamboos. Since the community is poor, they are dressed in a 5-yard cloth called Kanya. The present Oraon society is characteristically known by presence of institutions like Akhara, Sasan and Dhunkuria in each village. Akhara is a place of great social importance, forming a dancing ground and a place of entertainment. The graveyard is generally own as Sasan and is covered with stone slabs called Sasan dirt. There are many families who may put Sasan adjacent to their houses. Another significant aspect of Oraon neighbourhood is the presence of 'Dhumkuria'. This is a place for imparting social and moral training to each youth.

The activities of the Oraons centre on agriculture. Yet living in a sort of traditional society they calculate time by the appearance of noon and get up at the call of the cock at dawn. Women do household chores, carry pots of water from public wells, other duties of the family such as collecting fuel, dried leaves and help working mothers by acting as care taker of younger ones. The men work in the fields and if their presence in the fields is not essential, they work as hired labourers. The grown up children carry light agricultural implements to the fields and help their fathers. The boys are responsible for herding cattle and let them out to the grazing fields. The older members unable to work hard, stay at home with children and make ropes and nets.

The fundamental feature of social organization of the Oraons is based on totemism. The tribe is divided into several clans. The members of one clan use the name of flora and fauna of the place for their totem. They believe that such animals and plants, protect their ancestors. The different clans of the village form an organized community with their own 'punch'/council of elders. The authority of village elders is unquestioned even today. The traditional panchayat represents the common will of the people in matter of private or public disputes. The Oraons form a patrilineal society. Members of one clan are believed to be descendants from a common ancestor and sex relations between them are not permitted.

The primary unit of social organization is the nuclear family consisting of parents and their unmarried children. Exogamy is still the main feature of Oroans. Moreover, marriage between the members of the same gotra or clan is strictly forbidden. The restrictions include the marriage between the children of brothers and sisters and between the two sisters are also practised. Marriage is a must among the Oraons. There are three traditional rules regarding an Oraon marriage, these rules distinguish it from the other cultural groups of the village. Marriage in the same clan is a sin, as all are classified as relations. The Oraons have also adopted a 'Golet' form of marriage (marriage by exchange), where son and daughter are exchanged with another's son and daughter in marriage.

After marriage, the wife must go to live with her husband and his family. Eventually she is incorporated into the husband's group. A respectable Oraon marriage requires the offer of cattle to the bride's father in a number and quality satisfactory to him; this is called as bride price. Thus, clan, exogamy, patrilocal residence and bride price characterize the marriage system of Oraons. Forbidden marriage are sure to be punished by 'Dharmas' (Chief deity).

Most of them do not marry more than once, but if there is no issue from the first wife they take another wife. In some cases, young girl tends to run away with young Oraon man who cannot pay bride price. The normal marriage age for the Oraon girls is sixteen years and boys between 20 to 25 years. Though a man sometimes may not marry till the age of 30 if he cannot pay the bride price.

The Oraons continue to believe and practice the religion of their fore-fathers despite efforts of Christian missionaries. The traditional religion of the Oraons consists mainly in the worship of 'Dharmas' or a supreme being who is regarded by the universe as with the highest dignity. They also believe in ancestor spirits who occasionally punish the living for neglect of rituals. Besides this, the totemic object such as certain plants and animals are objects of reverence for certain clan.

Oraon men and women share a strong desire to have children in the family. The child is regarded as a boon and brings good fortune in many ways. The position of an Oraon woman depends upon her ability to bear children. They love all children irrespective of their sex. It is significant that children are economic assets and not only enhance dignity of the parents but also help them in agricultural operations and other economic pursuits. A pregnant woman is not subject to any restriction nor does she get any special features till she delivers the child. She is kept to her task upto the last day. The Oraons believe to do plenty of work during the nine months of pregnancy will produce industrious and strong child. There is also no restriction on her diet. The only precaution she has to take is that she should not attend any funeral procession nor touch a dead body. Family planning has not been socially recognized among them.

Among the Oraons, a newborn baby has no status in the society unless given the ceremonial name. It is the first definite step in which socialization of the child is accomplished. For Oraons this occasion is of extreme gravity in an individual's life. The name giving ceremony is known as 'Nam-pinjana', which is performed within 6 months of the birth. Until this ceremony is performed, the child is usually known by the day on which he or she was born, like if a boy who was born on Sunday, he will be called 'Eluvariu' and if it is a girl, she will be called 'Etwaria'. From the day of the 'Nam-pinjana' the child is called by the particular name decided by the devination. The ceremony itself is an expression of the child's social birth.

Infant among the Oraons is considered immature, unfashioned, unripe, and incomplete. The period of infancy is characterized as the period between birth and mourning. During this period, the parents take special care of their biological needs and make serious effort to give any kind of formal training. Infancy is considered to be a period of danger approximating sickness. Infancy is considered as a transition period in which Oraon parents contact the imaginary environment for the safety of the child's life.

THE MURIAS OF BASTAR OF MADHYA PRADESH

There is a special and recognized building or buildings for the unmarried young men and to sleep in and at times for the young women also in many cases together. There is complete liberty between sexes until married.

Murias of Bastar of Madhya Pradesh in India live in dormitories called ghotuls by them. The dormitories fall into two clearly defined groups. One is of the semi-military barracks type appears to aim at a strict segregation of the boys and is connected with war, hunting and magic. Second allows or even-encourages them to have relations with the unmarried girls and possibly aims at regulating the prenuptial interests of tribal youth. Both types of dormitories fulfil important social and religious functions. At first there is the communal house where the whole village live together. This develops into a group of individual houses segregating the unmarried boys, married men have their dormitory, the unmarried girls have theirs' and the only people who live at home are the mothers and very young children. Finally owing to the economic pressures of modern system of taxation family life is extended. The older boys and girls are committed with the task of educating the younger children, for which parents have neither the time nor inclination.

There is no fixed age at which children can claim admission to the dormitory; it depends mainly on their relation with their parents. When they reach the stage of going about with other children, forming gangs and playing with them, instead at home, there is a natural desire to go to the ghotul. Entry for boys is very informal infact they just slip in. A girl does not go until she covers her shoulders, the one who has passed infancy and wears woman clothing. In any case, there is no taboo on the younger children when young to go to the dorm. They may go and see dances but must return home for night. A child can sleep in a ghotul only after he is able to look after himself.

The ghotul is an ancient institution. It is a living university. There are no books or tests, yet one is taught life's education. Students are teachers here, and teachers, students. The ghotul is typically located outside the village.

The older boys and girls take lot of trouble over the young children. They teach them manners and to keep their mouth shut. They instruct them in dancing and the ghotul games. They watch them closely and punish any failure or slackness. They specially watch a child's regularity of attendance and whether a boy brings wool and the girl does her cleaning. Regularity, obedience and habit of hard work are taught and tested. Students are tested for skills in leaf weaving, vegetable growing, ash cleaning and woodcarving.

The young boys are called chilak and young girls are called motiyari among the Murias. Quarrels in the dormitory are strongly conditioned. The betrayal of the ghotul fellowship by repeating outside, anything that happens within its walls, especially any stories of the intimate relations of the chilaks and motiyaris or about some scandal about pregnancy, is one of the greatest ghotul crises. Ghotul solidarity is constantly emphasized by the use of the ghotul little names and proper names may never be used between members as it is punishable.

The dormitory has to be kept clean. Spitting is allowed but anyone who initiates inside the building is punished. Most ghotuls are actually kept beautifully clean and occasional lapses are severely penalized. It is the special duty of the girls to sweep and cow dung the building. The students decorate the ghotul walls with paintings and take turns to keep the surrounding clean and meticulous.

Failure to attend ghotul regularly is punished. Absence of 2-3 days, unless there is a very genuine excuse is fined specially if a motiyari absents herself, it raises the suspicion that the girl is having an affair with a married man or a member of another caste. On the other hand, if a girl enters the ghotul during her menstrual period, she must provide liquor and perhaps more substantial sacrifice to appease lingo pen whom she has offended. It is punishable or fine able for a motiyari to refuse to dance, or comb or massage a chelik, as also it is considered very offensive for a chelik to force a girl against her will.

The Muria wedding ceremonies are lengthy and elaborate. The fundamental things seem to be the preparation and instruction of the bride in the ghotul, the ceremonial fetching of the bride by the bridegroom and his party, the building of marriage booth with its associated magical materials and patterns, the procession goes around the marriage sole or booth seven times, the typing together of the bridal pair, the exchange of gifts and payment of bride price, liberal use of oil and turmeric to consecrate the bride and bridegroom, pouring of water over the bridal pair and the last is visit to the ghotul and the official bidding of the couple by the chelik.

But all these ritual duties are only the beginning of the task of the members of the ghotul. They have to entertain a large number of guests. The kotwaal arranges the wood and organizes the dances; the belosa sees to the supply of water and leaves, she and her motiari have to make leaf-cups and plates, which in itself is a very considerable task but in addition, they have to do all the cooking and serve the meals.

A ghotuls reputation largely depends on the excellence of its dancing. The younger boys and girls are carefully trained and practice night after night, repeating the same steps and rhythms till they get them right. Once a dancing expedition has started mistakes are regarded as ill omened.

The number and variety of Muria games is remarkable. They might be played indoors or in the compound. Some of these games are excellent exercises. They have the same kind of importance that drill has for army; they teach the ghotul members to move together and to move at once. Marriage games seem to be intended to practice the chelik and motiyari in the complicated ritual of a wedding, in which they play so conspicuous a part.

But perhaps, a majority of the games have religious importance. The ghotul itself is a religious institution and has its share in the worship of Gods, while many of the cheliks are trained as priests. One cannot commit a sin inside a ghotul. The ghotul is founded by lingopen, noblest of ghotul cult-heroes. Diwali and Dassera (Dushehra) are observed by ghotul members in their own special way. The dead also have an important part in the Muria religion. The departed are to some extent, associated with the fertility of the land and are remembered at sowing and harvest. In the religious life of the tribe, the chelik play an important part. Their success in hunting is the best of omens for the coming harvest.

At the end of the Mohua season, the chelik and Motiari celebrate the Irpu festival three days are spent collecting the Mohua flowers and making liquor. Then, they go dancing house to house, and, they eat and drink in honour of the Mohua tree. The Muria attitude towards the God's is a curiously ambivalent blend of familiarity and tenor, of humour, affection and abuse often they do not so much pray to the Gods, as talk things over with them, usually at the top of their voices. Every marriage attracts the neighbouring ghotuls. They all sit around campfires, sing, dance and have rice-liquour. The Muria get a great deal of fun out of dressing up. At weddings, they even appear as fancily dressed.

The humour of the Muria is probably more fully developed than that of any other tribe in central India. The ghotul is a natural school of wit, the constant association of young people forces them to device many forms of entertainment. The first and most elementary form of Muria humour is plain buffoonery. They love throwing dirty water at each other, sprinkling people with red ants, creeping up behind someone and clasping muddy hands round his face. If we turn to verbal wit, we find a similar tendency; in the songs are references of moustache peacocks and tusked hares and kotwar being fed on 12 years old gruel full of lizards and frogs.

The Muria have a simple, innocent and natural attitude to sex. In ghotuls, this is strengthened by the absence of any guilt and the general freedom from external interference. The Muria believe that sexual congress is a good thing, it does you good, it is healthy and beautiful, when performed by the right people at the right time out side the menstrual period and avoiding forbiddin days and in the right place within the ghotul walls where no sin can be committed. It is the happiest and the best thing in life.

The routine of a ghotul is a carefully devised preparation for intercourse, a tonic to deficient libido. First of all, the sense of touch is vividly stimulated by combing and massaging. After touch, smell is a powerful stimulant, charming is the freshness of the open hill and forest, but more charming is the smell of perspiration, oil and wet earth. No artificial scents are used. But the most usual method of attaining luminescence, is some form of dance. The ghotul is regulated by exact and far-reaching laws, which are very generally obeyed. There is little immortality in a ghotul.

The greatest sin is to injure some one by magic. It is very bad to hurt a man, specially an old man. To kill cattle without cause is bad, though there is nothing wrong in sacrificing a bull or cow for a funeral or at a festival. To give food to the hungry is the greatest virtue. Chelik and Motiyari must choose the right partners. They must strictly avoid the inner circle of forbidden relatives. Intercourse within the clan is forbidden, but is not regarded as very sinful as long as no one knows about it and it does not result in pregnancy. They have a strong sense of domestic morality and conjugal fidelity, and adultery is prohibited.

They believe in living the life to its fullness. That youth must be served, freedom and happiness are more to be treasured than any material gain, that friendliness and sympathy, hospitality and unity are of the first importance, and above all, that human love and its physical expression is beautiful, clean and precious.

FAMILY SYSTEMS IN FOREIGN SOCIETIES

In the fourth millennium B.C. in the Middle East, the Sumerians had founded cities such as Ur and Kish. They had considerable technical knowledge about agriculture and worked a variety of metals into weapons, ornaments and tools. In this civilization, polyandry was quite common. Then in about 2350

B.C., a Sumerian king, Uru Kagina, put an end to polyandry and reversed marriage customs. Men were permitted to marry many women depending on their wealth, king Solomon, ruler in ancient Israel in 955 B.C., was represented to have had 700 wives (Wedgwood, 1985).

THE PHILIPPINES

The central force in the family is the Filipino woman. Though, not typically the major breadwinner, she holds the family purse strings. The husband gives his wife his earnings, apart from his pocket expenses. In a very real sense, she is the boss of the house, yet the image conveyed is that the man is the master. While the husband is recognized as chief breadwinner and head of the family, the wife has definite spheres of competence in which the husband accepts her leadership. This is particularly true in household chores and family expenditures. But women are also regarded as shrewd and energetic traders. Many engage in small, independent commercial ventures. At higher socio-economic levels, maids are hired inexpensively to permit educated woman to pursue commercial and professional opportunities. The Filipinos female starts off on a nearly equal educational plane with her male counterpart. Monogamy is the widely stressed appropriate form of marriage. Two exceptions to monogamous legal unions among Christian Filipino families are consensual marriages and the querida system. Consensual unions, often occurring among the poor, who wish to avoid the wedding expenses, are more or less permanent relationships between a man and a woman without the sanction of a marriage ceremony. The querida system involves a married man, usually of higher status, seeing, supporting and possibly having children by a woman other than his wife. While a 'mistress relationship' is frowned upon, the civil code provides for the maintenance of his illegitimate children.

In a literal sense, the Philippines are a nation of children. Half of the population is under 17 years of age. Children are highly valued in traditional Philippine society as economic assets, as insurance in old age, as a demonstration of male potency, as sources of enjoyment, gifts from God, as extensions of themselves, etc. The child is expected to be quiet and submissive rather than aggressive and domineering. Children are taught filial loyalty and obedience to elders. In the Filipino family network, the responsibility is extended to family members, it places on individual achievement and getting ahead, alongwith the comfort and security found among relatives. The relatives may be more kin-oriented, but urban families posses in large measure the resources needed to assist an extra relative looking for work or going to school. However, in the Philippines the extended-family responsibilities and the lack of low-cost housing combined with the greater job and educational opportunities lead to a situation of a disproportionate number of urban extended-family situations. Household size is large in urban than in rural areas and the difference reflects the presence of extended kin.

THE AFRICA

The matrilineal system of the African countries differs considerably from that of the South East Asian groups. Even within India, the system differs from one group to another. Among these groups, difference is mostly observed in the type of residence after marriage. The pattern of duo-local residence exists among the Ashanti of the Gold Coast in Africa, Minangkhan of Sumatra and the Nairs of Central Kerala. However, the Khasis of Meghalaya, generally follow the residential pattern known as "matrilocal residence," where the husband resides with his wife's matrilineal kin or in other case couples settle down together in a new residence in and around his wife's maternal place (neo-local residence). It is the Minangkabaus of West Sumatra, Indonesia, comprosing the largest ethnic group in the world who follow a matrilineal system (Tanius, 1983).

Fula in Africa call the second wife "the jealous one," there are usually built in control mechanisms to ease the problem. The wives may be related especially as sisters (sorrote), if they are unrelated, they usually have separate dwellings. Women in these societies often prefer that, there be several wives, plural wives are a sign of status and, more important, ease the workload of individual wives (Bryan Strong, 1995).

THE AFRICAN AMERICANS

Among African Americans or Puerto Ricans, people have a long history of consensual marriages (heterosxual, conjugal unions that have not gone through a legal marriage ceremony). The tradition of consensual marriages probably began among Puerto Ricans, due to lack of economic resources, necessary for marriage licenses and weddings. Cohabitation symbolizes a committed union much like marriage for Puerto Ricans. Hence, they don't feel the need to marry legally should the woman become pregnant because they have already defined themselves as (consensually) married, the child is legitimate and the man who is living with the woman, the father. Although, non-martial union was never considered the cultural ideal, they were recognized as a form of marriage and they typically produced children (Manning and Landale, 1996). Such marriages are also common among Indian Ocean isles like Mauritius and Seychelles.

African Americans lay emphasis on inter-generational ties. They place a lot of importance to their children. They are mostly dual earners since long back, therefore, division of work between males and females is equal. They have egalitarian family roles. Kinship bonds are important, they provide economic assistance and emotional support in times of need (Taylor, 1994). They generally have extended family households.

THE UNITED STATES OF AMERICA

Polygamy is illegal in the United States as its traditional roots are in Christianity. Considering the high divorce rate in the United States, monogamy seems no longer to exist, it is better to describe the marriage system as serial monogamy or modified polygamy, because one person may have several spouses over his or her lifetime.

Among Latinos, la familia embraces not only the nuclear, but also the extended family. In la familia, abacus (grand parents) are especially influential as warm and affectionate figures to their grand children (Mirande, 1985). In Latino culture, compares (god parents literally co-parents) are important figures in the family. The compard (god father) and comrade (god mother) are considered to be responsible for the child's spiritual development and they are available as resources in time of need.

La familia is centered around the nuclear family, but it also, includes the extended family of grand parents, aunts, uncles and cousins, who tend to live close by, often in the same block on neighbourhood. There is close kin cooperation and mental acceptance especially at the times of need. Children are very important. Catholicism is also an important factor in the Latinos family life. Although, there is a tradition of male dominance, day-to-day living patterns suggest that women have considerable power and influence in the family (Griswold del Castillo, 1984).

Among Japanese Americans, despite acculturation and intermarriages, some families attempt to preserve the traditional concept of the i.e. Among American Chinese, elders continue to command respect and to influence younger family members (Hang, 1988). Among Japanese Americans the i.e. (pronounced "ee-eh") is the traditional family. The i.e. consists of living members of the extended family (such as grand parents, aunts, uncles and cousins), as well as deceased and yet-to-be-born family members (Ki Kumura and Kitano, 1988).

Among lesbians and gay men, fictive kin are important as a means of including one's partner and his on her relatives and friends as family. In one of the researches, a researcher found that seventy four percent defined a family as any group whose members loved and cared for one another (Footlick, 1990). Unrelated individuals who feel and are treated as relatives in a family are called affiliated kin or fictive kin (Strong, 1995). Among Lations, compadres (god parents) are considered family members. Among many traditional Native American tribes, the clan, group of related families, is regarded as the fundamental family unit (Yellow bird and Snipp, 1994).

THE SOUTH EAST ASIA

In Ceylon and throughout South-East Asia, the Sinhalese, had a customary law, it was (and is) the rule that if a man and a woman publically known to have cohabitated together and the woman bears a child, than the woman has a claim on the man for the support of the child (D'Oyly, 1929). Among their rural practice, all of a man's acknowledged children are equally his own whether or not be has at any time gone through a ritual of marriage with the child's mother. Likewise all of a woman's children have equal claims on her inheritance. Sinhalese still practice this customary law.

THE CHINA

According to anthropologist Janice Stockard (1989), a remarkable form of marriage, the spirit marriage, exists among canton, China, today. In this, marriage is arranged, between the two, by two families whose son and daughter died unmarried. After the dead couple is married, the two families adopt an orphaned boy and raise him as the decreased couple's son to provide family continuity. Another Cantonese marriage form, women do not live with their husbands until at least three years after marriage, as their primary obligations remains with their own extended families.

THE HUNZA OF HIMALAYAS

Among Hunsa or Hunza (Himalayas) conception and birth processes are known from an early age (Bircher, 1942). Children hear adult conversations on these issues, and therefore are not in the need of further education "when the capacities of procreation awake." No child marriages take place. Marriages take place at age 16-18; in case of a low age of the bride, the mother of the groom would sleep between the married ones until the girl is "ripe enough" for the marital act. A girl is marriageable from age 15.

THE MANI OR THE NEGRITO OF THAILAND

The Mani also called the Negrito of Thailand; a group in Trang Province of Andaman. Their social system does not accept incestuous relationships and is built on the principle of monogamy. When their children enter puberty, the parents build a new and separate hut for them to live in. A girl who has started menstruation is considered marriageable while a boy who has developed facial hair is said to be ready to take a wife.

The first steps towards selecting a partner among the Mani are left to the young people themselves. In the old days, a woman selected her marriage partner based primarily on the man's hunting prowess. Today, a woman tends to make her choice of a mate more on the basis of good looks and a modern style of dressing. A young man wearing sunglasses and jeans is considered more desirable than one not doing so.

However, young people cannot simply marry once they feel mutual affection for each other and declare their wish to become a couple. Before marriage and cohabitation is possible, a formal proposal has to be made and the consent of the girl's parents has to be sought. Should they oppose the union, the two young people cannot marry, no matter how much they love each other. In such a case, it would be considered bad if for the young man showed his annoyance at the decision of the girl's parents.

For the marriage party, both bride and groom were their beautiful dress. Relatives of both sides sit in front of the couple as they advise them to live well together and not to fight. After this session of matrimonial advice, all start eating the monkeys and langurs the groom has provided, leaving no leftovers. A few days later, relatives of the bride say their farewells and go back to their own homes.

To the Mani, a pregnant woman is a person of great importance. Once a woman is known to have conceived, she will not be allowed to engage in heavy work. As time for delivery draws closer, the group's care for her intensifies.

Shortly before the baby is due, the husband goes into the forest to look for a herb called tum toke that eases delivery. He then prepares and administers the herb on instructions from his wife. During this period, the women of the community sit near the hut where the pregnant woman lives, waiting and ready to help. Supervising the delivery is the duty of a female elder, generally the wife of the clan chief. During delivery, the woman in charge runs her hand over the stomach of the birthing woman. If the birth is difficult, she makes the mother-to-be chew more tum toke and sprinkles water on her while reciting incantations, until the baby is delivered. Occasionally, the husband helps in the delivery. If the husband does not know how to help in the delivery, he will instead offer assistance nearby, like in taking care of the fire, in bringing water and in going to fetch the medicines required. When the baby has arrived, the senior woman uses a thin slice of bamboo to sever the umbilical cord and will hold the baby until it has been disposed of. She also washes and dries the newborn baby. At the same time, it is the husband's duty to bury the afterbirth in a hole in the ground, ca. 50 cm (20 in.) deep, that he had dug up earlier for the purpose.

The Mani believes that loss of blood from the delivery, the mother's body temperature has fallen. Thus, after giving birth, the mother has to remain by a fire tended by her husband. Should the woman feel pain, a coconut sized stone is fire-heated and wrapped in a piece of cloth and is placed on her body to warm the painful body parts. Throughout the time when the mother is near the fire, she has to take boiled herbs known as *ching dok diao, fai doen kong and khun senah* before delivery. The three ingredients are boiled together and drunk in hot water as a kind of tea.

During this time, the mother is prevented from eating certain meats, such as monkeys, langurs and baboons as these are considered to have a "hot" property that could increase her blood pressure. The new mother is allowed to eat fish and vegetables only. Her time of having to be near a fire normally lasts about 7 days. When she is strong enough for travel, the family abandons camp and moves to a new place to live. It is believed that the blood during the delivery of a baby, after some days will bring illness to people living near it.

The mother pays close attention to her baby at all times. Initially it is breast-fed, but after 4-6 months, the mother feeds her child with honey, believing that honey helps digestion. Feeding the baby with honey is called *beukpaak*.

Still later, the child's parents start feeding their baby with more grown-up foods, such as prechewed, burned potatoes or yam, the daily staple of Mani diet. The mother takes the inside of a burned tuber and blows on it to cool it down. She then chews it to a mash and feeds it to the infant. During this period, the mother will alternate between feeding the baby with pre-chewed tubers and breast-feeding. Women have a duty to go into the forest in search of potatoes suitable for babies. As soon as the mother is healthy and strong enough, she returns to her usual duties around the village. When searching for food in the forest, she takes her newborn along with her. The baby is placed in a sling made of a loincloth and held around her neck and nestling safely on mother's chest.

When not out hunting and while the mother is cooking, fathers will also look after babies. Childcare among the Mani involves holding the baby to one's chest while embracing it. Mani babies are also protected from the harm threatened by evil spirits by the placing of a hua plai or kled un around their necks, other possible protective ornaments and amulets include turtle shell cut into squares and small animal bones with a hole pierced for a piece of string.

RURAL FAMILY AND URBAN FAMILY

Rural Family

Patriarchal joint family is the most dominant form in rural life. In this form there is greater homogeneity. It is more homogenous, stable, integrated and organically functioning than the urban family. The family ties are strong and lasting. The rural family also includes the distant relations. People cooperate and elder members hold control. Since they spend most of their time together, the psychological traits they develop are very similar. There is greater discipline and interdependence. The rural society is more disciplined. They themselves fulfil their educational, cultural and social needs of the people. It itself serves as a school, a recreation centre, and a hospital too. The interdependence binds them into a homogenous, compact, egoistic unit; it also strengthens solidarity and cooperation. They develop more collective family consciousness and less individualistic needs or emotions. Rural family is integrated and disciplined unit, the head of the family exercises almost absolute power over its members. He distributes the work and arranges marriages of the children. The participation is closer in various activities. They spend practically the whole day together. It has certain distinct characteristics like early marriages, family as a unit of social responsibility, family as a basis of norms of society, cooperative rather than contractual relations, dominance of family cult, ancestor worship and dominance of traditions, etc.

Though, now it is being changed under the influence of urbanization and westernization. It is now changing from a massive large joint family to small nuclear families. The rule of custom is being replaced by the rule of law.

Urban Society

It is segmented and varied society. On one side there are rich, very rich, middle class and poor, very poor on the other. Housing is also varied from bungalows to slums. People are shifting to cities in search of jobs and earnings. Cities have facilities, which attract them. The busy life, the luring and bright lights, fast moving buses, trains, electricity, metal roads all attract them. Mobility is more intense. They change occupation and residence easily. Density of population is more resulting into greater isolation from nature. There is more dependence on machines and technologies. Pollution is also high in cities.

CHARACTERISTICS OF URBAN SOCIETY

- Here people are less concerned about others. No community feeling.
- Society is not divided on the basis of caste, but economy.
- Families are separate, small and independent.
- Children get more priority, better care and better education.
- They are less bound by traditions, customs and rituals.
- More insecure because of high crime rate.
- Suspicious, worried and suffer from complexities. They have high aspirations, competitions and frustrations.
- More self-regulatory behaviour in civilized and culture societies. More inhibitions in expression, communication and social relations.
- Higher rate of technical adoption. Hence, life is fast. It is fast moving society.
- Leisure activities are different. These days confined to home; less social activities.
- Due to pollution, high rate of health problems. Though, medical facilities are better available. Life expectancy has increased but quality has deteriorated.
- Family relations are also changing. Parent-child relations are changing.

It is more democratic rather than authoritarian. There is less mutual respect. Relations in urban families are based on more competition and less cooperation. People think in terms of personal gains. The people and families enjoy more freedom and less control.

Family trends and loneliness is another feature of urban families. Now-a-days people prefer to have one or two children. They go for education and then service. Parents are left alone. In old age they suffer from loneliness. The situation is worse when one spouse dies. Sons and their wives wish to live separately, alone are the old people. Divorce rate is also increasing. Due to lack of adjustment skills, partners get separated and most sufferers are their children. Single-parent family passes through various socio-emotional crises. Now more families are becoming dual earner. Both have separate career. Children are the latch-openers. New forms of marriages have started beginning in big cities and are spreading in other cities also. Producing children without getting legally married, cloning-children and children in re-married families also suffer from various socio-emotional stress and crises. The result of such tensions is lack of proper development of children. Not only children but other members of families, relatives and also the whole society suffers because of the threat to the stability in society.

Urban society enjoys more facilities and comforts of life. They are aware of scientific, technological, social, economical and other advances. They can afford to purchase them also. Various means of transportation, entertainment and communication are available to them. Life is busy and people are less concerned about others. They are self-centered and lack community feeling. They are less bound by traditions, customs and rituals. They have self-regulated behaviour, hence have more inhibitions in expression, communication and social relations. They are more insecure because of high crime rate. Families are small, independent and nuclear. Children get better care, more priority and better education.

In brief, urban families are small, independent, nuclear, less stable, less traditional, more resourceful, not based on caste division, but on economic aspect. They are more status conscious, self-centered and competitive. They are modern, live mechanized life, and suffer from more socio-emotional stresses.

10

The Family

The concept of marriage and the concept of family are interrelated and interconnected both socially and sociologically. In the beginning of human society, there might not have been family or marriage system, but only a kind of unregulated sexual relations and not stable family relations. Later on due to development of human race, the marriage and family came in existence as an institution. Family as an institution is to be found even in the most primitive of human societies. It never originated but perpetuated.

Marriage and family are closely associated concepts. According to the Hindu philosophy and religion marriage or 'Vivaha' is meant to propagate "Kutumba" or "family." The formation of family depends on the incidence of marriage in human society. Family life is not the exclusive privilege of human beings. Even animals have families in their bio-social set-up. What distinguishes human family from animal family is the social sanction of marriage.

There are certain common objectives of marriage, which find fulfilment in the family. The first purpose of marriage is channelization of sex activity between husband and wife. But sex activity is not rigidly, universalized since in many tribal communities there is laxity of sex behaviour in terms of wife lending. Founding a family of procreation is the second universal objective. Sociologically, marriage is not complete until a child is born, in childless families adoption is institutionalized. Thirdly, marriage has a common objective of economic cooperation. The provisions of home and property considerations are important for the up-keep of the family formed by marriage. Division of labour between husband and wife varies in numerable ways in different social groups. Fourthly, it is a psychophysical phenomenon providing for the response of emotional and intellectual inter-stimulations of the partners involved. Lastly, a prominent objective of marriage in many social groups is the maintenance of kinship. Social relations between kinship group are strengthened by marriage and continuity in blood relationship is established; caste groups and racial groups advocate kinship prominence in marriage.

In every society; the age at which individuals are allowed to enter the state of marriage is recognized. But pre-puberty marriages are found in some traditional groups. In modern society, the age for marriage is legalized. Persons of immediate blood relations are forbidden to marry. Marital relations between parents and children are prohibited universally.

The positive aspects of marriage are found in the performance of rites, which vary, in different cultural groups. They are the protective symbols for the welfare of the couple. The negative aspects are found in the avoidance of bad omen, evil spirits against which they are protected.

Family is the most important primary group in human society. MacIver has defined family as "a group based on sex relationship sufficiently precise and enduring to provide for the procreation and upbringing of children." Anthropologist and sociologists have tried to trace the evolution of family life from the essential characteristics rooted in human nature. Westernmark and Charles Darwin have remarked that family obtained a form of social life by the operation of the possessive and jealous tendencies of the male who claimed monopolistic rights by customs. This accounts for the patriarchal pre-eminence in the origin of family. There are no evolutionary stages in the formation of family. Family living has not emerged from any single trait of male's dominance or female's privileges.

Family is distinguished from other organized social groups by its specific characteristics. Firstly, it is the most universal social organization. Membership in a family is recognized in two ways—parental family and marital family. Secondly, it is based on emotional stimulations of organic nature in terms of mating, procreation, parental care and affection. Thirdly, it influences the life of an individual from the initial stages of birth. It is the first fundamental agency of socialization to transmate organic habits and mental traits to human personality. Fourthly, it is the simplest social unit, limited in a size. It is enough if there are only 3 members husband, wife and child. Fifthly, it is the nucleus of all other social organizations. Sixthly, it imposes responsibilities through obligations and duties among parents and children. The members of the family have respective roles in their inter-personal relationships. Seventhly, family is governed by social norms of sex regulation through social sanctions of marriage. As a cultural unit, there are certain taboos forbidding sex relations between parents and children, brothers and sisters. Lastly, family is the most permanent institution as well as association.

Family is a set of parents and children or of relatives, a person's children, the members of a household, all descendents of a common ancestor, lineage, a race or a group of people from a common stock. It may include relatives and servants of the household also. The family and family life is included by the ideologies and discourses inherent in the society in which we live at a particular historical point. Family life is influenced by socio-cultural beliefs, which is perceived as acceptable and desirable in a given society, the familial point of view in which the family members jointly negotiate decisions based on their joint evolution of a set of shared beliefs, and the personal point of view of the person which has been accumulated from our life experiences with the outside world. Families describe a set of rules and belief system, which has to be followed in relation to each other. In North India, daughters don't touch their parents feet while in other parts of India the tradition is opposite, daughters touch the feet of their parents and other elders while paying respect to them. Such boundaries have been based on beliefs which had been set long back in the history. Society in which a person grows helps to establish a set of beliefs, enabling rules and procedures to be formed by its constituent family unit. The issue of power, decision-making, responsibilities, duties, obligations and commitments is pre-decided in a family unit. The role and tasks given to a member in the family is influenced by the gender role in the society.

Family performs various functions, such as—biological—reproduction, food, housing and clothing; psychological—affection, love, security; protection and care ; economic—division of labour, arrangement of income, organization and care of property; social function—to establish status, socialization, social control, assistance in choice of partner ; religious ; cultural ; and, educational functions.

The family is both the earliest and the most sustained source of social contact for the child. Even, though, many contemporary families have new and different structures, family relationships remain the most intense and enduring of all interpersonal and social bonds. Children carry the memories of past family interactions in their perceptions and feelings about family members, and in the standards they hold not only for family behaviour but also for the behaviour of people in general.

Family members share not only their memories of the past but their expectations of future shared events and experiences. It is largely this continuity over time that makes the family relationship qualitatively different from the shorter-lived relationships with play mates and friends, teachers, neighbours and ultimately co-workers and others.

SOCIALIZATION

In the child's earliest years, his sole interpersonal relationships may be with his parents, and parents generally present cultural beliefs, values and attitudes to their children in a highly personalized and selective fashion. Yet, even though parents' own personalities, family backgrounds, attitudes, values, education, religious beliefs, socio-economic status, and gender influence the way they socialize their children, their role in this socialization process—ensuring that their child's standards of behaviour, attitudes, skills and motives conform as closely as possible to those regarded as desirable and appropriate to her or his role in society is crucial.

Through socialization, social norms of the members of a

particular society in which you belong is learnt. Norms are society's rules of conduct for its members. Growing up in a society means learning its system of norms so that as an adult you will be able to function successfully with other similarly socialized people. The main responsibility of transforming one's social norms to successive generations lies on the family. In the family, there are norms that specify which persons in the society are eligible for marriage, when to marry, how many spouses you can have, whom to marry, where to live, what role you perform in the family set-up, how is child reared in the family, defines proper parental behaviour in front of and in relation to children, what to teach the child and what not to teach, and so on. Beyond the familial contribution and intertwined with it, there always lies a body of knowledge and practice shared by the society at large which the society transmits to all its new members. For adequate maintenance and sustainance of society is possible if all its members share a common code of principles, values, beliefs, attitudes and practices.

Family is an effective autonomous unit for a wide range of residential, consumption and social functions. What is family? In everyday conversations we discuss and assure what and how family should be. Pogrebin (1983) defined the essence of family as, "who it is, how it feels and what it does," suggests that families must be able to define themselves. In defining the family, Walters (1982) examines four aspects: biological factors, commitment, and attachment and mate selection. Commitment is the intention of a person to maintain a relationship while attachment is the bonding that causes feelings of at-homeness and ease when the other person is either present or easily accessible. Mate selection is a familial process, wherein, families stress the importance of selecting mates with similar attitudes, race, religion, social status and values.

Thorne (1982) has characterized families as places of sexuality, eating, sleeping and of close biological ties. Burgess and Locke (1945) defined the family as, "a group of persons united by the ties of marriage, blood or adoption; constituting a single household; interacting and communicating with each other in their respective social roles (husband and wife, mother and father, son and daughter, brother and sister); and creating and maintaining a common culture.

In the Cyclopedic Education Dictionary (1998) Spafford, Pesce and Grosser defined family as, "two or more persons (to include at least one person in whose name the housing unit is owned, based, or rented, and residing together within), usually family members who are related by birth, adoption, or marriage. However, non-related persons may also be considered part of the so-called extended family when residing together or sometimes even when they are not." A household "is any separate living unit occupied by one or more persons" (Wetzel, 1990). The Cyclopedic Education Dictionary (1998) defines a household as "containing biological or adopted family and any unrelated persons (unrelated sub-family members, other individuals or both) who may be taking residence there. The number of family households in a society is equal to the number of families. The number of family household members is not the same as the number of family members, however, in that the family household members include all persons living in the household, (adopted/biological) whereas, family members include only the head of the household and his/her relatives. In simple words, family household is any living unit containing at least two people related by blood, marriage or adoption.

Family provides the opportunities of a close intimate relationship, sharing emotionally and physically close and committed tie between two people. The word "intimate" is derived from the Latin word 'intimus', meaning 'inner' or in most (Perlman and Fehr, 1987). People who are intimate with one another, share their private thoughts, dreams, insecurities and triumphs and they know a great deal about one another. Family provides intimacy not only among the married couple but also in parent-child, grandparent-grandchild and sibling relationships.

Intimacy is also a virtue of close friendship. Intimate people are committed to each other's well being and at times are altruistic, self-sacrificing for the sake of other. Intimate relationship developed varies from culture-to-culture and family-to-family.

Family closeness and intimate relationships is also affected by the social change. Social change refers to fluctuations and modifications occurring in the larger groups, institutions and societies to which individuals belong.

Social change is defined as the process in which there is significant alteration in the structure and functioning of certain social system. Social charge denotes some observable alterations in the social phenomena over a period of time, a charge in social relationships and social structure of the society.

Man is generally described as a social animal. It is not possible for an individual to live without society. Individual is an unit of society. He lives in society after having been born into it. Individual cannot live without society. On the other hand, society is the vast field, in which the individual lives and acts. Society is nothing but a web of relationships between different individuals as social beings. The relationship between man and society is inseparable. One cannot exist without the other.

Families have faced challenges and changes starting with the ancient period. Families worked together helped out in times of trouble and distress, and celebrated special events together. Changes have been brought in family due to industrial and technological revolutions from agrarian society. Industrial and technological revolution has brought about new changes in the family system. Many families or members of the family have moved from rural areas to large cities. Earlier all family members worked together to provide from the family's needs. They were both producers and consumers. With the advent of factories and industries production shifted from the house to the factory. Now instead of being self employed people had to find work in factories.

Families became dependent on others and adopted the role of consumers. Mostly men went out in search of work with women being left behind to look after the home, elderly parents and young children. This brought a stress on the marriage relationship. Slowly the women folk also joined her husband at the place of his work leading to many families had to move away from the area where their relatives lived.

With the increase of technology production of goods increased. Material goods such as washing machines, refrigerators, cars, generators, tube wells etc. became easily available to make life easier. The need to possess various material goods to raise standards of living has resulted in demand of greater economic resources. As a result dual career families with working women have come up.

With the house lady working has resulted in a need for others especially husband, to help with household chores. The marriage relationship has changed. Couples unsatisfied with each other now separate. Parental interference in the couples' decision has minimized. The rate of divorce has increased and if unchecked would soar.

In a family all members affect one another. Bronfenbrenner's ecological system clearly demonstrates the effect on a child from others and others impact on the child in a social milieu. Nobody exists in isolation to others. What one member of the family does affects the rest of the family. Children also influence their parents and each other. Influence of the people children and parents interact with is also seen on the other members of the family. The rules, laws and social norms of the society also affect the whole family.

This social change has resulted in the breakdown of traditional family and has resulted in modern family. Traditional family is economically based, large, public, patriarchal family type while modern family is small, private, intimate and equalitarian type.

Families are characterized by closeness. Cohesion or closeness is a common goal for many families. Cohesion refers to the emotional bonding that family members have towards one another—the amount of connectedness among family members (Olson, *et al.* 1983). It is the feeling of closeness among family members, which leads to support during difficult times. Families approach problematic situations with a positive point of view. Families who take a confidant, optimistic approach to any problem the family faces are able to do because believe they have to stay together whatever may happen. They have confidence that their family will ultimately prevail and the crises would end.

A SOCIAL SCIENCE APPROACH TO THE FAMILY

The social science approach to the study of family involves the application of scientific methods to marital and familial functions, structure and interactions. Sociology as a discipline is concerned with the organization of society—its social structure and its social processes. The family sociologist is concerned with family functions, structures and changes. Psychoanalytical approaches concerned with the individual and his relation to social groups.

HISTORICAL APPROACHES TO FAMILY STUDIES

A systematic study of the family began after the middle of nineteenth century with the period of Social Darwinisn (1885-1900) and has continued through the period of emerging science (1900-1950) and the period of systematic theory building (1950). Middle of the nineteenth century emphasized Drawin's concept of biological evolution to changes within the family.

During the first half of the twentieth century various statistical techniques were developed and certain sociologist and psychologists studied personal adjustment of the individual, family influences on personal adjustment and the relationship between certain family problems and social problems in general. The most pronounced characteristic of family study during the period from 1990 to 1950 was the emphasis on interpersonal relationships in the family.

There are many notions about the origin and development of family. Some are obviously fanciful while others are symbolic some are supported by historical and other evidences. The notions of a definite origin lasted until very recently, but the concept of uniformity was challenged long ago.

According to the anthropologist Claude Hevi-Stress while the family is found practically everywhere, there is no natural law making the family universal. With the recognition that there was no single-family form came a desire to understand how various systems of family life arose. The early theories that attempted to elucidate the relationship between social change and the family were evolutionary, while later theories can be subsumed under the term structural functionalism. The idea of progressive development from savagery to civilization was much older than Charles Darwin's Origin of Species (1859). According to Henry Summer Marine, author of Ancient Law, the original form of family was patriarchal. Marine theorized that society was originally organized in male-dominated families which were more primitive and natural; female-centered families where more recent.

FAMILY THEORIES

Systems Theory

Psychiatrist Murray Bowen developed Family Systems

Theory in the 1950's based on his work in the family therapy field (Kerr, 1988). A family is a system in which its members are organized into a group forming a whole larger than its separate elements. A variety of intricate relationships evolve in the family system; alliances and coalitions are formed as energy and information exchanged. A system exists when there are components that have common properties interacting and influencing each other in ways that produce a whole larger than the sum of its independent parts (Goldenberg and Godenberg, 1991). For the family system to survive, it must be both flexible and stable. Otherwise, the family as a social system becomes dysfunctional (Melito, 1985). Change in any member affects and is affected by change in any other. The family's adaptability or ability to reorganize as it moves through successive stages is a key to healthy family functioning (McFadden and Doub, 1983).

Exchange Theory

Exchange theory has a theoretical perspective, whereby human beings seek to avoid costly behaviour and seek statuses, relationships, interactions, and feelings that are personally rewarding in order to maximize their "profits" (Nye, 1988). It is particularly useful in understanding precarious human relationships such as sexual involvement of singles, courtship processes, marital satisfaction and divorce as it offers a relatively simple focus on costs and rewards (Holman and Burr, 1980). It is less effective when the exchange process becomes more complicated, subtle, long-term or unconscious. Therefore, the exchange perspective would not be as useful when trying to interpret non-rational factors such as love, jealousy, self-esteem, values and social norms (Murstein, Cerreto and McDonald, 1977). It is most applicable in family power; the one who provides the most resources in the family has the most power (Adams, 1986). Couples may exchange different resources in a relationship such as beauty, money and sex for status. Such equity in relationships not only impacts the selection of a mate but also how two people will get along and how likely they are to remain together (Walster and Walster, 1978).

Developmental/Family Life Cycle Theory

A family life cycle approach is veiwed as a developmental

impasse that occurs as the family negotiates a transition from one stage to the next (Breunlin, 1983). Although families around the world differ enormously, there is evidence of the universality of the family life cycle (Hareven, 1974). Family life cycle also transcend varying family patterns. The differences in paths of development of single-parent and two-parent families are seen primarily not in stages encountered but in the number, timing and length of the critical transitions experienced (Ruben Hill, 1986). As the relationship grows so does the family with the passage of time. The family life cycle is composed of stages that extend from marriage to the death of a spouse. Most families go through similar stages in the family life cycle. These include the newly married stage, early and later parenthood stages, the empty next stage and retirement. Each stage has its own task, challenges, rewards and different roles. Chapter 11 will discuss this theory in detail.

11

The Family Life Cycle

Families exist in environments, which alter continuously. A family is an organic entity which maintains some form of identity and structure whilst at the same time continually evolves and changes. Apart from day-to-day variations and adaptations necessary for family life. Families may be faced at times with massive demands for change such when members arrive, births and marriages and depart divorce and death or desertion and separation. Development in a family is a life long process of socialization, adjustment and learning within families. Socialization is a process by which one learns the rules of a given society in order to function effectively within that culture. It must tune to make a person capable of fruitfully participating in a social group. The family is the most important socializing agent in the child's life. It is considered as the primary socializing agent and plays an influential role not only during childhood but throughout life in extended family and till adolescence in the western communities. Disruptions in this process by conflicts in the family may create problems for the young.

Within the stages of the family life cycle, each marriage and family has its own unique history (Aldous, 1978). Family life cycle focuses on the nuclear family. The family life cycle perspective uses a developmental framework to explain people's behaviour in families. According to it, families change over time, both, in who its members are and in terms of the roles played by them. At various stages, family has different developmental tasks to perform.

Duvall and Miller suggested that the family life cycle consists of eight stages beginning families, child bearing families, families with pre-school children, families with school children, families with adolescents, families as launching centres, families in the middle years and aging families. Variations on the traditional life cycle include disabled, adoptive, gay and lesbian, ethnic, immigrant, and single parent families, as well as step-families.

The family life cycle may divided into few or many stages on the basis of several factors. It is possible to think of a two stage family life cycle ; (1) the expanding family stage, which the family is taken from its inception to the time when its children are grown; and the contracting family stage, in which children are being launched by the family into lives of their own and in which the family continues to contract through the latest years until only one or both of the origin pair still remain at home.

Years ago, Sorokin, Zimmerman and Galpin (1931) discussed a four stage family life cycle based on changing family members constellation within the family. The stage include married couples just starting their independent economic existence; couples with one or more children; couples with one or more adult self-supporting children and couples growing old.

In plotting the changing financial income and outgo patterns throughout the family life cycle, Biglow (1942) elaborated on the school placement factor in a cycle he divided into seven periods: (1) establishment period, (2) child bearing and pre-school period (3) elementary school period, (4) high school period, (5) college period, (6) period of recovery, and (7) period of retirement.

THE EIGHT-STAGE FAMILY LIFE CYCLE

The Duvall eight-stage family life cycle is a refinement of the seven stage formulation developed for the first National Conference on Family Life (Duvall and Hill, 1948). It represents a combination of four factors used in determining family life cycle stages. These factors are plurality pattern, age of the oldest child, school placement of the oldest child and functions and status of families before children come and after they leave. The stages of family life cycle tend to overlap, yet each has its own clearly defined situation and problem. Evelyn Duvall has attempted to provide a clarification of the developmental task concept. It is Duvall's contention that, like the individual, families too have tasks that arise at a given stage in the family. The stages are as given below:

Stage 1. Married couples or the Beginning family.
Stage 2. Child bearing families.
Stage 3. Families with pre-school children (eldest child two and one half to six years).
Stage 4. Families with school children (eldest child six to thirteen years).
Stage 5. Families with teenagers (Oldest child thirteen to twenty years).
Stage 6. Families as launching centres (first child gone to last child's leaving home).
Stage 7. Middle-aged parents (empty nest to retirement)
Stage 8. Aging family members (retirement to death of both spouses).

The young person who is best prepared for both social and vocational responsibilities in adult life and also for the intimate, emotional demands of marriage, will be one who has been able to try out a variety of social and personal roles. Optimally, this means involvement both with opposite-sex peers and with close friends of the same sex in early years of adolescence. In later years, it also means opportunities to develop meaningful, trusting and mutually supportive relationships with an opposite sex peer.

The family life begins as soon as the mature and grown-up adults enter into a married life by vowing to live together accepting each other (of opposite sex) as a life partner. It is a big turning point in one's life. The enjoying, playing secured and dependent girls begin to live absolutely different life. The careless, carefree girl now begins to be dutiful, obedient and caring person. Boys too begin to be more responsible, restricting their social and sexual life. They too share their earnings and start helping others with more responsibility. Both begin to live upto the expectations of each others' families and the society also. Since whole life style changes, it is for them to adjust. Early they adjust, better the future of family. Due to lack of proper guidance some feel upset due to drastic changes in new life, others might get frustrated, bored or cheated. Some regret for being married. Better mental preparedness and understanding of necessity of marital life will ease out their problems, tensions and frustrations. After marriages couple follow various stages of family life; each stage with various characteristics, needs and functions. Most families with children go through all these stages. The kind of environment a baby has, the experiences that occurred during early childhood and the type of parents are influential factors in the kind of a person one becomes.

Stage 1. The Beginning Family

This is also called the period of establishment. It begins with marriage and continues until the first child is born. This stage is often called "Getting Acquainted Stage," when partners in the marriage venture, they are learning to know each other's habits and characteristics. It begins during courtship and may extend into marriage for a longer or shorter duration. The couple begins to recognize that marriage is a partnership and it takes two to build a home. As they learn to adjust to each other, to the daily routine at home and work, and to the in-laws, they find their happiness and love continue to grow.

With the commencement of marriage ceremony of the couple, they take up the roles of husband and wife, son-in-law and daughter-in-law and other relations according to the culture to which they belong. They are expected to look after their household tasks and manage their time and money.

During this stage they spend some time in honeymoon and later learn about each other. Couples learn to share and interact in each other's life. Sharing of common interests and goals desired to reach. They also have to learn to adjust to live with each other's habits and attitudes, which are not approved, by one of the partners. They learn to resolve conflicts and differences. Their problem from singlehood to married stage influences them through all the other family life cycle stages.

It is a period of adjustment and understanding; period of

building bonds and partnership; period of realizing realities and meaning of family life. The kind of relationship that husband and wife establish at this time will influence the quality of their future relations. The long-term goals which they formulate now, will influence their way of living and the manner in which they use their resources of time, money and energy, skills and income throughout their married life.

In many cultures, especially in India, bride comes in bridegroom's family of parents, brothers and sisters and also other extended relations. In traditional families all live together. Couples do not have separate establishment; others begin independent establishment after sometime. In modern families where males are working in different cities begin their establishment immediately. Establishment means living together as a unit making separate identity. Dowry or gifts in marriages help them to start their comfortable living. They have various needs and functions:

Needs of Adjustments

Home Setting

Finding a good house in good locality with sufficient accommodation and reasonable cost is the first necessity. Then setting the home interiors and managing budget.

Relationships with Neighbours and Family Members

Girls and boys both have to adjust with other's family members and also with some neighbouring families for social interaction.

Status

They have to establish and maintain their status. Arranging some social gathering or joining some clubs or other associations can help.

Economic

Generally, men earn and women manage the house but if need be girls and boys should be ready to accept this new earning role and adjust timings and work division accordingly. They have to learn about saving also.

Time Adjustment

Since new responsibilities are to be taken up by both, it is essential that both should be ready to change their habits and adjust timings.

Work Division

In family there are number of works to be done, husband and wife both should divide mutually in cultural context and economic need.

Intimate Relationship

More than any other need the most important need is to develop intimacy and love relations. They must understand each other, care for each other, sharing gains and losses, and satisfy each others (reasonable) psychophysical and social needs. They have to become best friends for each other, and satisfying each others' various psychological needs (security, respect, dependence, etc.)

Plan for Family

Couples have to decide about when to have their first child. They must meet and consult doctors in this regard.

The family members also bear responsibility in this regard, they should not criticize nor make heavy unreasonable demands, and neither they should make complaints against the wife to the husband. They should minimize interference and leave the pair to understand each other and develop intimacy. They should be spared for outing and recreational activities.

The Expanding Family

It covers a longer period than the beginning family. It begins with the birth of first child and ends when the last child leaves the home.

Stage 2. Child Bearing Families

Average family has at least two children. This stage lasts around two and half years. Marital satisfaction begins to lesser; children take up most of the parents' energy. Most of the mothers are deeply involved in child rearing even though they work outside the home. It brings with it adjustment to the new roles of mother and father. The tasks include caring for young children and meeting their needs. Relationships become more complex. Expectations from relatives, teachers, parents and others in the community also influence family roles. The couples have to find time to spend with each other, look after their personal needs, along with caring and nurturing young children. This at times becomes hard but the resultant joy and happiness which parenting brings helps the new parents to face the challenges. Young children become center of all their thoughts, feelings, dreams and goals. Grandparents and other relatives help with the heavy load of parenting responsibilities. Good patterns of communication lead to trust between family members. Family relationships grow stronger.

Becoming a parent is a role one acquires with no preparation and experience. Parents shape the lives of the next generations. They pass on the cultural heritage, religious beliefs and family traditions to their children. If the couple is ready for the care and responsibility passed of being a parent, their efficiency in their new roles as mother and father would increase. Parents provide a secure stimulating and monitoring environment to the child and together they form a close unit family. Parents are the role models for their children.

During this time parents find it necessary to make adjustment in their relations to each other and their children who are born. As soon as the baby arrives, the excitement is high during the first few days. Normally parenthood brings happiness and sense of fulfilment. It has been said that parenthood is the most important criterion of the individual's transition to maturity and adult responsibility. Though, it brings happiness but it can also be regarded as a crisis in life because it necessitates major changes in attitudes, values and roles.

With arrival of a child, the family is temporarily upset and all members of the family are under stress. Arrival of the first child is more upsetting because—both parents may feel inadequate for parental role, they had highly romanticized concepts of parenthood, because of the personal, social and economic discomforts, baby disrupts the affection and intimacy of the two (husband-wife) and changes in routine, increase in work and responsibilities is evident.

While both husband and wife must make marked adjustments in the patterns of their lives when they become parents, but mothers with professional training and experience often suffer more. They suffer severe crisis when they have to give up an important role. Men don't have to change roles when they become parents, but they may show resentment due to economic burden, being tied down, or getting less attention from wife. Gradually, as mother takes over the managing of the household and the baby, she needs to watch that father also plays his role with the infant. A breast-fed baby eliminates the complications of sterilization of bottles, and helps both mother and child to feel close to each other and establish a bond. Some fathers also take over the role of child rearing. Certainly, planned times for father to play with the baby are important.

Couples must plan their parenthood whether to have baby soon after marriage or after some time. So that coming child is awaited, loved and cherished by both parents. In Indian culture many pressures work. In-laws or parents always show eagerness to have the first baby soon. If delayed, relatives, friends and others will raise many questions. Couples, especially, women have to listen many sarcastic remarks. Age, health, and resources are other pressures. Since bringing up of the child demands various adjustments, couples should prepare themselves for this changed role. Couples especially make frequent complaints about being too busy, too occupied with small kid, disturbance in daily routine, number of discomforts like sleep, food, clothes etc. with the new child, wife loses charm and becomes disfigured, and social life standstill. There is no recreation except cries of baby, wife's neglect of husband or indifferent attitude, disagreement on many small or big issues and role-conflicts.

Another point that needs to be watched is a time for husband and wife to be alone, to continue some of their formal interests, and not to let the baby completely monopolize all of their activities and moments. Father can be just as jealous of a new baby as can an older sibling of both parents, who are not prepared for some of the changes taking place in the family pattern and the daily schedule.

In case of young couples that married early, the arrival of a baby complicates matters emotionally as well as financially. Both the husband and wife still have a great need for each other's love and affection, for approval and recognition. A third party who is constantly demanding attention may interfere. Child wants both his or her physical and emotional needs met immediately. A young couple often has mixed feelings towards having a child.

In the mean time, the baby, too has grown with feelings and needs. Through the closeness of kissing, cuddling and caring for, he or she finds a sense of trust. He or she gains emotional security through the recognition he gains as he or she attempts to talk, to turn over, to sit up and eventually to take his or her first step. He or she also experiences fear and anger from some of the unpleasant happenings in daily life.

Another year, married couple with the new baby reveals that time has passed and a second pregnancy has been announced. This time the news may not even be too welcoming yet, many young couples now a days seem eager to have several children close together and early in marriage. Though three years age gap between two children is ideal. They want their children to have the companionship of siblings near in age. Young couples are willing to sacrifice some of the luxuries of living in order to have a complete family early.

In the midst of the busy years of child bearing, the husband and wife work to maintain a satisfactory relationship in the sexual, recreational, emotional, intellectual and spiritual aspects of their married life. Together the couple plans rich experiences for their children as they work together in rearing their children.

Voluntary Childlessness

Increasing numbers of married couples today, are voluntarily childless especially in the developed nations of the world. It is true in higher and better-educated groups and especially in the Western societies. The reasons are many: some may do so because of careers, unwillingness to give-up good life, worries about the problems of new child, fear about lack of resources to provide to children, many parents decide to have only one child and some prefer to adopt rather than bear.

Stage 3. Families with Pre-school Children

This stage lasts about three and a half years. The family's oldest child is three to six years in this stage. As the family increases in number, the individuals who make up this group also grows and changes. The babies become creepers and crawlers, then toddlers who soon are climbing steps and furniture. Before long they begin to run or to jump, to skip and dance. Their world broadens. First, mother and then father were their main interests. Next, siblings who laughed and played with them become favorites. Relatives, neighbours, and outsiders, like the milkman, postman, servants help widen their horizon until soon they are chattering to and questioning many different kinds of people. Yet a secure home with two parents remains the pivot from which they swing into the outer world.

The most of polarity brings about some rapid changes in physical growth and sexual development in the child. Parents have to let go of some responsibilities while children take on more responsibilities. This transition for the child also results in transition in the family life cycle stage.

Stage 4. Families with Elementary School Period Children

It coves the time when children are 6 to 12 years of age. This stage lasts about six years and begins a series of overlapping experiences. The child takes his or her first-step out into the world and away from home. He or she also may experience some unpleasant emotions. Such feelings as fear of teacher, or a big dog, jealousy of a new baby or his classmates may cause frustration. Yet the newly found freedom of going to school and fascinating subjects, making new friends gives the elementary child a wider and more adventurous world to live. During this period, parents are primarily concerned with the education and health needs of children.

Stage 5. Families with Teenagers

It is the time when children are 12 to 18 years of age. When the child is in teenage period and this stage lasts about seven years. The parents are now occupied with helping children in solving their personal, social and vocational problems. They help them in becoming independent individuals. This is the time when adolescents are also coping with the changing biophysical bodily changes and trying to adjust between the peer pressure and parent's expectations. Such conflicting situations gives adolescents stress and generally conformity with peer group prevails over the family values.

Conflicts may arise when parents and adolescents don't agree on how much responsibility should be given up on taken on with children demanding more freedom. Patterns of clear and open communication involving children in family decision-making, positive attitude towards conflicts help in healthy home environment. Family members learn to respect each other's feelings and desires with sympathy and empathy develops.

Couples who married in their early teens and has children while both were trying to finish their education may discover that as their children approach teen age, they (the parents) are still in their late twenties or very early thirties. At this stage sometimes parents are not really prepared for the heavy living costs demanded by two or three teenagers. The parents who still may be establishing themselves in a business or profession may feel hard pressed for money. The financial pressure is another explanation of why many women return to work during the period of high expense. Even if the mother has to work, she should be aware of her growing children, what they do after school and on weekends. Father, too, has to spend qualitative time with the children to ensure the pattern of masculinity for his sons and to encourage his daughters in their feminine role.

It covers the time when children are in college. In the Indian subcontinent, children are still the responsibility of parents. The chief, parental duties are helping to select a college and finance their education. The parents' assistance may also be needed by their children to solve social problems. The late adolescent looks forward to college, to his or her vocational choice, marriage, or a combination of two or three goals. The parents begin to realize that their children are growing up and they will have to adjust to the quiet and perhaps lonely years ahead. This period is the time when a wife may become so involved in her growing children and her husband finds so hard to bring home extra income. As both parents work together for their common goals of giving their children a good start in life and achieving their own aspirations, they may become better work partners and find their daily lives filled with joy and satisfaction.

Stage 6. The Contracting Family

It is sometimes called the launching period. It begins when the first child leaves the home as a young adult and ends when the last child leaves home for a life of his or her own. This stage for some averages around eight years or less. It is marked by a young person's departure for marriage or full time employment. It is a period of adjustment for parents' and children both. The parents' help may be needed for a new vocational venture, a wedding, travel or many other activities. Here, the family circle is widened to include new relatives through marriage as well as through grandchildren. Parents begin to take a new role as grandparents. Marital satisfaction begins to rise for most of the couples with satisfaction of successfully launching their children. Usually parents recognize their offspring has grown up and accord him the rights and privileges of adulthood.

Stage 7. Families with Middle-aged Parents

As a couple moves on from the early child bearing stages through the child-bearing period and on to the launching stage, the two adults can look forward to their future together without responsibilities and cost of the children. As the last child leaves home permanently, either, through a job or marriage, the middle-aged couple seeks to total its assets including the abilities and interest of each of the partners. It is desirable for both husband and wife to develop interests that will be satisfying during the period of retirement. Most parents make the transition reasonably well (Anderson, 1988). In fact, marital satisfaction generally begins to rise for the first time since the first stage of marriage (Glenn, 1991), However, for some parents, it is the end of the family for children had been the focal point of much family happiness and pair.

While both men and women must make role changes as their children grow up and leave home, these changes are easier for men to make than for women, partly because the father's role is far less time and energy-consuming than the mother's and partly because men can compensate for radical changes in family life by deriving added satisfaction from their work which most women can not do.

Some of the adjustment problems that middle-aged men and women must face in their family lives are individual in nature, while others are more or less universal and a product of the culture in which the person lives. The most important of these are discussed below.

Adjustment to Changed Roles

When the children leave home to go to college, to marry, or to pursue a career—parents must face the adjustment problems of what is commonly referred to as the period of the "empty nest." In many homes, this period is almost, as long as the whole period during which the children were leaving the home. When the empty nest period occurs, it means a change of roles for both parents and a branching out from the family, which, in most cases, is more difficult for women than for men.

Whether the empty nest period will begin in the forties or fifties will depend on the size of the family and when the children leave home. If they go away to school or college, they will leave home earlier than if they remain at home while they are still students or while they are working until they marry.

Role changes necessitated by the empty nest period of family life effect women far more than men though men are not spared the effects of these role changes. According to tradition, the empty nest is a traumatic and unhappy period in life for the typical woman, though so far less for the typical man.

The departure of children is a cruel blow to some parents, especially those who are widowed or divorced. Otherwise, the effects are often positive. Whether the effects will be positive or negative will depend, to large extent, upon their marital relationships and family relationships.

The difficulties of adjusting to the departure of children from the home and to the role changes that this necessities are increased for parents who have few outside interests and have built their life around their children. Overly protective and possessive parents are especially prone to make their children the center of their lives. As their married children become increasingly involved in their own families, it becomes clear to parents that they feel more love and concern for their children than their children feel for them. This intensifies the parents' adjustment problems, especially those of the mother. Some get involved with grand children and get satisfaction.

Conditions that Complicate Empty Nest Adjustment

Loss of Parental Role

Like all habits, that of centering one's life around one's home and children is hard to break. Middle-aged people who are able to occupy their times with activities they find satisfying will be able to adjust to the loss of the parental role.

Lack of Preparation

Few are prepared for the role changes that take place in both their family and vocational lives.

Feelings of Failure

If marriages have not turned out as they had hoped or whose children have not come upon to their expectations, often blame themselves and feel they have been failures.

Feelings of Uselessness

The more child centered the home was earlier; the more useless the middle aged person will feel when parental responsibilities diminish or come to an end.

Many women need to discover a new lifestyle to keep themselves busy or they are busy with their own home and families or they may rejoin an employment according to their interest and capacity. Both may move to a smaller and more efficient home. Perhaps they can become more civic-minded. For the next 15-20 years if his health remains good, the husband probably will be bringing in his best income, at least if he is in the skilled or professional occupation group. In India, children after marriage tend to stay in the family home with the parents. Parents may be then absorbed in the upbringing of their grand children.

The not-so-empty Nest

The most of the families in India do not have the empty nest stage as after the son's marriage, the son along with his wife and children live with the parents. These days due to far-placed job opportunities from the hometown, advent of nuclear families due to varied reasons like non-adjustment with the in-laws, individualism and modernization, parents are being left alone in their old days. If unchecked, the not-so-empty nest would become empty.

Stage 8. Family with Aging Family Members

Old age, retirement, death and serious illness may hit a family at anytime, but more likely to happen to the couple who grows older. Facts show that women usually outlive their husbands, so there may be an adjustment to a single and lonely life. Somehow women usually adjust to retirement better because they have learned to engage in diverse task and hobbies through the years, they are not as apt to be suddenly left with nothing to do.

The desires of individual during this stage usually grow less intense and the need for care and protection increases. It is the period of adjustment to physical changes, to change in environmental conditions, to change in human relations and often to change in income. For those who can make the necessary adjustment and who have health and strength, human relations will be satisfying even if physical setting of home changes.

Adjustment to Changed Family Patterns

The pattern of family life undergoes marked changes during the period of middle age. The most obvious change is the withdrawal of children from the family, leaving husband and wife as the family unit. This change is usually more difficult for women to adjust to than for men because women's lives are centered around the home and family members, during the early adult years.

Good adjustment in old-age requires strong and varied interests, economic independence, which makes independence in living possible, many social contacts with people of all ages, not just the elderly, the enjoyment of work which is pleasant and useful but not overtaxing, participation in community organizations, the ability to maintain a comfortable home without exerting too much physical effort, the ability to enjoy present activities without regretting the past, a minimum of worry about self or others, enjoyment of day-to-day activities regardless of how repetitive they may be, avoidance of criticism of others, especially members of the younger generation and avoïdance of fault-finding, especially about living conditions and treatment from others.

Poor adjustment in old age is developed when you have little interest in the world of today or the individual's role in it, withdrawal into the world of fantasy, constant reminiscing, constant worry encouraged by idleness, a lack of drive leading to low productivity in all areas, the attitude that the only activities available are "make work" activities and, therefore, a "waste of time," loneliness due to poor family relationship and lack of interest in contemporaries, involuntary residence in an institution or with a grown child, constant complaining and criticizing of anything and every thing and refusal to take part in activities for the elderly on the ground that they are "boring."

Some important conditions which contribute to happiness in the old-age are a favourable attitude toward old age developed as a result of pleasable contacts with elderly people, happy memories of childhood and adulthood, freedom to pursue a desired life style without outside interference, a realistic attitude toward, and acceptance of, the physical and psychological changes that aging inevitably brings, acceptance of self and present living conditions even if these fall below expectations, an opportunity to establish a satisfying socially accepted pattern of life, continued participation in interesting and meaningful activities, acceptance by, and respect from the social group, a feeling of satisfaction with present status and past achievement, satisfaction with marital status and sex life, reasonably good health without chronic health problems, enjoyment of recreational activities planned for the elderly, enjoyment of social activities with relatives and friends, productive activities whether in housework or volunteer services, and a financial situation adequate to meet needs and wants.

ADJUSTMENT TO RETIREMENT

Retirement may be the termination of a pattern of life or transition to a new pattern of life. It always involves role changes, changes in interests and values, and changes in the whole pattern of individual's life. Retirement is not setting an alarm clock, reactivating public library cards, starting a second career—if any one wants to, taking the grand children to places on week days, wondering why your former colleagues do not phone once in a while, waiting for the postman to bring some excitement into your day, wondering why your former colleagues do not phone once in a while, reading a book all the way through at one sitting, getting special low rates discounts and running for pension, receiving invitations, reading newspapers and engaging in religious activities.

There are various kinds of retirements—voluntary or involuntary/compulsory. Adjustment to these depends upon the way you were prepared for it. To the younger person whose days are so often overly crowded with duties and responsibilities, the years of retirement appear like a golden period. When retirement actually comes, it seems less desirable that it appeared earlier. There are two types of attitudes towards retirement: some are willing to change life style and enjoy new roles. They do not relax, rather develop hobbies and become active in social or community affairs. Another type continues to work on different assignments. All their adjustment depends upon their health, financial position, happy marital and family status, and attitude of family members.

Women on the whole adjust better to retirement than men because: the change in their roles is not radical, working women hardly had comfortable life during career and fewer women had held executive positions, hence, do not feel power and prestige lost. Unmarried women adjust better to retirement because they had more social resources to fill their free time. Men on the other hand have less readily available means of getting satisfaction. Retirement is more traumatic to men than to women. These people require changes in relationships with offspring, spouse, and changes in sexual behaviour, parental dependency, and relationships with grand children.

PREPARATION FOR RETIREMENT

No organization requires retiring their workers, professionals before age unless it is very essential due to poor health or financial set back to the organization. The provident fund or pension schemes help in facing old-age problems. Preparation for retirement should take into account other problems such as utilization of leisure time and how to remain and maintain social activities. Family members may welcome the retirement of parents or may have negative or less favourable attitude towards retirement due to various reasons. Pre-retirement counselling may help in this regard. Since women continue to work on their old roles of home responsibilities, they do not find difficulty in this age, rather they may welcome as getting freedom from double roles.

Couples enter the retirement stage after one on both spouses retires from their career. Retirement ages may vary for many. Some work as long as they are physically able, while some choose an early retirement. Most of the couples plan ahead while they still are working to financially prepare for these years. Retirement is time for people to focus on themselves. Some pursue hobbies, interests, routine work, religious activities and travel.

Some are unable to adjust to their new role and freedom. They feel helpless and useless and develop a low self-esteem. Health and financial problems prevent them for looking at the future with hope. Retirement is end of paid employment.

HAZARDS OF PARENTHOOD

Parenthood is especially hazardous at certain times during a marriage. Parental satisfaction drops sharply as children grow older; it is lowest when they are in their teens and when they begin to leave home. They are more critical of their mothers. Parenthood involves several common potential hazards to good marital adjustment because—mothers devote more time to her children than to her husband, they clash over child-rearing methods—one parent blaming the other for being too strict or too protective or permissive, with more children than they wanted or being overworked or overburdened financially become disenchanted with marriage and relationships, birth of girl child and her responsibility, older children or adolescents who become hypercritical of parents get irritated with their behaviour and when parents have high aspirations for their children and make personal sacrifices to enable them to achieve their aspirations, they will be disappointed if children fail to live-up to their aspirations. Under such conditions husband-wife relations get strained and family environment becomes hazardous.

SINGLE PARENTHOOD

It is generally a result of divorce or death. Many times illegitimate babies are cared by mothers alone. In case of single men, relatives take care. But, now many fathers themselves manage to care. Those who can afford employ baby sitters or send their children to day care centres. In all such conditions, lot of adjustments are to be made like management of time, household activities, social-recreational activities and emotional balance are essential changes. One parent has to play the role of other parent also. Children kept under other's care may not satisfy many needs fully (neither of children nor of parents). Children reared by servants may be subject to disgrace, harassment, sexual abuse, neglect and other adverse effects.

FAMILY DESERTION AND NON-SUPPORT

Family desertion is a problem of the court and of the social agency. It is generally accepted to mean desertion by a husband of his wife or by a father of his children in cases in which the question of support arises. The two aspects are linked together, so that cases of non-support under separation or divorce agreements or decisions, which do not involve desertion, are rarely included in the time. On the other hand, desertion by the wife or mother or even desertion of aged parents is excluded because of the element of support.

In, so far as, it becomes known to courts of domestic relations or social agencies, family desertion is largely a phenomenon found among the low income groups, not necessarily because desertion as such is mainly due to economic pressure, but more probably because men in this group choose the informal freedom of desertion, rather than, the more conclusive and expensive methods of formal separation or divorce, when family discord has reached the breaking point.

A DEATH IN THE FAMILY

When a close relative dies, the child's sorrow is often complicated by feelings of guilt. A death of a member of the family a parent, a brother or a sister, a grandparent who has lived in the home stirs up feelings in a young child which are quite different from those aroused by the death of a person who is not well known to the child, or by an impersonal discussion of death. In the latter case, the young child's main concern is in the possibility of his own death and whether this will separate him from his parent. But when a member of the household or someone close to it dies, the child's previous relationship with that persons leaves a mixture of sweet and upset feelings which may last for many months.

First of all is the sense of loss. If a close brother or sister has gone, there is the repeated sharp sorrow which comes from wanting to share another experience with him or her and realizing again that he or she is not there. If a parent has recently died the child will continue to want to turn to him/her a 100 times a day, when he or she needs knowledge or assistance.

Child's mourning shows though one child is more apt than the other child, who loses her or his joy in his or her usual pursuits, look sad and easily breaks into tears. Another child, even in the same family, may appear on the surface almost unaffected.

That a child might feel guilty about the death of a close relative was recognized only lately before psychiatrists began to understand the hidden feelings of people of all ages who were miserable or nervous or mentally ill. It was first realized that an occasional adult would react to the death of a member of the family not just with mourning but also with a more complex depression that lasted for many months. He would cover himself with reproaches that he had not sought medical care early enough. His or her relatives would call these self-accusations entirely unjustified, the very opposite of the truth. It was discovered that such a person was feeling terribly guilty not so much about the things he or she had actually done or left undone which were largely imaginary, but about unkind feelings and wishes that he or she harboured at times towards the deceased.

DEATH OF A SPOUSE

The death of one partner ends the family life cycle. The remaining partner either lives alone or with some relative, children or friend. In many families, the husband dies first leaving the widow to finish her remaining years alone.

The death of a spouse leads the bereaved partner to deal with socio-emotional loss as well as adjust to a new life style. Personal freedom is affected. The loss of income, health and the ability to care for oneself are hard to accept.

The death of a spouse is very difficult because it means the loss of a companion, sex partner, partner in decision-making and ups and downs of life. For the elderly, bereavement is part of life more than for younger ones. The death of a spouse leaves the other partner lonely and gives single status to the spouse. Higher the attachment and dependency more difficult is the adjustment after the death. Women generally outlive their husbands. They not only face the loss of spouse but along with may face reduced income and other economic resources. In India, widowhood is extensively looked down upon especially in rural areas.

12

Typical and Atypical Forms of Family

In India, people learn the essential themes of cultural life within the bosom of a family. The basic units of society are the patrilineal family unit. The most widely desired residential unit is the joint family, ideally consisting of three or four patrilineally related generations, all living under one roof, working, eating, worshiping, and cooperating together in mutually beneficial social and economic activities. Patrilineal joint families include men related through the male line, along with their wives and children. Most young women expect to live with their husband's relatives after marriage, but they retain important bonds with their natal families. Despite the continuous and growing impact of urbanization, secularization, and Westernization, the traditional joint household, both in ideal and in practice is staill evident in the Indian society. Loyalty to family is a deeply held ideal for almost everyone. Large families tend to be flexible and well suited to modern Indian life, especially for farmers or agricultural workers children who live within extended urban households for educational and vocational purposes. The joint family is also common in cities, where kinship ties can be crucial to obtaining scarce jobs or financial assistance.

The joint family is an ancient Indian institution, but it has undergone some change in the late twentieth century. Although several generations living together is the ideal, actual living arrangements vary widely depending on region, social status, and economic circumstances. Many Indians live in joint families that deviate in various ways from the ideal, and many live in nuclear families, a couple with their unmarried children, as is the most common pattern in the West. However, even where the ideal joint family is seldom found (as, for example, in certain regions and among impoverished agricultural laborers and urban squatters), there are often strong networks of kinship ties through which economic assistance and other benefits are obtained. Not infrequently, clusters of relatives live very near each other, easily available to respond to the give and take of kinship obligations. Even when relatives cannot actually live in close proximity, they typically maintain strong bonds of kinship and attempt to provide each other with economic help, emotional support, and other benefits.

As joint families grow ever larger, they inevitably divide into smaller units, passing through a predictable cycle over time. The breakup of a joint family into smaller units does not necessarily represent the rejection of the joint family ideal. Rather, it is usually a response to a variety of conditions, including the need for some members to move from village to city, or from one city to another to take advantage of employment opportunities. Splitting of the family is often blamed on quarrelling women, typically the wives of co-resident brothers. Although women's disputes may, in fact, lead to family division, men's disagreements do so as well. Despite cultural ideals of brotherly harmony, adult brothers frequently quarrel over land and other matters, leading them to decide to live under separate roofs and divide their property. Frequently, a large joint family divides after the demise of elderly parents, when there is no longer a single authority figure to hold the family factions together. Household is any separate living unit occupied by one or more persons (Wetzel, 1990). Family household is a living unit containing of at least two people related by blood, marriage or adoption.

Different family structures are evident in our present day's society. The social and economic change brought about in the society is reflected in the different family structures existent today. Family structure depends on who lives in the household. The structure of the family influences many areas of a child's life. A family may include any combination of mother, father, children, grandparents or other relatives, sometimes, also includes step-parents or step-children. A family consists of two or more people who consider themselves related by blood, marriage or adoption.

Extended family typically, includes a family with many relatives, including such as grandparents, aunts, uncles, nieces and nephews, within the basic family unit of parents and children. In the majority of non-European countries, the extended family is often regarded as the basic family unit (Murdock, 1967). Emphasis is on cooperation, obligation, sharing and reciprocity. It encourages familism and collectivism to individualism, self-sufficiency and achievement.

IN INDIAN PHRASEOLOGY

In the most of India, people belong not only to co-resident family groups but to larger aggregates of kin as well. Subsuming the family is the patrilineage (known in northern and central India as the *khandan*, *kutumb*, or *kul*), a locally based set of males who trace their ancestry to a common progenitor a few generations back, plus their wives and unmarried daughters. Larger than the patrilineage is the clan, commonly known as the *gotra* or *got*, a much larger group of patrilineally related males and their wives and sons and daughters, who often trace common ancestry to a mythological figure. In some regions, particularly among the high-ranking Rajputs of western India, clans are hierarchically ordered. Some people also claim membership in larger, more amorphous groupings known as *vansh* and *sakha*.

Hindu lineages and clans are strictly exogamous, that is, a person may not marry or have a sexual alliance with a member of his own lineage or clan; such an arrangement would be considered incestuous. In North India, rules further prohibit marriage between a person and his mother's lineage members as well. Among some castes of the north, exogamy is also extended to the mother's, father's mothers, and mother's mother's clans. In contrast, in South India, marriage to a member of the mother's kin group is often encouraged.

Muslims also recognize kinship groupings larger than the family. These include the *khandan*, or patrilineage, and the *azizdar*, or kindred. The *azizdar* group differs slightly for each individual and includes all relatives linked to a person by blood or marriage. Muslims throughout India encourage marriage within the lineage and kindred, and marriages between the children of siblings are common.

Within a village or urban neighbourhood, members of a lineage recognize their kinship in a variety of ways. Mutual assistance in daily work, in emergencies, and in factional struggles is expected. Upon marriage, a woman becomes a member of her husband's lineage and then participates regularly in the worship of her husband's lineage Gods and Goddesses. Lineage bonds are also evident at life-cycle observances, when kin join together in celebrating births, marriages, and religious initiations. Upon the death of a lineage member, other lineage members observe ritual death pollution rules for a prescribed number of days and carry out appropriate funeral rites and feasts.

Some important kinship linkages are not traced through men but through women. These linkages involve those related to an individual by blood and marriage through a mother, married sisters, or married daughters, and for a man, through his wife. Anthropologist David Mandelbaum has termed these "feminal kin". Key relationships are those between a brother and sister, parents and daughters, and a person and his or her mother's brother. These relationships are often characterized by deep affection and willingly offered support.

The multitude of kinship ties is further extended through the device of fictive kinship. Residents of a single village usually use kinship terms for one another, and especially strong ties of fictive kinship can be ceremonially created with fellow religious initiates or fellow pilgrims of one's village or neighbourhood. In the villages and cities of the north, on the festival of Raksha Bandhan (the Tying of the Protective Thread, during which sisters tie sacred threads on their brothers' wrists to symbolize the continuing bond between them), a female may tie a thread on the wrist of an otherwise unrelated male and "make him her brother". Fictive kinship bonds cut across caste and class lines and involve obligations of hospitality, gift-giving, and variable levels of cooperation and assistance.

Neighbours and friends may also create fictive kinship ties by informal agreement. Actually, any strong friendship between otherwise unrelated people is typically imbued with kinship-like qualities. In such friendships, kinship terms are adopted for address, enhances affection in the relationship. In Gujarat, personal names usually include the word for "sister" and "brother," "Behn" and "Bhai" respectively so that the use of someone's personal name automatically sounds affectionate and caring.

All family members are socialized to accept the authority of those ranked above them in the hierarchy. In general, elders' rank above juniors, and among people of similar age, males outrank females. Daughters of a family command the formal respect of their brother's wives, and the mother of a household is in charge of her daughters-in-law. Among adults in a joint family, a newly arrived daughter-in-law has the least authority. Males learn to command others within the household but expect to accept the direction of senior males. Ideally, even a mature adult man living in his father's household acknowledges his father's authority on both minor and major matters. There is tremendous emphasis on the unity of the family grouping. Efforts are made to enhance a wider sense of harmony within the entire household. Husbands and wives are discouraged from openly displaying affection for one another, and in strictly traditional households, they may not even properly speak to one another in the presence of anyone else.

Psychologically, family members feel an intense emotional interdependence with each other and the family as an almost organic unit. Ego boundaries are permeable to others in the family, and any notion of a separate self is often dominated by a sense of what psychoanalyst Alan Roland has termed a more inclusive "familial self". Interpersonal empathy, closeness, loyalty, and interdependency are all crucial to life within the family in India.

In American phraseology, conjugal family is known as nuclear family. If other relative live within nuclear family, it is called extended family. Many blood relations living together is called as joint family or consanguineous family.

Maternal family is a social unit in which the female or the mother is the head of the family, the descent of lineage is traced through the female, the residence is in mother's abode and the property is inherited through female progeny. These features are characterized in terms of maternal authority—matrilineal, matrilocal and matriarchal. Husband has a secondary position in maternal family. Paternal family is characterized by the authority vested in father, descent through the male progeny, residence in father's abode and inheritance of property in male lineage. It is characterized in terms of paternal dominance, patrilineal, patrilocal and patriarchal. Wife is subordinate to husband. These two types of family are traditional families.

Family in simple societies served as an all inclusive, self-sufficient unit. In modern times, many changes have taken place in both, structure and function of family. There is a change over from joint family to nuclear family. These changes are due to industrialization, urbanization and education. Many social organizations have taken over the primary functions of family in terms of food, education, training, recreation, protection, worship and many other functions for which the traditional family was a self-sufficient unit. There is a change in the roles and status of members due to education, job opportunity and social legislation for women.

Change in functions does not mean its disappearance. There is a new outlook in modern society for marriage and family. Marriage by voluntary choice becomes more stable by mutual understanding of partners. Nuclear family ensures more satisfaction and security with limited responsibilities. Limited size of the family helps for greater economic growth for a comfortable living. Affection among members in nuclear families is unbounded to make it more stable. Family can never cease to exist. According to MacIver, "family is one of the conditions for social solidarity and strength". Following section of this chapter discusses the typical and atypical forms of family as existent in the present times.

TYPICAL AND ATYPICAL FORMS OF FAMILY

Traditional Nuclear Family

Traditional nuclear family is composed of two parents and one or more children, in which the father is the breadwinner and the mother the homemaker. Most children still live in families with two parents who have been married only to each other.

Family relationships are generally created into two ways: through marriage and through birth. Extended family relationships created through marriage are known as "conjugal" relationships. The word conjugal is derived from the latin word conjungere meaning "to join together." In-laws such as mother-in-law, father-in-law, daughter-in-law, son-in-law, brother-in-law, sister-in-law is through marriage.

Consanguineous relationships are created through biological (blood) ties, that is, birth. The word consanguineous is derived from the latin words "com" meaning joint and "sanguineous" meaning of blood. Child's relations with parents, grand parents, siblings, uncles and aunts are consanguineous relationships.

In cultures that emphasize kin groups, close emotional ties between a husband and wife are viewed as a threat to the extended family. The family of orientation (sometimes called the family of origin) is the family, in which you are born into and/or are subsequently part of, raised in the family that orients us to the world.

When a person marries, she/he leaves the family of orientation to create a new family of procreation that is composed of self, spouse and children, if any.

The family of procreation is formed when a couple has their first child. The family of cohabitation is the family we form through living or cohabiting with another person, whether we are married or unmarried. This family had traditionally been referred to as the family of procreation, but because many families have step-children, adopted children or no children, this older term is no longer an adequate description.

Much of our identity is formed in the crucibles of these two families. Sociologists William Goode (1982) suggests that there are several advantages of living in families. Families offer continuity as a result of emotional attachments, rights and obligations. Families offer close proximity and offer us an abiding familiarity with others. It offers us many economic benefits such as laundry, cooking, shopping and cleaning.

Families are classified according to the marriage regulations and forms as endogamous and exogamous. Families could also be classified according to the combinations of sexes in marriage as monogamous, polygamous, polyandry and group marriage families.

Structurally there have been two systems of families. A family in the past continues in the present also, namely, the joint family and a family which does not live in a joint family, namely, the nuclear family.

NUMBER OF SPOUSES

Most of the societies, now prefer monogamy as form of marriage, one man marries one woman at a given time. In today's American society, where divorce is more prevalent, the marriage type is serial monogamy, where in, at given specific time one man marries one woman only. Polygamy is the general term used to refer to all marriage forms that involve the taking of plural spouses. Under polygamy, the plural spouses may be either husbands or wives. Polygamy is sub-divided into two types, *polygyny* and *polyandry*. Polygyny is the more common form, involving the taking of plural wives. Polyandry, the taking of plural husbands, is rare.

Polygyny further subdivides into two basic types, sororal and nonsororal. The Latin word soror means sister. Under sororal polygyny the wives are sisters. Under nonsororal polygyny, the wives may be unrelated. In ancient times, sororal polygyny was practiced by Hebrews of scriptural times. Sororal polygyny is exceedingly widespread among the societies of the world. Polygyny does produce problems of adjustment for the people who practice it (as does any form of marriage), and sororal polygyny seems to minimize some of these problems. Co-wives who are sisters are more likely to get along with one another than the co-wives who are not sisters. Having grown up together, they are likely to have similar values, attitudes, and way of doing things. Jealousy between them is also less likely than in the case between unrelated women. This situation is often reflected in housing arrangements. The separation of the dwellings of the co-wives is likely to be more marked if they are not sisters.

A special form of sororal polygyny is the sororate, which is a cultural rule specifying that the preferred mate for a widower is the sister of his deceased wife. Under the sororate, the marriages are successive rather than concurrent.

Among the Buddhist people of the mountainous Ladakh District of Jammu and Kashmir in India, who have cultural ties to Tibet, fraternal polyandry is practiced, and a household may include a set of brothers with their common wife or wives. This family type, in which brothers also share land, is almost certainly linked to the extreme scarcity of cultivable land in the Himalayan region, because it discourages fragmentation of holdings.

RULES OF DESCENT

Rules of descent are social definitions that determine for the individual whom, among the myriad of biological kin, he considers himself related to. Rules of descent defines the family as a social group in contrast to the family as a biological group. There are four general rules of descent that warrant definition and description here. Patrilineal descent is assigned at birth to a group of kin who are related to the child through males only. To put it technically, descent is traced through the male lineage. The most important ties are those, which extend from father to son to grandson. Wives typically marry into their husbands' families and their children become members of the husband's family but not of the family into which the wife was born.

The second most common system of tracing descent is called bilateral. As the term implies, it involves tracing relationships through two sides of the family-through the mother's biological kin and the father's biological kin equally. Limiting it to very close relatives on each side regulates the size of the kin group. Such a system of tracing social relationships is in accord exactly with the facts of biological relationship. Some sociologists have suggested that a more accurate designation of this descent system would be multilineal. Since the incest taboos require that each person seek his mate outside his own family group, there is a continuous inter-penetration of family lines.

Matrilineal descent is the opposite of patrilineal descent. It traces relationship through females and the female line, discarding all of the father's relatives. Matrilineal descent is less common.

The fourth descent system is the double descent, where double descent exists, each person at birth is assigned to two kin groups, one traced through the paternal relatives and one through the maternal relatives. He becomes a member of his father's patrilineal group and a member of his mother's matrilineal group. This arrangement involves of course, discarding the father's matrilineal kin group and the mother's patrilineal kin group. There are, in the world, even more complex system of descent in which relationships are traced differently for sons and daughters and which zigzag between the sexes, from generation to generation. The rules of descent select from the ever-expanding group of biological kin those with whom close social relationships are to be maintained. Associated with rules of descent are rules of inheritance.

RULES OF INHERITANCE

Inheritance patterns are in some ways more complex than systems of descent and they have been studied less thoroughly. They are complicated by the fact that some possessions such as clothing, ornaments, and tools are used by only members of one sex while other possessions, such as money, are easily transmitted to either sex. Throughout most of human history and much over the world, inheritance rights have centered on land, dwellings, animals, and generally, the means of production. If such property passes to the heir or heir through males, the rule is said to be that of patrilineal inheritance, if the route is through females then it is matrilineal inheritance.

Inheritance patterns are further complicated because men and women may or may not inherit equally, and even within the same sex the siblings may or may not inherit equally. More often than not, the inheritance of major property items is through males to other males. The inheritance rights of women often are circumscribed and sometimes are non-existent.

The inheritance rights of males may vary with birth order, if all sons do not inherit equally, the most likely situations for the eldest son is to inherit a disproportionate part of the property. This arrangement is know as primogeniture. Less commonly found is ultimogeniture, where the youngest son is favoured.

RULES OF RESIDENCE

The nuclear family, it will be remembered, is virtually everywhere a common residential unit. At marriage the husband and wife take up residence together. Since they came from different families of orientation, this means that one or the other or both of them must move at the time of marriage.

The most common rule of residence is that which is called patrilocal. Under patrilocal residence the birde leaves the locale of her family of orientation and sets up housekeeping with her husband in the same dwelling with, or adjacent to, his family of orientation. Patrilocal residence is most common over the world. A special variant of patrilocal residence is the rule known as matri-patrilocal, where residence is with the bride's family for orientation for a prescribed period after which the couple takes up permanent residence with the groom's family. The couple may live with the bride's family for one year or until the first child is born.

Matrilocal residence involves the husband leaving the home of his family of orientation to take up residence with his bride in the locale of the family of orientation. Closely related to matrilineal descent and inheritance is another rule of residence known as avunculocal. Under avunculocal residence, the newly married couple takes up residence with the maternal uncle of the groom. Thus, the residence rule is built around males of the female line.

Under bilocal residence the couple is permitted to choose whether they will locate with the husband's kin or the wife's kin. The strength of the personal ties between the couple and their parents, the relative wealth of the two sets of parents and their power in the community, and the need for assistance from the young couple may be the determining factors.

The final rule of residence to be discussed here is neolocal. As the term implies, this rule involves the establishment of a new residence for the couple, apart from both families of orientation. This is the only rule of residence, which militates against the development of extended family units and encourages the isolation of the nuclear family.

AUTHORITY PATTERNS IN THE FAMILY

Strictly speaking, the distribution of authority between the husband and wife does not drive directly from the existence of incest taboos. The relationships between family authority patterns and rules of descent and residence, however, are such as to make brief discussion of them relevant here. We may describe three principal types as patriarchal, matriarchal and equalitarian.

A patriarchal family system is one in which power and authority are vested in the hands of males, with the eldest male usually wielding great arbitrary power. Patriarchal family systems have been very common through history and over the world. The ancient Hebrews, Greeks, and Romans, the Hindus and Mohammedans, and the Chinese and Japanese provide just a few examples.

The construction of a matriarchal family type is very simple. Logically, a matriarchy should involve the almost complete vesting of power in the hands of females. Even in societies, which are organized about women, in societies which follow matrilineal descent and inheritance and matrilocal residence, power tends to be held by males in the female lineage. Power is usually held by the women's brothers—from the viewpoint of ego, by the maternal uncle. Male dominance or at least a tendency toward it, appears to be one of those basic features of human existence that culture cannot completely contradict. A minority of societies are organized around the female lineage, but even among them, power, status, and property tend to be held by males.

The third type is the equalitarian family, implies a somewhat equal distribution of power and authority between husband and wife. This arrangement appears to be in accord with some of the basic facts of human existence. Few fair-minded people would question the fact that, except, perhaps for brute strength, there are many women in any society who are as strong, intelligent, clever, and ambitious as their husbands. Even in the most patriarchal of societies strong wives probably have dominated weak husbands.

Two different factors appear significantly in determining the pattern of organization of the family. One is the way in which descent was recognized. Whether on the male of female side, i.e. patrilineal or matrilineal. Secondly, according to the place of residence—near the husband's or wife's parents patrilocal or matrilocal. Whether members of the extended family life together according to the matrilineal descent, it is called, maternal family and by patrilineal descent, the paternal family.

The Maternal Family

The family is composed of an old woman, her sons, her daughters and the children of her daughters. Sons continued to live with their mothers even after marriage and are only visitors in the homes of their wives, who also dwelt with their own mothers. The control of the children is in the hands of their maternal uncles, namely, the brothers of their mothers and not their fathers.

The Paternal Family

In the paternal family, the family is organized according to the paternal descent, with the girls going to live with their husbands upon marriage in the dwellings of their fathers and mothers, married brothers, their wives and children. The relatives of husband controlled the children, with the presence of two grandparents and unmarried brothers or sisters of the father.

The Large Patriarchal Family

The large patriarchal family has been handed over from the ancient society. The patriarch exercises absolute power over the members of the family.

The Small Patriarchal Family

The small patriarchal family has its origin in the medieval period, composed of husband and wife generally with the presence of one or two grandparents, one or more unmarried brothers or sisters of the parents or other relatives. The dominance of the male as head of the family, whether father or grandfather, over the other members of the family is unquestionable.

The Modern Democratic Family

The modern democratic family is a product of the economic and social trends accompanying and following industrial revolution, which had led to the breakdown of the small patriarchal families. The modern family allows freedom to its members in their choices in several areas. After marriage the young people have more freedom from their parents. The husband and wife have equal rights in running the family in which the children participate freely according to their abilities and age level.

The Extended Family

In an extended family, several generations of one family live together sharing home and family activities. Grandparents, parents, aunts, uncles, and cousins live together in the same household.

The parents are eased of childcare and home responsibility with their parents and other relatives sharing the responsibility. Elderly members of the family are cared for and at the same time children benefit by having other adult role models. Grandparents and grandchildren share a special bondage. Sometimes relatives live near each other but not with each other but help each other in distress.

The Joint Family

The joint family is peculiar to almost all Indian communities. Literature shows as far back as records can be found; the joint family system always existed in India. For the needed manpower to till the fields, the joint family is the answer, in which all men folk worked together for the common welfare of the family. The joint family is one of the main units that formed the core of the traditional Hindu society. The joint family is defined as a group of people who generally live under one roof, eat food cooked at one hearth, hold property in common, participate in common family worship and are related to each other as some particular type of kindred. The joint family is family centered, characterized by intimacy and mutuality of interest. The joint family is a miniature world. But there is little initiative or independence for its individual members.

The joint family system although in existence from the ancient times has continually faced internal and external crisis, due to personality clashes. In the joint family, there is abundant scope for the clash of wills. The traditional mother-in-law conflict and many other strains occur when the women of the household are largely continued to each other's company and have little outlet for their emotions.

The Nuclear Family

The nuclear family includes a married couple and their children. This term was coined by the anthropologist Robert Murdoc in 1949 (Levin, 1993). Although in individual cases one or more additional persons may reside with them. The nuclear family is prevalent throughout the world mainly in the urban settings. Children are born to this couple or adopted by them. Often the husband is the only earning member while wife takes the responsibility of upbringing the children.

This type of family structure has strong bonds. The family is a close-knit unit and all activities centre around it. In this family, both the parents support and nurture the children. Children in the nuclear family receive their primary training in-group living through their parents in the family setting. Remaining dependent upon the parents during childhood they form intense emotional family bonds. Their parents serve as guides, educators and models to them. The nuclear family is the smallest social unit responsible for the preservation of the value system. The functions of the nuclear family are to see that each new member is socialized, accepts the value system and the nuclear family supplies conformity. Parents influence their children's future role expectations as husband and wife. Parents mutually support and benefit each other. They have more income for personal and family expenses.

The Single-child Family

Single-child families are more common among adults who marry late than among those who marry early, and, among those, where the wife is dedicated to her career. Some adults voluntarily limit the number of children they have. Many adults feel, from childhood experiences or the experiences of their friends, that one child is likely to be less disrupting to the marital relationship than two or more. Further, their careers or their personal and social interests often limit their children to one, feeling that by doing so they can still have the gratifications of parenthood and the gratifications of personal interests.

The Childless Family

Career oriented and highly educated men and women often decide to have no children so they can advance in their careers and enjoy the good life made possible by their joint earnings. Inspite of the traditional belief that every woman should be a mother to be truly feminine and not having a large number of children is foolproof evidence of a man's virility, an increasing number of married couples today are voluntarily childless. While this is true for all socio-economic levels, it is especially true among those of the higher and better-educated group, a trend more popular in Western countries. They may be unable to have children, don't ever plan to have children or have delayed having children. Such families have more financial resources at their hands. They don't have the expenses that go with child rearing. Usually such families have a pet to keep them busy.

The Families with Working Mothers

Families where mothers work outside the home and turn the children over to caretakers or put them in child-care centers are increasing in all socio-economic groups, especially in urban and sub-urban areas.

The attitudes of both parents toward the dual-earner arrangement and the mother's satisfaction with her work will modify the effects of maternal employment on children. If the working mother obtains personal satisfaction from employment, if she does not experience excessive guilt about being away from her children, and if she has adequate household arrangements to prevent her from being stressed by dual-role demands, she may be as good a mother or better than a home-making mother (Greenberger and Goldberg, 1989).

Mothers who derive a sense of satisfaction and self-efficacy from their home-making role and working mothers who enjoy their employment both show more positive relations with their husbands and with their children than unhappy home-makers who would like to be employed (Hoffman, 1989; Schultz, 1991). However, mothers and fathers both display more negative feelings and behaviour toward their children when their attitudes toward maternal employment and the wife's work status are not congruent.

Latchkey children refers to the children who regularly go home after school to an empty house or apartment. During this time they are left without adult supervision till their parents return from work. Some parents are able to provide check of their children by making phone calls and check on children's planned activities. Care may also be provided by grandparents, neighbours or family friends. Child should be made accountable to the parents and parents should set guidelines for the child's activities.

The Dual-Career Family

The increases of financial strain on the family has led more women to choose to work. The encompassing economic and social change has given rise to dual-career family.

In dual-career family, both husband and wife pursue careers outside the home while maintaining their parenting roles. In such a family structure, both the spouses develop their professional roles. Stereotyped sex roles get intermingled with mother going out to work and bringing home an income and father sharing in household keeping tasks and child-care responsibility, but if spouses don't share these tasks, then one spouse may feel over-burdened. Physical stress, tension and reduced leisure time results from trying to fulfil to many roles.

Families participate in two types of work—family work and paid work. Family work is the work we perform in the home without pay, it includes household maintenance, caring for children, the ill and the aged. Traditionally women performed this work and today also the over-whelming majority of family work is done by women. Paid work is the work we do for salary or wages. Traditionally, men had been responsible for paid work, but currently vast majority of women whether married or single, with or without children are also employed.

Work overload tends to occur when the total expected activities for one person to perform are greater than what the individual can handle comfortably. It may be like "too-many-to-juggle." In India, working women generally have more work load than men.

The Single Parent Family

The single parent family includes one parent and one or more children. The parent may either be a mother or a father. Such families, in India, are mostly a result of divorce, separation or death and incidents of unmarried woman with child through birth or adoption are now on rise. The challenges for a single parent who is mostly a woman are varied. As she not only has to look after the household responsibilities, give socio-emotional support to the children but also has to provide financial security to the child.

The most common means is through divorce. Generally, the mother is given the custody of the children. Quality of life is a major issue for single-parent families. Any type of disruption in family life can produce a crisis. Divorce is one of the most stressful experiences that one can have in adulthood. It can also be extremely upsetting to children. Life is hard for most single-parent families. Yet many people choose to divorce rather than remain in an unhappy relationship, even though they know they will have to make a multitude of difficult adjustments. For many people, this type of family arrangement is more efficient and harmonious than a household marked by tensions and strife between the adults.

The single parent is responsible for all the work that was earlier done by both the parents. Children in such homes become independent early as they take more responsibility for helping with family tasks. Children may have one role model to help them learn acceptable social roles. Single-parent family can also provide a warm, secure, loving home environment to the children. In India, single parent family are mostly supported by either paternal or maternal grandparents or other relatives. In such cases, children have others to relate to and look up as social role models.

The Unwed Mother's Family

Either by mistake or by choice sometimes girls become pregnant without declaring their marriage. If they don't get aborted and give birth to the child and also decide to keep child with them, will be a tough task, in terms of excessive burden of work and responsibilities along with social disgrace. The child will also face number of social and psychological problems. Incompleteness on one side and non-acceptance in society on other will add to his or her agony.

The Blended Family

The blended family consists of a husband and wife, of whom one or both have been married before. It also includes children from their previous marriages. New family roles are created as two different family structures combine to make a new family structure. Here both the parents are present who work together to meet the home needs of security, warmth, household responsibility and financial strain. Blended family is a new term for step-family. Popular belief holds that step family life is highly problematic for all involved. Researches have found, however, that this family form may be no better or worse than other family forms today, though the challenges are distinct. These include the need to deal with a complicated extended family network, difficulty in establishing parenting roles, an uncertain developmental life career and unique developmental tasks. Following death or divorce the family may have step-parent who replaces the missing parent such families are also called reconstituted families.

The Adopting Family

Adoption is the process by which an individual or couple legally become the parents of a child not biologically their own. Parents who cannot give birth to a child due to choice or for other reasons adopt a child. People who have no or less children also may opt for adoption. They may have concern for homeless children of the world and may wish to provide home for older, disadvantaged or disabled children.

Adoption of a child in a nuclear family, blended family, childless family or single parent family makes it the adopting family. In adoptive families, some or all of the children have no blood ties with the parents who have a legal responsibility for them and give them the family name. They have all the rights and privileges of natural children. An adopting family has different challenges to face. Parents and other family members have to adjust to a child whose background may or may not be known. Parents especially the childless couples who go in for adoption might be older and more enthusiastic on having a child after so long. The child who comes either from orphanage or another family takes time to be adjusted in the new family. Parents should emphasize that the child was wanted and specially chosen. The expression of love, warmth, affection and acceptance showed by the adopting family increases security among these children.

Some psychologists are of the view that adoptive children should not be told about adoption in the first place. And to inform the adoptive child only the information of asked. But some psychologists don't agree with this concept. They feel that the adoptive child be told of their origin. Most adopting families report feeling greatly enriched by the experience (Brodzinsky and Huffman, 1988). Adoption is a way of building families. Adopted children may feel uniquely loved. Adoptive families also have the same role tasks and social responsibilities of socializing their child in their culture. Though, at times they may face more difficulties and hostility from the child itself or other members of the family in accepting the adoptive child.

Cohabitation

Cohabitation refers to individuals sharing living arrangements in an intimate relationship, whether these individuals are married or unmarried. Cohabitation is also called living together and commonly refers to relationships in which unmarried individuals share living quarters and are sexually involved.

The Homosexual Family

A common misconception about homosexuals is that they are antifamily and prefer to maintain a single life style. People are often surprised to learn that many homosexual men and women form families that may include children. Because our society does not sanction homosexual relationship to legal means such as marriage, it is difficult for many homosexuals to find positive role models. It cannot be denied that homosexual families have a different family life and different problems than other families. In many respects, however, homosexual families are like heterosexual blended families.

These days gay and lesbians are also taking the role of parenting activity. Heterosexual fear that gay and lesbian parents may not be able to provide good role models to their children, fear of sexual abuse and worry that the children will become gay or lesbian. Lesbian mothers and heterosexual single mothers in a study by Kirkpatrick *et al.* (1981) were found that their lifestyles, child rearing practices and general demographic data were strikingly similar. Lesbian mothers and heterosexual single mothers have different sexual orientation. At times, lesbian mother may try to hide that she is cohabiting while heterosexual single mother would not hide if she is living with a man (Lewin and Lyons, 1982). These days some lesbians in committed relationships are choosing to create families through artificial insemination.

Studies of gay fathers indicate, "being gay is compatible with effective parenting" (Bozett, 1987; Harris and Turner, 1985/1986). Furthermore, it appears that gay men who disclose their orientation to their children and who have a stable gay relationship tend to provide better-quality parenting than those who remain married and keep their orientation hidden. Turner,

Scaner and Harris (1985) in their study concluded that most gay fathers have positive relationship with their children, the father's sexual orientation is relatively unimportant to the parent child relationship and gay father's endeavour to create stable home environments for their children.

Families headed by lesbians or gay men generally experience the same joys and pains, same hardships and fruits in rearing the family as heterosexual the only difference is that the former have to face the disapproval, insensitivity and discrimination from the society. Research finds children of gay male and lesbian parents to be well adjusted, with no noticeable differences from children of heterosexual parents (Patterson, 1992; Flaks *et al.*, 1995; Allen, 1997). Nor are they more likely to be gay as adults. But they may encounter challenges from peers.

Families headed by lesbian mother or gay fathers generally experience the same joys and pains as headed by heterosexuals except that they are likely to face insensitive discrimination from society (Kirkpatrick *et al.*, 1981; Lewin and Lyons, 1982; Bozett, 1987; Harris and Turner, 1985/1986).

The Elongated Family

Except in rural and small town areas, elongated families, consisting of the nuclear family plus relatives who live under the same roof, are relatively common today.

The Different Sized-family

In urban and sub-urban areas, small families with three or fewer children are more common than large families with six or more children, or medium sized families, with three to six children.

The Young-parent Family

Adults who assume the parental role in their late-teens or early-twenties constitute the young-parent family and have their last child before they are thirty. Such families more common among the less-educated adults than among those who attend college for professional training after schools.

The Overage-parent Family

Adults who marry late or who voluntarily delay parenthood

until the thirties are regarded as overage parents and, thereby, form the overage-parent family.

The Communal Family

In communal families, several nuclear families bond together to share the responsibilities for the care of the home and the children. They often share marital partners.

The Foster-parent Family

In foster-parent homes, the parents have no legal responsibility for the children nor do the children bear their names. Their role is primarily that of paid caretaker for children whose parents cannot or will not keep them or whose parents are dead or mistreat them.

The Inter-religious Family

Spouses come from different religious faiths though one often converts to the faith of the other either before or after marriage in inter-religious family.

The Inter-racial Family

In an inter-racial family, the two spouses come from different racial groups.

The Families with Renested Adult Children

Families with renested adult children are a modern phenomenon. This family type occurs when children who have been launched into adult lives of their own, return to the home base of their family of origin. The phenomenon of renested families occurs primarily when young adult children experience some type of economic or personal crisis, such as loss of job or divorce and turn to their family for support. Some renested families are formed when young adults return to their elderly parents home in order to take for care them.

The Generational Inverse Families

This family looks like a traditional extended family, but differs in the way that it is structured. Adult children had the household held in a custodial capacity towards their parents. The parents often move into the homes of their adult children and become dependent upon them for shelter and support. Such families are formed under these circumstances, when a widowed or divorced parent is in need of emotional support from the adult children, when the parent is physically unable to provide his or her own care, when it is economically necessary to pool the resources of parent and adult children in order for both to live comfortably or when the adult child is need of certain kinds of support, such as child care or house keeping service, that the parent is willing to provide in return for economic or emotional support.

Composite Family

It is a form of polygamous marriage in which two or more nuclear families share a common wife (polyandry) or husband (polygyny).

Serial Family

Woman or man having a succession of marriages, thus acquiring several spouses and different families over a lifetime but constituting only one nuclear family at a time. This type of family is more prevalent in the United States of America.

Binuclear Family

Binuclear family is a group of parents and children who used to live together but now live separately due to divorce or separation.

Non-family Household

Non-family household is any living unit containing one person living alone or composed of several unrelated people. These people are either never-married, separated, divorced or widowed.

Parents of all social contexts have in common is the joy and complexity of parenting as children progress through various stages of development. All families have in common is also the passage from one stage to another of family life cycle.

13

The Marriage and Divorce Laws in India

India is a country of diverse languages and religions. All major religions have their own laws that govern marriages and divorces within their own community, and separate regulations exist regarding divorce in interfaith marriages. Hindus, including Buddhists, Sikhs and Jains, are governed by the Hindu Marriage Act, 1955; Christians by the Indian Divorce Act, 1869; Parsis by the Parsi Marriage and Divorce Act, 1936; and Muslims by the Dissolution of Muslim Marriages Act, 1939, which provides the grounds on which women can obtain a divorce. Civil marriages and inter-community marriages and divorces are governed by the Special Marriage Act, 1956. This chapter contains a detailed description of these marriage and divorce laws.

THE HINDU MARRIAGE ACT, 1956

It is well established that marital relationships should be safeguarded from every possible angle, and that severance of a marriage should be allowed only when the marriage has irretrievably broken down. Prior to 1956 (that is, before the coming into force of the Hindu Marriage Act), divorce among Hindus was not recognized, except where allowed by custom. The Hindu Marriage Act, provides 15 grounds of divorce. Of the 15 grounds of divorce specified, eleven grounds are available either to the husband or the wife and 4 additional grounds for divorce are available to the wife only. In addition to the 15 grounds of divorce, the Hindu Marriage Act also provides for divorce by mutual consent. Marriage according to the Hindu law is a holy union for the performance of religious duties. It is primarily and essentially a sacrament. Apart from the religious aspect, it also has a secular element. Thus, the Hindu marriage is an admixture of religion and ethics with legal precepts and consequences.

The Hindu Marriage Act came into force on 18 May, 1955. It governs the Hindu marriages and has brought about important changes to the law on this subject prevailing earlier. This act applies to any person who is Hindu by religion in any of its forms, and also to Buddhists, Jains, and Sikhs. The conditions for a valid Hindu marriage are bigamy is not permitted as per the law, neither party should have a spouse living and polygamy permitted by ancient Hindu law is now prohibited. Bigamy is now a punishable offence under the Indian Penal Code. If a person wants to marry while the spouse is living, a divorce should be obtained. Divorce is granted by court on valid grounds.

The bride and the bridegroom should not be within degrees of prohibited relationship; otherwise the marriage would be void. The prohibited relationships are a lineal ascendant, e.g., father and daughter; son and mother, wife or husband of a lineal ascendant or descendant e.g., father-in-law and widowed daughter-in-law; widowed mother-in-law and son-in-law, widow of the brother or of father's brother or of mother's brother, or of grandfather's brother or of grandmother's brother and brother and sister; uncle and niece, aunt and nephew, or children of brother and sister or of two brothers or of two sisters.

Custom Saved

Under customary law certain marriages are valid though the above-mentioned rule is contravened. In South India, marriages between children of brother and sister and between a male and his sister's daughter are common and are valid by custom. Parties should not be sapindas of each other. Sapinda means "of the same body." Etymologically every one is a sapinda of everyone else since all human beings are descended from the Supreme Being. Sapinda relationship extends as far as the third generation in the line of ascent through the mother and fifth in the line of ascent through the father. Two persons are sapindas of each other if one is a lineal ascendant of the other within the limits of sapinda relationship or if they have a common lineal ascendant, that is, within the limits of sapinda relationship with reference to each of them.

Conditions for a Valid Hindu Marriage

Under Section 5 of the Hindu Marriage Act, a marriage may be solemnized between any two Hindus, if the following conditions are satisfied:

Marriageable Age

The amendment to this effect was issued in 1978, and as per this the bridegroom should have completed the age of 21 years and the bride the age of 18 years at the time of the marriage. The question of guardianship in marriage does not arise since the parties to be married are to be majors. If the condition as to minimum age is infringed, the validity of the marriage is not affected. If a marriage is performed between individuals who are below the prescribed minimum age, such marriages are void *ab initio*. Further, the parties to such marriage are punishable under Section 18(a) of the Act. However, if the customary rights and ceremonies of one of the parties to the marriage are performed, such marriage would not be void or voidable, though the parties to the marriage are punishable. But the parties (bride or bridegroom as the case may be) shall be punishable 15 days simple imprisonment or fine up to Rs. 1,000 or both.

Effect of Idiocy or Lunacy

If either party is a lunatic or an idiot, the marriage is voidable. It can be annulled by a decree of nullity and this is also a ground for divorce. Under Section 12 of the Act the party affected is entitled to file for a decree of nullity of marriage, on the ground that the other party was an idiot or lunatic at the time of marriage.

Effect of Impotence

A decree of nullity may be granted on the ground that the marriage has not been consummated owing to the impotence of the respondent. Both parties to the marriage should not be suffering from mental disorder of such a kind or to such extent, that such person is unfit for marriage and procreation of children. The burden to prove sufficient degree of mental disorder or unsoundness of mind at the time of marriage, is upon the who challenges its validity. Mere dullness of intellect is not sufficient to incapacitate a person from marrying. Under this Section, a spouse who is unfit (due to his mental disorder) to look after and bring up children, would be considered unfit for procreation of children, even if such person is not sterile and medically fit to give birth.

Both Parties to the Marriage should not have a Spouse at the Time of Marriage

The provisions of the Hindu Marriage Act prohibit bigamy. In case of a marriage solemnized between two Hindus during the subsistence of a former marriage, of either party to the marriage, such act would constitute the offence of bigamy and would be punishable under the provisions of the Indian Penal Code. Further such marriage (latter) would be void under Section 17 of the Hindu Marriage Act. In case such marriage, in contravention of this provision is performed, the first wife is entitled to institute a suit in any civil court, for declaring the second marriage of her husband as void, under Section 9 of the Code of Civil Procedure, 1908.

Both Parties to the Marriage should not be Subject to Recurrent Attacks of Insanity or Epilepsy

The Parties to the Marriage should not be within the Degree of Prohibited Relationship

However, if the custom or usage governing both parties permits marriages within the degrees of prohibited relationship, this prohibition would not apply to such marriages.

The Parties to the Marriage should not be Sapindas of each other

However, if the custom or usage governing both parties permits marriages within the degrees of prohibited relationship, this prohibition would not apply to such marriages.

Divorce

Under the Hindu Marriage Act, a party may file a petition for divorce and the marriage may be dissolved by a decree of divorce on the following grounds.

Adultery

Voluntary sexual intercourse with any person other than his/her spouse is called adultery. Though, initially a divorce could be granted only if such spouse was living in adultery, by the Marriage Laws Amendment Act, 1976, even a single voluntary sexual act, with any other person other than the spouse is a sufficient ground for divorce.

Cruelty

Initially cruelty was a ground only for judicial separation, but now forms a ground for divorce under the Amendment Act of 1976.

Desertion

This has been added as a ground for divorce by the Amendment Act, though previously it was a ground for judicial separation.

Conversion

In order to obtain a divorce on this ground, it should be proved that such other party has converted. Mere professing or theoretical allegiance to any other religion does not mean conversion. This ground has been added to the act for obtaining divorce, as according to the Hindu Law, a marriage is not dissolved by conversion by one of the parties. Therefore, contrary to the belief that conversion by itself resulted in divorce, a person now has to obtain a decree of divorce under the Act.

Unsoundness of Mind

Initially it was essential for a party to prove that his/her spouse was incurably of unsound mind for a continuous period of three years. However, now this duration has been omitted. In order to obtain a decree under this ground it has to be proved that the spouse is affected to such an extent that the party seeking divorce cannot be reasonably expected to live with him/her.

Virulent and Incurable Leprosy

If either of the two parties suffer from venereal diseases in communicable form, the divorce is given.

Presumption of death: Under the Act, a person is presumed to be dead, if he/she has not been heard of as being alive for a period of at least seven years.

In addition, Section 13(2) provides for further grounds for the wife to seek divorce are: bigamy; the husband is guilty of rape, sodomy or bestiality, after grant of maintenance under the Hindu Adoptions and Maintenance Act or Section 125 of Criminal Procedure Code, there was no resumption of cohabitation; if marriage was solemnized before 15 years of age and it was repudiated before 18 years. The above apart, under Section 13(B) dissolution of marriage by a decree of divorce may be sought by mutual consent by both the parties on the ground that they were not living together for one year or more. Under Section 15 after the decree of divorce had become final, the divorced person can remarry.

THE MUSLIM MARRIAGE LAW

Marriage under Islam is only a civil contract and not a sacrament. Under Muslim Law, a husband is entitled to have as many as four wives and all the wives are entitled to exercise marital rights with their husband. For a valid marriage under Muslim Law, the following requirements are essential: Proposal and acceptance—The consent should not be vitiated by the fraud or force. As the Muslim marriage is in the nature of contract, it requires free and unfettered consent of the parties' capacity to contract marriage. If the party is a minor, he/she should be represented by guardian. The following legal disability or impediment should not be present.

There is absolute prohibition of marriage in case or relationship of consanguinity which means the relationship of the person through his/her father or mother on the ascending side, or through his or her own on the descending side. Marriage among the persons related by affinity, i.e., through the wife is not permitted. Marriage with foster mother and other related through such foster mother is also void. Relative prohibitions are unlawful conjunction, marrying a fifth wife, marrying a woman undergoing iddat, marrying non-Muslim, absence of proper witnesses, woman contracting a second marriage during the subsistence of the first marriage. The following marriages are also prohibited: marrying pregnant women, marrying own divorced wife and marrying during pilgrimage.

Dower or mahr is an obligation imposed upon the husband at the time of the marriage as a mark of respect to the wife. The wife can receive it by instituting an action as if it was a debt due to her. Dower can be in cash or in kind and it is divided into two parts one called 'prompt' payable at the time of marriage before the wife can be called upon to enter into conjugal domicile and the other 'deferred' to be discharged when the specified event occurs and on demand made by the wife. Till the dower is paid the wife has the right to retain possession of her husband's property.

Iddat is the period of chastity, which a Muslim woman had to observe in divorce from her husband or on the death of her husband. During the period of iddat, she is not permitted to marry another man. The period of iddat is three months, if the marriage is dissolved by divorce and for four months and 10 days, if the marriage is dissolved by the death of her husband.

The custody of the child is called *Hizanat*. The mother is entitled to the custody of her male child until he has completed the age of seven years and regarding the daughter, the mother is entitled to the custody until she attains puberty belonging to Hanafis and until she is married in respect of others. This right of the mother is not lost by divorce.

Talak

A marriage under the Muslims law can be unilaterally put an end to by the husband by pronouncing talak (divorce). He can delegate this power to a third person or even to his wife so that she can by the exercise of this delegated power put an end to the marriage. The husband and the wife may by mutual agreement also put an end to the marriage.

The following conditions should be satisfied for a valid (Sahih) marriage are the parties should have attained the age of puberty or the marriage contract should be entered into by the guardian in marriage on behalf of the party concerned. The parties should be of sound mind. Otherwise, the guardian in marriage should act on behalf of the person of unsound mind in arranging the marriage contract.

Form of Marriage

There should be a proposal and its acceptance at one meeting. According to Shias, witnesses are necessary but according to Sunnis at least two male witnesses or one male and two female witnesses are necessary. The witnesses have to be sane and adults and the absence of witnesses can only render the marriage as irregular and not void.

Following disqualifications apply to the bride's side for a marriage to be irregular. She is undergoing iddat. A widow has to remain in seclusion for 4 months and 10 days from the death of her husband. If she is pregnant at the time of her husband's death then iddat lasts till delivery. A divorced woman whose marriage has been consummated should observe seclusion for three lunar months and if she is subject to menstruation, the period is three menstrual courses.

Effect of Difference of Religion

A sunni Muslim may validly marry even a non-Muslims Kitabia (e.g. Christian woman or Jew) and a Shia Muslim may do so provided the marriage is mutta (temporary) marriage. A Muslim male cannot validly marry a non-Kitabia. Among Shias such a marriage is void whereas the Sunnis take a more lenient view and regard it as irregular marriage. The woman may at any time embrace Islam and cure this irregularity.

Muhammedan law is based on the Quran mostly. It applies

to all Muslims, whether by birth or conversion. There are a few traditional forms of divorce and a few forms, which were added. For example, a Muslim woman cannot divorce her husband under traditional law because of cruelty without losing a part of her property. However, with The Dissolution of Muslim Marriages Act, 1939, she can. Muslim laws of divorce give the husband the right to divorce his wife without any misbehaviour on her part. Since Muslim law allows polygamy, seeking a divorce for adultery is almost out of the question. Divorce, on the grounds of cruelty and desertion came in with the dissolution of Muslim Marriages Act, 1939. Mutual Consent divorces exist in Muslim law and are called *Khul or Khulla* and *Mubaraa or Mubaraat*. In Khul, the wife has to part with some of her dower or some other property. Since Mubaraa is repudiation by mutual consent, no property has to be given. There are other forms of divorce. These are Ila, where the husband vows that he will not have sexual intercourse with his wife for four months or more, or an unspecified period. Zihar is another form of divorce where the husband compares his wife to a woman whom he cannot marry. For example, he says that his wife is like his mother. His wife then automatically gets the right to deny him sexual intercourse. He can atone it by doing suitable penance. Then there is Li'an or Laan, which is a false charge of adultery. Where the husband falsely accuses the wife of adultery, if she proves that she is not guilty of adultery, she is entitled to a divorce. Talak can be pronounced in three ways. Firstly, three separate pronouncements, each in the periods of purity, or the intervals between menstruation, and abstinence from sexual intercourse in the interim. The next form is one single pronouncement, followed by abstinence from sexual intercourse for the period of iddat. Both these forms are sanctioned, and both these are revocable till the period of iddat is completed. The third is the infamous triple talak. This is irregular and not highly approved. In this form of divorce, the man makes three pronouncements of divorce in immediate succession. This form of talak becomes irrevocable immediately.

THE INDIAN CHRISTIAN MARRIAGE ACT, 1872

The Indian Christian Marriage Act was passed to reduce into a smaller compass the two English Acts of Parliament and the three Acts of the Indian Legislature. This Act applies to the solemnization of marriages in India of persons professing the Christian religion. Indian Christians include the descendents of the natives of India converted to Christianity as well as converts. The Act comprehensively sets forth the persons by whom marriages may be solemnized, the procedure relating to registration of marriages, issue of certificates, time and place of marriage, etc.

Conditions for the Grant of Certificate of Marriage

Any person licensed under this Act to grant certificate may without notice to the Minister of Religion, certify the marriage if the following conditions are fulfiled: the age of the man intending to be married should not be under 21 years and the age of the woman intending to be married should not be under 18 years, neither of the persons intending to be married should have a wife/husband still living and the persons intending to be married should say to the other the following words: "I call upon these persons here present to witness that, I, ..., in the presence of Almighty God and in the name of our Lord Jesus Christ, do take thee, . . ., to be my lawfully wedded wife/husband" or words to this effect, in the presence of a person licensed under this Act and of at least two credible witnesses. On the application of either party to such marriage, on satisfaction of the above conditions and on the payment of a fee of four annas, the person licensed shall grant a certificate of marriage.

Conditions for Marriage

The Act applies when one or both the parties to the marriage is or are Christians. If the personal law applicable to either of the parties forbids the marriage, e.g. no ground of prohibited degrees of relationship, it cannot be validly performed under this Act.

The Christian Marriage Act is only concerned with the forms in which the marriage is to be solemnized and where the marriage is solemnized by a Marriage Registrar appointed under the Act, the following procedure is to be followed:

(a) Notice of Intended Marriage

One of the parties of intended marriage should give written notice of it to the Marriage Registrar of the District within which the parties have dwelt. Where the parties dwell in different districts the notice should be given to the Marriage Registrar of each district. The notice is affixed in a conspicuous part of the office of the Marriage Registrar and is entered in the "Marriage Note Book."

(b) Oath Before Registrar

One of the parties should appear personally before the marriage Registrar and make oath—there is no impediment of kindred or affinity or other lawful hindrance to the Marriage, the usual place of abode is within the district of such marriage registrar and if either of the party is minor (that is, one under 21 years of age) the consent of the persons competent to consent to the marriage (father and if he be dead the guardian of the person and if there be no guardian, the mother) has been obtained or that there is no person resident in India authorized to give such consent.

Marriage under Christian Law is in the nature of contract and hence there should be a free and voluntary consent between the parties. When there is a minor, as defined in the Act, the consent of father or guardian is necessary. Marriage is not permissible between the parties who are within the prohibited degrees of relationship under section 19 of the Act. There is no legal impediment for marriage between a catholic and a Protestant. By marriage, the husband and wife become one person, that is, the legal existence of the women is incorporated and consolidated into that of the husband.

The Indian Divorce Act governs divorce for Indian Christians. The problem with this is that the husband can only seek divorce if the wife has committed adultery. The wife has numerous grounds. Wife can seek a divorce if her husband converts, commits bigamy or rape, sodomy or bestiality. Apart from these, she has to prove two faults to get a divorce, like cruelty and adultery. The law regarding divorce, judicial separation and allied matters is contained in the Indian Divorce Act, 1869. Under section 18 of the Act either spouse can seek divorce on the grounds contained in section 19 which reads as follows:

Section 19

Grounds for decree of divorce are: The respondent was

impotent at the time of marriage and institution of the suit; that the parties are within the prohibited degree of consanguinity or affinity; That either party was a lunatic or idiot at the time of marriage and that the former husband or wife of either party was living at the time of marriage and the said marriage was then in force. Nothing shall affect the jurisdiction of the High Court to make decrees of nullity of marriage on the ground that the consent of either party was obtained by force or fraud.

Under Section 10

The wife can seek the marriage be dissolved on the ground—that her husband exchanged professing Christianity and gone through a form of marriage with another woman; incestuous adultery; bigamy with adultery; marriage with another woman with adultery; rape, sodomy or bestiality; adultery coupled with cruelty and adultery coupled with desertion without reasonable cause for two years or more. Under section 11, in cases of allegations of adultery, the adulterer should be made a party. Pendente alimony may be granted under section 36 of the Act.

THE PARSI MARRIAGE ACT, 1939

The Parsi Marriage Act of 1939 governs the Parsis of India in regard to the solemnization of the weddings and the dissolution thereof. The word 'Parsi' as used in the Act includes not only Parsi Zoroastrians of India, but also the Zoroastrians of Iran. For a valid marriage a Parsi should have completed 21 years of age. If a party to the marriage is under that age, the consent of the guardian should be obtained. The plaintiff should not be within the prohibited relationships specified in the Act. The marriage is solemnized according to a ceremony called "Ashirvad" by a priest. The presence of two other witnesses is also necessary. A Parsi marriage is monogamous. The officiating priest certifies the marriage and the marriage certificate is also signed by the parties (or guardians) to the marriage and the witnesses. It is sent by the priest, with a fee of Rs. 2 paid by the husband, to the Registrar of Marriages. The Registrar enters the certificate in a register kept for the purpose and the register is accepted as proof of the statements made therein.

Requisites to Validity of Parsi Marriages

No marriage shall be valid if—the contracting parties are related to each other in any of the degrees of consanguinity or affinity set forth in Schedule 1; such marriage is not solemnized according to the Parsi form of ceremony called "Ashirvad" by a priest in the presence of two Parsi witnesses other than such priest; or (c) in the case of any Parsi (whether such Parsi has changed his or her religion or domicile or not) who, if a male, has not completed twenty-one years of age, and if a female, has not completed eighteen years of age.

Certificate and Registry of Marriage

The officiating priest in the form contained in Schedule 11 shall immediately on the solemnization thereof, certify every marriage contained under this Act. The said priest, the contracting parties, shall sign the certificate and two witnesses present at the marriage and the said priest shall thereupon send such certificate together with a fee of two rupees to be paid by the husband to the Registrar of the place at which such marriage is solemnized. The Registrar on receipt of the certificate and fee shall enter the certificate in a register to be kept by him for that purpose and shall be entitled to retain the fee.

Grounds for Divorce

Any married person may sue for divorce on any one or more of the following grounds, namely: that the marriage has not been consummated within one year after its solemnization owing to the wilful refusal of the defendant to consummate it; that the defendant at the time of the marriage was of unsound mind and has been habitually so up to the date of the suit, provided that divorce shall not be granted on this ground, unless the plaintiff was ignorant of the fact at the time of the marriage, and has filed the suit within three years from the date of the marriage; that the defendant has been incurably of unsound mind for a period of two years or upwards immediately preceding the filing of the suit or has been suffering continuously or intermittently from mental disorder of such kind and to such an extent that the plaintiff cannot reasonably be expected to live with the defendant.

Divorce by Mutual Consent

Subject to the provisions of this Act, a suit for divorce may be filed by both the parties to a marriage together, whether such marriage was solemnized before or after the commencement of the Parsi Marriage and Divorce (Amendment) Act, 1988 on the ground that they have been living separately for a period of one year or more, that they have not been able to live together and that they have mutually agreed that the marriage should be dissolved provided that no suit under this sub-section shall be filed unless at the date of the filing of the suit one year has lapsed since the date of the marriage. The Court shall, on being satisfied, after hearing the parties and after making such inquiry as it thinks fit, that a marriage has been solemnized under this Act and the averments in the plaint are true and that the consent of either party to the suit was not obtained by force or fraud, pass a decree declaring the marriage to be dissolved with effect from the date of the decree.

Suits for Nullity

In any case in which consummation of the marriage is from natural causes impossible, such marriage may, at the instance of either party thereof, be declared to be null and void.

Suits for Dissolution

If a husband or wife shall have been continually absent from his or her wife or husband for the space of seven years, and shall not have been heard of as being alive within that time by those persons who would have naturally heard of him or her, had he or she been alive, the marriage of such husband or wife may, at the instance of either party thereto, be dissolved.

Punishment of Bigamy

Every Parsi who during the lifetime of his or her wife or husband, whether a Parsi or not, contracts a marriage without having been lawfully divorced from such wife or husband, or without his or her marriage with such wife or husband having legally been declared null and void or dissolved, shall be subject to the penalties provided in Sections 494 and 495 of the Indian Penal Code for the offence of marrying again during the lifetime of a husband or wife.

Remarriage when Unlawful

No Parsi (whether such Parsi has changed his or her religion or domicile or not) shall contract any marriage under this Act or any other law in the lifetime of his or her wife or husband, whether a Parsi or not, except after his or her lawful divorce from such wife or husband or after his or her marriage with such wife or husband has lawfully been declared null and void or dissolved, and, if the marriage was contracted with such wife or husband under the Parsi Marriage and Divorce Act, 1865 (15 of 1865), or under this Act, except after a divorce, declaration or dissolution as aforesaid under either of the said Acts. Every marriage contracted contrary to the provisions of sub-section (1) shall be void.

THE SPECIAL MARRIAGE ACT, 1954

The Special Marriage Act, 1954 which enable inter-religious marriages in India provides for divorce as well. As a registered marriage is considered as a "civil contract", the Act recognizes divorce by mutual consent as well, which is otherwise not available to marriage performed under Muslim and Christian personal law.

Wedding Legalities

It is necessary to keep in mind that as a rule all marriages have to be compulsorily registered. Those who undertake a civil marriage marry under the Special Marriage Act, 1954; do not need to take any further steps because in their case registration is itself the marriage ceremony. They require no formal marriage ceremony. But in the case of all religious/ceremonial marriages, and they are the majority in India, the additional step of getting the marriage registered with the registrar of marriages is compulsory.

However, the non-registration of a marriage does not affect its legality and validity. Couples who do not register their marriages can be fined and any one giving false information to the authorities can be penalized with a short jail term. Even then it is always advisable to register a religious/ceremonial marriage because there is then proof of its legality and validity.

In matrimonial disputes it is not uncommon for one of the

spouses to claim that no valid marriage took place. Religious authorities that solemnize marriages rarely maintain proper records. Once a marriage is registered with the authorities there is an assumption in law that a valid marriage took place.

Solemnization of Marriage under the Special Marriage Act, 1954

The objective of this Act is to replace the Special Marriage Act of 1872 and provide a special form of marriage that could be adopted by any person in India and all Indian nationals in foreign countries, irrespective of the faith to which either parties of the marriage profess. The parties to the marriage may adopt any ceremonies. However, certain formalities are prescribed before the marriage can be registered. In the case of Indian citizens abroad, Diplomatic and Consular Officers are appointed under the Act as Marriage Officers for the solemnization and registration of marriages between Indian citizens in a foreign country. Persons already married under other forms of marriage can register their marriages under this Act in cases where the marriage is solemnized in Jammu and Kashmir, both parties should be citizens of India and domiciled in the territories to which this Act extends, i.e. to the whole of India except the State of Jammu and Kashmir.

Procedure to be followed for the Solemnization of Marriages under this Act

Parties intending to solemnize their marriage under this Act should give a notice to the Marriage Officer of the district in which at least one of the parties to the marriage has resided for a period of at least thirty days immediately preceding the date of giving notice. The Marriage Officer on receiving such notice would enter a true copy of the notice in a book called the Marriage Notice Book, which would be open to inspection by any person who desires to inspect it, without any fee. The Marriage Officer in some conspicuous part of his office would publish a copy of the notice. In cases wherein either of the parties to the marriage resides within any other district, a copy of the notice would be sent to the Marriage Officer of such district and the copy would be published in a similar manner in the office of the Marriage Officer of that district. Any person may before the expiry of thirty days from the date of publication of such notice may object to the marriage on the ground that it would contravene Section 4 of the Act. On receipt of any such objection the Marriage Officer shall not solemnize the marriage until he has inquired into it. The Marriage Officer shall not take more than thirty days from the date of receiving objection to make inquiries and arrive at a decision. If no such objection is received the marriage may be solemnized after the expiration of the thirty days from the date of notice.

The parties and three witnesses are required to sign a declaration form before solemnization of marriage. The marriage may be solemnized at the office of the Marriage Officer or at a place within reasonable distance from the office. It may be solemnized in any form but would not be complete and binding unless each party says to the other in the presence of the Marriage Officer and the three witnesses in any language understood by the parties, "I . . . take thee. . . . To be my lawfully wedded wife/ husband." If the marriage is not solemnized within three calendar months from the date of notice, a fresh notice has to be given under the Act and the procedure mentioned above would have to be followed.

Conditions of a Valid Marriage under the Special Marriage Act, 1954

Chapter II of the Special Marriage Act deals with the solemnization of marriages. Under Section 4 of the Special Marriage Act, a marriage may be solemnized between any two persons if the following conditions are fulfiled: both parties to the marriage should not have a spouse at the time of marriage, both the parties to the marriage should be sound in mind and capable of giving a valid consent, both parties to the marriage should not be suffering from mental disorder of such a kind or to such extent, that such person is unfit for marriage and procreation of children, both parties to the marriage should not be subject to recurrent attacks of insanity or epilepsy, the male should have completed the age of 21 years and the female should have completed 18 years of age and the parties to the marriage should not be within the degree of prohibited relationship. However, if the custom or usage governing both parties permits marriages within the degrees of prohibited relationship, this prohibition would not apply to such marriages.

Certificate of Marriage

When the marriage has been solemnized, the Marriage officer shall enter a certificate thereof, in the form specified in the Fourth Schedule in a book to be kept by him for that purpose and to be called the Marriage Certificate Book and such certificate shall be signed by the parties to the marriage and the three witnesses. On a certificate being entered in the Marriage Certificate Book by the Marriage Officer, the certificate shall be deemed to be conclusive evidence of the fact that a marriage under this Act has been solemnized and that all formalities respecting the signatures of witnesses have been complied with.

THE FOREIGN MARRIAGE ACT, 1969

The Foreign Marriage Act, 1969, was passed by the Indian Parliament with a view to implement the twenty-third report of the Law Commission on the law relating to foreign marriages. The Foreign Marriage Act deals with the subject of solemnizing marriages abroad, where atleast one of the parties is an Indian citizen.

The salient features of the Act are it provides for an enabling form of marriage, which can be availed of outside India where one of the parties to the marriage is an Indian citizen. The form of marriage provided is not in supersession of but only in addition to or as an alternative to, any other form that might be permissible to the parties. It seeks to lay down certain rules in respect of the capacity of the parties and conditions of validity of marriage and also provides for registration of marriage on lines similar to those in the Special Marriage Act, 1954. The provisions of the Special Marriage Act, 1954, in regard to matrimonial relief's are sought to be made applicable, with suitable modification, not only to marriages solemnized or registered under the Foreign Marriage Act, but also to other marriages solemnized abroad to which a citizen of India is a party.

Under the Foreign Marriage Act, a marriage between parties, one of whom atleast is a citizen of India, may be solemnized by or before a Marriage Officer in a foreign country. The Central Government has been empowered to appoint such of its diplomatic or consular officers to be Marriage Officers for any foreign country. The conditions to be fulfiled for a marriage to be solemnized under the Act are as follows: neither party has a spouse living, neither party is an idiot or a lunatic, the bridegroom has completed the age of twenty one years and the bride the age of eighteen years at the time of the marriage, and the parties are not within the degrees of prohibited relationship. However, the fourth condition will not apply when the personal law or a custom governing at least one of the parties permits of a marriage between them.

Section 11 of the Act provides that marriages prohibited by any law in force in the foreign country or marriages appearing to be in contravention of international law or the comity of nations cannot be solemnized under the Act. In such circumstances, the Marriage Officer has to record his reasons for refusing to solemnize the marriage, in writing. The order of the Marriage Officer refusing to solemnize the marriage can be appealed against, before the Central Government. Further, under Section 17 of the Act, the Marriage Officer is also empowered to register marriages solemnized in a foreign country but not registered.

FAMILY COURTS IN INDIA

Family Courts in India have been set-up in several major cities and towns. Broadly, all matrimonial disputes like divorce, maintenance, alimony, custody of children, etc. are tried by the Family Courts. The concept of Family Court is to imply an integrated broad based service to families in trouble. It stipulates the Family Court structure should be such as to stabilize the marriage, to the family, and where a marriage has been broken down irretrievably, to it with maximum fairness and minimum bitterness, distress and humiliation Family Court system also visualizes assistance of specialized agencies and persons.

Jurisdiction of the Family Courts

The following disputes fall within the jurisdiction of the Family Court: proceedings between a husband and wife for declaring a marriage as null and void; proceedings between a husband and wife for restitution of conjugal rights; proceedings between a husband and wife with respect of judicial separation and divorce; disputes with respect to the validity of a marriage or as to the matrimonial status of any person; property disputes between a husband and a wife; disputes pertaining to the legitimacy of any person; proceedings with respect to maintenance; and proceedings in relation to guardianship of the person or the custody of, or access to, any minor.

Confidentiality

It is now a part of the concept of Family Court that confidentiality of the Court record should be maintained and if the parties so desire or the Court so thinks proper, the proceedings should be in camera. The Family Courts Act makes it obligatory on the part of the Court to hold the proceedings in camera if any party so desires. They may also be held in camera if the court so deems fit.

Procedure

The family Courts are free to evolve their own rules of procedure, and once a Family Court does so, the rules so framed over ride the rules of procedure contemplated under the Code of Civil Procedure. The Act stipulates that a party is not entitled to be represented by a lawyer without the express permission of the Court (However, in reality, it is invariably a lawyer who represents a party. This is done by filing a formal application seeking the Courts permission to be represented by a lawyer, and such permission, more often that not, is always granted). The most unique aspect regarding the proceeding before the Family Court are that they are first referred to conciliation and only when conciliation proceedings fail, is the matter taken up for trial by the Court. The Conciliators are professionals who are appointed by the Court. Once a final order is passed, the aggrieved party has an option of filing an appeal before the High Court. Such appeal is to be heard by a bench consisting of two judges.

14

Family Disorganization

Each family is unique in its style of living. While some characteristics of the family are fundamental, others keep on changing through different phases. Sometimes changes are sudden, causing disorganization and disruption in the structure of the family and its functions. Then there is crisis in the family. Every change brings with it the inevitable necessity for making adjustments. Many changes begin with small situations but become crises because of their being continued and upsetting influence on the emotional stability of the family members. A crisis is something unusual, demanding unusual solution of the problem.

Families are vulnerable to disorganization through the loss of children as well as a loss of parents. Family disorganization includes all situations in which one mate parts from the other. This could be because of death of partner, desertion, separation or divorce of the couple. Sometimes partners live together under one roof but they are emotionally not attached to each other. They quarrel, they fight, and they start living separate, then come back and then go again. They do not bother for each other. They are, in face, broken homes, broken psychologically. Development of their children is affected badly. They are phychologically and mentally disturbed.

The effect of continued home conflicts is more harmful to the children then the divorce in itself. The crisis arises out of the conflicts within the family. Whatever, the cause may be, but both partners loose confidence, faith and love for each other. Family lives together but due to conflicts cannot discharge their duties efficiently. Another cause of disorganization may be separation and legal divorce. Many counsellors advise people to separate and live independent happy life, if they cannot live together. The legal stamp on separation is called divorce. In both the situations family gets disorganized. Physical separation is easy but separating psychologically is a tough task. Not only partners but children too are the sufferers. The issue of their custody will have number of problems. If they live with one parent, they will loose the company of another. They are either deprived of certain opportunities or are pampered which is also harmful.

Marriage is an institution, which provides optimum and best environment, required for child's development. Several theoretical frameworks that have influenced the study of child development recognize the importance of the marital relationships. A marriage relationship needs regular loving care. It needs a commitment, time to spend together, share their thoughts and feelings. They need to encourage each other to grow and develop in their own areas. Love needs to worked on everyday basis. A marital relationship can be thought of as something that is alive.

It is important to remember that parents have a relationship with each other as well as with their children. When a couple offers each other emotional and physical support and comfort, the likelihood that they will provide the same kind of support and caring to their children is greatly increased. Research has shown that when partners are mutually supportive, they are more involved with their children and that their relationship with their children demonstrates affection, sensitivity and competent childrearing practices (Cowan and Cowan, 1992; Katz and Gottman, 1977).

Couples who share child care and household chores have more time for playful and pleasurable interactions with their children and increased their chances of witnessing developmental milestones like a child's first words or staggering steps.

In the past, divorce was neither acceptable nor practical. Couples did not have the option of divorce. A broken was seen as a personal failure and women were mostly economically dependent. Cultural appraisal of divorce is now changing. Now divorce is viewed as an alternative to an unhealthy marriage relationship. Though there is still pressure on the couple to stay married even if the relationship is turning sour and unhealthy. People may stay together for the sake of the children, to avoid the family and friends disapproval, fear of loneliness of being single, hope of return of marital bliss or happiness. They may continue to stay together, abuse each other until death does their part.

Conflict and love has coexisted among human beings for centuries. An ancient Sanskrit poem reflects this dichotomy:

In the old days we both agreed.
That I was you and you were me
But now what has happened
That makes you, you
And me, me?

Conflict is natural in intimate relationships.

TYPES OF CONFLICT

There are two types of conflict that affect stability of a relationship—basic *versus* non-basic conflicts and situational *versus* personality conflicts.

Basic *versus* Non-basic Conflicts

Basic conflicts resolve around carrying out marital roles and the functions of marriage and the family, such as providing companionship, working and rearing children. It threatens the foundations of marriage because they challenge fundamental rules.

Non-basic conflicts do not threaten the basic assumptions of marriage and may be negotiated. Basic conflicts challenge the fundamental assumptions or rules of a relationship whereas non-basic conflicts do not.

Situational *versus* Personality Conflicts

Some conflicts occur because of a situation and others occur because of the personality of either both or one of the partners.

Situational conflicts occur when at least one partner needs to make changes in a relationship. Such conflicts are also called realistic conflicts and are based on specific issues.

Personality conflicts are unrealistic conflicts based on the need of the partner or partners to release pent-up feelings or on their fundamental personality differences.

Differences and conflicts are part of any healthy relationship. The way we handle conflicts whether in healthy or unhealthy way, runs our relationships. Conflict may be used as a way of building and deepening our relationships. Major marital conflicts are related to sex and money.

Money Conflicts

Money conflicts occur because of power issues, disagreements over the allocation of resources or differences in values. Money is a major source of marital conflict. Couples disagree or fight over money, the way it is spent, allocation of the family's income, who decides the usage of money.

Sex Conflicts

Sex conflicts are also a major source of marital conflict. Sexual differences like one partner wants to have sex and other not, unsatisfied sex, orgasm not reached specially by woman lead to fights, poor oral sex, and so on. Generally, couples would fight and fight but not talk the real issue (the cause of unsatisfied sex) because of the taboo our society places on talking of sex and sexual behaviour and relationships. Problem situations in a marriage are pre-marital pregnancy, escape problems at home, past conflicts with parents and in-laws conflict. Teen marriages don't survive.

RESOLVING CONFLICTS

Conflicts can be resolved through agreement as a gift to freely agree with your partner as a gift, through bargaining about making compromises. A solution has to be fair to both to enhance the relationship. Sometimes differences can not be resolved, but they can be lived with. If a relationship is sound, differences can be resolved without undermining the basic ties.

For many married couples miscommunication and hurt feelings enter into their relationships and bring stress even on holidays. It's scarier to think of having daughter growing up thinking that all husbands control their wives with violence or threats of violence and a son who thinks that how men are supposed to treat their wives. If you can't change your situation for yourself, change it for your kids. Living with one parent in peace and security is so much better than living with two parents and fear.

A primary relationship is often stressful. Two people, each with different histories, different personalities, different needs, and different ways of doing things are trying to live under the same roof and get along with each other on a daily basis. One of the main difficulties that couples face revolves around expectation. Each person in the relationship brings expectations—a set of explicit expectation, a set of implicit expectation, a set of unrealistic expectation.

These expectations when in conflict with the other person's expectations and realities of life create stress. During the course of relationship, each partner may go through a series of transitions such as the death of a parent, the loss of a job or physical illness. Divorce becomes necessary if you have been stuck in a relationship that is less fulfiling than you want it, when it is beyond all measures of approachability.

FACTORS CONTRIBUTING TO DIVORCE

Researchers have identified several factors that often contribute to divorce. Background differences, personal immaturity and a lack of relationship skills can lead to divorce. Marrying into problem situations, escape problems at home, frequent financial conflicts increase the chances of divorce.

Difference in Backgrounds

Major differences in family and socio-economic backgrounds can result in differing views and expectations for marriage. However, similar and realistic expectations for marriage can help a marriage stay intact.

Personal Immaturity

The person's thoughts, feelings and goals leads to a person's maturity. Their personal readiness for marriage can affect the stability of their marriage.

Poor Relationship Skills

The need to communicate clearly, make decisions together, solve their problem, develop adjustment skills among the couple. If these relationship skills are lacking a marriage would break.

In Indian society, divorce is looked down as unrespectable. Divorce is regarded as a failure in personal relationships. Divorces are less frequent in India as compared to the western countries. Though, these days it is increasing. Some of the major causes of divorce are disparity in social or economic background of the two, bad habits like drinking, nagging, snoring, improper sex relations, physical incompatibility, adultery, troublesome relatives, disparity in religious faith or other ideologies, personality problems, cruelty, conflicting ambitions, values and needs of the couple and ill health or poverty.

Divorces are always traumatic in some way for everyone concerned. It is due to poor marital adjustment and it comes when husband and wife have been unable to find any other satisfactory solution to their problems. Many unhappy marriages do not end in divorce because of religious, moral, economic, children and/or other reasons. Some carry on family life, others start living separate or desert. Some enter into legal separation. The peak year for separation is the first year of marriage, and for divorce, the third year and by age these are twenties or thirties.

CONDITIONS BEHIND DIS-STABILITY OF MARRIAGE

Social Class

Desertion is more common among the lower social class, and divorce among the upper-middle and upper class.

Similarity of Background

Divorce is much more common among couples who have different cultural, racial, religious or socio-economic backgrounds.

Time of Marriage

Divorce rate is high when they marry in early age because they were immature; secondly, they feel that they can remarry easily.

Reasons for Marriage

Those who marry with romantic expectations, if get frustrated, may decide to separate.

Time at which the Couple become Parents

The shorter the interval between marriage and the birth of the first child, higher the divorce rate.

Economic Status

The lower the economic status of the family, the higher the rate of desertion and divorce.

Parental Model

Marital success or failure tends to run in families. Children of happily married parents are far less likely to be divorced.

Maintenance of Identity

Adults who can maintain their identity even after marriage, and who have opportunities for self-actualization are far less likely to be divorced.

Personal Adjustment

People with poor personal adjustment seem to be 'divorce-prone'. Many poorly adjusted adults try to find solution to their emotional problems in marriage. But, with new responsibilities they become more poorly adjusted.

Affection

In many cases it is cruelty, which parts them.

Realization that divorce affects all family members is important. When a marriage relationship breaks down, parents need to be aware of the impact on themselves and on their children. Adjustments in physical living arrangement, emotional, financial, social and parenting have to be made. Good communication skills can help the family members to understand the changes that are taking place. Recognizing that divorce is not a quick and easy way to end a relationship is important. Legal matter usually tarnishes and derogates the marital relationship that was existent.

EFFECTS OF DIVORCE

The effects of divorce vary from family to family. Both personal and general losses are involved. The loss of former love object affects the whole life situation. There is frustration and feeling of emptiness. Some feel divorce is a good escape from all sorrows of life. But, it is not easy to forget the past. For some, it leaves deep wound. Some after divorce decide to remarry. In India, men after divorce had the privilege to set up a new life, while women were expected to lead a solitary life and support themselves. But, now situation is changing.

The traumatic effect of divorce is usually greater than that of death because of the bitterness and emotional tensions and also the social attitude towards divorce. There are five phases of adjustment to divorce-denial that there was divorce; anger towards those involved; bargaining on the parts of children to bring parents back together; depression; and acceptance of divorce.

Divorce necessitates certain adjustments on the part of every member of the family: adjustment to the knowledge that divorce will take place, adjustment to the divorce itself, adjustment to the use by one parent of the child against the other parent, adjustment to peer group attitudes, adjustment to changed feelings, adjustment to living with one parent, adjustment to remarriages and adjustment to implications of family failure.

Children feel embarrassed. This is very damaging to their self-concepts unless they live with other such children. Children are most hurt by divorce when their love is divided and when they suffer from anxiety of the uncertainties and custody is fought in court and its decided to live with both alternately.

Though, many people feel that they will be benefited by divorce, they will build new life but face many problems. People have myth of romantic divorce as a case for marital problems. Couples expect less stress and conflict, greater freedom and many other delights. But, they do not prepare themselves for the traumas and stresses. Effects on family members are more pronounced during the first year of divorce. After that it is gradually resolved. Common problems divorced men and women face are discussed underneath

Economic Problems

After divorce, the husband and wife are both on reduced incomes because the husband's income must now support two households. Often the wife must take a job to supplement her alimony and child support.

Practical Problems

Even when the husband assumed few household responsibilities before divorce, the wife must now assume all household responsibilities, the practical problems of daily living—food preparation, bed-making, cleaning, marketing, etc.—formerly assumed by the woman, must, after divorce, be assumed by the man.

Emotional Problems

Few men and women are happy and carefree after divorce, though many are relieved that the stresses and strains of an unhappy marriage have ended. In many women, feelings of guilt, shame, resentment, anger and anxiety about the future are so dominant that they bring about personality changes.

Social Problems

Their social lives are limited mainly to relatives and friends of the same sex. They also face social disgrace.

Problems of Loneliness

Having been accustomed, since childhood, to the constant companionship of family members and then of a spouse, divorced men and women are lonely when they find themselves deprived of the constant companionship of a person of similar interests and values. Men, when the custody of the children is given to their wives, tend to be especially lonely over weekends and at holiday times.

Problems of Divided Child Custody

When custody of the children is divided between divorced parents, each experience adjustment problems for themselves and for the children. After being with one parent, for example, the other parent often encounters rebellion on the part of the children against home rules and responsibilities.

Sexual Problems

After divorce, both men and women are deprived of regular sexual outlets unless they remarry shortly after divorce or establish cohabitation.

Problems of Changed Self-concepts

Regardless of which spouse was responsible for the problems that led to divorce, both spouses tend to experience feelings of failure. These feelings inevitably colour their self-concepts unfavorably and lead to personality changes.

Divorce adjustment of mothers and fathers, parental reactions are related to child. The detrimental effects of divorce on children may be reduced if household routines are well organized and discipline of authorities is consistent. Living with a happy, a well-adjusted parent with whom she or he has a warm relationship and good communication enables a child to cope better with the parents divorce. Divorce may constitute either one or all of the following components.

The Emotional Divorce

In this, at least one partner is beginning to put emotional distance into the marriage, by stopping to care for the other. From the outside, the marriage may appear to be functioning adequately, but its heart is missing. This is called emotional divorce, which is usually the first state of marital disintegration.

The Legal Divorce

The legal divorce is the court-ordered termination of a marriage; both the partners may remarry and are legally independent of each other.

The Economic Divorce

The earner usually man gives alimony and child support.

Women usually experience the greatest decline in their standards of living.

The Co-parental Divorce

Spouses may divorce each other but they do not divorce their children.

The Community Divorce

When people divorce, their social context changes. In-laws become ex-in-laws and often they lose contact. Often friends may choose sides or drop out, or may not be as supportive as one wants.

The Psychic Divorce

The psychic divorce is accomplished when your former spouse becomes irrelevant to your sense of self and emotional well-being.

Legal divorce is a traumatic experience for all involved. Many changes result, which have a lifetime effect on parents and children. Family members struggle with the emotional trauma, new living arrangements, lower family income and new parenting arrangements. Both the spouses' have a feeling that divorce was their fault and blame themselves. They may feel hurt and rejected by the absent parent or spouse.

Children's emotional adjustment can be helped if both parents continue to be actively involved in their child's life. They need to let the child know that he or she is still loved even though the family is not together. Grand parents and other extended family members may be able to offer security and affection to the child. They both show interest in the child's friends, achievements and activities. Divorce may lead to less income. This is specially evident for woman if she is not working or working at low-income paid job. Since women tend to earn lower incomes, female-headed families tend to have less income to spend. The parent with custody of the children takes on the new role of single parent. The non-custodial parent has to adjust to the new role of being a visiting or part time parent. Family members have to adjust to the new living arrangements. The family may have to move, relocate in a new neighbourhood and find new friends. Children will have to adjust to living with one parent and visiting the other. Psychologist suggests that there is no predisposition towards parenting. Men are absolutely qualified to be the primary caregiver. Having dad staying at home is good for the children because they see both parents more.

Divorced women and children mostly need economic support. Following divorce, women are primarily responsible for both child rearing and economic support (Maccoby, Buchanan, Mnookin, and Dornbusch, 1993). Woman often experiences a dramatic downward turn in her economic conditions (Garrison, 1994; Morgan, 1991). The economic impact of divorce on women with children is especially difficult, as their employment opportunities are often constrained by the necessity of caring for children (Maccoby, Buchanan, Mnookin and Dornbusch, 1993). Gender discrimination in employment and lack of societal support for child care result poor economic resources for women and their children.

Alimony is the money payment a former spouse makes to the other to meet his or her economic needs from the one who earns more. Child support is the monetary payments made by the non-custodial spouse to the custodial spouse to assist in child rearing expenses.

There are two types of child custody—legal and physical. In joint legal custody, the children live primarily with one parent, but both share jointly in decisions about their children's education, religious training and general upbringing. The children live with both parents, dividing time more-or-less equally between the two households. In split custody, the children are divided between the two parents, mothers usually take the girls and fathers take the boys. In sole custody, one parent is responsible for the care of the child. It is women. It is given to women usually. It does not mean that non-custodial parent cannot see the child. Separation, divorce and remarriage bring about major changes in families. Changes occur in family structure. Family members role change. Financial changes take place. Close relationship within the family change.

MARITAL SEPARATION

The crucial event in a marital breakdown is the act of separation. Separation always precedes divorce but not all separations leads to divorce. A legal separation is a legal agreement for the couple to live apart, to divide their property, and to provide for their children. Sometimes a couple will move back together after a period of separation. Professional counselling may have helped them resolve their differences.

Separation in Early Years

Most divorces occur in the first ten years of marriage, many involve small children. Divorce radically changes the structure of a family and the relationship within it. The change involves loss, no matter how good the new situation turns out to be. Children and adults often need to mourn for the family as it was, and grieve for the parent who is missing.

Following the breakdown of a marriage, adults may want to invest in new relationships straightaway, and want to have no further contact with the previous partner. Children, on the other hand, need continuity of contact with both parents and will be wary of new relationships. Adults on the contrary, often want a fresh start, children often wish to keep as much as possible the same as it was.

However, in many situations, the adults are so affected by the stress and bitterness of separation that they are unable to plan their lives according to their children's needs, especially when these needs come into conflict with their own.

Effect on Children

Loss of parents through separation is potentially more damaging for children than a loss through death, because it is ongoing and unresolved. The long-term effects depend on arrangement made for continuity of contact with the non-custodial parents and whether the parents themselves have been able to adjust their lives successfully to the change.

The immediate effects of a separation depend on the atmosphere in the home before the break-up, and the quality of relationships between the child and each parent before as well as afterwards. Some children witness violence and emotional turmoil in the period leading up to separation. Many have poor explanations for what is happening and one parent may even ask for their support, thus forcing them to take sides.

The problems of families coping with difficulties at this time of acute distress are often compounded by drop in income, house moves and a change of school. Some children are more vulnerable than others while some gain maturity by taking on additional responsibilities. Very young children up to the age of five or six often appear to be very sad or frightened when their parents separate. Often they become clinging and demanding, holding on to security objects such as for toys and clothes. They may have disturbed nights, begin to bed wet, refuse to be left alone and protest about going to school.

Young children of seven or eight may react to family stress with a range of behavioural problems, which are usually temporary. Some may steal things at school, have temper tantrums, seek adult attention constantly and be irritable or depressed. They may cry at a little upsets and they may express their feelings through psychosomatic symptoms such as stomachaches. They also become disruptive and disobedient. Others will be unable to concentrate and withdraw into themselves, preferring to spend long periods alone than participating in-group activities. The pace and quality of their work may markedly deteriorate. At home, there may be increased quarrels and aggression between siblings. Absent mothers and fathers may be idealized or looked upon with hatred. Children, especially around the age of seven or eight, may express a very strong yearning for absent parent. They direct anger at their parents for separating and want them to reunite.

Role of Teachers

Teachers may be informed about a crisis at home, but their involvement is not always sought or welcome just as in the case of bereavement. Children may seek reassurance from teachers about what is happening at home. If children are obviously upset about events at home it is important that contact is established with parents and that basic arrangements for custody and access are known.

If teacher are aware of children whose parents are going through the painful process of separation, they may want to know whether any difficulties are likely to arise in school and how best to help, whether to enquire about family circumstances, and how to relate to both parents, particularly if the non-custodial parent visits the school.

During the initial stages of a family separation, children almost always want as much things and situations to remain the same as it always was, thus the continuing of familiar routines in school is very helpful. Children search for a cause. Many children blame themselves for family difficulties, as the only means of rationalizing the situation. Children need a lot of reassurance that it is not their fault.

Teacher's role during this crisis for the child is significant. They are available to talk without taking sides in matters. With all kinds of grieving, a trustworthy adult who listens, remains calm when the child is upset, but shares something of the child's feelings (without being critical), can help a child to identify and release emotions. It is not inevitable that children caught in the middle of marital separation are going to suffer long-term ill-effects, although they may be upset in the short term. The school can be a secure and stable place for children at the present as well as a bridge to a brighter future.

Separation in the Sunset Years

Separation is a result of marital discord. The unsuccessful marriage may lead partners to decide to live separate. They may go for legal divorce or not, but are emotionally apart and do not live together as husband and wife or as a family. It is generally, men who make situations worse beyond mutual compromise, but in modern society now women are equally responsible. This is occurring more in affluent society where women, too, have access to other men or are economically independent, whether or not they are earning or have enough inherited property. Many times, soon after marriage, partners do not find themselves compatible to each other and decide to separate. But, in other cases, they keep on trying to adjust and many years pass in their effort. But, finding married life meaningless they decide to separate in sunset years of life. Separation at this age is very painful. Generally, one gets the impression that separation or divorce is the best alternative to be followed to escape the problems. For them marriage was a 'net' or 'trap' and separation or divorce is "breaking loose from partner's clutches". But this is in fact a very worrisome attitude and can have dire consequences. It will bring with it all the problems of those Western societies, which have discarded the institution of marriage calling it too boring and old fashioned. The problems of depression, anxiety, drug addiction, criminality and suicide rates are said to be high in the divorced person as well as in their children.

The causes of separation may be many, such as lack of faith, sincerity, concern, mutual understanding, common goals or feeling of love but it has been noticed that increasing impatience, intolerance and frustration in both the partners become a reason for separation in the sunset years. Only men cannot be blamed for their indifference, cruelty and aggression, ego or chauvinism, which lead to separation.

Separating from one's life partner after a life long companionship makes the matter worse, when partners begin to experience loneliness and a feeling of guilt and regret for their act. Many, those who have lesser ego may reunite but sometimes because of their ego, they may feel like uniting again, but do not do so. Adjusting to new conditions, after separation, again is a new challenge. For women, living with parents or other relatives, or living in new neighbourhood or finding new house without anyone to share and care will again be a painful situation. Those who decide to remarry may not find it easy to adjust in new identities. Moreover, the old memories will also appear again and again, and disturb their new life. Therefore, a couple with marital harmony should with a healthy and optimistic attitude, try to face, recognize and treat the underlying causes of the discord and if needed, they may take professional help of a marriage counsellor. In fact, old age is a stage of life when husband and wife both need each other more than ever before. By caring for each other in health as well as in illness, by sharing all the joys and sorrows and by living with each other all the more as completed life partners can enhance the sense of integrity and well-being in each other and thus, the sunset year of life can prove to be a bliss. It has also been seen that, many a times they separate but soon after begin to miss each other. Thus, one should not make haste in taking such decisions.

Some couples have explained that they separated in sunset years because they were never happy and satisfied in life, but because of upbringing of children they remained together and as soon as this target is over, the binding force ends. They find no reason to stay together and separate for living own independent happy life, free from tensions and worries. In fact, they were never in love with each other, but lived only as an obligatory duty. Separation in early years and separation in sunset years both have different impact.

REMARRIAGE

Remarriage may follow the death of a spouse or a divorce. It is more often after divorce than death. Tendency towards remarriage is also increasing because of decrease in negative social attitudes towards divorce and single-hood. Longer the gap between divorce and remarriage, greater are the economic strains especially for non-working or low-pay working women. Generally, people think that remarriage will be successful but many remarriages are not as successful. In fact, most of the causes of divorce lie within individuals, their attitudes, behaviour and personality. Widows have better stable remarriage.

Adjustment in Remarriage

Adjustment is to be made by all—men, women, children and relatives. Adjustment demands breaking of old habits of action, forming new habits as well as new relationships. Remarriage involves adjustment with children and in-laws from the first marriage. Both have to adjust to each other as well as towards children. They must adjust to the role of stepparent. Stepparents and stepchildren take time in adjusting to their new roles. Younger the children better would be the adjustment.

Building of stepparent and stepchild relationships takes time. A stepchild may express fears, doubt, mistrust and insecurity. Anger and rejection may lead to child to purposely misbehave as a way of expressing these feelings. Although step parents can not take the place of absent parents, they can fill the gap the absent parents leave. Showing acceptance and affection and sharing experiences help intimate feelings to grow between the members of the blended family. The family needs time to develop bonds that build a sense of unity and togetherness, and love and security among its members. Cooperative attitudes can help provide the best environment for children to grow and develop. The blended family needs acceptance within the family structure as well as with other relatives and friends in the community to accept them as a family. They need to accept each other and the reality of their situation.

Stepfamilies are families in which one or both partners have children from a previous marriage or relationship. Stepfamilies are sometimes referred to as blended families. Each member the biological parent, the step parent and the child experiences the adjustment process in step family differently which depends on their past experiences and their understanding of the present circumstances. Stepmothers tend to experience greater stress in stepfamilies than do step fathers. Stepfathers are less involved in child rearing as compared to step mothers.

Adjustment becomes exceedingly difficult, if children have developed negative attitude towards stepparents. Children may resent to their disciplinary methods. They resent mothers more than fathers.

Many children feel embarrassment about having a stepparent. It is not that grave if many children known to them are of same type. Embarrassment is also caused by negative attitude of peers or teachers, especially when children bear different surname than the father. This complicates the problems of adjustment to the new pattern of family. If the stepparent has never been a parent before adjustment problems may be increased.

DESERTION

Desertion is the wilful leaving of one mate for another. It is one of the most common reasons for broken homes. In the case of desertion, the whereabouts of the deserting person is not known. The deserters are generally the man. Woman does it rarely, especially if they have children. This is more common among the poor people where they don't want to go for lengthy and costly divorce procedures.

BEREAVEMENT

Another form of disorganization is when one partner is separated due to death. Due to death of one partner, another loses not only company but his or her duty is doubled. In all such situations, insecurity prevails all around. After the death of the husband woman faces many psychological, social and economic turbulences. When wife dies, man feels completely helpless. He is unable to take dual charge—the charge of home and occupation. Generally, men go for second marriage then new series of problems begin. Accepting stepfather or stepmother is very difficult. In some families such crises are resolved in happier way. In Indian culture after the death of a spouse other relatives come forward for help. Many take and share responsibilities of the bereaved family especially those of children. Such persons are brother, sister, grandparents or uncles or aunts.

There are many other situations which cause crisis in the family and family gets disorganized like prolong illness of the bread earner or children, accident or unemployment. All these situations cause heavy burden on family. Under such circumstances family and its members pass through its very critical situations. Their basic needs are not fulfiled. They experience disgrace in society and school also. Due to heavy pressure, children are sent to other relatives homes where they may not get the appropriate status and treatment. Each crisis involves corresponding changes in the family. When one member falls sick others take the role assigned to him. If the sick person is an earning member, economic stress has to be borne, by making alternative arrangements.

Some times bad habits like alcoholism or getting involved in crimes also disrupts the family, when one person is sent to jail then real problems begin. The family loses bread earner or caregiver, it also suffers social disgrace and experience insecurity. Retrenchment or loss in business is other causes of economic crises, where family faces problems.

The same crisis precipitation events affect different families in different ways depending upon the hardships accompanying it, for example, economic losses are tolerated easily by rich families, deaths are tolerated in joint families. The shock of divorce is tolerated in educated and working women families. There are two types of resources to meet the crisis—family integration and family adaptability. The former means the bonds of coherence and unity running through family life in which common interest, affection and a sense of togetherness prevails. Adaptability refers to the family's capability to meet obstacles and accept changes to adjust to new situations amicably. Family must have agreement in its roles, structures, subordination of personality, ambitions to have family goals towards which the family moves collectively and satisfactorily. Having these the family is adequately organized.

15

Mass Media and Sex Education

Watching TV soap operas like Humlog, Buniyad was like watching old home movies or videos of our own families. In many cases we follow the emotional ups and downs of these sagas weekly. Many of our own ideas about families are not formed by real-world experiences but by TV experiences. Television has had a significant influence in shaping many of our ideas, values, and beliefs about the world, including marriage, family and other relationships (Gerbner, Gross, Morgan and Signorielli, 1986).

Indian television portrays around fifty families each week. The dominant TV family dramas are mostly joint families or nuclear families. The families represent some but not all of the different family forms found in our contemporary society. TV families are not true representative of the real life of the majority of Indians or in the Indian sub-continent. It may actually depict family life either imaginative or of Western culture. Television is now a part of family.

Apart from our own families, popular culture may be the most important vehicle by which norms, cultural rules and standards, and values about marriage and family are transmitted. A veritable industry exists to support the advice/information genre. They also transmit norms and information regarding a particular culture. Advice columnists act as moral arbiters as much as parents and other religious leaders. With the media awash in advice and information about relationships, marriage and family, one should evaluate what is presented closely and skeptically. One should look into the moralizing factors also.

Popular culture includes popular music, magazines, movies, hit vernacular languages Hindi/Punjabi film/album songs, and television programs which helps shape our attitudes and beliefs about the world in which we live. Popular culture conveys images, ideas, beliefs, values, myths and stereotypes about every aspect of life and society. It is an important source of information, misinformation and knowledge for us about our culture and traditions marriage, family and other intimate relationship. In fact, the mass media's influence is so significant because we don't often see how actual families (other than our own) interact (Meyrowitz, 1985). The more we rely on popular culture for information and descriptions about life, the more likely we are to mistake the world depicted by the entertainment media for the real world. Television has become an inseparable part of our life. We cannot afford to live without it. We have already started living with it. But now we have to learn how to live with it.

In the Indian context, we should see how sex and vulgarity are very well displayed on the mini screen as well as the big screen. We can see the extreme level of vulgarity in varied satellite network channels and, now increasing vulgarity in pop music albums and Hindi cinema. In action and adventure shows, sexual behaviour is often associated with violence or a display of power and is rarely depicted in the context of a loving or committed marriage relationship or as an expression of mutual affection.

When it comes to the issue of sexuality, television and movies tend to portray the glamorous side, largely ignoring consequences, such as unplanned pregnancy and sexuality-transmitted diseases. These days' soap operas running on various satellite network channels show extra-marital and pre-marital sexual relations, as if they are acceptable part of the society. Television is making unwed mother phenomena popular through serials. Women on screen seldom get pregnant or contract sexually transmitted diseases. Since many teens are heavily influenced by television for their information on sexuality, the consequences of such unrealistic portrayals can be devastating.

We should admit that media especially television is a very powerful medium, too powerful to resist. Those who are working behind the media have all the skills to attract the innocent minds. The television can inform us, entertain us and at the same time it can destroy us. The fact is that we cannot afford to ignore the power of television and the media. Valuable learning can be gained from the media. It is up to the adults to ensure that children's minds emerge enriched rather than endangered.

Certain themes run through sitcoms. In prime-time, television, love in marriage all adversity. "If you just love each other enough you will overcome any problem." Conflict is easily resolved through manipulation, and problems are solved through humour. Physical appearance and beauty are especially important (Moore, 1992; Yerby, Buerkel-Rothfus and Bochner, 1990). Comparatively less marital sex is depicted on television as compared to pre-marital or extra-marital sex. Such portrayals, however, are misleading, as most sexual interactions actually take place within marriage (Michoel, Gagnon, Laumann and Kolta, 1994).

SOURCE OF SEXUAL LEARNING

Sex education requires a recognition that often proves difficult for many adults. Most children become curious about their own bodies and those of others by age 2 or 3 years. When their questions are ignored or punished, they may learn negative sex attitude. Parents should provide as much information as the child can understand and be supplemented by appropriate books. But parents and other adults are not, however, the most frequent sources of sex information. Many fathers and mothers may be quite anxious about their own sexuality and fearful of their child's growing maturity. Sex education is often misrepresented and protested by small but effective groups of opponents. The opponents believe that sex education promotes sexual activity. A major criticism of sex education is that telling adolescents about intercourse, contraception and other intimacies will lead to an increase in sexual relations. Information is seen as removing an inhibitory barrier, encouraging sexual experimentation (Collier, 1981).

In India, people hesitate to discuss sexuality openly. While friends may discuss the subject with each other, they would not normally talk to their parents and elders about it. Parents, too, feel reluctant to discuss sexual matters with their children. Consequently, while children do pick up some information related to sexuality by asking each other, reading books (if they can find one) and through the television, the information that they gather tends to be incorrect and incomplete. This often causes them to indulge in unsafe and irresponsible sexual behaviour.

Sex education will enable the persons to live their life to their fullest capacity. They should be trained to meet their sexual needs appropriately. The various sources of sexual learning for any individual are parents, school, peer, media and partner.

Parents as a Source of Information

Children learn a great deal about sexuality from their parents. They learn not because their parents teach them but set out to be avid observers of their parent's behaviour. Much of what they learn concerns the hidden nature of sexuality (Robers, 1983). In most communities, sexuality arouses a silence, secretive life, bad to think about or talk about. Both young people and parents are embarrassed or distrustful to discuss these secret matters. It is mostly the mother who educates the child about sex.

School as a Source of Information

Sex education in schools and colleges also meets the goal of accurate information. Such information Klien (1984) found improves the teenagers' knowledge in areas such as human reproduction, effectiveness of various contraceptives and sexually transmitted diseases. This helps adolescents to communicate their feelings and talk.

Peer as a Source of Information

Adolescents gather a wealth of (mis) information about sex from one another. One acts out in similar way as the group. If the group is sexually active then there is a lot of pressure on the group members to behave in a similar way and to conform, therefore, continue being sexually active (DiBlasio and Benda, 1992; De Armand, 1983).

Media as a Source of Information

The media have a profound impact on our sexual attitude. Moffatt (1989) observed that media had a major influence on college students sexuality.

Partner as a Source of Information

The experience of interpersonal sexuality is ultimately the most important source of modifying traditional sexual scripts. Both men and women adjust their attitudes and behaviours in everyday interactions. If they are married, sexual expectations and interactions become important factors in their sexuality and an important aspect in marital satisfaction.

SEXUALITY—IT'S MEANING

According to the Sex Information and Education Council of the United States of America (SIECUS): "Human sexuality encompasses the sexual knowledge, beliefs, attitudes, values, and behaviours of individuals. It deals with the anatomy, physiology, and biochemistry of the sexual response system; with roles, identity, and personality; with individual thoughts, feelings, behaviours, and relationships. It addresses ethical, spiritual, and moral concerns, and group and cultural variations." (Haffner, 1990).

One of the primary misconceptions that society holds about human sexuality is that it means the drive to have sexual intercourse. While this may be part of the truth regarding sexuality, it is not the whole truth. Having a physical sexual relationship may be one facet of our sexuality, but it is not the only one or even the most compelling or important. Sexuality is, in fact, very much a social phenomenon (Way, 1982), in that all of us are social creatures who seek and enjoy "friendship, warmth, approval, affection, and social outlets" (Edwards & Elkins, 1988). Thus, a person's sexuality cannot be separated from his or her social development, beliefs, attitudes, values, self-concept, and self-esteem. Being accepted and liked, displaying affection and receiving affection, feeling that we are worthwhile individuals, doing what we can to look or feel attractive, having a friend to share our thoughts and experiences these are among the deepest human needs.

DEVELOPMENT OF SEXUALITY

An understanding of sexuality begins with looking at how the social and sexual self develops. These two facets of the total self must be examined in conjunction with one another, for sexuality is not something that develops in isolation from other aspects of identity (Edwards & Elkins, 1988). Indeed, much of what is appropriate sexual behaviour is appropriate social behaviour and involves learning to behave in socially acceptable ways.

From the time we are born, we are sexual beings, deriving enormous satisfaction from our own bodies and from our interactions with others, particularly the warm embraces of our mother and father. Research shows that the amount of intimate and loving care we receive as infants "is essential to the development of healthy human sexuality" (Gardner, 1986).

The lessons learned during the toddler stage are also important to healthy social-sexual development. The uninhibited pleasure that toddlers derive from exploring their own bodies is sometimes regarded with humor and at other times with embarrassment. If the adults around them accept these self-exploratory activities, children have a better basis from which to enjoy their bodies and accept themselves. This means that adults should impress upon him or her that there are appropriate and inappropriate environments for self-exploration.

In the pre-school and early school years, most children become less absorbed with self-exploration but maintain their curiosity about how things happen. They may disconcert parents by suddenly and directly asking simple (and not so simple!) questions about sexual matters. They are also fascinated to discover that the bodies of opposite-gender playmates are different from their own, and may investigate this fact through staring, touching, or asking questions. This type of behaviour is normal and needs to be treated as such. Strong, emotionally laden reactions on the part of parents can damage children, in that they can learn to feel guilt or shame about their body parts (Tharinger, 1987).

During this time period, children are also consolidating ideas about gender and gender roles, or what it means to be a male or a female. Between the ages of two and three, most children develop a sure knowledge that they are male or female. By age five, most are well on their way to understanding the kinds of behaviours and attitudes that go with being female or male in this society (Calderone & Johnson, 1990).

In the early school years, children's interest in the other gender may lessen in favour of new interests and relationships. Children may reject the opposite gender or show an interest in the opposite gender both are normal, for during the early school years children are learning about themselves as boys or girls. Friendships, playmates, games, and activities are important during this period to the continuing development of the sense of self within a social sphere.

With puberty, which starts between the ages of 9 and 13, children undergo great physical change brought about by changes in hormonal balance (Dacey, 1986). Both sexes exhibit rapid skeletal growth. Physical changes are usually accompanied by a heightened sexual drive and some emotional upheaval due to self-consciousness and uncertainty as to what all the changes mean.

'Adolescence' is the period from 12-18 years of age. This stage of development is marked by physical, psychological and emotional changes. The beginning of physical changes is called the onset of 'puberty', which starts around 11-14 years of age and is completed by 18 years. Puberty is marked by a sudden growth spurt and hormonal changes in the body, leading to development of secondary sexual characteristics such as breasts, body hair, moustache and change in the voice. These changes facilitate the origin of sexual feelings and sexual behaviour in all people. Naturally, these physical changes also demand emotional adjustment. Often, the adolescent does not know how to handle the changes that are happening in his or her body and the emotions that he or she is experiencing. At this age, the peer group, people of the same age becomes more important and the adolescent follows the rules and the codes of the group. These may often be contradictory to the rules and values laid down by the parents and family. Feelings of loyalty towards the peer group often become more important than those for the family. The adolescent also experiences a strong need to assert his or her independence, which may bring him or her in conflict with the parents. Sudden mood swings are also characteristic of this period. The adults, too, start demanding that the adolescent behave more appropriately. Youngsters are expected to behave in a more adult-like manner; yet, for some matters, the adults treat them like children. These conflicting expectations also add to the confusion of the adolescent, who may experience stress, also because of the changes that are taking place in his body. During this stage, most adolescents are prepared for a job, marriage and the related roles and responsibilities of adulthood.

Adolescence follows puberty and often brings with it conflicts between children and parents or caregivers. Adolescents may want to dress according to their own tastes, sporting unconventional clothes and hairstyles that may annoy or alarm their parents. Another is that adolescents often begin to place great importance on having their own friends and ideas, sometimes purposefully different from what parents desire. The influence of peers in particular seems to threaten parental influence. This is the time when incomplete or no information regarding sex would bare its great impact on the individual and, therefore, now is the time to import sex education.

SEX EDUCATION

The goals of sex education are to:

Provide Information

All people have the right to accurate information about human growth and development, human reproduction, anatomy, physiology, masturbation, family life, pregnancy, childbirth, parenthood, sexual response, sexual orientation, contraception, abortion, sexual abuse, HIV/AIDS, and other sexually transmitted diseases.

Develop Values

Sexuality education gives young people the opportunity to question, explore, and assess attitudes, values, and insights about human sexuality. The goals of this exploration are to help young people understand family, religious, and cultural values, develop their own values, increase their self-esteem, develop insights about relationships with members of both genders, and understand their responsibilities to others.

Develop Interpersonal Skills

Sexuality education can help young people develop skills in communication, decision-making, assertiveness, peer refusal skills, and the ability to create satisfying relationships.

Develop Responsibility

Providing sexuality education helps young people to develop their concept of responsibility and to exercise that responsibility in sexual relationships. This is achieved by providing information about and helping young people to consider abstinence, resist pressure to become prematurely involved in sexual intercourse, properly use contraception and take other health measures to prevent sexually-related medical problems (such as teenage pregnancy and sexually transmitted diseases), and to resist sexual exploitation or abuse. (Haffner, 1990).

The main thing is to give direct, honest and short answers that provide specific information. Information about intercourse, conception, contraception and the genetic implications can be simplified and explained in a language that an adolescent can understand.

Sex education is often misrepresented and protested by small and effective groups of opponents. Many people who criticize education believe that telling adolescents about intercourse, contraception and other intimacies will lead to an increase in sexual relations. Information is seen as encouraging sexual experimentation. But, sex education does not lead to an increase in sexual activity. Good sex education encourages people to use precautions. It also gives accurate information. It informs students about human sexuality, effectiveness of various contraceptives and sexually transmitted diseases, AIDS Acquired Immuno Deficiency Syndrome and unwanted pregnancy.

AIDS stands for Acquired Immuno Deficiency Syndrome. AIDS is one of the most serious public health problem that has ever faced the Indian population. AIDS is caused by the Human Immunodeficiency Virus (HIV). This virus may live in the human body for 5 to 8 years before actual symptoms appear. It primarily affects you by making you unable to fight other diseases. These other diseases can kill you. HIV is a very small germ called a virus. HIV makes the body weak and less able to fight sickness. People with HIV in their body go on to become sick with AIDS.

Our body has white blood cells, which fight against disease germs and kill them. These white blood cells protect us from falling sick. When a person has HIV in the body, the virus destroys the white blood cells, which, then can no longer fight against disease germs. This makes the person sick.

Signs and symptoms of HIV/AIDS infection are loss of about ten percent of weight, chronic diarrhoea and vomiting, prolonged fever without an identifiable source, development of pneumonia, development of certain types of cancer, abnormalities with skin, glands and eyes, acute transient illness with fever, muscle aches, headaches, rash or sore throat, experience of fatigue and malaise, lymph nodes may often enlarge around the time of sero-conversion, that is, the point where antibodies against HIV are produced for the first time, development of oral, anal and penile ulcers and herpes zoster, gastrointestinal symptoms including nauseas, coughing or shortness of breath and seizures and loss of normal thought process caused by brain infections.

A person becomes infected when HIV is introduced into his/her bloodstream. There are four main ways in which people become infected with HIV. HIV can be spread through sexual activities from male to female, female to male, male-to-male or female-to-female. HIV may be in an infected person's blood, semen, or vaginal secretions. It is thought that it can enter the bloodstream through cuts or sores-some so small you do not know they are there on tissue in the vagina, penis, or rectum, and possibly the mouth.

Very often people require blood transfusion. Reports indicate that around 5.5 per cent of those living with HIV in India acquired HIV through blood and blood products. You should be extremely careful in receiving blood transfusion from any hospital or health clinic in the country. Make sure that the blood given to you is properly tested and certified HIV negative. When you donate blood make sure that the doctor/nurse uses a sterile needle each time. Sharing needles or syringes, even once, is a very easy way to be infected with HIV and other germs. Sharing needles to inject intravenous drugs is the most dangerous form of needle sharing. Blood from an infected person can remain in or on a needle and then be transferred directly into the bloodstream of the next person who uses it. Sharing of needles and blades may also transmit HIV. If you plan to have your ears and nose pierced or get a tattoo, make sure you go to a qualified technician using sterile equipment. Similarly make sure that your barber uses a fresh blade to shave you. Don't be afraid or shy about asking questions even to a doctor, dentist or nurse.

A woman infected with HIV can pass it to her baby. The baby becomes infected while in mother's womb or as it is being born. There is also some risk of transmission through breast milk. If a woman is infected before or during pregnancy, her child has one chance in three of being born with the virus. There is no treatment to prevent this transmission completely.

There is presently no cure for AIDS. The most effective way to prevent HIV/AIDS is avoiding exposure to the virus, which you can contract by your own behaviour. Prevention is the only method to control the infection. Since many infected people have no apparent symptoms of the condition, it is hard to be sure who is or is not infected with HIV. So, the more sexual partners you have, the greater your chances of encountering one who is infected, and becoming infected yourself. Therefore stick to one mutually faithful partner.

16

Marital and Family Counselling

In day-to-day life many problems arise, person solves them at their own level but sometimes problems are such that they cannot solve them without the help of others. Other's help is required to achieve satisfactory results. Generally, these are the people within one's family, relatives or friends but their guidance may not be very suitable because all people are neither expert nor have complete knowledge.

In marital adjustment, the common varieties of problems do not require the professional services of a psychologist or marriage counsellor. These specialists are necessary for various troubles, but for most of us good first-aid techniques are sufficient to treat the minor ills of marriage. If, instead of foolish neglect, one will give marriage some attention and plenty of common sense, good results are bound to follow. One may not progress towards a solution quite so rapidly. Discussions may go on and on. Yet even in some instances when it is not possible to reach a rational decision, the spouse may benefit from the emotional catharsis involved in talking the whole issue out. This itself is eminently worth while. Where husband and wife feel great affection for one another, the method has still greater chance of success, for affection quickens sympathetic understanding. Love does not conquer all, but love combined with intelligence can conquer most of the problems of the marriage and can lead to a happy married life.

In Indian culture, there was no such trend to go to counselling centers but in Western culture family ties were not so closely knitted, people preferred to go to experts who were qualified, trained and experienced in this special field. They also keep the problem of the person confidential. In our Indian culture, families were close knitted, hence, as soon as problems arises many relatives and friends come forward voluntarily but in general elder members in the family take up this role. Elder either suppressed the problem and conflicts and tried to pull on the relationship with a hope or try to solve the problems. In most of such cases, couple's problems are not resolved, conflicts may be lingered resulting in marital disharmony. Now, with changing family systems in India, more and more people are seeking outside help, which is evident from mushrooming of marriage and family counselling centers in small cities also. Guidance and counselling provided by the experts can help to resolve problems and conflicts, find reasons of marital disharmony, help to eradicate or resolve conflicting reason or situation.

The guidance has been defined differently by social scientists. Various definitions of guidance includes the process of assisting to adjust, process of assisting an individual to find his place, establishing an effective relationship, attainment of self-direction by an individual, process of learning, helping and affecting changes in an individual, and process of helping every individual through his own efforts. According to Spears, the guidance helps to see clearly: where the person has been, where he or she is now, where he or she is going and what he or she has with which to get there.

Guidance is a process of dynamic interpersonal relationships designed to influence the attitudes and behaviour of a person. Guidance is a continuous process of helping the individual develop to the maximum of his capacity in the direction most beneficial to himself and to the society. Thus, it is clear that the purpose of guidance is to help individual in the identification of his abilities, aptitudes, interests and attitudes; to help the individual to recognize his aspirations; to help in obtaining experience for making free and wise choices; to help the individual in developing his potential to optimum level; and to help in focusing to become more and more self-directive. It further helps in developing harmonious relationship and social personal adjustment.

Counselling though with the same aim has some differences. In counselling, the counsellor gets more involved. Here, a relationship is established between the two persons in which one tries to help, another to understand his problem and later on to solve them. There are various types of guidance and counselling, generally divided into three types educational, vocational and personal. Besides these three, a new specialized area emerged which is very wide and useful today. It is known as marital and family counselling.

These days there are rapid changes in the social-personal relationship because of the freedom, exposure and developing technologies. Scientists have analysed three major changes that have affected the marriage—the decline in understanding between marriage partners; the loss of determination to stay married and the development of unrealistic marriage expectation.

Thus, there are three general objectives for marriage counselling. Counsellor helps by increasing understanding through communication; stimulating determination by emphasis on positive attitudes toward the partners; and, developing more realistic expectations through re-evaluation of marriage satisfaction. These are realistic and attainable goals for practical marriage counselling.

The family problems are increasing in the whole society, which is affected adversely by increased conflicts. The higher family conflicts, separation incidence and divorces necessitate the reorientation of people's thinking into marriage, marital relation and family relations. People prefer alternatives of marriage than marriage in itself. The family and marriage counsellors have many roles to play. The marriage counselling involves the physical and sexual aspects of relationship between husband and wife. It also takes care of the social aspect of their personalities so that their relationships are developed and maintained in a healthy way. Thus, in brief, we can say that marriage counselling is to help marital partners to adjust satisfactorily by developing understanding into the purpose of marriage—roles and responsibilities in martial life; and ways of developing love-based relationship and reality-based expectations.

PREMARITAL GUIDANCE AND COUNSELLING

In Western countries, sometimes couples consult a counsellor before marriage. This person may be a licensed marriage and family counsellor or a religious leader or the person who performs the marriage ceremony. The pre-marital counsellor will discuss the several areas of the marital relationship and how well acquainted the couples is with each other's personal qualities. The discussion would be regarding the similarly and differences among the couple, their expectations from marriage, their readiness for marriage, their ability to resolve differences, financial plans, raising up children, sexual adjustment and relationship with the in-laws. Sometimes counsellor may help the couple for planning for the future. In Seychelles, among the natives who are mostly Christians have to attend pre-marital counselling classes for a period of 2 years to six months before the ceremonial marriage takes place in a Church. A religious official performs a ceremonial wedding while a judicial officer performs a civil ceremony.

A guide is someone who leads the way. Guidance is something that is done with a person and not to a person. It is all that is said to guide and influence the behaviour in a positive way. It helps the person to grow and act maturely and learn to be the productive members in the society.

Pre-marital sex refers to the full range of sexual behaviour (everything from holding hands to intercourse) of never married young people and the term pre-marital intercourse refers to sexual intercourse between never-married young people. A pre-marital counsellor can assist couples in evaluating their relationship and also can identify marriage practices required by law. Evaluation of a relationship during engagement period helps to alleviate pains of a disrupting or unhappy marriage. They are wise to break the engagement at this point.

The younger girls and boys these days prefer going to marriage counsellors for guidance in various aspects of married life so that they can live happily after marriage. They want to know about the coming problems of adjustment and prepare themselves for healthy relationship. They also want to know about how to select partner for dating and marriage. Pre-marital counselling helps to prepare fully for married life.

Objectives of pre-marital counselling are to help them to express their feelings and attitudes, to help the couple to relieve fears, worries, and anxieties about marriage, to provide general and specific information, education and guidance about the problems and responsibilities of marriage, to encourage the couple to explore and communicate their individual needs, goals and values separately and preparing the couple to work together towards solution of their problems.

MARRIAGE COUNSELLING

In marriage counselling, the counsellor helps the individuals to explore their own problems and solutions. He first assesses the problem to know the depth of anxiety and the complexity of the situation. They talk to both the partners individually, and then hold sessions for developing insight into the problems and its situations.

Functions of marriage counselling are creating the climate in which the patient can talk about his/her problems, providing for ventilation and emotional catharsis, providing the reassurance of acceptance of the person's attitudes and perhaps some additional reassurance as well, diagnosing the real problem with the person, encouraging personal introspection and evaluation, helping the person to examine all of the possible alternatives and to decide on a specific action and motivating the person toward completing the chosen action. Marriage counsellors help in dating, mate selection, and personality changes favouring pre-marital qualities and later on finding solutions to arising problems in husband-wife relationships.

It is argued that pre-marital sex has an adverse effect on marriage. Sex in Indian society is permitted after marriage. Though, the society at present is seeing sexual revolution but still the cultural norms are adhered by most of the members of the society. Marital sex is the main problem in the marriage these days but talk on it is still not free from difficulty. People, now-a-days have started accepting that woman has sexual desires equal to man and they can also get orgasms. A recent Indian sex survey of married couples spanning over the 15 years between 1988 and

2003 by Dr. Narayana Reddy (2004) shows that the average Indian couple has sex every alternate day in their first five years of marriage, and every third day between five and 10 years of marriage. While the most adopted or preferred coital position is 'man on top' (34%), 35 per cent use more than one position during a session of love-making. And a very large majority (83%) feels that their spouses are equally enthusiastic in sex and participate actively. Also, its hardly the husband's prerogative to initiate sex. For a majority of couples (61%), its either spouse who starts it off, or both. And as many as 43 per cent indulge in foreplay for an average duration of 5 to 10 minutes; more than nine per cent extend it to 15 minutes or more. A significant 47 per cent of couples feel comfortable enough about their bodies to undress fully for sex and just 18 per cent want the lights off while making love. This survey shows that Indians are sexually very active and innovative, willing to be unconventional and experimental to seek their peaks of pleasure.

MARRIAGE ENRICHMENT PROGRAMS

Marriage counselling is to improve marriage with a focus on helping couples identify and resolve existing problems. Organized programs designed to help couples maintain or improve their marriage relationship are called marriage enrichment programs. Its main purpose is to keep the marriage strong and help them to grow. It helps couples in personal growth as an individual, growth as a couple and helps couple deal with financial problems.

Marriage counselling seeks to improve marriages, but usually focuses on helping couples identify and resolve existing problems. As part of the counselling, marital enrichment programs may be used to strengthen various areas of the relationship. Marital enrichment programs are organized programs designed to help couples maintain or improve their marriage relationships. The main purposes are to keep martiages strong and to help them grow. They usually seek to help couples in areas of personal growth, growth as a couple, and finance. Programs focusing on personal growth help each spouse to find ways to grow as a person. They focus on self-awareness or building self-esteem. They try to give individuals a purpose of life, a productive value to be of use. They may include skills for communicating personal feelings and ideas, new areas of personal interest. Programs aimed to make the marriage better or more rewarding, help the couple to grow together. They may aid in solving existing problems, aid in adjustment throughout lifespan or in improvement in the relationship. These programs may specialize in communication and conflict resolution skills. Programs also aim in helping couples deal with financial problems. Such problems often become major conflict area in marriage. The programs may deal with budgeting, spending, financial planning, retirement planning or the management of family resources.

FAMILY COUNSELLING

Family is a unit of members living together, interacting with each other. Since, there are various needs, demands and expectations of members, having different personalities, there are chances that some clashes will occur. There will be conflicts and tensions in relations, which all together upset all the members of the family. Family unity, cohesiveness or peace and organization will face threat. Such situations call for immediate attention. When own efforts at personal level do not succeed, the help of expert counsellors are required who objectively analyzes the problem, goes into the depth and helps in finding the solution. Where intense probing of problems are involved and solution requires changes in attitudes, perceptions and ways of thinking or changes in habits or personality component the work of counsellor begins. He or she listens, assesses and helps in planning solutions.

From beginning in marriage, the first major strain the family unit will have is the advent of the first baby. The second major strain is the last child's leaving the parental home. These two stages and all other stages in between these two, brings changes, which may be difficult to bear hence calls for counsellors help.

Parenthood

Counsellors help in preparing mentally to adjust to the new situation when a baby will arrive. In fact, family counsellor's role begins soon after the marriage in planning family like when to have baby, how much space in two children, signs of pregnancy, health and care during pregnancy, preparation for delivery, etc. Besides, counsellors prepare both husband and wife for getting ready to accept the changes likely to come in social and emotional relationships within family and outside the family.

The Maturational Crisis

The real crisis starts with the birth of the child when parents have to work hard. Counsellors prepare the couple in handling the child, caring the needs of the child and understanding non-verbal behaviour of the child. They also prepare for increased workload for sharing of responsibility and reduction in time that husbands and wives used to spend together. Counselling in infertility, sex-relations and behaviour are other areas.

Parent-child Relations

The growing child run into various types of conflicts with family members. Reasons may be many like children move in wider outside world and learn various new things. He or she develops new expectations where parents have their own cultural, economic and social limitations. Before any major crisis arises, it is advisable to get help from the counsellor. Parents and children both need such a help to have better understanding of each other, social-cultural changes and means of resolution.

Child's behaviour problems are generally, the result of home environment, which is rejecting, overprotecting, pampering, and insecure or too strict disciplinarian. These specific type of parental behaviour results into specific type of behaviour problems. Lack of contact, widens the gap in understanding each other's psyche. They may have high expectations from each other. When parents expect too much beyond child's reach, child devaluate himself.

Family homeostasis refers to the equilibrium, which is established between the various members of the family. To maintain this homeostasis parent of children especially adolescents seek counsellor's help for better understanding and relationships.

Other Relations

Many-a-times after a considerable duration even husbands and wives develop problems. There are family problems due to either domination of one partner and submissiveness of other partner. They are helped to see that they must learn to listen and try to understand their spouse's feelings and needs.

Conflicts develop in relationships with in-laws also. Counsellors may also help in this regard. Counsellors also go in depth of personality problems. Family counsellors have classified disorder families as:

The Perfectionist Family

This type of family is categorized by self-imposed demands for good behaviour. They give importance to marital relationship, childbearing, child-development and other family members even at the cost of personal and family living.

The Inadequate Family

This family depends upon others for encouragement, support and help in solving problems.

The Egocentric Family

This type of family remains confined within itself. It lacks social gatherings.

The Unsocial Family

This type of family lacks social contacts and social rapport.

The process of counselling involves interview, home visits and role-playing etc. It focuses also on strength and competencies. Characteristics of inadequately organized families are conflicting interpersonal relationships, conflicting divergences between husband and wife, cultural divergences between husband and wife, conflicts in aspirations, class membership pressures and economic pressures.

Family counselling helps in other areas also like premarital and extramarital relations (infidelity), extramarital pregnancies, young unmarried mothers, counselling with alcoholics (husbands or wives or children), drug addicts, widows, divorced (helping women to take care her children or building new relationships), never married women or men, middle-aged couples suffering from loneliness. They turn toward each other for strength and reassurance, comfort and inspiration for further living, retiring and empty nest, family with retarded child, how they react on his being institutionalized, death of a family member and counselling families with adolescent children.

In Indian culture, where marriage is considered a bond of several births, increasing divorce rate is alarming. The Indian society emphasizes on love to grow after marriage and the couple relationship be built on mutual interests and likings, caring and understanding which is developed by trust and security given by the marital relationship in itself. Where there is love before marriage, acceptance of the couple relationship by the family members of both the partners becomes necessary for establishing a fulfiling and satisfactory marital relationship. A happy marriage is the most satisfying relationship that life can bring to individual. Achieving a happy union lasting through a lifetime would require real adjustment and harmony at every level of intimate's daily experience, like sexual, emotional, intellectual, economic, social and religious.

Contemporary Indian family faces challenge from both within and outside forces. Differences in adherence to old traditions and in the acceptance of new ways of life and thought at different levels of the various sections of population develops a constraint in family solidarity from within and outside forces include industrialization, modernization, urbanization, educational and occupational opportunities, mobility patterns and other social forces have challenged the traditional conceptions of family life. The establishments of nuclear family because of economic necessities and personal reasons have a strong emotional involvement with the family of origin even after separation. Indian society has high moralistic character emphasizing strong familial bonds that would definitely check the rise of divorce rate. Inclusion of mass media into the integral part of the family, conveys the impression that urbanization, westernization and individualism is weakening the familial bonds, but a look into the reality, shows a far contracting image of family as compared to the one portrayed in the serial families. There is need for the parents to discuss the various role models and outcomes of mass media programs with their children to strengthen the right values and social norms in the children. Influence of western culture till date has not been able to eradicate joint family system or weaken the family ties. Interpersonal rivalries are common on the family front but the ties that bind the family are moral, religious and natural biological ties. Though disintegration of the joint family is evident but only to a small extent. On the whole, family is still intact in the Indian society.

Marriage counsellors while helping couples deal with their problems should take into consideration not only the couple's economic, sexual, and social reasons for conflicts but also their preparation for marriage, parental couple relationships, parental family cohesiveness, influence of mass media and courtship experience of the couple. Then marriage counsellors should suggest constructive adjustment techniques to the couple, ways to seek marital compatibility like inter-personal communication, mutual trust, development of partnership between the couple and acceptance of the partner, discussed in Chapter 7. Here we will outline the criteria for successful marriage, difficulties in marital adjustment and conclude with some necessities for a happy married life.

CRITERIA FOR SUCCESSFUL MARITAL ADJUSTMENT

Happiness of Husband and Wife

They are happy because they derive satisfaction from the roles they play. They are enjoying and playing their roles happily and have made sexual, emotional and personality adjustments.

Good Family Relations

Parent Child Relations

Good parent-child relationships reflect successful marital adjustment and contribute to it. If it is poor then there will be frictions and there will be no peace around.

Good Adjustment of Children

If parents have good relationship then children are also well adjusted, liked by their peers and successful at schools.

Good in-law Adjustment

Husbands and wives who get along well with their in-laws, especially parents, brothers and sisters in-laws, are far less likely to have frictional relationships.

Ability to Resolve Differences

Those who are successful have ability to find solutions to

disagreements with each other or with other family members. They try to understand each other's point of view.

Togetherness

Family enjoys spending time together. They will retain close ties till long. In most Indian families, siblings and cousins are closely tied and they visit each other frequently, attend family functions and sacrifice for each other.

Good Financial Adjustment

Generally, frictions occur due to financial strain. Better-adjusted people make good budget. Regardless of income they manage happily without making complaint against each other.

Good Social Relations

Being happy from inside, such people spread happiness around. They have cordial social relations. Move together to friends and relatives.

Good Physical Health

Good mental well-being results in good physical health.

Optimistic

Happily married person has very positive thoughts towards life. They are always optimistic while facing the hardships of life.

CONDITIONS CONTRIBUTING TO DIFFICULTIES IN MARITAL ADJUSTMENT

Limited Preparation for Marriage

Although sexual adjustments may be easier now than in the past because of more readily available sex information in the home, schools and colleges and premarital sexual experience, most couples have received little preparation in the areas of domestic skills, child rearing, getting along with in-laws, and money management. Therefore, lack in these latter important areas leads to difficulties in marital adjustment.

Roles in Marriage

The trend toward changes in marital roles for both men and

women and the different concepts of these roles held by different social classes and religious groups make adjustment problems in marriage more difficult now than in the past, when these roles were more rigidly prescribed.

Early Marriage

Marriage and parenthood before young people have finished their education and are economically independent derives them of the opportunity to have many of the experiences enjoyed by their unmarried contemporaries or even by their married friends who waited to be financially independent before marrying. This leads to constant envy and resentment that militates against good marital adjustments.

Unrealistic Concepts of Marriage

Adults who have spent their lives in school and college, with little or no work experience, tend to have unrealistic concepts of what marriage means in terms of work, deprivations, financial expenditures or changes in life patterns. This unrealistic approach to marriage inevitably leads to serious adjustment problems, which often lead to divorce.

Mixed Marriages

Adjustment to parenthood and to in-laws—both of which are important to marital happiness are much more difficult in inter-caste, inter-region, inter-racial or inter-religious marriages than when both marriage partners come from the same caste, region, racial or religious backgrounds.

Shortened Courtships

The courtship period is shorter now than in the past and thus the couple has less time to solve many of the problems related to adjustment before they are actually married.

Romantic Concepts of Marriage

Many adults have a romantic concept of marriage developed in adolescence. Overly optimistic expectations of what marriage will bring often leads to disenchantment, which increases the difficulties of adjusting to the duties and responsibilities of marriage.

Lack of Identity

If a man feels that his family, friends and associates treat him as "wife's husband" or if a woman feels that the social group regards her as "just a housewife" even though she is or has been a successful career woman, they are likely to resent the loss of their identity as individuals which they strove hard to achieve and were valued highly before marriage.

NECESSITIES FOR A HAPPY MARRIED LIFE

- Express your love verbally.
- Be physically affectionate.
- Express your appreciation and admiration.
- Have a caring relationship.
- Be faithful. Fidelity in marriage is must.
- Have healthy affectional and sexual pleasure in the relationship.
- Have some interest, habit and preferences that do agree with the partner.
- Have warmth sharing with each other.
- Spend time with each other. Communicate, talk and listen to each other.
- Feel committed and enjoy each other's company.
- Offer each other emotional support system.
- Respect and care for your partner's feelings and their family members.
- Tend to establish a sense of solidarity and modify competing interpersonal ties.
- Express your love materially also.
- Accept your partner's demands and put up with your partner's shortcomings.
- Maintain physical and mental attractiveness.
- Use discussion during conflicts and find solution to problems at hand.
- Tend to establish a sense of cordial familial relationship with your partner's family, relatives and friends.

- Have least expectations from your partner.
- Do unto each other as you would have the other do unto you.

(*Source:* Ratra, Amiteshwar, 2002, Few sources for a sound married life, Monovena, I.C. College of Home Science, CCS, Haryana Agricultural University, Hisar, Haryana, India.)

Glossary

Aahtkoat guna : 36 points.

Aarsimashaf: Reading of the Holy Quran by the newly weds in a Muslim wedding.

Aarti: A form of prayer, also a devotional song.

Aashirwad: Blessing.

Aath: A golden chain in the pierce of the middle of the ear with golden foil hanging from an almond shaped gold ornament below the shoulder.

Aathgath: A definition in Kashmir of the gift of salt and cash given to the newly weds.

Aathhoru: Almond-shaped ear ornament worn by Kashmiri women.

Aathwas: A Kashmiri wedding ritual.

Abstinence: Voluntarily refraining from indulgence in sexual intercourse.

Accessories: The items worn with clothing, such as shoes, handbags, head wear, belts, scarves and neckties.

Acquired Immune Deficiency Syndrome (AIDS): A disease caused by a virus that attacks the cells that normally help the body fight off infection and other diseases.

Active Interaction: Involves physical and verbal exhanges between two people who are doing something together.

Active Listening: Giving the sender some type of feedback.

Adan pradan: Give and take ceremony.

Adhibas tattva: Formal wedding invitation extended to the groom's family.

Adravanu: The Engagement.

Adultery: Voluntary sexual intercourse of a married person with someone else other than her/his spouses.

Affinity: Close relation.

Agape: An unselfish form of love involving unconditional caring and self-sacrificing.

Agarbatti: Incense sticks.

Aggressive: A type of behaviour that includes yelling, name-calling, criticizing, pushing, shoving, and possible violence.

Agni sakshi: With fire as witness.

Agwaani: Receiving the Baraat

Akandhpath: Continuous night and day prayer ceremony.

Akshatha: Showering the couple with rice.

Al Buddo Bhaat: Last meal of the Bride in her Maternal Home.

Alcoholic: The condition of being addicted to alcohol and losing the ability to control its use.

Alimony: Derived from the Latin verb meaning 'to nourish' or 'to give food to', the traditional condition in which the bread winning husband undertook the obligation to support his dependent wife and children even after divorce, now called, maintenance, monetary payments from one ex-spouse to the other for maintenance of her/his economic needs, a financial settlement paid to a spouse.

Alpana: Decorative patterns made of coloured rice paste and water.

Alternatives: The possible choices to consider when making a decision.

Altruistic: Unselfish regard for the welfare of others.

Amavas: No moon day.

Amra pallab: Mango stem with five leaves.

Anand karaj (Lavan Phera): Sikh wedding ceremony.

Androgyny: The social and psychological condition in which individuals can think, feel, and behave in ways that express both instrumental and expressive character traits. Androgyny is the combination of both masculine and feminine qualities in one individual.

Anna prasana: Food giving.

Antenuptial: Prior to marriage.

Anuradha: The 15th of the 28 constellations.

Anxiety: An uneasy feeling that causes people to believe that something terrible is going to happen.

Appagintalu Vadicantu Biyyam: Formal handing over of the bride to the groom's home.

Arasanikkal: Erecting the bamboo stick in front of the marriage.

Ardaas: Type of a prayer.

Arsanikal: Setting standards of a king.

Arundhati Nakshatra: Invoking the blessings of Arundhati and Vashisht.

Asault: Refers to a thereat to cause physical harm to a person.

Atta: Wheat flour.

Attachment: Bonding in the early months of life between an infant and the primary caregiver that endures over time.

Attar: Perfume.

Ayana: Prenupital blessing of the bride.

Azhagu Arathi: Arthi of groom by paternal grand mother.

Baale Birud for the Bride's: Honour of Cutting the Plantain tree stumps party at the Groom's house.

Babul: Father.

Bachelor Party: Celebrating the last days of bachelorhood.

Bagavanam: Tying of 'kappu'.

Baggi: Horse-pulled carriage.

Bahu Bhaat: Acceptance of the Bride into her new home.

Bajubandh: Upper arm ornament.

Bana Betai: Ritualistic bath.

Bangsas: Ancestral lines.

Baraat: Arrival of the groom's side.

Baraat Swagat: Groom is received and welcomed by the bride's father.

Baraati: Members of a marriage procession.

Baran dala: Usually a silver plate containg various ingredients with which the bride and the groom are accepted into their respective families.

Bariksha: A 'match' between boy and girl is arranged.

Bari-palang: Symbolic 'making of the bed'.

Basar ghar: Bengali ceremony after the wedding.

Bashar Ghar: Groom stays over at the Bride's Home.

Bath-Bride: Bride's ritual Bath.

Bath-Groom: The groom's bath.

Bathse: Personal invitations to family and close friends.

Batte Thadpa: Blocking the Path.

Bedi-lutna: Bride and groom leave the mantap after the wedding being.

Beneficiary: The person named in to receive the money.

Bereavement: A period of mourning after the death of a loved one.

Besan: Gram flour.

Bhaat: Gifts from the bride given by her 'mama'—maternal.

Bhabhi: Sister-in-law (brother's wife).

Bhagwan: God.

Bhandawar: Announcement of the wedding.

Bhog: Conclusion of a religious ceremony.

Bicchiya (Bichwa): Toe ring.

Bidaai: Sending off the bride.

Bidaai Ki Rasm: Bridal Send Off.

Bidai: The bride takes leave of her parental home.

Bindi: A symbolic dot on the forehead sported by Indian women.

Bisexuality: A sexual orientation in which sexual behaviour with the same sex and the opposite sex are viewed as equally pleasurable.

Blaming: A pattern in which people accuse others for everything that goes wrong as a way of preserving their own self-esteem.

Blended family: Consists of a husband and wife, of whom one or both have been married before. It also includes children from one or more previous marriages.

Body language: Involves expressing thoughts, feelings, and emotions through body movements, such as facial expressions, gestures, and body motions.

Boijotri: The groom is fetched by the Bride's maternal Uncle.

Bonding: Process of forming a close personal attachment in a relationship.

Bou baran: Post-wedding ritual performed at the groom's house in a Bengali wedding.

Bou bhat: Bengali ceremony where the bride is served food.

Brahma: The creator of the universe.

Brahmacharya: State of celibacy.

Bridegroom's Reception: Receiving the groom.

Career ladder: Each step or career builds on the experiences of the previous step (career).

Career: Refers to the work that a person does over a period of years.

Celibacy: Abstinence from sexual intercourse.

Ceremonial weddings: When friends and family witness the couple's vows taken before a religious official.

Chandlo Maatli: Mutual consent from both sides—Engagement.

Chane-ki-dal: Gram pulse.

Chapparashastra (Achandi): The mantap puja.

Chautanan: Post-wedding ceremonies.

Chedda Cheddi: Playful Teasing of the Bridal couple.

Cheka: Engagement.

Child abuse: Non-accidental, physical and/or mental injury, sexual abuse or exploitation, or emotional or physical neglect.

Child care: The full-time care and education of children.

Chiruya: Dry flattened rice.

Chooda: Wearing of bangles by bride in preparation of the wedding.

Choora: Set of red and white ivory bangles, with inlay work.

Chromosomes: Rod-shaped particles that carry hereditary information from each parent to the child.

Chronic illness: A medical problem that cannot be cured.

Chuda: Bangle ceremony.

Chuda Chadana: Adorning of the Bride with the Ivory Bangle by her maternal uncle and his wife.

Chudi: Bangle.

Chunni: A nose ring; also a long scarf.

Chunni Chadana: Dressing up and blessing of the Bride.

Chunri: A long scarf usually worn by women.

Church Ceremony: Exchange of holy wedding vows.

Citizen: A person who formally owes allegiance to a government. In return, he or she gains rights and responsibilities that are protected by the laws of the government.

Civil ceremony: When family members and a few friends witness a couple's wedding vows taken before a judicial officer.

Civil laws: Laws that govern a person's rights in relation to other people.

Clitoris: Most sensitive female sexual organ consisting of clitoral shaft, clitoral glans, and clitoral hood.

Closed marriage: A synonym for static marriage.

Coercive power: One of the six power bases, or sources of power. This power is based on the dominant person's ability and willingness to punish the partner either with psychological—emotional or physical violence, or with more subtle methods of withholding affection, acting in such a way as to punish your partner.

Cohabitation: Living together in an intimate sexual relationship without traditional, legal marriage. Also called living together or marriage without marriage.

Cohesion: Emotional bonding.

Cohesive: When group members join together because they feel they belong to the group.

Cohort: Persons from the same age group.

Coitus: Sexual intercourse.

Commitment (sternberg's triangular theory of love): The short-term decision that one loves someone and the long-term aspect—the commitment to maintain that love; one dimension of the triangular theory of love.

Commune: A group of adults and perhaps children who live together, sharing aspects of their lives. Some communes are group marriages, in which members share sex; others are communal families, with several monogamous couples, who share everything except sexual relations and their children.

Communication: An exchange of information between two or more people involving the sending and receiving of messages through spoken or written words, facial expressions, or gestures.

Commuter marriage: A dual career marriage in which the marital partners maintain separate residences in order to accommodate the career demands of both spouses.

Complementary qualities: A technique which focuses on a strength to make up for a weakness in another area.

Complementary roles: Each person in a relationship takes on a role that supplies what the other person lacks.

Compromise: A give and take method of resolving differences where both people give in a little to reach a solution that is satisfactory to both.

Conflict-habituated marriage: A marital relationship characterized by ongoing tension and unresolved conflict.

Conflict resolution: A communication skill that encourages a better understanding of the other person's point of view, helping to resolve conflicts in a positive way.

Conflict: When two people disagree on some issue.

Conjugal kin: The term used to define relationships acquired through marriage (spouses and in-laws), as opposed to consanguineous relatives (parents and grandparents), who are blood-related.

Conjugal power: Family power exercised between spouses.

Consanguineous kin: The term used to define blood-related kin (parents and grandparents), as opposed to conjugal kin (spouses and in-laws), who are related through marriage.

Consummate love: A complete love, in terms of Sternberg's triangular theory of love, in which the components of passion, intimacy, and commitment come together.

Coping behaviour: Planned behaviour that helps family members adjust quickly to changes that have taken place.

Courtly love: Popular during the twelfth century and later, courtly love is the intense longing for someone other than one's marital partner—a passionate and sexual longing that ideally goes unfulfiled.

Courtship: Period of social activities leading to engagement and marriage.

Crises: Experiences or events that cause people to make changes in their lives.

Crisis: A crucial change in the course of events, a turning point, an unstable condition in affairs.

Cultural Herigage: Learned behaviour that is passed on from generation to generation, such as behaviour guidelines, beliefs, celebrations, foods and religious traditions.

Custody: The right and responsibility of providing for the children's care until the children reach age eighteen.

Daan: Giving away.

Dahi Bhaat: Arrival of the bride in her in-laws home.

Dahi Koomro: Partaking of a Special Meal by the Bridal Couple.

Dahleej: Threshold.

Dampathi Muhurtha: Combined Muhurtha for the Couple.

Dan Zang: A Kashmiri wedding ceremony.

Darwaza Lagna: Arrival of the Baraat.

Darzi: A tailor.

Dasa: A system of prediction in astrology based on the individual's horoscope.

Dattar: Salt Ceremony.

Decision/commitment: A cognitive component of the triangular theory of love that addresses decision-making about the existence of and commitment to a loving relationship.

Decision-making process: A step-by-step method to guide thinking when a decision is needed.

Defendant: A person accused of wrongdoing.

Dejhoru: Ear ornament.

Democratic decision-making: Group members take part in the selection of one choice and help to carry out the plan of action.

Democratic: A style of leadership in which group members are involved in making decisions; each member's feelings, thoughts, and needs are considered.

Devar Samardhne: Puja seeking gods blessings for forthcoming wedding.

Devgon: A prayer ceremony as part of a Kashmiri wedding.

Devgun: Bathing ritual.

Devitalized marriage: A marital relationship in which a couple have lost the original zest, intimacy, and meaningfulness that were once a part of their relationship.

Devtas: The Gods.

Dhaan: Rice.

Dharemaipuna/Dhareyeruna: The actual unification of bride and groom.

Dhoop: Incense sticks.

Dhoti: An unstitched lower garment worn by men.

Dhruvnakshatra: Looking towards the Pole Star.

Dira gaman: Bengali post-wedding ceremony.

Divorce counseling: Counseling in which partners go together to negotiate conflicts, grievances, and misunderstandings. The goal of divorce counseling is to help a couple separate with a minimum of destructiveness to themselves and to their children.

Diya: Earthen lamp.

Dodhi Mangal: Bengali wedding ritual performed on the wedding day at the crack of dawn.

Dohlagan: Wedding ceremony performed during the morning.

Doli: Bride and groom leave for his home.

Doli Dinner: Celebrations of the bride's arrival into her new house.

Double message: A message which can be interpreted with two meanings.

Dowry: A sum of money or property brought to the marriage by the female.

Dress-Bride: Dressing up of the Bride.

Dress-Groom: Dressing up of the Groom.

Dual-career family: Both husband and wife pursue careers outside the home while maintaining their parenting roles.

Dual-career marriage: A marriage in which the woman and man are heavily committed to their careers.

Dual-earner marriage: A married couple with wife and husband both earning, but not necessarily employed in professional positions.

Dulha: A bridegroom.

Dulhan: A bride.

Dwar pooja: Prayers performed by the family priest, as the couple is led towards the wedding venue, in a Kashmiri wedding.

Economic divorce: The separation of the couple into separate economic units, each with its own property, income, control of expenditures, and responsibility for taxes, debts, and so on.

Emotion: A strong feeling arising without conscious mental or rational effort, such as joy, reverence, anger, fear, love, or hate.

Emotional divorce: Withdrawal of emotional involvement in marital relationship by at least one partner.

Empathy: The capacity to feel what another is feeling.

Empty-nest stage: Period in the family life cycle beginning when children leave home to become independent.

Endogamy: Marriage within one's social, religious, age, racial, ethnic, or educational group, marrying within one's own social group.

Engaged to be engaged: stage during which couples discuss the prospects of marriage and agree to a future engagement.

Engagement: Finalising the marriage.

Environment: A person's surroundings and everything in them, including both human and non-human factors.

Equal opportunity: All persons regardless of race, color, sex, national origin, age, or handicap cannot be discriminated against.

Erogenous zone: Areas of the body particularly responsive to sexual stimulation.

Eros: A romantic love style characterized by a powerful sense of sexual attraction between the two love partners.

Estrogen: Hormone present in both sexes but primarily considered a female sex hormone, maintains lining of vagina, produces breast growth, and controls menstrual cycle.

Ethnic group: Segment of society whose shared identity is based on common ancestry and common culture.

Ethnocentrism: Belief in the superiority of one's own cultural group.

Euphoria: A sense of freedom, well being, and relief.

Exchange theory: Theoretical perspective that sees relationships as determined by the exchange of resources and the reward—cross balance of that exchange. This theory predicts that people tend to marry others whose social class, education, physical attractiveness and self-esteem are similar to their own.

Exogamy: Marriage outside of one's social, religious, age, racial, ethnic, or educational group, arrying a partner from outside one's own social group.

Extended family: Wife, husband, unmarried children, plus one or more other relatives occupying the same household, vertical extension includes three or more generations while lateral extension includes same generations of kin such as aunts, uncles, cousins, and married siblings.

Extramarital affair: Secretive sexual involvement outside of marriage in which emotional commitment exists between the extramarital partners.

Familism: The valuing of traditional family living; also cherishing family values, such as family togetherness, cohesiveness, and loyalty.

Family: Two or more persons who share resources, responsibility for decisions, values, and goals, and have a commitment to each other over time, consists of two or more people living in the same husband that are related by blood, marriage, or adoption.

Family life cycle: Stages in the life of a family that extend from birth, marriage to the death of a spouse.

Family members: Any sexual expressive or parent-child or other kin relationship in which people live together with a commitment, in an intimate interpersonal relationship. Family members see their identity as importantly attached to the group, which has an identity of its own family cohesion. Intangible emotional quality that holds groups together and give members a sense of common identity.

Family of orientation or family of origin: Family that a person is born or adopted into consisting of self, parent(s), and any siblings.

Family of orientation: The family in which an individual grows up. Also called "family or origin".

Family of procreation: The family that is formed when an individual marries and has children, family established by self, spouse, and any children.

Family power: Power among family members.

Family routines: Small events that are repeated on a regular basis in the family and can strengthen the family.

Family system: All family members interact with one another and every member has an effect on every other family member.

Family systems theory: This theoretical perspective examines the family as a whole. It looks to the patterns of behaviour and relationships within the family, in which each member is affected by the behaviour of others. Systems tend toward equilibrium and will react to change in one part by seeking equilibrium by restoring the old system or creating a new one.

Family traditions: Established patterns of behaviour.

Family tree: A list of blood relatives. It is often used to trace hereditary factors such as diseases, life span, and traits from one generation to another.

Family values: Values that focus on the family group as a whole and on maintaining family identity and cohesiveness.

Fantasy: A defense mechanism where people use their imaginary thoughts as an escape to fill their personal needs.

Fixing the Muhurathakal: Erecting the pandal.

Flexible marriage: One that allows and encourages partners to grow and change both as individuals and in the relationship. Its synonym is open marriage.

Foreplay: Kissing, caressing, stimulation, of breasts, and/or oral genital stimulation to heighten the degree of sexual arousal, a prelude to sexual intercourse.

Formal dating: When one person invites another to a planned event. This type of date is structured and requires planning ahead.

Gaach Kouto: A blade of grass.

Gadwa: A round jug.

Gae Halud: Symbol for purification of body and limbs.

Gae Halud Tattava: Gifts sent from the groom's house for the bride as part of pre-wedding ritual in a Bengali wedding.

Gajra: A string of flowers worn in the hair.

Gal Halood/Haldi Uptan: Anointing of the Bride and Groom with turmeric paste.

Galsedi or Parichavan: A welcoming ceremony performed for the Groom by the bride's relatives.

Gana: An auspicious iron bangle with shells and beads.

Ganesh Pooja and Ganesh Sthapna: Blessings from Lord Ganesha.

Garbha lambhara: Impregnation.

Garhi-Bukhi: Puja for the Groom's and the Bride's mother.

Gath Bandan: Tying the nuptial knot.

Gauri Sangaman: The meeting of two Hindu deites, Gauri and Shiva.

Gay: A male homosexual.

Gender identity: The person's persistent, unambiguous definition of self as either female or male, how one feels about self as female or male.

Gender roles: Traits, behaviours, and attitudes socially prescribed for women and men in a given culture.

Gender stereotypes: Strongly held exaggerations or overgeneralizations about gender roles.

Gender: Attitudes and behaviour associated with and expected of the two sexes. The term sex denotes biology, gender refers to social role.

Gendered: The way every aspect of people's lives and relationships are influenced by gender, by whether we are male or female.

Gene: The basic unit of heredity that determines human characteristics or traits.

Genetics: The scientific study of how genes are passed from one generation to another.

Getting together: A courtship process different from dating, in which groups of women and men congregate at a party or share an activity.

Ghara: A pitcher.

Ghara Ghodoli: A Punjabi pre-wedding ceremony of filling water in a pitcher.

Ghataks: Matchmakers.

Ghidhari: Prayers to invite the dead ancestors to the wedding.

Ghodi: A mare.

Ghodi Sajana: Decoration of the mare.

Ghot: A small copper pitcher-shaped vessel.

Ghunghat: A veil.

Goal: Something a person wants to have or to achieve at a certain point.

Godh Barai: Brides lap is filled with gifts.

Gomedak: Precious stone of yellowish hue (onyx).

Gonda: A bag or pouch.

Gordastar: A turban.

Gors: Traditional Kashmiri priests.

Gota: The bright edging of a garment in silver or gold.

Gotra : Lineage.

Graha maitri: Pertaining to the household; native.

Graha Shanti: Prayer for harmony within the planets.

Grahapravesam: Entering of the couple into their new home.

Grahapravesham: The couple is welcomed into the home.

Granthi: A Sikh priest.

Grhya sutras: The Vedic treatise dealing with the performance of religious rites.

Grihasta: A married status.

Grihasta Ashram: State of life of married person in Hindu traditions.

Group dating: Several boys and girls spend time together, developing friendships with others in the group.

Group marriage: A family form in which several couples share a household and sexual relations.

Groups: Two or more people who interact and have an effect on each other.

Gruhapravesha: Welcoming the bride into her new home.

Guchedar Nath: Heavy tasseled nose ring.

Guidance: What one does with or for a person in order to enable adjustment to the environment.

Gulgule: A kind of sweetmeat.

Gumcha: Cloth draped around the shoulders.

Gurdwara: Holy shrine of the Sikhs.

Gur-ke-bheli: A brick of sweet molasses.

Guru Granth Sahib: The Sikh religious book and the present Guru.

Guru Granth Sahib rumala: A handkerchief or covering for the religious book.

Gutka: A Sikh religious handbook.

Haar: A necklace.

Haathon main mere: Put henna on my hands too . . . (lyrics of a song) bhi mehandi lagao.

Haldi and Tel: Turmeric (haldi) and oil ritualistic bath.

Haldi Ceremony: Purification and Beautifiction of bride.

Haldi choora: A pre-wedding ceremony which involves anointing the bride with turmeric paste.

Haldi Ka Din: The beautifying of the Bride with turmeric paste.

Haldi lapetan: Another name for the pre-wedding ceremony, where a paste of turmeric and sandalwood is applied to the bride-to-be.

Hasta Milap: Tying of the marital knot.

Hasthamilap: Tying of the wedding knot.

Hathevaro: Hand Fastening.

Havan: Sacred fire is lit.

Havan kund : The vessel in which fire is lit for the prayer.

Havan samigri: Ingredients for the prayer ceremony.

Havan-purnavati: Conclusion of the havan.

Heredity: The sum of the qualities that a person inherits from his or her parents.

Heterogamy: Marriage between partners who differ in race, age, education, religious background, or social class.

Heterosexuality: Preference for sexual activity with persons of opposite sex.

Heterosexuals: Individuals who prefer sexual partners of the opposite sex.

Holy Matrimony: Wedding Ceremony.

Homa or Havan: Sacred fire is lit.

Homam: Sacred fire.

Homogamy: Marriage between partners of similar race, age, education, religious background, and social class.

Homophobia: Fear, dread, aversion to, and often hatred of homosexuals.

Homosexuality: Preference of sexual activities with persons of same sex.

Homosexuals: People who prefer same-sex partners.

Hostility: When a couple continually argues or quarrels without settling conflicts or agreeing on solutions.

Hriday Sparshmantra: Couple takes a vow to be loyal to each other.

Human Immunodeficiency Virus (HIV): The virus that causes AIDS. The virus attacks cells that normally help a person fight off infection and disease.

Human resources: Personal qualities and characteristics that come from within a person, also the people who provide support in some way.

Hymen: A fold of mucous membrane, partly closing the vagina, which stretches or ruptures at first sexual intercourse if not previously stretched through strenuous exercise.

Hypergamy: A marriage in which a person gains social rank by marrying someone of higher rank.

Idealization: The tendency to perceive a loved one as more ideal than they actually are.

Identity: A sense of inner sameness developed by individuals throughout their lives.

Indra: The Hindu God of rain.

Infatuation: A strong feeling of attraction between a male and a female that tends to be self-centered or one-sided.

Infertility: A couple's inability to conceive a child after trying for a year or more, or the mother's inability to a child carry to full term.

Intercaste marriage: A marriage in which wife and husband are of different castes.

Intercourse: The insertion of the penis into the vagina, also called coitus.

Interfaith marriage: A marriage in which wife and husband are of different religions.

International laws: Laws that govern interactions with other countries or foreign governments.

Interracial marriage: A marriage in which the wife and husband are of different races.

Intimacy (Sternberg's triangular theory of love): Close connected, and bonded feelings in loving relationships, including sharing oneself with the loved one; one dimension of the triangular theory of love.

Intimacy: Feelings of closeness connectedness, and bonding which one experiences in loving relationships.

Intrinsic marriage: A marriage in which the emphasis is on the intensity of feelings about each other and the centrality of the spouse's welfare in each mate's scale of values. Intrinsic marriages are primary, intimate relationships.

Isaivu Pidimanam: Legal Agreement.

Jaimala: Exchange of garlands between bride and groom.

Jal dhala bhat: Rice cooked in water.

Janampatri: Horoscope.

Janavasam & Nichayathartham: Inviting the groom to the mandapam and sorting out.

Janeo: A sacred thread.

Janya: Sacred thread ceremony.

Jaymala: Bridal couple garland each other.

Jealousy: Emotional pain, anger and uncertainty arising when a valued relationship is threatened or perceived to be threatened, a negative response to a real or imagined threat resulting from the actual or potential loss of a relationship partner.

Jija: Brother-in-law.

Job: A position in which a person works to earn an income.

Joint custody: Following divorce, both parents legally share in the decisions and responsibilities of the children.

Joint family: Several generations of one family live together, sharing home and family activities.

Jon: Barley.

Jora Katai: Official collection of trousseau.

Jua & Muti Bund: Light hearted traditional ceremonies.

Kaccha Khana: A special meal for the Baraatis.

Kacchi Misri: Acceptance of Alliance.

Kahwa: Special Kashmiri tea seasoned with cardamoms and almonds.

Kaichi Utrrudal: Feast.

Kajal Lata: A small container for kohl or eye makeup.

Kajwat: A grinding stone.

Kaleva: Bride's brother invites his sister to her maternal home.

Kalgi: A crest.

Kaliras: Silver or gold ornaments strung to the bangles, worn by North Indian brides.

Kallan: Name of a South Indian community.

Kalpush: Part of a Kashmiri bride's headgear.

Kalyana Venu & Mama Venu: Gifts for bride by maternal uncle

Kalyanamaurappa: Arranging a 'match' between a boy and a girl

Kangan: A bracelet.

Kangana: Red thread ceremony.

Kanganam: Tying of sacred thread.

Kangna Bandhana: Tying of the bracelet on the couple.

Kangna Kholna: Untying of the bracelet.

Kanikadanam: Giving away of the bride.

Kanishran: A ceremony where the bride is bathed with a mixture of water, rice, milk and curd to the chanting of hymns.

Kankana shastras: Invoking blessings from the Gods.

Kankan-bandan: Groom and bride put bangles on each other.

Kanya daan: Giving away of the bride.

Kanya Nirakshan: Introduction or "Mooh Dikhai of the Bride".

Kanyadaan: Giving away the bride by her parents.

Kanyadanam: Giving away of the bride by her father.

Kanyadhan and Mangalyadharanam: Giving away of the bride.

Karik Muripa also known as Panda Pani: Cutting vegetables for curry, erecting the Pandal.

Karma: Deeds of a person.

Kasamdry: Ceremony signifying moral commitment to the marriage.

Kasar thala: A brass plate.

Kashi Yatra: Mock pilgrimage.

Kashiyathre: Groom prepares for pilgrimage to Kashi.

Kasumala: A necklace of coins.

Kelneeru: Purified water is brought home from the well or river.

Khol Barana: The marriage alliance is confirmed.

Kirtan: Religious recital.

Klalyanam Vivaham: Wedding ceremony.

Kodiyaal or Koru Arapuvavu: Advance party.

Kohvar: Bridal bed.

Kolam: Decoration of the house with rice flour paste.

Kombarek Kootuva: Leading the groom to the bridal chamber.

Korath: Groom is personally invited to come to the wedding.

Krool khanun: Decorating the door of the bride and groom's house by her/his paternal aunt.

Kshoura (part of the Muhurtha): Ritual Shave for the groom.

Kubipatta: Image of Saint Kuber worshipped in Bengal.

Kulam Vazhum Pillai: Handing over household resposibilities to the bride.

Kulchas: A kind of bread.

Kumarpet Ka Bhaath: A special meal prepared for the bride and her girl or Kumarpet Utaarna.

Kund: A square iron container in which oblations to fire are made.

Kundli: Horoscope.

Kunwar Kaleo: Morning after the wedding ceremony.

Kuri Maaduva: Betrothal Ceremony.

Kurta: A kind of shirt.

Kuvardhoti: A ceremonial gift for the bride from her in-laws prior to the wedding.

Laadi: A bride.

Laaja-Havan: Maternal uncle puts toe-rings on bride.

Ladis: Rows or strings.

Lagan Mahurat: Auspicious time set for the wedding.

Lagan or Lagna: The actual wedding ritual.

Lagan Saath: Auspicious time for the marriage.

Lagana: The first house of the horoscope.

Laja Homam: Offering puffed rice into the fire.

Lajahom: Bride Takes Vows to remain in her husband's home.

Lakshmi: Goddess of wealth.

Latchkey children: Children who regularly go home after school to an empty house or apartment.

Launching period: The time when young adult children leave home for post-high school education or a career.

Lava Chidakna also known as Pheras or Parikrama: Seven steps around the Fire.

Lavan: Hymn.

Legal divorce: The ending of a marriage through the legal process.

Legal separation: A legal agreement for the couple to live apart, to divide their property, and to provide for their children.

Legisatures: Law-making governmental bodies.

Lesbian: A female homosexual.

Libido: Sexual drive or desire.

Lifestyle: The way a person chooses to live.

Livun: A ceremony where sanctifying of Kashmiri houses takes place before the marriage ceremony starts.

Love style: A distinctive character or personality that loving or lovelike relationships can take.

Love: A deep and vital emotional resulting from significant need satisfaction, coupled with a caring for and acceptance of the beloved, and resulting in an intimate relationship. Love may make the world go round, but it's a lot of work too.

Ludus: The love style that focuses on love as play and on enjoying many sexual partners rather than searching for one serious relationship. This love style emphasizes the recreational aspect of sexuality.

Maanziraat: Ceremonial application of mehandi held before the actual marriage ceremony.

Madhuramvekal: Traditional ceremony held the day before the church.

Madva Bandhana: Constructing of the Wedding Mantap.

Magni or Sagai or Kudmai: Engagement.

Mahurat: Auspicious day or time for a particular ceremony or event.

Maira: Mama (maternal uncle) gives gifts to the bride.

Maiyan-pe-geayan: A condition in which the girl remains in old clothes and oil in the hair usually for one or two days before the wedding.

Mala badal: Exchange of garlands.

Manamal: A golden thread tied to the foreheads of both the bride and the groom.

Manavarai: Blessing of the couple.

Mandap: A raised canopy made for the marriage ceremony, or the wedding altar.

Mandap Aarohan: Decorating the mandap.

Mandava Mahurat: Blessings before the installation of the canopy.

Mandav-Saro: Planting of Mango Sapling.

Mandva Mahurat and Griha Shanti: Constructing of the Wedding Canopy.

Mangal ghot: A small pitcher-shaped vessel.

Mangal sutra: The wedding necklace.

Mangala Dharane: Tying of 'thali'—gold ornament which is sign of.

Mangalasnana: Ritualistic bath.

Mangalsutra: Gold chain tied on the brides neck by the groom.

Mangalyam: Stringing of matrimonial necklace.

Mangani or Mangni: Engagement.

Mania: The love style that combines strong sexual attraction and emotional intensity with extreme jealousy and moodiness, in which manic partners alternate between euphoria and depression.

Manjha: A pre-wedding ceremony where the girl is anointed with turmeric paste.

Mantras: Hymns.

Manu: The most prominent law-maker of the Hindus.

Marakkayar: A Muslim community.

Marchawangan pakore: Chillies covered in flour and fried.

Marital adjustment: The process couples use to modify their relationship as needs throughout their married life.

Marital roles: Responsibilities and expectations a person may be expected to fulfil after marriage, such as spouse, friend, wage earner, cook, caregiver, or housekeeper.

Marriage: The wedding ceremony.

Marriage counselling: Meeting with a professional to try to improve a couple's relationship.

Marriage enrichment program: With goals to increase self-disclosure, and intimacy and to develop communication and conflict resolution skills among the partners.

Marriage gradient: The sociological concept that men marry down in educational and occupational status and women marry up may be the bottom of the barrel.

Marriage: Legally binding contract between a woman and man which conveys certain rights and privileges including sexual exclusivity, legitimization of any children born of the union, and economic responsibilities.

Masturbation: Pleasurable self-stimulation of the genitals.

Matha tekna: Taking the blessings of the elders.

Maturation: The emergence of physical characteristics through the growth process.

Mature love: A long-lasting, caring, and giving type of love.

Mauli: A red coloured sacred thread.

Maulvi: A Muslim priest.

Mayara: Exchange of gifts between the two families.

Media: Sources of information and entertainment that include television, radio, movies, videos, newspapers, and magazines.

Mehandi: Henna.

Mehendi & Sangeet: Beautifying of the Bride.

Mehendi & Shukraana: Receiving of blessings and trousseaux by the bride.

Mehendi: Henna ceremony.

Mehenzeraat: Mehendi ki Raat—henna ceremony.

Meher: Dowry given to bride's family.

Mehndi: Gresh henna paste appplied in designs on brides ha.

Melkattu: Making of the Canopy for the wedding ceremony.

Mental health: The overall condition of a person's attitudes.

Messages: A communication skill in which partners avoid the word "you", speak directly to rather than about each other in order to avoid placing blame, and show ownership of problem.

Milni: Reception of the groom and his side by the bride's.

Mixed marriage: Any marriage with extreme differences although usually applied to race, religion, or nationality.

Mixed message: Two simultaneous messages that contradict each other; also called a double message.

Modern society: Social scientists refer to advanced industrial societies as modern because these tend to encourage individualism, social and personal change, and flexibility.

Monogamous: Having only one sexual or marriage mate at a time.

Monogamy: The sexually exclusive union of a couple.

Mooh Dikhai Ki Rasam: Introducing the Bride to her husband's family

Mooh-dekai: Bride is 'seen' by the grooms family.

Mook-dekai : Bride is seen by all and given gifts.

Mook-Dekai or Vadu Milan: Introducing the bride to her husbands family.

Mores: folkways believed to be of compelling social importance by group members.

Mou dikhai: Seeing the bride's face.

Mudha-Tikka: Engagement ceremony.

Muhuratham: Wedding ceremony.

Muhurtham or Lagnam: Wedding ceremonies commence.

Mujchatni: A dish comprising white radish mixed with green chillies and curds.

Mukut: A crown.

Murthasaese: Ceremony receiving the blessings of family, elders.

Myth: Belief that is held uncritically without examination.

Naandi: Pre-weding puja.

Naandi or Vratham: Ritual bath and adorning of bride and groom.

Nadi: Navel.

Nahn: Sacred Bath or Nahn.

Nai badye: Prime offering to the Lord.

Nakshatras: Constellations/stars.

Nalagu: Wedding Ceremony.

Naligadun: A wide belt that a traditional Kashmiri bride wears over her attire.

Namaskaram: Blessing of the bride and groom by the elders.

Nandi: Mythological bull.

Navgrahi Puja: Prayers to all the Planets.

Neer Edpa or Ganga Puja: Fetching Water from the River or Well.

Neo-local residence pattern: The newlyweds will leave their parents homes and set-up their own.

Nichaiyahtartham: Engagement.

Nichayadartham: Engagement ceremony.

Nikaah: Marriage Contract.

Nikaahnama: The Muslim wedding certificate.

Nikasi: Groom leaves for the wedding venue.

Nischaithambul: Engagement ceremony.

Nischaitharthum or Pradhanum: Engagement ceremony.

Nischathartham: Confirmation of commitment to be wedded.

Nischitartha: Auspicious date is fixed for the wedding.

Nischitattham: Engagement ceremony.

Niyams: Rules.

No fault divorce: The legal situation in which a partner seeking a divorce no longer has to prove grounds.

Nuclear family: A family group comprising only the wife, the husband, and their children.

Oonjal or Sambandhmale: Exchange of garlands between bride and groom.

Open marriage: A synonym for flexible marriage, in which partners allow and encourage each to grow and change over the years. Open marriages need not be sexually open; they can, by mutual agreement, be sexually exclusive.

Orgasm: Culmination of sexual excitement leading to sudden physiological and psychological release of sexual tension.

Oxytocin: Pituitary hormone that triggers maternal milk release and causes uterine contractions, helps the uterus return to its normal shape following children.

Padla: Bridal outfit gifted to the bride.

Pagadi: Turban.

Paindlipilla or Haldipaspu: Ritual bath and adorning the bride.

Pandal: A covering used for public meetings.

Pandalkal or Chapra: Blessing the pandol (canopy) at the wedding venue.

Pandit: Priest.

Pani Grahan Sanskar: Groom Pledges to look after His Bride.

Papdaipu: Ancestor worship.

Parchan: The bride is received in her new home.

Parenting: The rearing of children within a family to conform to the social group in which they were born.

Parikrama: Taking of the 4 steps around the fire.

Parwati: Hindu Goddess—wife of Shiva.

Pashmina: Cloth made of soft fine wool.

Passion (Sternberg's triangular theory of love): The drives that lead to romance, physical attraction, sexual consummation, and so on in a loving relationship; one dimension of the triangular theory of love.

Passion: A drive which leads to romance, physical attraction, and sexual involvement.

Passive interaction: When a person is involved only as an observer or listener.

Patri Patra: Bengali engagement ceremony or confirmation of a marriage alliance.

Patrika: A written marriage contract.

Peers: The other people in a person's age group.

Personality: The sum of all inherited and learned behavioural traits that combine to make a unique person.

Petting: Physical contact which may lead to sexual arousal and/ or orgasm but does not involve sexual intercourse.

Phalikalu Ceremony: Germination of 9 grains for prosperity.

Phera: Formal visit of bride to her parent's home.

Phera dalana: Taking a round.

Pheras: Circling the sacred fire and taking the holy vows of matrimony.

Phere: Circling the sacred fire.

Phir lath: A Kashmiri post-wedding ceremony.

Phool Sajjaya: Bride is decked with flowers on the third night after marriage.

Phool-Mudi: Flower and ring ceremony.

Pili-chithi: Written acceptance of marriage sent to bride's family.

Pithi: Blessings and purification of bride.

Polyandry: A marriage of a woman with plural husbands.

Polygamy: A marriage system in which a person takes more than one spouse.

Polygyny: Describes one man with multiple wives.

Ponn Pareyuuva: Seeking a Girl's hand in marriage.

Pool of eligibles: A group of individuals who, by virtue of background or birth, are most likely to make compatible marriage partners.

Poomanam Iduthal: Blessing of the couple.

Poovai Arithal: Arrival of the groom in the bride's house.

Potto Bastra: Welcoming the Groom.

Power: The ability to exercise one's will. Personal power, or autonomy, is power exercised over oneself. Social power is the ability to exercise one's will over others.

Pragma: A logical loving style concentrating on the practical aspects of the relationship involving a rational assessment of the partner.

Prasad: A blessing or offering to an idol.

Pregnancy: The condition of carrying a developing baby within the uterus.

Primary group: A group, usually relatively small, in which there are close, face to face relationships. The family and a friendship group are primary groups.

Psychic divorce: Regaining psychological autonomy after divorce; emotionally separating oneself from the personality and influence of the former spouse.

Puberty: An adolescent growth spurt that occurs at the time when reproductive organs mature. This sexual maturity in males and females takes place when certain hormones are released in the body.

Pucci Misri: Engagement.

Puddishuttal : Ceremony to ward off any evil.

Puja: A Prayer.

Purohit: A priest.

Qoran or Koran: The Muslim Holy Book.

Rangoli: Attractive patterns made of coloured paste of rice flour and water or flower petals.

Readiness for divorce: A state combining a willingness to take responsibility for one's own contribution to the breakup, seeing the alternatives to the marriage as somewhat appealing, and feeling comfortable with the decision to divorce without extreme vacillation over an extended period of time.

Receptions: Post-wedding party.

Registering the marriage: Legal agreement between both families.

Remarriages: Marriages in which at least one partner has already been divorced or widowed.

Remarried family: A family consisting of a husband and wife, at least one of whom has been married before, and one or more children from the previous marriage of either or both spouses.

Retirement: The end of paid employment.

Roka: Betrothal ceremony.

Rokna or Thaka: Acceptance of the Alliance.

Role sharing: A way of handling some responsibilities by working together to carry out a task.

Role: A way of acting to fulfil certain responsibilities in life, most often taught by the family, expected behaviour associated with a particular social position.

Roli: Powder prepared from a mixture of turmeric and lime used in painting the forehead or for prayer ceremony.

Romantic: One who takes an impractical view of love.

Romantic love: The exhilarating feeling that can spark a relationship that may then grow into mature love.

Romanticizing: Imagining or fabricating many qualities of a person the romanticizer wants to love, as well as many sentimentalized aspects of loving, marriage, parenthood, sexual expression, and so forth.

Romeo and Juliet effect: Circumstance in which parental interference increases the romantic attraction between two people leading to further rebellion against the parents.

Rot lagan: Marriage at night.

Roth Khabar: A Kashmiri ritual where bride's parents send roth, a bakery cake to bride's in laws on an auspicious Saturday or Tuesday.

Rukhsat: Farewell ceremony.

Ruksati: Bridal send off.

Rupia Peravanu: The Unofficial Engagement.

Saat pheras: Circling the sacred fire seven times and taking the holy vows of matrimony

Saath: Auspicious timing.

Safa : Head gear.

Safe sex: sexual behaviour that is more likely to leave each partner free of sexually transmitted disease and psychological scars associated with feelings of guilt.

Sagaai: The engagement ceremony

Sagai: The ring ceremony

Sagan: Pre-wedding ceremony; also an auspicious gesture.

Sagan-ka-thal: An auspicious plate.

Sagari: Decorating the Bride with Flowers by the Boy's relative.

Salary: A set amount of money that is paid for all the work that goes with a job description.

Sambandhi Virandh: Exchange of gifts between the two families.

Sampradhan: Ritual of giving away the bride.

Sangeet: Celebration with singing of Punjabi songs and dance.

Sankha Porana: A Bengali ritual of wearing conch shell bangles.

Sanmana Oota & Mamiseike: Dinner in honour of the groom.

Sanskars: Purificatory rites or rituals followed from time immemorial.

Sanzvaru: Decorating the bride.

Saptapadi: The seven vows.

Saptapathy: Seven steps around the sacred fire.

Sapthapathy or Saptpadi: Seven steps.

Sarbala: Care-taker of the groom.

Sari: An unstitched garment (usually 6 yards long worn with a blouse)—the traditional outfit worn by women in India.

Sarpench: Headgear worn by men.

Sarvana: Taking around the head.

Sasural: In-law's house.

Satavaro: Reception.

Satpathy: Seven steps around the fire.

Satraat: A Kashmiri post-wedding ceremony where the bride returns to her parent's house with her husband.

Seedha pallu: Drape of sari taken on the right side.

Seedhe haath tanni kadai: A ritualistic bath.

Seer Bakshanam: Sweetmeats prepared to be sent along with the bride.

Seer-Guthi: Applying vermillion or sindhoor on the brides head.

Sehera Bandi: Blessing for the groom by the elders.

Seherabandi: Tying of the groom's pagadi.

Sehra: Groom's headgear or veil usually made of flowers.

Sehra Bandhi: Decorating the Groom with traditional Headgear.

Sej: The wedding bed.

Sensuality: A more general term than sexuality, conveying a general awareness and readiness to respond to experiences from all of the sense organs.

Sesha: Blessing the couple.

Sex chromosomes: Male (XY) and female (XX) chromosomes that determine the sex of a child.

Sex-linked traits: Traits that are determined by recessive genes on the sex chromosome X.

Sex roles: A culture's definition of how males and females should behave.

Sex: The different chromosomal, hormonal, and anatomical components of male and females at birth.

Sexual abuse: Sexual contact or interaction between a child or teen and an adult, can be physical or non-physical.

Shaadi: Actual Wedding Ceremonies.

Shaadi Ki Rasm: Vows Taken by the Couple.

Shabad: Sikh prayer songs.

Shagan: Blessing with Gifts.

Shagun and Badia Ceremony: Goodwill gestures sent to the boy's side.

Shaka Paula: Adorning of the Bride by 7 married ladies.

Shamiana: Tent or covering.

Shankh: Conch shell.

Shastras: Holy books of Hindus.

Shilarohan: Mantras chanted to solidify the union like a rock.

Shiva: One of the Hindu Gods—the destroyer.

Shivratri: A Hindu festival celebrating the birth of Lord Shiva.

Shlokas: Prayers.

Shri Akhand Paath: Continuous reading of Guru Granth Sahib, Holy book.

Shubh Mahurat: Auspicious timing.

Shubho Dristi: A Bengali wedding ritual.

Significant others: People whose opinions about one are very important to one's self-esteem.

Sindoor: Groom applies the vermillion powder on his bride.

Sindoordaan: Applying the vermillion powder.

Single: Any person who is divorced, widowed, or never-married.

Single-parent family: A family consisting of a never married, divorced, or widowed parent and biological or adopted children.

Snathakam: The beginning of the wedding.

Social institution: A system of patterned and predictable ways of thinking and behaving—beliefs, value, attitudes and norms concerning important aspects of people's lives.

Social power: The ability to exercise one's will over others.

Socialization: Process by which one learns the rules of a given society in order to function effectively within that culture, the process by which society influences members to internalize attitudes, beliefs, values and expections.

Sole custody: One parent cares for children on a daily basis with assumption of all decisions and responsibilities.

Sprinkling of Water: Invoking blessings of the deities on the Couple.

Stepfamily: Remarriage in which one or both marital partners has child (ren) also called reconstituted or blended family.

Sternberg's triangular theory of love: Psychologist Robert Sternberg's formulation of love, in which a variety of types of love are constructed from the three basic dimensions of passion, intimacy, and commitment.

Storge: An affectionate, companionate style of loving.

Stri achai: A Bengali pre-wedding ceremony.

Stridana: A woman's worldly treasures.

Suhaag raat: Wedding night.

Swinging: A marriage agreement in which couples exchange partners in order to engage in purely recreational sex.

Symbolic interaction theory: Perspective on family life that takes as its starting point the meaning behaviour has for family members and the interplay between self-concept and family interaction.

Systems theory: Theoretical perspective that examines the family as a whole. It looks to the patterns of behaviour and relationship within the family, in which each member is affected by the behaviour of others. Systems tend toward equilibrium and will react to change in one part by seeking equilibrium by restoring the old system or creating a new one.

Tali: Neck ornament.

Tattvas: Gifts exchanged between the bride and the groom's families before and after the wedding.

Tekni: Horoscope.

Tel Baan: Ritual bath.

Temperament: Inborn qualities of reacting to the world.

Thaaka or Roka: Anouncement of the engagement.

Thali: A pendant for the auspicious wedding necklace.

The Ashirbaad: Engagement.

The Chandlo: Acceptance of the Alliance by both families.

The Lagna: Wedding Broken up into the below mentioned segment.

The Mudi: The engagement ceremony.

The Pithi: Beautifying the Bride and the Groom for the nuptia.

The Vows: Strictly Religious Part of Marriage.

The Wedding Procession: Groom's Proceeds to the Bride's Home.

Thimbu Kattudal: Tying of the matrimonial thread around the bride's.

Thiru Pootuthal: Matrimonial blessing.

Thirupootu Ceremony: Welcoming of the bride in her new home.

Tikka: Gifts for the groom.

Tilaak: Bride's brother visits groom's home bearing gifts for him.

Tilak: Giving gifts to the groom before the wedding.

Total marriage: A married relationship in which partners are intensely bound together psychologically.

Traditional family: Consists of a wife, husband, and their children living in their own household supported by the father's earnings while the wife concentrates on domestic activities and family life.

Trust: Permits the transfer or property or income from the investor to a second group (trustee) for the investor's beneficiaries.

Turmeric Bath: Cooling off of the bodies of the bride and groom.

Unconditional love: The parent's ability to love their children under any circumstance.

Unpaid family work: The necessary tasks of attending to both the emotional needs of all family members and the practical needs of dependent members, such as children or elderly partners, and maintaining the family domicile.

Upanayana: Invitation.

Uptan : Haldi Ceremony, beautification of bride.

Urdha-Morthu: Grinding daal—a traditional and religious cerem.

Uroos: A Muslim bride.

Utilitarian marriage: A union begun or maintained for primarily practical purposes.

Vaana: A formal commitment.

Vadava Vanu: Sending off of Bride and Groom.

Vadhu Pravesh: Bride enters her husband's home.

Valeena: Muslim wedding reception.

Valima: Wedding Reception.

Values: The ideals and beliefs that a person considers important and that influence his or her decisions and actions, basic beliefs with which a person determines her/his life goals, interests, and behaviour.

Vanwa: Oil Ceremony.

Vara Puja: Puja honouring the groom.

Varadh-Patra: Religious ceremonies performed in honour of dead.

Varamala : Exchange of garlands between bride and groom.

Varan: Belonging to work or duty.

Varapuja or Jaanvasam: Heralding the arrival of the groom and his family.

Varghodo: Groom's Procession.

Variv: Bride's in-law's house (as referred to in Kashmir).

Varmaala or Varmala: Wedding garland, the couple garlands each other.

Varna: Taking around.

Vatna: Mixture of gramflour, turmeric and oil.

Verbal communication: The use of words as in speaking and writing to send and receive messages.

Vethalepak: Engagement and exchange of gifts.

Vidaai: Bride leaves her parental home.

Vidai: Bridal send off.

Viday: Bridal send off.

Vidhai: Leaving of bride and groom for home.

Violence: Any physical act intended to harm another person.

Visitation rights: Arrangements for the non-custodial parent in a divorce settlement to visit the children.

Vital marriage: A marital relationship in which partners are intensely bound together psychologically.

Vivah: The marriage ceremonies commence.

Vivaha Nischayam: Engagement.

Vivah-havan: Sacred fire is lit.

Vivham (muhurtham): Marriage ceremonies.

Voluntary stable singles: Singles who are satisfied to have never married, divorced people who do not want to remarry, cohabitants who do not intend to marry, and those whose lifestyle preclude marriage, such as priests and nuns.

Voluntary temporary singles: Younger never—marrieds and divorced people who are postponing marriage or remarriage. They are open to the possibility of marriage, but searching for a mate.

Vows: Statements that specifically state a couple's commitment to each other.

Vratham: Blessings from departed elders.

Vridhi: A Bengali wedding ceremony where prayers are offered to the ancestors.

Wages: Payments and benefits received from an employer.

Wari: Gifts given to the bride from the groom's house.

Waza: Traditional Kashmiri cook.

Wedding Ceremony: The marriage ritual.

Wedding Morning: Morning functions.

Wedding Reception: Celebrating the wedding.

Wheel of love: In which love is seen as developing through a four stage, circular process, including rapport, self-revelation, mutual dependence, and personality need fulfilment.

Yedur Kansani: Women from both sides mingle and greet each other.

Yegnopavit: Ceremony where the groom adorns the sacred thread that all Brahmins must wear.

Bibliography

Acker, Michele and Davis, Mark, H., 1992, 'Intimacy, Passion and Commitment in Adult Romantic Relationships: A Test of the Triangular Theory of Love', *Journal of Social and Personal Relationships*, Vol. 9, No. 1, pp. 21-50.

Adams, B.N., 1986, *The family: A Sociological Interpretation* (4th ed.), San Diego: Harcourt Brace Jovanovich.

Ainsworth, Mary, D., Blehar, M.D., Waters, E. and Wall, S., 1978, *Patterns of Attachment: A Psychological Study of the Strange Situation*, Hills Dale, NJ: Erlbaum.

Alagna, S.W., 1982, 'Sex Role Identify Peer Evaluation of Competition and the Responses of Women and Men in a Competitive Situation', *Journal of Personality and Social Psychology*, Vol. 43, pp. 546-54.

Aldous, Joan, 1978, *Family Careers: Developmental Change in Families*, New York: Wiley.

Allen, Katherine R., 1997, *Lesbian and Gay Families*, pp. 196-218 in Terry Arendell (ed.), *Contemporary Parenting: Challenges and Issues*, Thousand Oaks, CA: Sage.

Anderson, S.A., 1988, 'Parental Stress and Coping During the Leaving Home Transition', *Family Relations*, Vol. 37, pp. 160-65.

Archer, J. and Lloyd, B., 1985, *Sex and Gender*, Cambridge: Cambridge University Press.

Assamese Marriage. http://imatch4u.com/assamese_wed.htm.

Baumrind, D., 1991, 'Effective Parenting During the Early Adolescent Transition', In P.A. Cowan and E.M. Hetrington (eds.), *Family Transitions* (pp. 111-64), Hillsdale, NJ: Erlbaun.

Baumrind, D., 1982, 'Are Androgynous Individual, More Effective Persons and Parents'? *Child Development*, Vol. 53, pp. 44-75.

Bell, A.P., Weinberg, M.S. and Hammersmith, S.K., 1981, Sexual Preference: Its Development in Men and Women, Bloomington, in Indian University Press.

Bell, R.R., 1981, *Worlds of Friendship*, Beverly Hills: Sage.

Bem, S.L., 1975, 'Sex Role Adaptability: One Consequence of Psychological Androgyny,' *Journal of Personality and Social Psychology*, Vol. 31, pp. 634-43.

Bengali Marriage Rituals. http://imatch4u.com/bengali_wed.htm.

Bengali Marriage. http://www.bangalinet.com/bengali_marriage.htm.

Bienvenu, M., Sr. 1986, *Strengthen Your Marriage Through Better Communication* (No. 642), New York: Public Affairs Committee.

Bishnupriya Manipuri Marriage System. http://imatch4u.com/manipuri_wed.htm.

Blanchard, R., 1988, 'Non-Homosexual Gender Dysphoria', *The Journal of Sex Research*, Vol. 24, pp. 188-93.

Blumstein, P. and Schwartz, P., 1983, *American Couples: Money, Work, Sex*, New York: William Morrow.

Bowman, H.A. and Spanier, G.B., 1978, *Modern Marriage*, McGraw Hill Book Company, New York.

Bozett, Frederick W., 1987, *Children of Gay Fathers*, In Gay and Lesbian Parents, Edited by Frederick W. Bozett, New York: Praeger.

Brecher, E.M., 1984, The Editors of Consumer Reports Books, Inc. Love, Sex and Aging: A Consumers Union Report, Boston Little, Brown and Company.

Brenton, M., 1985, *You and Your In-laws: Help for Some Common Problems*, New York: Public Affairs Committee, No. 635.

Breunlin, D.C., 1983, Theraphy in Stages: A Life Cycle View. In J.C. Mansen and H.A. Liddle (Eds), *Clinical Implications of the Family Life Cycle* (pp. 1-11), Rock Ville, MD: Aspen.

Bringle, Robert and Bram Brunk, 1985, Jealousy and Social Behaviour: A Review of Person, Relationship, and Situational Determinants. In *Review of Personality and Social Psychology*,

Vol. 6. Self, Situation and Social Behaviour, Edited by P. Shaver, Newburg Park, CA: Sage Publications.

Brodzinsky, David M., and Loreen Huffman, 1988, 'Transition to Adoptive Parenthood,' *Marriage and Family Review*, Vol. 12, Nos. 3-4, pp. 267-86.

Bronfenbrenner, U., 1980, *The Ecology of Human Development*, Cambridge, M.A.: Harvard University Press.

Bronfenbrenner, U., 1986, 'Ecology of the Family as a Context for Human Development: Research Perspectives,' *Developmental Psychology*, Vol. 22, pp. 723-42.

Bullough, V., Bullongh, B. and Smith, R.A., 1983, 'Comparative Study of Male Transvestities, Male to Female Transsexuals and Male Homosexuals', *The Journal of Sex Research*, Vol. 19 (August), pp. 238-57.

Burgess, Ernest, 1926, 'The Family as Unity of Interaction Personalities', *The Family*, Vol. 1, pp. 3-9.

Burns, C., 1982, What to do About Those Sticky, Picky, Touchy in-law Problems, *Glamour*, pp. 134-35, 159.

Burr and Wesley, R., 1976, *Successful Marriage—A Principles Approach*, The Dorsey Press, Illnois.

Buss, D.M., 1985, 'Human Mate Selection,' *American Scientist*, 73 (January-February), pp. 47-51.

Buss, David M. and Shackelford, Todd K., 2004, From Vigilance to Violence: Mate Retention Tactics in Married Couples, *Journal of Personality and Social Psychology*, Vol. 72, No. 2.

Calderone, M.S. and Johnson, E.W., 1990, *The Family Book About Sexuality* (Rev. ed.), New York: Harper Collins.

Carnelley, Katherine, B. and Janoff-Balman, Ronnie, 1992, 'Optimism About Love Relationships: General Versus Specific Lessons From One's Personal Experiences,' *Journal of Social and Personal Relationships*, Vol. 9, No. 1, pp. 5-20.

Cate, Rodney, M. and Lloyd, Sally, A., 1992, Courtship Newbury, Park, CA: Sage.

Cavan, Ruth Shonle, 1971, 'Attitudes of Jewish College Students in the United States Toward Inter-religious Marriage', *International Journal of Sociology of the Family*, Vol. 1, Special Issue, May, pp. 84-98.

Census of India, 1991, Paper-I of 1992, *Final Population Totals: Registrar General and Census Commissioner of India*, New Delhi.

Centes, R., Raven, B.H. and Rodrignes, A., 1971, Conjugal Power Structure: A Reexamination, *American Sociological Review*, Vol. 36, pp. 264-68.

Changing Family System Among A Matrilineal Group in India. http://www.iussp.org/brazil2001/s10/s12-_04_Das.pdf.

Chesebro, J., 1987, Communication, Values and Popular Television Series—A Four Year assessment. In the Newcomb (ed.), Television: The Critical View (4/e), New York: Oxford University Press.

Chognacki, Joseph, T. and Walsh, W. Bruce, 1990, Reliability and Concurrent Validity of the Sternberg Triangular Love Scale, *Psychological Reports*, Vol. 67, No. 1, pp. 219-24.

Christian Marriage Act. http://www.seasonsindia.com/marriage/christian_sea.htm.

Christian Marriage Law. http://www.krislon.net/matrimonial/lw/law-christian.htm.

Coleman, J.C. 1984. Intimate Relationships, Marriage and Family. Indianapolis. Bobs-Merrill.

Collier, J.L., 1981, *Whatever Happened to Sex Education*? Reader's Digest (May), pp. 128-31.

Conditions of a Valid Marriage Under the Special Marriage Act, 1954. http://law.indiainfo.com/personal/hindu_valid_marriage.html.

Cowan and Cowan, 1992, When Partners Become Parients. The Big Life Change for Couples, New York: Basic Books.

Crooks, R. & Baur, K., 1990, *Our Sexuality*, 4th Edition, Redwood City, CA: Benjamin/Cummings.

Crosby, John, F., 1991, *Illusion and Disillusion: The Self in Love and Marriage*, 4th Ed. Belmont, CA: Wadsworth.

Cuber, John and Peggy Haroff, 1965, *Sex and Significant, Americans. Rev.* Ed. Baltimore: Penguin Books.

Customs of Assam. http://www.webindia123.com/assam/people/customs3.htm.

D' Souza, A.A., 1979, *Happiness in Marriage*, Usha Publication, New Delhi.

Dacey, J.S., 1986, *Adolescents Today* (3rd ed.), Glenview, IL: Scott, Foresman & Company.

Das, Madhumita, Research Officer. National Family Health Survey-2, International Institute for Population Sciences,

Govandi Station Road, Deonar, Mumbai-400088, India.

Das, Man Singh, 1974, 'A Cross-Cultural Study of Intercaste Marriage in India and the United States', *International Journal of Sociology of the Family: A Special Issue of Inter-Marriage in Comparative Perspective*, Vol. 1, pp. 25-33.

Davidson, J. Kenneth, Sr. and Moore, Nelwyn, B., 1992, *Marriage and Family*, United States: WM.C. Brown Publishers.

De Lucia, J.L., 1987, 'Gender Role Identity and Dating Behaviour: What is the Relationship'? *Sex Roles*, Vol. 17, pp. 153-61.

De Fleur and Ball-Rokeach, 1989, *Theories of Mass Communication*, New York: Longman.

Derlega, Valerian, J., Metts, Sandra, Petronis, Sandra and Margulis, 1993, *Self-disclosure*, Newbury Park, CA: Sage Publications.

Desai, G.B., 1945, *Women in Modern Gujarathi Life*, Unpublished Thesis, Bombay: University of Bombay.

DiBlasio, F.A. and Benda, B.B., 1992, 'Gender Differences in Theories of Adolescents' Sexual Activity,' *Sex Roles*, Vol. 27, pp. 5-6.

D'oyly, 1929, Polyndry. Inheritance and the Definition of Marriage, p. 29. In E.R. Leach, 1955. Polyandry, Inheritance and Definition of Marriage: With Particular Reference to Sinhalese Customary Law, Man. No. 199, Dec. 1955, pp. 1-9. http://orion.oac.uci.edu/dbell/html/body_leach.html.

Driscoll, R., Davis, K.E. and Lipetz, M.E. 1972, Parental Interference and Romantic Love. The Romes and Juliet effect, *Journal of Personality and Social Psychology*, Vol. 24, pp. 1-10.

Edwards, J.P., and Elkins, T.E., 1988, Just Between Us: A Social Sexual Training Guide for Parents and Professionals who have Concerns for Persons with Retardation, Portland: Ednick, p. 7.

Families in Kerala. http://www.jadski.com/Kerala/f2 families inkerala.htm.

Family Courts in India. http://www.india4world.com/indian-law/family-courts.shtml.

Feeney, Judith, A. and Noller, Patricia, 1990, Attachment Style as a Predictor of Adult Romantic Relationship, *Journal of Personality and Social Psychology*, Vol. 58, No. 2, pp. 281-91.

Feeney, Judith, A. and Noller, Patricia, 1991, Attachment Style and Verbal Descriptions of Romantic Partners, *Journal of Social and*

Personal Relationships, Vol. 8, No. 2, pp. 187-215.

Feeney, Judith, A. and Noller, Patricia, 1992, Attachment Style and Romantic Love. Relationship Dissolution, *Australian Journal of Psychology*, Vol. 44, No. 2, pp. 69-74.

Feeney, Judith, A. and Raphael, Beverley, 1992, Adult Attachments and Sexuality: Implications for Understanding Risk Behaviours for HIV Infection, *Australian and New Zealand Journal of Psychiatry*, Vol. 26, No. 3, pp. 399-407.

Fehr, Beverly, 1988, Prototype Analysis of the Concepts of Love and Commitment, *Journal of Personality and Social Psychology*, Vol. 55, No. 4, pp. 557-79.

Flaks, D.K., I. Ficher, F. Masterpasqua, and G. Joseph, 1995, Lesbians Choosing Motherhood: A Comparative Study of Lesbians and Hetero Sexual Parents and their Children, *Developmental Psychology*, Vol. P. 31, No. 1, pp. 105-14.

Freud, Sigmund, 1972, Group Psychology and the Analysis of the Ego. London: Hogarth.

Fromm, Erich, 1956, *The Art of Loving*, New York: Harper and Row.

Gardner, N.E.S., 1986, *Sexuality*, In J.A. Summers (Ed.), The Right to Grow Up: An Introduction to Adults with Developmental Disabilities, pp. 45-66. Baltimore, MD: Paul H. Brookes, p. 45.

Garo Customary Laws.http://www.redtailcanyon.com/items/18057.aspx.

General Information Kanian.http://kanina.8K.com/peo-cul.html.

Gerbner, G.L., Gross, M., Morgan and Signorielli, 1986, Living with Television. The Dynamics of the Cultivation Process. In Perspectives in Media Effects, edited by J. Bryant and D. Zillman. Hillsdale, NJ: Lawrence Earlbaum Associates.

Ghurye, G.S., 1950, *Caste and Class in India*, Bombay: Popular Book Depot.

Giele, J.Z., 1988, Gender and Sex Roles. In N.J. Smelser (Ed.), Handbook of Sociology (pp. 291-323), Newburg Park, CA: Sage.

Glenn, N. 9, 1990, Quantitative Research on Marital Quality in 1980's, *A Critical Review Journal of Marriage and the Family*, Vol. 52, pp. 818-31.

Glenn, N.D., 1982, Inter-Religious Marriage in the United States: Patterns and Recent Trends, *Journal of Marriage and The Family*, Vol. 44, pp. 555-68.

Glenn, N.D., 1990, Quantitative Research on Marital Quality in the 1980's: A Critical Review, *Journal of Marriage and The Family*, Vol. 52, pp. 818-31.

Goldenberg, I. and Goldenberg, H., 1991, Family Therapy: An Overview (3rd ed.), Pacific Grove, CA: Brooks/Cole.

Goode, William, J., 1959, The Theoretical Importance of Love, *American Sociological Review*, Vol. 24, No. 1, February, pp. 38-47.

Goode, William, 1963, *World Revolution and Family Patterns*, New York: Free Press.

Gottman, John, M., 1994, *Why Marriages Succeed or Fail*? New York: Simon and Sepuster.

Gray-Little, B. and Burks, N., 1983, Power and Satisfaction in Marriage: A Review and Critique, *Psychological Bulletin*, Vol. 93, pp. 513-38.

Greenberg, B.S., 1980, Life on Television: Content Analysis of V.S., TV Drama. Norwood, NJ: Ablex Publishing Co.

Greenglass, E.R., 1985, A Social Psychological View of Marriage for Women, *International Journal of Women's Studies*, Vol. 8, pp. 24-31.

Gujarathi Wedding.http://imatch4u.com/gujarathi_wed.htm.

Gunter, B. and McAleen, J.L., 1990, Children and Television: The One-eye Monster? London: Routledge.

Haas, Adelaide and Haas, Kurt, 1990, Understanding Sexuality, St. Lowis. Times Mirror/Mosby College Publishing.

Haffner, D.W., 1990, *Sex Education 2000: A Call to Action*. New York: Sex Information and Education Council of the U.S. March, pp. 284.

Hareven, T.K., 1974, The Family as Process: The Historical Study of the Family Cycle, *Journal of Family History*, Vol. 7, pp. 322-29.

Haring-Hidore, M., Stock, W.A., Okun, M.A. and Witter, R.A., 1985, Marital Status and Subjective Well-being: A Research Synthesis, *Journal of Marriage and the Family*, Vol. 47, pp. 947-53.

Harries, M.B. and P.H. Turner, 1985-86, Gay and Lesbian Parents, *Journal of Homo Sexuality*, Vol. 12, No. 12, pp. 101-13.

Harrison, A.A. and Saeed, L., 1977, Let's make a deal: An Analysis of Revelations and Stipulations in Lonely Hearts

Advertisements, *Journal of Personality and Social Psychology,* Vol. 35, pp. 257-64.

Hatch, R.C., 1986, Marital Adjustment and Satisfaction as Related to Perceptions of Religious Practices and Orientations: An Examination of Graduate and Seminary Student Couples (Doctoral dissertation, Kansas State University, 1985), *Dissertation Abstracts International,* Vol. 46, pp. 2824A-2825A.

Hatfield, E. and Walster, G. William, 1981, *A New Look at Love,* Reading, MA: Addison-Wesley.

Hayes, Cheryl D. (ed.), 1987, Risking the Future: Adolescent, Sexuality, Pregnancy and Childbearing, Vol. 1. Washington, DC: National Academy Press.

Hayes, Robert, M., 1989, Homeless Children. In Caring for America's Children, Edited by Frank J. Macchiarola and Alan Gartner: New York: The Academy of Political Science.

Hazan, Cindy and Shaver, Phillip, 1987, Romantic Love Conceptualized as an Attachment Process, *Journal of Personality and Social Psychology,* Vol. 52, No. 3, pp. 511-24.

Heaton, Tim and Pratt, E.L., 1990, The Effects of Religious Homogamy on Marital Satisfaction and Stability, *Journal of Family Issues,* Vol. 7, No. 2, pp. 191-207.

Hendershott, A., 1986, The Relationship Between Religiosity and Marital Satisfaction. Paper Presented at the Meeting of the American Sociological Association, New York, NY.

Hendrick, Clyde and Hendrick, Susan, S., 1994, Attachment Theory and Close Adult Relationships, *Psychological Inquiry,* Vol. 5, No. 1, pp. 38-41.

Hendrick, Susan, S., Hendrick, Clyde and Adler, N.L., 1988, Romantic Relationships: Love, Satisfaction and Staying Together, *Journal of Personality and Social Psychology,* 54: 980-88.

Hendrick, Susan, 1981, Self-disclosure and Marital Satisfaction, *Journal of Personality and Social Psychology,* 40: 1150-59.

Hill, I., 1987, The Bisexual Spouse Different Dimensions in Human Sexuality (edition), Mc Lean, Va: Barlina Books, Inc.

Hill, Rubin, 1986, Life Cycle Stages for Types of Single Parent Families, *Family Relations,* Vol. 35, pp. 19-29.

Hindu Marriage Laws. http://www.krislon.net/matrimonial/law/law_hindu.html.

Hojat, M. and Crandall, R., 1987, Loneliness: Theory, Research and Applications (special issue), *Journal of Social Behaviour and Personality*, Vol. 2, No. 2, pp. 105-24.

Holman, T.B. and Burr, W.R., 1980, Beyond the Beyond: The Growth of Family Theories in the 1970's, *Journal of Marriage and the Family*, Vol. 42, pp. 729-41.

Honeycutt, J., 1994, *Memory, Gender and Relationships*, New York: Guilford Press.

Hoover and Hoover, 1979, *Concepts and Methodologies in Families*.

http://news.bbc.co.uk/1/hi/world/south_asia/332173. World: South Asia Eunuchs turn prejudice into cash. Friday, April 30, 1999.

Hurlock, E.B., 1976, *Developmental Psychology*.

Hwang, Sear-Shong and Benigno E. Aguirra, 1997, Structural and Assimilationist Explanations of Asian American Intermarriage, *Journal of Marriage and the Family*, Vol. 59, pp. 758-72.

Indian Wedding Rituals and Customs. http://shaadi_online.com/wedding-rituals.asp.

Ingoldsby, Brown, B., 1995, *Mate Selection and Marriage*, pp. 146-60 in Brown B. Ingoldsby and Suzanna Smith (Eds.), Families in Multicultural Perspective, New York: Guilford Press.

Jain Marriage. http://imatch4u.com/jain_wed.htm.

Jeffress, J.E., 1987, The Parent Dominated Wife, *Medical Aspects of Human Sexuality*, Vol. 21, No. 6, pp. 38, 43-45.

Johnson, Leona, 1998, *Strengthening Family and Self*, Tinley Park, Illinois: The Good Heart–Willcox Company, Inc.

Kalmijin, M., 1998, Differentation and Stratification—Inter-Marriage and Homogamy: Causes, Patterns and Trends, *Annual Review of Sociology*, Vol. 24, pp. 295-427.

Kamat, K.L., 2004, The Ghotul System of Education, Stories of Bastar Travel: The Ghotuls. Http://www.kamat.com/Kalranga/bastar/ghotul.html. Dec. 4, 2004.

Kannan, C.T., 1963, *Intercase and Inter-Community Marriage in India*, Bombay: Allied Publishers Private Ltd.

Kapadia, K.M., 1958, *Marriages and Family in India*, Bombay.

Kapadia, K.M., 1966, *The Matrilineal Family Marriage and Family in India*, K.M. Kapadia (ed.), Bombay: Oxford University Press, pp. 336-54.

Kapur, Promilla, 1973, *Sex the Consuming Rage, Love Marriage and Sex*, Vikas Publishing House Pvt. Ltd., Delhi, p. 225.

Kassop, Mark, 1987, Salvador Minuchin: A Sociological Analysis of his Family Therapy Theory, *Clinical Sociological Review*, Vol. 5, pp. 158-67.

Katz, Stan J. and Aimee E. Lin, 1988, False love and Other Romantic Illusions: Why Love goes Wrong and How to Make it Right, New York: Ticknor & Fields.

Kemper, T.D. and Janda, L.H., 1984, The Eye of the Beholder, *Psychology Today* (December), pp. 46-52.

Kennard, Jerry, 2004, So, is it a boy or a girls? http://menshealth_about_com/cs/genetics/a/thirdsex.html.

Kerr, M.E., 1988, Chronic Anxiety and Defining a Self, *Atlantic Monthly* (September), pp. 35-58.

Kirkpatrick, Lee A. and Shaver, Phillips, R., 1992, An Attachment—Theoretical Approach to Romantic Love and Religious Belief, *Personality and Social Psychology Bulletin*, Vol. 18, No. 3, pp. 266-75.

Kirkpatrick, Martha, *et al.*, 1981, Lesbian Mothers and Their Children: A Comparative Study, *American Journal of Orthopsychiatry*, Vol. 51, No. 3, July, pp. 545-51.

Klein, D., 1984, Knowledge, Attitude and Behavioral Changes as a Result of Sex Education, *Journal of Sex Education and Therapy*, Vol. 10, No. 1 (Spring/Summer), pp. 26-30.

Knox, Dand H., Jr., 1975, *Marriage: Who? When? Why?* Englewood Cliffs, NJ: Prentice-Hall.

Kramer, L., 1991, *The Sociology of Gender: A Text-Reader*, New Yorker: St. Martin's.

Kraus, J., 1977, Shotgun Weddings: Trends in the Socio-pathology of Marriage, *Australian and New Zealand Journal of Psychiatry*, Vol. 11, pp. 259-64.

Krokoff, L.J., Gottman, J.M. and Roy, A.K., 1988, Blue Collar and White-collar Marital Interaction and Communication Orientation, *Journal of Social and Personal Relationships*, Vol. 5, pp. 201-21.

Kyndiah, P.R., 1990, Khasis: Yesterday and Today, Meghalaya Yesterday and Today, New Delhi: Han-Anand Pub., pp. 95-104.

Lamanna, Mary Ann and Riedmann, Agnes, 2000, Marriages and Families: Making Choices in a Diverse Society. 7th Edition.

United States: Wadsworth Thomson Learning.

Lantz, H.R. and Synder, E.C., 1969, Marriage, John Wiley and Sons, Inc. New York.

Lederer, Williams and Jackson, Don, 1968, Mirages of Marriages, New York: Norton.

Lewin, E. and T.A. Lyons, 1982, Everything in its place: The Coexistence of Lesbianism and Motherhood. In Homosexuality: Social, Psychological and Biological Issues, Edited by W. Paul *et al*. Newbury Park, CA: Sage Publications.

Lott, B., 1987, Women's lives: Themes and Variations in Gender Learning. Monterey, CA: Brooks/Cole.

Maccoby, Buchanan, Mnookin and Dorn Busch, 1993, Post Divorce Roles of Mothers and Fathers in the Lives of their Children, *Journal of Family Psychology*, Vol. 7, No. 1, pp. 24-38.

Macklin, Eleanor D., 1987, Non-traditional Family Forms, pp. 317-53 in Handbook of Marriage and the Family, Edited by Marvin B. Sussman and Suzanne K. Steinmetz, New York: Plenum.

Macklin, Eleanor, 1978, No Marital Heterosexual Cohabitation, *Marriage and Family Review* (March), pp. 1-12.

Maneker, Jerry, S. and Rankin, Robert, P., 1993, Religious Homogamy and Marital Duration Among Those Who file for Divorce in California, 1966-71, *Journal of Divorce and Remarriage*, Vol. 19, No. 2, pp. 233-41.

Manning, Wendy D. and Narcy S. Landale, 1996, Racial and Ethnic Differences in the Role of Cohabitation in Premarital Child Bearing, *Journal of Marriage and the Family*, Vol. 58, No. 1, pp. 63-77.

Marcus, G.G. and Smith, R.L., 1982, Your Power, His Power: How equal? How Fair? How Balanced? *Glamour* (November), pp. 240-41, 278, 280.

Margaret Mead, 1953, "The Impact of Cultural changes on the Family" in Family in the Urban Community, Detroit: The Merrill-Palmer School, p. 4.

Margobin, L. and L. White, 1987, The Continuing Role of Physical Attractiveness in *Marriage Journal of Marriage and the Family*, Vol. 49, No. 1 (February), pp. 21-27.

Marriage and Morals (Naga), Naga Marriage. http://imatch4u.com/naga_wed.htm.

Martin, D. and Lyon, P., 1972, *Lesbian Woman*, New York: Bantam Books.

Mashal, M., 1985, Marital Power Role Expectation and Marital Satisfaction, *International Journal of Women's Studies*, Vol. 8, pp. 40-46.

May, Rollo, 1969, Love and Will, New York: Narton.

Mc Fadden, V.M. and Donb, G., 1983, Therapists new Role: Training Families for Health Survival. In J.C. Hansen & H.A. Liddle (Eds.), The Family Therapy Collection (pp. 134-60), Rockville, MD: Aspen.

Mc Whirter, N., 1988, *Guninners Book of World Records* (Editor), New York: Sterling Publishing Co., Inc.

Mead, Margaret, 1966, *Marriage in Two Steps*, Red Book, July.

Mehta, Rama, 1970, *The Western Educated Hindu Woman*, Bombay: Asia Publishing House.

Melito, R., 1985, Adaptation in Family Systems: A Developmental Perspective, *Family Process*, Vol. 21, pp. 89-100.

Melville Keath, 1977, *Marriage and Family today*, Randon House, New York.

Meyrowitz, J.I., 1985, No Sense of Place: The Impact of Electronic Media on Social Behaviour, New York: Oxford University Press.

Michael, R., Gagnon, J., Laumann, E. and Kolata, G., 1994, *Sex in America: The Definitive Survey*, Boston: Little Brown.

Mikerlincer, Mario and Erev, Irit, 1991, Attachment Styles and the Structure of Romantic Love, *British Journal of Social Psychology*, Vol. 30, No. 4, pp. 273-91.

Miller, Brent, 1986, Family Research Methods, Beverly Hills, CA: Sage Publications.

Minuchin, Salvadoor, 1981, *Family Therapy Techniques*, Cambridge, MA: Harvard University Press.

Mizo Marriage Rituals. http://imatch4u.com/mizo_wed.htm.

Mofatt, M., 1989, *Coming of Age in New Jersey: College and American Culture*, New Brunswick, NJ: Rutgers University Press.

Moore, K.L., 1989, Before We are Born. Philapelphia: Saunders.

Murdock, George Peter, 1967, Ethnographic Atlas: A Summary, *Ethnology*, Vol. 6.

Murdock, George, 1949, *Social Structure*, New York: Free Press.

Murstein, B.I., Cerreto, M. and McDonald, M.B., 1977, A Theory and Investigation of the Effects of Exchange. Orientation on Marriage and Friendship, *Journal of Marriage and the Family*, Vol. 39, pp. 543-48.

Muslim Marriage Ceremony. http://imatch4u.com/muslim_wed.htm.

Muslim Marriage Law. http://www.krislon.net/matrimonial/law/law_muslim.htm.

Muslims Theory of Marriage. http://www.seasonsindia.com/marriage/islam_sea.htm.

Myths Surrounding Quran and Divorce. http://law.indiainfo.com/personal/myth-quran.html.

Nanda, S., 1990, Neither Man Nor Woman, the Hijra of India, Belmont, CA: Wadsworth.

National Family Health Survey, India, 1992-93. International Institute for Population Science (IIPS), Bombay, August, 1995, pp. 73-85

National Family Health Survey, 1998-99, Key Findings, International Institute for Population Sciences, Mumbai, India.

Nock, S.L., 1987, Sociology of the Family, Englewood Cliffs, New Jersey: Prentice Hall.

Noller, P. and Fitzpatrick, M.A., 1990, Marital Communication in the Eighties, *Journal of Marriage and the Family*, Vol. 52, pp. 832-43.

Nye, F.I., 1988, Fifty Years of Family Research 1937-87, *Journal of Marriage and the Family*, Vol. 50, pp. 305-16.

Office of the Registrar General and Census Commissioner, 1992, Census of India, 1991, Series I, India, Part IV-B (ii) of 1992. Religion. New Delhi. Office of the Registrar General and Census.

Olson, Walter, 1998, Free to Commit, *Reason Online Magazine*, October. http.//www.reasonmag.com/9710/col.olson.html.

Ortega, S.T., Whitt, H.P. and Williams, J.A., 1988, Religious Homogamy and Marital Happiness, *Journal of Family Issues*, Vol. 9, pp. 224-39.

Patterson, Charlotte, 1992, Children of Lesbian and Gay Parents, *Child Development*, Vol. 63, pp. 1025-42.

Pearlin, Leonard I., 1975, Status Inequality and Stress in Marriage, *American Sociological Review*, Vol. 40, pp. 344-57.

Peck, M. Scott, 1978, The Road less Traveled: A New Psychology of Love, Traditional Values and Spiritual Growth, New York: Simon and Schuster.

Perlman, D. and Fehr, B., 1987, The Development of Intimate Relationships. In D. Pealman and S. Duck (Eds.), Intimate Relationships: Development, Dynamics and Deterioration (pp. 13-42), Newburg Park, CA: Sage.

Pistole, M. Carole, 1989, Attachment in Adult Romantic Relationships: Style of Conflict Resolution and Relationship Satisfaction, *Journal of Social Personal Relationships*, Vol. 6, No. 4, pp. 505-12.

Pogrebin, L.C., 1983, *Family Politics on an Intimate Frontier*, New York: McGraw-Hill, p. 26.

Radhakrishnan, S., 1956, Religion and Society, 2nd Edition, Third Impression, London: George Allen and Unwin Ltd.

Raikar-Mhatre, Sumedha, 1997, Divorce and Christian Marriages in India Till Cruelty do us part. http://www.goacom.com/news/news97/may/marriages.html.

Rajput Marriage. http://imatch4u.com/rajput_wed.htm.

Rao Prakasa, V.V. and Rao, V. Nandana, 1982, *Marriage, the Family and Woman in India*, Heritage Publishers, New Delhi.

Ratra, Amiteshwar, 2002, Preparedness, Marital Quality and Maintenance Behaviour in Working and Non-working Women. Unpublished Thesis, Hisar, Haryana: Chaudhary Charan Singh Haryana Agricultural University.

Ratra, Amiteshwar, 2002, Few Should's for a Sound Married Life, Monovena, I.C. College of Home Science, CCS Haryana Agricultural University, Hisar, Haryana, India.

Raven, B., Centers, R. and Rodrigues, A., 1975, The Bases of Conjugal Power. In R.W. Cronwell and D.H. Olson (Eds.), Power in Families (pp. 217-34), Beverly Hills: Sage.

Reddy, M.M. Krishna, 1998, Marriage Population and Society: Demographics Perspectives of a Social Institution, New Delhi: Kanishka Publishers, Distributors.

Reddy, V. Narayan Karan, 1978, Marriage in India: A Psycho-Sociological Study, Gurgaon, Haryana: The Academic Press.

Registration of Marriage Celebrated in Other Forms. http://www.krislon.net/ matrimonial/law/law-celebrated_forms.htm.

Ress, Ira, 1980, Family Systems in America, 3rd Ed., New York: Holt, Rinehart and Winston.

Reven, B., Centers, R. and Rodrignes, A., 1975, The Bases of Conjugal Power. In R.W. Cromwell & D.H. Olson (Eds.), *Power in Families*, pp. 217-34. Beverly Hills: Sage.

Rhyne, D., 1981, Bases of Marital Satisfaction Among Men and Women, *Journal of Marriage and the Family*, Vol. 43, pp. 941-55.

Ridley, C.A., Peterman, D.J. and Avery, A.W., 1978, Cohabitation: Does it Make for a Better Marriage?, *The Family Coordinator*, Vol. 27, pp. 129-36.

Roberts, Elijabeth, 1983, Childhood Sexual Learning: The Unwritten Curriculum. In C. Davis (Ed.), Challenges in Sexual Science. Philadelphia: Society for the Scientific Study.

Rose, S.M., 1985, Same and Cross Sex Friendships and the Psychology of Homosociality, *Sex Roles*, Vol. 12, pp. 63-74.

Rubin, A.M. and J.R. Adams, 1986, Outcomes of Sexually Open Marriages, *Journal of Sex Research*, Vol. 22, pp. 311-19.

Rubin, Zick, 1973, Liking and Loving: An Invitation to Social Psychology, New York: Holt, Rinehart and Winston.

Rulin, L.B., 1976, *Worlds of Pain: Life in the Working Class Family*, New York, Basic Books.

Russell, C., 1974, Transition to Parenthood, *Journal of Marriage and the Family*, 36: 294-302.

Saluter, Arlene, 1994, Marital Status and Living Arrangements: March 1993. Bureau of the Census Current Population Reports. (Population Characteristics Series, p. 20, No. 478), Washington DC: US Government Printing Office.

Saxton, Lloyd, 1970, Love in a Paired Relation. In: The Individual, Marriage and the Family: Current Perspective, Edited by Lloyd Saxton, Belmont, California: Wadsworth Publishing Company Inc.

Schaap, Cas, Brunk, Bram and Kerkstra, Adam, 1988, Marital Conflict Resolutions. In Perspectives on Marital Interaction, Edited by Patricia Noller and P. Marry Anne Fitzpatrick, Philadelphia: Multilingual Matters.

Sexuality Education for Children with Disabilities, 1992, National Information Center for Children and Youth with Disabilities, NICHCY News Digest.www.Nichcy.Org.

Sharpsteen, Don, J. 1993. Romantic Jealousy as an Emotion Concept: A Prototype Analysis, *Journal of Social and Personal Relationship*, Vol. 10, No. 1, pp. 69-82.

Shatzmiller, Maya, 1996, Marriage, Family and the Faith. Women's Conversion to Islam, *Journal of Family History*, Vol. 21, No. 3, pp. 235-46.

Shaver, Phillip and Hazan, Cindy, 1987, Being Lonely, Falling in Love: Perspectives from Attachment Theory, *Journal of Social Behaviour and Personality*, Vol. 2, No. 2, Pt. 2, pp. 105-24.

Shaver, Phillips, R. and Brennan, Kelly, A., 1992, Attachment Styles and the 'Big Five' Personality Traits: Their Connections with Each other and with Romantic Relationship Outcomes, *Personality and Social Psychology Bulletin*, Vol. 18, No. 5, pp. 536-45.

Shaver, Phillips, Rindy Hazan and Bradshaw, D., 1988, Love as Attachment: The Integration of Three Behavioural Systems. In the Psychology of Love, Edited by Robert Sternberg and Michael Barnes, New Haven, CT: Yale University Press.

Shostak, A.B., 1987, Singlehood. In M.B. Sussman and S.K. Steinmetz (Eds.), *Handbook of Marriage and the Family* (pp. 355-67), New York: Plenum Press.

Simpson, Jeffrey, 1990, Influence of Attachment Styles on Romantic Relationships, *Journal of Personality and Social Psychology*, Vol. 59, No. 5, pp. 971-80.

Sinha, K., 1970, Meghalaya: Triumph of the Tribal Genius, Delhi, Publication Division of ISSD, pp. 138-43.

Social Organization. http://orissagov.nic.in/people/tribe/tribesocial.htm.

Solemnization of Marriages Under the Special Marriage Act, 1954. http://law.indiainfo.com/personal/solemnization.html.

Solemnization of Special Marriage. http://www.krislon.net/matrimonial/law/law-solemnization.htm.

South Indian Wedding. http://www.sanathanadharma. Com/articles/wedding.htm.

Spafford, Carol Sullivan; Pesce, Augustus, J. and Grosser, George, S., 1998, Cydopedic Education Dictionary, Abany: Delmar Publishers.

Spanier, G.B., 1983, Married and Unmarried Cohabitation in the United States, 1980, *Journal of Marriage and the Family*, Vol. 45, pp. 277-88.

Stanush, M., 1991, After the Romance, *Austin American Statesman*, February 14, pp. E1, E6.

Staples, Robert, 1999, Interracial Relationships, A Convergence of Desire and Opportunity, pp. 129-36 in Robert Stapes (Ed.). The Black Family. Essays and Studies, 6th ed., Belmont, CA. Wadsworth.

Stein, P.J. (Ed.), 1981, *Single Life: Unmarried Adults in Social Context*, New York: St. Martin's Press.

Sternberg, Robert and Barnes, Michall, 1985, Real and ideal others in Romantic relationships. Is Four a Crowd? *Journal of Personality and Social Psychology*, Vol. 49, pp. 1589-96.

Sternberg, Robert and Graje, K.S. 1984. The nature of love, *Journal of Personality and Social Psychology*, Vol. 47, pp. 312-27.

Stinnett, Nich and Defrain, John, 1985, *Secrets of Strong Families*, Boston: Little, Brown.

Stockard, Janice, 1989, *Daughter of the Canton Delta. Marriage Patterns and Economic Strategies in South China*, 1860-1930. Stanford, CA: Stanford University Press.

Stover, Ronald, G. and Hope, Christine, 1996, Marriage, Family and Intimate Relations, New York, Harcourt Brace Jovanovich College Publishers.

Strong, Bryan and Christine De Vault, 1995, The Marriage and Family Experience, 6th Edition, Minneapolis/St. Paul. West Publishing Company.

Sullivan, Harry Stack, 1947, Conceptions of Modern Psychiatry, Washington DC: William Alanson, White Psychiatric Foundation.

Sullivan, Oriel, 1997, The Division of Housework Among Remarried Couples, *Journal of Family Issues*, Vol. 18, No. 2, pp. 205-23.

Tanius, M., 1983, Matrilineal Society and Family Planning: A Minangkaban Case Study, Population Change in South East Asia. Wilfredo, F. Arece and G.C. Avarez (Eds.), Singapore, ISAS, pp. 358-90.

Teachman, Jay D., 1983, Early Marriage, Premarital Fertility and Marital Dissolution, *Journal Family Issues*, Vol. 4, pp. 105-26.

Teti, Doughas M. and Michael Lamb, 1989, Socio-Economic and Marital Outcomes of Adolescent Marriage, Adolescent Childbirth and their Co-occurrence, *Journal of Marriage and the Family*, Vol. 51, pp. 203-12.

Tharinger, D.J., 1987, Sexual Interest. In A. Thomas & J. Grimes (eds.), Children's Needs: Psychological Perspectives, Washington, DC: National Association of School Psychologists, p. 5356.

The Foreign Marriage Act. http://law.indiainfo.com/personal/foreign-marriageact. html.

The Indian Christian Marriage Act, 1872. http://law.indiainfo.com/ personal/christian.html.

The Law.http://www.emory.edu/English/bahri/divorce.html.

The people. http://shillong.med.nic.in/depts/artc/people.htm.

The Special Marriage Act, 1954. http://www.krislon.net/matrimonial /law/law_act_1954.htm.

Thompson, Linda and Alexis Walker, 1989, Gender in Families: Women and Men in Marriage, Work and Parenthood. In Contemporary Families: Looking Forward, Looking Back, Edited by Alan Booth. Minneapolis: National Council on Family Relations.

Thorne, B., 1982, Feminist Thinking on the Family: An Overview. In B. Thorne and M. Yalom (Eds.), Rethinking the Family: Some Feminist Questions (pp. 1-24), New York: Longman.

Thonghom, Suvat, 1995, The Mani: The Negrito of Thailand. Edited and Expanded by George Weber. http://www.Andaman.org/book/chapter 36/text36.htm.

Tribal Issues of East Singhbhum, Jamshedpur. http://jamshedpur.nic.in/tribal.htm.

Turner, P.H., Scadden and Harris, 1985, Parenting in Gay and Lesbian Families. Paper Presented at the First Meeting of the Future of Parenting Symposium, Chicago, IL (March).

Turner, Ralph, H., 1970, The Family Interaction. New York: John Wiley and Sons Inc.

Untitled Document, Article Courtesy: Janki Dass from 'Women of Punjab' by Yash Kohli. http://www.sikh_heritage.co.uk/heritage/wop/women of Punjab.html. pp. 22-28.

Vande Berg, Leah, R. and Streckfuss, Diane, 1992, Prime-time Television's Portrayal of Women and World of Work: A Demographic Profile, *Journal of Broadcasting and Electronic Media*, pp. 195-207.

Vatsyana, 1948, *The Kama Sutra* (translated), Delhi: Rajkamal.

Wadhwa, Soma, 2004, Fleshed out: A Peep into the Bedroom of

Married Couples: How, Why, What they do, *The Weekly Newsmagazine Outlook*, Dec. 20, 2004, pp. 62-74.

Walster, E. and Walster, G.W., 1978, *A New Look at Love*, Reading, MA: Addison-Wesley.

Walters, L.H., 1982, Are Families Different from other Groups?, *Journal of Marriage and the Family*, Vol. 44, pp. 841-50.

Way, P., 1982, The Need to Know: Sexuality and the Disabled Child. Eureka, CA: Planned Parenthood of Humboldt County.

Wedding Rituals Marathi. http://www.calonline.com/matro/marathi.asp.

Weinberg, Martin S., C.J. Williams and Douglas W. Pryor, 1994, Dual Attraction: Understanding Bisexuality, New York: Oxford University Press.

Weitzman, L., 1985, The Divorce Resolution: The Unexpected Social and Economic Consequences for Women and Children in America, New York: Fee Press.

Weitzman, L.J., 1984, Sex-Role Socialization, A Focus on Women in J. Freeman (Ed.); Women: A Feminist Perspective, (3rd ed.) (pp. 157-237), Palo Alto, CA: Mayfield.

West, D.J., 1983, Homosexuality and Lesbianism, *British Journal of Psychiatry*, Vol. 143, pp. 221-26.

Westermarck, E.A., 1891, *The History of Human Marriage*, London: Macmillan.

Wetzel, J.R., 1990, American Families: 75 Years of Change, *Monthly Labor Review*, Vol. 113 (March), pp. 4-13.

White, G., 1980, Inducing Jealousy: A Powder Perspective, *Personality and Social Psychology Bulletin*, Vol. 6, No. 2, pp. 222-27.

White, M.K., 1990, *Dating, Mating and Marriage*, New York, Adine de Gruyter.

Yancey, George and Sherelyn, Yancey, 1998, Intenracial Dating, *Journal of Family Issues*, Vol. 19, No. 3, pp. 334-48.

Yerby, Buerkel-Rothfus and Bochner, 1990, Understanding Family Communication, Scottdale, AZ: Gorsuch Scarisbrick.

Index